AMERICAN PATENT LAW

Students and established scholars of intellectual property law often look for historical context when trying to understand the development and present-day contours of IP rules and systems. *American Patent Law* supplies this context, offering readers a comprehensive account of the evolution of the US patent system and patent doctrine beginning in 1790. From the technologies for harvesting wood and shoemaking in the earliest periods to computer software and biotechnology of the present, each chapter of the book covers the characteristic technologies of each historical era. The book also describes how businesspeople in each era acquired and enforced patents and used patents as the foundation of various business arrangements. This book is a landmark in the history of technologies, the US patent system, and the way private actors have deployed patents across American history.

ROBERT MERGES is a professor of law at Berkeley Law (University of California), where he co-directs the Berkeley Center for Law & Technology. He has been writing about patents and patent law for over thirty years.

American Patent Law

A BUSINESS AND ECONOMIC HISTORY

ROBERT P. MERGES
University of California, Berkeley

CAMBRIDGE
UNIVERSITY PRESS

CAMBRIDGE
UNIVERSITY PRESS

Shaftesbury Road, Cambridge CB2 8EA, United Kingdom

One Liberty Plaza, 20th Floor, New York, NY 10006, USA

477 Williamstown Road, Port Melbourne, VIC 3207, Australia

314–321, 3rd Floor, Plot 3, Splendor Forum, Jasola District Centre, New Delhi – 110025, India

103 Penang Road, #05–06/07, Visioncrest Commercial, Singapore 238467

Cambridge University Press is part of Cambridge University Press & Assessment, a department of the University of Cambridge.

We share the University's mission to contribute to society through the pursuit of education, learning and research at the highest international levels of excellence.

www.cambridge.org
Information on this title: www.cambridge.org/9781009123419

DOI: 10.1017/9781009129206

First published 2022

A catalogue record for this publication is available from the British Library.

Library of Congress Cataloging-in-Publication Data
NAMES: Merges, Robert P., author.
TITLE: American patent law : a business and economic history / Robert P. Merges, University of California, Berkeley.
DESCRIPTION: Cambridge, United Kingdom ; New York, NY : Cambridge University Press, 2022. | Includes bibliographical references and index.
IDENTIFIERS: LCCN 2021057922 (print) | LCCN 2021057923 (ebook) | ISBN 9781009123419 (hardback) | ISBN 9781009125796 (paperback) | ISBN 9781009129206 (epub)
SUBJECTS: LCSH: Patent laws and legislation–United States–History.
CLASSIFICATION: LCC KF3114 .M463 2022 (print) | LCC KF3114 (ebook) | DDC 346.7304/86–dc23/eng/20220208
LC record available at https://lccn.loc.gov/2021057922
LC ebook record available at https://lccn.loc.gov/2021057923

ISBN 978-1-009-12341-9 Hardback
ISBN 978-1-009-12579-6 Paperback

This book is dedicated to the community of scholars that is the University of California at Berkeley. Being among you is one of the great satisfactions of my life.

Contents

Figures

Tables

Preface

Many if not most books bear the imprint of biography, in their origin if not their content. This is definitely true of the book you're looking at. I took a fair number of undergraduate history courses at my American university, and so thought I knew something of the field. But when I arrived at Trinity College, Dublin, for a year of study in Irish history, the academic advisor assigned to me looked in horror at the scattershot selection of "micro-history" courses I had taken. Though a senior at Trinity, I was assigned straightaway to a freshman course whose title was "History of Ireland from 600 to 1550 AD." The primary textbook was the *Cambridge History of Ireland, Volume 1: 600 to 1550*. When I asked what course was set for the spring, I was told: "Irish History II: 1550–1730." I had already guessed the main textbook – the *Cambridge History, Volume 2*, covering precisely the same years. The advisor never said it, but her attitude was: I don't know what that mishmash is on your transcript, but here we study history. So go start.

I was not displeased with my American university experience; it afforded me the chance to take a very wide assortment of classes, from chemistry to economics, from finance to intellectual history. But my Irish introduction to *longue-durée* (long duration) study as the cornerstone of history stuck with me.

Years later I often found myself casting about for a source to consult on some aspect or another of patent law and economic history. For almost any era or topic, there were helpful sources. But to get the full picture, I had to string together snippets of context and scattered insights regarding the coevolution of patent law and the American economy. It often felt like trying to reconstruct a fascinating news story from the strips of jumbled, shredded newsprint that had been packed around some item in a shipping box. Frustrating.

So, it occurred to me that my field, patent law, could use a single-volume history that covered the founding era up through current times.[1] As has happened to me more than once, I went in search of a book that I imagined should be found in the literature on my field. On not finding it, I ended up supplying it myself.

I will add, quickly: There are some outstanding history monographs in this field, and I draw on all of them in this book. Several show real mastery over important episodes, technologies, and economic eras: Chris Beauchamp on the telephone; Oren Bracha on intellectual history; Zorina Khan on the nineteenth century; Herb Hovenkamp on classical Gilded Age economic theory; Kara Swanson on the history of patent examiners, women inventors, and more; and Edward Walterscheid on the entire founding era. But there was not, to my knowledge, a single comprehensive volume that tried to integrate the insights and observations of these many deep but only loosely connected works. With this book, I can say I have now tried. I describe the place of patents in business and the American economy from the beginning in 1790 up to the present time.

If I sound as if writing this book was like scratching a long-standing itch, I don't want to give the impression that it was an irritating process. In fact, I enjoyed it immensely. But that was because I had so much support, help, and backing. I could immerse myself in the secondary historical literature, as well as census and GDP data, old patents, Patent Office reports, and patent cases, because I was not teaching classes for a year. And this sabbatical was made possible by my colleagues at the Berkeley Center for Law and Technology: Peter Menell, Pam Samuelson, Molly van Houweling, former Executive Directors Robert Barr and Jim Dempsey, and the talented, dedicated, and supportive staff, Richard Fisk, Jann Dudley, Irys Schenker, numerous student interns, and all the other members of the BCLT community. I could not have taken time off from my teaching and other obligations without all their help. They form an integral part of my corner of a great world university. In recognition, I dedicate this book to the place and values that bind us together: U.C. Berkeley – a lively, thrumming community, trying to live out its own enlightened progressive aspirations, that I have had the great fortune to be part of for over 25 years (and counting).

The list of others who helped me in immediate forms must begin with Su Li, Ph.D., Berkeley Law class of 2021. Su helped enormously with the many graphs and tables in this book, gathering data, formatting the results, and poring over the small details in many of the figures and illustrations. A law student with her empirical skills, and the patience and diligence to apply them so helpfully, was the perfect gift from the Writing Gods during the gestation of this book. I was probably not worthy of this level of help. But I am very glad I got it anyway.

[1] I might have been inspired by a book from one of my Trinity instructors, L. M. Cullen's Economic History of Ireland Since 1660 (London: Batsford Publishers, 1972).

The library staff at Berkeley Law, led and guided by esteemed colleague Katherine Vanden Heuvel, were indispensable to my research. They answered dozens of queries for books, articles, and online resources. I always had what I needed, in surprisingly short time, so forward progress was never stymied. It is a privilege and a luxury for any researcher to have a staff of skilled professionals two floors down or one email away, and I am profoundly grateful to yield up a long round of applause for those at Berkeley who perform this vital scholarly function.

I also owe a vast debt to the many colleagues, former students, and friends who I have met in the past ten years or so on my visits to and research about mainland China. Visiting China during these dynamic years of economic development, and watching the concurrent growth of a modern, progressive intellectual property system there, made me more curious than ever about the rapid years of "economic take-off" in the United States from roughly 1870 to 1910. Though the differences could fill a large book, there seemed to me significant similarities between the two periods of rapid growth. And – most strikingly for a scholar of intellectual property – the Chinese government seemed intent on developing a world-class intellectual property system. Not primarily as the result of pressure from the United States and other countries but because of national self-interest. Here was evidence, in a contemporary setting, of a state undergoing rapid economic development and simultaneously feeling an urgent need to upgrade institutions for granting and enforcing IP rights. Watching it all, I was inspired to return to a similar moment in history when the United States was on the rise, and to explore more fully the co-development of the US patent system along with its economy.

To name a few names: Professors CUI Guobin and JIANG Ge of Tsinghua Law School; Professors YANG Ming, and ZHANG Ping, of Peking University Law School; my Berkeley colleagues, Mark Cohen and HAO Yuan of our Asia IP Law initiative; former students Professor CHEN Xiankai of Jinan University, BIAN Renjun of Peking University, SONG Haiyan of NBA-China, and LIU Fang (Helen Liu) of the Anjie Law Firm, Beijing; JIANG Nandi of Rouse Law firm, Beijing; HONG Yan, also of Tsinghua Law School; Jacob LI of National Tsinghua Law School, Taiwan; Jesse LU of the National Cheng-Chi University Law School, Taiwan; K. C. (Kungchung) LIU of Singapore Management University; LEE Jyh-An of the Chinese University of Hong Kong; former Judge HSIUNG Sungmei of Deloitte Law Partners, Taipei; and my friend SONG Haining, Fangda Partners, Beijing. I have no doubt missed many others, but, as with all my friends, I hope they will forgive my mental density and accept sincere apologies.

When it comes to acknowledgments, two provisos come to mind. Save the best for last; and keep it short. So, in that spirit I say: most of all, thanks to my family – wife Jo and children Robert and James (the true historian in the family). You keep me loose, absorb my horrific puns, and generally humor me in my digressions and other foibles. You are the pack this dog loves to run with. Love you, one and all.

1

Introduction

Overview and Themes

CHAPTER OUTLINE

Over the years, a number of brilliant historical studies have appeared in my primary field of patent law. The nonprofessional but exceptionally devoted historian Edward Walterscheid comes first to mind.[1] His history of the earliest years of patent law (1790–1836) is an invaluable resource. Zorina Khan's economic history of

[1] Edward C. Walterscheid, To Promote the Progress of Useful Arts: American Patent Law and Administration, 1787–1836 (Littleton, CO: Fred B. Rothman & Co., 1998).

intellectual property law during the "long" nineteenth century (1789–1910)[2] is a tour de force of empirical and analytic rigor. Christopher Beauchamp's history of the Bell telephone technology and legal controversy is a similarly outstanding book.[3] Beauchamp's article on the "first" patent litigation explosion is also one I refer to over and over.[4] The same goes for Oren Bracha's intellectual history of copyright and patent from 1790 to 1909, an essential reference for me.[5] Likewise, research by the historian Kara Swanson on the evolution of the US Patent Office and the profession of patent agent/lawyer, among other topics, is the best and most thorough account of these crucial topics.[6]

Good as they are, none of these works try to cover the story of patents and patent law from 1790 (the first Patent Act) to the present. I have often thought that the field could use such an overview. I know I would have been glad to have it for a number of research projects in the past. Not seeing such a book, and Armed with a fat file of historical materials collected over the years, I (to quote one historian describing another) "found it necessary to refashion" myself into something I had admired since my college days – a *longue-durée* historian.[7] Or to try, at any rate. So here we are.

1.1 PATENTS: PRIVATE RIGHTS AS INSTRUMENTS OF ECONOMIC POLICY

The government – our government – grants patents. But patents are mostly sought, held, and used by private businesses. As acts of a sovereign state, each patent grant comes wrapped in all manner of policy issues: to best serve society, how many patents should the government issue, what should they cover, how long should they last before expiring, and so on. But to their owners – companies and individuals – patents are only important insofar as they make some money or serve some other instrumental goal. Behind every patent is an owner who spent money to acquire it and who has (or had) some plan for it.

2 Zorina Khan, The Democratization of Invention: Patents and Copyrights in American Economic Development (Cambridge: Cambridge University Press, 2009).

3 Christopher Beauchamp, Invented by Law: Alexander Graham Bell and the Patent That Changed America (Cambridge, MA: Harvard University Press, 2015).

4 Christopher Beauchamp, *The First Patent Litigation Explosion*, 125 Yale L.J. 848 (2016).

5 Oren Bracha, Owning Ideas: The Intellectual Origins of American Intellectual Property, 1790–1909 (New York: Cambridge University Press, 2016).

6 Kara Swanson, *The Emergence of the Professional Patent Practitioner*, 50 Tech. & Cult. 519 (2009); Kara Swanson, "The Surprisingly Engrossing History of Patent Examiners," Slate.com (May 7, 2014); Kara Swanson, *Rubbing Elbows and Blowing Smoke: Gender, Class and Science in the Nineteenth-Century Patent Office*, 108 Isis: J. Hist. Sci. 40 (2017); Kara Swanson, *"Great Men," Law, and the Social Construction of Technology*, 43 L. & Soc. Inq. 1093 (2018).

7 The importance of long duration histories is the main theme of a much-discussed book by two historians. See Jo Guldi and David Armitage, The History Manifesto (Cambridge: Cambridge University Press, 2014). See also Deborah Cohen and Peter Mandler, *The History Manifesto: A Critique*, 120 Am. Hist. Rev. 530 (2015); David Armitage and Jo Guldi, *The History Manifesto: A Reply to Deborah Cohen and Peter Mandler*, 120 Am. Hist. Rev. 543 (2015).

In this book I tell the story of American patent law from the vantage point of patent owners. Beginning with the first Patent Act in 1790, I lay out the general economic trends that formed the background to invention and technological development. I describe some devices and techniques that characterize each era: technologies for harvesting and using wood, in the earliest period; the new machinery of the mid-nineteenth century, exemplified in fields such as wood working and shoemaking machines; the technologies of large-scale industry in the late nineteenth and early twentieth centuries, starting in steel and continuing to electrical power generation, telephony, and a host of other industries; characteristic products of the industrialization era, including electric lighting, bicycles, and agricultural equipment; then the chemical and auto industries, from the 1920s on; and ending with synthetic fibers, computer hardware and software, and biotechnology.

Throughout the book I also highlight new entrants and their use of patents. In this I am not so concerned with particular industries. Therefore, we touch on diverse fields such as farm equipment, coffin hardware, paper-making, auto parts, and vegetable canning. The primary point of these case studies is to show something of the state of each industry at a given time, the development of a specific invention, the patenting of that invention, and how patents fit into the business enterprises that owned and deployed them. I share my curiosity about what kinds of patents inventors were getting and what kinds of business enterprises the inventors were part of. I show how they and their colleagues *used* patents to pursue business goals – and how these patent strategies changed over time as industries and markets unfolded.

Only rarely did Congress have in mind a particular inventor or business when debating and passing patent legislation. But it did have in mind an overall picture: small grants of government power, to dispersed individuals, who would raise money to create, improve, and implement new inventions. This was just one part of an overall governmental imperative to rapidly grow and develop the economy. Indeed, as we will see (in this chapter, and at length in Chapter 2), invention patents were mentioned frequently through the first half of the nineteenth century as a cure for the shortage of labor in the new American nation. Patented inventions, it was hoped, would help to better leverage the labor of each working citizen. In parallel, liberal land grants – the land patent system – would attract immigrants, reducing the labor shortage on the supply side. Patents for land and inventions were thus important policy instruments in the early economic development state. Together, they represent a distinctive economic strategy.

This might be described as a democratic property strategy. By strategy here I mean an approach, almost a style. It was not a fully worked out government program whose steps and components were described in detail and implemented in a master sequence. This was instead a loosely theorized concatenation of distinct but compatible policies. Both invention and land patents intelligently leveraged the light but durable framework of the early federal government.[8] In an era when the reach of

[8] Acting to implement one of Hamilton's suggestions in his Report on Manufactures, early treasury official Tench Coxe actually proposed using land grants as a reward for new

visionaries such as Alexander Hamilton far exceeded the modest grasp of the new federal state, both types of patents injected federal development policy into all corners of the economy. But they did so by combining a small dose of federal power, the power to back up the federal right in court, with a large measure of private funding and initiative. Patents of both types were federally *granted* – bestowed or conferred on qualified individuals by act of the government. Once granted, these rights covered valuable assets whose use and development were in the hands of private parties. For each patent type, the most essential federal presence in the post-grant period was the local federal district court.[9] It was in court that these rights could be enforced – if and when their owners decided to enforce them. The private ordering that they facilitated, together with reliance on a generalized and privately activated enforcement mechanism, were important aspects of these property grants.

Invention and land patents are unquestionably individual property rights. But why do I call policies behind these rights a "democratic property" strategy? The answer is breadth and reach. Both invention and land patents were granted to widely dispersed individuals in all corners of the country. Acquisition costs were low, and with work and good luck a land or invention patent might form the nucleus of a profitable farm or business.[10]

Patents, and technology promotion generally, are rightly associated with Alexander Hamilton and the Report on Manufactures. Yet because invention patents were available to all comers, and were inexpensive to acquire, they were much more congruent with early land development policy than with many of Hamilton's grand, government-directed schemes. In fact, the patent world came in some respects to represent Jefferson's vision of small, independent property owners making their own way without top-down constraints or guidance from the government. There never was any mention of a "yeoman inventor," to go along with Jefferson's idealized portrait of the yeoman farmer. Yet one could sometimes detect in the world of technology the Jeffersonian pattern of dispersed ownership spread among scattered small claimants. Because of this, the democratic property strategy

inventions. Edward C. Walterscheid, *Patents and Manufacturing in the Early Republic*, 80 J. Pat. & Trademark Off. Soc'y 855, 864 n.32 (1998):

> [Tench Coxe's] suggestion that land be used as the premiums [with which to reward inventors under a proposed "bounty" or reward system] was not based on European practice, but instead seems to have been derived from the recent requests made to the Continental Congress for land grants as a reward for invention.

9 These grants did necessitate an administrative structure, to be sure, but the agencies that ran both invention and land patent systems were profit centers: they brought in more money than they spent.

10 In light of the structural exclusion of slaves, most women, and other groups, this development strategy might more accurately be described as relatively democratic given the low standards of the times. See Section 1.1.2.

imparted a Jeffersonian twist to the essentially Hamiltonian idea of promoting technological innovation.

In keeping with the democratic spirit, acquisition costs for land and invention patents were intentionally kept low. Moderate acquisition costs were, however, accompanied by an additional requirement: To gain full title, the applicant had to prove an expenditure of time and effort sufficient to demonstrate a good faith intention to develop the asset underlying the right – a piece of land, or a new invention, as the case may be. Both land and invention patents (and federal mining claims as well) often have a two-stage vesting model. Stage one encourages a tentative legal claim, which is no more than a right to exert preliminary effort developing the asset. To secure actual title, land had to be "improved": The would-be owner had to clear land, plant, harvest, etc., and also build a house, barn, or the like. This two-step procedure tries to steer expenditures and effort into actual development of the underlying asset, instead of speculative buying with quick resale to others. Only after proof of good faith development efforts at Stage One will formal title issue at Stage Two.

Why is speculation disfavored? What kinds of tactics are considered "unproductive" and so disfavored in Stage One? To answer that, a brief digression will help.

1.1.1 *A Short Digression on "Rent-Seeking"*

When I say rent-seeking I mean the effort one expends to shape or capture government favors that add to one's profits. Government lobbying is typical. Strictly speaking, lobbying by itself is not an automatic sign of inefficiency, nor are the things lobbyists ask for. Inefficiency only results when a piece of legislation does nothing to stimulate additional production, and so contributes nothing to greater economic output or the encouragement of beneficial activity. A change in this direction creates what economists call a "rent," which generally means a profit-making opportunity. I use the term in a narrower sense. For me it typically signifies a government-backed claim that is used by its holder to get money without contributing anything of real value.[11] The "seeking" usually takes the form of spending time

[11] This is not a universally accepted definition of a rent, but it is the most common one. For an overview of the issues, see Roger D. Congleton and Arye L. Hillman, eds., Companion to the Political Economy of Rent Seeking (Cheltenham: Edward Elgar, 2015). Before the modern study of political economy and rent-seeking, many of the same unproductive activities were called speculation. Like rents, however, speculation in general can be productive, as more risk-oriented or foresightful investors buy assets on the belief that they will rise in value. Nevertheless, particularly in the nineteenth century, a "speculator" was usually not considered productive. This is a consistent theme in the legal histories of J. Willard Hurst. See J. Willard Hurst, Law and the Conditions of Freedom in the Nineteenth Century (Madison: University of Wisconsin Press, 1967), at p. 6. Hurst said that nineteenth-century American citizens believed "[t]he legal order should protect and promote the release of individual creative energy to the greatest extent compatible with the broad sharing of opportunity ... [and] they wanted ... at least some affirmative legal preference of settlers over speculators." For a critique of Hurst's

and money to acquire a valuable government favor. Rent-seeking is almost always a pejorative in economic writing. That's because by definition the rent by itself adds little or nothing to productivity. And what is worse, the competition to capture the rent wastes money that might otherwise be spent on welfare-enhancing things like making new products or lowering the cost of existing ones.[12] Rents don't help society in any real sense. They do not increase overall welfare. And yet they are valuable to their holders – for use extracting value from other, typically productive, economic actors.[13]

In the general, non-IP, literature, a classic example of a rent is a government import quota, which restricts imports in favor of domestic producers.[14] Assuming a robust market for imported products, there is real value in holding an official government license to import goods.[15] If the quota is divided up into allotments, the number of imported products authorized by each allotment determines its value. The bigger an allotment's share of the total import quota, the more valuable that allotment is. The point to seize is the *competition* for the allotments. Each one is valuable; more than one firm wants each one; so, firms will spend time and money trying to increase the chance they'll get one, and the size (proportion of the overall quota) of any allotment they do get. The allotment is a rent; the competition for it is the "seeking." Voila, rent-seeking 101.

historical work, especially in the way it leaves out minorities and the dispossessed, see Hendrik Hartog, *Four Fragments on Doing Legal History, or Thinking with and against Willard Hurst*, 39 L. & Hist. Rev. 835 (2021).

12 There is a sizeable economic literature modeling rent-seeking as a game among contestants spending money in competition for a rent or a larger share of a rent. See, e.g., Ngo Van Long and Frank Stahler, *A Contest Model of Liberalizing Government Procurements*, 25 Euro. J. Pol. Econ. 479 (2009) (showing via an economic model how opening a country's government procurement process to foreign participants – which should increase competition and lower costs – may actually lead to a net waste of resources as firms collectively spend more on lobbying than the value of a procurement contract).

13 Judge (and Professor) Richard Posner, describing one of two focal policies animating the law of trade secret protection, said this about similarly unproductive effort: "The second [view of trade secret law] emphasizes *the desirability of encouraging inventive activity by protecting its fruits from efforts at appropriation that are, indeed, sterile wealth-redistributive – not productive – activities.*" *Rockwell Graphic Sys., Inc.* v. *DEV Indus., Inc.*, 925 F.2d 174, 178 (7th Cir. 1991) (Posner, J.) (emphasis added). The Judge here differentiates between two types of activity: one productive ("inventive activity") and one unproductive or "sterile" ("appropriation"). The latter type of activity is not worth encouraging, and in fact should be discouraged. It redistributes, instead of adding to, existing wealth. What *is* worth encouraging is "productive . . . activities": activities that increase collective, and not just individual, welfare. Said differently, rent-seeking investments increase one's slice of an existing pie. Productive investments make more pies.

14 This example comes from a foundational article, Anne O. Krueger, *The Political Economy of the Rent-Seeking Society*, 64 Am. Econ. Rev. 291 (1974).

15 Notice I said this holds for "the classic treatment of international trade." Contemporary debate in this area embraces the costs to workers of replacing domestic with foreign production, possible ecological impacts (e.g., if the foreign manufacturers of a product produce more carbon than domestic ones do), and other factors such as national security that add complexity to trade theory.

It is easy to see how the patent system might be used to generate rents that fit the same pattern. A "patent" on all soft drinks, for example, would give its holder enormous economic power. The makers of Coke, Pepsi, and a host of other soft drinks would spend big to capture such a rent. Whichever government agency were in charge of granting this soft drink patent would be inundated with lobbyists, each armed with elaborate arguments and campaign contributions to match. From an economic point of view, little good can come from this spending. Every dollar paid to lobbyists is a dollar less to spend on consumer discounts, product improvements, and the like. The asset being sought is a government-backed right to lower competition. The higher cost to consumers and the competition *for* this "patent" right would both contribute to economic waste.

This is (I hope!) a fanciful scenario. The legal requirements of patentability – novelty, nonobviousness, adequate disclosure, and the like – were fashioned over time to prevent issuance of our hypothetical soft drink patent, and anything like it. Yet there are still at times opportunities for seeking smaller rents under the rubric of the patent system. The legislative extension of a patent otherwise due to expire is a simple case: The extra profit that would be earned during the extension period is an attractive prize, one that might well justify considerable expenditures for lobbying. A more common case is when an inventor tries to obtain a patent that covers more than he or she actually taught or disclosed, that is, an unduly broad patent. A number of patent requirements are in place to police this, but they do not always work as intended. Some overly broad patents slip through the system despite best efforts to stop them.

These expansive patents, combined with features of patent litigation, create good conditions for rent-seeking. Rents take the form of court decisions and private settlements that overvalue patents relative to the true merits of the inventions they cover.[16] The extreme cases are the vague and overbroad patents that should never have been issued in the first place. Owners of these patents, often firms specializing in patent assertion and litigation, sometimes use them to extract considerable profit from innovative and efficient companies. Aggressive use of the patent system, including by those whose inventive contributions might be seen as minor, has been

[16] On the analogy of the import quotas from the classic rent-seeking literature, the overbroad patents are like the import quota allotments. The cost of filing and pursuing useable, overbroad yet plausibly valid patents, or buying such patents held by others, the cost of re-shaping them (where possible) using various patent system maneuvers (amending pending applications, patent re-issues, etc.), the cost of figuring out which big companies might be infringing the patents, the cost of filing suit against several such companies, the costs of litigation and/or negotiation of settlements – all these expenditures are the equivalent of the allotment-seeking lobbying costs in the import quota example. It makes no difference, from the perspective of rent-seeking theory, that in litigation money is spent trying to use court procedures to capture a valuable prize (a damages award or negotiated settlement). These are still expenditures made to influence a government process (here, litigation) in pursuit of a government-backed right (a final judgment or court order, or the threat of one). In short, rents.

part of the patent system from the beginning. In the latter nineteenth century, there were enough specialist firms of this kind that they earned their own moniker: patent sharks. At the beginning of the twenty-first century, the popular name was patent troll. Whatever the era, whatever the label, the substance is the same. Patents are used not to further the traditional goal of promoting innovation. They act as a wasteful tax on true innovators, transferring money from active, productive firms to firms whose sole purpose is acquiring and making money from patents.

Anyone who reads IP cases, or falls into a debate over IP policy, knows this: In the realm of IP, the line between a rent and a beneficial incentive can be very thin.[17] In those eras when the patent litigation-centric business model thrived, the perception of excessive, and excessively costly, patent litigation has signaled to some at least that legal reforms are in order. But those called sharks and trolls of course protest, so reform is usually a drawn-out, contested event. To the extent patent litigation-centered firms spend money defending the status quo, these expenditures too should be counted as part of their rent-seeking outlay.

1.1.2 *Productivity-Enhancing Conditions on Property Grants*

For federally granted rights, an applicant seeking title must first show some preliminary effort or investment. For land and mining claims, this means some minimum improvements (a building, planting of fields, beginning of mining operations, etc.). For an invention, the applicant must show enough research has been done to establish that the claimed invention is basically operative (i.e., meets the utility requirement) and that the inventor provides an informative description (in the patent specification) of the invention sufficient to teach others in the relevant field how the new invention works (enablement requirement). These are finely balanced policies. The required initial investment separates a land or invention patent from a mere "paper right." A speculator cannot just acquire rights on the cheap and quickly resell them to those willing to do the real development work. On the other hand, the upfront investment level cannot be set too high; asking too much would put the rights out of reach of many people. The trick to policy design is to encourage and

[17] This is true also of the line between land speculator and productive settler. See Seymour V. Connor, *Land Speculation in Texas*, 39 Southwest. Rev. 138 (1954):

> As a matter of fact the difference tween the land speculator and the land-owner seems to be one of degree rather than kind, and a really satisfactory definition for land speculation is hard to make. Was the pioneer not speculating who moved west with the frontier, buying forty, sixty, or eighty acres, clearing tract, living on it until civilization caught up with him, and selling out to move farther west.

In this example, the clearing of land and then living on it (presumably by cultivating it) constitute productive investments that were encouraged by the land patent regime. Selling the land at a profit does not take away the social benefits of these improvements, which puts this activity outside the definition of unproductive speculation.

support many individuals to develop the underlying assets (land and inventions) without transferring too much wealth to speculators and without excluding too many individuals of modest means from the chance to profit from their inventions. This in a nutshell is the democratic property strategy.

Each patent grant, however modest, represented a small dollop of federal power placed in the hands of a private citizen. While invention patents had been given as early as the fifteenth century (in Venice), and land grants were an ancient prerogative of monarchs and republics, there is a distinctly American flavor to the systematic grant of both to any ordinary citizen who meets the modest statutory requirements. The grants gave many people, most from humble origins, the right to invoke the power of the federal government to enforce their rights. The private ordering decisions that were enabled post-grant, and private control over whether and when to enforce their rights, made them property grants; the low barriers to acquisition and wide availability of the rights made them democratic.

Or, perhaps I should say, *relatively* democratic. Compared to government backing for elite-sponsored enterprises such as the Livingston steamboat (see Chapter 2), invention patents after 1820 were more democratic. But when viewed from the perspective of a black inventor, or in many cases a woman inventor,[18] the patent system was of a piece with most other legal rights – it was off limits, out of reach.[19] Patents were awarded to white citizens of even modest means, but until Emancipation in 1865, a slave, considered a non-citizen, could not obtain a patent in his or her own name. The short-lived Confederate Patent Office did permit patents on slave-created inventions, however; but with the predictable caveat that the same person who owned the slave also had ownership of a slave-invented patent.[20]

18 Deborah J. Merritt, *Hypatia in the Patent Office: Women Inventors and the Law, 1865–1900*, 35 Am. J. Legal Hist. 235 (1991) (noting the relative dearth of female inventors in patentee lists from the nineteenth century). See also Leila McNeill, These Four Black Women Inventors Reimagined the Technology of the Home, Smithsonian (February 7, 2017) (scholars "can identify only four African-American women who were granted patents for their inventions between 1865, the end of the Civil War, and the turn of the 19th century.").

19 See generally Kara W. Swanson, *Race and Selective Legal Memory: Reflections on "Invention of a Slave,"* 120 Col. L. Rev. 1077 (2020) (describing the origin and meaning of an 1858 U.S. Attorney General opinion concluding that no black person, slave or free, could be named as an inventor on a US patent); Shontavia Jackson Johnson, *The Colorblind Patent System and Black Inventors*, 11 Landslide (Am. Bar Assoc.) No. 4 (2019), available at www.americanbar.org/groups/intellectual_property_law/publications/landslide/2018-19/march-april/colorblind-patent-system-black-inventors/ (noting the many unacknowledged contributions of slaves to technical innovation, including the cases of the Eli Whitney cotton gin and the McCormick reaper, discussed in Chapters 2 and 3 of this book, respectively); Keith Aoki, *Distributive and Syncretic Motives in Intellectual Property Law (with Special Reference to Coercion, Agency, and Development)*, 40 U.C. Davis L. Rev. 717 (2007) (documenting widespread prohibitions on participation of slaves in property ownership, civil litigation, etc.).

20 See Patricia Carter Sluby, The Inventive Spirit of African Americans: Patented Ingenuity (Westport, CT: Praeger Publishing, 2004), at pp. 227–228.

The trend set in the nineteenth century persists today, with black and women inventors still underrepresented in the patent rolls.[21]

1.1.3 *Patents and Business Enterprises: Adaptive Change over Time*

If anything in this book is more than a rehash of prior histories, or a litany of pet topics, it is this: a deep dive into the relationship between patents and business enterprises. In the earliest period, patents and related government franchises often covered entire economic markets (or even industries). Legal protection for a technology, in other words, translated (often intentionally) into an industry-wide exclusive franchise. The best example is the various steamboat franchises and patents, which gave legal rights not simply to a technology but to an actual market. (These are covered in Chapter 2, in the section on "Courtier Capitalism.")

In these "franchises" or "privileges," the scope of the exclusive grant was tied not just to technical features but also to entire new technologies, and hence the market that these technologies defined. Livingston's grant from the State of New York, for example, covered, quite broadly, "the sole and exclusive right and privilege" of making, using, and navigating "all and every species or kinds of boats, or water craft, which might be urged or impelled through the water, by the force of fire or steam."[22] A New York State court, in a decision from 1812, even took pains, while upholding the validity of a concurrent state franchise, to distinguish the New York State grant from a true federal patent right:

> [T]he respondents [Van Ingen, trying to break into the New York steamboat business] show no patent, and the appellants [Livingston et al.] have not obtained their grant, as inventors of the steam-boat, and, therefore, the privilege is totally unconnected with the patent power. It seems to be admitted that [the U.S.] congress are authorized to grant patents only to the *inventor* of the useful art.[23]

21 See Colleen V. Chien, *The Inequalities of Innovation*, Emory L.J. (2020), available at https://papers.ssrn.com/sol3/papers.cfm?abstract_id=3157983; Lisa D. Cook and Chaleampong Kongcharoen, The Idea Gap in Pink and Black (Nat'l Bureau of Econ. Res., Working Paper No. 16331) (September 2010) (identifying African American and women inventors using various methods, discussing under-representation of these groups in patent lists, but noting that black and women innovators have a better record in commercializing innovations than the patent data would suggest). Women inventors may have been rare, but they made important contributions, as we see in Chapter 3 with the story of Margaret E. Knight, a major inventive force in a number of nineteenth-century industries. Aside from her pioneering paper bag machine (about which Chapter 3 has much to say), she contributed other patented inventions in papermaking as well as other industries, including the shoe industry and the automotive field. See Henry Petroski, *The Evolution of the Grocery Bag*, 72 Am. Schol. 99, 101 (2003); Zorina Khan, *"Not for Ornament": Patenting Activity by Nineteenth Century Women Inventors*, 31 J. Interdisc. Hist. 159, 184 (2000).

22 Camilla A. Hrdy, *State Patent Laws in the Age of Laissez Faire*, 28 Berkeley Tech. L.J. 45, 78 (2013) (citing and quoting the New York grant).

23 *Livingston* v. *Van Ingen*, 1812 WL 1156 (N.Y. 1812) (defending right of states to grant privileges to entrepreneurs, and even to grant "patents of importation," i.e., protection for technologies

This was right in line with the pattern laid down in Great Britain in the early years of its patent system: The focus was on technologies, conceived of as coextensive with the new markets they opened up.

This betrayed a conception of state franchises as applying to a technology-market-industry triad. The goal, as a policy matter, was to confer exclusivity over the *market* that would be created (and defined) by a new technology. Though technological parameters were used to define the protected market, the focal point of the government franchise (or privilege) was to confer exclusivity over the market itself. Government and a well-connected private party combined forces,[24] under the auspices of a government grant, to directly stimulate the development of a market for a new product type – such as the steamboat – whose diffusion and improvement was thought to provide self-evident advantages for society at large.

The conception and scope of early privileges made them most often coextensive with the market for a new type of product or service. Although some post-grant transactions were likely contemplated (including perhaps various financing arrangements and exclusive regional operators or licensees), the market-wide scope of the right makes it unlikely that anyone imagined the right might form an input into a

imported from overseas (and perhaps from other states)), overruled in part by *North River Steamboat Co.* v. *Livingston*, 1825 WL 1859, at *3 (Ct. Corr. Err., N.Y. [New York State highest court] 1825) ("The state grant is in force, only when and where, the right to navigate from state to state [i.e., the federally derived navigation right], is not exercised."). The *North River Steamboat* case reconsidered the prior *Van Ingen* ruling in light of the intervening landmark U.S. Supreme Court decision in *Gibbons* v. *Ogden*, 22 U.S. 1, 221 (1824) (commerce clause in U.S. Constitution implicitly pre-empts any state regulation of interstate commerce; federal navigation statute is supreme over conflicting state acts).

24 Historians have argued that the screen between public and private spheres was quite diaphanous in the early federal period. See, e.g., Gordon S. Wood, *The Origins of Vested Rights in the Early Republic*, 85 Va. L. Rev. 1421 (1999). Wood says:

> [A]ll government in the colonial period was regarded essentially as the enlisting and mobilizing of the power of private persons to carry out public ends . . . If the eighteenth-century city of New York wanted its streets cleaned or paved, for example, it did not hire contractors or create a "public works" department; instead it issued ordinances obliging each person in the city to clean or repair the street abutting his house or shop. In the same way if the colony of Connecticut wanted a college, it did not build and run the college itself, but instead gave legal rights to private persons to build and run it – in short, creating what were called corporations. Most public action – from the building of wharves and ferries to the maintaining of roads and inns – depended upon private energy and private funds. Governments were always short of revenue and instead tended to rely mostly on the legal authority they possessed. They issued sanctions against private persons for failure to perform their public duties, and they enticed private persons into fulfilling public goals by offering corporate charters, licenses, and various other legal immunities together with fee-collecting offices. Thus were private and public spheres blurred.

Ibid., 85 Va. L. Rev. 1421, 1431, citing Hendrik Hartog, Public Property and Private Power: The Corporation of the City of New York in American Law, 1730–1870, at 62 (1983) ("Governments [in this early period] did not act so much as they ensured and sanctioned the actions of others.").

larger product or might be combined with other rights in a joint venture, or any similar transactions. The right was thought of, in an implicit way, as akin to a permit to operate a business – under the grant, the only permissible business of its type, as defined by the technology employed. Patents, to put it simply, were meant to confer a right to operate not just a single business organization but an entire *type of* business.

It took time for this notion of patents to fade away. Signs of change began in the early nineteenth century, an era when large-scale, automated textile factories began appearing on the banks of New England rivers. The authorization to raise capital and own assets on this scale came not in the form of a government franchise but in the form of a state corporate charter. These newly formed companies sometimes acquired patents, some of which were quite valuable. The large textile firms were in this respect a prototype for later companies. The textile firms accumulated multiple, related patents on various machines, components, and systems used in their factories. They acquired and deployed patents as business assets, using them to maintain competitive advantage over certain features of textile production, and to protect profit margins, so some of the firm's earnings could be plowed back into research on new and better machinery.

One critique of invention patents originated in response to this trend. "Corporatization," it was said, betrayed the democratic character of the patent system.[25] Big companies displaced individual inventors as patent owners after 1880. According to this view, once patent ownership passed from individual inventors to large corporations, the patent system had abandoned its founding charter. Patents were converted from incentives aimed at individuals and small companies to a tool of corporate power and control.

No doubt, the nineteenth century presented the patent system with numerous challenges, as described in depth in Chapter 4. But in my view the "corporatization" critique depends on a distorted picture of the pre-corporate era. Patents, particularly those on valuable inventions, were from the start co-owned by investors, turned over to partnerships, and used as the central locus of networks of regional franchise owners. Patents were used as the scaffolding around which private enterprises were built. There is a persistent Jeffersonian myth surrounding patents, the idea of the "small inventor" creating a new technology and closely holding a patent to earn a profit. But this was never really the dominant pattern, even in the earliest years of the system. It's true that patents did not become common corporate property until the late nineteenth century. But that's because there were very few corporations until then. (And as mentioned, the private corporations that were chartered, such as textile manufacturing plants in Massachusetts, held many patents). Once the notion of a Jeffersonian golden age is set aside, it is easier to see that patents and patent

[25] See, e.g., Jay Dratler, Jr., *Incentives for People: The Forgotten Purpose of the Patent System*, 16 Harv. J. Legis. 129 (1979).

ownership developed over time in keeping with the needs, requirements, and constraints of the changing national economy. They were – like their cousins, federal debt and federal land patents – protean assets born from the new Republic and intended to promote commerce and economic growth. Invention patents exemplified the democratic property strategy of the mid-nineteenth century, but they were never a static presence in the American economy.

From my perspective the increase in corporate patent ownership in the late nineteenth century was more a fulfillment of patent law's founding charter than a betrayal of it. It was part of the move to much higher levels of capital investment, which in turn fed the growth of large-scale corporate research. Corporate ownership did support increases in enterprise scale and scope, but it did not by itself inevitably produce industry-spanning market monopolies. Finally, the emergence of patent-related tactics as an aspect of competitive corporate strategy was not in itself anything new. Private enterprises prior to 1880 put patents into action in a number of ways: to structure an enterprise, to coordinate regional partners, to protect market share or profit margins, and so on. Chapters 2 and 3 show this quite plainly.

Disillusion with patents as tools of big industry takes attention away from the place of patents among the ranks of small companies, especially new entrants (startup companies). In industries as diverse as auto parts, audio recording, and synthetic materials, they also helped upstart companies gain a secure foothold in highly competitive industries. The durable role of patents in service of new firm entry continued, even as ever-larger patent portfolios raised concerns as a barrier to entry during the rise of antitrust enforcement, first in the Progressive Era (c. 1910) and then the high point of antitrust enforcement after 1930. After the coming of the Federal Circuit in 1982, patents received a boost that was noticed by venture capitalists and other investors. Therefore, patents' place in the world of business changed again: They became important assets in the dynamic world of venture-backed startup companies. Increased patent value also brought a familiar phenomenon: another wave of rent-seeking litigation in the form of patent trolls presented major challenges after the late 1990s. But by 2020, many patent reforms had begun to do their work, following the same pattern as the late nineteenth-century cycle of excessive litigation followed by reformist legal change. Litigation once again appeared to be in slight retreat, and the patent system seemed poised to return to a more constructive, if perhaps more modest, role in the American business enterprise.

1.1.3.1 An Example of Adaptive Change: The Law of Patent Assignments

Patents, as I said, provided the core kernel around which a series of private arrangements could be structured. They provided part of the legal infrastructure for private ordering. The following chapters are full of examples, but to illustrate what post-patent-grant private ordering actually looks like, and how patent doctrine facilitates that ordering, consider the example of patent assignments. Patent assignments made an important contribution to the financing of inventions and regional patent-based franchises from the earliest years of the patent system. Though the blunt purpose of assignments is to transfer an ownership interest, there were a few steps to making general assignment law adjust to the needs of early American inventive enterprise. So, the rise of a distinct body of *patent* assignment law makes for a nice case study.

The first step was to enable partial assignments of patent rights. In an era before corporations were common, partial ownership turned patent rights into something like corporate stock. In general, a partial patent assignment formed a co-ownership arrangement, which gave each co-owner an undivided partial share in the entire patent right. Without a corporate structure, without even a partnership contract, a patent provided an off-the-rack organizational structure. An ownership and governance structure was created automatically, in the form of co-ownership rules, when part of a patent was assigned.

Allocating partial ownership shares to investors is a good way to raise capital for overall operations. It was common from the very earliest days of the patent system for patents to issue to the inventor and an assignee – which signifies that the inventor drew an investor even before the patent grant. We will see this and many variations in the business uses of patent in the chapters ahead. Multi-tiered enterprises (with patents broken into half interests, quarter interests, thirty-seconds interests, etc.), built around patent-based partnership agreements, were very common. Partial owners both financed new technologies and, depending on the terms of patent partnership agreements, lent a hand to the management of the enterprise as well.

The other type of partial assignment conferred ownership of an exclusive territory. Patent owners often assigned exclusive rights to limited regions (such as Massachusetts only, or to only the cities of Boston, Cambridge, and Watertown). These made each regional assignee the sole owner of the patent in the assignee's limited region. Regional assignments in effect created franchises: a central patent-owning partnership granted exclusive territories to independent regional investor/operators. A federal court procedural rule that grew up around this practice gave regional owners the right to enforce their patent interest in their exclusive territory. (Thus, the owner of the rights to Massachusetts had standing to sue anyone infringing the patent in a federal court in Massachusetts.)

And so, the two types of assignment served different ends. Partial interests in the complete patent were assigned to raise money and give investors an ownership stake in the core asset of the partnership (the patent). Exclusive regional assignments facilitated formation of decentralized, autonomous franchises. Through this simple example we see the diversity of business arrangements that sprang into shape from the very beginning of federal patent grants.

The law of assignments is a good example of the interaction between the needs of business enterprise and the specific doctrinal and administrative adjustments of the patent system.[26] There are many other examples of this process at work throughout this book: One of the book's central themes is the persistence and pervasiveness of adaptive legal change.

As with so much in the US economy, the place of patents in the business enterprise changed in the late nineteenth century. General incorporation laws ended the days when partial patent arrangements and partnerships dominated the business landscape, growing mechanization led to more complex technologies, and an increase in efficient scale called for larger capital investments in many industries. It became increasingly rare for an enterprise to be founded on a single patent, and more common for growing corporations to assemble portfolios of patents. Regional franchise arrangements, so common in the 1860s and 1870s, were slowly replaced by single corporations with national reach, thanks to general incorporation laws, as well as the new nationwide reach of technologies for communication (the telegraph) and transportation (railroads). For a brief period in the latter nineteenth century, free-lance inventors enjoyed a heyday providing technical solutions across an array of industries. But the rise of companies with unprecedented economies of scale and scope brought with it the advent of the centralized corporate research and development (R&D) division. Companies such as General Electric, AT&T, and DuPont strove to create an assembly line of useable research tailored to the needs of each industry. Though new companies continued to enter the economy with innovative products, large, centralized R&D labs became a highly significant participant in the patent system.

Patent law underwent waves of adaptive change in tandem with the development of technology and shifts in the structure of business enterprises. I am most interested in how the patent system, as an institution, became transfigured over time. A simple economic theory says that property rights adjust over time with alterations in the value of underlying assets: The rights that cover an asset change along with shifts in value of the asset itself. There is little doubt that new ideas, inventions, and technology in general have vastly increased in value since the 1790s. Therefore, there is no surprise that patents have become more numerous and more powerful since that time as well.

But this is an abstraction, a generalization. I am interested in the details: in the specific ways that patent doctrine and administration have changed over time. In this spirit I trace the development of important features of the patent system. I study the origin of formal patent examination in 1836, and the creation of the "invention test" in 1851, a new patent requirement that sprang up to weed out trivial patents. Both came during an era when patenting activity was increasing, and in response to

[26] An example of an administrative, as opposed to doctrinal, adjustment was the development of Patent Office record-keeping related to assignments – a public registry that could be searched by anyone wanting to know who owned a patent, whether the inventor had assigned to co-owners, and, later, whether the patent had been used to secure a loan (i.e., was mortgaged) or served as collateral for an ancillary debt (i.e., was subject to a lien).

profit-making from weak or improvidently issued patents. Later, courts worked out the law of improvement patents and improvised the double patenting rule, to adjust to the more numerous and fine-grained patent rights that accompanied the diffusion of mechanization and the more complex technologies and products that followed. Throughout, the law has reacted to patent-related businesses that profit from valuable rights while contributing little or nothing to innovation – to rent-seeking, as defined earlier. In several eras, the patent system has been consumed with the need to end rent-seeking and steer investment back into real research.

Important public policy issues pervade the grant and enforcement of every patent. The scope and duration of each right restricts the free actions of third parties, while the lure of rights may contribute to or detract from the society-wide supply of knowledge, ideas, and information. Certainly, government suppression of information is a classic public law issue, concerning as it does the relationship between the individual and the state. By the same token, intellectual property, including patent law, significantly affects an individual's access to information, broadly conceived. The literature on intellectual property is full of many things, but one surely is this: Intellectual property is a branch of public law. The federal government grants these rights, and the economic power the rights confer must be policed and patrolled carefully by that same government. Classic public law material.

All true. But patent owners are also deeply interested in patent law, not because it encapsulates all manner of important policies, but because it shapes the parameters of an asset type on which some businesses depend. These businesses do all sorts of things with this asset: They acquire and bundle it with other assets to create a legal embankment, designed to slow down or keep out competitors; they use it and possibly others like it to bring a lawsuit against a competitor whose products threaten to undermine the asset owner's revenues; they write contracts allowing others to use the asset in productive ways, in exchange for royalties; they pledge it as collateral for loans; they offer it for sale on a specialized market; they trade rights to it in exchange for the right to use similar assets held by others; and so on. Each tactic is chosen to advance a particular strategy.

From the vantage point of a patent owner, then, patents are classic instruments of private law. A patent is an asset that promotes private ordering: the complex collaborations and organizational structures that are formed around a handful of simple but sturdy legal tools. I find both the public and private law aspects of patents equally interesting and equally important in the field. But if I am biased (and what author isn't?), on this score I would probably lean toward the private law side. First, because it's been a bit slighted in the main run of scholarship. And second (a possibly related point), it's the side of patent law that has always interested me the most.

1.1.4 *Founding Era Political Economy*

Lobbyists were not unknown in the early days of the American Republic. We see in Chapter 2 several historical figures mounting impressive influence campaigns to further their capital-intensive industry-building schemes. Robert Livingston and his steamboat head up that particular regatta. But to the founding generation, "political economy" did not mean the economic study of resource expenditures on political benefits. It meant the study of ways to deploy state resources to advance a nation's economy.[27] If the presence of lobbyists in the early years is no surprise, the nation- and economy-building strategy of the founders is. To a degree not often equaled elsewhere at the time, the early US government adopted policies that cleverly rationed its small but promising power. It granted individual ownership rights, backed by federal authority, to widely dispersed citizens with diverse economic plans and prospects. Later, from this rough-and-ready early period, small but specialized government agencies emerged – the Land Office and the Patent Office.

Eighteenth-century governments had certainly tried to use land policy to contribute to economic growth. The young United States was hardly unique in this respect. Notable examples were the British efforts at land reform, first in Ireland and later in Scotland.[28] The Irish schemes covered vast acreage, assigning ownership (usually to nobles) of large tracts, with a plan for owners to rent out plots for family farms.[29] The idea behind Scottish policy was to break the hold of feudal relationships and traditional economic culture by converting rent into a contractual rather than duty-based obligation, promoting commercial agriculture, and building a network of roads connecting the Highlands with market centers. Economic relations based on British-style land holding and use patterns were supposed to help open the economy to

[27] See generally, Joel Mokyr, The Enlightened Economy: An Economic History of Britain 1700–1850 (New Haven, CT: Yale University Press, 2010). Another critical policy arena was trade and importation. See R. Davis, *The Rise of Protection in England, 1689–1786*, 19 Econ. Hist. Rev. (2nd ser.) 306 (1966); P. O'Brien, T. Griffiths, and P. Hunt, *Political Components of the Industrial Revolution: Parliament and the English Cotton Textile Industry, 1660–1774*, 44 Econ. Hist. Rev. (2nd ser.) 395 (1991).

[28] The land schemes known as "plantations" in Ireland beginning in the sixteenth century were prototypes for politico-economic reform via land policy. See, e.g., Annaleigh Margey, *Plantations, 1550–1641*, Chapter 22, vol. 2, in Jane Ohlmyer, ed., Cambridge History of Ireland (Cambridge: Cambridge University Press, 2nd ed., 2018), at pp. 555 et seq. It goes without saying that many ancient communities were uprooted to make way for these plantations; a sad story for another day.

[29] On Ireland, see Annaleigh Margey, Plantations, at p. 568:

> [In the Irish plantation scheme in the Munster region of Ireland from the 1580s,] the estate or seignory sizes were ... [set] at 12,000, 8,000, 6,000 and 4,000 acres. Each seignory was to be settled by an "undertaker", who undertook to bring ninety-one Englishmen to the estate within seven years. The completion date was set as Christmas 1594. The [plantation] commission proposed rents at differing rates across the province, depending on the estate size.

For Scotland, see Christopher Dudley, *Party Politics, Political Economy, and Economic Development in Early Eighteenth-Century Britain*, 66 Econ. Hist. Rev. 1084 (2013). As with the early United States, there were obviously strong elements of conquest and native displacement in these policies as well. Also much death and suffering, making the settlers' title of "undertaker" into a grim double entendre.

commercialization and industrialization.[30] Despite the grant of large tracts, these development plans were not just for the benefit of land-owning nobles. They were also designed to influence the economic prospects of small farmers as well. In this and in other ways, there is evidence that British colonial strategy was, overall, more decentralized than parallel policies of other imperial powers such as Spain. This had implications for general settlement patterns and immigration, among other things.[31]

Yet even in the overall context of eighteenth-century land policies, the American approach stands out.[32] It had a distinctive mixture of three characteristics: it was quite democratic (for its time), handing out small parcels to millions of new owners;[33] it was linked explicitly to promoting foreign immigration; and it was, by dint of the vast reaches of unclaimed (from the settler's viewpoint) government land,[34] huge in scale. These three features of US policy amplified the economic

[30] See Christopher Dudley, *Party Politics, Political Economy, and Economic Development in Early Eighteenth-Century Britain*, 66 Econ. Hist. Rev. 1084 (2013), at pp. 1089–1090.

[31] See Stanley L. Engerman and Kenneth L. Sokoloff, *Once Upon a Time in the Americas: Land and Immigration Policies in the New World*, in Dora L. Costa and Naomi R. Lamoreaux, eds., Understanding Long-Run Economic Growth: Geography, Institutions, and the Knowledge Economy (Chicago: University of Chicago Press, on behalf of the National Bureau of Economic Research, 2011), at p. 18 (discussing the related area of immigration policy):

> [An] important factor behind the maintenance of the strict limitations on immigration, in our view, was the greater centralization or concentration of political authority [in Spanish colonies]. Not only did the imposed controls apply to immigration to all of the Spanish colonies in the Americas, but centering the government structures for Spanish America in Mexico City and Lima meant that outlying areas with different conditions and demands for labor … were largely deprived of autonomy or even influence in policy.

On the comparison of later land and development policies in Latin America and the United States, see Hernando de Soto, The Mystery of Capital: Why Capitalism Triumphs in the West and Fails Everywhere Else (New York: Basic Books, 2000), at p. 7 (detailing the advantages of effective and generally available government agencies for granting title to homes and goods, chartering corporations, etc.). On land and the economic gains from secure title, in South America and elsewhere, see Lee J. Alston, Gary Libecap, and Bernardo Mueller, Titles, Conflict, and Land Use: The Development of Property Rights and Land Reform on the Brazilian Amazon Frontier (Ann Arbor: University of Michigan Press, 1999).

[32] Stanley L. Engerman and Kenneth L. Sokoloff, *Land and Immigration Policies in the New World*, at p. 27:

> It is perhaps worth highlighting how different the attention to, and prevalence of, land ownership was in the northern part of North America as compared to Europe. Tenancy and farm labor were clearly much more common in Britain and France than in their American colonies on the mainland.

[33] Gregory Ablavsky, Federal Ground: Governing Property and Violence in the First U.S. Territories (Oxford: Oxford University Press, 2021), at p. 104 (describing small-parcel land sales policy embodied, e.g., in the Harrison Land Act of 1800, which was explicitly designed, in the words of its sponsor, "to give more favorable terms to that class of purchasers who are likely to become actual settlers"; this Act set the maximum purchase size at 640 acres or one "section" of federal land).

[34] See Stuart Banner, How the Indians Lost Their Land: Law and Power on the Frontier (Cambridge, MA: Belknap Press, Harvard University, 2007).

influence of government grants to private citizens. In 1796, the *minimum* parcel size a citizen could buy was 640 acres (260 hectares).[35] By 1832, Jacksonian times, this was down to 40 acres (16 hectares). The per-acre price dropped from $2.00 per acre in 1796 to $1.25 after 1820. Taken together, this meant that the minimum buy-in cost for a piece of the young country fell from $1280 in 1796 to $50 in 1832. Economic historians Stanley Engerman and Ken Sokoloff summarized it this way, "That the westward movement [in the United States] accelerated over the nineteenth century, and that more individuals from lower income groups were able to acquire land, was to no small degree attributable to the liberal land policies."[36]

Patent policy was quite similar, in a number of ways. Cheap land and invention patents were both consciously intended to alleviate the shortage of labor. Land sales attracted immigration, affecting labor on the supply side. Patents stimulated creation and diffusion of labor-saving technology, which reduced the number of workers required to achieve a given level of output. They came at the problem from different angles, but both were aimed at compensating for an initial (founding era) factor endowment problem: very low population density, when projected over the unexplored territory the new nation planned to develop.

But there were other, deeper similarities between initiatives for cheap land and equal-opportunity patenting. Both embodied what might be called a property-based governmental strategy – a combination of public and private elements calculated to best spur growth under the conditions of the time.[37] The public component came straight out of the Constitution: The Constitution lists both land sales and invention patent grants among the powers held by Congress.[38] Thus, federal land and invention certificates represented concrete manifestations of the Congressional desire for economic development. Alexander Hamilton's plan for government debt made

35 Figures in this paragraph are from Stanley L. Engerman and Kenneth L. Sokoloff, *Land and Immigration Policies in the New World*, at p. 29.

36 Stanley L. Engerman and Kenneth L. Sokoloff, *Land and Immigration Policies in the New World*, at p. 31.

37 There was never a pitched policy battle over patent policy as there was for land policy. See Gregory Ablavsky, Federal Ground: Governing Property and Violence in the First U.S. Territories, at p. 51. ("[T]he intense fights over land distribution in the post-Revolutionary U. S. were contests about democracy and political economy.") By contrast, the democratic tilt of patent law was not the product of a single top-down policy choice. It resulted instead from a series of incremental choices and trends, each of which was highly influenced by ambient Jacksonian principles (low application fees, opposition to industry-spanning privileges, a generally egalitarian spirit, etc.).

38 See U.S. Constitution, Article I, Section 8, clause 8 (Intellectual Property Clause): "Congress shall have the power … To promote the progress of science and useful arts, by securing for limited times to authors and inventors the exclusive right to their respective writings and discoveries."); Article IV, section 3, par. 2 (land clause): "The Congress shall have power to dispose of and make all needful rules and regulations respecting the territory or other property belonging to the United States; and nothing in this Constitution shall be so construed as to prejudice any claims of the United States, or of any particular state."

Treasury certificates into a tradable financial asset, thus introducing increasing liquidity into the national economy. In much the same way, federal land and invention patents were traded on crude secondary markets, at times feeding speculative activity.[39] More importantly, both were federally backed assets around which deals could be made and partnerships could be structured.[40] By analogy with federal debt instruments, patents introduced hard, federally backed assets into the stream of commerce, thus stabilizing and stimulating economic development.

There is a final commonality uniting land and invention patents. They both made good use of another of the limited instrumentalities of federal power – the federal courts.[41] In battles over land claims where one or more claimant held a US land patent, the federal courts had jurisdiction. They consistently carved out a broad

[39] On the market for regional patent rights, see Chapter 3. There were also markets for government land rights, some of which took the form of "land scrip" – government certificates conferring the right to select a parcel from available federal lands (a "location" or "entry" right). See, e.g., *Jay* v. *Dollarhide*, 3 Cal. App. 3d 1001, 1015, 84 Cal. Rptr. 538, 546 (Ct. App. 1970) ("[U]nder [certain federal] acts respecting the ... public lands, land rights were bought and sold on the market as 'land scrip,' passing by assignment"). See generally, Paul Wallace Gates, *The Role of the Land Speculator in Western Development*, 66 Pa. Mag. Hist. Bio. 314 (1942); W. W. Robinson, Land in California: The Story of Mission Lands, Ranchos, Squatters, Mining Claims, Railroad Grants, Land Scrip, Homesteads (Berkeley: University of California Press, 1948), at chapter VIII ("Land Scrip"), pp. 177–189. See also ibid., at pp. 179–181, detailing the story of one large block of scrip, "Valentine Scrip," representing land claims on over 13,000 acres in California: "Speculators got some [of the Valentine] scrip, to peddle along with other types of scrip." Valentine received his scrip in a special Act of Congress, but much of it originated with government grants to military veterans and the individual states in the United States. The latter grants were made under the Morrill Act, P.L. 37-503 (37th Cong., 2d sess.), 12 Stat. 503, codified at 7 U.S.C. §301 et seq. (1862) (later replaced by a similar Act). They allowed States to sell land rights and use the money to establish "land grant" (state, or public) colleges for the study of agriculture and related fields. See Gregory J. Vincent, *Reviving the Land-Grant Idea through Community-University Partnerships*, 31 South. U. L. Rev. 1, 9 (2003) (history of Morrill Act). It was thought unwise to permit a state to directly own property in other states, so § 302 of the Morrill Act prohibited this. But assignees of land rights could choose property anywhere in the United States, which meant that Morrill Act scrip necessarily passed through a market before being turned into specific land claims. See ibid.: "In no case shall any State to which land scrip may thus be issued be allowed to locate the same within the limits of any other State, or of any Territory of the United States, but their assignees may thus locate said land scrip upon any of the unappropriated lands of the United States subject to sale at private entry at $1.25, or less, per acre ... " Note also the price ceiling: a form of government regulation on the behavior of speculators, in service of democratic policies favoring low-cost land.

[40] For more on patents and different forms of business enterprise, see Chapters 2 and 3. For more on the market for federal land titles and efforts to rein in property speculation, see Gregory Ablavsky, Federal Ground: Governing Property and Violence in the First U.S. Territories, at pp. 77 and 104.

[41] See Gregory Ablavsky, Federal Ground: Governing Property and Violence in the First U.S. Territories, at chapter 3, "The Rise of Federal Title," pp. 79–105.

swath of federal influence where state law (which covers most property issues) arguably was in conflict.[42] As for invention patents, cases involving them represented a significant portion of the federal caseload in the early years of the Republic. Patent disputes stood alongside cases on import duties, maritime trade (admiralty), bankruptcy, and federally related land claims as the main aspects of the new economy under the direct supervision of federal law.

So, both land and invention patents were federal assets. They were backstopped by federal courts. This highlights another point of contact between the two types of government grants. For both, rights were vested in individuals and enforced by individuals. They were unquestionably *private* entitlements. The power of the federal state was embodied in the grant, but decisions about whether, when and where to enforce them were left to their owners. Enforcement brought government power to bear, but through the instrumentality of the courts. Not all patents are enforced; patent owners choose to litigate only a small portion, usually. Private enforcement conserves on government resources: Government time and power are devoted only to patents valuable enough (in the eyes of their holder) to be worth the expensive privilege of federal litigation. At a time when federal power was in limited supply, and federal presence was thin on the ground in some places, yoking the courts to invention promotion and economic development made sense. In keeping with the limited resources of the federal government, court power was invoked and deployed selectively. Yet there *was* a federal district court in almost every commercially important city. That court, and the federal prestige it represented, stood behind every land title and patent issued by the government in Washington.

My main point is this: Federally backed titles, granted to individuals, were important threads in an economic development strategy woven around the twin themes of *decentralization* and *democratization*. The legal historian J. Willard Hurst captured the essence of this nineteenth-century strategy when he wrote:

> Impatient confidence in productivity, and hence in any positive or restrictive uses of law which would free more units of production, was natural to our situation. We came from a scarcity-conscious Old World into a rude new land where our own

[42] *Gibson* v. *Chouteau*, 80 U.S. 92, 99 (1871):

> With respect to the public domain, the Constitution vests in Congress the power of disposition and of making all needful rules and regulations. That power is subject to no limitations. Congress has the absolute right to prescribe the times, the conditions, and the mode of transferring this property, or any part of it, and to designate the persons to whom the transfer shall be made. No State legislation can interfere with this right or embarrass its exercise …

See generally, Gregory Ablavsky, Federal Ground: Governing Property and Violence in the First U.S. Territories, at chapter 3, "The Rise of Federal Title" (detailing the work taken on by governors of the Territories (e.g., the Northwest Territory) in resolving conflicting claims to land title, deriving from a mélange of state law, colonial era grants from European powers, and Native American land claiming rules and practices).

> capital scarcity was a fact continuously weighing on us ... We continually experienced the tangible accomplishments of individuals, small groups, and local efforts, with a heady sense of living in a fluid society in which all about him all the time one saw men moving to new positions of accomplishment and influence. Our background and experience in this country taught faith in the capacities of the productive talent residing in people. The obvious precept was to see that this energy was released for its maximum creative expression.[43]

Hurst emphasizes that nineteenth-century law and government were instrumental in furthering this "release of energy." Consider patents. Each federal patent, covering land or invention, represented a small dollop of federal governmental power, conferred on and held by a private party. The latent power of the federal courts backed the right, but those courts were called into action at the behest of private rightholders involved in private disputes. Invention (or occupancy for land), capital formation, and enforcement actions – under the property strategy, all this flowed from private initiative. The great emphasis in patent history is on the patent as incentive, the lure of reward to spur invention. But by emphasizing how patents contributed to enterprise formation, investment, and business strategy, this book lends depth and detail to the incentive story. It tells something of the private (law) life of patents.

1.1.5 *Public Rights in Private Hands*

It's not that I intend to give short shrift to public law issues. It's impossible to do so while telling even a barebones version of the history of US patent law. This is evident from just two of many episodes: (1) crusades against patent litigation abuse, beginning in the nineteenth century and culminating in the patent troll controversy of recent years; plus (2) the extended period when antitrust law looked closely and skeptically at all manner of patent-related contracts (1930s to early 1960s), a time when patents were rarely discussed in elite courts without being linked to the public policies embedded in the distinctly public law field of antitrust.

I realize businesses are at most "persons" but never "people." The problems of raising money, rolling out a product, and trying to keep ahead of the competition – business problems – do not stack up well against protection of fundamental civil rights,[44] or the reach and limits of the state as against the individual. Making payroll is just not as romantic as battling Leviathan on behalf of the citizenry.

[43] James Willard Hurst, Law and the Conditions of Freedom in the Nineteenth-Century United States (Madison: University of Wisconsin Press, 1967), at p. 7. Hartog interrogates the presuppositions behind Hurst's use of "we" in passages such as this. Hendrik Hartog, *Four Fragments on Doing Legal History, or Thinking with and against Willard Hurst*, 39 L. & Hist. Rev. 835 (2021).

[44] This puts me in limited company. For many who support the view of patents as property (as against the notion of patent law as a specialized regulatory system), property rights under the US constitution have the same status as other rights. See, e.g., Richard Epstein, Takings: Private Property and the Power of Eminent Domain (Cambridge, MA: Harvard University

At the same time, at least for some of us, private law has its charms. From the first Patent Act businesses and lawyers seized on the newfound federal grants and began to deploy private law tactics in service of business strategies. Thus, the New England inventor Ithiel Town established a web of regional affiliates to construct and service local wooden bridges built according to the effective Town design. Later, the early lathe inventor Thomas Blanchard elaborated on the regional franchise structure to build an even denser network of affiliates. Patents were central to both the Town and Blanchard enterprises. For both, their regional affiliates owned exclusive rights granting them autonomy in their local territories. The affiliates were free to manage their region as they wished, deciding which local workshops to license and when to enforce the patent right against local infringers.

Patent law quickly fashioned a set of rules, many adapted from private law precedents, to facilitate these business models. The legal infrastructure drew from contracts, property assignments, partnerships, and federal court enforcement rules. But the kernel was the patent right, a small dollop of state power handed out to private enterprises all around the country. My admiration for the creativity and elegance of the structures formed around this stout little right must shine through at times. So, try as I might in this book to convey the dual nature of patents – a fit subject for both public and private law – I may fail in my attempts at balance. If I find myself giving "long shrift" (i.e., extra attention and care) to the private law side of patents, at least you the reader have been warned.

My subject is patents, but my emphasis in on business and the economy. I draw from the vast literature on the history of technology for case studies and general context. I look often to litigated cases. Each published report of a patent-related dispute is the residue of a business strategy (sue the new entrant; defend an incumbent product line; get compensated for inventing a widely used technique; etc.), and not infrequently it also tells in rich detail about the nature of an invention, as well as the patent owner's business model, investors, and contracts (regional partial owners, licensees, joint venture partners, etc.). I look, of course, to other legal materials such as legislative histories and treatises, and at contemporaneous trade publications for background on the people involved.

Most importantly, I read patents. Each tells a story: a problem faced, a solution tried, a claim staked. Collectively, they are the essence of the patent system – the

Press, 1985). Not quite, in my book; freedom of speech and voting rights, together with other civil rights, take precedence over property interests. So for me patents (and other property rights) can be regulated, and the patent system amended over time, without (in the vast number of cases) triggering a constitutional obligation to compensate patent owners under the constitution's "takings" principle. See Robert P. Merges, *What Kind of Rights Are Intellectual Property Rights?*, in Rochelle Dreyfuss and Justine Pila, eds., The Oxford Handbook of Intellectual Property Law (Oxford: Oxford University Press, 2017), at p. 33 (IP rights are definitely property rights, but "the property label does not dictate outcomes under regulatory takings doctrine"). Compare Adam Mossoff, *Patents as Constitutional Private Property: The Historical Protection of Patents under the Takings Clause*, 87 B. U. L. Rev. 689 (2007) (reaching the opposite conclusion).

many corpuscles that circulate through the bloodstream of the system, and that give it purpose and life. Throughout this book I pick out representative patents from each era and tell part of the story of the era through the life of that patent, that inventor. I do my best to describe the state of the technology and industry, the business that formed around or used the patent, and what the patent did for the business.

Here is a list of the inventors, inventions (with dates), and business enterprises described in the various case studies in this book:

Jeremiah Purdy	Maple sap bucket (1817)	Independent inventor
Ithiel Town	Lattice truss wooden bridge (1820)	Head partner of regional franchise network
D. D. Allen	Adjustable shoe peg cutting tool (1852)	Independent inventor
Henry Bessemer	Bessemer steel making process (1865)	Licensor to most major steel companies
Samuel F. B. Morse	Telegraph system and equipment (1840)	Assigned to Western Union, dominant telegraph company
Ashurst	Seed drill (1884)	Assigned to regional manufacturer Havana Press-Drill Co., in 1885
E. A. Wright	Double-action cultivator	Assigned to Eagle Mfg. Co.
Merrill and Horner	Coffin lid plate (1863)	Basis of regional franchise network among coffin makers
Hilborne Roosevelt	Hanging mouthpiece (for telephone) (1879)	Assigned to Western Electric Mfg. Co., manufacturing arm of the Bell Telephone System
George Westinghouse	Air brake for train (1869)	Assigned to Westinghouse Train Brake Co.

Elmer W. Sperry	Gyroscopic compass (1918)	Assigned to Sperry Gyroscope Co.
Edward Dayton Rockwell	Bicycle Bell (1892)	Assigned to New Departure Bell Co.
Wellington Kidder	Printing Press (1884)	Assigned to Campbell Printing Press Mfg. Co.
Margaret Knight	Paper bag making machine (1871)	Assigned to Eastern Paper Bag Co.
Charles P. Ginsburg and Shelby Henderson	Quadruplex tape recorder (1958)	Assigned to Ampex Corp.
Ray Dolby	Noise reduction systems	Assigned to Dolby Laboratories, inc.
Robert W. Gore	Polytetrafluoroethylene (Gore-Tex) (1974)	Assigned to W. L. Gore & Assocs.
John Paul Hogan and Robert L. Banks	Commercial polypropylene (1958)	Assigned to Philips Petroleum, Inc.
Miguel Angel Ondetti and David W. Cushman	Angiotensin Converting Enzyme (ACE) inhibitor (1977)	Assigned to E. R. Squibb & Sons, Inc.
Samuel A. Stranahan	Anti-shimmying device for cars	Assigned to General Motors Corp. in 1929
Gerhart S. Suppinger	Salt tablet dispenser (1936)	Assigned to Scientific Tablet Co., which became G.S. Suppinger, Inc.

Thoger Jungerson	Jewelry casting technique (1938)	Held by Jungerson as cornerstone of patent licensing and enforcement business
Walter M. Cross	Automatic Coal Feeding Furnace (1930)	Assigned to Honeywell, Inc.

These patents and business enterprises do not amount to a statistically representative sample of all US patents. But there are enough of them, from enough eras, covering enough different industries, to constitute a useful body of qualitative data. Each helps illustrate a point in the text. And taken together, they give a helpful overview of inventions and patenting since the first Patent Act.

1.2 WHAT SHAPES PATENT HISTORY? INTRINSIC FEATURES OF TECHNOLOGY AND ECONOMICS, OR GROUPS OF INFLUENTIAL PEOPLE AND THEIR SOCIAL PEERS?

It is no doubt already apparent to the trained eye what kind of history this is. It tells how patents functioned, and how those functions changed over time. It describes how adaptive changes in the law accommodated economic development and technological evolution. Patents and patent law served a valuable purpose, to support economic growth and encourage new technologies. The patent system changed over time, adjusting to changing conditions to continue in this purpose. Put simply, patents had an important function in the overall scheme of the developing US economy.

I don't study historical method, but I know enough to know that some practitioners shy away from this kind of functional account. It tends to make history just one long Carousel of Progress.[45] Functional accounts like mine can feel a bit

[45] The reference is to a long-time exhibit at Walt Disney theme parks, originally constructed by General Electric for the 1964 World's Fair in New York. See "Carousel of Progress," www.en.wikipedia.org, available at https://en.wikipedia.org/wiki/Walt_Disney%27s_Carousel_of_Progress. Similar "wow, look where we have come from and where we are going" shows and events were also sponsored by other companies. See, e.g., "General Motors Parade of Progress," available at www.gmheritagecenter.com/gm-heritage-archive/Featured_Innovations/1936_Parade_of_Progress.html (describing 1930s bus tour and road show sponsored by GM, promoting future products). See generally, David Nye, America's Technological Sublime (Cambridge, MA: MIT Press, 1994) (describing sites and projects celebrated and depicted to create feelings of awe and admiration, including the Brooklyn Bridge, Boulder Dam, and human-made environments such as Las Vegas); ibid., at pp. 289, 291 (describing Disneyland in these terms).

celebratory: project X succeeded because it had to; an invention was widely adopted because that is the only scenario that would have made sense; etc. A second critique is that these celebrations of progress pave over a lot of unpleasantness and exclude a lot of deserving people. They are at best selective; and at worst, propaganda; providing cover for a harsh and unjust back story, and thus in effect for a dark economic reality. Behind the progress story are facts like these: Inventions are helped along, and sometimes actually created, by unnamed and unsung contributors who at best merit a footnote. In many (especially older) histories, the true contributors are literally relegated to the footnotes or margins. And, to take another example, inventions are adopted without the consent, and sometimes to the detriment, of many people too low in social status to participate in decisions or show up in histories.

Another problem some have with functionalist histories is inevitability. The economy changed, new technologies emerged, and *of course* patent law adapted seamlessly and sped the entire project on down the track. It's that "of course" that rankles bona fide historians. They well know that historical events, even entire historical trajectories, are contingent. Things could have been different and maybe better. It just did not turn out that way. The economy might have bubbled along anyway even if patent law had taken different turns, or even if patents had been abolished altogether. The economy might have been stronger under different legal configurations, or in the absence of patents. History is a single-run experiment with all sorts of critical variables – variables whose fractional contribution to the final outcome cannot be known for sure.

Against these concerns, I offer two brief points in support of my version of functionalism, then enough on methodology. In my view, the strong form view of functionalism lacks subtlety and so justifies the criticism it has drawn.[46] A more reasonable version of purpose-based theories includes room for a study of *dysfunction* as well.[47] Certainly, some features of the patent system contributed to periodic

[46] Early functionalist sociologist Bronislaw Malinowski overplayed his hand with this definition in an *Encyclopedia Brittanica* entry from 1926:

> The functional view of culture insists therefore upon the principle that in every type of civilization, every custom, material object, idea and belief fulfills some vital function, has some task to accomplish, represents an indispensable part within a working whole.

Bronislaw Malinowski, "Anthropology," in Encyclopaedia Britannica (13th ed., Supp. vol. 1) pp. 131–140 (Chicago: Benton, 1926), at p. 131.

[47] See Robert K. Merton and Alice S. Rossi, Social Theory and Social Structure (New York: Free Press, 1968), at pp. 46, 47 ("[Functionalism] no more assumes that all social mechanisms are functional than the theory of biological evolution involves the comparable assumption that no dysfunctional developments occur ... [We must ask,] under which circumstances do these [identified] social mechanisms fail to operate, with resulting inefficiency, confusion, and conflict?"). See also ibid., at chapter 3 ("Manifest and Latent Functions"), which describes the sometimes "underground" or "hidden" (non-overt) functions served by some social practices. One might be tempted to assign a latent function to patent law: keeping alive a social practice that bestows distinction and attention on the act of technological innovation. This more "cultural" role might either supplement or replace a more immediately materialist

bouts of rent-seeking, during which firms were encouraged to spend more money on clever patent schemes than on the productive work of invention and product introduction (innovation). As I mentioned earlier, the "patent troll" wars that started in earnest around the year 2000 speak to the continuing threat of rent-seeking inefficiency. This book describes each episode of litigation fever the patent system has weathered: a good example of the decidedly non-perfectionist (un-Whiggish)[48] version of functionalism on offer here.

A useful and defensible version of functionalism begins with the idea of adaptive change, of interrelated aspects of society co-evolving over time. It is dynamic, not static; it trains attention on interrelationships. A précis might say: "System Part X changed, and the change influenced Part Y; then Y changed, in accord with one of its purposes of responding to change in Part X; this change in Y in turn promoted better functioning of Part X."[49] For me, this more modest variant of functionalism fits: It captures the drip-drip-drip of new inventions, and the shifting

role, i.e., the idea that patents encourage research investments that otherwise would not be made. For one version of this more cultural interpretation of patent law's function, see George Basalla, The Evolution of Technology (Cambridge: Cambridge University Press, 1988), at p. 124:

> The significance of patents is not that they offer strong and indisputable incentives for invention. The most that can be said is that at some times and under certain circumstances patents have probably been beneficial in promoting economic growth and inventiveness. In fact, the effectiveness of the patent system is less important than the fact that every industrialized country in the West has made patenting a national institution, complete with supporting bureaucracy, legislation, and state funding. When combined with the zealous pursuit of patents by industry, the existence of professional careers in patent law practice ... the popular enthusiasm for the idea of the patent, and the economist's and historian's interest in probing the meaning of patents, the result is an obsession with technological novelty that is without precedent. No other cultures have been as preoccupied with the cultivation, production, diffusion, and legal control of new machines, tools, devices and processes as Western culture has been since the eighteenth century.

48 The reference is to "Whig history," a type of historical writing describing events as a steady progression toward freedom, enlightenment, and progress in general. See Herbert Butterfield, The Whig Interpretation of History (New York: Norton, 1931). For an assessment, see William Cronon, "From the President: Two Cheers for the Whig Interpretation of History," Perspectives on History: Newsletter of the American Historical Association, September 1, 2012, available at www.historians.org/publications-and-directories/perspectives-on-history/september-2012/two-cheers-for-the-whig-interpretation-of-history (appraisal of Butterfield's book and the history-as-progress historians it critiqued, written while historian Cronon was President of the American Historical Association).

49 See generally Siegfried Karsten, *Dialectics, Functionalism, and Structuralism, in Economic Thought*, 42 Am. J. Econ. & Soc. 179 (1983), at p. 179 (emphasis in original):

> [Functionalism and Structuralism] emphasize *communication*, *feedback*, and *continuity*. The aim of these methodologies is to facilitate the analyses of changes in interrelationships which constitute the processes of evolution. The economist is concerned with the theoretical analysis of socioeconomic processes. His task can be facilitated by describing and analyzing structural-functional relationships of the *economy* and its parts.

currents of patent law in rough synch with developments in business and finance. For my story, technologies, business enterprises, and patent law fit together in a tight functionalist braid. I do not say the patent system was perfect, inevitable, or even demonstrably beneficial by any empirical measure.[50] I do say that the three elements of the braid I mentioned changed shape over time in response to each other. And that the purposive thrust of the system was always aimed, in a general way, at productivity-enhancing new technologies, technology-embracing enterprise, and economic growth. Episodic dysfunction – typically excessive litigation by those who contributed little to actual innovation – there was; but it was always recognized as incongruent with the true aims of patent law, and remedial policies were adopted accordingly.

But who or what crafted patent law's "purposive thrust," and who was it that "aimed [the patent system] . . . in a general way" at the goal of furthering economic growth, and, finally, who was it who determined what would and would not count as "furthering" in the first place? These issues, buried in the more uni-dimensional "steady progress" stories of the past, form the core of the academic program called social construction. This program is broad and diverse, united only by a general similarity of principles and methods within the ranks of it members. Crudely put, the main principle is that groups of people exert tremendous influence over the structure of ideas, institutions, and even objects: that collectively, people (through society) construct much of the shared mental and physical reality that forms the primary context for human life.[51]

On one level, for legal matters this must be correct. Law is an inherently social construct; the rules governing society are written, shaped, and applied by groups of people. It is undeniable: Patent law and the patent system were created, shaped, and altered over time by various groups of people. It is, like other law, literally a social construct. But this is not the same as saying it is purely contingent, haphazard, or

One critique of functionalism takes the view that it presumes social equilibrium, and hence is not sufficiently dynamic, but I obviously disagree. See Walter Goldschmidt, *Functionalism*, in David Levinson and Melvin Ember, eds., Encyclopedia of Cultural Anthropology (New York: Henry Holt and Company, 1996), at p. 510.

50 For more than most reasonable people need to know about this topic, see Robert P. Merges, Justifying Intellectual Property (Cambridge, MA: Harvard University Press, 2011).

51 For origins, overview and assessment of this program, see Darin Weinberg, Contemporary Social Constructionism: Key Themes (Philadelphia: Temple University Press, 2014), at p. 4:

> Nowadays, using the term "social construction" is usually meant to convey that something that has been considered beyond the scope of social influence is actually the product of specific sociohistorical or social interactional processes. Hence, social constructivism thrives particularly vigorously among social scientists interested in the studies of such matters as beauty, gender, morality, pathology, race, science, and sexuality. Whereas it was once believed that these phenomena were determined by fixed natural or metaphysical laws and were therefore sociohistorically invariant, social constructionists have repeatedly demonstrated the extent to which their characteristics are, in fact, culturally relative or historically specific.

random. This institution was formed in part through the influence of some hard guiderails, things that are not the products of purely social processes: in particular, science and the natural world.[52]

For example, as discussed at length in Chapter 5, chemical science became more reductionist, more precise, and more refined in the late nineteenth century. Science-based enterprises arose to exploit the new knowledge; a special branch of patent law developed, shaped by the basic features of chemistry and the commercial needs of the emerging chemical industry. Chemical structure became the basis of patent claims. Patent specifications written for chemists were tested against the rising level of chemical expertise; the nature and sequencing of chemical research dictated new rules regarding the timing of patent applications; and so on.

Science and technology aside, the more fluid guiderails of business needs and economic forces also limit the range of viable patent system designs. In this matter, however, precision is important. In the late eighteenth and early nineteenth centuries, for example, labor-saving technologies were viewed quite differently in Great Britain and the United States. Britain feared them, as liable to increase unemployment among hired hands and unlanded laborers, and hence possibly contribute to political instability. In contrast, if commentators in the young American Republic agreed on anything, it was that there was a drastic labor shortage in the New World. So, in the United States, inventions that conserved on labor were celebrated, promoted, and invited into existence. This was perhaps not inevitable. It is quite easy to show that a powerful and influential social group – elites in politics, finance, and trade – crafted and advanced this agenda. A different social configuration could have privileged different types of technology or advocated against the evils of new technologies altogether. But the overall goal of improving the material

[52] My insistence on "hard guiderails" would be contested by the "strong program" or "strong form" of social constructionism, which was first applied to the generation and acceptance of scientific knowledge – the field with (supposedly) the hardest guiderails of all, the laws of nature. See, e.g., Steve Woolgar and Bruno Latour, Laboratory Life: The Construction of Scientific Facts (Princeton, NJ: Princeton University Press, 1986). The strong program includes social construction of technologies, as opposed to science; see Wiebe E. Bijker, Of Bicycles, Bakelites, and Bulbs: Toward a Theory of Sociotechnical Change (Cambridge, MA: MIT Press, 1997). As applied to new technologies, social constructivists emphasize (1) the need to study failed projects as well as successful ones (to counter the implicit functionalist-triumphalist narrative: i.e., technologies are created and adopted because they work, not because they were pushed by influential people); and (2) the need to describe in terms of social forces the very judgment of what "works", why one technology is considered a "success" and another a "failure." See Trevor J. Pinch and Wiebe E. Bijker, *The Social Construction of Facts or Artifacts: Or How the Sociology of Science and the Sociology of Technology Might Benefit Each Other*, in Weibe E. Bijker, Thomas P. Hughes, and Trevor J. Pinch, eds., The Social Construction of Technological Systems: New Directions in the Sociology and History of Technology (Cambridge, MA: MIT Press, 1987), at p. 22 ("Historians of technology often seem content to rely on the manifest success of the artifact [i.e., technology or invention] as evidence that there is no further explanatory work to be done.") and p. 24 ("The success of an artifact is precisely what needs to be explained.").

conditions of the new country's citizens seems reasonable. It was also widely recorded that labor costs were higher in the United States compared to Britain. Putting all this together, it was certainly understandable that American economic policy encouraged labor-saving technologies. It is true that influential people such as Alexander Hamilton pushed this point. But it's also true that he had a lot of evidence for it.

The patent system is in this way a creature of society, to be sure. But given the goal of furthering production and consumption, the shape and contours of the early US patent system were quite evidently influenced by basic economic conditions such as the labor shortage. As those conditions changed, so did the patent system. The timing and many of the details of adaptation were no doubt influenced and mediated by interested social groups. But the changes themselves were meant to contribute to a goal that seems more firm and less contingent: the need to generate more economic activity in the new country. Over time, change came to doctrine, statutory law, and administrative practices. But the change that occurred was shaped by the shared goal of promoting economic growth.[53]

Patent law was created to serve a purpose, and it transformed as changing conditions dictated. The legal changes were meant to adapt patent law to preserve its primary goal of promoting new technologies, and in this way contribute to economic growth. The overall context of invention changed but not the founding purpose. The system was (and still is) supposed to be an engine of innovation and economic development. Substantive patent law has been chasing that basic objective from its earliest days.

This is not the same as saying that the early patent system was *optimal* in any sense. How could it be, when from the outset it officially ignored technological contributions from enslaved people and Native Americans?[54] This was not only

[53] Notice that I am implicitly arguing that the exclusion of black inventors, most women, etc., was not the main function of patent law but a byproduct of the carrying out of its main purpose (innovation) in a social context shaped and constrained by racist and sexist presuppositions. I could be wrong. From the perspective of a theory that is concerned primarily with distributional concerns, patent law could be seen as just one small part of the fine mesh of institutions and rules whose primary purpose was to concentrate wealth in one group, one class, of people. After all, almost everyone in society is a consumer. If patents redistribute wealth from consumers (necessarily including black people and women) to inventors/entrepreneurs (limited almost exclusively to white men), this – and not some contribution to the stock of new technologies – could be seen not as a byproduct but as the whole point of the exercise. The obvious solution, for one wanting to preserve the patent system, is to make it more open to everyone, and thus put an end to distributional distortions.

[54] See, e.g., Kara Swanson, *Race and Selective Legal Memory: Reflections on Invention of a Slave,* 120 Colum. L. Rev. 1077 (2020) (giving a history and careful reading of infamous opinion by the US Attorney General in 1877 that an enslaved person could not apply for or hold a patent and neither could the slaveowner); Kara Swanson, *Intellectual Property and Gender: Reflections on Accomplishments and Methodology*, 24 Am. U. J. Gender, Soc. Pol'y & L. 175, 182, 185–186 (2015). See also Henry E. Baker, The Colored Inventor: A Record of Fifty Years (New York: Crisis Publishing Co., 1913), at p. 1, available at https://babel.hathitrust.org/cgi/pt?id=emu

wasteful, though it certainly was that: there is irony in an officialdom bemoaning the labor shortage while willfully ignoring the potential good ideas of hundreds of thousands of the country's inhabitants. It was also morally wrong, in an era steeped in natural law principles, to strip excluded inventors of the possibility of ownership. This also encouraged other wrongdoing: It invited those who worked alongside enslaved people, Native Americans, and women to steal their ideas. Historians have now discovered a fair number of patents listing "inventors" who were no such thing. In short, when I state that the patent system was designed to promote economic development, was meant to be "democratic," and was "functional," I mean that it pursued these goals within a socioeconomic system that was cruel, unfair, and wasteful.

Recognizing this, my basic point remains: that technologies and economic forces inevitably leave a strong imprint on the patent system. So, in my view, a functionalist account – informed by an understanding of the broader socioeconomic context – is the best fit for the topics in this book.

1.2.1 *Positive, Normative, or What?*

Some readers like to know the author's point of origin or general attitude. Am I just going to describe the functions of patents in the business enterprise – a purely "positive" project? Or am I going to evaluate what I see in good-bad, right-wrong terms – a normative kind of book? I lean throughout on the former. But despite efforts to stay on the positive straight and narrow, I admit I stray into the normative lane from time to time. A few words about why.

Teaching patent law, writing student casebooks, I read new patent cases every week. I also look frequently at old, classic cases. For purposes of grasping the patent law issues

.010000667530&view=1up&seq=1 (pamphlet published by NAACP publishing house, written by first black patent examiner, recounting over 800 patents known at that time to have black inventors):

> It is not so apparent, however, to the general public that along the line of inventions also the colored race has made surprising and substantial progress ... And it is highly important, therefore, that we should make note of what the race has achieved along this line to the end that proper credit may be accorded it as having made some contribution to our national progress.

For more on nineteenth-century women inventors, see B. Zorina Khan, "Not for Ornament": Patenting Activity by Nineteenth-Century Women Inventors, 31 J. Interdisc. Hist. 159 (2000). For evidence of continuing racial and gender disparities in the number of patent applications and issued patents, see Colleen V. Chien, *The Inequalities of Innovation*, 72 Emory L.J. (2022). See also Kara Swenson, *Centering Black Women Inventors: Passing and the Patent Archive*, 25 Stan. Tech. L. Rev. 305 (2022) (tracing individual stories of black women inventors whose ideas were stolen by white men who filed patents and claimed inventorship; exploring the significance of these missing inventors from the patent archive).

in a case, the preliminary paragraphs (styled "Facts") are indispensable. They describe the invention at the center of the case: the industry (are we in oil discovery or seed drills, shoemaking or leather tanning, nail-making or organic chemistry?), the technology (what goes where in the making of things, etc.), and the specific invention (what it does, how it works, what the patent on it covers). The facts of a case set the context for the legal problem(s) presented. They frame the application of legal rules.

But from the vantage of someone interested in business dealings, case facts carry an entirely different message. They are chock full of fascinating tidbits. Unlike the legal discussion, case facts scatter small clues and make sideways references to matters of business. How the parties to the case made their money, how the invention fits into the patent owner's business, transactions leading up to the case, how and why the fight got started between the two parties – and more. I have always paid attention to facts like these. And taken notes; thus, this book.

But even a straight account can have normative dimensions. For one, the choice of topic within a subject itself conveys a normative slant: If I took the time to write on private ordering centered around patents, I must think it's important (and probably beneficial, too). Put differently, the choice of what to describe – what features to render positively – casts a normative shadow on the resulting work. In this spirit, you may find in these pages some instances of "this is I like, this not so much." I am a well-known fan of patent pools, for example, seeing in them an elegant contractual solution to some knotty problems in the management of dispersed and fragmented patent rights. So, while I try to accurately describe antitrust attacks on patent pools, mostly from the 1920s to 1960s or so, I don't pretend I have no dog in this fight. I do, and she is a fine dog too.[55] So you can find in my sources extensive discussion of the evils of patent pools, but you won't find me joining in. Likewise with certain other features of patent law – the law of patentable utility in the chemical field (Chapter 5), which I describe as a clever solution to the timing of property entitlements; and the benefits of the "invention" (now, nonobviousness) requirement (Chapter 3), which in my view helps patent law police the important threshold between technically new (but trivial) inventions and those worth rewarding with a patent. There are other places where the normative theme is more subdued, but you can hear it if you listen closely.

1.2.2 *Patent History and the Economics of Property Rights: The Demsetz Theory*

The economic study of institutions is a prime example of functionalist analysis. This branch of economics looks at property rights, contracting, and non-governmental cooperative governance arrangements as efficiency-directed responses to various economic forces and conditions. One of the cornerstones of this body of work is

[55] This implicit comparison of my patent pool research with a dog in a fight not only stretches past the point of metaphorical credibility. It also gives new meaning to the phrase "pet theory," so to speak.

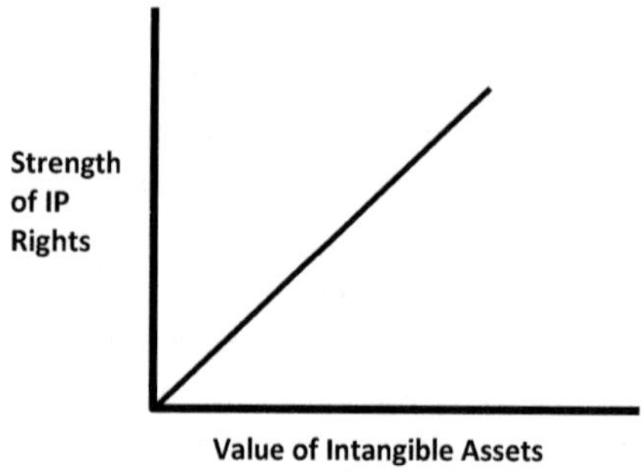

FIGURE 1.1. Simple or naïve version of the Demsetz view of property rights

the economic approach to property rights pioneered by Harold Demsetz.[56] Demsetz theorized that property rights over an asset change in response to the economic value of the asset. For example, in his foundational paper, Demsetz describes a shift in European taste in the nineteenth century that brought beaver skins into fashion for coats and hats. In response to the increasing value of beaver pelts, native people in northern Canada began recognizing greater exclusive rights over hunting areas. Put simply, the increased value of the pelts led to stronger property claims over the grounds that produced them.[57]

The very simplicity of the Demsetz explanation is part of its appeal; economists, as much as anyone, appreciate a tidy narrative. But most "just so" stories come and go. Yet the Demsetz model has achieved real staying power. In the intellectual property field alone, it is cited and discussed quite often.[58] The basic statement of this generative theory can be represented this way (Figure 1.1).

[56] See Harold Demsetz, *Toward a Theory of Property Rights*, 57 Am. Econ. Rev. 347 (Pap. & Proc.) (1967).

[57] See Harold Demsetz, *Toward a Theory of Property Rights*, at p. 352:

> We may safely surmise that the advent of the fur trade [in response to consumer tastes] had two immediate consequences. First, the value of furs to the [native peoples] was increased considerably. Second, and as a result, the scale of hunting activity rose sharply. Both consequences must have increased considerably the importance of the externalities associated with free hunting [such as beaver depletion from too much hunting]. The property right system began to change, and it changed specifically in the direction required to take account of the economic effects made important by the fur trade. The geographical or distributional evidence collected by [a historian] indicates an unmistakable correlation between early centers of fur trade and the oldest and most complete development of the private hunting territory.

The externality of overall beaver population depletion is countered by awarding exclusive hunting territories. In one's own territory, one bears the cost of over-hunting, so one does less of it. See Garrett Hardin, The Tragedy of the Commons, 162 Sci. 1243 (1968) (resource depletion due to common, non-exclusionary, use rights).

[58] As of April 2020, "Demsetz" in proximity to "property rights" had appeared in the law review literature 159 times, with 65 occurring since 2010. Westlaw Database Search (Demsetz w/5 "property rights").

But note: The theory in this simple (almost caricatured) form is usually not the final word among legal theorists of property. This is not surprising. Demsetz left open a fairly obvious question: *How* do property rights adjust to shifting economic conditions?[59] This is just one reason many writers use Demsetz as a jumping-off place for their own related, but usually less one-dimensional, accounts.[60] The two most common emendations to this "naïve theory of property"[61] are (1) recognition that governments grant property, and therefore the allocation and strength of rights depends not only on efficiency but also on private investments in lobbying; and (2) the granting of rights itself imposes costs, seen most easily when many dispersed rightholders have claims over small parcels or components that must be assembled into a single unit for some activity to move forward. Factor (1) is deemed "political economy"; and (2) is transaction costs.

1.2.2.1 Political Economy, Part II

Political economy in the Founding Era was synonymous with government economic policy. But in contemporary academic usage, it means something else. It means the analysis of private efforts to capture government resources or spending.

Political economy considerations in this modern sense are a frequent theme of IP scholarship. Corporate generators of intangible assets, who are also owners of large-scale IP holdings, have every reason to push for changes to IP law that make rights stronger and longer lasting.[62] Strictly speaking, lobbying by itself is not an automatic sign of inefficiency, nor are the things lobbyists ask for. Inefficiency only results

59 Consider this:

> I do not mean to assert or to deny that the adjustments in property rights which take place need be the result of a conscious endeavor to cope with new externality problems. These adjustments have arisen in Western societies largely as a result of gradual changes in social mores and in common law precedents. At each step of this adjustment process, it is unlikely that externalities per se were consciously related to the issue being resolved. These legal and moral experiments may be hit-and-miss procedures to some extent but in a society that weights the achievement of efficiency heavily, their viability in the long run will depend on how well they modify behavior to accommodate to the externalities associated with important changes in technology or market values.

Demsetz, A *Theory of Property Rights*, at p. 350.

60 Other work on economic institutions points out that efficient institutions are the exception, rather than the rule. See Douglass C. North, Institutions, Institutional Change and Economic Performance (Cambridge: Cambridge University Press, 1990), at p. 110 ("Because polities make and enforce economic rules, it is not surprising that property rights are seldom efficient.").

61 So-called in Thrainn Eggertsson, Economic Behavior and Institutions (Cambridge: Cambridge University Press, 1990), at p. 271 (deeming the simple Demsetz model "the naïve theory of property rights").

62 See, e.g., Jonathan Barnett, Innovators, Firms, and Markets: The Organizational Logic of Intellectual Property (New York: Oxford University Press, 2021), at p. xiii (Preface) (noting each company adjusts its IP lobbying to reflect its "demand for IP," which is based on what will best further its business model); Jessica D. Litman, *Copyright Compromise and Legislative History*, 72 Cornell L. Rev. 857, 862 (1987) (Copyright: "During more than twenty years of negotiations,

when a change in IP law contributes nothing to greater economic output or the encouragement of beneficial activity. As defined earlier in this Introduction, this is rent-seeking. A rent in this sense, as mentioned, signifies a government-backed claim that is used by its holder to get money without contributing anything of real value.

The naïve version of Demsetz fails to include the costs of influencing government in order to capture a rent. Examining government restrictions conferring private payoffs, and tracing money spent by multiple firms lobbying to make restrictions more profitable, make up much of the research on political economy. A government-granted property right (such as a patent) is one example of such a restriction: A patent owner can restrict others from using the claimed invention. The payoffs from these investments may distort the simple government response mechanism implicit in the simple Demsetz theory. In that theory, increases in underlying asset values are more or less instantly and automatically translated into a more tightly specified property right. Political economy considerations – including especially rent-seeking expenditures – add a considerable degree of complexity to the simple Demsetz story.

1.2.2.2 Transaction Costs

Political economy modifies the Demsetz story in the period leading up to the grant of rights. Instead of directly translating changed conditions into changes in property, government mechanisms can be influenced and manipulated in ways that alter the efficient configuration of rights. Transaction costs add complexity at another point in the story – after the rights are granted. Because transaction costs influence a number of historical events and practices we will discuss, it is important to explain what these costs are and how they affect the operational efficiency of property (patent) grants.

Property rights concentrate the rights and duties relating to an asset in the hands of a single party – the owner.[63] There are benefits to this arrangement, with the most oft-discussed being the incentive to invest in creating or managing the asset.[64]

the substantive content of the [1976 Copyright Act] emerged as a series of interrelated and dependent compromises among industries with differing interests in copyright.").

63 This is what Demsetz is referring to when he talks about the way property rights "internalize externalities." See Demsetz, *Theory of Property Rights*, at p. 350:

> [P]roperty rights develop to internalize externalities when the gains of internalization become larger than the cost of internalization. Increased internalization, in the main, results from changes in economic values, changes which stem from the development of new technology and the opening of new markets, changes to which old property rights are poorly attuned.

See also Henry E. Smith, *Property as the Law of Things*, 125 Harv. L. Rev. 1691 (2012) (exclusive property rights cordon off distinct assets whose use then requires an owner's permission; this "exclusion strategy" concentrates decision-making power over an asset in a single legal actor).

64 Another advantage is informational: The only thing a potential user of an asset needs to know before using it is who the owner is. Property confers broad powers on the owner, and it does so uniformly, with few exceptions or limitations. See Thomas W. Merrill and Henry E. Smith,

But there are also costs. Ownership of an asset means that anyone who wants to use it must deal with the owner or risk the chance that the owner will enforce the right. The most apparent transaction cost is therefore the cost of contracting with an owner. (This includes finding him or her, negotiating a license, etc.) In the original Demsetz example, contracts of this sort are not central to the analysis.[65] The property right in his prime example – exclusive rights to hunting grounds for beavers – may not have been alienable (assignable by contract), and in any event each was big enough to support hunting activity. It was not necessary to assemble multiple rights-parcels into a single larger parcel in order to hunt effectively. Thus, there was no reason for Demsetz to discuss the costs of contracts for this purpose.

But, particularly in more advanced economies, multi-component products are the norm. The complex, modular designs of products such as computers, mobile phones, game consoles, televisions, and software are often accompanied by extensive and dispersed patenting. There may be a separately owned patent on each component, subcomponent, or product feature. So, unlike the Demsetz scenario, a manufacturer must get licenses to, or otherwise deal with, multiple patents and patent owners.[66] This form of transaction cost adds a considerable layer of coordination in the post-property-grant stage. And if these costs are high enough, they will (or should) influence patent policy. The famous *eBay* injunction case from 2006 is perhaps the best example.[67] Concerns with transactional "holdout" and overcompensation to patent owners drove the Supreme Court to relax the existing

Optimal Standardization in the Law of Property: The Numerus Clausus Principle, 110 Yale L.J. 1 (2000) (discussing the way standardization of property makes it unnecessary for potential users of an asset to delve into the details of the rights held by an owner, and thus why legal systems frown on customized use-rights in place of traditional property).

65 Demsetz does discuss private agreements to internalize an externality (such as overhunting, which imposes costs on an owner's neighbors in the form of lower productivity for all), in the manner of Ronald Coase. See Demsetz, *Theory of Property Rights*, at pp. 356–357:

> [T]he externalities that accompany private ownership of property do not affect all owners, and, generally speaking, it will be necessary for only a few to reach an agreement that takes these effects into account. The cost of negotiating an internalization of these effects is thereby reduced considerably.

See generally, Ronald Coase, *The Problem of Social Cost*, 3 J. L. & Econ. 1 (1960).

66 Put generally, the problem is one of transaction costs. Oliver Williamson (and now many others) places these costs at the center of his economic theory. Transaction cost economics (TCE), the field pioneered by Williamson, takes as its primary concern the problem of costs and hazards in the transfer of resources from one economic unit to another. See Oliver E. Williamson, The Mechanisms of Governance (New York: Oxford University Press, 1996), at p. 3. One specific set of transaction costs – the difficulty of assembling many separate rights with many dispersed owners into an efficient-sized bundle – is known as an anticommons. See Michael A. Heller and Rebecca S. Eisenberg, *Can Patents Deter Innovation? The Anticommons in Biomedical Research*, 280 Science 698 (1998); but see Jonathan M. Barnett, *The Anti-Commons Revisited*, 29 Harv. J. L. & Tech. 127 (2015) (little empirical evidence in support of anticommons theory).

67 *eBay Inc.* v. *MercExchange, L.L.C.*, 547 U.S. 388 (2006).

pro-injunction rule. Transaction costs featured heavily in the crucial passage of the *eBay* decision. In overturning the rule that proven patent infringement must always result in an injunction (order to stop operations), the Court explicitly incorporated transaction cost considerations into decisions about a crucial dimension of patents, the availability of injunctions as remedy for patent infringement. This then serves as a good example of the ways in which post-grant transaction costs can factor into the overall specification of patent rights. The *eBay* case (see Chapter 6) thus illustrates how the simple Demsetzian theory has been supplemented in the IP field to include transaction costs.

Even when it does not directly shape patent doctrine, post-grant contracting is highly relevant to any assessment of patent law and innovation. A solid body of scholarship attests to this. The contemporary literature emphasizes not just the isolated costs and incentives of a lone researcher who undertakes inventive work. Close observers notice also whether this lone researcher needs to acquire other IP rights to do her work. And whether a lone researcher, now with patent in hand, has added to a formidable tangle of multiple rights (a "thicket") in her industry.[68] There is, also, a line of writing that looks to the effect of IP protection on the overall structure of various industries. Does patent protection facilitate supplier-buyer transactions, or other types of "vertical" contractual relations? If so, does this make small, specialized firms more viable in certain industries? Does a proliferation of patents act as a barrier to new firm entry, either in general or at various stages in the development of an industry? These are the kinds of questions being asked by the newer patent research.[69]

A modification of the Demsetz story that includes sensitivity to transaction costs obviously fits with the private law emphasis of this book. What is "private ordering" but a series of exchanges, transactions, and relationships? Conceiving of a transactional overlay on the naïve Demsetz theory fits especially well in a history that emphasizes the role of patents in the business enterprise over time. The ordering that was sought – from early franchising to mergers to later patent pools – was achieved through private dealings. In those dealings the patent right was always at the core. But from this core there was assembled a complex superstructure of private arrangements. As I explain, I try not to lose sight of the superstructure in describing the rights at the core. By this move, I hope to show not only the importance of post-grant transactions but also their relevance for policies related to patent law.

[68] On this, see the important contribution by Mark A. Lemley and Carl Shapiro, *Patent Holdup and Royalty Stacking*, 85 Tex. L. Rev. 1991 (2007).

[69] See, e.g., Robert P. Merges, *A Transactional View of Property Rights*, 20 Berkeley Tech. L.J. 1477 (2005); Jonathan Barnett, Innovators, Firms, and Markets: The Organizational Logic of Intellectual Property (New York: Oxford University Press, 2021); Daniel Spulber, The Case for Patents (Singapore: World Scientific Publishing, 2021).

1.3 THE AGES OF AMERICAN PATENT LAW

United States patent history is conventionally pegged to the major milestones in patent legislation: the 1790 and 1793 Acts, the 1836 Act and birth of the examination system, the 1870 Act, consolidating nineteenth-century developments, and so on. I certainly cover each of these. No history of patent law could do otherwise. But my periodization is more tied to economic trends and the evolution of American business practices.

The Founding Era is often truncated in 1836, with the near-simultaneous deaths of John Adams and Thomas Jefferson. This works well for political history. But American business, and the role that patents played in it, had undergone a fundamental change by about 1820. The earliest period included some well-connected industry promoters (such as Robert Livingston and his steamboat company), as well as true inventors of various stripes – from the modest to the significant (such as Eli Whitney and his cotton gin).[70] By 1820, government-backed projects based on industry-wide patent "privileges" were becoming less common. More often, patents were sought and owned by purely private enterprises. Because of difficulties in transportation and communication, new technologies were often owned by a central entity and licensed to regional manufacturers and distributors. This established the template for more elaborate patent-based franchises later in the nineteenth century. The point here is that after 1820 or so inventors such as Ithiel Town (wooden bridges) and Henry Blanchard (for wood-turning lathes) used their patents as the foundation for nationwide licensing enterprises – an important change that came after the immediate post-1790 era.

The Civil War (1860–1865) represented a profound break with the Founding Era and opened the way to a vast number of political and social changes. Even so, the War itself represents more of a lull in technological activity than a high-water mark. It was the post-War build out of railroads, and the coming of the telegraph, that accelerated economic changes in the nineteenth century. The patent-based franchise model reached its peak in the period from 1870 to 1890 or so, with partnerships as the still-dominant form of business enterprise. But the transportation and communication revolutions, together with fundamental changes in finance and the coming of general incorporation laws, marked the beginning of the end of the dominant franchise model. Nation-spanning companies, set up to exploit the emerging giant industries of electrical power generation, railroad technology, and the telegraph, opened the new era of "corporatization." In the world of technology and patents, the most important change was the advent of the centralized, in-house research and development (R&D) lab.

[70] The backstory, and socioeconomic impact (including on slavery), of the cotton gin, are discussed in Chapter 2.

These new corporate divisions reduced reliance on "outside" (independent) inventors, rationalizing and centralizing the research function as part of the revolution in the "scale and scope" of the business enterprise – to use the terms of business historian Alfred Chandler.[71] Patents held a very different place in the Chandlerian firm than they had previously. There were a number of crucial changes to the fabric of patent law as it adjusted to the presence of these new firms. The inventive work of employees was routinely found to fall within the ownership umbrella of the large employer firms. In addition, courts came to recognize that large companies frequently assembled patents into large portfolios, showing how much had changed since the era when an enterprise could be founded on a single patent. This recognition culminated in the *Continental Paper Bag Patent* case from 1909,[72] when the Supreme Court implicitly recognized the corporate conception of patents as strategic options. Under this view, a patent did useful work simply by adding to a corporate portfolio. So even if the particular technology a patent covered was not being actively implemented by the patent-owning firm, the overall stimulus to corporate research was reason enough for a court to enforce it.

After corporatization was well-entrenched, patents continued to serve various functions. They were, for example, useful tools of business strategy in the early twentieth century. Patent consolidation provided impetus to the formation of massive companies such as AT&T (successor to Alexander Bell's early telephone companies), General Electric, and Westinghouse. Henry Ford famously fought an early auto industry patent – the automobile Selden patent, often cited as an example of patent-based rent-seeking. Yet patents were not unknown in the early auto industry. They facilitated entry in the auto parts industry and came to be a significant set of assets owned by the eventual Big Three auto companies. The patent pool arrangement these companies devised to solve patent blockages represents one of the earliest and most successful uses of this transactional device.

Political developments intersect most noticeably with the history of patents beginning with the Progressive Era at the turn of the twentieth century. Progressive Era antitrust law – one of the distinct innovations of this political moment – developed a deep and lasting interest in how business firms licensed and otherwise used their patents. Some early cases penetrated the thin veneer of patent licensing, which served as a cover for price fixing among competing manufacturers. Other cases ended the practice of controlling distributors and even end-users of a firm's product through the device of a conditional patent license. The evident absurdity of Thomas Edison's efforts to extend his patented film projector

[71] See Alfred D. Chandler, The Visible Hand: The Managerial Revolution in American Business (Cambridge, MA: Belknap Press, Harvard University, 1993); Alfred D. Chandler, Scale and Scope: The Dynamics of Industrial Capitalism (Cambridge, MA: Belknap Press, Harvard University, 1994).

[72] *Continental Paper Bag Co.* v. *Eastern Paper Bag Co.*, 210 U.S. 405 (1908).

into a dominant position in filmmaking and distribution is but one well-known example.

Progressive Era policing of patent licensing gave way to much more aggressive – and far less defensible – attacks on all manner of manufacturer-distributor (or "vertical") contracts. This was a defining aspect of patent policy beginning in the 1930s and extending well into the 1960s. Because of it, patents became linked in the public mind with antitrust law. Patent ownership seemed to many like simply an excuse to perpetrate power abuses on contractual partners. An anti-patent turn in Supreme Court cases culminated in some dubious rulings from the 1940s: the "flash of genius" test for inventions, from 1944; and a vertical restraint case pitting a small patent-owning cannery company against the emerging industry giant Morton Salt – a "Goliath vs. David" story from 1942. (See Chapter 5.) These cases, combined with an accumulation of uncodified doctrines and practices, provided a convenient reason for a major new statement of American patent law – the 1952 Patent Act.

Even while antitrust dominated much of the patent policy discussion between 1920 and 1982, however, patents were part of a separate set of developments that received less attention. Numerous innovative entrants relied on patents to gain a foothold in established industries. Elmer Sperry's gyroscopic compass and related technologies are a good example, as are Ray Dolby's innovations in amplification and filtering of sound recordings, and Wilbert Gore's discovery of the plastic polymer behind Gore-Tex fabric. Patents also played an important role in the development of entire new industries, such as those based on the evolving field of chemistry. The emergent chemical industry was then responsible for a noteworthy episode of adaptation, as numerous patent law doctrines were molded to suit the needs of chemical invention. Overall, then, the period from 1920 to 1982 reveals two parallel sets of events in patent history. While antitrust debates dominated the headlines, patent law quietly and unobtrusively played a part in the emergence of numerous innovative firms.

The final era covered in this book is easy to define and demarcate. The year 1982 marks not only the advent of a new legal regime for patents – the Federal Circuit era – but also a return to older principles of economic policy. The most important policy was the most basic: innovation returned to favor. The anti-corporate spirit of the 1960s and 1970s rubbed off on corporate research and new technology generally. This was also the dawn of the modern environmental movement. The mass production technology of the 1970s was recognized as the greatest contributor to the increasingly visible pollution of water, air, and soil. So, in those years, before hybrid engines and cheap solar panels, environmentalists tended to see technology as the problem and not the solution.

But against these developments, some counter forces were at work. Prime among them was the pressure from Japanese competition. In books, white papers, and press conferences, the shapers of policy voiced unanimous anxiety about the rapid gains of the Japanese innovation system.[73] Many at the time felt – in a way quite reminiscent of worries over Chinese competition forty years later – that these gains came at the expense of and due to the failures of the American innovation system. Ronald Reagan became US President in 1980 after staking out a simple platform: address US "competitiveness." A cornerstone of his policy was a return to faith in innovation and private initiative – both of which pointed to a renewed interest in patents. This interest culminated in two major patent initiatives: passage of the Bayh-Dole (university patent licensing) Act in 1980 and creation of the Federal Circuit in 1982. Though ostensibly created to pursue "predictability" and "efficiency," the Federal Circuit from the start was well aware of the not-so-secret agenda that had breathed life into the very old idea of a special patent court. The agenda was to strengthen patent rights.

The agenda was fulfilled. The volume of patenting continues to increase rapidly. Corporate mergers and acquisitions (M&A) often have important patent or IP components, meaning these rights contribute in a measurable way to firm value. Support for patents among investors such as venture capitalists lends credence to the idea that patents matter in the startup world as well. And finally, there is a growing "secondary market" for patents, another clever private law adaptation in the use and deployment of flexible patent assets.

But during the same era, an unforeseen side-effect materialized: modern-day rent seeking, in the form of the patent troll. From the mid-1980s until roughly 1995 or so, the problem of excessive and unproductive patent litigation grew, driven by Federal Circuit case law that made patent rights more and more valuable. By 2006, efforts to rein in the trolls were well under way. That year marked one of the more strenuous course corrections, the *eBay* case, which made it more difficult for a patentee to stop a competitor in their tracks with an injunction. Another decisive push in the direction of patent reform came in 2011, with passage of the America Invents Act. This gave birth to cheaper patent challenges, housed in the Patent Office. These challenges (chiefly the Inter Partes Review proceeding) reduced the settlement leverage trolls had counted on in prior years, when only costly federal litigation could weed out an invalid patent. Passage of the AIA, however, highlighted another important change in the patent landscape, this one related to political economy. Corporate backing for patent reform shaped two distinct arms of the reform movement: the pharmaceutical arm and the information technology arm. This revealed a split in the interests of different high-stakes patent owners, one that may alter the future flight path of the American patent system.

All of this, of course, was yet to come when the earliest barebones patent legislation was passed in 1790. Let's start there.

[73] For one of many examples, see National Research Council, Committee on Japan Framework Statement and Report of the Competitiveness Task Force, Maximizing U.S. Interests in Science and Technology Relations with Japan (Washington, DC: National Research Council Press, 1997).

2

Founding Era Patent Law, 1790–1820

CHAPTER OUTLINE

2.1 MACRO ISSUES

There is an enormous amount of romanticism concerning the origins of the US patent system. Tales abound of steamboats on the Schuylkill River during the Constitutional Convention, Thomas Jefferson drafting the patent law with a quill pen, and the passage of the 1790 Patent Act moments after the first Congress was called to session.[1] There is a bit of truth in all these legends, and the legends themselves become semi-factual: The energetic push for a patent law forms part of the narrative and culture of America's distinctive (yet sometimes conflicted) enthusiasm for new technologies. Many who have written about the early US patent system seem to have taken a page from a well-known western film, which includes the line, "when the fact becomes the legend, print the legend."[2]

But before the legend there were facts, so we start there. In 1790, people living in the territory of the United States numbered only about 4 million. Population growth during the Founding Era looks like this:

Year	Population
1790	3,929,000
1795	4,607,000
1800	6,297,000
1805	6,258,000
1810	7,224,000
1815	8,419,000
1820	9,618,000

Source: Statistical, at p. A1–8, available at www2.census.gov/library/publications/1975/compendia/hist_stats_colonial-1970/hist_stats_colonial-1970p1-chA.pdf?#.

[1] On the presence of an early prototype steamboat in Philadelphia in 1787, the year of the Constitutional Convention, see Andrew Sutcliffe, Steam: The Untold Story of America's First Great Invention (New York: St. Martin's Press, 2015). On Jefferson's actual role in the early patent system, see, e.g., Edward C. Walterscheid, *Patents and the Jeffersonian Mythology*, 29 J. Marshall L. Rev. 269 (1995).

[2] *The Man Who Shot Liberty Valence* (1962), John Ford, Director.

This was a mostly rural population; there were few big cities. The land they lived on was, from their perspective, mostly frontier. This shaped their actions and outlook, and in many ways explains their views about technology. For the simple fact was that, again from their perspective, they had inherited a vast landscape yet had very few hands with which to work it. This basic fact – of a severe labor shortage, in light of the size of their self-set task of settlement and development – was the single greatest influence on early American attitudes toward technology.

If the nature of the land was different from that of European origins, two other facts of their lives were not; they were, in fact, important legacies that shaped the early US economy. First was familiarity with a market economy. The mostly British and northern European immigrants to the eastern United States brought with them a familiarity with buying and selling that shaped their new economy from the outset. It was already a market economy in many ways. The second legacy had more colonial origins, but it formed an important part of the setting in which they lived. This was a high degree of ethnic diversity. Over time, exposure to different ethnic skills, tools, and practices gave these people a wider array of options in solving the problems of everyday life. This began, of course, with the many technologies that Native Americans had perfected over the years. The melding of native technologies with those from a diverse array of European peoples is a distinctive feature of the early material culture of the new republic. A habit of drawing from diverse sources, together with real and pressing challenges in their environment, may have made these early Americans more willing to experiment than they otherwise would have been.

2.1.1 *The Labor Shortage Problem*

Over and over, almost everyone who related an account of the newly formed country talked of the American shortage of labor. In his *Report on Manufactures* from 1791, Alexander Hamilton (Secretary of the Treasury, and future Broadway idol) described the problem and provided a typical list of causal factors:

> The smallness of ... population [of the United States] compared with their [i.e., the states's] territory – the constant allurements to emigration from the settled to the unsettled parts of the country – the facility, with which the less independent condition of an artisan can be exchanged for the more independent condition of a farmer, these and similar causes conspire to produce, and for a length of time must continue to occasion, a scarcity of hands for manufacturing occupation, and dearness of labor generally.[3]

The "dearness of labor" was a constant theme in communications from British travelers to their friends and family back home. This was true not only in the United

[3] Alexander Hamilton, Report on Manufactures (1791), available at www.constitution.org/ah/rpt_manufactures.pdf (citing to pagination in Collected Works of Alexander Hamilton, Henry Cabot Lodge, ed., 1904, Collected Works available at http://oll.libertyfund.org/titles/hamilton-the-works-of-alexander-hamilton-federal-edition-12-vols, at vol. 4), at p. 194.

States, but in the New World generally. The brutal effective "solution" to this problem was, in the Caribbean and southern United States, slavery. But in the North, slavery was comparatively rare (though not at all unheard of). The typical (not wealthy) New England family ran its own farm with its own labor. It was these yeoman farmers, together with new immigrants, who pushed the development frontier ever westward, sometimes, but not usually, with the help of forced slave labor.

The western frontier affected the labor situation in two ways. As Hamilton put it, many early Americans were eager to substitute "the less independent condition of an artisan" for "the more independent condition of the farmer." This reduced the labor force available in the workshops that were the center of the artisanal crafts: blacksmithing, candle making, silver making, printing, shoe making, and the like. It was recognized very early in the colonial era that the institution of the traditional craft apprenticeship brought over from Europe (mainly England) would need to be adapted to the differing conditions of the New World. The length of apprenticeships was reduced in the United States, as were the stringency of conditions attached to apprentice status. Also, apprentices who had graduated to become journeymen did not constitute a large captive workforce as they did in Europe: They more typically left after their training and became in effect Masters, or at least Masters of their own fate. They accomplished this by simply moving to a new town, often on the frontier, and opening their own shop. And, as Hamilton says, some chose to become farmers, giving up altogether on a career as an artisan.

The other way that the frontier affected the labor situation was that it expanded the range within which the labor market was defined. By opening more territory for economic development, westward expansion decreased the already-thin ratio of people to land – at least until immigration could catch up.

"The frontier" has such mythical status in the United States that it is important to sort out precisely how constant westward expansion on the part of European settlers induced invention, and later, industrialization. In general, what might be called frontier agriculture was a growth industry. According to economic historian H. J. Habakkuk,

> [T]he possibilities of gain were favourable not only to the expansion of agriculture, but to growth of those types of industry developed to process the raw materials produced by the expanding agricultural sector, industries producing heavy agricultural equipment, and industries producing the simpler manufactures for the local market where transport-costs kept out imports.[4]

There was not much "heavy agricultural equipment" yet in the founding period – that would come later, with McCormick's reaper and the gas-powered tractor. But the other categories Habakkuk mentions, raw material processing and "simpler

4 H. J. Habakkuk, American and British Technology in the Nineteenth Century: The Search for Labor-Saving Inventions (Cambridge: Cambridge University Press, 1967), at p. 39.

manufactures," are present in abundance in the patent rolls of the time. Indeed, large-scale mill designs and improvements in simple tools make up an important component of founding era patents.[5] Mills of various sorts were perhaps the most important large-scale capital infrastructure in the colonial era, with Oliver Evans's integrated "hopperboy" grist mill being the most famous.[6] In fact, the first colonial patent was for a mill design. Despite their importance, however, mills were exceptional in one respect: They grew out of the practice of a trade, or out of problem-solving exercises by generalist inventors such as Evans. Far more typical were inventions by artisans. These originated in a certain context, the artisan workshop, so it behooves us to take a moment to understand this context, and in particular the labor practices common within it.

2.1.1.1 Continental Labor Traditions and the Early American Economy

A shortage of labor was one important feature of the early American economy that shaped the rate and direction of inventive activity.[7] Another was the artisan tradition, and more specifically the organization of artisanal labor. The United States inherited the traditional structure of craft occupations from Britain, but that structure soon shifted under the very different conditions of the new world. Traditionally, skilled craft occupations such as glassmaking, silver- and gold-smithing, watchmaking, printing, furniture and cabinet making, bookbinding, and a host of other crafts were organized in trade guilds. Guilds provided a structure within which the craft "mysteries" could be protected and handed down, in part insuring quality control and consistent quality standards.[8] They also gave their members collective

[5] For a comprehensive and invaluable list of pre-1836 patents, see Michael Risch, 64 Fla. L. Rev. 1279, 1309 (2012):

> 516 patents related to mills, 496 involved steam, and 236 improved plows. Another 381 patents were for some improvement on stoves. A total of 180 patents involved pumps, and 66 patents related to tanning leather. New machines for washing clothes and dishes (mostly clothes) accounted for another 267 patents. Movement was also important during this time: 213 patents related to propelling something and another 79 harnessed horse power. So was cutting things, with 471 patents relating to this task. Spinning thread was also popular, showing 192 patents, in addition to 188 cloth patents in the index. Manufacturing materials were relevant as well, claiming 145 brick-related patents and 126 wood-related patents.

[6] For the definitive account, see Christopher Beauchamp, *Oliver Evans and the Framing of American Patent Law*, 71 Case W. Res. L. Rev. 445, 447 (2020). ("If the complicated birth of United States patent law can be told through the story of a single figure, that person is Oliver Evans. Evans was one of the leading inventors and engineers of the early Republic. He was also its most prominent patentee.").

[7] That phrase serves as the title of a very influential early volume on the economics of innovation. See Richard R. Nelson, ed., The Rate and Direction of Inventive Activity: Economic and Social Factors (Cambridge, MA: National Bureau of Economic Research, 1962).

[8] See Stephen R. Epstein, *Craft, Guilds, Apprenticeship, and Technological Change in Preindustrial Europe*, 58 J. Econ. Hist. 684 (1998); W. Patrick McCray, Glassmaking in Renaissance Venice: The Fragile Craft (Aldershot: Ashgate Publishing, 1999).

economic and political power, in some cases serving to limit new entrants and hence economic competition.[9] While guilds restricted generic craft knowledge to the guild membership, there was also room for invention and variation within a craft; shop-specific techniques could be cleaved off from generic guild knowledge and protected in some primitive ways from wide diffusion.[10]

Within an individual workshop, craftspeople were organized into a three-part hierarchy. Masters were at the top (with the workshop's owner, or proprietor, at the very top if there were more than one master); journeymen, those who had completed seven or more years of training but were not yet masters, came next; and apprentices were at the bottom. In Britain, the apprenticeship term had been formalized as a seven-year training period by the Statute of Artificers in 1563.[11] Under that system, given the relatively large population of journeymen in Britain, it was difficult to ascend to the rank of Master. Guilds restricted entry, which benefitted entrenched craftspeople (masters and journeymen alike) but crimped the prospects of young apprentices.[12]

The situation in the young United States was different: " . . . [A]s elsewhere in the New World, the productive systems inherited from Europe were inadequate to the altered balance in factors of production, and they had to be adjusted."[13] This was evident with respect to apprentices and artisanal training. In the United States, ample reserves of open land together with a general labor shortage gave craftspeople many more options than they had in Europe. The prospect of becoming an independent yeoman farmer with a new plot of land constrained the power of masters over their apprentices and journeymen. Apprentices were quick to leave their masters, and they together with journeymen fanned out to populate new towns in the expanding frontier. The result was both an increase in opportunities (and social standing) for craftspeople and a wide diffusion of craft knowledge in the hinterlands of the expanding Republic. Both these factors contributed to the inventive spirit of the young country. Both played a part in the rapid mechanization and industrialization of the early nineteenth century.

9 See Ted Sichelman and Sean O'Connor, *Patents as Promoters of Competition: The Guild Origins of Patent Law in the Venetian Republic*, 49 San Diego L. Rev. 1267 (2012) (finding historical evidence that the first known patent statute, in Venice in 1474, was aimed in part at assisting new entrants trying to operate outside the powerful Venetian guilds).

10 On this, see Robert P. Merges, From Medieval Guilds to Open Source Software: Informal Norms, Appropriability Institutions, and Innovation (November 13, 2004). Available at SSRN: https://ssrn.com/abstract=661543. or http://dx.doi.org/10.2139/ssrn.661543. For a similar treatment of scientific researchers, see Robert P. Merges, *Property Rights Theory and the Commons: The Case of Scientific Research*, 13 Soc. Phil. & Pol'y 145 (1996).

11 5 Eliz. 1 c. 4 (1563).

12 W. J. Rorabaugh, The Craft Apprentice: From Franklin to the Machine Age (New York: Oxford University Press, 1986), at p. 8.

13 Daniel Vickers, *The Northern Colonies: Economy and Society*, in Stanley L. Engerman and Robert E. Gallman, eds., The Cambridge Economic History of the United States: The Colonial Era (Cambridge: Cambridge University Press, 1996), at p. 223.

Another, more speculative, effect can be advanced here too. Historians speak of indentured servitude, and even sometimes apprenticeship, in the language of property.[14] Though apprenticeship was not as restrictive as indentured servitude, apprenticeship contracts were strictly enforced; recovery of a "runaway apprentice" was a common occurrence. And undoubtedly an apprentice bound to a workshop was considered an asset belonging to that shop – in a rough sense, a form of quasi-property.[15] Because technology was conceived of explicitly as a substitute for labor, particularly artisanal labor, when it came to inventive property the legal treatment of human labor may have sprung to mind (or suggested itself implicitly) as a fitting analogy. And – here is some speculation – that may explain why the original patent term in the United States was set with explicit reference to the length of apprenticeship contracts. The 1790 Act set the patent term at fourteen years, with explicit reference to the training time for two apprentices. Though stated as a *maximum* patent term, with the implied right of the three presiding patent officials to reduce the term when they thought prudent, in fact fourteen years seems to have become quite standard almost right away. In any event, what is interesting for our purpose here is that the term was set by analogy to the prevailing term for bound apprentice labor.[16]

Perhaps the apprentice term was simply a convenient precedent, and it means little.[17] But perhaps there is something submerged within it. It is curious at least, and

[14] See W. J. Rorabaugh, The Craft Apprentice, at p. 20: "The traditional private-property rights of the master to the labor services of his apprentice clashed with a public need for soldiers [during the Revolutionary War]." "While Congress did not wish to overturn traditional property rights of the master, it also recognized that the enlistment of apprentices might be the only way some states could fulfill their military quota." Ibid., at p. 21.

[15] See generally, Alan D. Watson, *A Consideration of European Indentured Servitude in Colonial North Carolina*, 91 N. C. Hist. Rev. 381, 390 (2014):

> Regardless of number, indentured servants constituted valuable assets, actually "chattels personal," no different from clothes and livestock, which prompted a committee of the Irish House of Commons in the 1730s investigating servitude in North Carolina to observe that masters had a right to sell or assign servants "as we do our cattle." For the protection of their property, masters recorded indentures … As property, servants' contracts, in essence the servants, might be bought and sold multiple times, used as security in debt proceedings, exchanged for the purchase of a boat, hired out, particularly in the case of estates of deceased, and bequeathed to heirs.

[16] The practice began in England. C. Michael White, *Why a Seventeen Year Patent?*, 38 J. Pat. Off. Soc'y 839 (1956), at p. 841: "The early English patent length was correlated with the time needed to put the invention into general practice throughout the country – the training period for two sets of apprentices." Edward C. Waltersheid, *The Early Evolution of the United States Patent Law: Antecedents (Part 3)*, 77 J. Pat. & Trademark Off. Soc'y 771 (1995), at p. 779: "It was assumed [in England] that the mode of practicing the invention would be taught to native apprentices who in turn would follow the trade."

[17] There is evidence, for example, that the apprentice training requirement common in England had already dropped out of American colonial patents. See Edward C. Walterscheid, *Early Evolution of the United States Patent Law: Antecedents (5 Part I)*, 78 J. Pat. & Trademark Off. Soc'y 615 (1996), at p. 628 ("While it was obviously intended [in colonial era patents] that the patentee should work the industry or enterprise for which the patent was granted, only infrequently did a patent contain any specific requirement for working within a particular

perhaps quite telling, that the technology that public officials hoped would substitute for some of the missing new world labor was awarded property status equivalent to the term of service of human apprentices. On these terms, the average invention might have been seen as meriting a patent when it could do the work of two apprentices of average skill. And, just like young apprentices were free to pursue their own fate after their term was up, a patented invention, once its term expired, could not be stopped from going out into the world to move about freely and find employment where it could. The apprentice analogy, in other words, contained both a property element and a post-property-expiration element of free movement. It explains not just the patent term but also the importance of populating the public domain with useful economic assets after that term is over.

2.2 THE ORGANIZATION OF BUSINESS IN THE FOUNDING PERIOD

So far, I have stressed the macro-level economic context of the founding period. I turn now to a related topic: the organization of business in this era. Population, trade policy, and access to capital are all crucial to investing in innovation. But so is the way businesses are put together. What kind of enterprises were common? How big were they? Where did inventors fit in? These are the topics I take up now.

Let us start with a brief overview of the types of patents that were issued in the founding era. The chart that follows groups them in general categories. The number and type of invention in each category tells us something about the business structures that commonly generated each type of invention.

Class	Description	Count	Percent
126	Stoves and Furnaces	245	6.58
460	Crop Threshing or Separating	132	3.54
241	Solid Material Disintegration	120	3.22
144	Woodworking	107	2.87
172	Earth Working	104	2.79
83	Cutting	100	2.68
19	Textile Fiber Preparation	87	2.33
57	Textile Spinning and Twisting	73	1.96
68	Textile Fluid Treating	59	1.58
114	Ships	57	1.53
100	Presses	55	1.48
415	Rotary Fluid Motors and Pumps	52	1.40

Most Common Patent Classes, 1790–1839; from Michael Risch, *America's First Patents*, 64 Fla. L. Rev. 1279, 1308 (2012) (used with permission).

time. There seems to have been almost no requirement to teach the trade or art to others such as had been a fairly common feature of early English patents . . . ").

With this general taxonomy of patents in mind, let us consider the three most common business models operating during the founding era.

2.2.1 *Public-Private Projects: Courtier Capitalism and the Federal Armories*

In a very young economy, with limited private capital, government partnerships were a crucial means for jump-starting economic activity. These partnerships took two primary forms. One was direct requests for state backing of privately conceived investment projects. The other was federal military armories, which were government facilities whose contractors and employees benefitted from federal funding. We review them both.

2.2.1.1 Courtier Capitalism

At first, citizens of the newly organized United States often emulated European, and particularly British, practices. This was certainly true when it came to patents. Beginning in the colonial era, inventors sometimes sought patents from the individual states. This carried over to the Confederation period, and indeed continued during the debate over constitutional ratification.

As in Britain, patents were but one of several forms of government backing available to aspiring entrepreneurs. In this era, before the corporate form had become generally available, corporations were created with special, one-off government grants. This was the vehicle by which state-supported ventures were launched. Some corporations covered very large ventures; the British East India Company and the Virginia Company are two prominent examples. But many were of smaller scope, covering, for example, the right to build a bridge in a certain place.[18]

Whatever their scope, corporate franchises of this sort could only be obtained through governmental influence – what came to be known later as lobbying. Adroit deployment of political connections, together with a persuasive sales pitch, were keys to success. It also never hurt to give ample shares of stock to the politicians one was courting.

Yet despite the appearance of corruption, state sponsorship of innovative enterprise in this era was arguably effective. First, capital was limited in the new country. Alexander Hamilton had, in a brilliant stroke, converted the young nation's debt into a liquid form of capital that helped credit grow.[19] But the task confronting the

[18] See, e.g., *Charles River Bridge* v. *Warren Bridge*, 36 U.S. (11 Pet.) 420 (1837) (contesting exclusive right to build a bridge at a certain point on the Charles River in Boston).

[19] Hamilton's contemporary Noah Webster wrote in 1791, shortly after the new Treasury Department both "nationalized" state debts and began issuing US government Treasury bonds:

> The establishment of funds to maintain public credit has an amazing effect on the face of business and the country. Commerce revives and the country is full of provision. Manufactures are increasing to a great degree, and in the large towns vast improvements are making in pavements and buildings.

founding generation was formidable, and few of the large-scale projects of the day could have been achieved without the collective power of the state to help raise the money. The Erie Canal in New York State is the preeminent example,[20] but many other improvements, schemes, and projects followed the same pattern. In this context, "projectors" of great projects regularly plied public officials.

Early patentees were well represented in the ranks of "courtier" capitalists. Some, like John Fitch of steamboat fame, sought to consolidate state patent grants into a single federal grant. Fitch also hoped that the federal stamp of approval would give him an advantage in the long-running, multi-state battle over steamboat patents – a battle that Robert Fulton and Robert Livingston won in the end.[21] Other patentee-courtiers hoped to supplement the grant of an ordinary patent with supplemental funding from the federal Congress. Oliver Evans, famous for his integrated grist mill design, is a good example. Still others prayed for special treatment, which they said was necessary because standard patent coverage was not sufficient for them to recoup their investments or to fully develop the relevant technology. For their purposes, a patent was simply one among several instruments they might use to obtain the state backing they sought.

Courtier patentees laid the groundwork for the steady stream of special Congressional petitions that in time led to various codifications and a general regularization of certain Patent Office procedures.[22] For present purposes what matters is that special pleading in Congress supplemented the operation of the regular patent process, particularly for large-scale projects.

Letter of Noah Webster to James Greenleaf, October 13, 1791, in Harry R. Warfel, ed., Letters of Noah Webster (1953), at p. 104. US government debt found a ready market in Europe, which allowed the US government to borrow money at pre-set interest rates of 3 and 6 percent (for short- and long-term bonds, respectively), which funded investment projects in the new and fast-growing country that yielded returns estimated at from 10 to 20 percent per year. Robert E. Wright and David J. Cowen, Financial Founding Fathers 25 (2006).

20 See Brian Phillips Murphy, Building the Empire State: Political Economy in the Early Republic (2015), at p. 2: (Describing Robert Livingston as a political as well as business entrepreneur) (footnote omitted):

> The animating energy of colonial government had long come from collaboration between official entities and local private interests. In Livingston's mind the propriety of that relationship had in no way been discredited by the Revolution. Restoring those pre-revolutionary practices would favor Livingston's family and others with capital to invest and influence to exercise, and for the next thirty years Robert planned and profited from political-economy practices he helped set.

21 See Timothy Milford, *"Patent Property": The Fulton Lawyers and the Franchising of Progress*, 58 Am. J. Legal Hist. 87 (2018) (describing the work of lawyer/courtier-lobbyists Cadwallader D. Colden and Thomas Addis Emmet in obtaining state and federal support for Robert Fulton's steamboat enterprise).

22 The growth of petitioning, and its influence on various features of administrative agencies and procedures, are well recounted in Maggie McKinley, *Petitioning and the Making of the Administrative State*, 127 Yale L.J. 1538 (2018). A good history of legislative petitions and the development of British patent law can be found in Phillip Johnson, Privatised Law Reform: A History of Patent Law through Private Legislation, 1620–1907 (London: Routledge, 2018). I know of no equivalent comprehensive history for the United States.

2.2.1.2 Federal Armories

The United States was born after war with the reigning Great Power of the day, Britain. It therefore seems natural that a reliable source of state-of-the-art weaponry would be high on the to-do list of the young country. This was achieved with two federal armories: the government-run weapons factories at Springfield, Massachusetts, and Harpers Ferry, Virginia.[23] For several reasons, the armories turned out to be not only a steady source of weaponry; they were also an important stimulus to invention and innovation in the early Republic. First and foremost, they were great centers of technical talent. In all the ways that concentrated pockets of technical specialists encourage them to learn from and stimulate each other, early armory workers pushed forward the technological frontier at a rapid pace.[24] Despite the concentration of talent, the technologies and management techniques originating in the armories spread to other industries and other regions. This was due partly to the migrations of the skilled artisans, who moved back and forth between the armories and moved into new regions as the economy expanded. Finally, the technologies themselves were quite generalizable – a result of the fact that many were in the form of machines and machine tooling. Though originating with weaponry, many of the armory innovations turned out to have applications in all sorts of manufacturing industries. This meant that the armory technologies diffused rapidly and widely, which in turn helped to fuel the wave of industrialization that accelerated throughout the nineteenth century.

The management of the armories was far different from that of a modern government agency. To begin, the workers who made weaponry came from a long line of independent artisans.[25] They had their own craft traditions, passed down from other gunsmiths in apprentice training.[26] While they were employees in the sense that the government paid their salaries, they had more freedom to come and go than

23 The latter is also remembered as the target of John Brown's pre-Civil War "raid" or liberation effort. See James M. McPherson, Battle Cry of Freedom: The Civil War Era (New York: Oxford University Press, 1988), at pp. 205–208; Steven Lubet, *Execution in Virginia, 1859: The Trials of Green and Copeland*, 91 N.C. L. Rev. 1785 (2013) (trial of surviving ex-slaves who participated in the Harpers Ferry skirmish).

24 See Merritt Roe Smith, Harpers Ferry Armory and the New Technology: The Challenge of Change (Ithaca, NY: Cornell University Press, 1977), at p. 59 ("The roster of early armorers at Harpers Ferry reads like a Who's Who of Pennsylvania gunmaking."); David A. Hounshell, From the American System to Mass Production, 1800–1932 (Baltimore: Johns Hopkins Press, 1985), at p. 39 (describing how interchangeable parts innovator John H. Hall absorbed "best practices" at the federal armories).

25 See Merritt Roe Smith, Harpers Ferry Armory.

26 On artisanal tradition, craft secrets, and the passing of the "mystery" of a craft from master to apprentice under supervised conditions, see W. J. Rorabaugh, The Craft Apprentice, at p. 33. See generally, Pamela O. Long, Openness, Secrecy, Authorship: Technical Arts and the Culture of Knowledge from Antiquity to the Renaissance (Baltimore: Johns Hopkins Press, 2002), at chapter 3, "Handing Down Craft Knowledge," pp. 72–101.

typical employees in the twentieth century. Especially at the Harper's Ferry armory, they were also part of a rural, non-industrialized community. Many kept their own farms and, in some cases, operated as independent artisans (fixing guns, for example) on the side. Another way they were treated as independent artisans, rather than subservient employees, was that when they made useful inventions in the course of their work at the armories, they retained patent rights.[27]

Several armory-related patents proved to be important. For example, an artisan named Sylvester Nash developed a turning lathe to replace the traditional grindstone, for use in the crucial task of shaping gun barrels.[28] Numerous other inventors, including Eli Whitney, were at work on the same task, because machine lathing was faster and turned out a more uniform part – a key goal of the early armory technicians, whose ultimate goal (eventually achieved) was the fabrication of truly interchangeable parts. The inventor Nash was sent to Harpers Ferry to teach the artisans there how to construct his new lathe. A few months after he arrived, he took a side trip to Washington to file an application for a patent on his invention. Under the registration system, there was no patent examination, of course, and his patent duly issued on April 11, 1818.[29] As was becoming common around that time, Nash sold the regional rights to his invention to the Harpers Ferry Armory. He then returned to Springfield, where he eventually sold the remaining rights in his patent to the Armory there, which used it in combination with several other advanced designs for lathe components, thus achieving superior results in gun barrel turning.[30]

Another celebrated invention growing out of the armories was a duplicating lathe created by Thomas Blanchard. Blanchard was already a noted inventor when, in 1820, he was asked to put his mind to a problem in gunmaking. The stock or blunt end of a rifle is used to brace the "kick" from firing the weapon against the shooter's shoulder. In the early nineteenth century, wood turning lathes were part of the technological landscape, but they still required human labor and skill to make an effective gunstock. The extant lathes could spin a rectangular block of wood, but the craftsperson had to apply a blade or saw to carve the stock to the desired shape. Blanchard recalled a known technique for making round hat-shaping wooden pieces (called hat blocks). He decided to adapt that technique for making gunstocks. The result was an ingenious machine. It used a model gunstock made of hardened wood. Blanchard designed a series of cams that moved a blade in and out as it

[27] The best treatment of the retention of patent rights by those whom tradition deemed artisans can be found in Catherine L. Fisk, *Removing the 'Fuel of Interest' from the 'Fire of Genius': Law and the Employee-Inventor, 1830–1930*, 65 U. Chi. L. Rev. 1127 (1998).

[28] See Merritt Roe Smith, Harpers Ferry, at p. 117.

[29] See Henry Ellsworth, Comm'r of Patents: A Digest of Patents Issued by the United States from 1790 to January 1, 1839 (1840), at p. 582, available at https://catalog.hathitrust.org/Record/002009332?type%5B%5D=title&lookfor%5B%5D=digest%20of%20patents&ft=ft.

[30] Merritt Roe Smith, Harper's Ferry Armory, at pp. 123–124.

followed the model. These in and out motions were transferred to a blade that progressed along the wooden piece to be carved in precise sequence with the progress of the cams over the model. The result was in effect an automatic 3-D tracing machine. It copied the shape of the model and used it to direct the cutting blade to shape the raw piece of wood. The result: a new gunstock, in the identical shape of the model that had been traced. This has been called "a truly elegant invention,"[31] but it was more than that. It was itself a model or "microcosm" of American mechanization, converting labor-intensive step in one the making of a partially mechanized turning-only lathe into a fully autonomous mechanical operation. The business model Blanchard adopted to exploit the lathe, based on exclusive territorial patent rights, was also a model of a typical early patent-based enterprise. (See later in this chapter for a more detailed description.)

Despite the significance of Blanchard's invention, perhaps the most important innovation launched in the armories was the system of truly interchangeable parts in the manufacture of a complex product. This was the work of John H. Hall. Hall's particular invention was a breach-loading rifle – a rifle where the bullet is loaded at the end near the trigger, rather than the far end where the bullet exits the barrel (a so-called musket-loader).[32] But more important than the famous "patented Hall breach-loading rifle" was the method of making it. Hall's goal – and in truth the "holy grail" of early nineteenth-century manufacturing – was to be able to disassemble a handful of rifles, dump the parts on a table, and have an assembler put together a fully functional rifle from whichever combination of parts was chosen.[33] Hall was the first to succeed, and full interchangeability became a hallmark of what was called "the American system."

2.2.2 *Patents and Capital Investment: Big City Finance and New Industrial Ventures*

Toward the end of the founding period, we begin to see a new strain of industrialization, one less dependent on the active participation of the state. Private capital, typically originating in one of the financial centers of the new republic, funded ambitious mills and production plants. These culminated in the famous "Waltham

[31] David Hounshell, From the American System, at p. 35.

[32] See Merritt Roe Smith, Harpers Ferry Armory, at pp. 188–189 (describing the ploy by Dr. William Thornton, then Commissioner of Patents, to obtain a one-half interest in Hall's breach-loading rifle patent, on the pretense that Thornton had earlier conceived a breach-loading rifle along the lines of the Hall design).

[33] See David Hounshell, From the American System, at p. 41. ("Hall's ability to manufacture interchangeable rifle parts rested not only on his skills in designing metal- and wood-working machinery but, perhaps more important, on his extensive use of gauges and on his rationalized design of fixtures.")

Plan" of financier Henry Cabot Lowell, often cited as the first true large-scale factory in the United States.[34]

A prototype for the larger scale Waltham works was the textile factories started by Samuel Slater beginning at the end of the eighteenth century. First in partnership with the Brown and Almy merchant partnership firm of Providence, Rhode Island, and later with the backing of his own family members, Slater erected mills for spinning cotton. He employed his British experience (he was an immigrant from England) to assemble leading spinning technologies – machines for brushing raw cotton ("carding"), machines for gathering cotton into small bundles to be fed to spinning machines ("roving"), and water-powered machines for spinning cotton (the famous "Arkwright Frame").[35] Slater combined these technologies with merchant sources of capital to construct the first true industrial-scale factories in the United States. Located first in Pawtucket, and later in other towns in Rhode Island, Slater's mills were a kind of transitional economic form: After spinning, yarn was then "put out" to home-based weavers, who operated in a network of family production units. Slater's system combined the machine spinning of thread with the traditional "proto-industrial" setup for weaving, a good example of a transitional technology.

Slater had made no patentable advance, it seems, in the design of his machines. In fact, his early ventures are often seen as an example of the transfer of established technology from Britain – an activity strictly prohibited by British law.[36] This was part of what might be called a transatlantic diffusion pattern. It might also be termed industrial espionage or "piracy," depending on your point of view.[37] For our

[34] See David A. Hounshell, From the American System; Peter Temin, *The Industrialization of New England, 1830–1880*, in Peter Temin, ed., Engines of Enterprise: An Economic History of New England (Cambridge, MA: Harvard University Press, 2000), at pp. 109, 117.

[35] Barbara M. Tucker, *The Merchant, the Manufacturer, and the Factory Manager: The Case of Samuel Slater*, 55 Bus. Hist. Rev. 297 (1981).

[36] Doron Ben-Atar, *Alexander Hamilton's Alternative: Technology Piracy and the Report on Manufactures*, 52 Wm. & Mary Q. 389, 395 n. 33 (1995) (quoting from Slater's journal which stated that Slater was enticed to the United States by the promise of a premium or bounty for those who could bring British textile know-how to the United States.). Students of patent history will recognize the pattern: this is the same practice pioneered in Elizabethan Britain, induced immigration by foreign-born artisans in fields such as textiles, metallurgy, mining, and ordnance (weaponry). See Christine MacLeod, Inventing the Industrial Revolution: The English Patent System, 1660–1800 (Cambridge: Cambridge University Press, 1988), at p. 11.

[37] See David J. Jeremy, Transatlantic Industrial Revolution: The Diffusion of Textile Technologies between Britain and America, 1790–1830 (Cambridge, MA: MIT Press, 1981). Jeremy describes the strict British legal prohibitions on export of textile technologies such as the Arkwright frame, and the successful American efforts to obtain the technologies by enticing expert craftspeople to emigrate to the United States. For the most part it appears that the know-how was transferred not in the form of illicit export of machinery, but in the permissible (or at least hard to police) form of the memories and skills of the emigres. Ironically, the Venetian government had tried to prevent diffusion of glassmaking skill to other European countries in the early modern period, but apparently those techniques leaked out in various directions, to the benefit of the glassmaking industry in Britain as well as other countries. See Christine MacLeod, Inventing the Industrial Revolution, at p. 11. Another irony is that, along with artisan

purposes, the point is that it was Slater's knowledge of British techniques that allowed him to raise capital. Only later, according to some records, did Slater obtain some US patents.

By 1813, entrepreneurs were shaping a more patent-centric form of capital-backed industrial plant. The Boston Association founded its famous textile factory in Waltham, Massachusetts, in that year. Partly spurred by the British embargo of 1809 (which helped spark the War of 1812), wealthy merchant families from Boston raised capital for the first "cotton to cloth" textile factory. The new venture, the Boston Manufacturing Company, had as its lead investor Henry Cabot Lowell, from one of the wealthiest and most diversified merchant family firms in Boston. Unlike Slater's Rhode Island mills, the Boston mill handled weaving as well as spinning.[38]

The Boston Company owned patents awarded to their chief engineer and noted inventor, Paul Moody.[39] (The main street in Waltham is still called Moody Street.) The Company deployed these patents in a number of ways, adumbrating later patent portfolio management techniques we will see in this book.[40] One deployment strategy was licensing: "In 1817, the company's net income from patent licenses was $34,000; five years later it was $345,000, a tenfold increase."[41] That $345,000 figure is worth roughly $9 million in contemporary dollars, which represents a significant annual return on the initial R&D investment in the machine shop.

skills, the movement of people around Europe also led to the diffusion of the idea of granting patents. See ibid.

38 Jonathan T. Lincoln, *Beginnings of the Machine Age in New England: Documents Relating to the Introduction of the Power Loom*, 7 Bull. Bus. Hist. Soc'y 6, 6 (1933) (describing the differences between the "Rhode Island" system of Slater and the "Waltham Plan" of Lowell's Boston Manufacturing Company).

39 See Henry Ellsworth, Comm'r of Patents: A Digest of Patents Issued by the U.S. from 1790 to January 1, 1839 (1840), available at https://catalog.hathitrust.org/Record/002009332?type%5B%5D=title&lookfor%5B%5D=digest%20of%20patents&ft=ft (listing eight patents issued to Paul Moody, all relating to textile machinery).

40 Machine building was, to use the terminology of later business analysts, a "core capability" of the new textile firm. When investment shifted from Waltham to Lowell, Massachusetts, one of the first buildings constructed was the Lowell Machine Shop, a larger version of the one at Waltham. Chaim Rosenberg, Life and Times of Lowell, at p. 295. As was the case in Waltham, the Machine Shop not only made machinery for internal use. It also sold finished machines to other textile firms in the area. The Lowell shop eventually employed 1,000 people in the construction of machines for both internal (Lowell Company) use and sale to others. In addition, the machine shop helped achieve the "agglomeration effects" that are often associated with intensive innovation (as in Silicon Valley, California, in later years). The Boston Company spurred local inventive activity by acquiring state-of-the art machinery from regional machines shops. Local inventor/artisans included Shepherd Leech from Easton, Massachusetts (roller lathe and cutting machines); Luther Metcalf's carding machines; and F. Stowell of Worcester, who provided other machines. Chaim Rosenberg, Life and Times of Lowell, at p. 241.

41 Carl E. Prince and Seth Taylor, *Daniel Webster, the Boston Associates, and the U.S. Government's Role in the Industrializing Process, 1815–1830*, 2 J. Early Rep. 283, 291 (1982).

To back up its licensing demands, the Company employed statesman and noted orator Daniel Webster as its chief outside counsel; Webster represented the Company in six patent infringement suits related to the Moody patents.[42] Another strategy was to use patents as leverage to acquire equity in other firms. In 1822, the Merrimack Manufacturing Company was established in East Chelmsford (later renamed Lowell), Massachusetts. In exchange for shares in the new Merrimack Company, the Boston Company of Waltham paid cash but also gave a license to the Moody patents that the Boston Company owned.[43]

It appears that this was a general practice. Patents played some role in capital formation in a number of early New England textile companies. Patents – together with state corporation charters – were the primary form of direct government involvement in this industry. Textiles thus differed from the earlier form of "courtier capitalism," which featured more direct government backing. As one historian put it,

> Except for machinery patents, no Waltham-Lowell corporation ever asked for a monopoly. In place of the dubious security such favors brought, stockholders had been able to rely on the technological and financial superiority of the enterprises themselves.[44]

Bypassing government as a direct funding source was partly the result of a maturing capital market. According to Douglass C. North:

> The early development of a capital market in the Northeast around foreign trade and the cotton trade, as compared with its relatively primitive state in the other regions, was another important influence on manufacturing development. The growth of savings institutions and financial intermediaries in the Northeast aided a wide variety of early manufactures. The development of the New England textile

[42] See Chaim Rosenberg, The Life and Times of Francis Cabot Lowell (Maryland: Lexington Books, 2011), at p. 269.

[43] See Robert F. Dalzell, Jr., Enterprising Elite: The Boston Associates and the World They Made (New York: W. W. & Norton Company, 1987), at p. 48. The terms were reported as follows: Boston Manufacturing received $75,000 for assigning the Moody patents to the Merrimack (Lowell) company and for releasing Moody from his employment contract in Waltham so he could join the new company in Lowell. See Nathan Appleton, Introduction of the Power Loom: and Origin of Lowell, 1799–1861 (Lowell, MA: B.H. Penhallow Press, 1858), at p. 24.

[44] Robert F. Dalzell, Jr., Enterprising Elite, at p. 86. See also Caroline F. Ware, The Early New England Cotton Manufacture: A Study in Industrial Beginnings (Boston: Houghton-Mifflin, 1931) (access to capital was one of the major factors that helped the cotton textile industry launch in early nineteenth-century New England). As this example shows, even the northern industrial part of the United States was deeply connected to cotton. Despite the geographic separation from cotton growing, the northern economy was also implicated in the institution of slavery. See generally, Sven Beckert and Seth Rockman, eds., Slavery's Capitalism: A New History of American Economic Development (Philadelphia: University of Pennsylvania Press, 2016).

> industry was implemented by the shift of capital from shipping into textiles ... The abundance of financial intermediaries in Boston and the Northeast provided the large amounts of loan capital essential to rapid expansion of the textile firms.[45]

Investments in textile mills were not risk-free, of course, but they were seen as a good bet, given the growth prospects. In a famous case in trusts and estates law, the trustees of a $50,000 fund were sued in 1830 by the trust beneficiaries, Harvard College and Massachusetts General Hospital, for breach of trust. The trustees invested in Lowell's mills in Waltham and Lowell, Massachusetts. But Harvard and Massachusetts General challenged these investments as imprudent and excessively risky. The court disagreed, noting that other prudent investors in the area had made the same investments.[46] The court seemed to recognize that with a diversified investor base and access to superior technology, the harnessing of private capital to machinery-based production was a sound investment.

2.2.3 *Small Scale Capitalism*

The fluid boundary between ordinary patents – those sought under the Patent Act – and special government-backed monopolies, such as the state steamboat franchises mentioned earlier, perhaps contributed to the early conception of patents as "privileges." It is important not to overestimate the number or prominence of these special monopolies, however. A remarkable feature of the patent system throughout the nineteenth century was its trend toward "democratization."[47] In Chapter 3, on the patent system in the Jacksonian era (1821–1849), we see the full flowering of the movement for democratization. But even in the founding period it was present. Unlike courtier entrepreneurs, most patent applicants in the founding period were not politically connected, and most patents were not sought for large projects like mills and transportation systems. Sampling from the list of patents issued in 1817, we find the following inventions:[48]

45 Douglass C. North, The Economic Growth of the United States, 1790–1860 (New York: Prentice-Hall Publishers, 1961), at p. 169.

46 *Harvard College* v. *Amos*, 26 Mass (9 Pick) 446, 461 (1830) (finding, under the "prudent investor" rule, that the trustees were not liable, because other reasonable investors had made the same investments).

47 The masterwork on this theme is the invaluable book by B. Zorina Khan, The Democratization of Invention: Patents and Copyrights in American Economic Development, 1790–1920 (New York: Cambridge University Press, 2005).

48 John Quincy Adams, Secretary of State, Letter from the Secretary of State [to Congress] Transmitting a List of the Names of Persons to Whom Patents Have Been Issued for the Invention of any New and Useful Art [in the year 1817], January 13, 1818, H. Doc. 48, 15th Congress, 1st Session, available in Am. State Pap., Serial Set Vol. No. 7, Session Vol. No. 3, at pp. 5–14.

Invention title	Inventor name and address
Cutting and heading nails at one operation	Isaac Northrop, Oneida County, New York
Straw cutting machine	Elihu Hotchkiss, Battleboro, Vermont
Scythe factory machine, improvement in	Benjamin and John Tyler, Claremont, New Hampshire
Cast iron cooking stoves	Albertus Swain, Hudson, New York.
Machine for raising the nap on woollen cloth	Eli Starr and Nathan Couch, Hudson, New York.
Improvement on Rumsey and McComb's water wheel	Theodore Burr, Burr Haven, Dauphin County, Pennsylvania
Improvement in window and door frames	John Jordan, Rockbridge County, Virginia
Machine for giving motion to saw gates	Samuel Herrick, Clermont County, Ohio
Sap bucket	Jeremiah Purdy, Cherburne, Chenango County, New York.
Threshing machine, for threshing small grain	Nathan Read, Belfast, District Maine

The democratic nature of the US patent system is aptly captured in this brief, unsystematic sample. Look first to the geographic range of inventor addresses. Frontier or recently developed areas are well represented. Oneida and Chenango counties in New York were not quite frontier, but they were also far from the power centers of Philadelphia, New York City, Boston, and Washington, DC. The patent issued to Isaac Northrup for cutting and heading nails was issued in January of 1817. At that time his home, Oneida County, New York, had a population of roughly 51,000; it had grown rapidly from the time of the 1810 census, when population was listed at 31,000.[49] No doubt a good part of this population growth was due to the construction of the Erie Canal, which began the same year Northrup received his patent. The canal originates to the east, in Albany, New York, and passes through Oneida County. Population growth, stimulated by the construction of the canal, obviously fed the demand for new building construction (homes, businesses, etc.), in turn driving the demand for low-cost nails. Thus were Northrup's inventive faculties directed to a growing market.

Much the same story can be told for Jeremiah Purdy's prosaic invention, a sap bucket. Purdy hailed from a county south and west of Oneida, Chenango County, New York. The population of this county was officially 31,215 in 1820, but the county has been subdivided since then. Purdy's small town of Cherburne (later renamed Sherburne) was not incorporated until thirteen years after he received his patent; the current population of roughly 1,300 means that probably this is and always was a

[49] All population figures are from the US Census website, Census.gov. See, e.g., www.census.gov/library/publications/1821/dec/1820a.html (data for 1820 census).

small town.[50] There was economic activity in the area, however. An extension of the Erie Canal, the Chenango Canal, was begun in 1824, and this created a "spur" that fed into the main canal. Purdy was perhaps involved in the maple syrup trade, as there are plentiful sugar maples in this part of New York State.[51] Whatever its ultimate purpose, Purdy's sap bucket was a simple contrivance made, not surprisingly, from wood. The full specification of the patent was lost in the Patent Office fire of 1836, but one drawing from Purdy's US Patent Number 2850X remains.

This would seem to be some sort of transfer bucket, which receives sap from gathering buckets that hang off the maple trees. Perhaps Purdy envisioned a modular design, where the square ends of the bucket were removed and the sap was left to flow down the tubular length of wood into the metal pan that is set over the fire in a sugar house. (Roughly 40 gallons of raw sap is required to make one gallon of syrup.)

Whatever his business goals, Purdy obviously thought it worthwhile to push forward in the design of tools for use in connection with his cash crop. And, perhaps, to find a market for that design – with the help of his patent. Regional trade patterns would make it likely that agricultural products such as maple syrup from towns surrounding the new canals would supply the population of the growing Erie Canal region. The simple point here is that even a citizen of a small, inland, wooded area was encouraged to harness his inventive faculties in an effort to improve a modest area of technology to help serve a growing economic market.

The proximity of both Northrup and Purdy to the new canals is telling. Economic historian Kenneth Sokoloff studied a large sample of all US patents issued between 1790 and 1846.[52] One of his key findings was that inventive activity showed a strong correlation with proximity to navigable waterways:

> Although the importance of specific mechanisms remains unclear, the evidence suggests that the extension of the waterway network during the period [1790–1846] stimulated significant increases in inventive activity. It is observed finally that the analyses of the temporal and cross-sectional patterns reinforce each other in implying that inventive activity was positively related to the growth in markets, and that the results deepen our understanding of early American industrialization.[53]

50 Geographic Identifiers: 2010 Demographic Profile Data (G001): Sherburne village, New York. U.S. Census Bureau, American Factfinder.

51 A detailed historical account of the founding of Cooperstown, New York, emphasized the importance of maple syrup as an important agricultural cash crop during the early settlement period of the state's rolling frontier areas. See Alan Taylor, William Cooper's Town: Power and Persuasion on the American Frontier (New York: Knopf Publishing, 1996), at p. 104 (describing overland winter sleighs transporting maple syrup and potash (derived from the ashes of burnt trees, used for making soap, glass, and bleach for dying cloth) to the local regional market town, Albany.)

52 Kenneth Sokoloff, *Inventive Activity in Early Industrial America: Evidence from Patent Records, 1790–1846*, 48 J. Econ. Hist. 813 (1988) (sample of roughly 4,500 US patents, representing around 30 percent of the roughly 15,000 patents issued during this period).

53 Sokoloff, *Inventive Activity*, at 817.

Proximity to the Erie canal system, together with the timing of my small sample – 1817 – explains to some extent why rural inventors were entering the patent system.[54] An import embargo and tariffs associated with the War of 1812 also played a part. These economic policies caused a spike in domestic US economic activity of all kinds, and our small inventors were simply part of that trend. Low Patent Office fees, detailed in Section 2.3.1, meant that it would not break them financially to take a chance at gaining legal protection.

2.2.3.1 Regional Patterns of Production and Invention

Geography, transportation, and local demand played an important part in early American industrialization. Canals were only one part of the story. Many districts could not be reached by navigable waterways, which meant that older forms of overland transport continued to connect these districts with the larger population centers. Turnpike construction, in New England and elsewhere, represented one solution to the problem of economic isolation. But transport costs remained high. In addition, the tradition of local workshops, and artisans to staff them, meant that despite falling transport costs, local or regional production was still quite common.

Tools were a crucial component of technology in the rapidly developing United States. Most every settler-farmer needed an axe, a pick, and/or a shovel. Other common tools were hammer, plows, hoes, perhaps a saw, and other basic hand tools.[55] Yet mass production and easy transportation were as yet not on the scene. As a consequence, production of these simple items tended to take place at the regional level. There were multiple, dispersed workshops for these and other simple tools. This pattern originated with the much-celebrated village blacksmith – the earliest "technologist" in many new settlements. But in many cases a local blacksmith evolved into a regional producer of tools. Thus, there were many regional workshops

[54] As Sokoloff points out, however, patenting was not evenly dispersed across the states of the new Union:

> [L]arge inter-regional differences first materialized between 1805 and 1811, when major increases in patenting occurred in many parts of Southern New England and New York but were essentially confined to metropolitan centers in other areas. Rural counties in these two regions raised their patent rates by well over 800 percent between 1799–1804 and 1805–1811, while analogous jumps in patenting in the rest of the Northeast, such as the leap in Northern New England from a base of 15.1 in 1812–1822 to 33.0 in 1823–1829 and 65.5 in 1830–1836, were not realized until the 1820s or later.

Sokoloff, Inventive Activity, at 828.

[55] The best source on tool ownership patterns in the late eighteenth century is Judith McCaw, "So Much Depends Upon a Red Wheelbarrow: Agricultural Tool Ownership in the Eighteenth-Century Mid-Atlantic," Early American Technology: Making and Doing Things from the Colonial Era to 1850 (Chapel Hill: University of North Carolina Press, 1994), at p. 328. McCaw finds axe ownership most common, with one quarter to one third of the households studied (in counties in New Jersey and Pennsylvania) owning more than one axe. Ibid., at p. 349. But there is surprising variation in patterns concerning plow and wagon ownership. See ibid., at p. 346.

specializing both in the design of tools and in constructing and perfecting production machinery for making them in commercial quantities. These workshops were the training ground for many practical trades people. They were the source of the cultural archetype, the Yankee tinkerer, or restless American experimenter. And in the end, they were the source of many nineteenth-century inventors and patentees.

2.2.3.2 The Importance of Wood

Another feature of invention lists from the founding era is the preponderance of inventions having to do with wood. The superficially primeval forests that blanketed the non-coastal United States had in fact been cultivated and, in some sense, managed by Native Americans for centuries.[56] Yet even with these human interventions, most land newly settled by Europeans and their offspring had large numbers of mature trees. Wood from these trees was the single greatest raw material in the early founding period. That is why so many patents from this era center on tools and implements for harvesting trees as well as the things that can be done to and with wood.

If a shortage of labor was the most important feature of early US economic history, abundant wood was not far behind. This was very different from the natural environment known to emigrants from western Europe: there in most cases the first-growth forests had been depleted or completely eliminated long before the new world opened to settlement. The first settlers had to learn how to adapt to their new environment, which stimulated a good deal of copying (mostly from Native peoples), adaptation (of old-world tools for new-world tasks), and outright invention.

British farming in the eighteenth century was characterized by a long-settled landscape, restricted farmland, and an abundant population of free rural labor. The early United States presented just the opposite. The land was, by British standards, undeveloped; it was available on easy terms from the colonial states and the new federal government; but there was a shortage of hands to work it.[57] The predictable result was adoption of farming techniques that British visitors saw as wasteful.[58] The earliest settler often planted Indian corn among the rows of mature trees. This required little tending and supplied food for the period during which a

56 My primary business is with technology, invention, and economic development. Even so, it must be recognized that the land and resources underlying US economic development were in most cases wrongfully acquired from the Native population that first inhabited the landscape. US economic development begins with this as one of two "original sins," the other being, obviously, slavery. See Stuart Banner, How the Indians Lost Their Land (Cambridge, MA: Belknap (Harvard University) Press, 2007) (describing in encyclopedic detail the many ways land was unfairly acquired from Native Americans: by (1) fraud, deceit, intentional incapacity (through alcohol), buying land from tribes that did not really have a claim over it, or from "representatives" with no legal authority to sell it, etc., (2) treaty, (3) removal, (4) war, and (5) genocide).

57 See Daniel Vickers, *The Northern Colonies: Economy and Society*, at pp. 222–223.

58 Ibid.

house and barn might be constructed. Land was often cleared using the "girdling" technique learned from the Native people: A deep band was cut into a tree, which interfered with the flow of nutrients from roots to limbs. This killed the tree, but it took time. With many acres to clear, this was an effective technique for all but the first few acres in the new homestead.

The immediate area of house and barn was cleared with an axe. This was the most ubiquitous tool on the American frontier, and it became over time the stuff of myth and legend.[59] It is also a fine example of the adaptation of European technology to the new American setting. American settlers took the conventional British axe and made it sturdier, heavier, and more efficient.[60] They took the narrow, graceful British axe head and made it thicker, heavier, and with a much longer cutting edge (or "bit"). They took the straight, narrow wooden handle, made it thicker and longer, and put a curve into it to give the tree chopper more leverage. The heavier axe head in turn created challenges: It was more likely to come loose or fly off the handle (hence that figure of speech), so they employed more elaborate techniques to keep it in place. These included wooden wedges driven between the axe head and handle, and head-handle attaching hardware of various sorts.

Numerous early patents provide a record of the incremental inventions that blazed a new trail (so to speak) in axe technology. The digest of patents issued between 1790 and 1839 lists nineteen patents that include "axe" in the title.[61] Axe design also tells a story of functional variation. Axes were specialized for various jobs. The "hewing axe" was the biggest axe, used for felling large, ancient trees. Other more specialized axes were developed for splitting wood, cutting notches for fitting wooden pieces together (mortise and tenon construction), the broadaxe (for finishing boards), the bull axe (an axe with a large hammer on the opposite end of the

59 See James Fenimore Cooper, The Chainbearer (1845) at 97, available at www.gutenberg.org/files/34916/34916-h/34916-h.htm:

> The American Axe! It has made more real and lasting conquests than the sword of any warlike people that ever lived; but they have been conquests that have left civilization in their train instead of havoc and desolation. More than a million of square miles of territory have been opened up from the shades of the virgin forest, to admit the warmth of the sun; and culture and abundance have been spread where the beast of the forest so lately roamed …

See also David E. Nye, America's Second Creation: Technology and Narratives of New Beginnings (Cambridge, MA: MIT Press, 2004), at p. 45 ("In the eighteenth century the axe became inseparable from the narratives of settlement, and by the early nineteenth century Americans understood that their distinctive axe was the icon of the American woodsman.").

60 See Henry J. Kauffman, American Axes: A Survey of Their Development and Their Makers (Brattleboro, VT: Stephen Greene Press, 1972).

61 Henry Ellsworth, Comm'r of Patents: A Digest of Patents Issued by the U.S. from 1790 to January 1, 1839 (1840), available at https://catalog.hathitrust.org/Record/002009332?type%5B%5D=title&lookfor%5B%5D=digest%20of%20patents&ft=ft.

axehead from the blade, used for driving large wooden pins in construction of sailing ships), and so on.[62]

2.2.3.3 Patents and Regional Franchises

In capital-intensive industries such as textile machinery, we have seen how large-scale capital from financial centers such as Boston provided the money to develop new technologies and industries. As mentioned, the legal instrument that made this possible was the business corporation. For smaller-scale inventors and businesses, the legal instrument that served this purpose was the federal patent. To an extent not appreciated by many today, patents supported the capital investment needed to develop an invention.[63] In addition, patents served as the foundation of a business model where the manufacturing and distribution of a patented invention was carried out by a network of regional investors and business partners. Before the advent of general incorporation laws, when each corporate charter required its own legislative Act, and before many state courts had developed elaborate bodies of law to handle complex commercial transactions, the familiarity and prestige of a federal property right – in the form of a patent – served as the solid ground on which a business structure could be built.

Evidence from a Connecticut fraud case decided in 1815[64] shows the value of a patent, and why patents were relied upon as the basis of business arrangements. The plaintiff argued (emphasis added):

> That the defendant offered to the plaintiffs to assign and sell to them a patent-right and licence to build, erect, use and improve, and also liberty to dispose of a certain machine for cutting, making and manufacturing combs, in consideration of the sum of 500 dollars to be paid by the plaintiffs to the defendant; and the defendant, that he might induce the plaintiffs to puchase said right and licence, confidently affirmed and declared to the plaintiffs, that he owned and possessed, as the sole proprietor thereof, a good and valid exclusive patent-right for cutting, making and manufacturing combs, and for improvements in machines for making the same, *secured by letters patent under the authority and laws of the United States*; and he

62 See Kauffman, American Axes, at Glossary, pp. 143–145.

63 Scholars have commented on the use of patent acquisition and licensing in the nineteenth century. See Adam Mossoff, *Patent Licensing and Secondary Markets in the Nineteenth Century*, 22 Geo. Mason L. Rev. 959 (2015); B. Zorina Khan, *Trolls and Other Patent Inventions: Economic History and the Patent Controversy in the Twenty-First Century*, 21 Geo. Mason L. Rev. 825, 837–839 (2014); Naomi R. Lamoreaux, Kenneth L. Sokoloff, and Dhanoos Sutthiphisal, Patent Alchemy: The Market for Technology in US History, Bus. Hist. Rev., Spring 2013, at pp. 3, 3–5, 34–36. On the use of patents to build regional franchising networks, see the excellent paper by Sean M. O'Connor, Origins of Patent Exhaustion: Jacksonian Politics, 'Patent Farming,' and the Basis of the Bargain (February 19, 2017) (University of Washington School of Law Research Paper No. 2017-05), available at SSRN: https://ssrn.com/abstract=2920738 or http://dx.doi.org/10.2139/ssrn.2920738.

64 *Bull* v. *Pratt*, 1 Conn. 342 (Conn. 1815).

> further falsely and fraudulently affirmed and declared to the plaintiffs, that the same was of great value, and that he had good right to sell the same, or any part thereof, as and for a good and valid patent-right, and thereby induced the plaintiffs to purchase a pretended right in and to the same.[65]

In the case, Defendant Pratt apparently copied a machine design from another patentee, Tryon. The court held that when Defendant Pratt assigned the patent he knew to be invalid, plaintiff Bull, Pratt's assignee, had a legitimate claim of fraud. Pratt's patent was acquired under the "registration" system of the 1793 Act, which required no examination by the Patent Office prior to granting a patent. Contemporaries complained that some unscrupulous people used patent models, deposited in the Patent Office, as the basis of "copycat" patents.[66] This and other misuses of the patent system led to the adoption of the patent examination system under the 1836 Act.

Patents served as the nucleus of private law arrangements not only because they were backed by the federal government. They could also be assigned, in whole or in part. This feature of flexible alienability proved to be extremely important. Partial patent assignments were quite common in the early stages of invention development in the founding era; Typically, a financier took a fractional interest in a patent in exchange for investment capital.[67] The patent property was both a vehicle into which investment could be directed and an asset that provided some security for the investment. Partnerships with a patent or patents at their center were the most common form of business organization aimed at developing and commercializing a new technology. At this early stage, patents acted as a catalyst for private law transactions. They were solid state-backed assets around which a new business could form and evolve.

As mentioned, transport costs and limited scale manufacturing made it difficult to centralize product assembly and distribution during this era. Even a simple device,

[65] 1 Conn. at 346–347.

[66] See *Davis* v. *Palmer*, 7 F. Cas. 154, 159 (C.C.D. Va. 1827) (No. 3,645) (Marshall, Circuit Justice) (instructing the jury that if "the imitator attempted to copy the [patented] model" and made an "almost imperceptible variation, for the purpose of evading the right of the patentee," then "this may be considered as a fraud on the law"), cited in Adam Mossoff, *Who Cares What Thomas Jefferson Thought about Patents? Reevaluating the Patent "Privilege" in Historical Context*, 92 Cornell L. Rev. 953, 993 n. 193 (2007).

[67] A typical case on this point is *Tyler* v. *Tuel*, 10 U.S. (6 Cranch) 324 (1810). There an inventor appeared to assign to a partnership, formed by the inventor and an investor, all rights to his patent, reserving from the partnership, and for himself, only rights to certain counties in Vermont: assignment included all rights "excepting in the counties of Chittenden, Addison, Rutland and Windham, in the state of Vermont ... "). 10 U.S. 324, 325. The patent, in other words, was the primary asset of the two-person partnership. The inventor-partner reserved to himself an exclusive territory that he would supply himself. The partner was expected to find and develop licensees in all other regions.

such as Eli Whitney's cotton gin, had to be manufactured in each region of use. Whitney learned this lesson through bitter experience. As a consequence, inventor-financier partnerships often turned to regional franchising.[68] Under this arrangement, rights to an invention were parceled out geographically. One partnership might operate in southern New England; another in the remainder of New England; others in the mid-Atlantic states; and still others in the south and on the western frontier (western Pennsylvania, Ohio, etc.). Each "master regional partner" in turn subdivided its territory into smaller units, hiring agents to market the patented design to local businesses. Manufacturing might be carried out by the regional "master partner," or instead by numerous local workshops in each major part of a regional territory.

ITHIEL TOWN'S LATTICE TRUSS BRIDGE DESIGN The franchising model required only that a patented design be brought to each region. Material, labor, and transport for distribution all came from local sources. Royalties under exclusive regional licenses flowed from the local/regional assignee back to the inventor-financial partnership at the heart of the whole operation. It was an early but effective version of the "market for ideas."

A patented bridge design from 1820 shows this market at work. A Connecticut architect and engineer, Ithiel Town, created a design for a wooden bridge with a distinctive feature: a diamond-shaped pattern of wooden boards or slats that served as the bridge's "side walls," running on both sides for the length of the bridge. This design effectively distributed the weight-bearing function of the side walls (which help to hold up the road surface of the bridge, preventing it from sagging). Town's patent information and lattice structure are reproduced in Figure 2.1, as well as a photograph of a Town-style bridge still standing today.[69]

According to a later historian,[70]

> The Town lattice rapidly came into favor for bridge building because the straightforward design could be erected quickly by the average carpenter; it utilized sawn planks instead of heavy hewn timbers; and it did not require massive abutments to resist the thrust of an arch.

[68] See, e.g., *Treadwell* v. *Bladen*, 24 F. Cas. 144 (Case No. 14,154) (C.C.E.D. Pa. 1827). (Patent on an improvement in "a machine for saving labour" in making biscuits: "On the 23d of May, 1826, Edward Treadwell, in consideration of $700, assigned to Elizabeth Watson the patent right, so far as the same applies to the city and county of Philadelphia, and all other towns and villages bordering on the river Delaware from Easton to Newcastle inclusive.")

[69] Lola Bennett, *From Craft to Science: American Timber Bridges, 1790–1840*, 35 APT [Assoc. of Preserv. Tech.] Bull. J. Preserv. Technol. 13 (2004), at p. 16: "Of the thousands of Town lattice trusses built in the nineteenth century, about 150 examples can still be found in the United States."

[70] Lola Bennett, *From Craft to Science*, at p. 16.

FIGURE 2.1. Covered bridge with Ithiel Town-designed triangular trusses

The Town design "proved to be extremely practical for long-span bridge construction."[71] It was, one historian has written, "an entirely new type of bridge truss," "a real invention, not resembling any design advanced for wooden spans in the thousands of years before its time that bridges had been built."[72]

It was also widely publicized:[73]

> In the decades following the granting of the 1820 lattice patent, inventors, engineers, and theorists responded-by building it, altering it, condemning it, and using it as an inspiration to create new structures and to devise methods of structural analysis. The dissemination of the lattice concept was enhanced by the growth in technical publishing that took place during the nineteenth century and that facilitated the border-crossing exchange of ideas. The international shipment of U.S. publications was not unusual during an era of popular and professional

[71] Harvie P. Jones, *The Town Lattice Truss in Building Construction*, 15 Bull. Assoc. Preserv. Technol. 39 (1983), at p. 39.

[72] Richard Sanders Allen, Covered Bridges of the Northeast (Chicago: Stephen Green Press, 1957; Dover Publishing ed., 2006), at p. 15.

[73] Gregory K. Dreicer, *Building Bridges and Boundaries: The Lattice and the Tube, 1820–1860*, 51 Tech. & Cult. 126 (2010), at pp. 128–129.

> curiosity about all aspects of American life. Moreover, the lattice bridge design was well suited for graphic reproduction. In comparison to the existing frame systems, it possessed a clarity and uniformity that helped make it an engineering pinup of the railway age.

But Town was a busy architect who had no interest in starting a company to build bridges.[74] Instead, he obtained a patent for his innovative truss design and, after proving the concept, set about promoting his design and licensing it as widely as possible. As he himself wrote in a widely circulated pamphlet describing the design:

> Those who wish to purchase rights, and to obtain particular directions for building bridges according to this improvement, (the description of which is annexed,) will please to write to me at the City of Washington in the District of Columbia, where myself or an agent will at all times attend promptly to the business.[75]

Though primary records of Town's bridge-related income are hard to come by, he appears to have set the royalty rate at one dollar per foot of bridge: "Town built only a few bridges himself, but he aggressively promoted his design through agents who sold the rights to use his patent at one dollar per foot of bridge."[76] He also employed a widespread enforcement strategy:

> Agents for the sale of the patent rights flourished in every shire town, collecting a royalty of $1 per foot of bridge to be built. Should the agent find an eager-beaver builder who had already put up a Town lattice bridge without payment of royalty, he would usually settle for $2 a foot.[77]

The sale of blueprints instead of whole bridges made sense, given the high transport costs of the era and the ready availability of wood throughout the United States, as it

74 See Mary Woods, *The First American Architectural Journals: The Profession's Voice*, 48 J. Soc. Arch. Historians 117, 119 (1989) ("The architects who founded the American Institution [of Architects] were major contributors to the country's architectural development in the 1820s and 1830s: William Strickland, Ithiel Town, Isaiah Rogers, James Gallier, T. U. Walter, and Alexander J. Davis."). R. W. Liscombe, A *"New Era in My Life": Ithiel Town Abroad*, 50 J. Soc. Arch. Hist. 5 (1991) (describing Town's European travels, visiting famous architectural sites).

75 Ithiel Town, A *Description of Ithiel Town's Improvement in the Construction of Wood and Iron Bridges*, 3 Am. J. Sci. Arts (1821), available at https://babel.hathitrust.org/cgi/imgsrv/download/pdf?id=hvd.32044102952934;orient=0;size=100;seq=184;num=158;attachment=0, at pp. 158, 165–166.

76 Lola Bennett, *From Craft to Science*, at p. 16.

77 Richard Sanders Allen, Covered Bridges of the Northeast, at p. 15. To some of these "eager beavers," who probably were just copying a bridge they had seen somewhere, Town's agents no doubt appeared as rent-seeking opportunists. On the other hand, the doubling of the normal bridge royalty would be reasonable in light of the 1793 Act, which provided for a standard remedy of triple the normal royalty. See Patent Act of 1793, ch. 11, § 5, 1 Stat. 318–323 (repealed 1836) (providing damages "at least equal to three times the price, for which the patentee has usually sold or licensed to other persons, the use of the said invention.").

then existed. In addition, the dissemination of Town's pamphlet, together with the growing number of bridges that could be inspected, meant that Town's *ideas* sometimes preceded the arrival of his licensing agents. The structure of US patent law, then as now, dispensed with the need to prove that a bridge builder learned about the lattice truss design directly from Town, or that a builder knew that Town had a patent.[78] If a Town agent discovered a bridge built to the Town specification, the builder was liable under the patent law. Town's royalty stream, in other words, was not dependent on his agents making deals in advance of bridge construction. This principle encouraged the diffusion of ideas in the young country. But royalties did depend on chasing down infringers: It put the burden of enforcing a patent on the shoulders of the patent owner. In return, patent law did away with any defense that infringing acts were done in ignorance of the patent.

2.2.4 *Patent Transactions and the Franchising Model*

Variations on Town's use of local licensing agents quickly appeared in the US economy. Because the patent statute allowed a patent owner to assign rights to a specific region, a patent owner could appoint a "master regional partner" who owned the exclusive right to practice the patentee's invention in a specific region. The following diagram illustrates the use of patent transactions in the typical regional franchising model in the founding era. The specific instance shown here is drawn from transactions related to the Blanchard shoe-making lathe patent of the 1820s and 1830s, used to make the wooden forms around which shoes were constructed (called shoe lasts).[79]

For Blanchard and others, this simple business structure, formed around a federal patent and exclusive regional assignments, served as the basic commercialization and distribution vehicle in the early nineteenth century. As we will see, it became even more elaborate (and gave rise to abuses) in its more mature form later in the century.

[78] See *Ames* v. *Howard*, 1 F. Cas. 755, 757 (C.C.D. Mass. 1833) (Story, J.) ("I am by no means prepared to say, that any notice is in cases of this sort ever necessary to any party, who is actually using a machine in violation of a patent-right."); see also Robert P. Merges, A *Few Kind Words for Absolute Liability in Patent Law*, 31 Berkeley Tech. L.J. 1 (2016) (explaining the traditional rule, as well as criticism of it)); Patrick R. Goold, IP Accidents: Negligence Liability in Intellectual Property (Cambridge: Camridge Univ. Press, 2022) (proposing alternative to strict liability, a negligence standard).

[79] The example is drawn from Carolyn C. Cooper, Shaping Invention: Thomas Blanchard's Machinery and Patent Management in Nineteenth-Century America (New York: Columbia University Press, 1991), at pp. 172–173. The inventor is Blanchard; the corporation is the Blanchard Gunstock Turning Factory; the regional agent is Colonel Henry Orne; and the localities are Danvers and Lynn, Massachusetts, and "elsewhere," presumably also in Massachusetts. The early Blanchard model expanded in later years as the marketing of shoe-making machinery became more sophisticated. See Ross Thomson, The Path to Mechanized Shoe Production in the United States (Chapel Hill: University of North Carolina Press, 1989), at p. 163.

2.2.4.1 Fractional Patent Shares as Quasi-Stock

In addition to supporting franchising, patents also acted as quasi-securities.[80] Fractional patent rights served much the same function as shares of stock. In this era, many businesses were single-product affairs. Also, some patents covered multi-step, "end-to-end" production processes. (Oliver Evans's "hopperboy" patent for an integrated grist mill, for example.) So, a patent covering a product or factory design served as a reasonable proxy for the entire business built around the patented item. Fractional shares of a patent, then, represented shares of a business enterprise. These fractions were sold off or assigned into a partnership by the inventor, often as a joint enterprise with the inventor's first or primary investor. This investor usually received the first partial assignment from the inventor. The different fractional patent shares were later subdivided, combined, bought, and sold, much in the way of shares of stock in an incorporated company.[81]

An 1845 case, *Valentine* v. *Marshal*,[82] shows how it all worked. The court states the pattern of assignments among the facts of the case:

> The action was commenced at April term, 1843, for the violation of a patent right granted on the 24th of April, 1840, to Daniel Fitzgerald, Jesse Fitzgerald, and Elisha Fitzgerald. The plaintiffs allege they are sole legal owners thereof. The declaration avers that on the 27th of November, 1840, the patentees assigned the said patent, &c., to Nestor Houghton, which assignment was duly recorded according to law. That on the 16th of April, 1841, Houghton assigned the same to Henry Valentine, plaintiff, and Winthrop Eaton, which assignment was duly recorded May 21, 1841. That on the 20th of April, 1841, the last-named assignees assigned to Alexander Cassilli, plaintiff, one-fourth part of said letters patent. That on the 31st of December, 1841, the said Winthrop Eaton assigned to said Henry Valentine one half of three-quarters (being his whole remaining interest), and plaintiffs made proof of the assignment.[83]

Figure 2.2 shows the transactions in diagram form.

[80] The US experience tracks a short-lived precedent from Britain. In the 1690s two British developments converged: (1) a primitive stock market was founded, in part to help channel excess capital accumulated due to the closing of foreign investment opportunities in the European wars of the era; and (2) the exception, encoded in the Statute of Monopolies, for corporate entities. Clever promoters put these together, by packaging of dubious patents in corporate form for offer on the stock market. See Christine MacLeod, *The 1690s Patents Boom: Invention or Stock-Jobbing?*, 39 J. Econ. Hist. 549, 550 (1986) ("[In] the early 1690s ... the patent system was subject to the same forces which played havoc with the embryonic Stock Exchange. There was a spectacular outburst of patenting, but not necessarily of inventing; the ready availability of capital promoted both worthless 'projects' and a few technically valuable experiments."). See also Phillip Johnson, Privatised Law Reform, at supra, pp. 85–91 (explaining the origins of British limits on patent ownership to no more than five co-owners).

[81] Indeed, in modern times fractional interests in a patent may be considered a security. See *State* v. *Williams, Blue Sky L. Rep.* (CCH) ¶ 71,280 (Wash. Super. 1975), aff'd 17 Wash. App. 368, 563 P.2d 1271 (1977).

[82] 28 F. Cas. 869 (C.C.S.D.N.Y. 1845).

[83] 28 F. Cas. 869, 869 (C.C.S.D.N.Y. 1845).

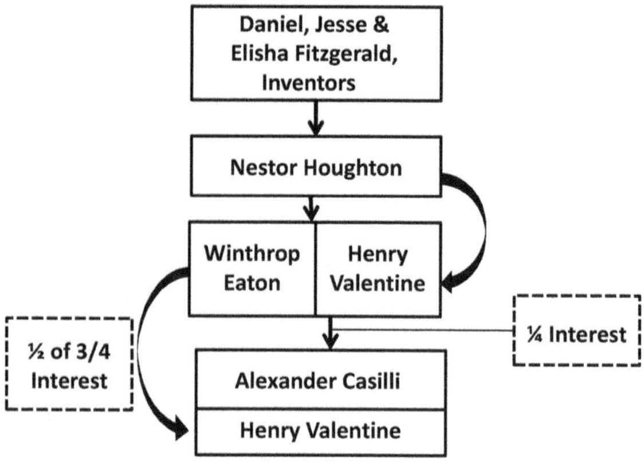

FIGURE 2.2. Complex fractional patent shares assignment pattern

The result of these transactions was to concentrate full ownership in the hands of Casilli and Valentine, in the ratio of 1:4, one-fourth for Casilli, three-fourths for Valentine. (Recall that Valentine retained his half of the original three-fourths interest, so when Eaton assigned the other half of the three-fourths interest to Valentine, that gave Valentine a three-fourths total interest in the patent). Unfortunately, the court dismissed the suit because the Eaton-Valentine assignment was not recorded in a timely fashion, and the court found no other convincing evidence for it.[84] Casilli and Valentine could have re-filed the suit after proper proof, or joined Eaton as a plaintiff, but there is no record of that. My point here is not about legal proof or procedure, however; it is just to show how in the nineteenth century fractional interests in patents were traded and assembled like blocks of corporate stock.

It is interesting to think about the Figure 2.2 transactions, and the possible role and function of the first assignee, Nestor Houghton. Was he a speculator, buying up patents for resale to others? Perhaps he had invested early, even at the patent application stage, providing capital to the inventors so they could complete the invention and file a patent.[85] Was he a matchmaker, a middleman, leveraging a network of inventors and/or patent lawyers on one hand, and industrial investors on the other? There is certainly evidence that some patent assignees received "finders fees" for putting inventor/patent sellers together with buyers of patent rights.[86]

[84] 28 F. Cas. 869, 869 (C.C.S.D.N.Y. 1845).

[85] On investors who sought assignment of patent applications, see *Boston Mfg. Co.* v. *Fiske*, 3 F. Cas. 957 (Case No. 6,394) (C.C.D. Mass. 1820) (action by the Lowell textile factory company; the court held that acquisition of a patent application gave the assignee Manufacturing Company standing to sue for infringement after the application issues as a patent).

[86] See *Burr* v. *Gregory*, 4 F. Cas. 813, 813–814 (C.C.S.D.N.Y. 1828) (action for enforcement (via specific performance) of a contract to award a 3/15ths interest in a patent to a "matchmaker" who put the inventor into contact with an inventor; case dismissed due to lack of federal

Whatever his specific purpose, Houghton's presence in the chain of transactions helps illustrate that there was a vibrant, liquid market for early-stage "startup" financing in the early nineteenth century, and that patent rights were the preferred vehicle for these investments. We will have more to say about the development of this market, and some of its abuses, in Chapter 3.

2.3 PATENT LAW AND ADMINISTRATION IN THE FOUNDING ERA

After quickly canvassing basic economic trends in the founding era, we turned to the business aspects of patents. Our attention moves now to the government agencies involved in granting and enforcing patents – that is, the parts of the US government responsible for administration of the patent system.

2.3.1 *Basic Attitudes toward Patents*

Economic development was understood as the crucial object of the founding era government. Patent protection was an integral part of this policy. As George Washington wrote in his first annual report to Congress in 1790:

> The advancement of Agriculture, commerce and Manufactures, by all proper means, will not, I trust, need recommendation. But I cannot forbear intimating to you the expediency of giving effectual encouragement as well to the introduction of new and useful inventions from abroad, as to the exertions of skill and genius in producing them at home; and of facilitating the intercourse between the distant parts of our Country by a due attention to the Post-Office and Post Roads.[87]

Under the 1790 Act, there is some evidence that patent examination was quite rigorous; according to patent historian P. J. Federico, the grant rate appeared to be less than 50 percent.[88] Perhaps this reflected the influence of Thomas Jefferson, who as Secretary of State was one of three members of the 1790 Act Patent Board. But this changed rapidly with the coming of patent "registration" under the 1793 Act. And in any event, the application fee of $5 under the 1790 Act ($30 after 1793), though nontrivial, was far lower than that of the other major patent-granting

jurisdiction as there were no patent issues in the case, only contract issues, which are a matter of state and not federal law).

87 President George Washington, Message to Congress, January 8, 1790, available at National Archives Online, https://founders.archives.gov/documents/Washington/05-04-02-0361. (The reference to "encouragement" for "inventions from abroad" bears the influence of Alexander Hamilton, who advocated "patents of importation"; but such patents have never been permitted under American patent law, which then and now bars patents for inventions that are known from published sources anywhere in the world).

88 P. J. Federico, Operation of the Patent Act of 1790, 18 J. Pat. Off. Soc'y 237, 244 (1936) (49 of 114 applications were granted in 1790 and 1791; other applications were pending when the 1793 Act was passed).

countries of Britain and France, where patents cost roughly $585 and $300 (for a fifteen-year patent) in the nineteenth century.[89] In litigation, the win rate for patent owners was roughly 50 percent (on a very small sample) between 1800 and 1820.[90] But, especially after 1793, this rate may well be affected by the patent registration system. Litigation was almost the only way to weed out invalid patents.

For various reasons – small sample size especially – these figures do not capture the overall enthusiasm of Americans for their patent system in the founding era. Consider this statement from Justice Joseph Story in a case from 1818:[91]

> [I]t must be remembered, that patents in England receive a strict construction, because they are there considered as being in derogation of common right. Whereas, in the United States, they are more justly regarded as bounties upon the productions of genius, and as means of great and extensive benefit to the public. As such, they ought here to receive the most liberal construction; and no patent should be held void, if it in fact fulfil the ultimate design of the patent law; if it furnish in the specification a description essentially certain, to enable the public to avail itself of the invention after the patent term shall have expired. This is the object of the law; and to this, as the great end of all its provisions, ought the attention of the judiciary and juries to be directed.[92]

An 1833 opinion,[93] again from Justice Story on circuit in Massachusetts, also proclaimed a generous attitude toward patents:

> Patents for inventions are not to be treated as mere monopolies odious in the eyes of the law, and therefore not to be favored; nor are they to be construed with the utmost rigor, as *strictissimi juris*. The constitution of the United States, in giving authority to congress to grant such patents for a limited period, declares the object to be to promote the progress of science and useful arts, an object as truly national, and meritorious, and well founded in public policy, as any which can possibly be within the scope of national protection. Hence it has always been the course of the American courts, (and it has latterly become that of the English courts also,) to construe these patents fairly and liberally, and not to subject them to any over-nice and critical refinements. The object is to ascertain, what, from the fair sense of the

89 B. Zorina Khan, The Democratization of Invention, at p. 50 (citing sources placing the total fees under the 1790 Act at no more than $5); 32 (regarding costs for British patents); and 43 (France).

90 Ibid., at p. 82.

91 Because many patent cases originated in two major urban centers, Boston and Philadelphia, the two Supreme Court justices assigned to ride circuit in those regions – Story for Boston, Bushrod Washington for Philadelphia – authored many early patent law opinions. See Edward C. Walterscheid, *To Promote the Progress of Useful Arts: American Patent Law and Administration, 1787–1836 (Part I)*, 79 J. Pat. & Trademark Off. Soc'y 61, 74 (1997) ("Of the 58 lower-court cases, a remarkable forty were decided by two Supreme Court justices sitting as circuit court judges. In other words, most of the reported judicial interpretation of the Patent Act of 1793 was by two individuals, Justice Bushrod Washington and Justice Joseph Story.").

92 *Barrett* v. *Hall*, 2 F. Cas. 914, 922 (C.C.D. Mass. 1818) (Story, J.).

93 *Ames* v. *Howard*, 1 F.Cas. 755 (No. 326) (C.C.D. Mass. 1833) (Story, J.).

words of the specification, is the nature and extent of the invention claimed by the party; and when the nature and extent of that claim are apparent, not to fritter away his rights upon formal or subtile [sic] objections of a purely technical character.[94]

The association of patents with "mere monopolies" – a reference to the British Statute of Monopolies – had been broken. The US patent system was both "national" and "meritorious," terms that were close to synonymous for the arch-federalist Story. But implicit in the passage is also the thought that the patent system is a *success*, in part because the courts were not looking for ways to invalidate or limit patents.

Certainly, Justice Story saw the merit in the invention at issue in the *Ames* case, a significant cost-saving improvement in paper-making machinery.[95] The key for inventor John Ames was that Story understood the nature of Ames's improvement and its relationship to the other components of the paper-making machine. Ames's patent said: "What I do claim, as new and as my invention, is the construction and use of the peculiar cylinder above described, and the several parts thereof in combination for the purpose aforesaid."[96] The defendant, Charles Howard, accused of infringing the Ames patent, argued that he was not in fact infringing. For Howard, the phrase "the several parts thereof in combination" referred to the parts of the novel *cylinder* – which apparently opened the door for the defendant to argue that some details of its cylinder construction were different from Ames's. But Story, affirming a trial court instruction to the jury, agreed instead with Ames. The "parts … in combination" meant the parts of the entire paper-making machine, and not the parts of the cylinder. Story: "It is not then the cylinder alone, or its several parts, which are claimed per se; but they are claimed in their actual combination with the other machinery to make paper. In this view of the clause full effect is given to all the words, and the sense is at once natural and consistent."[97]

94 1 F.Cas. 755, 756.

95 On the construction and importance of the paper-making machine invented by the patent owner, John Ames, see Judith McCaw, Most Wonderful Machine: Mechanization and Social Change in Berkshire Paper-Making, 1801–1885 (Princeton, NJ: Princeton University Press, 1987), at p. 101. See also ibid., at p. 164:

> The introduction of the cylinder machine in Berkshire County owed most to Ames. He patented his version of the device in 1822 and subsequently became New England's first paper-making machine builder. At least two of the earliest Berkshire mills to buy paper machines purchased them from Ames.

96 *Ames* v. *Howard*, 1 F. Cas. 755, 756 (C.C.D. Mass. 1833).

97 1 F. Cas. 755, 757 (C.C.D. Mass. 1833). The "combination claim" recognized by Story is similar in some ways to a claim to an improvement (discussed infra). A claim combining Part A, Part B, etc., and then the Ames cylinder as a separate part, is infringed only by someone who uses the Ames cylinder in combination with the other parts. Part A and Part B standing alone, or in combination with a non-Ames cylinder (or alternative part that does the work of the cylinder), do not infringe. This limits patent coverage to Ames's contribution, the cylinder – much like the limitations inherent in an improvement patent.

This interpretation would apparently include a wider array of specific cylinder constructions (as long as they followed the basic principles of Ames's design). It is an example of the liberal American view on improvement patents (described later), but more broadly, of the characteristic attempt by American courts to seek out the innovative core of an invention and protect the main principle if possible.

2.3.2 *Rejecting Patents of Importation: Establishing the Important Economic Functions of the Public Domain*

A simple heuristic for characterizing US patent policy in various historical periods, mentioned in Chapter 1, is to differentiate between Hamiltonian Moments and Jeffersonian Moments. In general, the founding period was more Hamilton than Jefferson; it was more favorable to inventors and a robust patent law. But as with other periods, the span of years between 1790 and 1820 were hardly monolithic. Within a generally Hamiltonian portion of historical time, there were Jeffersonian moments. The original 1790 Act Patent Board, as we have seen, was no pushover when it came to patent applicants. And some very early federal court cases followed British precedent, applying a formalistic and somewhat restrictive patent jurisprudence.[98]

[98] See, e.g., *Woodcock* v. *Parker*, 30 F. Cas. 491, 492 (C.C.D. Mass. 1813) (Story, J.) (appearing to construe a specification as claiming an entire machine when arguably it only claimed a single, improved element, the "spring plate"):

> In the present case, if all parts of the machine, except the spring plate, (which the plaintiff claims as emphatically his own invention,) existed before, and were applied to produce the same effects in the same manner; and the plaintiff has established the spring plate to be his exclusive invention, still his patent ought to have been confined to such improvement, and not to have comprehended the whole machine. [Patent invalid.]

A short time later, Story's Supreme Court colleague Justice Bushrod Washington signaled a similar formalistic approach in *Cutting* v. *Myers*, 6 F. Cas. 1081, 1082 (C.C.D. Pa. 1818) (B. Washington, J.), a case involving the Robert Fulton steamboat patent. Justice Washington, on circuit, granted the defendant's demurrer (motion to dismiss the case) on a very technical ground, viz:

> [The patentee/plaintiff's filings] contain no allegation that a patent did issue to [Robert Fulton]; or secondly, that it was tested [i.e., signed] by the president [Jefferson, as the patent issued prior to Madison's swearing-in that year]. As to the first, the allegation is, that a patent was made out in due form of law under the seal, and in the name of the United States, by which there was granted to the said [Fulton] &c. But the law proceeds to declare that the patent so made out shall be delivered to the petitioner, and that no person can receive it until he has taken the oath, and made the disclosure prescribed in the third section of the act. Now there is no allegation in these counts that the patent was more than made out, or that it was ever delivered to [Fulton], and consequently, there is nothing averred from which the court can imply that those conditions [i.e., the oath and associated "disclosures"] were performed, without which [Fulton] was incapable of receiving a patent.

But if these were minor checks on the momentum of the Hamiltonian thrust, another issue represented a more forceful pushback. This was the rejection of patents of importation. In keeping with his mercantilist instincts, Hamilton specifically called for such patents in his Report on Manufactures. This idea was backed (or perhaps initiated) by Hamilton's assistant, the pro-manufacturing advocate Tench Coxe. Jefferson, however, was opposed, as were a substantial number of other political figures.[99] Delegates to the Constitutional Convention had rejected a broader intellectual property clause than the eventual clause 8 of Article I; the rejected version included patents of importation as well as bounties or rewards for encouragement of new inventions and industries. The same fate befell a series of bills leading up to the 1790 Act: Importation patents were eliminated from the coverage of the Patent Act.

This was a victory for Jeffersonian forces. Thomas Jefferson himself was suspicious of patents. It was Madison's support for limited term patents and copyrights that led to the inclusion of Article I, Section 8, clause 8. And, because Hamilton is closely associated with industrial development and economic policy generally, it might be supposed that eliminating patents of importation proved costly to the young country.[100] But, it seems, the opposite is true. For reasons some founders understood, and maybe for some they did not, limiting patents to those technologies that were new to the world (not just the United States) may have promoted economic growth more than import patents would have done.

The first reason is that, at least after the immediate post-Revolution period, economic prospects were good enough in the young United States that special rewards such as patents may not have been necessary to induce crafts people to bring overseas inventions into the country.[101] Thus the classic reason for patents of importation – pioneered in Britain under Queen Elizabeth I – was mostly absent.[102]

[99] See, e.g., Letter, Jefferson to Madison, July 31, 1788, in J. P. Boyd, ed., The Papers of Thomas Jefferson (Princeton, 1956) 13:442–443 (arguing against any form of government-backed monopoly right, including the limited-term monopolies authorized by the intellectual property clause).

[100] See Edward C. Walterscheid, *To Promote the Progress of Useful Arts*:

> The United States, however, would become the first country wherein novelty, or more correctly the type of anticipation that precludes novelty and hence patentability, would be predicated on what was known or used not merely within its borders but anywhere in the world. That the United States should take this approach was all the more remarkable because it occurred at a time when the new nation desperately needed to develop a manufacturing base through the transfer of technology from Europe and particularly Great Britain. Yet the Congress in enacting the Patent Act of 1790 deleted provisions which would have expressly authorized patents of importation. The statutory language was sufficiently ambiguous, however, that it would take several decades before judicial interpretation firmly established that novelty meant new anywhere in the world and not merely in the United States.

[101] See, e.g., David J. Jeremy, Transatlantic Industrial Revolution.

[102] See Christine MacLeod, Inventing the Industrial Revolution, at p. 12 (describing the role of William Cecil, Lord Burghley, in promoting British patents as a way to accelerate growth in the Elizabethan period).

All that was needed was a generous immigration policy; then, as now, it paid off economically to make the United States a beacon of opportunity to all people regardless of their place of birth.[103] Skilled immigrants brought with them not only the mental blueprints needed to build foreign inventions but also the crucial "tacit" knowledge[104] that is hard to write down but essential to actually make many machines and inventions work well.[105]

The second reason patents of importation might have been a bad idea is that they would have effectively weakened the standard of patentability. Though the early patent system required only that inventions be novel and useful, a *worldwide* (vs. US-only, or local) definition of novelty required that a patentee had to do more than copy and import. He or she had to create something not known or used anywhere (at least insofar as that was provable). As Justice Story said, drawing a contrast with two features of English law:

> How, indeed, can it be possible, that an English court should deem some intellectual labour, beyond the novelty of the combination, necessary for a patent [i.e., something akin to "inventive step" or nonobviousness], when it is the acknowledged law of England (different in that respect from our own), that the first importer of an invention, known and used in foreign parts, may be entitled to a patent as the inventor in England? What of intellect is employed in the mere importation of a known machine? An inventor, in the sense of the English law, is the first maker, or constructor, or introducer, in England.[106]

As Story recognized, a worldwide novelty standard required more "intellectual labor" than local novelty. This had two benefits. It widened the circle of available, unpatentable technology. Overseas inventions were accessible, patent-free, to

[103] In this respect, it is worth noting that US patent law fairly rapidly abandoned its early policy of disfavoring patents for foreign-born but US-based inventors.

[104] For the origins of this concept, see Michael Polanyi, The Tacit Dimension (New York: Anchor Books, 1967). For a more contemporary elaboration in the context of patents, see Peter Lee, *Transcending the Tacit Dimension: Patents, Relationships, and Organizational Integration in Technology Transfer*, 100 Cal. L. Rev. 1503 (2012).

[105] There was in addition what would today be termed a "textualist" objection to patents of importation: Those who introduced them would not be "inventors" as called for by the Constitution. See Jeanne C. Fromer, *The Intellectual Property Clause's External Limitations*, 61 Duke L.J. 1329, 1353–1354 (2012) (footnotes omitted):

> Although a draft of the Patent Act of 1790 provided for patents of importation, the final version of the law that Congress passed during its first session did not authorize them. The provision was removed on March 5, 1790, after debate in the House of Representatives. Representative Thomas Fitzsimons explained that it had been removed because of "the Constitutional power being Questionable." Correspondence reveals that James Madison – and possibly others – doubted the constitutionality of patents of importation … Madison did not believe that Congress could constitutionally provide for patents of importation because these patents seemed to lie outside of the means specified in the IP Clause, which allows patent rights to be conferred on inventors, not on importers of already-created inventions.

[106] *Earle* v. *Sawyer*, 8 F. Cas. 254, 256 (C.C.D. Mass. 1825) (Story, J.).

everyone in the United States. And it also pushed inventors who wanted patents to create something truly novel. It is not evident from Story's words why he felt mere importation was not enough to warrant a patent. In the immediate context he was distinguishing a British case as exhibiting a low standard for patentability. But perhaps he felt the young country, aspiring to take its place in the community of nations, should set its sights higher than the British courts had. Or maybe he felt a patent should be reserved for things that exhibit some sustained thought or clever insight. ("What of intellect is employed in the mere importation of a known machine?"). It is impossible to say with our current historical data whether the extra rigor Story seemed to demand played any part in the rapid industrialization of the United States, but it certainly did correlate with an uptick in inventive activity in the newly launched Republic.

2.3.3 *Improvement Patents and the Allocation of Inventive Property*

There is some evidence that in Britain, patents were intended to stimulate and support a new trade or industry.[107] One rationale for this was that if a patent did not open employment in a new trade, it might in fact be a threat to current employees in an established field. This was a concern, as were any developments that undermined employment in heavily populated Britain.[108] The case law from eighteenth-century England presents some evidence to the contrary, but given the cost of acquiring a British patent, it would only be rational to pursue patents on fairly major machines or techniques.

From the earliest cases, the American courts spoke favorably of improvement patents. The low patent fees encouraged patenting of more incremental inventions. And there seems also to have been a spirit of "all hands on deck": every crafts person, machinist, and inventor was welcome to contribute what they could to the great task of economic development. Certainly, the invention of the early machines we have discussed – the Blanchard lathe, Moody's textile spinning and weaving machinery, rifle boring, and many others – invited tinkering and optimization. This is typical, as Habbakuk describes:

[107] Christine MacLeod, Inventing the Industrial Revolution, at p. 13.

[108] Ibid., at p. 13: "It followed that the patenting of mere improvements was frowned upon – whether to an existing trade or a patented invention since they were liable to interfere with the livelihoods of established workers." A pair of later cases give some credence to the argument. They rely on highly technical grounds to invalidate improvement patents that might have been valid under a more generous regime. *Tetley* v. *Easton*, 22 Law Times Rep. (No. 557) 134 (Queen's Bench, November 25, 1853); *Holmes* v. *Northwestern and London Railway*, 22 L.J. Rep. 57 (Ct. Comm. Pleas, 1853). In both cases, the British courts invalidated patents for stated improvements. The defect in each case was that the inventor's specification did not specifically disclaim what was old in the art. The essence of the holding in each case was overclaiming: appearing to claim what was old along with the novel improvement.

> The initial effect of most of the great inventions was to save labour per unit of output at the expense of some increase in capital or at least without much saving. The saving of capital came later from such improvements as [in textiles] the increase in the number of spindles on each mule and the increase of the speed of the spindle ... When the [new] capital-intensive labour-saving machines had been installed, there usually proved to be possibilities of technical improvement in their construction and use. For the economy as a whole, one important form of capital-saving consisted of labour-saving improvements in the manufacture of machines ...[109]

American courts adapted patent law to meet these developments. Joseph Story's son recounts how the new judge was challenged in the early patent cases:[110]

> Cases began to arise involving all the principles applicable to Patents; and to the adjudication of these, the existing rules were not only to be practically applied as they never before had been, but new rules and modifications were demanded. The questions were often so novel, that counsel were forced to argue, and the Court to decide, without chart and upon general principles. I have often heard my father relate, that in several of the early cases tried before him, the gentlemen engaged in them apologized for the mode in which they had been conducted, saying, that the law was so without precedent and forms, that they knew not how to proceed ...
>
> The condition of the law relating to patents, when my father came to the Bench, has already been adverted to. In its principles and practice it was nearly formless in America, and the English decisions were so contradictory and unsatisfactory as to afford little aid. The strong inventive genius of New England began to develop rapidly after the [Revolutionary] war, and his Circuits were crowded with patent cases. It became his office, therefore, almost to construct the law on this subject, and the system which is now developed is mainly owing to his effort. This law then in England was a mere shuttlecock between equity, with its liberal doctrines, and the common law, with its fear of monopoly.

With more specific patents, the question of patenting improvements arose early in US cases. An 1804 opinion by Bushrod Washington, another early shaper of US patent law, Washington addresses the issue in the context of a patent on a tilt (or trip) hammer, a large hammer that is lifted by a water-powered cog wheel.[111] The spinning wheel has protrusions that lift the hammer and then drop it on an anvil or other surface, bringing great force to bear on whatever is being hammered. The

[109] H. J. Habakkuk, Labor-Saving Inventions, at pp. 52 and 55.

[110] William Wetmore Story, The Life and Letters of Joseph Story (Boston: Little Brown Publishers, 1851), pp. 236–237; and ibid., volume 2, p. 584. The early Fessenden patent treatise concurs in this view. See Thomas Green Fessenden, Essay on the Law of Patents (Boston: Charles Ewer Publisher, 2nd ed., 1822) at dedication page ("To the Hon. Joseph Story ... To whose learned and luminous decisions the author is indebted for a great and valuable part of the present edition of his treatise ...").

[111] *Reutgen* v. *Kanowrs*, 20 F. Cas. 555 (C.C.D. Pa. 1804) (Case no. 11,710).

inventor Kanowrs (identified as "a German, and poor"),[112] conceived of a design where the hammer and anvil surfaces had complementary concave shapes, which was ideal for rounding or cutting off bolts to a specific length. The defendant, named Graunt, began using the one tilt hammer that Kanowrs had constructed, when he (Graunt) leased the same farmland Kanowrs had formerly occupied. (In fact, the owner of the farmland leased to Kanowrs and later Graunt had helped with the design of the Kanowrs trip hammer.) But the second lessee Graunt had added an additional feature: swedges or cutting edges (presumably in the hammer surface), which might have assisted in cutting bolts to a certain length. Justice Washington discussed both the Kanowrs trip hammer and its relationship to the infringer's adaptation of it. The chief legal issue was infringement, which Washington said boiled down to this question:

> [H]ave the defendants, or either of them, used a machine similar to the one mentioned in the plaintiff's patent and specification. The specification states the parts to be, a strong platform, of a given form, with two upright posts, for a hammer to move in, and to be operated by a cog-wheel, connected with the handle of the hammer; the force; water, or any thing else; corresponding concaves in the hammer and anvil. The machine used by the defendant, Graunt, is of that description; but in addition, swedges are used. The question is, is the defendant's improvement of swedges, an improvement on the principle, or the form, or proportions of the plaintiff's machine; if the first, he has as much right to use his improvement, as the plaintiff has to use his original invention. If otherwise, and the defendant has used the original invention, thus altered, it is a violation of the plaintiff's right.[113]

A trip hammer so different from the Kanowrs model that it operates on a new "principle" might receive its own patent. But a mere improvement in "form" or "proportions" would simply be an infringement of Kanowrs' patented design.

In another case, Justice Washington recognized the importance of incremental innovation, valuing a basic invention for its contribution to a more effective later improvement.[114] And elsewhere Justice Story used a simple example to

[112] 20 F. Cas. 555, 555 (at Synopsis).

[113] 20 F. Cas. 555, 556. The key is the significance of Graunt's addition of swedges to the Kanowrs design of double-concave hammer surfaces. This explicit weighing of the relative virtues of the patented item (Kanowrs' design) and the accused patent infringer's variation on it (Graunt's addition of swedges) is a constant feature of nineteenth-century patent cases.

[114] The case is *Gray* v. *James*, 10 F. Cas. 1019, 1020–1021 (C.C.D. Pa. 1817) (Case no. 5,719):

> [I]f another person can superadd to that invention something which will remove all its defects, and render it useful, it immediately becomes valuable, not on account of its own qualities, but because of its capacity to receive the improvement and with its aid to become useful. The original discovery, and the improvement, became articles of traffic between the two discoverers, as soon as the improvement was made which it was their mutual interest to give value to. Is the defendant's improved machine valuable? This is admitted. But why is it so? Because he has availed himself of Perkins's original discovery on which to ingraft his own, and without which his own would have been useless to himself and to the world. But how did he possess himself of Perkins's discovery? By an unlawful invasion of property to which Perkins was exclusively entitled. Had he, as he

discuss the importance of dividing entitlements for basic inventions and improvements:[115]

> The original inventor of a machine is exclusively entitled to a patent for it. If another person invent an improvement on such machine, he can entitle himself to a patent for such improvement only, and does not thereby acquire a right to patent and use the original machine; and if he does procure a patent for the whole of such a machine with the improvement, and not for the improvement only, his patent is too broad, and therefore void … Mere colorable differences, or slight improvements, cannot shake the right of the original inventor. To illustrate these positions; suppose a watch was first invented by a person, so as to mark the hours only, and another person added the work to mark the minutes, and a third the seconds; each of them using the same combinations and mode of operations, to mark the hours, as the first. In such a case, the inventor of the second-hand could not have entitled himself to a patent embracing the inventions of the other parties.

But the inventor of the second-hand might well obtain a patent for this improvement in clocks.

Reading the early cases on patentable improvements, it is hard not to see the analogy with land settlement.[116] Under purchases policies of the US Land Office (discussed later in this chapter), each settler was sold a specific parcel. The vast public lands were divided and subdivided into plots of various size, depending on the needs (and budgets) of individual settlers. Something similar was at work in patent law. The vast intellectual landscape of early nineteenth-century technologies was divided up into individual claims. Judges (and later the Patent Office) tried to assess and award the proper allocation of patent power that had been earned by the inventive work of each patentee. As patents had been broken loose from the world of

was bound to do, sought to acquire a title to this property by contract, is it to be believed that it would have been treated by the parties as of no value? It is obvious that it would not. This course of reasoning is intended to show, that when it was stated by the court to the jury that the charge of worthlessness against Perkins's machine came with a bad grace from the defendant, who was making so profitable a use of it, it was no answer to say that it is useful merely on account of the improvement which others had made to it; because, if it was useful in that respect, and without the original discovery the improvement could not have been made, it followed that the original discovery was useful and valuable.

115 *Odiorne* v. *Winkley*, 18 F. Cas. 581, 582 (C.C.D. Mass. 1814) (Case no. 10,432).

116 The connection between land settlement and patents was made explicit in one proposal (never adopted) to award bounties or premiums to inventors in the form of land grants. See Edward C. Walterscheid, *Patents and Manufacturing in the Early Republic*, 80 J. Pat. & Trademark Off. Soc'y 855, 864 n.32 (1998):

> [Tench Coxe's] suggestion that land be used as the premiums [with which to reward inventors under a proposed "bounty" or reward system] was not based on European practice, but instead seems to have been derived from the recent requests made to the Continental Congress for land grants as a reward for invention. See, e.g., [Frank] D. Prager, "The Steamboat Pioneers Before the Founding Fathers," [37 J. Pat. Off. Soc'y 486, 493–494 (1955)]; and E. [Burke] Inlow, The Patent Grant (Baltimore[: Johns Hopkins Univ. Press] 1950) at p. 45, citing from Journals of the Continental Congress (1785) XXVIII:349.

FIGURE 2.3. Plat map of a portion of Guthrie County, Iowa
Source: Library of Congress, LCCN Permalink, https://lccn.loc.gov/2008629002.

political influence and speculator/courtiers, and as the scope of individual patents was recast from entire businesses to incremental technical contributions, inventive space was divided and subdivided. The map in Figure 2.3, of a typical land allocation in the United States, shows the basic unit, the section, and its divisions and subdivisions in one Iowa county (Guthrie).

This plat map could as well stand in for a patent landscape drawn in the early nineteenth century. The improvement patent was the legal tool used to subdivide inventive space. It had, in some ways, the same democratizing effect as public land sales by the US Land Office. Individual claims were superimposed on the vast technical frontier, and ownership was allocated accordingly. Visionaries such as Alexander Hamilton may have pushed in 1791 for an innovative manufacturing sector to the US economy, distinct from the dominant agrarian sector. But it took the growth and maturation of the patent system, and perhaps some conceptual borrowing from the legal framework of the agrarian sector, to implement an innovation policy along democratic lines.

2.3.4 *Assignments*

Though it would seem natural enough to provide for free assignability of patents, given the frequent analogy between patents and real property, in fact this was somewhat of an American innovation. And it proved to be a productive one. In branching off from the traditionally restrictive British assignment law,[117] the US legal system opened the way to myriad business arrangements. We saw two of these earlier: fractional interests in an entire patent, and the exclusive regional franchise. In this section I describe the legal rules that enabled entrepreneurs to pioneer these novel forms of business.

The 1790 Act set the pattern by permitting issuance of a patent to a "petitioner ... [or] his, her or their heirs, administrators or assigns ... " Permission to grant a patent to an assignee was followed by giving explicit enforcement powers to an assignee in Section 4: "If any person or persons shall [infringe] ... without the consent of the patentee or patentees, their executors, administrators or assigns ... [the infringer] shall forfeit and pay [damages] to said ... assigns ...."[118] There are no reported court decisions under this short-lived statute, but the successor Act in 1793 repeated the same liberal treatment for assignees:[119]

> [I]t shall be lawful for any inventor, his executor or administrator to assign the title and interest in the said invention, at any time, and the assignee having recorded the said assignment, in the office of the Secretary of State, shall thereafter stand in the place of the original inventor, both as to right and responsibility, and so the assignees of assigns, to any degree.

The key language relates to "at any time" and "to any degree." The first phrase permits assignment of patent applications (as "interests," since there is not yet title) – which was from the earliest days an important avenue for inventors to attract early-stage investors. The "to any degree" phrase means that sub-assignments, sub-sub assignments, and so on are permissible. This opened the way to trading in regional franchise rights, as well as "late round" investments by those wishing to acquire rights from one or more earlier investors. The complex assignment pattern we saw earlier in the case of *Valentine* v. *Marshal*[120] serves as an example of how this legal rule enabled the fractional patent interests that supported capital formation.

To return to the 1793 Act, the recording provision, though helpful in giving notice of assignee rights, was early on found not to be mandatory.[121] Assignments could still

[117] British restriction date from the early eighteenth century. They were enacted in response to a speculative "bubble" (the South Sea Bubble) in which fortunes were lost and capital flows interrupted. See Phillip Johnson, Privatised Law Reform, at pp. 85–91 (explaining the origins of British limits on patent ownership to no more than five co-owners).

[118] 1790 Act section 1, Ch. 7, 1 Stat. 109–112 (April 10, 1790).

[119] Patent Act of 1793, Ch. 11, 1 Stat. 318–323 (February 21, 1793), Section 4.

[120] 28 F. Cas. 869 (C.C.S.D.N.Y. 1845). See discussion in this chapter.

[121] *Holden* v. *Curtis*, 2 N.H. 61, 63 (1819):

> But the act of Congress does not, in direct terms, declare the assignment void if unrecorded. Its language resembles that in most statutes, concerning the record of deeds of real estate; and, in relation to these last, it is every where held, that, without recording, the title passes between the parties, and is void only as to creditors, and those who afterwards purchase from the grantor without notice.

be valid without recordation, though recording, then as now, gives an assignee superior rights over those who acquire title later. Finally, by mentioning "interests" in patents the statute suggested that title-related transactions other than full assignment – including mortgages, pledges, liens, and the like – were also permissible and could be recorded in the Patent Office.[122]

2.3.4.1 *Why Assignment Is Important*

Assignment creates an ownership interest in the assignee. It is a transfer of at least part of the inventor/patent owner's legal title. This is important, because ownership confers rights and creates flexibilities that a mere contract cannot duplicate. The legal treatment of partial assignees as part owners of a patent was crucial to the effectiveness of the business arrangements that grew up around federal patent grants.

One reason ownership matters is that a property interest can generally be further assigned or alienated, while successive transfer of rights under a contract is more problematic. Courts often differentiate between a true assignment (partial or complete) and a "mere license," or contract to use a patented invention.[123] To simplify, there is a more liquid market for assignments because they are property, whereas it can be difficult to pass a contract from one person to another. (This stems from the

[122] This was made explicit in the 1836 Patent Act, and all Acts subsequent, by adding the words "grant and conveyance":

> [E]very patent shall be assignable in law, either as to the whole interest, or any undivided part thereof, by any instrument in writing; which assignment, *and also every grant and conveyance of the exclusive right* under any patent, to make and use, and to grant to others to make and use, the thing patented within and throughout any specified part or portion of the United States, shall be recorded in the Patent Office within three months from the execution thereof, for which the assignee or grantee shall pay to the Commissioner the sum of three dollars.

Patent Act of 1836, Ch. 357, 5 Stat. 117 (July 4, 1836) (emphasis added).

[123] See, e.g., *Troy Iron & Nail Factory* v. *Corning*, 55 U.S. 193, 216 (1852) ("A mere license to a party, without having his assigns or equivalent words to them, showing that it was meant to be assignable, is only the grant of a personal power to the licensees, and is not transferable by him to another."). On the general superiority of title to contract rights, see *Wilder* v. *Adams*, 29 F. Cas. 1216, 1217–1218 (C.C.D. Mass. 1846) (No. 17,647) ("[T]here is, in selling by license under another, a recognition or admission of title in that other, not to be contravened lightly between the parties. If a lessee [or licensee] be not actually evicted by some better or higher title in a third person, he is bound to pay rent as long as he continues to enjoy quietly the premises leased to him, [even] though by one whose title may be invalid."); *Fletcher* v. *Peck*, 10 U.S. 87, 123 (1810) ("A grant is a contract executed ... "). But compare *Lightner* v. *Boston & Albany Railroad Co.*, 15 F. Cas. 514, 514 (C.C.D. Mass. 1869) (No. 8,343) (patent licensed to two companies that later merged; newly formed company, product of the merger, was still licensed under the patent despite the fact that it was a new entity; "A mere authority to use a patented invention will not always and perhaps not usually be transferable. Whether it is so or not will depend in each case on the terms or nature of the contract.")

fact that contracts are often seen as person-to-person legal relationships, whereas property interests are "good against the world.")[124]

The second reason ownership matters so much is that only an owner (or the equivalent)[125] can file a patent infringement suit in a US federal court.[126] This was a crucial step in the development of patent law in support of the regional franchising business model. Decision-making authority and control over the timing and conduct of litigation are crucial elements in the power to enforce a patent.[127] By granting this power to each regional assignee (at least in equity suits), the early cases enhanced their power considerably. This in turn increased the value of regional assignments and therefore the entire business model based on them.

Exclusive territorial assignments were crucial for the development of regional franchises. A regional assignee can initiate litigation against an infringer in the

[124] See generally, Thomas W. Merrill and Henry E. Smith, *Optimal Standardization in the Law of Property: The* Numerus Clausus *Principle*, 110 Yale L.J. 1 (2000). As applied to intellectual property see Robert P. Merges, *A Transactional View of Property Rights*, 20 Berkeley Tech. L.J. 1477 (2005).

[125] That is, an exclusive licensee, under some circumstances. The law regarding licensee standing to enforce a patent is complex. But an assignee (even of a fractional share), is an owner, and so has the right to bring suit without question. See, e.g., *Waterman* v. *Mackenzie*, 138 U.S. 252 (1891).

[126] For equity suits, see *Ogle* v. *Ege*, 18 F. Cas. 619, 620 (C.C.D. Pa. 1826) (No. 10,462) (Story, J.):

> As to the first ground for dissolving the injunction, I shall content myself with observing, that whether an assignee of part of a patent, circumscribed as to the interest by local limits, can maintain a suit at law in his own name, or united with the patentee or not (a question unnecessary to be decided in this case); there can exist no doubt but that he may support a suit in equity to enjoin third persons from infringing the patent, and for an account.

Because equity jurisdiction included money damages (in the form of an "accounting" of the patentee's loss due to infringement), equity alone was enough to provide robust enforcement power. Later cases clarified that title ownership was the key to all patent enforcement, whether in law or equity. See, e.g., *Waterman* v. *Mackenzie*, 138 U.S. 252, 255 (1891):

> Every patent issued under the laws of the United States for an invention or discovery contains "a grant to . . . " one entire thing, [which] cannot be divided into parts, except as authorized by those laws. The patentee or his assigns may, by instrument in writing, assign, grant, and convey, either (1) the whole patent, comprising the exclusive right to make, use, and vend the invention throughout the United States; or (2) an undivided part or share of that exclusive right; or (3) the exclusive right under the patent within and throughout a specified part of the United States . . . A transfer of either of these three kinds of interests is an assignment, properly speaking, and vests in the assignee a title in so much of the patent itself, with a right to sue infringers. In the second case, jointly with the assignor. In the first and third cases, in the name of the assignee alone. Any assignment or transfer, short of one of these, is a mere license, giving the licensee no title in the patent, and no right to sue at law in his own name for an infringement.

[127] This is still the case today. See, e.g., Josh Lerner and Robert P. Merges, *The Control of Technology Alliances: An Empirical Analysis of the Biotechnology Industry*, 46 J. Indus. Econ. 125, 127 (1998) (pointing to "decisions about patent litigation" as one of the important terms of control negotiated in biotechnology industry licensing agreements).

assignee's territory. The owner of an exclusive right in a region need not wait for permission or participation on the part of the original inventor/assignor. This is true even if that inventor/assignor retains rights in all regions except those given to the assignee. Put simply, with regional ownership goes regional enforcement authority. One effect of regional assignments, therefore, was to *decentralize* patent enforcement decisions. The party with local knowledge could decide whether an infringement suit made sense. While it is possible for assignor/assignees to write a contract that governs post-assignment litigation decisions, the default rule is that the regional assignee decides.[128]

For assignees of fractional interests in the entire patent (rather than exclusivity in a certain region), the rule is different. An assignee of an undivided partial interest in a patent cannot unilaterally commence litigation. It takes all the owners to bring suit (in part to prevent duplicative litigation).[129] This unanimity rule prevents the types of conflicts that occur in corporations with majority and minority share blocs,[130] but creates some risk that a partial owner can extract extra benefits from the other owners in exchange for permission to bring suit.[131] But even though this structure might have invited conflicts among owners of partial interests, there is no record of any actual holdout behavior or power struggles among the holders of fractional patent

[128] On this, see *Bedford* v. *Hunt*, 3 F. Cas. 37 (C.C.D. Mass. 1817) (Case No. 1,217), where there was a regional assignment from the inventor/owner Bedford, but Bedford is the named party:

> [Patentee Bedford] afterwards sold out to different individuals the right to use this patent in particular towns. The real plaintiff in this case was William Chadwick, to whom such a right had been sold by Bedford; and within whose limits the defendant had manufactured boots, &c. after the manner described in the patent, and vended the same, without having purchased, either of the plaintiff or of Chadwick, the right so to do.

Perhaps to be safe in an era before regional assignees were definitively authorized to file suit, or perhaps because Bedford insisted on participating in cases involving his patent, the inventor/original owner Bedford is the named party in the suit brought to enforce the regional rights of the assignee/franchisee, Chadwick.

[129] In *Whittemore* v. *Cutter*, 29 F.Cas. 1120, 1120 (1813) (No. 17,600) (Story, J.):

> The [1793] statute gives to the assignee all the right and responsibility, which the original inventor had in the undivided portion of the patent, which is conveyed; and an action may well be maintained by all the parties, who at the time of the infringement are the holders of the whole title and interest.

[130] Ronald J. Gilson and Alan Schwartz, *Corporate Control and Credible Commitment*, 43 Int'l Rev. L. & Econ. 119, 125 (2015) (reviewing the literature discussing ways a majority shareholder can extract benefits from the corporation at the expense of minority shareholders).

[131] See *Willingham* v. *Lawton*, 555 F.2d 1340, 1344 (6th Cir. 1977) (patent co-owners are "at the mercy of each other"). Economists call this "holdup." There are contractual solutions to the problem if all co-owners will agree to be bound. See, e.g., 14B Am. Jur. Legal Forms 2d § 196:42 ("Agreement between co-owners of invention not to transfer patent rights"). See generally Robert P. Merges and Lawrence A. Locke, *Co-Ownership of Patents: A Comparative and Economic View*, 72 J. Pat. & Trademark Off. Soc'y 586, 598–599 (1990) (discussing contracts among co-owners to mitigate the problems created by co-ownership rules).

shares. The interests of all co-owners were perhaps aligned enough to prevent any paralyzing fights.

2.3.5 *Patent Administration in the Founding Era*

From the point of view of patent administration, the conventional narrative progresses from the pinnacle of perspicacity to the canyon of oblivion. We go from leadership by a certified genius – Thomas Jefferson himself no less – to a basement-dwelling under-clerk mindlessly stamping the Patent Office seal on every application slipped under the door. The 1790 Act famously featured three cabinet-level officials reviewing every patent application. And then we whipsaw to the 1793 Act, universally known for eliminating patent examination and inaugurating the Registration Era. The arc of the early story ends with the hardheaded Jacksonians instituting the professional examining corps in 1836, and thus creating the modern Patent Office.

Tempting as it is to reprint the legend, I will instead choose in this instance to recite the facts. They come in this case in a package of three primary points. First, although formal review of patent applications did end with the 1793 Act, that legislation did not result in a pure registration system. Beginning with the redoubtable William Thornton, Commissioner of Patents from 1802 to 1828, Patent Office officials had ways of questioning or criticizing issued patents they felt were invalid. Though without the binding force of legal judgments, this "invalidity jawboning" surely weakened some patents. Second, patent revocation proceedings, though applicable only to issued patents, meant that registration was not always the only legal consideration of a patent outside of infringement litigation. Revocation was a procedure to weed out weak patents, not in the same way as initial examination but not quite in litigation either. Third, there were several legal rules not connected with patent examination that were in effect punishments for trying to commercialize weak patents. The most important was a fraud cause of action against a patentee who had assigned or attempted to assign a blatantly invalid patent. By allowing assignees of dubious patents to bring a suit for fraud, these cases made it riskier to assign flimsy patents to third parties. Given the importance of patent assignments in early nineteenth-century business models, closing off the "assignment market" in this way surely damaged the value of patents perceived as weak or invalid. Thus, although patents could be registered as of right under the 1793 Act, there were still ways that the legal system signaled poor patent quality. Registration was not always tantamount to a reliable and robust title.

2.3.5.1 Jawboning Weak Patents: The Thornton Effect

There is a good deal of folklore concerning the first Commissioner of Patents, Dr. William Thornton (Figure 2.4). He was, like the hero of the novel *Captain Blood*, a

FIGURE 2.4. Dr. William Thornton, first commissioner of patents

"bachelor of medicine and several other things besides ...."[132] Thornton was an apothecary, hypocritical abolitionist,[133] amateur linguist, steamboat enthusiast,[134] and most notably, an architect, responsible for large sections of the US Capitol Building in Washington and other Federalist period buildings in east coast cities.[135] Probably his most legendary feat was to convince British troops not to torch the Patent Office building when they were marauding through Washington during the War of 1812.[136]

132 Rafael Sabatini, Captain Blood, at p. 1.

133 Gordon S. Brown, Incidental Architect: William Thornton and the Cultural Life of Early Washington, D.C., 1794–1828 (Athens: Ohio University Press, 2009), at p. 67 (describing Brown's resettlement plan for freed slaves but also his ownership of slaves in Washington and the Caribbean).

134 On Thornton's involvement with steamboats, see James Thomas Flexner, Inventors in Action: The Story of the Steamboat (New York: Collier Books, 1962; originally published, 1944), at pp. 159, 162; on steamboats and Thornton's treatise on linguistics see Daniel Preston, *The Administration and Reform of the U.S. Patent Office, 1790–1836*, 5 J. Early Rep. 331, 334 n. 6 (1985) (citing Thornton Papers collection).

135 See Architect of the Capitol, www.aoc.gov/architect-of-the-capitol/dr-william-thornton (Thornton was named first Architect of the Capitol, a position that still exists, when his basic design was accepted by President George Washington in 1793).

136 The story goes that on August 19, 1814, Thornton camped out at the Patent Office and when the British troops arrived, he implored them to spare the building because of its importance as a repository of knowledge and cultural treasures. See Library of Congress, "This Day in History," August 19, available at www.loc.gov/item/today-in-history/august-19/ ("Upon entering the city, the British set fire to the White House, the Capitol, and many of the other public buildings. The Patent Office, however, was saved from destruction by the Superintendent of Patents, Dr. William Thornton, who convinced the British of the importance of its preservation.").

From the perspective of patent administration, Thornton's contributions were perhaps less colorful. But they were more than trivial. Under the 1793 Act, Thornton's job was purely ministerial. Aside from a few formalities (such as submission of a specification and payment of the $30 fee), there was – in theory – nothing substantive to the job at all. But Thornton saw it otherwise. Between his forceful personality and the gaps in the law pertaining to patents at this early stage, he influenced patent administration in a significant way.

For the first seventeen years of the 1793 regime, Thornton performed something like a patent examination function. Despite the apparently simple admonition of the 1793 Act to register patents as soon as formal requirements were met,[137] Thornton is on record as informing some patent applicants that he was not inclined to issue the patents they requested.[138] But even after Thornton was ordered to end this "informal examination" – apparently in a rebuke from Thornton's boss, Secretary of State Robert Smith (serving under President James Madison)[139] – Thornton continued to find ways to pass judgment on patent quality. He wrote private letters to applicants, informing them that their claimed invention was not new, or was

[137] Section 1 of the 1793 Act says: "[W]hen any person ... shall allege he or they [have made an invention] ... [and] that shall present a petition to the Secretary of State, signifying a desire of obtaining an exclusive property in the same, and praying that a patent may be granted therefor, it shall and may be lawful for the said Secretary of State, to cause letters patent to be made out ... "

[138] See Edward C. Walterscheid, To Promote the Progress of Useful Arts: American Patent Law and Administration 1790–1836 (Littleton, CO: Fred B. Rothman & Co., 1998), at p. 260 ("[A]t least through 1810, [Thornton] had taken it upon himself the authority to refuse to issue patents in some circumstances, although just what those were is unclear." (footnote omitted)). Another source lists some of the grounds on which Thornton effectively sought to deny patents. See Daniel Preston, Administration and Reform, at p. 344 (footnote and sources omitted):

> Although he could not deny anyone a patent, Thornton did what he could to discourage applicants when he felt their inventions were unworkable or not original. If he thought a device would not work (particularly perpetual motion machines), he demanded a working model of it before he would issue a patent. If the application were for a machine, tool, or compound already patented, the superintendent would so inform the applicant and warn of the likelihood of a lawsuit. Knowing that such warnings were often "unthankfully received," he gave them anyway, lest the applicants "unknowingly involve themselves and their families in ruin, sometimes by infringing on the rights of others, sometimes by selling Patents under the guarantee of originality, sometimes by attempting perpetual motions and other impossibilities." Likewise, he warned them against "Deceptions, by which many begin by deceiving themselves, and end by deceiving their fellow Citizens."

[139] See Edward C. Walterscheid, To Promote, at p. 261 (citing an 1811 pamphlet issued by Thornton, aimed at patent applicants, and stating that the Patent Office had no discretion to reject patent applications). Of course, it could also be that Thornton said one thing for public consumption in his pamphlet and acted otherwise; there is an unbroken record at least through 1831 of Thornton strong-arming applicants and bad-mouthing patents. It was in 1831 that he was rebuked once again, this time by Attorney General John M. Berrien, serving under President Andrew Jackson. See Edward C. Walterscheid, To Promote, at p. 261 n. 58 (quoting from Berrien's 1831 letter reminding Thornton that the Secretary of State's office "acts rather ministerially than judicially in granting patents").

impractical.[140] And on at least one occasion, Thornton publicly criticized the lack of novelty of a patented invention that was at the time earning substantial royalties. This led to a suit for libel by the inventor, which Thornton apparently won.[141] The basis of the libel suit was Thornton's public letter, published in two national magazines and reprinted in part as a handbill, criticizing both the minor invention in controversy and the 1793 Act that permitted the patent to issue. The notoriety of the case and the cogent arguments Thornton put forward undoubtedly contributed to the reform movement leading to the Patent Act of 1836.[142]

2.3.5.2 Court-Based Attacks on Patents

Aside from patent infringement actions, where validity could be raised as a defense, there were two other court-based avenues of attack on patents. One came from the statute: under Section 10, anyone who thought a patent might have been "obtained surreptitiously, or upon false suggestion," could file a repeal action in the federal district court where the patent owner resided. A three-year time bar, measured from patent issuance, applied to these repeal actions. The historical record shows that this provision was used on occasion, but the surviving opinions attest to the murky language that set the parameters of the repeal action. This may explain the relative rarity of the cases, though historical records do reveal some that were unreported. Section 10, the repeal action provision, said that it was lawful "for the judge of the said district court, if the matter alleged shall appear to him to be sufficient, to grant a rule, that the patentee, or his [successor] show cause, why process should not issue against him to repeal such patent ...."[143] The two primary cases on the topic diverged on the meaning of the "show cause" language, especially in relation to a later sentence in the section: "And if sufficient cause shall not be shown to the contrary, the rule shall be made absolute, and thereupon the said judge shall order process to be issued against [the] patentee."[144] It went on to say that "in case no sufficient cause shall be shown to the contrary [i.e., cause to doubt the need for

[140] Edward C. Walterscheid, To Promote, at p. 263 n. 63 (quoting letters of this nature written by Thornton to various applicants in 1806, 1809, 1812, 1814, 1818, and 1821).

[141] Edward C. Walterscheid, *The Winged Gudgeon: An Early Patent Controversy*, 79 J. Pat. & Trademark Off. Soc'y 533 (1997). The "gudgeon" invented by Michael Withers was a cup-shaped or hollow cylinder holder into which a rod could be placed; it was used in grist mills for holding mill shafts in place. The "wings" were projections that came out from the cup-shaped piece, at a ninety-degree angle from the lip of the cup. They were used for tightening the cup down onto the shaft. Withers's specific invention was to file down or "bevel" these projections on two sides, making it easier to turn the cup-shaped piece to tighten it or loosen it on the mill shaft. Gudgeons were known in the art, as were the wings or projections, as was beveling – but only on one side of the projection. Withers's "point of novelty" then was the trivial contribution of two-sided beveling on the gudgeon wings.

[142] Edward C. Walterscheid, *Winged Gudgeon*, at p. 541.

[143] Patent Act of 1793, Ch. 11, 1 Stat. 318–323 (February 21, 1793), Section 10.

[144] Ibid.

repeal], or if it shall appear that the patentee was not the true inventor or discoverer, judgment shall be rendered by such court for the repeal of such patent."[145]

Justice Story, in a case called *Stearns* v. *Barrett*,[146] thought that Section 10 required the judge to look at the repeal filing and decide whether to open a proceeding or not. The judge was asked to duplicate the procedure for the British *scire facias* ("make known") procedure, employed by British common law courts to invite a patent challenger and patentee to present evidence about patent validity. Section 10 did not, in other words, permit a judge to summarily declare a patent invalid. "I have come to the conclusion," Story wrote, "that the proceedings upon the rule nisi are not conclusive; and that the process, to be awarded upon making the rule absolute, is not a final process, but a judicial writ in the nature of a *scire facias* at the common law ... The process is called in the statute a process to repeal the patent, merely as a description of its nature and use; and not because it necessarily and absolutely, per se, repeals the patent ... "[147]

Judge Van Ness of the Southern District of New York disagreed. He looked to the history and purpose of the statute, finding in it not the basis for a jury trial (as in Britain) under the *scire facias* process, but instead a summary proceeding to be decided, with finality, by the judge alone. For Judge Van Ness, the differences between British and American practice at the patent issuance stage were crucial. In Britain, as part of a process he called tedious, there could be up to two formal hearings regarding patent validity prior to issuance.[148] In that context, a common law *scire facias* proceeding made sense; there would normally be an extensive record, which the patent applicant could put in evidence before a judge. But, the judge emphasized, the US context was different: "As patents under our law are issued as a matter of course to all who will apply for them, swear they are inventors, and pay thirty dollars, it was natural, and in a great degree requisite, to protect the public against frauds and impositions, that some expeditious summary mode of investigating their merits and trying their validity should be provided."[149] Speed and efficiency, he repeated, were the key requisites under the American circumstances:

> I can find nothing in [Section 10], nor in the context, nor in the report of the proceedings of the congress that enacted the law, leading to the conclusion that a *scire facias* ... were anticipated or intended by congress as preliminary steps to the process of repeal, which the section directs the district judge to issue. I remain of the opinion that all the judicial authority intended to be given by the tenth section is vested exclusively in the district judge; that the proceeding under it was meant to be summary, and that no other can be had, without more detailed legislative

[145] Ibid.
[146] 22 F. Cas. 1175, 1178 (C.C.D. Mass. 1816) (No. 13,337) (Story, J.).
[147] Ibid.
[148] 16 F. Cas. 96, 97.
[149] Ibid.

> provision on the subject ... The course pursued here is prompt and efficacious, as is obviously required by the nature of the case.[150]

Van Ness was right – a rare instance where Justice Story (perhaps too much the anglophile in this case) was less persuasive. Efficient judicial review – created in some ways as a clear substitute for Patent Office examination – made sense in light of the structure of the 1793 Act. Even more than this, however, the opinion in *McGaw* points to a larger issue. Under it, courts and the Patent Office worked more as partners in a seamless, unitary administrative process in the patent field. This was characteristic of government operations in the founding period, when economic development was the common force driving much government action.

2.3.5.3 The Administrative Structure of the Patent System in the Founding Era

The patent system was one of the earliest instruments of economic development put in place by the young United States. It represents a distinctly pre-twentieth-century policy, one of the strands in the sturdy rope that pulled the early Republic forward into prosperity.[151] But this system was the product of a much smaller and weaker state than the one we currently inhabit.[152] Government priorities were different as well. Herbert Hovenkamp has accurately described the situation:

> At the beginning of the 19th century the United States was severely underdeveloped. Government intervention in the economy took the form of monopoly grants

150 16 F. Cas. 96, 101.

151 Legal historian J. Willard Hurst described the entire nineteenth-century American legal tradition in these terms. J. Willard Hurst, Law and the Conditions of Freedom in the Nineteenth-Century United States, at p. 6 (The most important "working principle" of American law in the nineteenth century was that "the legal order should protect and promote the release of individual creative energy to the greatest extent compatible with the broad sharing of opportunity for such expression"). Just to repeat: The celebratory tone elides the lost potential of contributions from people who were shut out of the patent system at the time.

152 As far as I know, the earliest patent scholarship on the topic in this section is John Duffy, *The FCC and the Patent System: Progressive Ideals, Jacksonian Realism, and the Technology of Regulation*, 71 Colo. L. Rev. 1071, 1079–1080 (2000):

> [W]hile the Progressive-era regulatory agencies have gone from fashionable innovations to antiquated relics during the twentieth century, the patent system continues to thrive with much the same structure that it was given in 1836 ... [A]gencies created in the twentieth and later part of the nineteenth centuries were influenced by then-fashionable political and regulatory philosophies, which radically overestimated the abilities of public agencies. In contrast, the modern American patent bureaucracy was established during the Jacksonian era, which was nothing if not realistic about the abilities of government officers and institutions ... [In addition,] the patent system provides further cause to check the enthusiasm of today's [regulatory agency] reformers. For agency abolitionists who seek to idealize the common law, the patent system provides a well-documented failure of the common law to regulate effectively without the assistance of an administrative agency.

> to encourage economic development, as well as tax breaks and other subsidies dedicated to the creation of infrastructure. The early American state also took a much heavier role in fostering innovation through the patent system, encouraging the actual development and deployment of patented devices and processes. Under the leadership of Chief Justice Marshall the Supreme Court facilitated the use of monopoly grants. It also furthered a strongly national and pro-regulatory interpretation of the Commerce Clause, designed to facilitate national development and limit state free riding and other self-interest.[153]

It is against this backdrop that one needs to view the founding era Patent Office.

THE EARLY PATENT OFFICE: A PROTO-ADMINISTRATIVE AGENCY The early history of the administrative patent function is a choppy one. The initial 1790 Act, with its heavyweight "examiner corps" of the Secretaries of State and War, and the Attorney General, quickly gave way to a pure registration system. From 1793 to 1836, you sent the proper documents to the State Department, and you got a patent (subject to the caveats mentioned earlier). Fights between rival inventors as to who was first were resolved by the District Courts. And patent validity was not usually reviewed until the patent owner tried to enforce the patent. The resulting system, whereby federal judges determine patent validity in the context of a defense to patent infringement, was and is a distinctive aspect of US patent practice.[154]

With the advent of real patent examination in 1836, the administrative side of US patent law began to take shape. But the early period continued to influence the post-1836 scene, particularly with respect to the important role of courts in the system.[155]

[153] Herbert Hovenkamp, *Appraising the Progressive State*, 102 Iowa L. Rev. 1063, 1067–1068 (2017) (footnotes omitted).

[154] In most other countries, validity (even post-patent issuance) continues to be the province of the national patent office, with courts typically limited to patent enforcement issues (infringement, remedies, etc.). See Robert P. Merges and Seagull Haiyan Song, Transnational Intellectual Property Law (2018), at chapter 2, pp. 35–39 (introduction to European and Chinese patent systems).

[155] See Edward C. Walterscheid, To Promote, at p. 61:

> The Patent Act of 1836 is generally acknowledged to be the foundation for the modem patent examination system in the United States. It created the Patent Office, a corps of examiners, modem interference practice, administrative appeal practice, and the modern patent numbering system. But what is frequently forgotten or ignored is that the patent system it created came into existence predicated on – and in no small measure in reaction to – decades of prior administrative practice under a detailed statutory scheme which had received rather extensive judicial interpretation. Almost ten thousand patents had been issued by 1836. There thus was a significant background, both legal and administrative, against which to view the Act of 1836.

Patent counts pre-1836 are always a matter of some speculation because of the fire that destroyed all Patent Office files in 1836. Another scholar puts the correct number of pre-1836 patents at 15,000. See Kenneth L. Sokoloff, Inventive Activity in Early Industrial America, 813 (1988). Then again, a painstaking study that tried to find and read all pre-1836 patents turned up just 2,500. See Michael Risch, *America's First Patents*, 64 Fla. L. Rev. 1279, 1281 (2012).

A good example is the patent repeal procedure reviewed earlier in this chapter. One way to view that procedure is that it substituted courts for patent examiners, using existing resources (district court judges) in place of building an additional administrative apparatus.

The use of courts as federal outposts was simply a function of the very limited availability of federal institutions. The same is true of the copyright system; under the 1790 Copyright Act, works subject to copyright had to be deposited in the federal district court where the registering author resided.[156] With so little federal power in toto, there was little concern at this time with separation of powers. When I speak of a unitary conception of federal authority, this is what I have in mind.

In total, at least 2,500 patents were issued under the 1790 and 1793 Patent Acts. And, as we will see in Chapter 3, while the creation of a formal patent bureaucracy in 1836 changed the way inventors acquired patents, the basic design of the patent system remained intact. As before, the essential feature of the system was to award a form of property right to individual inventors. In this sense, the patent system had much in common with another crucial early policy for economic development: distribution of public land to individual proprietors. The bureaucracy created for this latter task was the General Land Office. Because land policy had a similar design, and was administered through a parallel, early agency, it is worth taking a look at the land distribution system in some detail.

THE GENERAL LAND OFFICE Though organized land sales had always been a part of the colonial and early Federalist period, a formal and bureaucratized land distribution function – the General Land Office – was only formed in 1812. It was established as part of the Treasury Department, which made sense. Its function was to stimulate economic development, but the sale of land was also an important source of funding for the young US government.[157] Over time, the Land Office opened many district branches in areas of active settlement, and became one of the most powerful and immediate arms of the nineteenth-century economic development state.

In 1812, Land Office districts were concentrated in the "Old Northwest" (largely Ohio and Indiana), as well as Missouri (as far west as St. Louis) and the region around New Orleans (a function of the Louisiana Purchase).[158] District offices surveyed all the public lands made available by westward expansion. This function was aided immeasurably by the development of standardized surveying instruments and techniques. The most notable was the use of the standard twenty-two-yard

[156] Act of May 31, 1790, ch. 15, 1 Stat. 124, at § 3, 1 Stat. 124, 125.

[157] See Malcolm J. Rourbaugh, The Land Office Business, 51, 52, 59, 61 (1968) (hereafter Rourbaugh, Land Office) (describing organization of General Land Office and land sales revenues after its formation). See also Gregory Ablavsky, Federal Ground: Governing Property and Violence in the First U.S. Territories (Oxford: Oxford University Press, 2021), at p. 104 (describing small-parcel land sales policy embodied, e.g., in the Harrison Land Act of 1800).

[158] Rourbaugh, Land Office, map at pp. 28–29.

measuring chain, which measured the grids that formed the basis of all federally issued land plots starting with those issued in northeastern Ohio.[159] This standardized tool set the boundaries of the land plots that were surveyed, recorded, and subdivided for sale. It is the foundation of the land "section" of 640 acres, which is still the basic measure of land area in the rural United States.[160]

Land was sold to settlers in section and partial section sizes. Purchases were financed with loans that were often subsidized. District agents were paid partly in salary and partly through sales commissions.[161] Prices varied, especially because developers (and perhaps) speculators often bought large (town-sized) parcels and subdivided them for final sale. Official prices were low, by design; a typical price was $1.40 an acre, with the district offices responsible for handing out title and collecting payments.[162] The policy had its intended effect: the handing out of many small parcels to many small purchasers.[163] By 1832, for example, the General Land Office was giving out 40,000 land patents per year throughout the country.[164]

Despite the order imposed by standardized lot sizes and a centralized bureaucracy, land settlement was chaotic. Conflicting and overlapping claims were common. Land was often first settled by squatters, or by those who took title via

[159] Andro Linklater, Measuring America: How the United States Was Shaped by the Greatest Land Sale in History, 5 (hereafter Linklater, Measuring) (New York: Penguin Books, 2002). Indeed, the corner of the baseline for the first plots surveyed in Ohio was called The Place of Beginning, and bears an historical marker to this day. Ibid.

[160] Linklater, Measuring, at p. 183. See also Gregory Ablavsky, Federal Ground: Governing Property and Violence in the First U.S. Territories, at p. 104 (Harrison Land Act of 1800 was explicitly designed, in the words of its sponsor, "to give more favorable terms to that class of purchasers who are likely to become actual settlers"; this Act set the maximum purchase size at 640 acres or one "section" of federal land).

[161] Rourbaugh, Land Office, at p. 31.

[162] Ibid., at p. 87.

[163] There were also large grants, both to town developers beginning in the early nineteenth century and for railroad rights of way later. See Robert L. Rabin, *Federal Regulation in Historical Perspective*, 38 Stan. L. Rev. 1189, 1195–1196 (1986) (footnotes omitted):

> The federal contribution to this pro-growth, booster spirit was foremost in the area of land grant policy. Between 1850 and 1870, the U.S. government offered grants-in-aid for railroad construction of alternate sections of right-of-way on either side of a rail line. The total acreage granted has been estimated to have reached the awesome figure of 180 million acres – an area larger than the entire Old Northwest. In addition to this dramatic gesture in support of the railroads, the government initiated a series of land sales and grants for settlement purposes, the most renowned being the Homestead Act of 1862, which granted a standard allotment of 160 acres of land to settlers who agreed to a set of homesteading conditions …
>
> From the first surge of enthusiasm for westward expansion and commercial development, an infectious, pro-growth spirit was evident and there was no noticeable disposition at any level of government to maintain a hands-off policy regarding entrepreneurial activity.

[164] Rourbaugh, Land Office, at p. 257.

grant from Native Americans[165] or a foreign government. Preemption Acts often permitted squatters who had developed land to purchase it; the 1841 Act, for instance, offered occupants the right to buy up to 160 acres for $1.25 per acre.[166]

Because conflicting titles were common, various dispute resolution mechanisms were put in place to sort things out. Early on, the Treasury Department established Boards of Commissioners empowered to hear evidence of conflicting land claims and award title to the proper claimant.[167] These regional boards were interposed between the local district offices and the General Land Office in Washington. Despite great efforts to staff them with experts and clothe them with authority, decisions of the commissioners (and related disputes) often found their way into the federal courts.[168]

The general rule was that the award of a land patent was strong evidence of the accuracy of the factfinding that led to it. As the Supreme Court said in 1839,

> A [land] patent is evidence in a Court of law of the regularity of all the previous steps to it ... The Court are [sic] bound to presume [the regularity of] the acts of commissioners intrusted by laws of Congress to inquire into claims to lands ... and the decisions of these commissioners are in Courts of law binding and effectual.[169]

In another case, plaintiffs claimed land included in a town site in Alabama. The district land office refused to issue title to plaintiffs, and instead sold the town lots according to normal practice under the General Land law. The Court agreed with the actions of the land office:

> From the earliest date of the legislation of Congress on this subject, there have been appropriations to the public use, made by withdrawing from this mass [of acreage] certain portions of territory for public seminaries, towns, salt springs, mines, and other objects; and the particular land in controversy was appropriated under a

165 Sometimes by purchase, more often by sheer conquest of one sort or another. See Stuart Banner, How the Indians Lost Their Land: Law and Power on the Frontier (2007). Cambridge, MA: Harvard University Press.

166 The Preemption Act of 1841, 27th Congress, Ch. 16, 5 Stat. 453 (1841), available at www.minnesotalegalhistoryproject.org/assets/Microsoft%20Word%20-%20Preemption%20Act%20of%201841.pdf.

167 Rourbaugh, Land Office, at pp. 38–39. According to legal historian David Ablavsky, the sorting out of criss-crossing and conflicting land titles devolved to Land Office officers (and courts), which assisted in no small part in the general recognition of federal authority in far corners of the United States. Gregory Ablavsky, Federal Ground: Governing Property and Violence in the First U.S. Territories, at p. 1. It appears that maintaining careful and authoritative records of land sales and holdings added to the federal government's authority in this sphere. See *Galt* v. *Galloway*, 29 U.S. 332, 342–343 (1830) ("As the records of this office are of great importance to the country, and are kept under the official sanctions of the government, their contents must always be considered, and they are always received in courts of justice as evidence of the facts stated.").

168 See Jerry L. Mashaw, *Reluctant Nationalists: Federal Administration and Administrative Law in the Republican Era, 1801–1829*, 116 Yale L.J. 1636, 1696–1719 (2007) (discussing extensive body of Land Office decisions).

169 *Bagnell* v. *Broderick*, 38 U.S. 436, 446 (1839).

> previous law, to wit, the act of April, 1820, for the site of a town. We, therefore, think, that it was not included in the right to appropriate vested in the complainants . . .[170]

A second case was to the same effect. It shows how much discretion the local commissioners were given – on the theory, very likely, that they were closest to the facts of each case. In a case that shows the important role of General Land Office as final arbiter over local title disputes, the Supreme Court held that local land commissioners had adopted a reasonable interpretation of the Congressional Act aimed at settling title to lands in Mississippi that were acquired as part of the Louisiana Purchase:

> The certificate granted in the case before us, is sufficient evidence that the commissioners west of [the] Pearl river [in Mississippi] adopted a more liberal construction [than that given the Act in question by other local district offices]; such as we think they were warranted in adopting, and such as, we think, is manifestly sanctioned by Congress, in the Act of 1806 [pertaining to distribution of land acquired in the Louisiana Purchase]. It is the opinion of this Court, that the commissioners were authorized to hear evidence as to the time of the actual evacuation of the territory by Spanish troops, and to decide upon the fact. We are bound to presume that every fact necessary to warrant the certificate, in the terms of it, was proved before the commissioners; and that, consequently, it was shown to them . . . Upon the whole, it is the unanimous opinion of this Court, that the Supreme Court of the state of Mississippi has not misconstrued the Act of Congress, from which the rights of the parties are derived; and that the judgment of the Supreme Court be affirmed.[171]

The result here was to eject the defendant from any effective title to the land in question. This notwithstanding the defendant's acquisition of title at a regular Land Office land auction in 1819 – one year before the date of the plaintiff's official land title (or patent). The reasoning was that local Land Office commissioners had awarded the plaintiff a certificate in 1807, showing that plaintiff's claim took effect at the time remaining Spanish forces evacuated the area in controversy. The certificate was based on a finding that plaintiff's claim was operative on the official Spanish evacuation date in 1798. Thus, the local district Land Office, when it converted the 1807 certificate into formal title to plaintiffs in 1820, had in effect ratified the award of the certificate in 1807. This precluded the defendant's purchase at a regular land auction in 1819.[172] The same theme of deference to local acts and local knowledge – as mediated by the federal dispute resolution apparatus – is evidenced in other cases as well.[173]

[170] *Chotard* v. *Pope*, 25 U.S. 586, 590 (1827).
[171] *Ross* v. *Doe ex dem. Barland*, 26 U.S. 655, 668–669 (1828).
[172] *Ross* v. *Doe ex dem. Barland*, 26 U.S. 655, 656–663 (1828).
[173] See, e.g., *United States* v. *Arredondo*, 31 U.S. 691, 727 (1832):

> The [US has] . . . submitted to the principle which prevails as to all public grants of land, or acts of public officers, in issuing warrants, orders of survey, permission to cultivate or

The limited cases reviewing actions of the land office did not (as was customary) state anything akin to a modern standard of review. Nonetheless, as we have seen, the Supreme Court usually affirmed the actions of the various land offices when they were challenged.

INVENTIONS AND LAND: THE PROPERTY STRATEGY This brief comparison of Patent Office and General Land Office yields several useful insights. First, notice the similarity in evolution and structure. Regional district offices grew under the Land Office, as did the central administration. Patent examiners grew in number, and supervisory examiners began to appear. Officials experienced in the granting procedure were drafted onto expert dispute resolution boards – proto administrative courts, in many ways – and then true federal courts sat in review in cases that warranted their oversight.

Most importantly, it is not only the goal of the patent system (public encouragement of economic growth) but also the *mechanism* it employs that makes it comparable to the Land Office. Patents are individual property rights granted by a centralized government to widely dispersed creator/owners. These exclusive grants give private patent owners the right to invoke the power of the state to exclude others from making or using those things covered by the owner's claims. A patent, as with other IP rights as well as legal title to individual parcels of land, gives a small dollop of state power to a private owner. Patent grants are in this sense a highly *decentralized* policy mechanism. Conferred by a central (federal) authority, yes; but enforceable only if and when a private owner decides.

INSTRUMENTAL (NOT REIFIED) PROPERTY This emphasis on property grants makes it tempting to argue, from our vantage point, that intellectual property rights reflect a classical liberal vision of political economy – that patents were born in an essentially libertarian state, giving them an essentially libertarian character. From this may follow a number of propositions, including that patent property may not be revoked except by an Article III judge.[174] Tempting views, these, but historically,

> improve, as evidence of inceptive and nascent titles, which is; that the public acts of public officers purporting to be exercised in an official capacity and by public authority, shall not be presumed to be an usurped, but a legitimate authority, previously given or subsequently ratified, which is equivalent. If it was not a legal presumption that public and responsible officers claiming and exercising the right of disposing of the public domain, did it by the order and consent of the government, in whose name the acts were done, the confusion and uncertainty of titles and possessions would be infinite, even in this country; especially in the states whose tenures to land depend on every description of inceptive, vague and inchoate equities, rising in the grade of evidence, by various intermediate acts, to a full land legal confirmation, by patent, under the great seal.

174 See, e.g., *Oil States Energy Servs., LLC* v. *Greene's Energy Grp., LLC*, 138 S. Ct. 1365, 1380 (2018) (Gorsuch, J., dissenting):

> Until recently, most everyone considered an issued patent a personal right – no less than a home or farm – that the federal government could revoke only with the concurrence of

none too accurate. The better view is to see patents as one of many expedient policies wheeled into place under the felt necessities of their time of origin. They were one way to join the limited powers of the newborn state to private effort and private capital. They were one device by which a cash-strapped but landed country tried to jumpstart the engine of economic development. They were in this sense the opposite of a libertarian instrument. They were in no way born of a desire to hold back the power of the state, leaving room for the private sector. The state at this time had little power *to* hold back. One thing the state did have was the authority of a nationwide court system. By allowing individual patent owners to deploy this enforcement network in service of privately owned rights, the government encouraged investment and economic development. Patents were born of an intense spirit of pragmatism. To see them any other way, especially as an expression of some high theory about preventing Leviathan or a runaway state, is anachronism pure and simple.

I think in fact that this early pragmatic strain found expression in other legal fields touching on property rights. The best example is the power of the state to *take away* property: eminent domain. Though today this is a fraught, politically inflected battleground, in the Federalist period and throughout much of the nineteenth century it was just another policy tool of a pro-development state. State governments were not at all shy about taking private property in service of economy-building projects such as mill-dams, canals, roads, and later rail lines.[175]

To summarize: There was no consensus at all around a sanctified view of property let alone around a small "night-watchman" state. The consensus was around doing whatever it took to promote economic development. If that meant giving out property rights (as with patents), fine; if it meant taking away property rights (with compensation), that was fine too.

The approach to economy-building was pragmatic, not grounded in a single economic ideology. To summarize some of the key points from this chapter: The small population of the new Republic was mostly perched along the Atlantic

> independent judges. But in the statute before us [on Inter Partes Review under the America Invents Act of 2011] Congress has tapped an executive agency, the Patent Trial and Appeal Board, for the job. Supporters say this is a good thing because the Patent Office issues too many low quality patents; allowing a subdivision of that office to clean up problems after the fact, they assure us, promises an efficient solution. And, no doubt, dispensing with constitutionally prescribed procedures is often expedient. Whether it is the guarantee of a warrant before a search, a jury trial before a conviction – or, yes, a judicial hearing before a property interest is stripped away – the Constitution's constraints can slow things down. But economy supplies no license for ignoring these – often vitally inefficient – protections.

This view is wrong: bad policy, on top of inaccurate history. There is very little room in the US patent system for "vitally inefficient" procedures or the logic that would support them.

175 The best account of this is by my colleague, the eminent legal historian Harry Schieber. See Harry N. Scheiber, *Property Law, Expropriation, and Resource Allocation by Government: The United States, 1789–1910*, 33 J. Econ. Hist. 232 (1973).

coastline. Given the policy of land appropriation, and liberal immigration, plus the mindset that the vast North American continent needed settlement, labor was perceived to be scarce in comparison to the vast job to be done. Adapting the inherited European practice of granting patents was one way to do it. Balancing the desire to stimulate new invention against limited governmental resources, Congress in 1793 instituted the patent registration system. Despite chronic problems with rent-seeking and patent quality (taken up in Chapter 3), businesspeople rapidly learned to use federal patent grants as a basic scaffold on which to build businesses. Patents became in some instances like shares in a technology-based business. In others they were the basis of regional franchises. Though pressure continued to build for reforms in the system, the business function of patents was well established by the end of the founding period. Although the years leading up to the 1836 Patent Act saw many calls for change, both the "hidden" patent quality checks of the 1793 Act (reviewed earlier) and the existence of already-familiar patent-based business models meant that there was a fair degree of continuity between the founding period and the Jacksonian era that followed.

3

The Jacksonian Era and Early Industrialization, 1820–1880

CHAPTER OUTLINE

The era that followed the founding period was characterized overall by very rapid population and GDP growth. The US population nearly doubled in twenty years from 1820 to 1840. It took until 1863 for GDP per capita to grow that much, and the economy actually shrank after that due to the devastation of the Civil War.[1] By 1872, the post-War slump was over, however, and the US economy entered what one historian has called the "takeoff stage."[2] Figure 3.1 tells the basic story of this era.

Patenting activity increased dramatically during this period. Figures 3.2 and 3.3 show patent applications and issued patents per year from 1840 to 1880.

3.1 THE CHANGING CONTEXT OF INVENTION

We saw in Chapter 2 that by 1820, in industries such as textile manufacturing and papermaking, the factory machine shop (or its equivalent) was often the location where invention took place. This was a general pattern. As one historian put it,

> [M]achine shops became the schools and machines the books of an American technology that many at the time considered the embodiment of democratic values. The self-taught mechanic was Everyman, capable of improving the technology with which he worked. An expanding manufacturing economy and growing

[1] These figures do not capture the full economic picture because of distortions in data about the southern US slave economy and its overall contribution to economic growth. See Sven Beckert and Seth Rockman, eds., Slavery's Capitalism: A New History of American Economic Development (Philadelphia: University of Pennsylvania Press, 2016).

[2] Walt W. Rostow, The Stages of Economic Growth: A Non-Communist Manifesto (Cambridge: Cambridge University Press, 1960). Uniform, universal, stage-type models of economic growth have fallen out of fashion since 1960, but whatever the terminology, there appear to be some important factors that contributed to specific national instances of rapid growth. See, e.g., Joel Mokyr, A Culture of Growth: The Origins of the Modern Economy (Princeton, NJ: Princeton University Press, 2018) (explaining the early European Industrial Revolution as a product of political competition among fragmented European states, the spirit of inquiry and culture of shared information among scientists across Europe, and other localized factors); Wayne M. Morrison, China's Economic Rise: History, Challenges, and Implications for the United States (Washington, DC: U.S. Congressional Research Service, June 25, 2019), available at https://crsreports.congress.gov/product/details?prodcode=RL33534 (emphasizing political and economic reforms in China after 1978 as the key factors in rapid Chinese economic growth).

Year	GDP	Population	GDP/capita
1821	17,223	9,899.00	1,739.80
1822	17,875	10,189.00	1,754.30
1823	18,522	10,488.00	1,766.00
1824	19,620	10,795.00	1,817.50
1825	20,498	11,115.00	1,844.10
1826	21,227	11,449.00	1,854.10
1827	21,886	11,797.00	1,855.20
1828	22,182	12,158.00	1,824.50
1829	23,025	12,525.00	1,838.30
1830	25,142	12,901.00	1,948.80
1831	27,217	13,277.00	2,050.00
1832	29,057	13,676.00	2,124.70
1833	29,951	14,086.00	2,126.30
1834	30,455	14,504.00	2,099.80
1835	32,071	14,917.00	2,150.00
1836	33,021	15,340.00	2,152.60
1837	33,323	15,790.00	2,110.40
1838	34,702	16,224.00	2,138.90
1839	35,593	16,656.00	2,137.00
1840	35,691	17,120.00	2,084.70
1841	36,490	17,612.00	2,071.90
1842	37,656	18,124.00	2,077.70
1843	39,522	18,641.00	2,120.20
1844	41,768	19,157.00	2,180.30
1845	44,412	19,708.00	2,253.50
1846	48,020	20,313.00	2,364.00
1847	51,289	20,987.00	2,443.90
1848	53,018	21,706.00	2,442.60
1849	53,755	22,464.00	2,393.00
1850	56,252	23,261.00	2,418.30
1851	60,780	24,095.00	2,522.50
1852	67,799	24,999.00	2,712.10
1853	73,343	25,911.00	2,830.60
1854	75,875	26,856.00	2,825.30
1855	79,039	27,727.00	2,850.60
1856	82,213	28,497.00	2,885.00
1857	82,634	29,298.00	2,820.50
1858	85,978	30,068.00	2,859.50
1859	92,203	30,780.00	2,995.60
1860	93,146	31,513.00	2,955.80
1861	94,805	32,215.00	2,942.90
1862	106,586	32,889.00	3,240.80
1863	114,782	33,607.00	3,415.40
1864	116,084	34,376.00	3,376.90
1865	119,408	35,182.00	3,394.00
1866	113,929	36,052.00	3,160.10
1867	115,883	36,970.00	3,134.50
1868	120,403	37,885.00	3,178.10
1869	123,679	38,870.00	3,181.90
1870	127,371	39,905.00	3,191.90
1871	133,430	41,010.00	3,253.60
1872	144,596	42,066.00	3,437.40
1873	156,931	43,225.00	3,630.60
1874	159,785	44,429.00	3,596.40
1875	159,500	45,492.00	3,506.10
1876	166,103	46,459.00	3,575.30
1877	174,368	47,400.00	3,678.60
1878	179,970	48,319.00	3,724.60
1879	200,947	49,264.00	4,079.00
1880	217,601	50,262.00	4,329.30

FIGURE 3.1. Population, GDP, and GDP per capita, 1820–1879

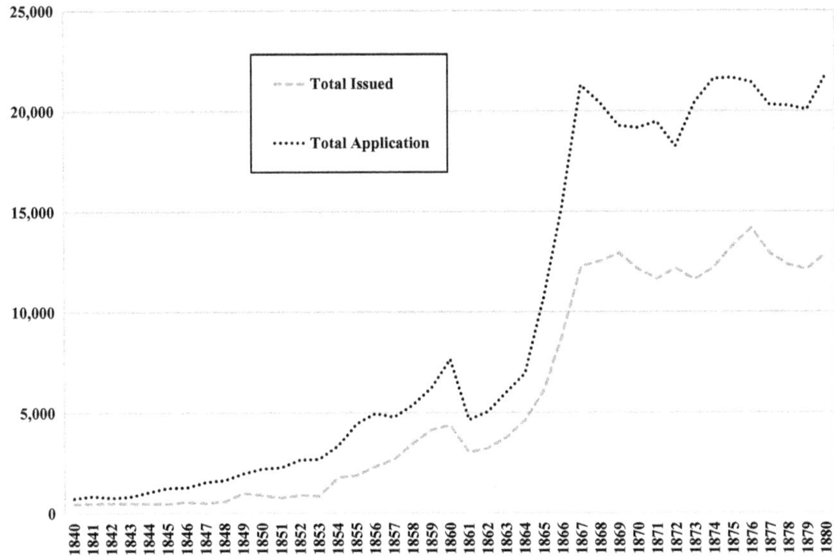

FIGURE 3.2. Patenting activity, 1840–1880

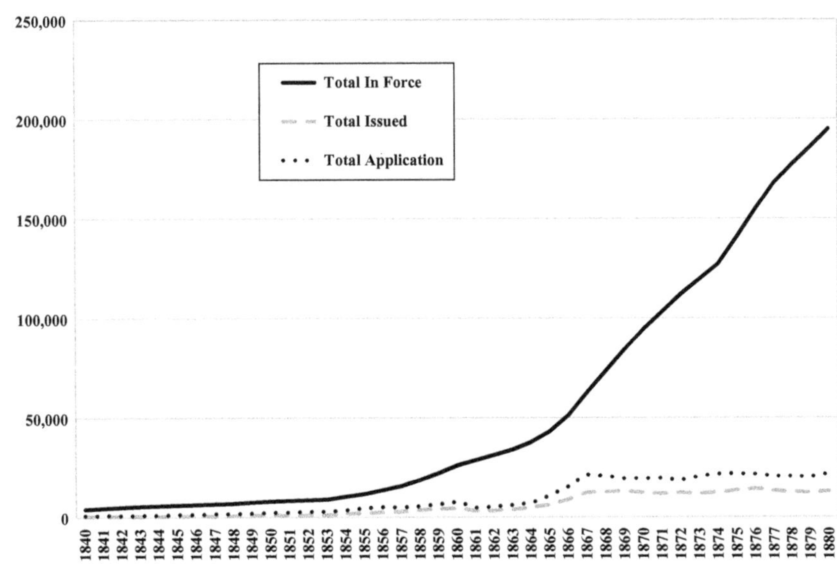

FIGURE 3.3. Patents in force, 1840–1880

technological enthusiasm embodied in the nation's patent system provided further stimulus for invention.[3]

The "self-taught mechanic" was in fact a ubiquitous figure among nineteenth-century inventors. He (or, sometimes in those days, she) often emerged out of a craft tradition. The development of better tools and machines had always been part of the world of millers, blacksmiths, shoemakers, and the like. But what was different, what ramped up the self-reinforcing cycle of invention, was the emergence of specialists: mechanics who developed new tools and machines, and who also *made a living* (or tried to) from the creation, marketing, and sale of their newly designed tools and machines. The regularization and commercialization of inventive activity was one of the chief developments in the years between 1820 and 1880.

Many self-taught mechanics made tools or improved machinery in their own work. The rapid pace of economic growth meant that when someone made a useful improvement, they might well consider whether there might be a broader market for it beyond their own workshop. Many such efforts failed, of course; that is the nature of entrepreneurship. Others succeeded modestly, and a few early nineteenth-century inventions ended up forming the foundation of long-lasting innovative firms. That is the story of the Fairbanks scale, set out in Section 3.1.1. To begin, however, we should start with a more typical invention, which led to a more modest business.

A detailed study of changes in shoemaking between 1810 and 1900 provides many possible examples of early nineteenth-century invention-based businesses.[4] Traditionally, shoemaking was a pure craft: Each individual pair of shoes was formed by a long series of individual steps performed by a single shoemaker in a local shop. But this began to change around 1820. Higher demand, better transportation networks, and a steadily creeping awareness that there was money to be made from specialization led to an upsurge in shoemaking inventions. Market size, the structure of production, and tool (later machine) inventions all worked together to increase standardization and lower costs.[5] In this context, some shoemakers realized that they could patent a good idea and make money from it. Some even became serial inventors, contributing improvements in one specialized aspect of shoemaking or in several disparate ones.[6]

[3] Paul Israel, From Machine Shop to Industrial Laboratory: Telegraphy and the Changing Context of American Invention, 1830–1920 (Baltimore: Johns Hopkins University Press, 1992), at p. 2.

[4] Russ Thomson, The Path to Mechanized Shoe Production in the United States (Chapel Hill: University of North Carolina Press, 1989).

[5] See Ibid., at pp. 34–45.

[6] See Ibid., at pp. 182–197 (covering patenting in the shoemaking machinery sector, which emerged gradually from tool and implement patenting after 1860 or so). According to Thomson, "From 1837 through 1911, 4,266 shoe patents were issued to 2,416 American residents. Twenty-nine percent of these inventors were issued more than one shoe patent." Ibid., at p. 186.

The patent system helped open the opportunity for inventive specialization. Mechanics in and around the shoe industry understood that an invention for one's own shop or company could be turned into an economic asset providing returns beyond the boundaries of an individual enterprise. As historian Russ Thomson says, "these [shoe-related] innovations could be recognized as property . . . [T]he inventor could be remunerated by everyone using the innovation in the form of patent royalties or payment for new [machines] . . . [So] the returns to invention extended beyond the reduced costs secured by use of the new technique in the inventor's own shop."[7] There may not have been a direct connection, but it seems likely that the growing market for parts of shoes (the sole, the upper, etc.) and tools specialized for making each part led naturally to an active market for patented inventions. In other words, industry specialization, and the market that fostered it, yielded specialization in the market for tool and machinery designs.[8] The effort and problem-solving skill it took to design a new tool or machine part could – through the mechanism of a patent – be turned into a saleable asset separate and apart from the pairs of shoes made using the new tool. This pattern, which has been called "the propertization of labor,"[9] fits well the emergence of shoemaking invention as a specialized economic role. The institutions that emerged before 1820 – regional agents to market rights, fractional patent share investors, and the lawyers who structured the assignments and contracts – helped to support the class of specialized inventors who came to prominence between 1820 and 1880.

Consider one example. Shoes from time immemorial have been constructed in two main parts: the sole and the upper. The traditional way to attach the two is to sew them together. But shoemakers in the nineteenth century found it quicker to attach them with tacks, nails, or, in what came to be the dominant design, short pieces of wood called pegs.[10] A series of holes is punched in sole and upper, and wooden pegs are driven into the holes to secure top piece to bottom. Pegs can be pre-cut, or they can be cut to order from long pieces of thin wood as the pegging proceeds.

In 1852 an inventor named D. D. Allen invented a specialized tool for cutting pegs. It is mounted on a workbench, and the shoe is brought to the peg-cutter. Each

7 Ibid., at p. 38.

8 On the connection between IP law and the viability of firms specializing in new designs, machines, chemical compositions, etc., see Robert P. Merges, A *Transactional View of Property Rights*, 20 Berkeley Tech. L.J. 1477 (2005). A comprehensive treatment of the relationship between firm entry, patents, and industry structure is Jonathan M. Barnett, Innovators, Firms, and Markets: The Organizational Logic of Intellectual Property (Oxford: Oxford University Press, 2021).

9 See Robert P. Merges, Justifying Intellectual Property (Cambridge, MA: Harvard University Press, 2011), at pp. 289, 293.

10 Thomson, Path to Mechanized Shoes, at p. 34 (quoting a *Scientific American* article from 1869 declaring that the shoe peg "worked perhaps as great a revolution in a most important branch of industry as was ever effected by a single device"); p. 35 (pegged shoes represented 75 percent of total shoes in 1860); and p. 36 (wholesale price of pegged shoes was roughly 35 percent less than the price of traditional sewn shoes).

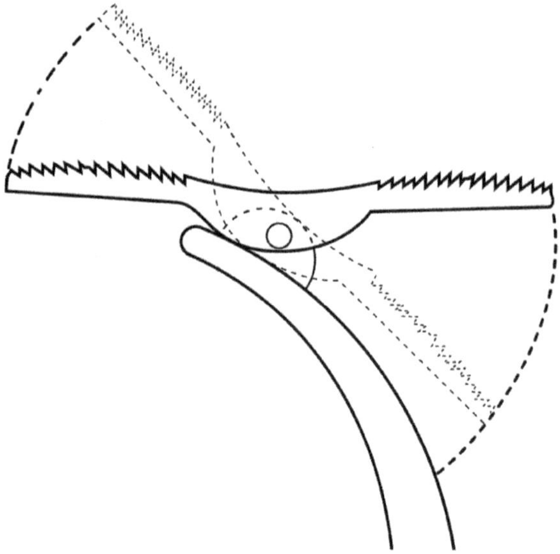

FIGURE 3.4. US patent 9,340, "Self-Adjusting [Shoe] Peg Floater," issued to D. D. Allen October 19, 1852. Used to cut wooden pegs projecting from shoe soles; pegs attach the shoe bottom (sole) to the upper. The shoe bottom is placed facing the peg-cutter; pegs are cut by the rotating blade, first side E (for pegs on the front of the shoe being made) then side D (for pegs in the heel)

length of wood that is inserted in the holes can be cut with Allen's tool, forming custom-length pegs quickly. The cutter has two parts: one for the pegs on the front of the shoe, one for the pegs on the back, near the heel. The operator moves each peg in front of the cutter and pushes down on the rotating part of the cutter, which cuts off the peg when it scissors it between the rotating blade and the fixed blade underneath.

The claim to Allen's US patent 9,340 (Figure 3.4) describes the invention simply:

> I claim the adjustable float or cutter C, D, E, connected to a shank B, by means of the pin or pivot b, which turns loosely in the bearing or standard a, so as to permit the float to adjust itself to the proper positions to cut the pegs from the heel to the toe of the boot in the manner herein set forth.[11]

Inventions like this became quite commonplace in the nineteenth century. Even for this highly specialized tool, Thomson says, "at least five peg cutters were patented from 1852 through 1860."[12] The same was true in all spheres of shoe production: Shoe lasts (wooden forms around which shoes were made), leather-cutting machines, and ultimately sewing machines were all the subject of intensive

[11] US Patent 9,340, at p. 2.

[12] Thomson, Path to Mechanized Shoes, at p. 39.

inventive effort. The shoe industry placed New England at the forefront of burgeoning industrialization while becoming one of the first industries to pioneer mass production and nationwide branding. But increasingly, the individual tools and steps in shoe production were combined, and the separate workshops specializing in each step were consolidated. By the 1890s, the transitional period of shoe tool innovation was ending, and the modern shoe factory was just beginning.

Just as shoemaking tools gradually gave way to entire *machines* for making shoes, independent mechanics specializing in inventions gradually gave way to centralized research labs, housed in large, nation-spanning firms. This trend, accurately summarized in the book title *From Machine Shop to Industrial Laboratory*, is one we return to in depth in Chapter 4.

3.1.1 *Invention, Entrepreneurs, and Firm Growth in the Early Nineteenth Century*

D. D. Allen's "peg floater" is typical of many incremental inventions, such as those relating to improved tools. A few rare inventors moved into promising fields, made an important "foundational" invention, and went on to form a thriving firm characterized by continuous technical improvement, expanding markets, and widening product offerings. There were success stories such as these throughout the nineteenth century, though the later ones – Thomas Edison, George Westinghouse, et al. – received the most attention (due to the advent of mass media). But a good example of an earlier protean figure is the inventor of the platform scale, Thaddeus Fairbanks.

The platform scale was fairly simple but extremely useful. (You can still see it in operation in many post offices and doctor's offices.) It was convenient, because it could weigh goods without removing them from the wagon or cart they were in. The item to be weighed was placed on a platform, which was set into a shallow pit in the ground. Under the platform, two levers (long arms on a hinge) of different lengths responded to the weight on the platform; the shorter lever moved down in response to the weight and transferred the downward motion to the second lever. This second lever was attached by a length of wire to a beam several feet above the platform floor, where it could easily be seen. This was the weighbeam: a short, usually metal, arm that had notches cut into it. Small weights were hung from these notches until the weighbeam came level. Because of the mechanical advantage ("multiplier effect") created by the two levers, small weights on the weighbeam offset even a very heavy weight sitting on the platform. By knowing the proportion between the small weighbeam weights and the actual weight on the platform, the weight of an item can be determined. Figure 3.5 (taken from a Fairbanks patent issued in 1831) shows the basic idea.

The Fairbanks workshop was as an outgrowth of the grist mill and sawmill in St. Johnsbury, Vermont, founded by Erastus Fairbanks, father of inventor Thaddeus.

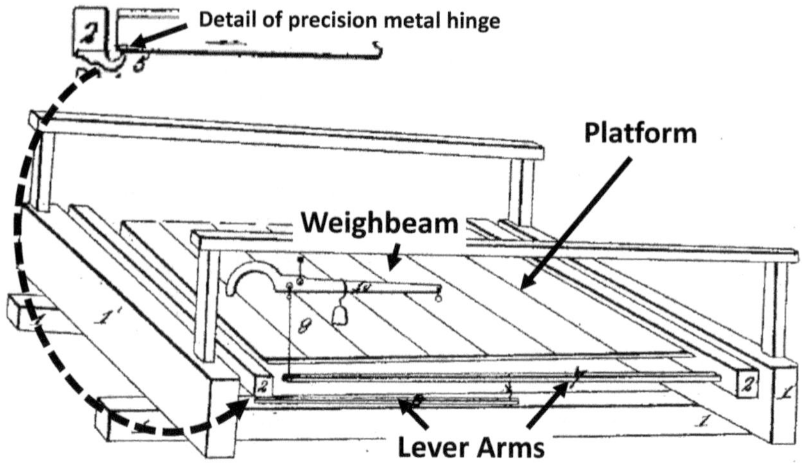

FIGURE 3.5. Fairbanks platform scale, from US patent 6573X, issued June 13, 1831

Thaddeus and several of his brothers were partners with their father in the St. Johnsbury mill, and also in an iron foundry Thaddeus had established by 1823.[13] Because of the difficulty and cost of overland transport, at its founding in the late 1820s, the Fairbanks firm (organized as a partnership between Erastus Fairbanks and several of his sons including the inventive Thaddeus) could directly supply finished products – initially plows, wagons, and stoves – only in the immediate areas around Vermont. This was also the initial territory into which Thaddeus sold his novel platform scale, which he developed first to weigh grain and lumber in connection with the family mills. But it was soon apparent that the platform scale was a very good idea, so the ever-hustling Fairbanks family filed for a patent and began to develop the scale business.

Word spread quickly about the advantages of the Fairbanks scale. Because of the serious limitations of the transportation network at the time, it was a challenge to expand, given the location of St. Johnsbury in north central Vermont – a landlocked and mostly rural state. Overland transport was, however, available to move scales to the important city of Burlington, Vermont, seventy miles west, as well as Portland (Maine) to the east. Newly developed canals made it possible to move scales from Burlington to New York, via Lake Champlain and the Hudson River, though overland routes were used to serve Boston.

[13] This and many other facts and details of the early days of the Fairbanks Scale operation can be found in an excellent PhD thesis from 1995. See Allen Rice Yale, Jr., "Ingenious and Enterprising Mechanics: A Case Study of Industrialization in Rural Vermont, 1815–1900," PhD Thesis, Dept. of History, Univ. of Conn., 1995, available at Univ. Microfilm Inc. Thesis files, UMI Number: 9543982, accessed via ProQuest (paywall), April 2021 (hereafter "Yale Thesis").

But Fairbanks devised a business model that took account of the limited and expensive transportation network of the time. For its earliest scales, wood was the primary input; so, Fairbanks itself only manufactured the precision iron components of the scale. Customers in rural areas acquired their own wood. The final installation of the scale was left to a traveling agent who worked for Fairbanks:

> Only a very small portion of the large platform scales was manufactured in the shops in St. Johnsbury. The bulk of these scales were fabricated out of wood provided by the customer at the site of construction. The Fairbanks scale was first developed toward the end of America's wooden age. Because of the abundance of forests and the relative scarcity of iron and steel, the larger scales, like many items fabricated in America at that time, were made predominantly of wood. Only the iron components of the larger scales were fabricated at the scale works. During this period the accuracy of the scale depended on the skills of the itinerant installer who assembled and sealed the scale [at the customer's location].[14]

So, with a mix of fully made scales and key scale parts, Fairbanks could serve most of the eastern part of the country. As for the more distant parts – the "west" (beyond mid-Pennsylvania) and the south – the logistical infrastructure of the 1830s made these out of reach. Yet the Fairbanks scales surely had a market in these regions. The solution was to emulate pioneers such as Ithiel Town: license or assign territorial patent rights to local manufacturers. This was entirely possible, because when Thaddeus invented the platform scale (sometime around 1830), he, on behalf of the Fairbanks family firm, filed what became a long succession of patent applications, resulting in an important early patent.

The Fairbanks patents enabled an 1833 agreement that included some features of the business model pioneered by earlier inventors such as Eli Whitney and Ithiel Town. The agreement was between the Fairbanks partners (Thaddeus, Erastus, etc.) and a wealthy investor from Vermont named Mellen Chamberlain.[15] Under the agreement, Chamberlain provided capital to the expanding business, while also leveraging his apparently extensive business contacts[16] to find local manufacturers who could manufacture Fairbanks scales in locations closer to the western markets:

[14] Yale Thesis at p. 35.

[15] See Yakup Bektas, *Displaying the American Genius: The Electromagnetic Telegraph in the Wider World*, 34 Brit. J. Hist. Sci. 199, 207 (2001) (describing "Mellen Chamberlain (1793–1839), a well-to-do native of Vermont" who worked to commercialize the Morse telegraph).

[16] It appears Chamberlain got around. He was "about to begin a tour to southern Europe and the East" in June of 1838, which explains why he was in Paris that year to witness some of the earliest demonstrations of F.B. Morse's telegraph. happened to be in Paris when Morse and Smith were promoting the telegraph." See Yakup Bektas, *Displaying the American Genius*, at 207. One reason Morse may have assigned foreign rights to Chamberlain (which excepted England and France) was because of Chamberlain's successful efforts to commercialize the Fairbanks scale. Ibid., at p. 208 n. 32 (describing Chamberlain's assignment and promotion deal with the Fairbanks firm).

> The regions far distant were dealt with in a broad territorial assignment. On August 15, 1833, the Fairbanks firm assigned exclusive rights "to *make*, sell & convey our Platform scales… in all that section of country west of the Allegheny mountains including Alabama & excepting Michigan territory" [Italics in original].[17]

According to the most detailed study of the early years of the Fairbanks Scale Company:

> [T]erms of the [1833] agreement are not clear, but [the assignee, Mellen Chamberlain] may have given Fairbanks notes worth $10,000 in exchange for an assignment of patent rights or a license to manufacture Fairbanks scales. The result of this agreement was the establishment of the partnership of Chamberlain and Fairbanks.[18]

According to the same history, and consistent with the pattern established by patent owners such as Ithiel Town, Chamberlain subdivided his interest by selling fractional shares of the patent to an investor and a sub-assignee-manufacturer in Pittsburgh:

> Chamberlain, in turn, sold 1/10th of his rights to Moses Atwood of Pittsburgh and another l/10th to L. R. Livingston. During the first few months Chamberlain received scales shipped through Boston, but by the end of 1833 he was receiving patterns, gauges and other equipment needed to manufacture scales. Subsequent accounts indicate that L. R. Livingston made scales for Chamberlain. In 1838, Livingston subcontracted the manufacture of Fairbanks scales to Otis Young of Pittsburgh.[19]

Because of the subsequent transactions (described as sub-assignments, i.e., rights were "sold"), it is almost certain that Chamberlain's interest in the Fairbanks patent came via assignment and not license. Whatever form the legal interest took, Chamberlain moved quickly to begin making and marketing Fairbanks scales in the western region:

> [B]y the end of 1833 he [assignee Chamberlain] was receiving patterns, gauges and other equipment needed to manufacture scales. Subsequent accounts indicate that L. R. Livingston made scales for Chamberlain. In 1838, Livingston subcontracted the manufacture of Fairbanks scales to Otis Young of Pittsburgh. By 1834 Chamberlain and Fairbanks had agents throughout the Ohio and Mississippi Valleys with scales in Pittsburgh, Akron, Louisville, Lexington, St. Louis, Nashville, Memphis, and New Orleans.[20]

Because Chamberlain was not a manufacturer, it is likely that he passed on the patterns, gauges, etc., to his licensee-sub-assignee Livingston.

In any case, as of the 1830s, a rough picture of the Fairbanks business model and distribution map looks like Figure 3.6.

[17] Yale Thesis, at p. 137.
[18] Ibid.
[19] Ibid.
[20] Ibid.

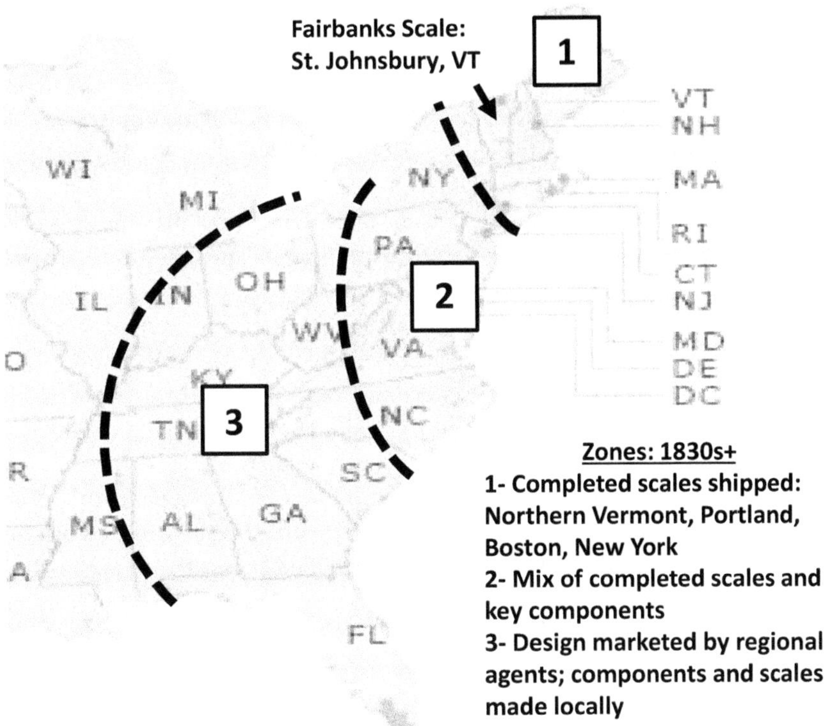

FIGURE 3.6. Fairbanks scale works distribution strategy, 1833

As it happened, this was a short-lived arrangement. Within a decade, Fairbanks seems to have shifted to a strategy that would not become commonplace until later in the nineteenth century. The company centralized production in its own factory in St. Johnsbury.[21] It came to rely on a large network of employee field agents and independent sales representatives. It shipped Fairbanks all over the growing United States, and then all over the world. And it relied heavily on a what was then a new promotional device: nationwide advertising. In all these ways, Fairbanks took on the contours of a late nineteenth century Chandlerian firm – only it did so much earlier than many other companies.

What motivated Fairbanks Scale to centralize production by 1840? One answer is that railway lines came to New England early, and these provided far superior overland distribution compared to wagon and horse. In fact, the Fairbanks works

[21] With respect to the western territories that had been exclusively assigned to investor Chamberlain, Fairbanks accomplished this centralization by buying back Chamberlain's interest from his estate after he died. See Yale Thesis, at p. 119 ("[I]n 1840 Fairbanks had bought back from Chamberlain's estate its patent rights to sell Fairbanks scales in the western states.").

was a major investor in several regional railway lines that served St. Johnsbury.[22] In addition, railway lines were major buyers of Fairbanks scales. For weighing freight and passenger bags, the Fairbanks platform scale was ideal. More railroads meant a bigger market for Fairbanks scales. It also meant more efficient distribution of scales to distant customers, and eventually, to customers located all over the country.

A further factor favoring centralization of manufacturing in Vermont may have been quality control. A frequent complaint about remote manufacturing affiliates was that it was difficult for the "home office" to monitor quality. From all appearances, Fairbanks was quite particular about the details of its manufacturing, and was proud of the quality of its scales. Perhaps the "western" licensees-sub-assignees chosen by Chamberlain were not making scales that were up to Fairbanks's standards. In any event, the "outsourcing" ended and from the 1840s on it appeared that Fairbanks was willing to negotiate the vicissitudes of nineteenth-century bulk transportation in order to maintain its high-quality standards.[23]

The Fairbanks network of agents – both in-house and independent – staffed offices in fifty cities by 1847. This grew to 226 cities by 1866, which is strong testimony to the popularity of Fairbanks scales and the fast growth of the company.[24] Besides their sales duties, these agents also kept an eye out for potential infringers. When they saw something suspicious, they reported back to company headquarters in St. Johnsbury:

> [Fairbanks] had to determine if any of its competitors were in fact infringing on its patents, and, if so, bring suit to halt the infringement. It was always a concern of the company and its agents that Fairbanks' patent rights be protected. Frequently it was Fairbanks' traveling agents who informed the company of suspected cases of patent infringement. They occasionally examined a competitor's scale, and evaluated it in terms of patent infringement.[25]

Though it was founded in the early nineteenth century, Fairbanks nevertheless evolved rapidly. As mentioned, its structure by the mid-1840s resembled most closely the large companies with centralized production and national advertising that came to prominence in the later nineteenth century.

Yet it is worthwhile reviewing the role of its patents in the early Fairbanks story. The early 1830s patent allowed Fairbanks to experiment with an Ithiel Town-regional exclusive franchise model. That business model turned out not to be optimal for the firm. But the patent allowed Fairbanks to give it a try. Nationwide,

[22] Details in Yale Thesis, at p. 111.

[23] For a sense of these challenges, and an appreciation that no customer was too remote to be turned away by Fairbanks, see Ronald R. Switzer, *Fairbanks Weighing Devices on the Steamboat Bertrand*, 55 Neb. History 254 (1974) (describing four Fairbanks scales that were lost when the steamboat "Bertrand" sank in the Missouri River en route to Fort Benton, Montana in 1865).

[24] Yale Thesis, at p. 144.

[25] Ibid,, at p. 122.

dividable rights gave Fairbanks a number of options. When decentralized production did not fully satisfy the firm's needs, it re-centralized production. From that point on – again emulating classic Chandlerian firms from later in the nineteenth century – Fairbanks concentrated on continuous innovation, backed by a formidable patent portfolio. Thaddeus himself was credited as an inventor on over forty patents by 1888, and the Fairbanks company had acquired roughly 160 patents by 1914.[26]

Patents were, of course, only part of the Fairbanks story. The other nuts and bolts of private law played their part in helping Fairbanks implement business strategy. Partnerships, sales agent contracts, corporate acquisitions, joint ventures, consulting contracts, and so on provided flexible tools that Fairbanks used to further the interests of the firm and adjust business structures in response to changing conditions.

As with other private law tools, the Fairbanks patents opened various strategic options and alternative avenues. Of course, this was only one company. But consider: The same basic tools were available potentially to all companies such as Fairbanks, and all inventors like Thaddeus Fairbanks. The weigh scale industry was not targeted by a government development program. It was not the focus of an invention prize or an innovation subsidy. These might have helped, but in the context of the times, they were far from a practical reality in many industries. What was practical for the central government was to deliver some valuable entitlements and to set up a court system whose duties included the enforcement of these entitlements and the private contracts built on them. The Fairbanks story shows that these instruments of private ordering could be quite helpful, one might say powerful, in their own way.

Even though there was much the federal government did not do to promote innovation in this era, it did provide an infrastructure sturdy enough to give assistance to innovative and savvy young companies such as Fairbanks. This much, of course, is well known: It is the prime embodiment of the Gilded Age, laissez-faire mentality so well documented by various scholars. What is new here, in these pages, is to introduce patents to the discussion of the private law instruments – the legal toolbox – deployed in service of nineteenth-century private ordering.

The early Fairbanks patents let the firm explore the benefits of outsourcing. When that did not work to the satisfaction of the firm, it was able to quickly change course. When it did so, its patents changed function too: from forming the basis of a regional franchise network to providing a portfolio of flexible corporate assets capable of supporting diverse corporate strategies. Patents, as with other instruments of private law, provide a flexible and adaptable set of tools. It is easy to miss the subtle contribution these tools make; their overall, cumulative effect is difficult to estimate and hard to assess, because it is dependent on how private actors *deploy* these instruments. And the value added (if any) from these arrangements and rearrangements.

What can be said is that in the right hands the tools of private ordering – including patents – open up possibilities for structuring a business. And, equally

[26] Ibid., at p. 346.

importantly, they can assist in restructuring and re-ordering when new information prompts a change in structure. (The strategic uses of corporate patent portfolios for centralized firms are discussed later in this chapter and especially in Chapter 4.) Patents, particularly when deployed in private agreements, are not as visible as other policy instruments such as prizes, subsidies, and so on. Patents do support contacting in various ways, but they do so subtly, which makes it hard to see their impact. The stories of Ithiel Town and the Fairbanks scale company are meant to show how these business people used patents in the economic context of their times. It is a theme that recurs throughout this book.

3.1.2 *Key Industries*

The shoe industry of D. D. Allen's "floating peg" invention is representative of a number of fields where mechanization proceeded step-by-step.[27] The same is true for the Fairbanks scale firm, though in that case the pioneering nature of the product and the firm's quick-acting management style accelerated the pace of mechanization considerably. In both cases, however, improvements in transportation and communication helped drive market demand, which in turn stimulated increasing mechanization.[28] It is impossible to understand the rapid growth and shifting business models of the nineteenth century without studying the companies and trends behind the rapid improvement in transportation and communication systems.

These improvements were driven by a number of factors. First of these, of course, was government policy: tariffs in the case of steel; corporate charters and land grants for the railroads; and government procurement policy for the telegraph. In most cases these policies found expression through the activities of private companies: large-scale, capital-intensive, and fully integrated companies. These companies were very different by nature from specialty product firms such as D. D. Allen's shoe equipment enterprise and the Fairbanks scale company. Yet despite differences, the

[27] As mentioned, Russ Thomson documents this process in shoemaking in thorough and interesting detail in his book, *Path to Mechanized Shoes*. For a more general treatment of the mechanization/industrialization process, see the classic study by Maxine Berg, The Age of Manufactures, 1700–1820: Industry, Innovation and Work in Britain (London: Routledge, 2nd ed., 1994), at pp. 20–27 (calling the early stages of the process "proto-industrialization" to highlight the emergence of industrial-era institutions and practices out of a background of pre-modern, traditional economic relationships).

[28] Though the nomenclature is not crystal clear, it would seem that all three of these nineteenth-century technologies are instances of General Purpose Technologies (GPTs). See Timothy F. Bresnahan and Manuel Trajtenberg, *General Purpose Technologies: Engines of Growth?*, 65 Econometrics 83 (1995). In any event, they are certainly examples of what economists Robert Cooter and Aaron Edlin call "fertile technologies." See Robert Cooter and Aaron Edlin, *Fertility: Chapter* 5, in The Falcon's Gyre: Legal Foundations of Economic Innovation and Growth (Robert Cooter, ed., Berkeley, CA: Berkeley Law Books, Book 1, 2014), at pp. 5.1 et seq., available at www.law.berkeley.edu/library/resources/cooter.pdf.

large infrastructure-building firms in the telegraph, steel, and railroad industries found they had uses for patents too.

Though only the telegraph industry was crucially dependent on patents, invention and patenting played a part in all three. In steelmaking, several critical inventions made up part of the constant process refinements that improved yields and spurred higher output. In railroads, independent inventors made numerous important contributions, and the overall volume of patent litigation in the industry led to the single largest industry-sponsored patent reform movement in the nineteenth century. Perhaps most importantly, these three industries bred some of the first nationwide mega-corporations: they were prototypes of the companies that pioneered large in-house corporate research and development (R&D) divisions in the early twentieth century, and that dominate patenting activity to this day.

3.1.2.1 Steel

Let us begin with the steel industry. Iron was the most important metal product in the early period of industrialization. While crude iron had been available for thousands of years, increased regional production and localized fabrication made it the metal of choice for agricultural implements (plows, horseshoes, tools, etc.), household items (window sash weights, clothes irons), and even some industrial products such as iron bridges. Local blacksmiths worked with crude pig iron, fashioning it into useful items for local markets, and in some cases adding extra carbon content to create handmade steel. (Steel is iron, with roughly 2 percent of extra carbon added.)

Despite its widespread use, iron had some significant limitations. Aside from its propensity to rust, it was also weaker and more brittle than steel. The problem was that steel was difficult to make before the 1860s. It could be produced by adding carbon to iron through various techniques, but these were labor intensive and required significant skill. The most common, at the industrial scale, involved mixing molten iron with oxidizing agents, to produce the proper level of carbon content for steel. This "puddling," as it was called, produced the iron for the Eiffel Tower in Paris and the frame for the Statute of Liberty in the United States. But this process yielded a variable grade of steel (as individual batches differed in content) and was impossible to scale up efficiently.

Though the growing demand for iron led to increased production through the 1860s, the world awaited a better and more efficient process for making high volumes of quality steel.[29] This arrived in 1865 with the invention of a high-temperature process that worked with forced air – the creation of British inventor

[29] See Peter Temin, *The Composition of Iron and Steel Products, 1869–1909*, 23 J. Econ. Hist. 447 (1963); Thomas J. Misa, A Nation of Steel: The Making of Modern America, 1865–1925 (Baltimore: Johns Hopkins Press, 1995).

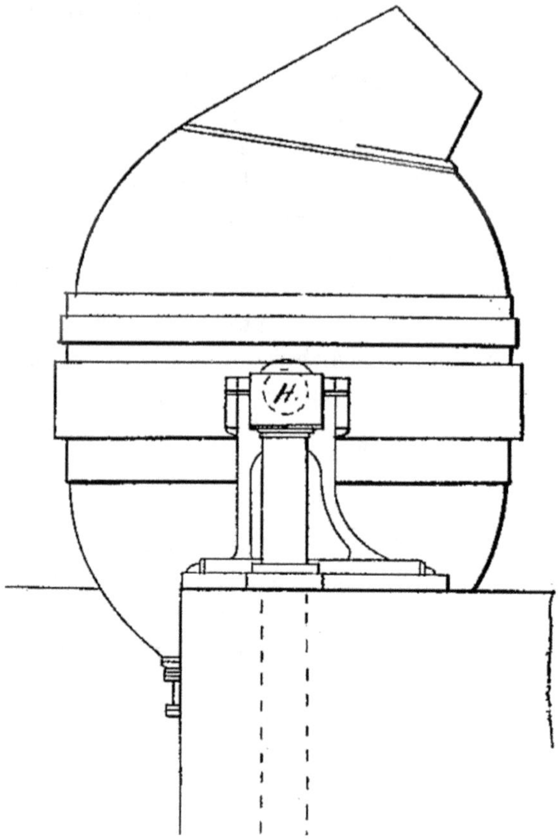

FIGURE 3.7. Bessemer process vessel: Air injected on the underside, superheating the liquid iron and making steel more efficiently. US patent 49,055, issued to Henry Bessemer, July 25, 1865

Henry Bessemer.[30] (See Figure 3.7.) The Bessemer Process, together with some crucial refinements, revolutionized steel production. According to one measure, steel production increased 90 *times* between 1863 and 1880.[31]

The basic Bessemer process used a cylindrical chamber and pumped-in air to create the conditions for efficiently converting iron into steel. Despite its importance,[32] it took several additional inventions to make the Bessemer Process truly

30 Bessemer's patents were licensed in the United States by Alexander Lyman Holley, who was himself an important inventor of improvements on the basic Bessemer Process. See Jeanne McHugh, Alexander Holley and the Makers of Steel (Baltimore: Johns Hopkins University Press, 1980).

31 Data at "U.S. Steel Ingots and Castings Production 1863–1919," available at http://data.nber.org/databases/macrohistory/rectdata/01/a01208.dat.

32 James H. Swank, History of the Manufacture of Iron in All Ages (Philadelphia: American Iron and Steel Institute, 2nd ed., 1892; reprinted New York: Burt Franklin Publisher, 1965), at 407: "The

useful. The first refinement came from a fellow Briton, Robert Mushet, who saw that the right mixture of ingredients into the Bessemer chamber would more perfectly regulate the carbon content of the resulting steel product.[33] A second refinement was along the same lines, but applied to the removal of phosphorus, which is present in high concentrations in some varieties of iron. This was the work of British steel engineers Percy Gilchrist and Sidney Thomas[34] and, virtually simultaneously, Jacob Reese of Pittsburgh in the United States.[35] Subsequent improvements by the American engineer Alexander Lyman Holley completed the perfection of the basic Bessemer design.[36] Taken together, these collective

establishment of the Bessemer steel industry in many countries is justly regarded as constituting a much more important revolution in the production and use of iron and steel than had been created by any preceding influence or combination of influences in any age of the world's history." See also *Bessemer Steel and Its Effect on the World*, 78 Sci. Am. 198 (1898).

33 Mushet added what was called "spiegeleisen," an alloy of iron and manganese. See British Patent 2,219, issued in 1856. On Mushet's contribution, see James H. Swank, History of Iron, at 400:

> [In] 1856, [Mushet] took out a patent for his process of adding to melted cast iron, which had been decarburized and desiliconized by a pneumatic blast, a melted triple compound of iron, carbon, and manganese, of which compound spiegeleisen was the cheapest and most convenient form.

According to industry historian Swank,

> Without the assistance rendered by Mr. Mushet . . . Mr. Bessemer's invention would not have been of much value. It may also be added that many and valuable improvements have been made in the application of the Bessemer process since its introduction in Europe and America.

Ibid., at 396.

34 James H. Swank, History of Iron, at 405:

> An important improvement upon the Bessemer process is the work of two English chemists, Sidney Gilchrist Thomas and Percy C. Gilchrist, both of London. It renders possible the use in the converter of cast iron which contains a large percentage of phosphorus, no method of eliminating from it this hostile element having previously been in use. The first patent . . . relates to the application of a lime lining to the Bessemer converter and to the use of lime in combination with its melted contents. The Thomas-Gilchrist process is now employed with success in the manufacture of Bessemer steel in [other countries] . . . [and] been introduced in this country in connection with the Bessemer process, but only in a small way.

35 James H. Swank, History of Iron, at 405:

> Mr. Jacob Reese, of Pittsburgh, Pennsylvania, also claims priority over Messrs. Thomas and Gilchrist in the invention of the basic process, and this claim was long a subject of controversy in the United States. It rests upon patents which / were granted to Mr. Reese in this country in 1866.

36 See Peter Temin, *The Composition of Iron and Steel Products, 1869–1909*, 23 J. Econ. Hist. 447, 458–459 (1963):

> [A]n American engineer, Alexander Lyman Holley, deserves a large share of the credit [for perfecting the Bessemer Process, leading to a rapid increase in steel production]. Holley was responsible for many of the inventions that made the manufacture of Bessemer steel a success in the United States and which helped to lower the supply curve for Bessemer steel. His two most important innovations were the Holley bottom and the "American" floor plan. The first of these [was an easily removable bottom to the

contributions helped propel US steel production to unprecedented levels in the late nineteenth century.[37]

This tangled patent landscape was resolved only with the formation of a single company that took ownership of all the relevant patents.[38] Notice the difference between this situation and the relatively clean patent posture for new technologies earlier in the century. Though priority contests were certainly not unheard of,[39] the typical new technology in the early era was covered by a single patent. Patents were largely coextensive with discrete products; they conferred rights over the market for that product. The Bessemer Process patents show how things had changed by the 1860s. First, they covered an industrial process – a relatively rare subject for patents in the earlier era.[40] Second, they produced a classic "blocking patents" scenario, where rights over two interlocking patents were needed to put in effect a complete

> Bessemer converter, which allowed a bottom to be repaired without shutting down the converter] ... The second innovation altered the floor plan of a converting plant to facilitate the rapid movement of the metal and to separate the repairs of the bottoms from the activities concerning the metal.

For a sampling of Holley patents, see US Patent Reissue No. 5,318, "Improvement in Ingot Molds," issued to Alexander Lyman Holley, March 11, 1873; US Patent Reissue 5,217, "Improvement in Stoppers for Ingot Molds," issued to Alexander Lyman Holley, March 11, 1873.

37 See Robert C. Allen, *International Competition in Iron and Steel, 1850–1913*, 39 J. Econ. Hist. 911, 916 (1979):

> [For steel rolling mills,] [t]otal factor productivity increased 35 percent [between 1860 and 1909], with most of the increase occurring after 1879. The increase in total factor productivity was primarily due to the rise in labor productivity, and secondarily (given its smaller share) to the rise in fuel productivity ... One suspects that the rise in fuel productivity, which occurred between 1860 and 1890, was due at least in part to the shift from iron to steel ... The rise in labor productivity after 1879 was associated with a sharp rise in capital per worker ...

Recall that the Bessemer Process used blown air, rather than fuel-generated heat, to make steel – which was an important reason that fuel productivity increased.

38 James H. Swank, History of Iron, at 406:

> These [Bessemer and Kelly] patents and the Thomas-Gilchrist patents were purchased in 1879 for [the U.S.] by the Bessemer Steel Company Limited, but controversy concerning the exact scope and significance of Mr. Reese's patents did not end until 1888, when the ownership of all the patents for the United States was finally vested in the company mentioned.

39 And indeed, at least in the United States, Bessemer faced a priority issue himself:

> In 1856 Mr. Bessemer obtained in [the United States] two patents for his invention, but was immediately confronted by a claim of priority of invention preferred by William Kelly, an ironmaster of Eddyville, Kentucky, but a native of Pittsburgh, Pennsylvania. This claim was heard by the Commissioner of Patents and its justice was conceded, the Commissioner granting to Mr. Kelly a patent which at once operated as an impediment to the use of the patents granted to Mr. Bessemer. The effect of this action by the Commissioner was to prevent for several years any serious effort from being made to introduce the Bessemer process into this country.

James H. Swank, History of Iron, at 396–397.

40 Michael Risch, *America's First Patents*, 64 Fla. L. Rev. 1279, 1320 (2012) ("About 12% of the patents we studied [1790–1839] were methods.").

new technology. And third, multiple patent owners in the end joined together to overcome the logjam of patent rights – a development necessitated by the relatively splintered rights held by separate inventors. As we will see later, these were all characteristic of the middle to late nineteenth century patent scene. Numerous patent doctrines were at this time being developed to cope with the more highly variegated ownership claims over these more complex technologies (see below), and this is an excellent example.

3.1.2.2 Railroads

After an initial period characterized by regional rail lines and small railway companies (such as those promoted by the Fairbanks Scale firm, described earlier), the railroad industry grew steadily throughout the nineteenth century. Figure 3.8 shows the growth in railways, by track miles over the years.

By the later nineteenth century, the railroad industry was dominated by large, vertically integrated firms.[41] These firms did not only laid track and made schedule shipments. They also performed service on and made routine improvements to locomotives, freight cars, passenger cars, switching technology, rails, and all other aspects of railroad technology.[42] Moreover, innovations diffused rapidly to rivals, and this was an accepted part of the business.[43] Far from preventing this flow of information, the chief technology players at the major railroads saw themselves as part of a larger, cross-firm enterprise – an instance of what has been called "collective invention."[44] They shared a common culture that included an implicit norm regarding new techniques: I share with you, you share with me. Sometimes this meant eschewing patents altogether. At other times, it meant wide licensing of those railroad inventions that were patented.[45] In either case, there was pride in an innovation that others could use, and perhaps even a boost to firm or individual reputation when a new invention spread across the railway industry.

It is not uncommon for patents to coexist with an open access or widespread sharing norm. It is always important to remember that a patent owner is not *required* to enforce his, her, or its patents. There may be good reasons to obtain patents (and other IP rights) while effectively waiving them in many cases.[46] In this sense, patents

[41] Steven W. Usselman, Regulating Railroad Innovation: Business, Technology, and Politics in America, 1840–1920 (Cambridge: Cambridge University Press, 2002, at p. 88) (example of the Baltimore and Ohio Railroad as it vertically integrated).

[42] Steven W. Usselman, *Regulating Railroad Innovation*, at p. 68 (describing multifarious operations of the Pennsylvania Railroad: buying and laying rails, buying and servicing locomotives, purchasing various supplies, etc.).

[43] Steven W. Usselman, *Regulating Railroad Innovation*, at p. 64.

[44] See Robert C. Allen, *Collective Invention*, 4 J. Econ. Beh. & Org. 1 (1983). See also Eric von Hippel, Democratizing Innovation (Cambridge, MA: MIT Press, 2005).

[45] Steven W. Usselman, Regulating Railroad Innovation, at p. 65.

[46] See generally, Robert P. Merges, *To Waive and Waive Not: Property and Flexibility in the Digital Era*, 34 Colum. J.L. & Arts 113 (2011). See also Robert P. Merges, A *New Dynamism in*

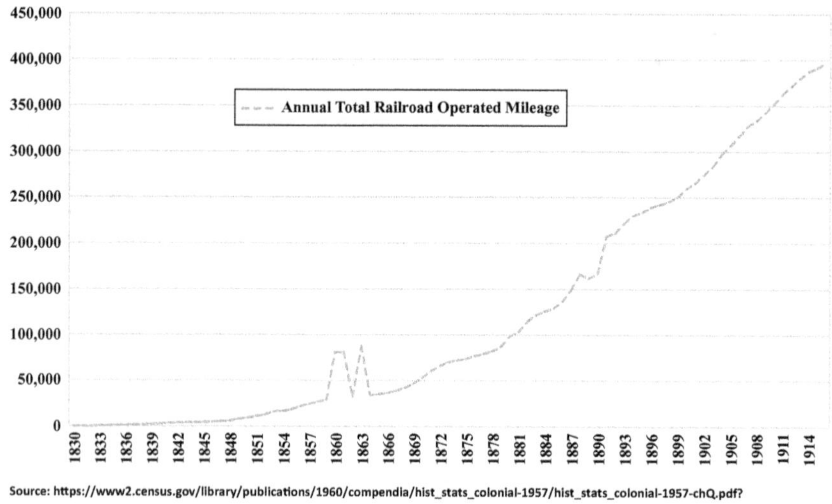

FIGURE 3.8. Total cumulative railroad track mileage 1830–1914

(and other IP rights) may be seen as options. The owner may choose to exercise the right only against certain strategic rivals, permitting all others open or low-cost access. An example from the early locomotive days shows the point. It involves the inventor of numerous important refinements in train locomotives, Matthias W. Baldwin. According to a definitive account of the Baldwin locomotive works,

> Baldwin ... took pride and interest chiefly in the technological and inventive aspects of his work. His technical creativity primarily accounted for the seventeen patents he received between 1833 and 1866. Following common practice at the time, Baldwin made most of these patents available to others in return for royalties. But in at least one case, and probably in a second as well, he balked at allowing others to use particular designs that he felt provided an important competitive advantage for his firm.[47]

One of the patents that was not licensed covered Baldwin's "half crank" invention, a way of transmitting engine power to the driving wheels of the locomotive by placing the engine-connecting shafts on the inner side of the driving wheels, rather than on the outside as is traditional. This permitted locomotives to climb very steep grades. An illustration of the half crank, "inside drive" design, is shown in Figure 3.9.

the Public Domain, 71 U. Chi. L. Rev. 183 (2004) (describing emerging strategies for dedicating intellectual property rights to the public domain to serve private ends).

47 John K. Brown, The Baldwin Locomotive Works, 1831–1915 (Baltimore: Johns Hopkins Press, 1995), at p. 61.

FIGURE 3.9. A Baldwin Locomotive c. 1890
Source: Library of Congress Photo Repository

According to a memoir by another locomotive designer named George Escol Sellers, Baldwin refused to license the half-crank patent to perhaps his greatest rival, the celebrated multi-talented inventor Seth Boyden.[48]

In the absence of vigorous patent enforcement, investments in new technologies were repaid by virtue of profit margins and growing revenues, which did not depend on excluding others or reaping direct royalties. Locomotive technology, for example, was simply too complex for many firms to get into the industry. The Baldwin Locomotive Company of Philadelphia was a world leader in building the great engines that pulled rail cars. But these engines were built on a semi-custom basis; no two were exactly alike. Baldwin engineers were famous for their craftsmanship and innovations, but patents did not play much of a role in protecting the firm's

[48] See Early Engineering; Reminiscences (1815–1840) of George Escol Sellers (Eugene S. Ferguson, ed.) (Washington, DC: Smithsonian Institution, United States National Museum, Bulletin no. 238, 1965), at p. 188:

> [Sellers writes:] Mr. Boyden is well known as the father of malleable iron castings, of which he made an entire success, and afterwards his great invention of manufacturing felt hat bodies by machinery . . . I have made this digression [from railway technology] to show the versatility of Mr. Boyden as an inventor . . . [At one point Boyden] came to Philadelphia [to visit Sellers] bringing with him a movable card model of his proposed valve gear [for a new locomotive engine] . . . He stated to me that before calling on us he had seen Mr. Baldwin, had tried to interest him in longstroke engines, with his [Boyden's] valve arrangement, and that Mr. Baldwin had declined to sell the right to use his half-cranks on the engines he [Boyden] had agreed to build for the Morris and Essex Railroad.

This is the same Seth Boyden whose train brake company was involved in a dispute with George Westinghouse over a new generation of air-powered train brakes, described later in this chapter. See *Boyden Power-Brake Co.* v. *Westinghouse*, 170 U.S. 537 (1898).

investments. There were few rivals to begin with, and it was hard to profit from copying a Baldwin innovation. The massive capital requirements and decades of accumulated know-how kept profits high and served as effective barriers to technology copying. After the initial period of locomotive design, patents were not essential. In this respect, the nineteenth-century locomotive industry is somewhat similar to the aircraft industry of the late twentieth and early twenty-first centuries. Boeing and Airbus compete vigorously in the large passenger jet market, yet only rarely do patent disputes factor in. A somewhat similar dynamic held sway during the oligopolistic "big three" period in the American automobile industry.[49]

With respect to the railway companies, things began to change by the 1870s. This era saw a host of "outside inventors" descending on the railroads.[50] They promoted a long series of improvements and enhancements, some centering on safety devices invented in response to highly publicized rail disasters. But many came from mechanics and tinkerers of all varieties, swept up in the fascination with rail and steam that (then and now) seems to hold many in its thrall. The number of patents awarded for various aspects of railway technology grew steadily throughout the nineteenth century,[51] and many originated outside the workshops of the railroad lines and locomotive companies.

This was in some ways a continuation of the patterns we noted from earlier in the century. Independent inventors, not affiliated with any particular company (or even, in many cases, any particular industry), sought profits from their patented contributions.[52] A dispersed workforce of creative inventors participated in a nationwide "idea market," just as we saw in earlier chapters in the cases of Ithiel Town and Eli Whitney. But there was one big difference. Rather than relying on regional production and distribution, the later nineteenth-century railroad inventors were limited to a few large potential customers. And those customers were operating on a much greater geographic scale than was true of most enterprises earlier in the century. Though railway lines remained partially regional through most of the nineteenth century, they were moving inexorably toward a nationwide scope of operations. Independent inventors thus faced a changed landscape. They had to market their patented inventions to very large companies that were rapidly centralizing their

[49] The aircraft and auto industries were pioneers in the creation of patent pools. These are organizations that pull together the patents of multiple companies, combining technologies and splitting patent royalties. Patent pools retain the benefits of patents while lowering the costs of combining many patented inventions in the making of a complex product. See Chapter 5, sec. 5.2.3.1, infra.

[50] Steven W. Usselman, Regulating Railroad Innovation, at p. 64 and chapter 3.

[51] The classic source is Jacob Schmookler, Invention and Economic Growth (Cambridge, MA: Harvard University Press, 1966) (well-known account of "demand-pull" influences on invention, with nineteenth-century railroad inventions a prime example).

[52] Naomi R. Lamoreaux and Kenneth L. Sokoloff, *The Rise and Decline of the Independent Inventor: A Schumpeterian Story?*, in F. Scott Kieff and Troy A. Paredes, eds., Perspectives on Commercializing Innovation (New York: Cambridge University Press, 2012), at pp. 359–391;

management and operations. Gone were the days when patent owners could carve up the nation into separate regional markets. Rapidly fading were the days when the regional exclusive franchise (based on regional assignments) was the primary focus of the patent-based enterprise. The railroad was a harbinger. The market for patents centered on a few large firms, and this would soon be true for many other industries as well.

In volume, uptake, and impact, the period from 1860 to 1880 represented the last great era of "outside" invention – the sourcing of new technologies from dispersed, independent inventors. This is because, at the same time the railroads were licensing-in outsider patents, companies in other industries were beginning to hire engineers and scientists as employees whose primary job was to develop improvements and new technologies. The large, integrated, in-house R&D lab was just being born – a primary focus of Chapter 4.

While outside inventors made numerous contributions in the later nineteenth century, the patent system itself really burst into prominence when courts began awarding huge damage awards in patent suits against the railroads.[53] In the wake of several especially noteworthy decisions, patent matters rose to the highest levels of discussion within the railroad companies. Although the corporate response took some time to coalesce, by the 1880s the industry was fully mobilized. Two specialized industry organizations supervised and carefully monitored the progress of important infringement suits, including several at the Supreme Court. Meanwhile, a legislative response took shape. Railroad executives lobbied hard in Congressional hearings against the extension of patents that had been costly to the industry. Lobbying also centered on a bill to overturn a particularly costly doctrine that had arisen in the courts. The "doctrine of savings" used a firm's estimated cost savings due to the use of a patented device as the basis of damage calculations. In the hands of a sympathetic judge or jury, it could lead to very expensive judgments. The industry labored to pass a bill to overturn the doctrine – and very nearly succeeded. But when the Supreme Court in 1878 adopted a more favorable interpretation of the "savings doctrine," the industry stopped pushing the proposed legislation.[54]

For all the industry concern, there is little evidence that the wave of outside inventors (and related patent suits) appreciably injured the railroad industry. The econometrician Jacob Schmookler documented railroad industry investment, additions to railroad track mileage, and stock prices for the period 1837 until 1950. All three measures showed robust increases throughout the nineteenth century.[55]

[53] See, e.g., *Chicago & N.W. Railway Co.* v. *Sayles*, 97 U.S. 554 555-556 (1878) (summarizing district court proceedings from 1865 through 1875); In re Caewood Patent, 94 U.S. 695 (1876) (concerning patent for "swedge block" used to repair and straighten worn railway rails).

[54] *Chicago & N.W. Railway Co.* v. *Sayles*, 97 U.S. 554 (1878) (reversing lower court opinions and reining in "doctrine of savings").

[55] Jacob Schmookler, Invention and Economic Growth (Cambridge, MA: Harvard University Press, 1966), at p. 116.

Of special note is the fact that particularly sharp *increases* in these measures were recorded at the same time patents were arriving as a major force on the railroad scene (roughly, between 1860 and 1890). Whatever the effects of patents on the railroad industry, they did not bring it to a halt. Of course, growth might have been even more robust in the absence of patents. But realistically, they did not appear to slow the development of the industry in any significant way. What they did do was to reward some smaller, "outside" inventors, and in at least one case (George Westinghouse, described in Chapter 4), act as a foothold for a new entrant that later grew into a major industrial force.

3.1.2.3 The Telegraph

What the railroad was to transportation, the telegraph was to communication. It revolutionized the transmission of information, and in the process created or made more viable a number of important industries. And, as is often said, telegraphy linked together the wide American nation in ways that accentuated and accelerated the growth of national markets and (in some ways) a national sensibility.

Unlike railroads, which crept up slowly on the American economy, the radical newness of the telegraph was understood from very early on. This was one way in which it was different. There were two others. It was the first new industry that was based on developments in science. In contrast to shop-based, mechanical technologies, telegraphy is based on electrical current. Its prime component cannot be directly observed, felt, or touched. An inventor working with electric current must depend on instruments to measure its features, and on theoretical understanding to predict its effects.[56] This field was therefore one of the first to depend vitally on scientific knowledge and training.

The second difference was the rapid increase in the scale of the industry. Railroads began primarily as short lines, concentrated in a few regions. In mechanical fields, such as textiles and shoemaking, things started with craft-based technical expertise and regional manufacturing-distribution firms. But apart from the very earliest days, telegraphy reached a large scale very quickly. The relatively low cost of stringing telegraph wire, together with the rapid realization that the larger the network, the larger the profits, meant rapid diffusion of this milestone technology..

Although many inventors around the world were working on telegraphic communication, Samuel F. B. Morse was recognized as the pioneer.[57] He received his

56 David Hochfelder, The Telegraph in America, 1832–1920 (Baltimore: Johns Hopkins University Press, 2012), at p. 2.

57 Paul Israel, From Machine Shop to Industrial Laboratory: Telegraphy and the Changing Context of American Invention, 1830–1920 (Baltimore: Johns Hopkins University Press, 1992), at p. 37 (deeming Morse a "team leader" in the collaborative process of inventing the electromagnetic telegraph).

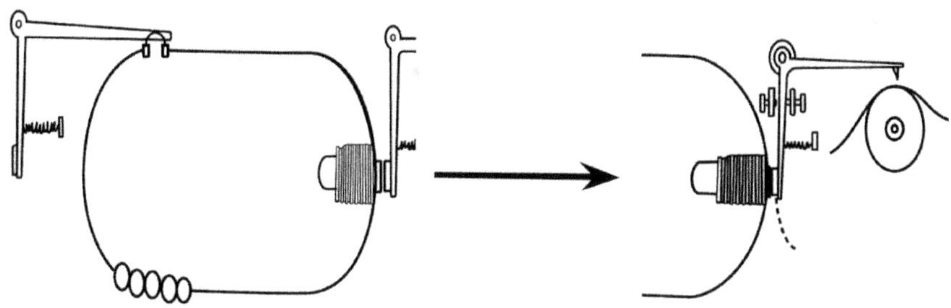

FIGURE 3.10. US patent RE 117, issued to Samuel F. B. Morse, original issue date June 20, 1840, reissued June 13, 1848, "Improvement in Electromagnetic Telegraphs," drawings p. 4. The device on the left generates the signal by breaking the current in the circuit; the "register" on the right receives the signal and records it on a spool of paper (shown far right). The arrow between the two can represent a vast distance

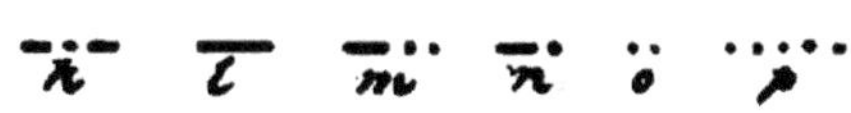

FIGURE 3.11. Excerpt from Morse's "System of Signs" – codes for the letters k, l, m, n, o, and p: Morse Code. US patent RE 117, "Improvement in Electromagnetic Telegraphs," drawings p. 1

basic patent in 1840. The Morse system was relatively simple, requiring a steady current and an electromechanical transmission and receiving mechanism. Morse also created a library of codes for numbers and letters – now known of course as Morse code.[58] Figures 3.10 and 3.11 from Morse's basic patent (as reissued in 1848) capture the flavor of his design. In its earliest days, the telegraph industry was as fragmented as early railroads. Following the conventional regional franchising model described in Chapter 2, Morse assigned regional patent rights to a number of partners. In addition, several competing telegraph technologies were championed in some regions. Most regional companies were underfunded in the early days. And finally, incompetent managers and grasping investors added to the confusion.[59] The answer to all this, as industry pioneers understood, was consolidation:

> The challenge facing the telegraph pioneers was how to make order out of this chaos and create a functioning, profitable network in a tempest of entrepreneurial enthusiasm. The solution they discovered, the creation of a single, unified system,

[58] For a description, see David Hochfelder, Taming the Lightning: American Telegraphy as a Revolutionary Technology, 1832–1860 (Cleveland, OH: Case Western University Press, 1999).

[59] Joshua D. Wolff, Western Union and the Creation of the American Corporate Order (Cambridge: Cambridge University Press, 2013), at p. 14 ("Minimal capital requirements [for investors], an array of contending patents, and managerial incompetence created a[n] [early] telegraphy industry that was fiercely competitive and generally dysfunctional.").

> was anything but novel – there was already a unified national network in the form of the U.S. Post Office. But creating a unified national system in private hands was novel ...[60]

While novel, a consolidated industry structure was not too long in coming. According to the eminent historian of big business, Alfred D. Chandler, Jr.,[61]

> Because of the importance of through traffic, the patterns of competition, cooperation, and consolidation were compressed into a much shorter time period in the history of the telegraph than they were in that of the railroads. By the mid-1850s, the managers of telegraph companies began to work out the cooperative arrangements required to send messages [across the country] ... [After a brief period when there was an inter-regional "pool" of telegraph traffic,] [s]oon there was only the "big three" [companies]. In 1866, these three merged into a single company, Western Union, thus creating the first nationwide multiunit modern business enterprise in the United States.

Although the telegraph industry – like railroads – eventually brought the lion's share of technology development in-house – for example, by creating industrial research labs – this did not happen right away.[62] Perhaps because railroading and telegraphy originated in an older milieu, they underwent a fairly long transitional period in which internal engineering improvements coexisted with a thriving sector of "outside" inventors. An important intermediate form of corporate research was an 1877 contract between Western Union and Thomas Edison, a sort of outsourced R&D lab solution.[63] It required Western Union to pay for all telegraph-related research at Edison Labs, while giving Western Union ownership of Edison's pre-existing telegraphy patents.[64]

Firms founded after 1880 or so, the end of this transitional era, mostly skipped over these hybrid research arrangements. For companies such as General Electric, Westinghouse, and DuPont, outside invention was rare. Almost from their inception, all they knew when it came to invention was the dominance of the in-house R&D lab.

60 Joshue D. Wolff, Western Union and the Creation, at p. 14.

61 Alfred D. Chandler, Jr., The Visible Hand: The Managerial Revolution in American Business (Cambridge, MA: Belknap Press of Harvard University, 1977), at p. 197.

62 See, e.g., Steven W. Usselman, Regulating Railroad Innovation (Cambridge: Cambridge University Press, 2002), at p. 246 (describing the Pennsylvania Railroad's locomotive testing plant, constructed and initially operated by Prof. F. M. Goss of Purdue University, originally built for the St. Louis World's Fair in 1904, then reconstructed at the Pennsylvania Railroad's vast works in Altoona, Pennsylvania).

63 Lewis Coe, The Telegraph: A History of Morse's Invention and Its Predecessors in the United States (Jefferson, NC: McFarland Pub., 1993), at p. 118.

64 Paul Israel, *Telegraphy and Edison's Invention Factory*, in Working at Inventing: Thomas A. Edison and the Menlo Park Experience (William S. Pretzer, ed.) (Downsview, Ontario: Monarch Books of Canada, 1989), at pp. 66, 70.

3.1.3 *Developments in Finance*

To complete our overview of the 1820–1880 period, as it pertains to research and patent issues, we move now to an important related topic. Inventions and, especially, development of new technologies take money. Thus, availability of both working funds and long-term investment capital is crucial to innovation and long-term economic growth. We stop now to consider the ways in which the development of US finance impacted the world of patents and research.

A general problem with economic development is that money accumulates in sectors that thrive, but it sometimes fails to flow into high-growth sectors of the future. Put simply, money gets stuck. Part of the story of the late nineteenth-century US economy is that practices emerged that helped to "unstick" money. As economic historian Lance Davis put it, "certain institutional innovations in the period 1870–1914 acted to reduce ... barriers [to capital mobility]."[65] One mechanism was a more efficient flow of funds between banks in different regions. Davis found that there was a wide regional divergence between bank loan interest rates in 1870, but that it had closed substantially by 1914.[66] This indicates that money was effectively moving from the highly developed eastern United States into fast-growing areas in the West. Growth comes not just from long-term lending but also from the provision of working capital (lines of credit, inventory financing, and the like). A study of nationally chartered banks, which had high reserve requirements and extended mostly short-term credit, shows that in the period 1870–1914, "getting a [federal] bank of the minimum size increases production per person [in a county] between 6% and 11%."[67] And federally-chartered banks were by no means the only source of credit; the number of state-chartered banks increased rapidly in the early nineteenth century as well.[68] Banks were an important source of investment and

[65] Lance E. Davis, *The Investment Market, 1870–1914: The Evolution of a National Market*, 25 J. Econ. Hist. 355, 356 (1965). See generally Robert G. King and Ross Levine, *Finance and Growth: Schumpeter Might Be Right*, 108 Q. J. Econ. 717 (1993).

[66] Ibid., at 369–370 (footnote omitted):

> Between 1870 and 1914, a national short-term capital market gradually evolved. The movement started in the major eastern cities and moved first to the large cities in the other regions. From that point the market grew to encompass those smaller city and country areas with the best banking facilities and finally those areas with the least-developed banking structures.

[67] Scott L. Fulford, *How Important Are Banks for Development? National Banks in the United States, 1870–1900*, 97 Rev. Econ. & Stats. 921, 922 (2015).

[68] Peter L. Rousseau and Richard Sylla, *Emerging Financial Markets and Early U.S. Growth*, 42 Explor. Econ. Hist. 1, 5 (2005):

> Starting with only three banks in 1789, 28 new banks obtained state charters in the 1790s and another 73 were chartered in the decade that followed ... The profitability of these early banks, for which annual dividends of more than 8% were common, sparked a rapid expansion that reached a high-water mark of 834 state banks by 1840. After declining in the depression of the early 1840s, the number of state banks nearly doubled again by 1860, when there were some 1600 state banks.

working capital. They helped fund new businesses, including many based on patents, and also stimulated demand through inventory financing, consumer credit, and the like. Banks also occasionally received patents as collateral or security for business loans to entrepreneurs.[69]

As explained later in this chapter, most nineteenth-century enterprises were conducted as partnerships (and in some instances, trusts). The Fairbanks firm described earlier, for example, was organized as a partnership. But already by the mid-nineteenth century there were enough corporations to supply an active market in equities. According to one economic historian,[70]

> A rough estimate [of the total U.S. equity market] can be derived . . . indicating that the US equity market came to $40 million around 1803 and $890 million in 1850. If we assume constant continuous growth (which works out to be 6.6% per year over the period), we arrive at an estimate of $171 million for the size of the US equity market in 1825.

This represents a relatively small equity sector. Part of the reason (aside from a shortage of capital in the economy generally) was that corporate stocks or shares were relatively rare. As with other business organizations of the time, many patent-based enterprises were not corporations. Those that were not could not resort to the

69 See, e.g., *Bank of Washington* v. *Nock*, 76 U.S. 373, 376 (1869). Inventor Nock designed a lock for mailboxes used by the U.S. Postal Service. The bank advanced money to Nock to begin manufacturing locks, the loan to be paid out of funds Nock received from the Postal Service. The government was slow to pay, however, which brought Nock's indebtedness up to an uncomfortable level. This occasioned an assignment of Nocks' patent to the bank, to be held in trust, as further security for the advances:

> [Nock,] having now received about $3000 of advances, by an instrument dated June 6th, 1840 . . . reciting . . . his desire to secure, "by an assignment of the patent, in manner hereinafter expressed," payment [of existing and future advances] transferred the patent to the bank, upon trust, in case of his failure to pay the bank the money advanced or to be advanced, as it became due, [and in the event of Nock's default] to sell the patent after sixty days' notice by advertisement, and reimburse itself.

The holding in the case turned not on disposition of the patent, but on the bank's assertion that it had a lien on proceeds from a legal judgment Nock obtained against the Postal Service. The Supreme Court upheld the District of Columbia court's ruling that there was no such lien so the bank could not collect out of the proceeds of Nock's judgment against the Postal Service. A definite school of hard Nocks story. See also *Waterman* v. *Mackenzie*, 138 U.S. 252, 252 (1891) (cornerstone case on standing to sue for patent infringement; facts show a patent-related financing scheme in the form of a loan with a repurchase option, implemented by way of a conditional patent assignment; patent owner assigned the patent to an assignee, and gave that assignee a promissory note for $6,500, with the stipulation that the assignor could reclaim the patent by paying off the note on a future date: "[If assignor] shall well and truly pay the said note, according to its tenor, then this assignment and transfer shall be null and void, otherwise to be and remain in full force and effect.").

70 Ibid., at 9 (citing Raymond W. Goldsmith, Comparative National Balance Sheets: A Study of Twenty Countries 1688–1978 (Chicago: University of Chicago Press, 1985)). The volume of equity (securities) trading is estimated from newspaper listings of stock offerings and transactions. Ibid., at 7.

formal equity market to raise capital. They instead usually organized as partnerships. The patent-based regional franchise partnerships described earlier, and then in more depth later this in this chapter, are of course examples.[71]

Though ownership of patent-based enterprises took various forms, as going concerns they needed working capital to grow. Here the development of banking and credit markets made an important contribution. The rapid expansion of bank credit after the Civil War (1861–1865) coincided with the economic takeoff of the late nineteenth century. It has been estimated that the output of the average workshop or factory more than doubled between 1866 and 1886.[72] In the 1870s alone, one study found, investment in steam power led to large increases in productivity and large increases in the scale of factory production.[73] Although equity investment (investment in the ownership of firms) was important, the availability of credit was equally so.

From the perspective of investment in new technologies, credit expansion was important for several reasons. First, cash for new machinery could be borrowed, and repaid out of the higher revenues produced by the new machine. Credit thus stimulated the market for machinery – a portion of which was patented. Second, and perhaps more important, bank credit freed up internal funds within an enterprise. Retained earnings, paid-in capital, and other internal funding sources could then be deployed on essential long-term investments. Many of these involved new production techniques, new lines of business, and in many cases new inventions. Outside capital, in other words, freed up internal funding for investment in what we now call product research.[74] As a result, bank entry is associated with more rapid economic growth due to industrialization.[75]

[71] Alfred D. Chandler, The Visible Hand: The Managerial Revolution in American Business (Cambridge, MA: Belknap Press of Harvard University, 1977), at 43 ("Until the 1840s, the investment in sailing ships, steamboats, canal boats, stagecoaches and wagons remained small enough to be easily funded by a small number of partners.").

[72] Anthony O'Brien, *Factory Size, Economies of Scale, and the Great Merger Wave of 1898–1902*, 48 J. Econ. Hist. 639 (1988).

[73] Jeremy Atack, Fred Bateman, and Robert Margo, *Steam Power, Establishment Size, and Labor Productivity Growth in Nineteenth-Century American Manufacturing*, 45 Explor. Econ. Hist. 185 (2008) (finding that the ratio of capital to output increased during the 1870s as a result of investment in steam engines).

[74] See Matthew Jeremski, *National Banking's Role in U.S. Industrialization, 1850–1900*, 74 J. Econ. Hist. 109, 114 (2014):

> [T]he majority of loans [between 1850 and 1900] provided operational liquidity, bridged seasonal needs, and helped purchase small capital improvements. They thus were more likely to fund the purchase of steam engines rather than the construction of large factories. Maybe more important for the period, however, the availability of working capital loans would have freed up an establishment's own funds for investment.

[75] Ibid., at 136–137: "[Liberalized banking legislation in the 1860s led] to a 30 percent increase in banks and a 10 percent increase in total bank capital [in the Northeast and Midwest]. These additions greatly increased the access to funds for new entrepreneurs and the ability to expand for existing manufacturer businesses."

The "substitution effect" of bank credit thus freed up internal investment capital for R&D projects. This was crucial. Economists going back to the early twentieth century emphasize that internal funding of R&D is often necessary for successful innovation. Because R&D is inherently speculative, it is very difficult for outside investors to effectively evaluate the chances of success. The line between a "true believer," who is really onto something, and a self-deluded (or fraudulent) speculator in over his or her head is a very thin line indeed. In recent years, we have seen the rise of "repeat players" with special expertise in evaluating innovative technologies and business plans – venture capitalists.[76] And, to be sure, there were savvy investors who pioneered the venture capital industry, but not until the twentieth century.[77] Overall, many inventions in the nineteenth century sprang from the internal resources of small and medium-sized companies. For this reason, and because of the general advantages of increased credit, inventive activity thrived along with expanded banking and lending.[78]

In this period, US population increased by a factor of five (from roughly 10 million to almost 50 million), but GDP grew even faster. The economy was almost twelve times bigger in 1880 than it was in 1820. This is what economists call "economic takeoff," and what lay people call simply "boom times." As with most economic growth, the explanation has everything to do with increased productivity. It was in this era when the rapidly expanding industrial sector drove economic growth. And – whether as cause, effect, or some of both – patents were part of the story.

Two key drivers of productivity gains were railroads and telegraphs. The first revolutionized transportation, which linked together formerly isolated pockets of commerce into a single national market. The second brought distant buyers into direct contact with sellers, reducing opportunities for interregional arbitrage and helping to create a single, unified market. Related innovations – ranging from the advent of national consumer brands to rapid improvement in iron and steelmaking technologies – followed quickly. All these developments fed activity in the patent field. And the enabling technologies of railroads and telegraphs were themselves two of the pioneering technologies that became major focal points for nineteenth century patent law.

[76] Samuel Kortum and Josh Lerner, *Assessing the Contribution of Venture Capital to Innovation*, 31 RAND J. Econ. 674 (2000).

[77] See, e.g., Spencer Ante, Creative Capital: Georges Doriot and the Birth of Venture Capital (Boston, MA: Harvard Business Review Press, 2008) (French business school teacher and early venture capitalist who began teaching at Harvard Business School in 1926).

[78] The pattern persists. See William Mann, Creditor Rights and Innovation: Evidence From Patent Collateral, Working Paper, Andersen School of Management, UCLA, April 27, 2015, available at http://ssrn.com/abstract=2356015 (In the United States in 2013, 40 percent of patent-holding firms had pledged their patents as collateral at some point, and these firms performed 28 percent of total R&D and received 22 percent of all patents). See generally Ronald J. Mann, *Secured Credit and Software Financing*, 85 Cornell L. Rev. 134 (1999) (describing frequency of secured credit financing in the software industry, along with common financing terms and challenges, such as remedies in the event of bankruptcy).

This rapid set of developments strained the infrastructure of American institutions in numerous ways. Steam boiler explosions – common due to the primitive state of boiler technology – put pressure on the court system, and ultimately yielded federal safety and inspection legislation.[79] The rapid build-out of railway lines, combined with lack of coordination between fast-growing railroad companies, led to accidents and pricing disputes. The earliest industry-specific federal regulatory agencies were set up in response. Telegraphic communication and related issues also created novel problems that called for novel solutions, and finally, the growing volume and diversification of patent filings put pressure on the Patent Office to keep pace. The period between 1840 and 1880 was one of rapid transformation in the economy. Patterns of commerce in 1840 were not appreciably different than they had been in 1820 in many respects. But by 1880, something approaching the twentieth century economy was taking shape. The years covered in this chapter thus represent a crucial transition from the founding era to the era of "corporatization" (1880–1920) we take up in Chapter 4.

3.2 PATENTS AND BUSINESS ORGANIZATIONS

As with the Founding period (Chapter 2), patents influenced the way businesses were structured and operated between 1820 and 1880. Though the sole proprietors and partnerships of the founding era continued, two new organizational forms rose to importance. The first was the business trust, understood by historians as an important transitional form on the way to the general-purpose corporation. And the second was, of course, the corporation itself. Patents were an important asset in each of these new business forms. But why, given the widespread adoption of the regional franchising model described in Chapter 2, did these new forms appeal to businesses holding patents?

The answer turns on the changing nature of business and technology in this era. By 1880, the US economy had developed a large number of truly national firms. As mentioned, improvements in transportation and communication were primarily responsible for this shift away from regional production and distribution. At the same time, rapid industrialization caused a quantum shift in the sophistication of industrial technologies. Beginning with railroads and telegraphs, the growing economy produced rapid improvements in materials, production machinery, and consumer goods. The old model of a single firm based around a single patent or group of patents was becoming outdated. This was the first stage in a major shift – the shift from patents as a single, enterprise-wide foundation stone to patents as numerous, individual assets held in bulk by large companies. It was the beginning of the era when patents are best

[79] Richard N. Langlois, David J. Denault, and Samson M. Kimenyi, "Bursting Boilers and the Federal Power Redux: The Evolution of Safety on the Western Rivers" (1994). Economics Working Papers. Paper 199401, available at www.researchgate.net/publication/23742739_Bursting_Boilers_and_the_Federal_Power_Redux_The_Evolution_of_Safety_on_the_Western_Rivers.

understood as individual components of large corporate portfolios. The era of the large-scale business enterprise put pressure on existing patent doctrines and institutions. So, a host of new doctrines, practices, and institutional features were born to respond to the changing needs of the industrial-economic system.

3.2.1 *Elaboration of Regional Franchises*

In the years leading up to 1880, the regional franchise model pioneered in the founding period reached its final form. This was the period when the market for local patent rights flourished. The combination of national property rights with regional production, distribution, and marketing continued to make sense in many industries until well into the nineteenth century. The growth in the overall market size made it efficient to divide and subdivide regional rights to a finer and finer degree. Patent agencies sprang up in all parts of the country, to offer patent rights to local representatives, and in some cases to earn royalties themselves as master regional assignees running a network of sub-assignees and licensees. The growing national market meant that national magazines and newsletters were being launched, to great success. Thus, it was that *Scientific American*, a magazine created and run by the Munn Patent Agency, came to be a major clearinghouse for patent rights throughout the country. Similar publications served the same function; they prospered in part by running advertisements from patent owners looking for regional representatives to introduce patented technologies into as many new markets as possible.

The proliferation of the regional franchise model occasioned two important challenges for the legal system. First were disputes between competing holders of local rights, usually in adjacent localities. Customers shopping for the lowest price might find a product in region A, buy the product there, and then bring it into region B, a separate territory run by a separate regional affiliate/franchisee of the patent owner. This problem of cross-selling (really a species of arbitrage) was and is a major headache for any business model that depends on awarding exclusive local selling territories. Where patents were involved, courts gradually built up the doctrine of patent "exhaustion," which permitted buyers of patented goods to take them from one region into another. Much of the law of exhaustion dates from this historical period.

A second challenge was the abuse of the local patent agent model. Despite the efforts of the patent system to issue quality patents, a fair number of patents were granted on common household items. Unscrupulous patent agents used these weak patents to file many infringement cases against user/customers and small businesses, hoping to obtain settlements from these relatively unsophisticated defendants.[80]

[80] On this episode, see Gerard N. Magliocca, *Blackberries and Barnyards: Patent Trolls and the Perils of Innovation*, 82 Notre Dame L. Rev. 1809, 1811 (2013) ("Called 'patent sharks,' [these unscrupulous patent agents] bought dormant agricultural patents and then sued farmers who were unknowingly using protected technology."). See also Earl W. Hayter, *The Patent System and Agrarian Discontent, 1875–1888*, 34 Miss. Valley Hist. Rev. 59 (1947) (describing the role of

This, the first "patent troll" business model, brought dishonor and scandal to the patent system. It also invited numerous patent reforms, including in the areas of design patents and damages (discussed earlier in connection with the railroad industry). If some of the courtier patent lobbyists were guilty of rent seeking in the founding period, the "patent farmers" who arose in the nineteenth century played the same role in the later era. The cycle of rent seeking followed by patent reform continued in this era, as it does down to the present day. Given the nature of patent rights, the line between meritorious invention and grubby rent-seeking is a difficult one to draw and enforce. This is the reason the Patent Office kept a very close eye on that line, and still does.

3.2.1.1 Territorial Franchises and Patent Exhaustion

Exclusive territorial assignments continued to be the primary method of commercializing patents until the late nineteenth century. Patentees created ever more complex and finely sub-divided territorial arrangements. Consider, for example, the series of transactions related to some important early patents on the wood-turning lathe (or planing machine), invented by Woodworth in the 1820s. Under the original patent term, one set of regional rights looked like this:

> Woodworth's patent bears date the 27th of December, 1828, and runs for fourteen years. On the 29th of July, 1830, the patentees conveyed to Isaac Collins and Barzillai C. Smith the right to construct, use, and vend to others, the planing machine invented within several States, including Pennsylvania, except the city of Philadelphia. On the 19th of May, 1832, Collins and Smith transferred to James Barnet the right to construct and use, during the residue of the aforesaid term of fourteen years, fifty planing machines, within Pittsburg and Alleghany county, for which he agreed to pay four thousand dollars. Barnet agreed not to construct or run more than fifty machines during the term aforesaid, and Collins and Smith bound themselves not to license during the term, nor to construct or use themselves during the term, or allow others to do so, in the limits of Pittsburg [sic] and Alleghany county.[81]

This patent was extended by a special act of Congress in 1845 (a late, and increasingly rare, version of courtier capitalism as described in Chapter 2):

> The patentee, by deed dated the 14th of March, 1845, and also by a further deed dated the 9th of July, 1845, conveyed to James E. Wilson all his interest as administrator in the letters patent under the extension by the act of Congress. And Wilson, on the 4th of June, 1847, for the consideration of twenty-five thousand dollars, gave to Bloomer, the plaintiff, a license to construct and use, and vend to others to

the Granger movement in anti-patent lobbying on behalf of beleaguered farmers). See this chapter on the emergence of modern patterns of patent-related political economy.

81 As described in *Bloomer* v. *McQuewan*, 55 U.S. 539, 554 (1852).

> construct and use, during the two extensions, "all that part of Pennsylvania lying west of the Alleghany Mountains, excepting Alleghany county, for the first extension, which expires on the 27th day of December, 1849, and the States of Virginia, Maryland, Kentucky, and Missouri, excepting certain parts of each State."[82]

With this complex set of rights in place, the chances of conflict among assignees and licensees obviously increased. This was the backdrop to an important Supreme Court case. *Bloomer* v. *McQuewan*[83] pitted the assignee under the original term of the Woodworth patents – the partnership called McQuewans[84] and Douglas – against a regional assignee of the Congressionally extended Woodworth patents. The field of battle was the city of Pittsburgh: Elisha Bloomer, the plaintiff-assignee, claimed that Barnet needed to sign a new license agreement to continue to run his fifty planing machines in Pittsburgh. Barnet and his assignors, McQuewans and Douglas, begged to differ; they said the original license to Barnet still stood, and that no new license was necessary.

The case was unusual in that it revolved around patents extended by a special Act of Congress. But it set the stage for later cases where the issue was a conflict among territorial assignees. The question in these later cases was whether "cross-selling" between exclusive territories would be permitted or not. Though different in fact, the similarity between cross-selling cases and the facts of *Bloomer* (viz. they both involve conflicting claims of right under multiple assignments and licenses) meant that the tracks laid down in *Bloomer* would be important ones for the future. In its holding, the Supreme Court ruled in favor of Bloomer, which meant that Barnet needed a new license to the now-extended patent from Bloomer:

> The franchise which the patent grants, consists altogether in the right to exclude every one from making, using, or vending the thing patented, without the permission of the patentee. This is all that he obtains by the patent. And when he sells the exclusive privilege of making or vending it for use in a particular place, the purchaser buys a portion of the franchise which the patent confers. He obtains a share in the monopoly, and that monopoly is derived from, and exercised under, the protection of the United States. And the interest he acquires, necessarily terminates at the time limited for its continuance by the law which created it. The patentee cannot sell it for a longer time. And the purchaser buys with reference to that period; the time for which exclusive privilege is to endure being one of the chief elements of its value. He therefore has no just claim to share in a

82 *Bloomer* v. *McQuewan*, 55 U.S. 539, 554–555 (1852).

83 55 U.S. 539 (1852).

84 John and Allen McQuewan were partners with Samuel Douglas, thus the partnership name of McQuewans [plural] and Douglas. Because partnerships could not sue as a distinct legal entity, the first named party in the lawsuit was John McQuewan, so the case name is "McQuewan [singular] v. Bloomer." See case caption, 55 U.S. 539.

further monopoly subsequently acquired by the patentee. He does not purchase or pay for it.[85]

And yet, the Court said, the situation is different for end users – people and companies that had purchased a planing machine from Barnet. As to them, the extended patent was irrelevant, and they need not pay Bloomer for the right to continue using planing machines bought from Barnet during the original patent term:

> But the purchaser of the implement or machine for the purpose of using it in the ordinary pursuits of life, stands on different ground. In using it, he exercises no rights created by the act of Congress, nor does he derive title to it by virtue of the franchise or exclusive privilege granted to the patentee. The inventor might lawfully sell it to him, whether he had a patent or not, if no other patentee stood in his way. And when the machine passes to the hands of the purchaser, it is no longer within the limits of the monopoly. It passes outside of it, and is no longer under the protection of the act of Congress. And if his right to the implement or machine is infringed, he must seek redress in the courts of the State, according to the laws of the State, and not in the courts of the United States, nor under the law of Congress granting the patent. The implement or machine becomes his private, individual property, not protected by the laws of the United States, but by the laws of the State in which it is situated. Contracts in relation to it are regulated by the laws of the State, and are subject to State jurisdiction.[86]

This was, technically, dictum: part of the deciding opinion not required to resolve the case at hand. (There were no end users in the case.) But the instinct of the Court was to address the issue, because it was obvious that the regional franchising model – and the problem of cross-selling – was impacting consumers. Thus, the Court created "out of whole cloth" a rule that both preserved the viability of regional franchising and yet protected consumers from having to pay two sets of assignees or licenses for the right to use the same patented item.[87]

Notice that the *Bloomer* opinion refers to state contract law as the proper forum for resolving disputes after an end user (customer) purchases a patented item. A contract of sale might include terms such as a payment schedule or warranty. Disputes over these terms are not patent-related disputes, the Court says, because the purchased item has "passed outside" of the federally backed patent right. It was this concept of passing outside, of going beyond "the limits of the monopoly," that gave rise to the label of "patent exhaustion." The practical impact of this doctrine is that

[85] *Bloomer* v. *McQuewan*, 55 U.S. 539, 549 (1852).

[86] *Bloomer* v. *McQuewan*, 55 U.S. 539, 549–550 (1852).

[87] See Sean M. O'Connor, Origins of Patent Exhaustion: Jacksonian Politics, "Patent Farming," and the Basis of the Bargain, Univ. of Washington Law School Legal Studies Research Paper No. 2017-05 (March 8, 2017), available at https://papers.ssrn.com/sol3/papers.cfm?abstract_id=2920738, at 7 ("[Justices] Taney and Clifford constructed their rhetoric for the cases [beginning with *Bloomer*] out of whole cloth.").

where a consumer purchases a patented item outright, buyer-seller rights are determined from the sales contract (or some other state law right), and buyer-seller disputes may not be heard in federal courts as a patent case. This makes sales contracts (and related state law) the paramount legal regime for structuring consumers' post-purchase rights and remedies.[88]

While the exhaustion principle leaves contract law as the key post-purchase governance regime for seller-consumer transactions, this does not mean that contracts are unimportant higher up the distribution chain. Contracts were a crucial adjunct to patent rights in structuring assignor-assignee and owner-licensee transactions. The simplest form of regional franchise was based exclusively on patent assignments, it is true. Local ownership via an outright territorial assignment gave each regional assignee freedom to operate within the relevant region. But in many situations, patentees and their master partners (initial assignees) desired some sort of control over the patent-based regional enterprises. Quality control, allocation of responsibility for regional patent enforcement, maximum production limits, and (in this earlier era) sometimes minimum resale price provisions – these and other restrictions were and are commonly imposed on licensees.

3.2.2 *The Backdrop to Contracts: Barebones Co-Ownership Rules*

Elaborate contract terms are to be expected in sophisticated business arrangements such as regional patent franchises. It is in the parties' interest to clarify rights and obligations. But an additional impetus for contracting is that the default legal rules that apply to co-owners of a patent – if left unmodified by contract – dictate outcomes and structure incentives in ways that will often deeply undermine the business relationship between co-owners.

Under the statutory default rules for co-ownership, each co-owner was (and is still today) independent. There was no need to obtain permission from a co-owner to manufacture or sell under a co-owned patent. And money made from selling a patented item did not (and does not) have to be shared with other co-owner(s). The legal form of this ownership structure is called tenancy in common.[89]

Put simply, patent co-owners have no obligations to one another, unless they enter into a contract specifying rights, duties, and decision-making procedures. This is partly an expression of the preference for simplicity in property arrangements. Legal theorists recognize that property rights are intentionally limited to a few

[88] The exhaustion doctrine underwent further elaboration in the latter part of the nineteenth century. For a case study, see the discussion of regional franchise rights in the case of *Adams* v. *Burke*, later in this chapter.

[89] See *Pitts* v. *Hall*, 19 F. Cas. 758, 760–761 (C.C.N.D.N.Y. 1854) (No. 11,193); Robert P. Merges and Lawrence A. Locke, *Co-ownership of Patents: A Comparative and Economic View*, 72 J. Pat. & Trademark Off. Soc'y 586, 589 (1990).

simple structures.[90] These theorists argue that this arrangement makes it easy for people dealing with owners to understand the rights of those owners. Once an asset is identified, and its owner located, there is no need for a lengthy inquiry into exactly which uses of the asset are controlled by the owner,[91] or under what conditions the owner is allowed to sell or rent out the asset. An outright owner is understood to have broad, plenary power over the asset that is owned. One dealing with an owner can have confidence that the owner may sell an asset to almost anyone, or contract for any use of it, for almost any purpose. The great benefit of property, as a legal entitlement, is thus its breadth and simplicity.

Cases on patent co-ownership in the absence of contractual modification exemplify this theme. They show that, to keep entitlements simple, co-ownership does not force co-owners (and their assignees) to bargain or agree with the other co-owners regarding permitted uses, revenue splits, etc.:

> In the case of joint patentees, where no agreement of copartnership exists, the relation of copartners certainly does not result from their connection as joint patentees; and, when one joint owner of a patent transfers his undivided interest to a stranger, the assignee does not become the partner of his co-proprietor. In both cases, the parties interested in the patent are simply joint owners, or tenants in common, of the rights and property secured by the patent; and their rights, powers, and duties, as respects each other, must be substantially those of the joint owners of a chattel.[92]

This simple structure entails minimal obligations, and free assignability of interests (without permission from, or accounting to, other co-owners).[93]

90 Thomas W. Merrill and Henry E. Smith, *Optimal Standardization in the Law of Property: The Numerus Clausus Principle*, 110 Yale L.J. 1 (2000).

91 Henry E. Smith, *Property as the Law of Things*, 125 Harv. L. Rev. 1691 (2012).

92 *Pitts* v. *Hall*, 19 F. Cas. 758, 760–761 (C.C.N.D.N.Y. 1854) (No. 11,193). See also *Drake* v. *Hall*, 220 F. 905, 908 (7th Cir. 1914):

> The distinctions between co-ownership of property and copartnership relation therein, and that mere joint ownership and control of property does not constitute relationship as copartners therein, are well settled … It is of the essence of copartnership relation that an agreement appear, express or implied, for sharing the profits of a business. The requisites of a partnership are that the parties must have joined together to carry on a trade or adventure for their common benefit, each contributing property or services, and having a community of interest in the profits … Without proof of such import in the agreement or conduct of these parties the contention of copartnership relation between them thus became untenable.

93 See *Kabbes* v. *Philip Carey Mfg. Co.*, 63 F.2d 255, 256 (6th Cir. 1933) ("Moeller owned a half interest in the patent. The assignment which he made, not being attacked, is presumed to be valid. Thereunder his half interest passed to the defendant, and the defendant, being the owner of a half interest in the patent, is entitled to use it without interference from the plaintiff."); *Rainbow Rubber Co.* v. *Holtite Mfg. Co.*, 20 F. Supp. 913, 915 (D. Md. 1937) ("[O]ne co-owner of a patent right, whatever his undivided interest may be, may exercise that right as he pleases, regardless of the consent of any co-owner. Thus, no recovery of profits or damages can be had against such a co-owner if, without the consent of the others, he makes, uses, or sells the patented invention. That is to say, he may, at will, make, use, or sell the patented invention or license others to do so, and neither he nor his licensees may be enjoined from so doing. No

One simple way to achieve a small degree of control was to add conditions onto the assignment of a patent interest. A condition subsequent, as it is known, can divest an assignee of title if the assignee violates the stated condition.[94] But this is a very limited device for retaining management control of an enterprise, for two reasons. First, it is often difficult to foresee all the potential conflicts in running an enterprise, which makes it difficult to specify with precision all the conditions that will result in the dissolution of the assignment.[95] Second, conditions are construed strictly, because they produce a result disfavored by the legal system generally: the stripping of an owner of his or her unfettered ownership rights.[96] For these reasons the

recovery of profits or damages may be had against his licensees at the suit of any other co-owner of the patent."). The rule continues in force today. See *Ethicon, Inc.* v. *U.S. Surgical Corp.*, 135 F.3d 1456, 1465 (Fed.Cir.1998); *Beane* v. *Beane*, 856 F. Supp. 2d 280, 295 (D.N.H. 2012) ("By virtue of his co-inventorship, Alan [Beane] became a co-owner of the patent . . . and was entitled to use that patent without [brother] Glenn's consent or, indeed, without even accounting to him for any resulting profits. See 35 U.S.C. § 262."). Note that sometimes, co-owners of real property can petition a court for either a division of the property or a "forced sale" of the property and a split of the sales proceeds. See, e.g., *Williams* v. *Coombs*, 88 Me. 183, 33 A. 1073, 1074 (1895) ("[T]his [co-owned real] property could not be divided without greatly impairing its value, [so] a sale of the whole property would be much more beneficial to both parties, and … the [request] of the bill [complaint] that the court decree a sale of the property should be granted."). No such "forced sale" remedy is available in patent cases, however.

94 See, e.g., *Bliss* v. *Reed*, 106 F. 314, 318 (3d Cir. 1901); *Bassick Mfg. Co.* v. *Ready Auto Supply Co.*, 22 F.2d 331, 333 (E.D.N.Y. 1927) (citations omitted):

> The fact that some of the assignments of the … patents [at issue in the case] are made subject to said agreements [i.e., conditions subsequent] does not qualify the character of the title transferred, because the right to obtain a reassignment of the legal title given therein, under certain conditions in said agreements expressed, is a condition subsequent, and the title of the plaintiff cannot be assailed except by showing that such reassignment has been made [as a result of the agreed-upon contingency]… There was no evidence offered to show any such reassignment.

D.M. Sechler Carriage Co. v. *Deere & Mansur Co.*, 113 F. 285, 288 (7th Cir. 1902) (condition subsequent does not mean the grant under the assignment is anything less than an assignment).

95 An assignment can be undone using the legal action called rescission. But rescission is only possible when "that which was undertaken to be performed in the future was so essential a part of the bargain that the failure of it must be considered as destroying or vitiating the entire consideration of the contract, or so indispensable a part of what the parties intended that the contract would not have been made with that condition omitted." *Lauer* v. *Raymond*, 190 A.D. 319, 326, 180 N.Y.S. 31 (App. Div. 1920). Thus, a disagreement based on changed conditions, or a general conflict over the best way to manage a patent-based business, would not be sufficient to rescind a past assignment. For a condition subsequent case in the patent context, see *Halstead* v. *Gen. Ry. Signal Co.*, 51 N.Y.S.2d 372, 374 (Sup. Ct. 1944), aff'd, 268 A.D. 1060 (App. Div. 1945) (rescission of invention assignment agreement based on condition subsequent).

96 *Lowe* v. *Copeland*, 125 Cal. App. 315, 318–319, 13 P.2d 522, 524 (Cal. Ct. App. 1932) (alleging condition subsequent in patent assignment agreement):

> A condition subsequent refers to a future event upon the happening of which the obligation becomes no longer binding on the party in whose favor the condition was created if he chooses to enforce it… Forfeitures under such provisions, however, are not favored; and any inconsistent acts or dealings by the party claiming the forfeiture will be regarded as a waiver.

condition subsequent was of very limited utility in structuring the rights of participants in an ongoing enterprise. With or without conditions, then, structuring a business around simple patent assignments, without more, was fraught with difficulties. The default legal structure that follows from simple co-ownership was too cumbersome to be left in place.

As a result, businesspeople who wanted to form an enterprise based on shared interest in a patent resorted to two reliable legal instruments: contracts and trusts. Each has its advantages. What unites them is a structure for making business decisions that binds the business owners into a single management unit – exactly what is missing from the default co-ownership rules.

This channeling into contractual enterprise forms has significant benefits. It forces co-owners to supersede the default co-ownership structure by writing contracts to govern the management of the co-owned asset. As one court explained,

> A personal chattel vested in several different proprietors cannot possibly be enjoyed advantageously by all, without a common consent and agreement among them. To regulate their enjoyment in case of disagreement, is one of the hardest tasks of legislation, and it is not without wisdom that the law of England and of this country in general declines to interfere in their disputes, leaving it to themselves either to enjoy their common property by agreement, or to suffer it to remain unenjoyed, or to perish by their dissension, as the best method of forcing them to a common consent for their common benefit.[97]

Put in more theoretical terms, the harsh co-owner rules are "penalty defaults."[98] They are default rules: rules that apply unless they are changed by agreement of the parties. And they are "penalties" because in the absence of such agreement they make life difficult for one or more of the parties. The logical response to a penalty default is to contract your way out of it, which is exactly what most patent-based businesses did in the nineteenth century. Two voluntary contract-based structures were most effective, and we see evidence that they were widely used in the period from 1820 to 1880. These were the partnership, as structured by a partnership agreement; and, particularly later in our period, the patent ownership trust. We take up each in turn now.

3.2.3 *Partnerships*

Enterprises relied heavily on contracts (agreements) to organize their activities: "In the early nineteenth century, most multi-owner firms in Britain and the United

[97] *Pitts* v. *Hall*, 19 F. Cas. 758, 761 (C.C.N.D.N.Y. 1854) (No. 11,193).

[98] See Robert P. Merges and Lawrence A. Locke, *Co-ownership of Patents: A Comparative and Economic View*, 72 J. Pat. & Trademark Off. Soc'y 586, 599 n.33 (1990) (citing Ian Ayres and Robert Gertner, *Filling Gaps in Incomplete Contracts: An Economic Theory of Default Rules*, 99 Yale L.J. 87, 95–100 (1989) (coining the term "penalty default" and describing how it promotes voluntary contracting).

States were organized as partnerships . . . "[99] A partnership, especially in those days, could be organized around a fairly simple contract. The essential features of a patent-based contractual partnership were: (1) a statement of joint ownership or interest in the patent or patents, together with (2) at least a partial list of rights, duties, and obligations of the respective parties.

In *Penniman* v. *Munson*,[100] a group of Vermont businesspeople came together on a venture in 1841. Thomas Mills purchased rights to make and sell a stump remover in the town of Colchester (near Burlington). Mills then entered into a two-part agreement with two others, Udney H. Penniman and William B. Munson. Mills, Penniman, and Munson agreed to purchase rights under the patent from the local patent agent (Ormsbee) for the parts of Chittenden County outside Colchester. In addition, as to Colchester itself, Mills conveyed two one-third interests in Mills' rights to Penniman and Munson. The contract also said each of the three were to pay a third of the total cost of the patents ($600, or $200 each) and to share equally in the profits or loss if any.[101] This agreement – to share in the profit and loss; and to treat the relevant patent as "held as a joint or common stock, for the purpose of selling and disposing of the same on joint account"[102] – was found to convert the joint assignment into a true partnership:

> It is probable, that the mere act of conveying to them undivided interests in the patent, did not create among them the relation of partners, for individuals may have a joint interest in property, and still not be partners; but when, after that purchase was made, *they agreed to convert their separate rights into a common interest*, for the purpose of selling the same, and to divide the net proceeds equally between them, there can be no doubt, that a partnership was thereby created, or such a relation formed, that each has the right to call the others to account, for the avails they respectively have received. The bill states the facts from which the law creates that relation between them, and under this proceeding their agreement will be enforced, as decreed by the chancellor, that the orators [equity plaintiffs] and the defendants shall share equally in the original expenditure, for the purchase of the patent right, and in the net profits and losses on its resale, by either or all of them.[103]

99 Eric Hilt and Katharine O'Banion, *The Limited Partnership in New York 1822–1858: Partnerships without Kinship*, 69 J. Econ. Hist. 615, 615 (2009). See also Naomi R. Lamoreaux, *The Partnership Form of Organization: Its Popularity in Early-Nineteenth-Century Boston*, in Conrad E. Wright and Katheryn P. Viens, eds., Entrepreneurs: The Boston Business Community, 1750–1850 (Boston: Massachusetts Historical Society, 1997), at pp. 269–295.

100 26 Vt. 164 (1853).

101 26 Vt. 164, 164–165 (1853).

102 26 Vt. 164, 168 (1853). The reference to patent shares as "common stock" is a reminder that patents in this period often served the same function as equity stock in a later era – a legal instrument used to allocate partial ownership shares in the enterprise.

103 26 Vt. 164, 169 (1853) (emphasis added). *Burnley* v. *Rice*, 18 Tex. 481, 493 (1857) ("Part owners are not partners."), citing *Lawrence* v. *Dale*, 1817 WL 1628 (N.Y. Ch. 1817), aff'd sub nom. *McNeven* v. *Livingston*, 1819 WL 1801 (N.Y. 1819).

The importance of the holding in the specific case was that Munson, who had worked out a further territorial assignment deal that left him with a nice personal profit, had to share the proceeds from the later deal with his partners.[104] He was not free to act for his own self-interest. The profit-splitting aspect of the partnership agreement created a management structure that prevented self-dealing and made the partnership, as a distinct entity, the focus of exploitation and administration of the patent rights. In the broader picture, the case illustrates the benefits of the partnership form, and the alignment of rights and duties that follow from it, as opposed to simple co-ownership.

Courts at times seemed to stretch to find a partnership arrangement when the facts presented little for it evidence beyond bare co-ownership. Protesting that the parties' limited agreement was meant strictly as simple co-ownership failed in the face of evidence of a shared enterprise.[105] And partnerships were recognized even based on informal, oral agreements – written agreements were not strictly required.[106] Telling other people that a patent is managed jointly was also treated

[104] The additional deal concerned the rights for the remainder of the state of Vermont. Munson stated a price for the state that was higher than what the patent owner demanded. The idea was that Munson (and a secret co-conspirator) would use his partner's payments as the total purchase price, and wind up with a one-fourth interest in the Vermont-wide rights to the patent, without paying anything for those rights). 26 Vt. 164, 165.

[105] See *Manhattan Brass & Mfg. Co.* v. *Sears*, 45 NY 797 (1871). The owner of a patent conveyed an interest to another in an assignment agreement that called for the parties to manufacture the patented article. The court held that there was a partnership, because the agreement evidenced an intent to share in the enterprise's profits, and (to a limited extent) to share in its losses as well. The agreement also provided that each party should have the right to inspect the enterprise's books. Even though, the court noted, the parties intended something less than a comprehensive arrangement, it was a legal partnership nonetheless, notwithstanding that the assignment agreement characterized the parties as simple co-owners of the relevant patent.

[106] See, e.g., *Gates* v. *Fraser*, 6 Ill. App. 229, 229–230 (Ill. App. Ct. 1880):

> [I]t was verbally agreed between [inventor Gates] and Fraser at the time of making application for the patent [for end-pieces (or "shoes") on crushing or stamping machines, e.g., for crushing rock], that each should pay half the expenses of procuring the patent, and that they were to be equal partners in all losses and expenses, and gains and profits relating thereto, and in all royalties or patent fees to be derived therefrom ... [T]he patent proved to be of considerable value, and the shoes made according to the same have been extensively used in mining machinery ... [and] the entire business connected with the patent has consisted in licensing others to make and sell the same, which licenses have been verbal ones to the different firms and corporations with which complainant and Fraser have been connected in business since the patent was granted.

The court held that royalty income to Fraser, on licenses he had independently negotiated with several firms, must be split with his partner Gates, despite the absence of a written agreement. Defendant Fraser had argued that the oral agreement violated the Statute of Frauds, but the court was not having any of that: "[P]artners hold partnership funds and effects under an implied trust, each standing in the relation of trustee for the other ... It is against conscience that one who has money which equitably belongs to another, should be suffered to shield himself against its payment under the Statute of Frauds." 6 Ill. App. 229, 233 (Ill. App. Ct. 1880)

as an indication of a partnership rather than simple co-ownership, according to some cases.[107]

Yet even as some courts stretched to fit patent-based enterprises into the form of a partnership, there were inherent limits to these contract-based business organizations. An early case showed the reasons. The steamboat partnership between Robert Livingston and Robert Fulton, formed in 1802, "provide[d] for the construction of a passage-boat, moved by the power of the steam-engine, to be used on the Hudson, and that the patent for such a boat should be taken in the name of Fulton, and the property thereof equally divided [between Livingston and Fulton], and also the emoluments of it; and that the number of boats, offices, and agents, should be augmented or diminished, as the parties should think proper ...."[108] But the partnership agreement said nothing explicit about the rights of an assignee to license third parties under the patent. Thus, when Fulton, the more active partner, formed a company and located an assignee to operate steamboats on the Ohio River, the court held this was a personal assignment of Fulton's half-interest in the patent, rather than a contract binding on the Fulton-Livingston partnership. Because of this, the court was unwilling to hold Livingston liable under the assignment granted by Fulton in favor of a company to build and operate the Ohio River boats.[109] Cases

107 See, e.g., *Reutgen* v. *Kanowrs*, 20 F. Cas. 555, 556 (C.C.D. Pa. 1804) ("[T]he plaintiff frequently acknowledged the joint right of the defendant, to the invention, as partnership property; and that the patent was to be taken in their joint names . . . "). Other cases said a partnership may be inferred merely from the conduct of the parties:

> Undoubtedly the patentees may by agreement thus change the nature of their ownership and use of the patent into a copartnership business, and proof of such arrangement would furnish support for the decree. In another view, it may be that *proof of their agreement* ***or conduct*** *as copartners in the manufacture and sale of goods under the patent*, would authorize relief between the parties for an accounting of profits and losses arising in such business. Without proof, however, of one or both of these conditions in the appellant's use of the patent, as charged in the bill, no accountability arises, and the issue is thus narrowed to such inference of fact as may be derived from the evidence.

Drake v. *Hall*, 220 F. 905, 906 (7th Cir. 1914) (emphasis added).

108 *Lawrence* v. *Dale*, 1817 WL 1628 (N.Y. Ch. 1817), at *4, aff'd sub nom. *McNeven* v. *Livingston*, 1819 WL 1801 (N.Y. 1819). The Livingston defendants (Robert Livingston and his brother) were joined to the lawsuit by Lawrence, the aggrieved Ohio River assignee, who wanted relief under the contract and a repayment of money they had invested with Fulton for Fulton to supervise and build the Ohio River steamboat – work that the plaintiff Dale said was poorly done and left the boat in an unusable condition. Ibid.

109 In the manner of many later regional franchises, the Fulton-Livingston patent had been offered to potential assignees outside New Jersey and New York, in this case by an early patent agent named Latrobe. 1817 WL 1628, * 1. Livingston apparently approved of the use of the Latrobe agency, or at least did not object; but the resulting Fulton assignment for the Ohio River area was found not to implicate the partnership or Livingston personally: "A joint interest in a patent may exist in full force, and yet have no connection with a special covenant to construct a boat for the benefit of an assignee. Such a power is no necessary part of the joint concern. The Livingstons may have an interest in all the branches of steam navigation arising under the patents, and even in the personal services of Fulton bestowed on their common concern, without being bound by his special undertakings. There must be some other authority to bind

of a later vintage emphasized the limitations of the partnership form, which were inevitably found to be the result of partnership contracts that circumscribed the scope of partnership activities.[110]

3.2.4 *Preserving Capital Formation, While Integrating Management*

Partnerships centered on patents were often memorialized by contracts designed to prevent individual partners from self-dealing, or opportunistic behavior. Contracts created rules and structures that made it much more likely that a patented invention would be efficiently exploited. Unlike co-ownership, where competing regional franchises (each licensed by a different co-owner) were possible, a partnership was more likely to select a single regional franchisee. This maximizes profits and enhances returns to the patent's owners. In this way and others, concentrating the management or exploitation of a co-owned patent in a single entity made sense.

Partnerships melded the benefits of patent co-ownership with unified management and control of the patent-based enterprise. while preserving the benefits of patent co-ownership.[111] Put another way, partnerships responded to the vulnerability that followed from raising capital by means of partial patent assignments. So long as investors at the time of their investment demanded partial ownership of a patent in exchange for investment funds, splintered ownership interests were bound to follow. While fresh funds invigorated the target enterprise, split ownership threatened it. The solution was to preserve the patent-ownership form of investment while creating a single legal entity to which each investor and principal owed his or her primary loyalty.

A partnership centralizes decision-making and management in a single entity, preventing the parties from working at cross-purposes. At the same time, a partnership is a unified focal point for others who want to do business with a patent-based enterprise. So long as a customer, input supplier, or patent agent knew who the official representative of a patent-based partnership was, the partnership form lowered the risk of dealing with an enterprise with multiple owners, perhaps

them than what is to be deduced from the [Fulton-Livingston partnership] articles of 1802." Ibid., at *5.

110 See, e.g., *Richardson* v. *Provost*, 35 S.C.L. 57, 60 (So. Car. Ct. App. (Law) 1849) (Partners in a patent for pressing cotton were not general partners, so a debt incurred by one (who – it is distressing to report – "purchased a negro" with the loaned money) was not payable by the other.).

111 Using more modern terminology, we might say that partial patent rights served some of the same functions as corporate securities, with partnership agreements then acting like corporate charters to structure incentives and allocate duties among the co-owners so as to maximize the joint surplus of the enterprise. Another rough analogy would be to a modern syndication arrangement, such as those common in the entertainment industry, where the owner of TV broadcast rights for a popular program will find and grant licenses to local TV stations in many regions. Syndication is usually based on licensing, however, rather than exclusive regional ownership rights.

claiming inconsistent control rights, that had formed around the nucleus of a patent. Co-ownership splits patents up, spreading the benefits of property ownership among a group of investor/managers. Nineteenth-century partnerships tried to offset the forces of dispersal and fragmentation that could follow from barebones co-ownership. A binding agreement among partners could unify the potentially splintered co-owners into a single, more effective legal-economic entity.

While fresh funds invigorated the target enterprise, split ownership threatened it – and partnerships provided one solution. The limits of this solution, however, were noticeable and formidable. Chief among them was that the partnership contract was often interpreted as creating a rather limited and static structure. Unforeseen problems, inadvertent omissions from the contract, and related issues meant that partnerships formed on specific terms, for a limited purpose, were not able to hold together enterprises whose scale and dynamic opportunities were undergoing rapid development and change. Something more was needed. At first, that something more was the patent trust.

3.2.5 *The Patent Trust as Transitional Vehicle*

Trusts were employed to organize business enterprises throughout the nineteenth century.[112] Businesses usually have assets that need to be managed, and they often have passive investors as well. These needs map well onto the constituent parts of a basic trust: The *res* or asset is entrusted to an administrator (trustee) who manages the asset in the interests of one or more beneficiaries. Because the trust is a very flexible legal instrument, it may be adapted for all sorts of different enterprise types.

Trusts worked well for patent-based enterprises. The patent (or patents) at the core of the business is an obvious asset around which a trust can be formed. Passive investors – so common in enterprises that begin with an inventive concept, which then needs to be put into practice – are natural in the role of trust beneficiaries. And most importantly, a trust can gather together multiple enterprise owners in a single legal entity with a single manager. The combination of diversified ownership with a single legal focal point is exactly what patent-based businesses needed in the nineteenth century.

A "practical guide" to patent matters, published in 1873, put the matter well:

> [If you follow my advice,] you likely will not assign undivided interests in your patent without providing in the assignment or in a separate written contract that your interests shall be operated together, and that there shall be an accounting to each other on the basis agreed upon, and also other provisions necessary to fully include your agreements. The title to your patent might be placed in the hands of a trustee (to prevent transfers of any interests therein), and a separate written agreement made with reference to the whole matter. This latter method will likely afford

[112] John Morley, *The Common Law Corporation: The Power of the Trust in Anglo-American Business History*, 116 Colum. L. Rev. 2145 (2016).

> the greater security and to my knowledge it has been approved and endorsed by parties who have adopted it.[113]

Nineteenth-century cases confirm that the trust arrangement was indeed "approved and endorsed" by numerous businesspeople involved in patent-based enterprises. The complexity of trust arrangements varied. Some were as simple as an assignment with a trustee/power of attorney, granting the assignee-trustee the plenary right to dispose of patent interests on behalf of the original patent owner.[114] Others were more complex, providing, for example, for the creation of a trust to hold foreign patent rights and distribute the income from them to the trust beneficiaries.[115]

[113] Harvey L. Hopkins, Law and Facts on Patents and Inventions. A Practical and Legal Business Guide for Developing, Patenting, Perfecting, Manufacturing and Operating Inventions. Compiled from a Life of Experience. What to Do and What Not to Do (Chicago: Charles A. Johnson Publisher, 1887), available at https://babel.hathitrust.org/cgi/pt?id=osu.32437122273150&view=1up&seq=5, at p. 66.

[114] For an example, where the grantor was an inventor of seed drills and the grantee/holder of the power of attorney was a patent agent (West) with an investor partner (Westcott), see *Wescott* v. *Wayne Agric. Works*, 11 F. 298, 299 (C.C.D. Ind. 1882):

> In consideration of the premises I [Moore] hereby further make, constitute, and appoint the said Charles W. West and John M. Wescott my true and lawful attorneys in law and in fact, with power irrevocable, giving and granting to them full and exclusive and unreserved power and authority for me ... to assume and take upon themselves the entire and exclusive management and control of the aforesaid letters patent, and of each and every of them, and to dispose of all the right, title, and interest which I have under the same ... for such price or prices, upon such terms, and to such persons, and for such place or places as they, my said attorneys, shall deem proper ... and acknowledge all such deeds and instruments of writing as shall be necessary or proper for the granting or licensing to others the said rights under the said letters patent ...

The case arose when Westcott purported to assign an interest in the Moore patents to a partnership, Kinsey and Morris, which partnership then conveyed a one-twelfth interest in the patents to the Wayne Agricultural Works, itself an apparent partnership operating a machine shop that built seed drills. Westcott apparently believed he had received a one-half interest in the Moore patents, and so he was in a position to make a personal transfer of part of that interest to Kinsey and Morris. The court held that the Westcott transfer was invalid, and thus that the Wayne Agricultural Works had no interest in the patents, because Moore had not vested ownership of different parts of his patents to West and Westcott personally but instead had granted his (Moore's) rights to the trust entity as administered by West and Westcott together:

> [T]he power that Moore granted to West and Wescott was a joint one – a personal confidence was reposed in their mutual judgment and discretion ... I think it was the intention of the parties to invest West and Wescott with the entire legal title to the patents, jointly, as trustees, with full power to dispose of them at their discretion. This was done to enable them to "take upon themselves the entire and exclusive management" of the business, for the purposes specified ...

Wescott v. *Wayne Agric. Works*, 11 F. 298, 301–303 (C.C.D. Ind. 1882). The case thus illustrates (1) that a patent trust was a separate entity, distinct from the individuals participating in the trust; and also (2) the pitfalls of this arrangement, which unlike a corporation was not registered or publicized, making it difficult for third parties to know who to deal with, when acquiring partial interests in a patent or patents.

[115] See *Smith* v. *Moore*, 129 Mass. 222, 222–223 (1880) (concerning patents for high-pressure metal casting):

In each case, the business goal was to combine different resources (inventions, capital, skills) into a focal point entity to best develop a patented technology.[116]

A business involving shoe-making equipment serves as an example of a more sophisticated trust – one which closely approximated a corporation. According to the opinion in a tax case stemming from this enterprise,

> Previously to May 10, 1866, Gordon McKay had acquired, by invention, assignment or license, interests in letters patent of the United States for improvements in machinery for sewing the soles of boots and shoes to the vamps [uppers], and had been carrying on the business of manufacturing machines under these letters patent, and licensing shoe manufacturers to use them.[117]

McKay eschewed the regional franchising model. His business was centralized in Lawrence, Massachusetts, and instead of assigning regional rights to his patents he took on investors to back his shoe machine factory and licensing activities. These investors he gathered together in the form of a trust, issuing transferable trust certificates as evidence of their part ownership of the enterprise:

> On May 10, 1866, McKay executed an instrument under seal, in which, after reciting the foregoing facts [regarding patents, machinery, factory, land, etc.], he declared that he had held and should continue to hold the business and property in trust for the benefit of all persons who were or might become interested therein,

> [The parties created an] association called "The American Compression Casting Association" for the purpose of introducing the inventions in Europe and obtaining patents therefor. The plan of the parties was that the legal title to the patents should remain in the plaintiffs, as trustees, for the benefit of the shareholders in the association. They accordingly executed a "declaration of trust," which was the basis upon which the association was formed and was to be conducted. It provided, among other things, that the trustees should hold the property for the use of the association, should divide among the shareholders the profits of the business when directed by the executive committee, that no member of the association should have any right to make any bargains or receive any money on behalf of the association except as authorized by the declaration of trust . . .

When a buyer of the European rights was located in the United States, the inventors and owners of the US patents, the Smith brothers, tried to claim the proceeds for themselves (cutting the defendant "association" or trust out of the deal) – a move that failed under the court's analysis:

> When, therefore, the agent of [the buyer of European rights] offered to pay the eight hundred pounds in Boston [to the association/trust], the defendants were the proper persons to receive it; and when it was paid to them, they received it, not for the use of the plaintiffs, but for the use of the association and its members . . .

129 Mass. 222, 225.

[116] On this, see *Blakeney* v. *Goode*, 30 Ohio St. 350, 351–353 (1876) (expert machinist agreed to assist inventor/patent owner in perfecting and implementing an invention in exchange for half the proceeds from the inventor's patented invention; held, though the inventor/patent owner had the sole right to assign partial ownership rights in the patent, the contract between the parties created a trust, so income earned by the inventor/patent owner from his assignments must be shared with the partner/beneficiary, as specified in the trust).

[117] *Gleason* v. *McKay*, 134 Mass. 419, 419 (1883).

> upon the terms and conditions therein set forth. Upon the execution of this instrument by McKay, all the persons then interested in the property or business signed an agreement in the following terms: "In consideration that the said Gordon McKay has agreed and does hereby bind himself and agree to deliver to each and every party having an interest in the property set forth in the foregoing certificate and declaration of trust, a certificate and declaration similar to the foregoing, expressing the several interests of each party, in case all of the persons interested in said property shall sign this agreement, we do hereby severally bind ourselves and agree to receive from said McKay such certificate and declaration of trust, as the sole evidence of our respective interests in the above-described property ..."[118]

On the foundation of the trust, a management structure was built: "After the ... issue of the [trust] certificates, the shareholders, on May 28, 1866, held a meeting, as provided for by the declaration of trust, and chose an executive committee and adopted by-laws for the regulation of the business of the association."[119] The "executive committee" manages the assets of the trust: "Since said date, the business of the association has been conducted by its executive committee under the provisions of said declaration and by-laws, McKay holding the legal title of all its property as trustee, under said declaration ...."[120]

The holding in the *McKay* case was that sale of the trust certificates could not be taxed in Massachusetts as commerce in "commodities."[121] For our purposes, however, the case shows the flexibility of the trust to hold property (including patents) for the benefit of multiple investors. The simpler structure of patent assignments and regional franchises is giving way here to a more sophisticated arrangement – one capable of amassing more property and more capital. The growing scale of business (here, the booming shoe manufacturing industry) is matched by a larger and more diversified enterprise structure. This is a pattern we see repeated throughout the period. It marks the coming of the true corporation, and with it, an enterprise

[118] 134 Mass. 419, 420.

[119] Ibid.

[120] Ibid.

[121] 134 Mass. 419, 421, 425:

> Whenever a member sells his shares, or any of them, new certificates are issued to the purchaser, and such purchasers thereupon become members of the association. Said shares are frequently sold, and such sales reported at auction sales in Boston, and are subject of transfer upon assignment of certificates of shares, as set forth in said certificates; and, upon such assignment, the assignee is entitled to receive new certificates, and to demand and receive of the association his proportionate share of the net profits of the association, under said declaration and by-laws. ***
>
> The peculiar feature that the interest of each member may be transferred without the special assent of the other members, is created by agreement of the partners under their natural rights at common law. We do not see how this peculiar feature can be called a commodity, subject to a special excise, any more than the agreement of copartnership itself, or any clause or part of it, or any other agreement, right or mode of transacting any business, can be called a commodity, and so liable to taxation at the will of the Legislature.

structure flexible enough to accommodate the larger patent portfolios of the late nineteenth and early twentieth centuries.

But general incorporation laws were not common before 1890. Legal trusts were used extensively before then to achieve some of the same goals. Because the trust form was flexible, it proved useful as a framework for conducting business. Trustees served the functions of corporate officers; trust agreements substituted for corporate charters and bylaws; trust certificates anticipated the widespread use of corporate stock; and so on.

As we have seen, trusts were useful in the patent context because they helped to mediate the cumbersome management structure that followed from complex patent ownership arrangements. Trusts re-centralized firm management in the wake of complex patterns of assignments, licenses, and sub-licenses. Put another way, a trust agreement, like a partnership, integrated the multiple, dispersed owners of a patent into a single legal entity. By the mid- to late-nineteenth century, partial ownership shares in patents had become customary in American business. But the legal structure of patent co-ownership – in particular the "no duties to co-owners" rule of the tenancy in common – was increasingly out of sync with the need for centralized management of patent-based firms. The interim solution was the patent-based trust. A well drafted trust agreement provided ownership shares in a single entity with a distinct, identifiable management structure: the trustees. Under this arrangement, co-owners could participate in the profits from a patent-based firm without clashing and conflicting with each other. The divided ownership structure of the early nineteenth century worked well when regional management of different regional markets made sense. Patent ownership roughly coincided with efficient management. But later in the nineteenth century, when the first truly national markets began to appear in the United States, the splintered ownership structure no longer worked well. Conflicts among regional co-owners undermined the potential profits from adopting a single, national business strategy. The patent-based trust was the solution.

As we will see, what was true of corporations generally was also true of technology- and patent-intensive firms: the trust gradually gave way to flexible, multi-divisional firms along the lines described by Alfred Chandler. The rise of the Chandlerian firm after 1870 coincided with the widespread adoption of centralized, corporate R&D divisions. And with this came the advent of the large corporate patent portfolio. The patent-based trust was just a step along the way, a transitional form mediating between the old sole proprietor/partnership model of Ithiel Pool and Thomas Blanchard, the regional franchise, and the giant, research-intensive firms such as General Electric, DuPont, and Westinghouse.

The three characteristics of this transitional period were (1) an increase in the incidence of firms based around more than one patent; (2) a combination of regional markets and patent assignments, along the traditional lines, with increasingly efficient nationwide communication and transportation infrastructure; and (3) the means for vastly superior capital formation, together with liberalized incorporation statutes after 1890, which opened the way for a huge jump in the feasible scale of business firms.

3.2.6 *The Coming of the Corporation*

In the corporate law field, the advantages of the corporate form center on limited liability. The corporation is a legal vessel for productive activities that allows investors to cap their exposure to liability at the level of their individual investment. For many years, limited liability dominated the work of scholars trying to explain the emergence and importance of the corporate form. A related theory also stressed liability issues. This was the idea that corporations were useful because they sequestered the assets of a business from the personal assets and affairs of investors. Investors who owed money in their personal capacity, for example, present no risk for the companies they invest in. Personal debts do not flow from an investor to the firm. This is the "asset partitioning" function of the corporation.[122]

The history of patent-based enterprises tells a slightly different story, one that is more about the upside of collectively owned enterprise and less about what happens when companies or investors owe more than they can pay. In the patent context, there certainly are advantages that come with limited liability.[123] Some patent infringement suits against partnerships in the nineteenth century wound up finding

[122] Henry Hansmann and Reinier Kraakman, *Organizational Law as Asset Partitioning*, 44 Eur. Econ. Rev. 807 (2000).

[123] See, e.g., *Berry* v. *Vantries*, 1824 WL 2423, at *4 (Sup. Ct. Pa. 1824), where the manager of an ironworks was found personally liable for the tort of conversion of a nail-cutting machine. The lawsuit began when the owner of a patent on the nail-cutting machine had sold the machine to a third party, Vantries; the patent owner, a former employee of the ironworks managed by the original defendant Berry, was found to have rightly sold his machine to Vantries, so that when Berry refused to give the machine to Vantries, Berry was liable for conversion:

> [T]he manager [Berry] of an iron-works of a factory such as this, although he is, in contemplation of law, the agent of the [factory's] owners, stands in a relation very different from that of a mere servant. He is not an executive agent, divested of all discretionary power, but the *locum tenens* [placeholder, representative] of the owners, and invested with all their authority. Instead of executing commands, his business is to give them, and to judge of the propriety of every measure taken for the benefit of his employers; and *in this, as respects third persons, at least, he acts at his peril* ... [Berry] attempted to defend himself on the ground of his having acted as an agent, and *it was requisite, in addition, to prove, that he acted as an agent under circumstances sufficient to excuse him*.

1824 WL 2423, at *4 (second and third emphases added). See also *Renton* v. *Chaplain*, 9 N.J. Eq. 62, 73–74 (Ch. 1852) (creditors of one partner, Carter, in a joint partnership forced a sheriff's sale of that partner's assets including patent rights; Plaintiff Renton, purchaser of the levied assets at the sheriff's sale, sued for an injunction under the patent to prevent Carter's partner, defendant Chaplain, from constructing machinery implementing the patented invention; court implicitly acknowledged Chaplain's potential liability, but refused to grant an injunction on the grounds that Chaplain's exploitation of the patent would not harm Renton, purchaser of Carter's interest in the patent).

individual partners personally liable.[124] But overall, the advantages of the corporate form parallel those of the partnership and the business trust: multiple investors, together with a single management entity. This combines capital formation (the investors) with efficiency (a single decision-making structure, and a single point of contact for third parties).

The superiority of the corporate form is that it provides these benefits in a way that is far less restrictive than partnerships or trusts. Partnerships and trusts are both defined by the contracts that form them. They are thus prey to all the problems of contracting over matters that are fast-moving and undergoing rapid change – often key characteristics of enterprises based on patented innovations. With the coming of general incorporation statutes, the American legal system made it simple to form a business enterprise with a very high degree of ongoing flexibility. In the place of a formative contract, as with the partnership or trust, the corporation has a charter and bylaws. But these quickly became, after the 1890s, merely procedural rules for *how* the business made decisions. Corporate charters were and are incredibly general as to the types of business the corporation can conduct. They read, in practical effect, "this company can do whatever its management team and board of directors decide is best for making money for the stockholders."

This flexibility has plenty of general advantages, for obvious reasons. A company can explore new markets, design new products, shift its core strategy radically, or go into a completely different business than its current one, all within the confines of the expansive corporate structure. Corporate rules are for the most part procedural,

[124] This fits the pattern of "weak entity shielding for partnerships" described in the corporate law literature. See Henry Hansmann, Reinier Kraakman, and Richard Squire, *Law and the Rise of the Firm*, 119 Harv. L. Rev. 1333, 1403 (2006). See also Naomi R. Lamoreaux and Jean-Laurent Rosenthal, *Entity Shielding and the Development of Business Forms: A Comparative Perspective*, 119 Harv. L. Rev. F. 238, 245 (2006) (discussing partnership form in France and how it compared to partnerships in the United States). See also Naomi R. Lamoreaux, *Constructing Firms: Partnerships and Alternative Contractual Arrangements in Early-Nineteenth-Century American Business*, 24 Bus. & Econ. Hist. 43 (1995). For a contrasting case, showing stronger entity shielding in the case of a corporation, see *Ambler* v. *Choteau*, 107 U.S. 586, 590–591 (1883), where an inventor (Ambler) was defrauded by a partner (Whipple), and the partner Whipple assigned patent rights in a series of transactions that brought the patents into the hands of a Missouri corporation whose directors were sued by Ambler for its role in Whipple's fraud:

> [Ambler contested] the use of the patented invention in Missouri by the Missouri corporation, of which the defendants are stockholders and directors. It is not in any manner alleged or claimed that the defendants have profited by what Whipple has done, except through the title acquired by the conveyance to [an intermediate assignee] Blunt & Insley, and from them, with the consent of Whipple [and his partner in the fraud] the faithless trustees, to the corporation. No effort is made to set aside these conveyances. It is conceded that [the intermediate assignee] actually paid Whipple [and Whipple's partner] $70,000 for the assignments which were made [to the corporation].

On these facts, the Court found that the stockholders and directors of the corporation owed nothing to Ambler, the defrauded patent owner.

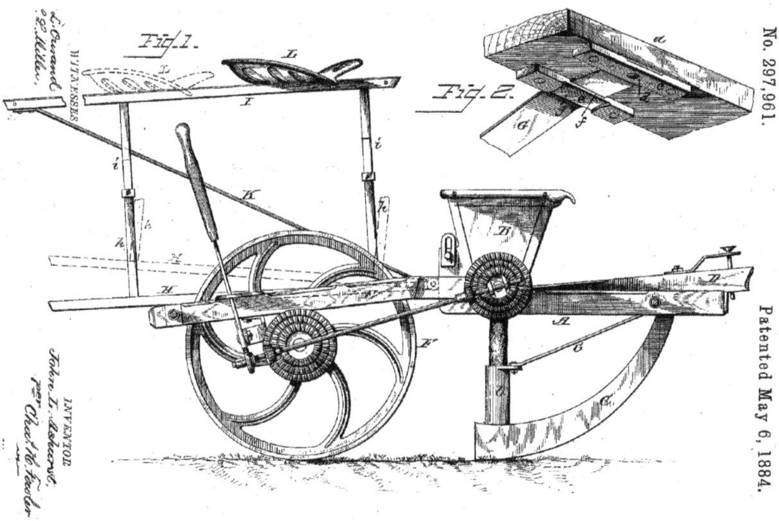

FIGURE 3.12. Ashurst grain drill. Ashurst's seed drill, US patent 297,961, Assigned to Havana Press-Drill Co., Inc. in 1885. (Operator sits on seat, L; Bow-shaped runners in front open shallow furrow in the ground; seeds are dropped from the hopper (B) through a shaft; dropping controlled by the hand lever behind the rear wheels; then seeds are pressed into the ground by the rear metal wheels (F), assisted by the weight of the operator)

and their overall purpose is to maximize income rather than adhere to any rigid plan for doing so.

This flexibility was appealing to patent-based enterprises, as it was to many others. Thus, with the advent of general incorporation laws, we see evidence that principals began exchanging patent rights (as well as many other assets) for shares of stock in new corporations. Take a typical case from 1883, involving one Ashurst, a machinist and holder of regional rights to a patented seed drill (an agricultural implement for planting seeds quickly in straight rows; see Figure 3.12). Ashurst agreed to assign to the newly formed Havana Press Drill Co., Inc. his regional rights to the patent, plus completed machines on hand, in exchange for stock and working capital (in the form of two loans):

> [Ashurst agreed to] assign all his rights in the patents of the Blunt press drill for the state of Kansas to the proposed corporation, such rights to be good during the life of the company, [and] the company should issue to Ashurst 150 shares of its stock, fully paid up. And it was further agreed that Ashurst should execute to the company his two promissory notes for $2,750 each, due in two and three years after date, with 6 per cent. interest, and deposit with the company 60 shares of the stock as collateral security; and that, on this being done, the company should execute notes to the bank for like amounts, and upon like terms. And it was further agreed that the

> bank and Ashurst should sell to the company all drills then on hand, wherever they were, at $30 each, royalty paid, payable December 1, 1884, and March 1, 1885 . . . [125]

Compare this arrangement to the typical patent-based enterprise from earlier in the nineteenth century. It has a number of advantages: (1) a unified corporate structure to make decisions regarding the patent rights, free of the cumbersome co-ownership rules prevalent in earlier times, or the need to specify by contract the permissible operations of the enterprise;[126] and (2) ownership by Ashurst not just in certain discrete assets (the patents) but also in a share of all revenue generated by the corporation. This gives him a claim not just on patent-related royalties but on a pro rata share of all revenue the patents and other assets of the corporation generate individually and collectively. This in addition of course to limited liability: Creditors supplying drill parts, employees with wage claims, and even people injured by the drill presses must look almost exclusively to the assets of the drill press company for compensation. Ashurst and the other principals need not in general worry about losses beyond the value of their stock holdings.[127]

[125] *Havana Press-Drill Co.* v. *Ashurst*, 148 Ill. 115, 123–125, 35 N.E. 873, 874–875 (1893).

[126] Other cases show that corporations were sometimes formed as a vehicle for re-integrating various splintered interests in a patent. The corporation served as a single owner and decision-making entity. See, e.g., *Hills* v. *McMunn*, 232 Ill. 488, 489–493, 83 N.E. 963, 964–965 (1908) (corporation organized around a patent (U.S. 639,884, "Pile," December 22, 1899) issued to inventor Behrend; corporate organizer agreed with an investor to acquire (a) Behrend's personal three-fourths interest in the patent, together with (b) the remaining one-fourth interest, which was owned by two other investors). In the case the court ordered the defendant McMunn to deliver to plaintiff Hills stock in a substitute corporation McMunn had organized in place of the corporation plaintiff established. 232 Ill. 488, 500, 83 N.E. 963, 968. (The defendant objected to the plaintiff's corporation because of its (perhaps unfortunate) name, the Slick Steel Piling Company; defendant preferred U.S. Steel Piling Company.) See *Hills* v. *McMunn*, 135 Ill. App. 338, 339 (Ill. App. Ct. 1907), rev'd, 232 Ill. 488, 83 N.E. 963 (1908); US Patent 639,884 (describing modular, water-tight construction pilings to be driven into soft ground for construction of dams, bridges, etc.). Defendant McMunn seems to have been involved in other inventive companies, including a company making shoe brakes for railroad cars. See Articles of Association of The American Brake Company. (St. Louis: Missouri Secretary of State, August 9, 1880) (listing S. W. McMunn as a founder), cited in U.S. Dept. of the Interior, National Park Service, National Register of Historic Places Registration Form for the American Brake Company Building, 1920 North Broadway, St. Louis, MO, at p. 7, available at https://dnr.mo.gov/shpo/nps-nr/07000172.pdf.

[127] In the actual case, one founder of the Havana Press-Drill Company, named Rhodes, accumulated almost all the company's stock; Rhodes had the Ashurst patent license plus certain other patents (including one invented by Ashurst) assigned to himself personally and then licensed the patents (including a sub-license of Ashurst's Blunt patent license) to another company, the Stoddard Manufacturing Company of Ohio. 148 Ill. 115, 128, 35 N.E. 873, 876. The court ordered that the lower court should "award to [Ashurst] such portion of the royalties derived from the use of [his] patent [by Rhodes] as under all the circumstances shall appear to be just and equitable." 148 Ill. 115, 140, 35 N.E. 873, 881. Because Ashurst was a minority shareholder in the Havana Drill Press Company, the holding can be seen as compensation for corporate insider self-dealing. The irony here is that the asset that Rhodes misused against the minority shareholder was a patent originating with that same minority shareholder, Ashurst.

Let me return to point (2) from the previous paragraph. Corporate ownership, in the form of shares of corporate stock, gives shareholders such as Ashurst the right to a pro rata portion of all corporate income. This is important to patent owners and inventors who participate in corporations. Ownership of a patent gives such a person a claim to a single, discrete asset. Where that asset is essential to the firm, ownership of it provides leverage to demand a royalty payment commensurate with the centrality of the asset. But where the asset plays a less distinct role – where it is one of many undifferentiated and intermixed assets that generate firm value – ownership of individual firm assets might well lead to some problems. There are two reasons: (1) it is more difficult to place a value on an undifferentiated, intermixed asset than an essential, discrete asset, making royalty payments more uncertain and possibly more contentious; and (2) firm management may have techniques for reducing the revenue that stems from or is associated with any intermixed asset. Both factors may cause problems. If each key asset of a firm were owned by a consortium of owners, fights could break out between these ownership groups. There could be arguments over which of several key assets were the really important ones for generating firm value. And in addition, if the management team of the enterprise were also owners, in their individual capacities, of key firm assets, they could try to skew firm activities to enhance the revenue attributable to the assets they owned. This might be at the expense of ownership groups not represented in the management team. And, as a manager pushes for a personally profitable product mix or production process, overall revenue might suffer.

Why emphasize the difference between ownership of essential, discrete assets and ownership of undifferentiated, intermixed assets? Because this well describes the transition that took place in the latter part of the nineteenth century with respect to the place of patents in the average business enterprise. In the early years of the century, and throughout the era of patent-based regional franchises, many enterprises were founded on the basis of a single patent. Often, the patent would be extended by Congress or the Patent Office; and sometimes one or a few improvement patents would also be involved. But in many cases, a single enterprise was coextensive with a single patent or a very small number of patents.

This changed. By the later nineteenth century, more and more enterprises were coming to hold a greater number of patents than was true in the early nineteenth century. Though not nearly as large as the vast corporate patent holdings that came to dominate industry in the twentieth century, we can say that the transition was under way from the era of the single patent to the era of the patent *portfolio*.

A single patent in the founding era (Chapter 2) is a good example of an essential firm asset as described here. For enterprises based on a single patent, the patent covered the single product sold by the enterprise. And the patent protected against competition in the market for that product. A single patent, in other words, was coextensive with a single product and a single economic market. Under these conditions, patent owners and investors had every reason to base the entire enterprise on a single patent. Because the patent was the foundation of all firm revenue, providing for multiple partial ownership shares in the patent was a perfectly plausible way to allocate returns from the overall firm. The firm *was* the patent; ownership shares in the patent were thus a serviceable proxy for ownership shares in the *firm*.

But the corporate form makes more and more sense as the era of patent portfolios gains momentum. A single patent that is part of a patent portfolio is like any undifferentiated, intermixed corporate asset, described earlier. When a company holds multiple patents, and as it develops multiple product lines, the value of any single patent becomes harder to determine. This was a feature of the later nineteenth century, and, as a consequence of growing technological sophistication and increased patent activity, the scope of the average individual patent changed over time. There were more patents, and each was on average narrower than in the past. It became less common for an individual patent to cover a discrete product. Patents came more and more to cover *parts* of products, or features of products, rather than entire products themselves. (Beware: This is generalization, not an iron law.)

With this in mind, it makes sense that an inventor or owner of a single patent might want to hold a claim on the entire economic value of a firm rather than on one asset employed by the firm. This is an additional reason (beyond limited liability) that we see patent owners who participate in the founding of firms later in the nineteenth century acquiescing in the corporate form and taking shares of stock. The coming of more complex, multi-faceted business enterprises killed off the predominance of the old patent-based enterprise.

The *Ashurst* case and others like it were cameo appearances of the coming trend. One principal in the Havana Seed-Drill Company, along with Ashurst, was John W. Rhodes. Rhodes received two patents on seed drill components, both modifying features of the basic Ashurst design. One was for an arm handle, with gearing, to raise the forward runners in the seed drill out of contact with the ground. The design included a dis-engaging gear mechanism that stops the feeding of seeds into the chute when the arm is raised (see Figure 3.13). Another was for a wider, multi-wheel seed drill, which distributes the weight of the rider over each set of wheels, to push all the dropped seeds into the soil (Figure 3.14).

Finally, Ashurst himself patented a further improvement to his basic seed drill design (shown above, Figure 3.13, US patent 297,961. The Ashurst improvement covered an alternative way to lift the front runners off the ground – by sliding the driver's seat backward, putting all the driver's weight over the rear wheels and pulling the runners up off the ground (Figure 3.15).

These seed drill patents tell a story. They show the growing sophistication of even simple machines (e.g., the gearbox in the Rhodes 355,715 patent). They show how patents were obtained more frequently on components rather than entire products (the sliding seat, the lift handle, etc.). As a consequence, they illustrate one reason why the Havana Drill-Press enterprise was organized as a corporation. The enterprise, and the entire industry, was moving beyond the stage where a single patent

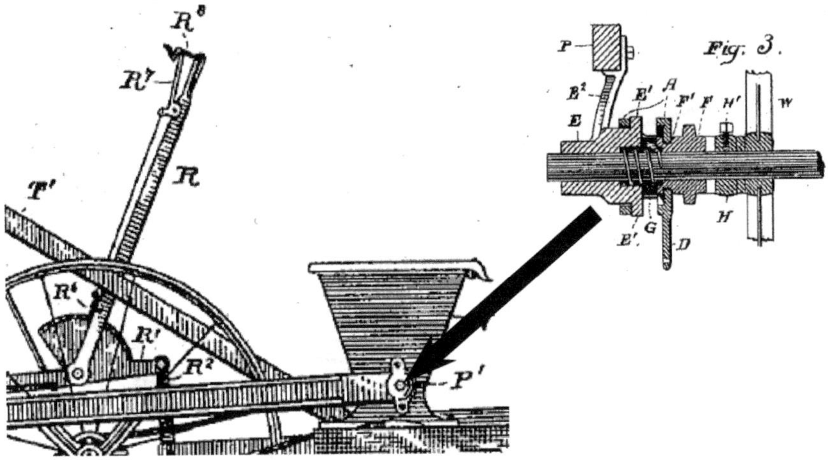

FIGURE 3.13. From US patent 355,715, "Planter," issued to John W. Rhodes, January 11, 1887. Handle R lifts the seed hopper and runners underneath it (not shown), while gearbox of Figure 3 disengages seed feeding mechanism

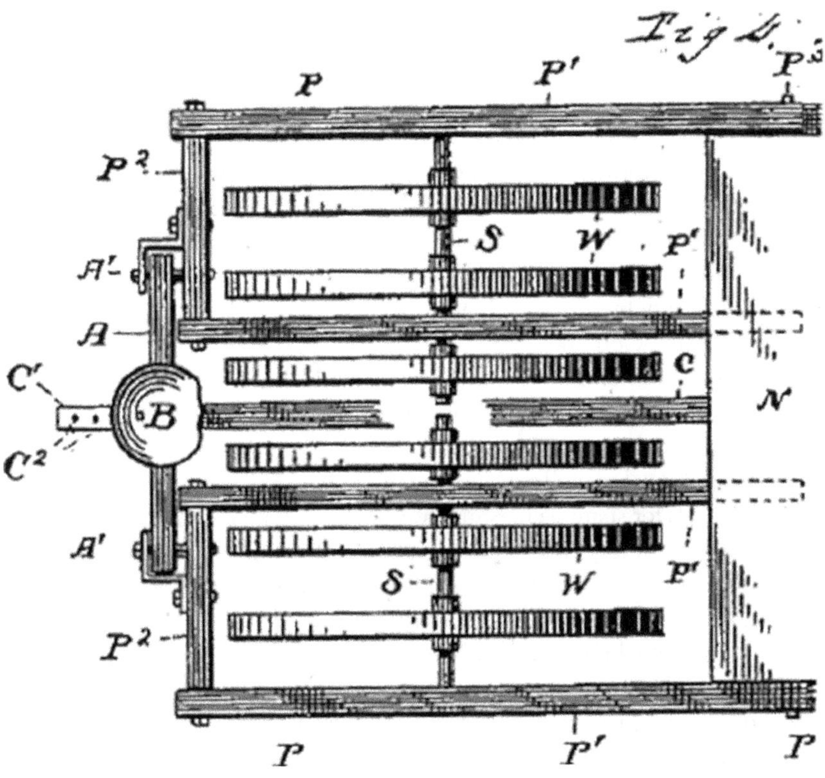

FIGURE 3.14. Multi-wheel seed drill, seen from the top (US patent 355,716, issued to John W. Rule, January 11, 1887). The driver sits in seat B. The framework over the wheels (W) distributes the weight of the driver to push each set of wheels down evenly to plant the dropped seeds in the soil

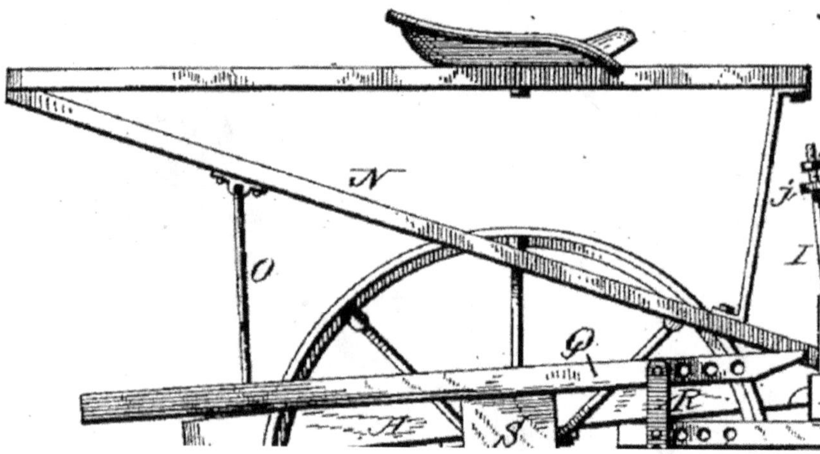

FIGURE 3.15. Ashurst sliding seat lift mechanism for lifting the runners (not shown). US patent 325,583, issued to John L. Ashurst, September 1, 1885

was an adequate basis for organizing the principals, allocating income, etc. As patents moved toward portfolios, enterprise moved toward the corporate form.

3.2.6.1 Summary: Early Corporatization

The movement to corporations as the locus of business enterprise was only beginning in 1880. Momentum increased in the years following, as we will see in Chapter 4, but the basic logic of corporatization was already in place.

To summarize that logic, look to Figure 3.16, which shows various assets (tools, machinery, a factory building, employment contracts, and a small patent portfolio) being placed inside Corporation X.

The individual owner of one of these assets could receive payment in cash or its equivalent. But if he or she wanted to participate in the enterprise in an ongoing fashion, the obvious way to do that would be to receive shares of stock in Corporation X. Figure 3.17 illustrates a share block of this nature.

Trading patents for share ownership gives the inventor a claim on a pro rata share of the corporate earnings. This allows the inventor to profit from the overall activities of the firm, and not just those directly related to the patents he or she contributes. As we will see, the more complex the enterprise becomes, the more difficult it becomes to value any individual patent and its contributions to corporate earnings. Taking a block of shares does require some rough initial valuation: A very minor single patent may be worth only a few shares of stock, while a crucial patent portfolio may be worth many shares. But after the initial assessment, specific accounting for the value added of each patent is no longer necessary. In general, as I have been emphasizing, the larger the corporation the more impractical it becomes to organize the entire

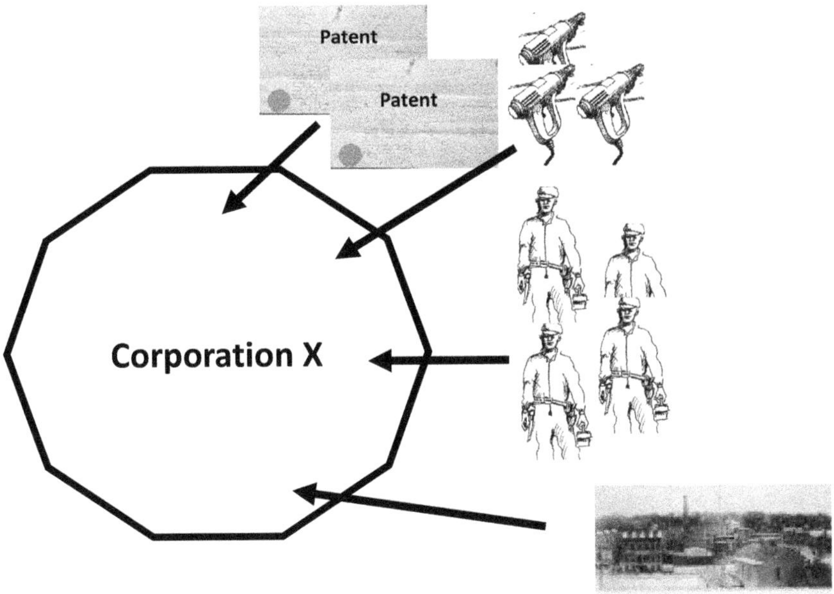

FIGURE 3.16. Assets placed inside a corporation

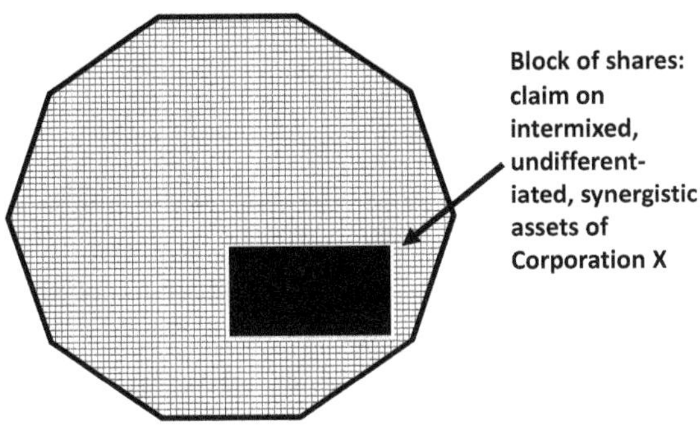

FIGURE 3.17. Shares of stock in corporation X

enterprise around split shares in a single patent. Again, the rise of the patent portfolio goes hand in hand with the trend toward corporatization.

3.3 LEGAL DOCTRINE AND PATENT SYSTEM ADMINISTRATION

As we saw in Chapter 2, a changing economic context caused changes in the structure and operation of patent law. Not surprisingly, this highly functional branch of law tended to adapt as the economy developed. In the period under study,

1820–1880, patent law divided ownership claims more finely than in the Founding Era. There were many more patents than in the earlier era, and technologies were becoming more complex. Greater specialization of production led to an increase in the number of separate process steps and product components. In response, patents became more tightly specified. The development of this branch of the law thus followed the basic economic theory of property: As discrete technological assets (tools, machines, products, and systems) became more valuable, it became more worthwhile to measure off and delineate property rights with greater precision. The responsiveness of the patent system then in turn helped perpetuate the cycle of increasing value, by providing a greater number of property rights covering economically relevant assets. Patent precision increased along with economic activity and did its part to push the economy forward.

Increasing precision in patent law took place in four doctrinal areas: (1) the increasing specificity of patent claims, which helped in the development of the legal category of "improvement patent"; (2) patent validity, where a more rigorous standard of patentability (the "invention test") was added on top of the simple novelty standard; (3) creation of the "double patenting" doctrine, to prevent overlapping clam coverage in an increasingly crowded patent landscape; and (4) development of rules to resolve disputes between holders of adjacent regional franchises, and to keep consumers from being swept into territorial franchise disputes, known as the "patent exhaustion" doctrine. We take up each in turn.

3.3.1 *Claims*

Precision is enhanced when an inventor expresses more definitely what he or she asserts as the specific owned invention. From the earliest time in US patent law, this formal assertion of right has been called a claim. But the nature of claims was at first quite vague and general. In section 3 of the 1793 Act, for instance, the patent applicant is called on to both describe and distinguish the invention: the applicant "shall deliver a written description of his invention, and of the manner of using, or process of compounding the same, in such full, clear and exact terms, as to distinguish the same from all other things before known." The very first US patent, issued in 1790, includes a dim shadow of what might be called a claim, in the form of a brief summary of the nature of the invention in describing the right being granted by the government:

> [T]hese [letters patent] are therefore in pursuance of the [1790] Act ... to grant to the said Samuel Hopkins ... for the term of fourteen years the sole and exclusive Right and Liberty of using, and vending to others, the said Discovery, of burning the raw Ashes previous to their being dissolved and boiled in Water ... [128]

[128] US Patent X1, granted to Samuel Hopkins, July 31, 1790, at p. 1.

Other patents include similar summaries of the invention.[129]

And from early days, a detailed specification drafted under the guidance of the early patent acts was spoken of (loosely) as a claim. Fessenden, in his 1822 treatise, speaks of "the party, who claims a patent."[130]

By 1836, even with fairly primitive claim formats, we begin to see greater efforts to distinguish the invention claimed in a patent from other related inventions and prior art. A handwritten claim from 1836 demonstrates the point:[131]

It reads:

> What I claim as my own invention and not previously known in the above described machine is the elastic revolving belt saw and the manner of using the same and do not therefore claim as my invention any of the other several parts of said machine, nor their particular combinations.

The inventor here is saying what his patent does *not* cover – an important step forward in claim specificity. (Such "negative" claim limitations are not always favored today.) He disclaims, for example, coverage of the belt saw itself; wisely, because this type of saw (as distinguished from the even earlier reciprocating, or back-and-forth, saw) was already known. A glance at one of the patent diagrams helps explain what is being disclaimed (Figure 3.18).

The arm braces holding the top wheel, and the wheels holding and directing the band saw could be copied by others so long as they were used for a different purpose, e.g., for a belt of leather or cloth for polishing objects. In other words, only the specific combination of support, wheels, and band saw, are covered by the claim.

Another very common claim format incorporated element references in a drawing directly into the claim. Consider the diagram below, from a patent for an early

[129] See, e.g., *Whitney* v. *Carter*, D. Ga., reported in Thomas Green Fessenden, An Essay on the Law of Patents for New Inventions (Boston: Charles Ewer Publishers, 2nd ed., 1822), at p. 132 (distinguishing the product accused of infringement from the invention as described (hence claimed) in Whitney's patent: "[T]he defendant also uses teeth, formed of circular plates, instead of teeth made of wire [on the rollers used to separate cotton seed]. And it was contended that this was a departure from the specification, and an improvement on the original discovery . . ."), available at https://babel.hathitrust.org/cgi/pt?id=hvd.32044050955889&view=1up&seq=7. See also Fessenden, 2nd ed., 1822, at pp. 130, 142 (apparently quoting or paraphrasing a British case concerning a fire grate that permits wood to be added from the bottom rather than the top):

> The defendant, in his specification, had summed up the amount of his claim, stating, "my invention consists in this, that the fuel necessary for supplying the fire shall be introduced at the lower part of the grate, in a perpendicular or in an oblique direction : as to the manner of performing it, it is set forth in the annexed descriptions and drawings."

[130] Thomas Green Fessenden, An Essay on the Law of Patents, at p. 43.

[131] B. Barker, "Band Saw Mill," US Patent X9303, issued January 6, 1836.

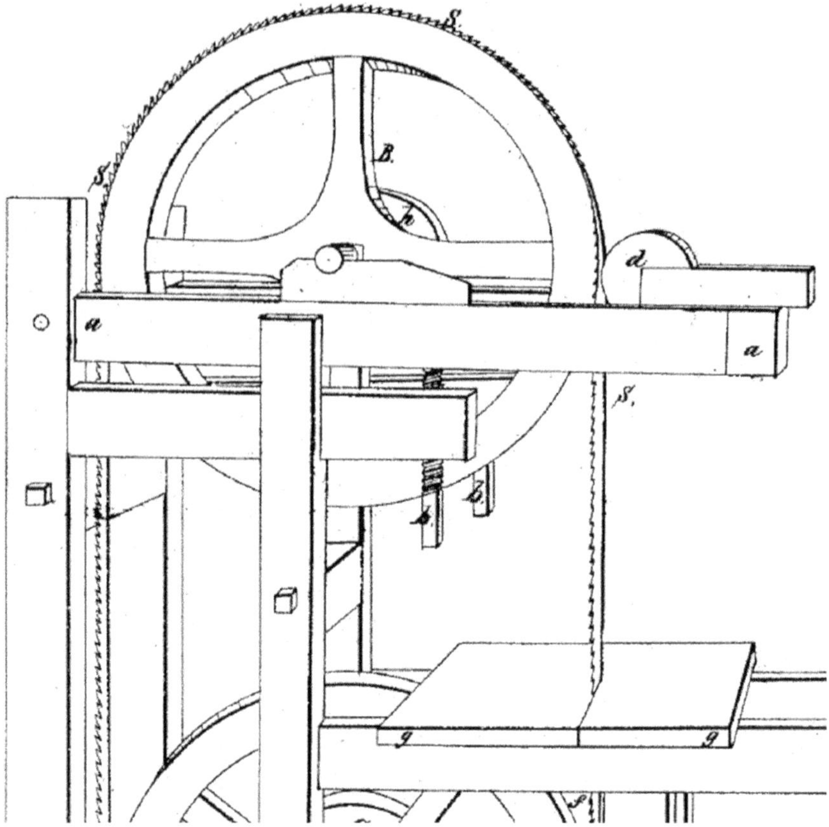

FIGURE 3.18. Band saw, US patent X9303, January 2, 1849

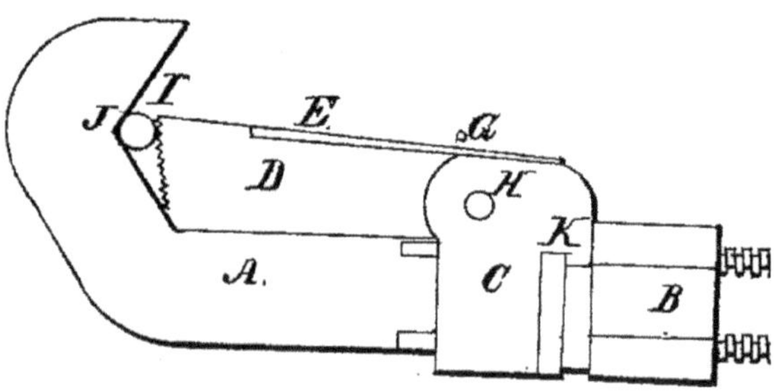

FIGURE 3.19. Drawing from US patent 6,002, 1849

version of the adjustable wrench.[132] As is customary, the various parts of the wrench are identified with letters in Figure 3.19 (A, D, E, a, etc.).

[132] F. H. Batholomew and Solyman Merrick, US Patent 6,002, "Screw-Wrench for Grasping Cylindrical Forms," issued January 2, 1849.

The single claim at the end of the patent reads:

> What we claim in the above described wrench, and for the purpose of holding and turning cylindrical substances, is – The combination of the lever D with the main bar of the Wrench, also with the slide C, the nut B and the spring E, substantially as herein described.

The greater precision of this claim form comes from incorporation of the diagram elements. This tends to incorporate the features of the diagram elements into the claim, providing greater specificity than more sweeping verbal formulations. It resembles the contemporary claim format that explicitly lists the specification examples of a recited claim element and provides coverage for these examples and their "equivalents."[133]

Later in the century, multiple claims – delineated by numbers – begin to appear more frequently.[134] US patent 276,198, entitled "Machine for Cutting Wooden Plates," issued to inventor Seth H. Smith on April 24, 1883, is representative. (Note the continuing importance of wood as a material, see Chapter 2.) It covers a machine for carving small wooden product containers out of a single block of wood. Despite the title, the invention was as useful for cutting shipping containers (for butter and other products) out of a wooden block as it was for making dinner plates.[135] A detail of the machine is shown in Figure 3.20, with element F being the cutting blade carving the wood, Element C being the shaft that turns the cutting element, and the open rectangle below the cutting area being the space through which the block of wood is passed so the blade (F) can carve it.

The patent concludes with these four claims:

> 1. A plate or dish cut or scooped from a block of wood in concavo-convex form, as an article of manufacture.

[133] See 35 U.S.C. § 112(f) (authorizing so-called means-plus-function claims in this format).

[134] See, e.g., *Greenwood* v. *Bracher*, 1 F. 856, 857 (C.C.D.N.J. 1880) (interference between two rival patent owners):

> John Bigelow made application to the commissioner of patents for letters patent for certain improvements in sweat-leathers for hats and caps, and that the patent was refused, because the subject-matter had already been incorporated in two several letters patent granted to Thomas W. Bracher, the defendant in this suit – one dated July 23, 1878, and numbered 206,296, and the other dated December 3, 1878, and numbered 210,489; that afterwards, to-wit, on the eighteenth of February, 1879, the commissioner declared an interference between the parties in order to determine the question of priority of invention, the subject-matter involved in the interference being the claim of the first recited Bracher patent and the first claim of the Bigelow application, and the claim of the second recited Bracher patent and the second claim of the said Bigelow application, the claims respectively being identical ...

[135] See *Oval Dish Co.* v. *Sandy Creek N.Y. Wood Mfg. Co.*, 60 F. 285, 287 (C.C.N.D.N.Y. 1894) ("The invention of this patent ... relates to a machine for cutting continuously from a block of wood concavo-convex shells, plates or dishes, serving as packages for butter, berries and for other purposes ... ").

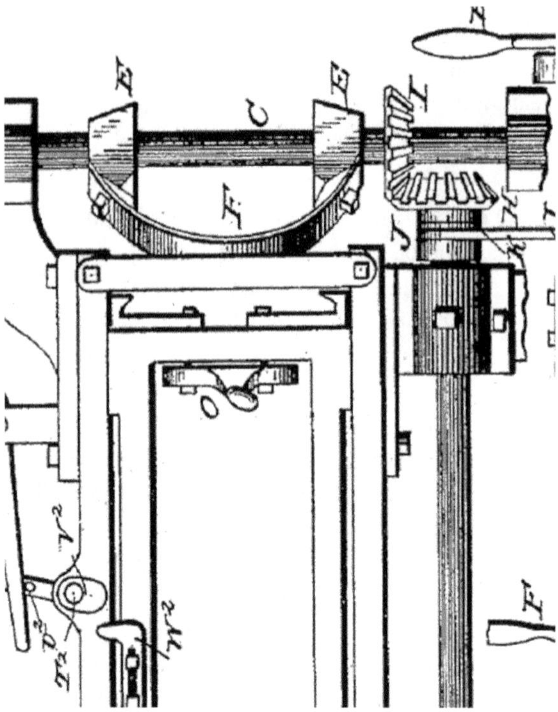

FIGURE 3.20. US patent 276,198, "Machine for Cutting Wooden Plates," issued in 1883

2. A plate or dish cut or scooped from the face of a block of wood in concavo-convex form and segmentally in cross-section, as an article of manufacture.
3. A plate or dish consisting of a shell cut or scooped from the face of a block of wood in concavo-convex form and with horizontal upper edges, as an article of manufacture.
4. A plate or dish consisting of a shell cut or scooped from the face of a block of wood in concavo-convex form, segmentally in cross-section, and with horizontal upper edges as an article of manufacture.

Here we see far more refinement in each claim as compared to the earlier claim forms. Claim 1 covers any scooped-out wooden holder made with the machine as described. Claim 2 narrows the coverage: It covers wooden holders that are of uniform size. A separate cutting element (not shown) cuts the long wooden block into uniform sizes, so the scooped out wooden holders are all identical in their overall length as well as the length of the scooped-out portion. Claim 3 narrows the claim still further, by requiring the scooped-out dishes to have horizontal upper edges. This means in effect that the scooped-out portion must be narrower than the overall width of the wooden blocks; otherwise (as covered by Claims 1 and 2) the scooped-out blocks might have sides that are curved because the cutting element cuts all the way to the edge of the wooden block. Claim 4 then combines the limiting features of Claims 2 and 3; it calls for a block of uniform length that also has horizontal sides.

The rationale for this claim structure – which has become the conventional one in most patents around the world – reflects the increasingly crowded technology landscapes into which the patent was born. When the inventor Seth Smith filed his patent application, it was already becoming difficult to know with certainty the features and dimensions of all similar machinery described in printed literature or in actual use in industry. By claiming the broadest possible version of his invention (Claim 1), Smith gave himself a chance at a very broad patent. But by claiming successively narrower versions (i.e., by adding qualifications – called claim limitations), he gave himself a chance that at least one of the claims would survive if a somewhat similar machine or wooden dish were found in the prior art. As any art grows in volume, it increases the "validity risk" of patents in the field. Smith hedged against this risk with successively narrower claims.[136]

To summarize: Claims became more and more precise over the course of the nineteenth century, as technology became more complex and the number of patents increased. An excellent summary of these developments is found in a table from patent scholars J. Jonas Anderson and Peter S. Menell (Table 3.1).[137] By "reference characters," these authors mean patent drawing element numbers referred to in a claim:

[136] In an infringement suit brought under this patent, several pieces of prior art were put into evidence in an attempt to invalidate the patent claims. See *Oval Dish Co.* v. *Sandy Creek N.Y. Wood Mfg. Co.*, 60 F. 285 (C.C.N.D.N.Y. 1894). In the end, the court found that none of the prior art was similar enough to invalidate the patent. (It held the same with respect to a related patent in the suit, US Patent 273,773, issued to Seth Smith on March 13, 1883, also for a wooden plate.) The court found that the accused infringer did not make and sell wooden dishes with horizontal upper edges, so only Claims 1 and 2 of the 198 patent were infringed:

> [T]he dishes made by [one of defendant's] machine[s] did not infringe the third and fourth claims of the [Smith] patent for the reason that they did not have horizontal upper edges. Subsequently a machine was used by the defendant which possessed every element of complainants' combination. The only material differences are that defendant's cutting knife was made to oscillate instead of revolve and the facing knife to reciprocate vertically instead of revolve around a shaft. Both move in the same plane and do identically the same work. That this construction was adopted for the purposes of evasion is very apparent. It is thought that the changes adopted by the defendant were equivalents for the parts which performed the identical functions in the combinations of the claims ... The complainants [Smith's assignee] are entitled to a decree for an injunction and an accounting upon the claims of ... the first and second claims of [Patent] No. 276,198.

60 F. 285, 292. The language of "equivalents" used here expressed was the basic test for infringement: equivalents embodiments meant infringing embodiment. This is consistent with the more purposive style of analysis found in older US cases (nineteenth century through the Federal Circuit era) and is quite distinct from twenty-first century invocations of the more technical "doctrine of equivalents." See Robert P. Merges and John F. Duffy, Patent Law and Policy: Cases and Materials (Durham, NC: Carolina Academic Press, 8th ed., 2021), at chapter 8.

[137] J. Jonas Anderson and Peter S. Menell, *Informal Deference: A Historical, Empirical, and Normative Analysis of Patent Claim Construction*, 108 Nw. U. L. Rev. 1, 13 (2013). Used by permission of the authors.

TABLE 3.1. *Evolution of claim practice*[54]

Year of issue of patents; percentage of claims having reference characters; and average number of claims

1860	73%[a]	1.3
1880	82%[a]	3.3
1900	22%	7.7
1920	0%	7.2
1940	0%	6.9

[a] Many of the claims not having reference characters were process claims

Note especially the steady growth in the average number of claims in a patent over time.

3.3.2 *Invention Test*

The earliest Patent Acts required only that an invention be new and useful; there were no further hurdles to patentability. The Supreme Court added a new, more rigorous test in 1851 in the case of *Hotchkiss* v. *Greenwood*.[138] The Court, reviewing a patent on clay/porcelain doorknobs secured with a wedge-shaped shaft or shank, upheld a jury instruction that led to the invalidation of the patent. Evidence at trial established that clay and porcelain were known to be useful materials; and that the tapered or "dovetail" shank for doorknobs was well known as a way to prevent doorknobs from being pulled off their shafts. (The dovetail shape was wider at the end embedded in the doorknob, and the thin end of the shaft was screwed into the door.) In so holding, the Court authorized a new test: that a claimed invention be the product of a certain degree of skill or ingenuity. Mere novelty and usefulness, standing alone, were no longer to be enough. The Court said:

> [U]nless more ingenuity and skill in applying the old method of fastening the shank and the knob were required in the application of it to the clay or porcelain knob than were possessed by an ordinary mechanic acquainted with the business, there was an absence of that degree of skill and ingenuity which constitute essential elements of every invention. In other words, the improvement is the work of the skilful mechanic, not that of the inventor.[139]

[138] 52 U.S. (11 How.) 248 (1850).
[139] 52 U.S. (11 How.) 248, 267 (Nelson, J.).

From 1850, an invention had to display a certain degree of "ingenuity and skill" in addition to being technically new (nothing identical had appeared in the prior art before) and useful. It had to be the work of an "inventor," rather than the product of a "skillful mechanic." Though this opinion has since become the universally accepted fountainhead for the new "invention" requirement (renamed "nonobviousness" in the 1952 Patent Act), there were antecedents. The 1793 Act included a provision on improvements, stating "that simply changing the form or the proportions of any machine, or composition of matter, in any degree, shall not be deemed a [patentable] discovery."[140] And, too, there were some pre-*Hotchkiss* cases that strongly implied that "novelty" meant something at least slightly more stringent than simply "nothing precisely like the claimed invention appears in the prior art."[141]

Putting aside the prior hints and whispers in the direction of the new test, the question remains: Why did the invention test crystalize in 1850? What was going on that made the Supreme Court feel the need to add an explicit new test to the list of patentability requirements?

The most likely answer is the very technological and economic changes described earlier in this chapter. In a definitive review of the origins of the invention test, legal scholar John Duffy said this:

> Modern theory predicts that the nonobviousness requirement plays its most important role where society and technology are experiencing rapid change. In a more static society, theory predicts that the obviousness doctrine would be less important. Thus, this Article shows that history and theory are mutually reinforcing, for the nonobviousness requirement did not develop until the rapid technological and social changes of the nineteenth century demanded it.[142]

Referring to Figure 3.2, showing the growth in issued patents over time, notice the increases under way in the late 1840s. To this add the concerns that led to the 1836 Patent Act, mostly centered on weak patents and excessive litigation. It all adds up to a felt sense that the "big two" traditional requirements (novelty and utility)

[140] Act of February 21, 1793, ch. 11, §2, 1 Stat. 318, 321 (repealed 1836).

[141] See Edward C. Walterscheid, *Novelty & the Hotchkiss Standard*, 20 Fed. Circuit B.J. 219, 260–261 (2010):

> Rather than being the direct antecedent of the *Hotchkiss* standard, the "form or proportions" language of the 1793 Act and the case law interpreting it created a judicial predisposition or readiness to viewing patentability as requiring something more than simple novelty and utility. That predisposition continued even after the "form or proportions" language had been deleted from the patent statute.

[142] John F. Duffy, *Inventing Invention: A Case Study of Legal Innovation*, 86 Tex. L. Rev. 1, 2–3 (2007).

were not up to the job of keeping patents legitimate. There was a felt need to provide a new tool for weeding out undeserving patents. And so, the invention test was born.[143] One historian of patent law wrote of this, "It may well be that the development of nonobviousness [invention] as a condition for patentability constitutes the most significant legal innovation that occurred in the history of U.S. patent law."[144]

3.3.3 *Double Patenting*

Claim refinement and the invention test were not the only scenes of doctrinal innovation in nineteenth-century patent law. As inventors more commonly filed multiple patents on different aspects of an invention – part of a general trend toward a more crowded patent landscape – judges in patent cases paid more attention to potentially overlapping patents. Thus, what is now called the doctrine of double patenting was born. This is a simple rule: one invention, one patent.[145] It should be evident that there was no need for such a rule until a substantial number of inventors began to file multiple related patents with potential coverage overlaps.

A Supreme Court case concerning some patents issued in 1879 and 1881 is widely credited as the first definitive case on double patenting.[146] An inventor named Edgar Wright from Davenport, Iowa, had invented an improved plow (or "cultivator"). Wright's new feature was a thin metal bar coiled into the shape of a spring at one end. The bar could be positioned two ways: (1) to exert downward pressure on the crossbar during plowing (to keep the plows digging into the ground), or (2) to exert upward pressure on the crossbar when it was in the raised position. Both patents were based on the same specification and drawings, a portion of which is shown in Figure 3.21.

The 1879 patent claimed both the downward and upward effects of the metal piece; another application was split off (in a "divisional") from the first one and

[143] See Duffy, Inventing Invention, at 17–18 ("As patents became easier to obtain, patent rights broader, society less static, and inventors more numerous, the need for obviousness or some similar doctrine grew more dire.").

[144] Edward C. Walterscheid, Novelty & the Hotchkiss Standard, at p. 219 (2010).

[145] An important variant later developed, one that balanced the prohibition on multiple patents against a desire to encourage an inventor to rapidly perfect and improve on a basic design. This variant permits an inventor to file a new patent application covering an obvious variant on an earlier-filed application. The new-variant application can issue as a separate patent, but that patent must expire on the same day as the patent that issues on the earlier-filed application. This is effectuated by a terminal disclaimer: a renunciation of any patent term that would exceed the term of the first-issued patent. See *Perricone* v. *Medicis Pharm. Corp.*, 432 F.3d 1368, 1373 (Fed. Cir. 2005) (double patenting designed to "prevent claims in separate applications or patents . . . so alike that granting both exclusive rights would effectively extend the life of patent protection."); 35 U.S.C. § 253 ("[A]ny patentee or applicant may disclaim or dedicate to the public the entire term, or any terminal part of the term, of the patent granted or to be granted.").

[146] *Miller* v. *Eagle Mfg. Co.*, 151 U.S. 186 (1894).

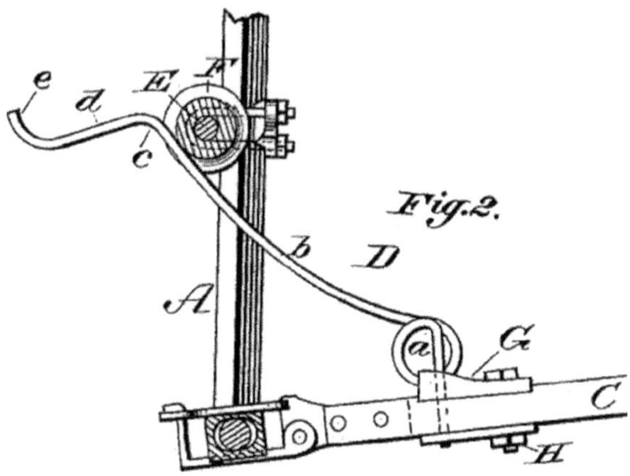

FIGURE 3.21. Double-action spring in *Eagle Mfg. Co.* Double Patenting Case: From US patent 222,767, "Wheel Cultivator," issued to E. A. Wright, December 16, 1879. The key feature is the metal rod/spring marked "D"; it can be configured to exert either downward or upward pressure on the crossbar (C), which raises and lowers the plows (not shown)

claimed only the upward-pressure effect. The initial application was very similar to another invention whose inventor sought a patent. So, the Patent Office declared an interference to see which patent application had priority. Wright won the interference and was issued a patent in 1879. The second application, claiming only the upward-pressure effect of the metal piece, issued in 1881. It was the 1881 patent that was invalidated by the Supreme Court in the *Eagle Manufacturing* case. The basic logic is simple: The second patent would in effect grant two extra years of patent protection for an important function of the basic crossbar-pressure improvement claimed in the first patent.

Under the circumstances, the Court said, the important task was to compare the two patents. The rationale was simple: If a prior patent to a *third party* invalidates a later patent to the same invention, such a prior patent issued to the *same party* should invalidate the later patent as well:

> The first patent, issued in 1879, covered both the lifting and depressing actions or operations, while the second patent covered only the lifting effect. The spring device which was designed to accomplish these effects or operations, is the same in both patents. The drawings in each of the patents are identical, and the specification in each is substantially the same. Under these circumstances can it be held that the second patent has any validity, or must it be treated as having been anticipated by the grant of the 1879 patent? If, upon a proper construction of the two patents, which presents a question of law to be determined by the court, (Heald v. Rice, 104 U. S. 737 [1881],) and which does not seem to have been passed upon and decided by the court below,they should be considered as covering the same invention, then the later must be declared void, under the well-settled rule that two

> valid patents for the same invention cannot be granted either to the same or to a different party.[147]

Despite what the Court said, the rule against double patenting was anything but "well-settled." In the cases cited in *Eagle Manufacturing*, in fact, duplicate patents by a single owner are at most a tangential issue.[148] Of course, there is a long tradition of cloaking judicial novelty in the trappings of ancient tradition. (Judges are the opposite of inventors in this way: They never tout the merits of an innovation because they never admit to one.)

In any event, the need behind *Eagle Manufacturing* was apparent, and becoming more so by the year. As we have seen, the single patent covering a single product sold on the market was a fading trope by 1880. Multiple products, with multiple components, and greater specialization were on the rise. So too were patent portfolios: multiple patents on different aspects or features or components of complex products. In this environment, there were more boundaries between more patents than ever before. Rules were needed to police the boundaries, to prevent overlapping coverage that would effectively extend patent protection beyond the limited term of a single patent. Double patenting was one of those rules.

[147] 151 U.S. 186, 197.

[148] Consider, for example, the earliest of the cases cited, *Troy Iron and Nail Factory* v. *Odiorne*, 58 U.S. (17 How.) 72 (1854). *Troy Iron* was unusual, and it is somewhat doubtful that it has much precedential value at all. The parties to the lawsuit were operating under a private stipulation that they would agree to a finding of no liability if the accused infringer could prove he independently invented the plaintiff's patented machine, i.e., proved construction of a full machine prior to the patent owner's patent filing date. The invention in the case was a machine for making "hook headed spikes" – spikes with an elongated head, often used to pin down or secure rails or other metal parts to a wooden surface. (They are still used to hold the lower edge of railway rails to wooden rail ties.) The key date in the stipulation was the plaintiff's patent filing date: Construction of a machine for making hook-headed spikes at any time before the plaintiff's patent filing date would let the defendant off the hook, so to speak. 58 U.S. 72, 73. The Court was persuaded by the accused infringer's evidence that its fabricator (named Savary) had in fact, before the plaintiff's filing date, constructed such a machine. The Court did note that Savary had his own patent: "The machine complained of was built by Richard Savary, for the Boston Iron Company, in the spring of 1839, and obtained, by the [accused infringer] … Savary was the patentee of a machine to make ship and boat-spikes, and, at the suggestion of the agents of the Boston Iron Company, added an attachment of an apparatus to make a hook-head to spikes." 58 U.S. 72, 73. But the Court's attention was focused on the *timing* issue (per the stipulation), rather than comparison of the claims of the plaintiff's and Savary's patents. As the Court said, "The time at which this [hook-making] apparatus was attached to [Savary's] machine (substantially complete in its operative parts,) is the time when the machine complained of was 'constructed,' in the sense of the stipulation." Ibid. Because the construction date preceded the filing date, the defendant won the case. Note further that even if the Court had compared plaintiff's invention to the patent under which the accused infringer's machine had been constructed (the Savary patent), this would not have been a true double patenting analysis: The two patents in question were not owned by a single person.

3.3.4 *Exhaustion*

The final change in doctrine also concerns boundaries, but of a different sort. Just as claims police the boundaries between ownership stakes across technological landscapes, the exhaustion doctrine polices geographic boundaries. As we saw earlier in this chapter, exhaustion comes into play when adjoining regional patent franchises come into conflict. This usually happens as a result of cross-selling: when a regional franchisee claims it lost a sale that it rightfully should have made, because another regional franchisee sold to a buyer in the exclusive territory of the first franchisee. Sometimes cross-selling happens when a rival franchisee makes sales directly into a franchisee's territory. At other times it happens when a sale is made in the proper location but the consumer carries the patented item into a region controlled by a rival franchisee. In both cases the injury is the same: The aggrieved franchisee claims loss of a sale that by rights it feels it should have made.

An excellent case study comes in the form of a Supreme Court dispute from 1873 called *Adams* v. *Burke*.[149] This was a classic case of cross-selling, which began with a legal complaint in 1863.[150] The date is significant, because the case involved a patent on a component of a burial coffin. The Civil War years were years when death was ubiquitous, and so it is perhaps not surprising that a good deal of inventive initiative was directed at what might be called the technology of burial and remembrance. Anthropologists have described trend this as the "beautification of death," and it is closely associated with the mid- to late-nineteenth century:

> The "beautification of death" movement reached the pinnacle of its expression in the elaborate, ostentatious mourning rituals practiced by middle-class Victorians in the second half of the 19th century. Hallmarks of the period include elaborate mourning clothes, ornate grave markers with sentimental inscriptions, and highly decorated burial containers ... Adoption of the term casket, connoting a jewelry box, epitomized the sentimental approach to heaven and death associated with the movement.[151]

Mourners found comfort in these technologies of presentation, and the rapidly growing commercial sector took notice:

[149] *Adams* v. *Burks*, 1 F. Cas. 100 (C.C.D. Mass. 1871) (No. 50), aff'd sub nom. *Adams* v. *Burke*, 84 U.S. 453 (1873).

[150] *Adams* v. *Burke*, 84 U.S. 453, 453 (1873): "Bill in equity [by James Adams against Alpheus Burks] for an injunction to restrain alleged infringement of letters-patent [No. 38,713] for an improvement in coffin lids granted James S. Merrill and George W. Horner, May 26, 1863, and for an account."

[151] Francine W. Bromberg and Steven J. Shephard , *The Quaker Burying Ground in Alexandria, Virginia: A Study of Burial Practices of the Religious Society of Friends*, 40 Hist. Archeol. 57, 64 (2006) (sources omitted). See generally, James J. Farell, Inventing the American Way of Death, 1830–1920 (Philadelphia: Temple University Press, 1980); Jessica Mitford, The American Way of Death Revisited (New York: Vintage; Reprint edition, 2000).

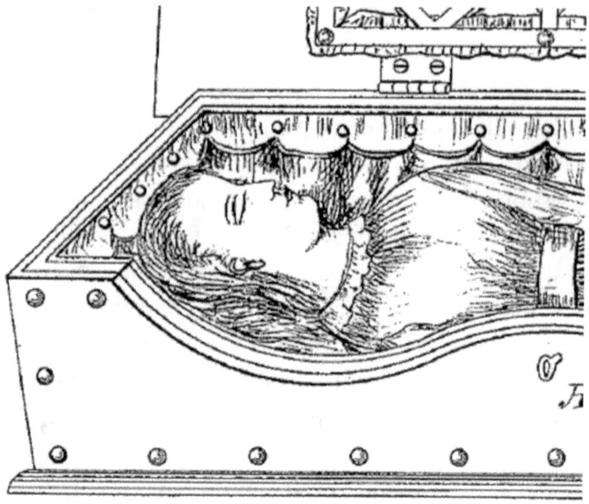

FIGURE 3.22. Depiction of young woman in US patent 54,321 (1866)

> As the industrial revolution progressed, home and heaven were increasingly idealized to provide comfort in the face of the upheaval and uncertainties of the changing times. The increased sentimentality with regard to the concepts of death and dying created a market for the trappings of the beautification of death. At the same time, improvements in technology and transportation enabled the trappings to become affordable to all segments of the population. Catalogs advertising mass-produced hardware and burial receptacles became more common as the 19th century progressed ....[152]

Even patent diagrams captured the trend, as shown in Figure 3.22.

One dimension of the beautification movement was centered on casket hardware. According to one historian,

> The combined forces of mass production and the professionalization of the funeral director eventually gave rise to a fully commercialized funeral industry. Mass-produced coffin hardware, including coffin handles, hinges, plaques, lid fasteners, lid lifters, and tacks, were made specifically for use on coffins. The ornate styles of mass-produced coffin hardware paralleled the sentimental styles so typical of other objects associated with 19th-century mourning. The symbolic representation of the beautification of death inherent in mass-produced coffin hardware can be appreciated in contrast to the plain or restrained styles common to hand-finished handles and plaques made before the mid 19th century ... Handles, nameplates or escutcheons, and tacks used on coffins were not 19th-century innovations, but the degree

[152] Francine W. Bromberg and Steven J. Shepherd, *Quaker Burial Ground*, at 64 (citations omitted). See also Martha V. Pike and Janice Gray Armstrong, eds., A Time to Mourn: Expressions of Grief in Nineteenth Century America (Stony Brook, NY: Museums at Stony Brook Publishing, 1980).

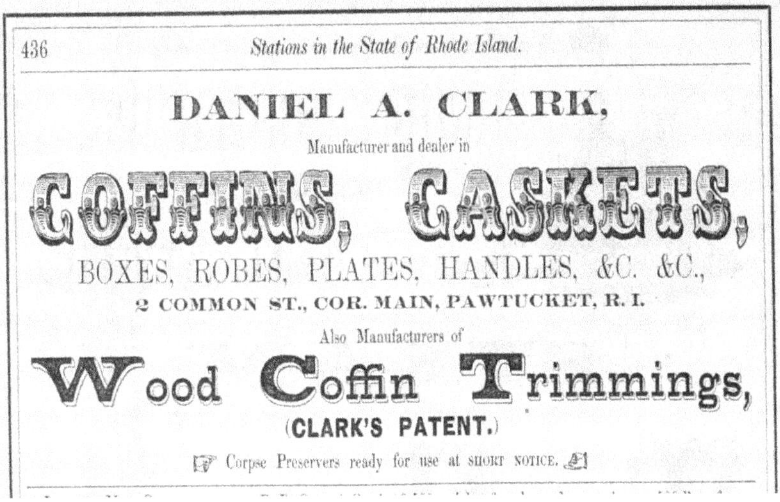

FIGURE 3.23. Typical coffin-related business notice (note the reference to the patent), from Webb's New England railway and manufacturers' statistical gazetteer (Webb Brothers & Co., Providence, 1869, available at https://catalog.hathitrust.org/Record/009607251)

> of coffin embellishment peaked during that period with the use of both highly ornamented and specialized, mass-produced items . . .[153]

There was an active market for novel and attractive coffin hardware, and this was the genesis of the patent at issue in the case of *Adams* v. *Burke*. As with most patented technologies at the time, exclusive regional rights were assigned to various franchisees. Production and distribution then took place at the local level; the assignee of the regional patent rights used the patented design to fabricate and sell its own products. An advertisement from the time shows the regional patent market at work (Figure 3.23).

These inventions served a large and growing market. True to the post-Jacksonian democratic spirit, coffin makers tried to serve all segments of the market. No sooner was there a "high end" innovation than it was copied for less expensive coffins. The need for an inexpensive casket that furthered the goal of beautification was the motivation for the patent at issue in *Adams* v. *Burke*.

The *Adams* case was centered on a patent issued to two inventors, Merrill and Horner, in 1863. The specific improvement of the Merrill and Horner patent at issue in *Adams* v. *Burke* involved what was called an inscription plate on a coffin. This

[153] Edward L. Bell, *The Historical Archaeology of Mortuary Behavior: Coffin Hardware from Uxbridge, Massachusetts*, 24 Hist. Arch. 54 (1990), at p. 57.

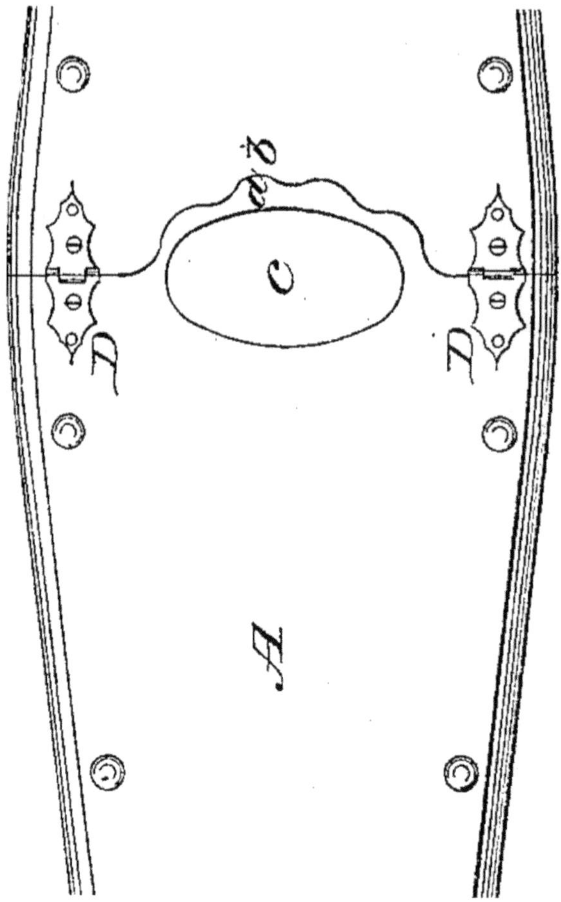

FIGURE 3.24. Merrill and Horner, US patent 38,713 (1863), at issue in Adams v. Burke

metal plate was inscribed with a suitable memorial message and was viewable on the top cover of the coffin during a wake or funeral service. The specific configuration of the Merrill and Horner design allowed the plate to be prominently displayed over the chest of the corpse, by virtue of a "cutout" and hinge arrangement, as you can see in Figure 3.24.

The inscription plate, marked C, remains prominently visible when the top of the casket is opened for viewing the corpse. This is an excellent example of a hardware invention that added to the "beautification of death" mentioned earlier. The name of the dead person, together with perhaps an inscribed bible verse or short description ("loving husband and father," etc.), remained prominent during the viewing of the corpse.

Merrill and Horner, inventors of the patent, were from Maine. As was customary, they marketed the rights to their invention to various regional assignees. A local undertaker (and an inventor himself, see later) named Jacob Seelye[154] bought the regional rights for Cambridge and Boston, Massachusetts. Seelye and his partner, named Lockhart,[155] then sub-licensed rights to the Merrill/Horner patent to various Boston-area coffin makers and undertakers, including Alpheus Burke, or Burks, an undertaker within their exclusive Cambridge-Boston region. To summarize, under the typical regional franchise model of the day, the patent rights followed this path:

Merrill/Horner → Seelye and Lockhart → Alpheus Burke

James Adams, an undertaker in the outlying suburban town of Natick, Massachusetts, also took an assignment. It's not clear who from; it could have been another regional assignee, parallel to Seelye and Lockhart, or it could have been directly from Merrill and Horner, the patent owners. The point is, Adams had an exclusive right (via assignment) for Natick and another town, both roughly seventeen to twenty miles outside Boston. According to the Circuit Court opinion:

> The complainant [plaintiff] in this case [James Adams] is the assignee of a territorial right, for the towns of Natick and Sherborn in Massachusetts, in the patent issued to Merrill & Horner, for a new and useful improvement in coffin lids. The defendant [Alpheus Burks – corrected to Burke in the Supreme Court opinion] is charged in the bill with an infringement of the complainant's rights under the patent, in the town of Natick. The defendant by plea sets out in defence that Merrill & Horner have assigned to Lockhart & Seelye of Cambridge, all their right, title, and interest in the invention secured by the letters-patent, for, to, and in a circle whose radius is ten miles, having the city of Boston as its centre. (Such a circle would not, upon any construction of the terms of the grant, include the towns of Natick and Sherborn.) Defendant's [Burke's] plea further sets out that he is an undertaker, and that in his business as an undertaker he has used and sold no coffins containing the invention secured by the letters-patent, except such coffins containing said invention as have been manufactured by Lockhart & Seelye, within a circle whose radius is ten miles,

[154] See City of Cambridge, MA, The Mayor's Address and the Annual Reports Made to the City Council (Cambridge, MA, Welch Bigelow & Co., 1868), available at https://babel.hathitrust.org/cgi/pt?id=uiug.30112108225043&view=1up&seq=6, at p. 156 (listing Jacob C. Seelye as an undertaker in the city of Cambridge).

[155] The Cambridge business directory of 1859 lists several people named Lockhart who were "coffin makers," and from the listings it appears that numerous members of the Lockhart family were also carpenters. See 1859 Cambridge Directory at 110. (Fun fact: The Lockhart listings are on the same page as the listing for "Longfellow, Henry W., on Brattle Street in Cambridge" – the famous Henry Wadsworth Longfellow, author of "The Blacksmith," "Hiawatha," and other popular nineteenth-century verse). Meanwhile, the only listings for Seelye is for a Jacob C. and Norman M. Seelye, both listed as "sewing machine maker" in the business directory. Perhaps neither is the Seelye involved in the coffin lid partnership; but perhaps one or both took an interest in the patented invention as an investment. See Cambridge Directory (Cambridge, MA: John Ford at the [Cambridge] Chronicle Office, Publisher, 1857–1883), available at https://catalog.hathitrust.org/Record/100499157.

> having the city of Boston as its centre, and sold within said circle by said Lockhart & Seelye, without condition or restriction.[156]

The problem was that, although Burke purchased patented coffins from Seelye and Lockhart in Cambridge, Burke then apparently *sold* the coffins to people in Natick. The alleged cross-selling, in other words, occurred when Burke re-sold the coffins to buyers in Natick. The case asked the question: Could Adams, the Natick assignee, prevent cross-selling by Burke, who purchased from Seelye and Lockhart under the exclusive Boston-area assignment?

The Circuit Court said no, Adams had no power to stop Burke from selling to customers from Natick and Sherborn. Judge Shepley in his opinion pointed out the absurd implications of the theory Adams had advanced:

> If [Adams is right], the purchaser of a manufactured patent article of wearing apparel might be liable for the use of the patented article in every town and city through which he might travel, in which there might be an assignee of a [distinct] territorial right, although he had purchased it of one having a lawful right to make and sell it, so as to convey an absolute and unrestricted title.[157]

Given how common regional patent assignments were at the time, the court's point was clear for the contemporary reader to see. To prevent chaos in the market, once a legitimate purchase was made in any region, the owner of the patented item was free to take it across regional lines and otherwise use it without fear of infringing the rights of other regional patent assignees. The Supreme Court affirmed this commonsense result,[158] which helped free consumers from the potential headaches of the regional, patent-based franchise business model.

3.3.4.1 Completing the Story

The visible inscription plate design of the Merrill and Horner patent was not the end of coffin-related invention in the era. There were a number of subsequent improvements. A good example is a patent issued to Merrill's Cambridge-area assignee, Jacob C. Seelye. Seelye was not content merely to serve as an agent of Merrill and Horner. Somewhere along the line, he had an idea to simplify and improve on the Merrill coffin lid design. Instead of providing for a "cutout" in the coffin lid, which made the inscription plate visible but required an elaborate, curving wood cut,

[156] *Adams* v. *Burks*, 1 F. Cas. 100, 100 (C.C.D. Mass. 1871), aff'd sub nom. *Adams* v. *Burke*, 84 U.S. 453, 21 L. Ed. 700 (1873).

[157] *Adams* v. *Burks*, 1 F. Cas. 100, 101 (C.C.D. Mass. 1871), aff'd sub nom. *Adams* v. *Burke*, 84 U.S. 453, 21 L. Ed. 700 (1873).

[158] *Adams* v. *Burke*, 84 U.S. 453, 457 (1873) ("[W]e hold that in the class of machines or implements we have described, when they are once lawfully made and sold, there is no restriction on their *use* to be implied for the benefit of the patentee or his assignees or licensees ...") (emphasis in original).

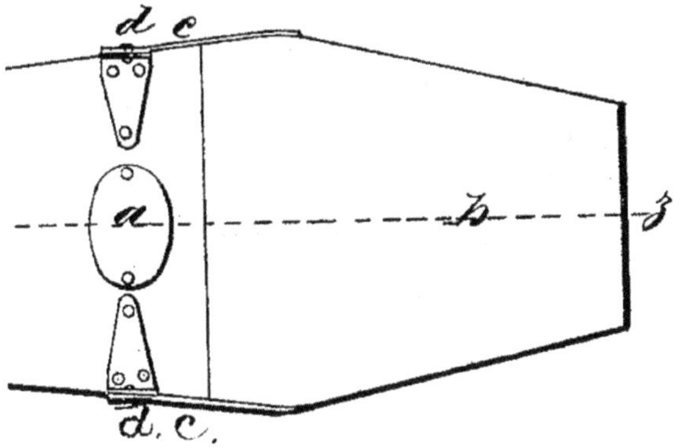

FIGURE 3.25. US patent 48,842, to Jacob C. Seelye, "Improvement in Hanging Coffin Lids," which Seelye said was "simpler and cheaper" then the Merrill design

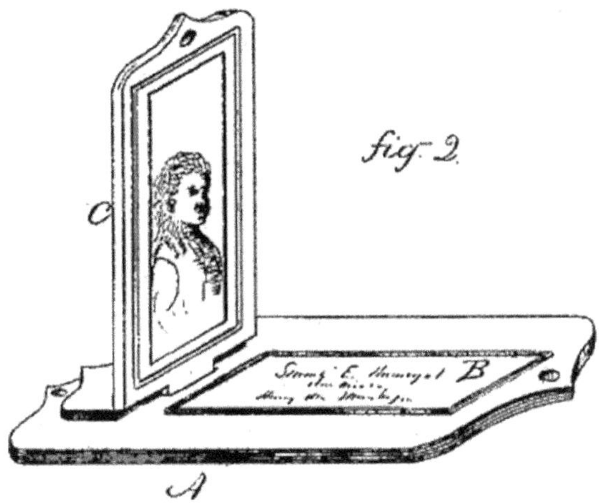

FIGURE 3.26. Illustration from US patent 135,155, to George B. Ransom (January 21, 1873)

Seelye provided the same overall effect with two extended rods that held the coffin lid (the part covering the corpse's head). The rods were attached to hinges (marked "d" in Figure 3.25) that allowed the lid to be swung open for viewing while keeping the inscription plate (marked "a") visible. This avoided the fancy wood cut of the Merrill design, while allowing for attractive hinge hardware, inscription plates, and open casket funerals or wakes.

Not to be outdone, an inventor named George B. Ransom received US patent 135,155, on an "Improvement in Coffin Plates," in January of 1873. The patent diagram shows a two-part, "pop-up," coffin plate, where a photo can be displayed along with an inscription (Figure 3.26).

The Ransom patent and the facts in *Adams* v. *Burke* demonstrate the necessity of the exhaustion principle. Exhaustion was an important pro-consumer principle, created to protect purchasers from potential liability that might attach under the regional patent franchise business model. The growing volume and complexity of issued patents (e.g., the Ransom patent) in the context of finely divided regions (such as those in *Adams* v. *Burke*) necessitated some way to cut off claims that would interfere with the normal use of purchased items. Exhaustion did just this.

3.3.5 *Patent Office Administration*

Between 1820 and 1880 the Patent Office participated in the most important job of the new national government: building the institutional infrastructure to support and promote economic activity. It did this job in parallel with other early federal agencies such as the Post Office; the General Land Office (succeeding a division of the Treasury Department), which surveyed land and issued title to settlers; the Customs Service; and the Treasury Department's Coastal Trade Office. In these early years, the overriding policy of rapidly building out a robust national economy provided a unifying force that blurred the lines between legislature, courts, and the executive function, and even (at times) between citizen and state.[159]

Although patent examination began with the 1836 Act, there was at first only one patent examiner (called an "examining clerk" in the Act).[160] There were only two examiners until the 1840s, and the Patent Office did not take on its modern aspect, with examination divisions and specialist examiners, until the 1870s. The graph in Figure 3.27, captures the growth of the Office.

Recall that in the early years, the Patent Office was part of the State Department. This may have been a nod to Thomas Jefferson, the first Secretary of State, with a known interest in patent matters; or it may have been that no one knew where else to put the patent function. In any event, as far back as 1812, some members of the government recognized that State was a poor fit for patents. A report from that year recommends creation of a "Home Department" where the Patent Office might reside.[161]

The Patent Office was eventually relocated to the Interior Department in 1849. The few examiners there were between 1836 and 1849 worked out of the State

[159] Jerry L. Mashaw, *Recovering American Administrative Law: Federalist Foundations, 1787–1801*, 115 Yale L.J. 1256, 1260, 1277 (2006).

> [T]he first independent agency at the national level was not the ICC [Interstate Commerce Commission, created in 1887], but the Patent Office, created ninety-seven years earlier ... [In this early era,] the national government's primary attentions were directed to defense and development. Land grants, protection of intellectual property, the creation of post offices and post roads, and the promotion of the carriage of goods by sea were all crucial to the creation of the new national market.

[160] Patent Act of 1836, Ch. 357, 5 Stat. 117 (July 4, 1836), at section 2.

[161] Rep. Adam Seybert, Chair, Report of the Special Committee on the State and Condition of [the Patent Office], communicated to the House of Representatives June 12, 1812, H.Rep. No. 326, 12th Cong., 1st Sess., available at Am. State Papers (1834), at pp. 112 et seq.

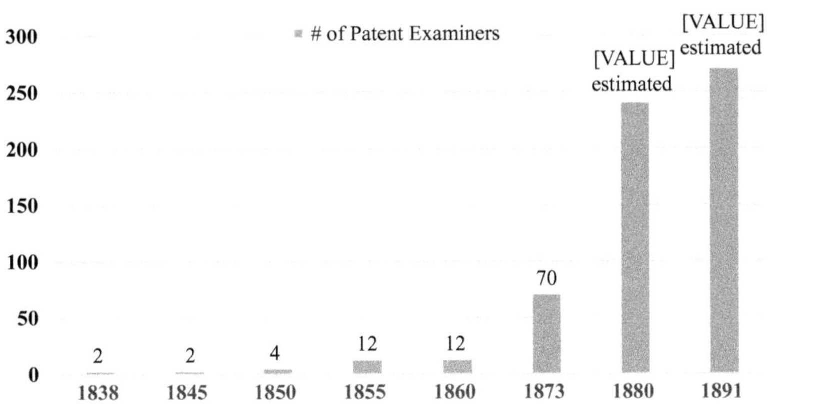

Notes:
Beginning in 1850, the Annual Report lists "Examiners" and "Assistants." Both are counted as "patented examiners" in this table.
1880 estimate: from p. v, Annual Report of the Comm'r, asking for 10 new examiners which would add a 25th examining division; inferring that each division has 10 examiners.
1891 estimate: from the Commissioner's Report for that year, which is arguing the need for more space (a chronic problem, mentioned in every annual Report from 1850 on).

FIGURE 3.27. Number of patent office examiners, 1838–1891

Department.[162] The first examiners were drawn from a pool of people who were invariably described as "men of science": mostly university-trained natural scientists with some breadth of background and no shortage of technical interests. It was Senator John Ruggles of Maine, sponsor of the 1836 Act, who said that the patent examiner job required "extensive scientific attainments."[163] Once selected, examiners achieved – due to the dearth of scientifically trained professionals – something close to celebrity status in the nineteenth century. The first patent examiner was Charles M. Keller, who had been superintending the scale models that accompanied most inventions in the early days of the system.[164] One of Keller's early successors was a medical doctor, electrical experimenter, inventor, and later promoter of the patent system, Charles Grafton Page,[165] who joined the Patent Office in 1842. Though Page made unusually important contributions to early electrical research,[166] his scientific training made him typical of the earliest generation of patent examiners. As Page's biographer put it, "all [the early examiners] were regarded as worthy 'scientific men.' … [I]n sum a most

[162] See National Archives, Department of the Interior. Patent Office (1849–1925), Organization Authority Record, available at https://catalog.archives.gov/id/10480220.

[163] Robert C. Post, *"Liberalizers" versus "Scientific Men" in the Antebellum Patent Office*, 17 Tech. & Cult. 24, 28 (1991).

[164] Ibid., at p. 27.

[165] Robert C. Post, Physics, Patents and Politics: A Biography of Charles Grafton Page (New York: Science History Publications, 1976), at 47 ("[H]ow does one deal with a man whose pursuits ranged from experimental physics to practical pharmacy and the application of electromagnetic power to useful purposes, and who all the while held down a regular job with the State Department's Office of Patents?").

[166] He made one of the first inductive electrical coils and was one of three primary contributors in the development of the magneto. See Robert C. Post, *Antebellum Patent Office*, at p. 67.

FIGURE 3.28. The Old Patent Office Building, constructed between 1836 and 1865 (now the National Portrait Gallery, Smithsonian Institution)

impressive cast of characters."[167] The job was attractive in part because it paid well, bestowed prestige, and left time for independent scientific research.[168]

The presence of eminent scientists is just one way the Patent Office in these early years was something of a hybrid. It was, of course, a government agency, granting patents over meritorious inventions, handling patent appeals, and awarding priority when multiple inventors claimed the same thing, but was also a cultural institution. The patent models that many inventors deposited were not just a source of patent-related prior art. They were also cultural artifacts, and many tourist visits to Washington in the mid-nineteenth century included a trip to the Patent Office to see them. The Smithsonian Institution in Washington was to become the preeminent museum in the Capitol. But the Smithsonian was not properly established until 1846,[169] so until that time the Patent Office served as a museum of technology – and in some ways a shrine to American creativity and initiative. The Patent Office building was one of the largest

[167] Robert C. Post, *Antebellum Patent Office*, at p. 59.
[168] Ibid., at p. 55:

> The pay [$1500 per year under the 1836 Patent Act] was certainly on a par with a good professorship ... [A]nd the hours were but six or seven daily, depending on the season. [Page] would have time to resume the pursuit of his personal research, while getting paid for the exercise of his expertise. Page was now [, after his hiring,] a true professional scientist.

[169] The endowment was granted by British citizen James Smithson in 1836, but it took official Washington ten years to figure out how to implement Smithson's vision. See www.si.edu/about/history.

in the city and became a Washington institution. Among other things, it served as a hospital during the Civil War (with poet Walt Whitman writing of the anomaly of dying troops jammed in among the patent models),[170] as well as the site of President Lincoln's second Inaugural Ball.[171] Figure 3.28 shows the Patent Office Building, built between 1836 and 1865.

By the time the grand structure was complete, the role of the Patent Office and its examiners had changed. The years after the Civil War marked the end of the "heroic" period of the early system, and the onset of a rapid period of industrial and economic development. Patent examination and the other functions of the Patent Office were regularized and bureaucratized. The examiner corps went from individual public figures to a large group of professional experts. All the major features of modern patent processing entered the scene between 1850 and 1880: (1) the stratification of Patent Office personnel into clerks, examiners, and Principal Examiners;[172] (2) a sharp reduction in special Congressional acts for patent extensions, with the settling of the patent term first at fourteen years plus an optional seven-year extension (1836 Act),[173] then a fixed term of seventeen years from the date of patent issuance (in 1861);[174] (3) formalization of the patent appeals process, with

[170] Walt Whitman, Specimen Days and Collect (Glasgow: Wilson and McCormack, 1883), available at https://catalog.hathitrust.org/Record/012349652, at pp. 30–31:

> I must not let the great hospital at the Patent office pass away without some mention. A few weeks ago the vast area of the second story of that noblest of Washington buildings was crowded close with rows of sick, badly wounded and dying soldiers. They were placed in three very large apartments. I went there many times. It was a strange, solemn, and, with all its features of suffering and death, a sort of fascinating sight. I go sometimes at night to soothe and relieve particular cases. Two of the immense apartments are fill'd with high and ponderous glass cases, crowded with models in miniature of every kind of utensil, machine or invention, it ever enter'd nto the mind of man to conceive; and with curiosities and foreign presents. Between these cases are lateral openings, perhaps eight feet wide and quite deep, and in these were placed the sick, besides a great long double row of them ... Sometimes a poor fellow dying, with emaciated face and glassy eye, the nurse by his side, the doctor also there, but no friend, no relative[:] such were the sights but lately in the Patent- office.

[171] Which Walt Whitman wrote about in the *New York Times*. See www.civilwarmed.org/whitman/.

[172] The informal allocation of labor between senior and junior patent examiners was instituted at this time. See Annual Report of the Commissioner of Patents for the Year 1873, at p. xi:

> The only remedy for the evil here pointed out [i.e., inadequate examination] is for such a reorganization of the Office as will secure supervision of the work of examining. The Examiner's duty should be to examine and report to some superior officer, who should review his work and determine the question of patentability. The very fact that one's work is to be reviewed, and approved or disapproved, will secure thoroughness, when the absence of such supervision engenders haste and carelessness.

[173] Patent Act of 1836, 5 Stat. 117, 119, at section 5.

[174] Act of 1861, 12 Stat. 246, 249, at section 16. Regularization of the patent term was a response to pressure from businesses and consumer groups who felt that the patent extension process had become lax and corrupted. See Christopher Beauchamp, *The First Patent Litigation Explosion*, 125 Yale L.J. 848, 886–887 (2016) (footnotes omitted):

the right for inventors to appeal adverse decisions to the federal court in Washington, DC;[175] and (4) the regularization of patent reissues under formal Patent Office procedures (replacing the ad hoc process that had prevailed).[176]

The growth in patent volume also led to a greater emphasis on effective communication of patent-related information. As prior art searches became more common, with the growing volume of patents, the Patent Office experimented with various patent classification schemes. The 1858 Commissioner's Report lists a fairly simple one, with five major patent classifications:

I. — Agriculture, including implements and operations
II. —Metallurgy and manufacture of metals
III. —Manufacture of fibrous and textile substances

> Extensions were a notable aspect of patent management for several decades in the middle of the nineteenth century. [E]xtension practice … reached its peak in the third quarter of the century … Between 1836 and 1851 only thirty-eight patents were extended by the Patent Office board and only a handful by Congress … After the Commissioner of Patents gained sole authority to grant extensions in 1848, the approval rate rose above 50%. By the late 1850s the doors had been flung open: between 1857 and 1877, around 80% of extension applications were approved. Many more patents were extended in that period: often around 5% to 8%, and sometimes as high as 11%, of the patents expiring each year. Over two hundred extensions per year were granted in 1872 and 1873. The welter of extensions came to an abrupt end soon thereafter, though, because the Patent Act of 1861 abolished administrative extensions for all grants made after that date. The Commissioner of Patents granted the last extension in 1877 …

For an account of the lobbying – including wining and dining – accompanying extension campaigns, see Ibid., at 924 (footnotes omitted) ("Congressional interventions, above all in the form of private bills extending patents, were highly influential and highly controversial in the politics of patents. Vast sums were reputedly poured into extension battles by the owners of the Woodworth, McCormick [reaper] and various rubber patents. In 1854, a congressional committee … painted a lurid picture of the '[a]gents, attorneys, and letter-writers' employed to bombard legislators in patent extension cases. '[C]ostly and extravagant entertainments' were laid on for 'ladies and Members of Congress and others' in support of extension bills."). For more on special petitions, see Patent Administration in Chapter 2. *See* Robert P. Merges and Glenn Harlan Reynolds, *The Proper Scope of the Patent and Copyright Power*, 37 Harv. J. Legis. 45 (2000) (criticizing "private patent bills").

[175] Annual Report of the Commissioner of Patent for 1855, at p. 4 (emphasis in original):

> In case of the *rejection* of an application, the law and the practice of the office permit an appeal to the Commissioner, and finally to one of the judges of the circuit court of the District. But such appeals are attended with much trouble and expense, so that, in most cases, especially where the applicant resides at a distance, a rejection by the examiner is, in point of fact, final.

[176] See Kendall J. Dood, *Pursuing the Essence of Inventions: Reissuing Patents in the 19th Century*, 32 Tech. & Cult. 999, 1001 (1991). The informal origins of reissue practice, and its codification in 1832, 1836, and thereafter are recounted in Craig Allen Nard, *Legal Forms and the Common Law of Patents*, 90 B.U. L. Rev. 51, 67–68 (2010). See also Andrew P. Morriss and Craig Allen Nard, *Institutional Choice & Interest Groups in the Development of American Patent Law: 1790–1865*, 19 Sup. Ct. Econ. Rev. 143, 144 (2011) ("Interest groups therefore turned to Congress on occasion to 'lock in' changes in the law that they had achieved through the courts."); Robert P. Merges, *One Hundred Years of Solicitude: Intellectual Property Law, 1900–2000*, 88 Cal. L. Rev. 2187 (2000) (describing the same pattern).

IV. —Chemical processes, manufactures, and compounds
V. — Calorifics, comprising lamps, stoves, &c.[177]

There were also sub-classes in common use; beginning in 1836, there was an "increase[e] [in the] the number of classes from 16 to 22, [with] one miscellaneous class, class 22." As patent volume grew, so did the refinement of classifications: up to 145 classifications in 1872.[178] At the same time as finer classifications were created, there came a demand for more complete prior art information. In 1866, regular printing of patent specifications was instituted.[179]

By 1880, the focus of patent examination had also shifted to the individual patent claim. In the Annual Commissioner's Report for that year, Commissioner E. M. Marble said:

> In order to thoroughly examine and decide the intricate questions which arise, the ablest and most experienced examiners must have sufficient time for mature consideration on each claim. The number of claims presented in each application will average not less than four.[180]

The same report details the emergence of the still-familiar back-and-forth nature of patent prosecution, with its attendant workload for the examiner:

> It is the duty of the Commissioner of Patents to furnish an applicant with any and all information which in his judgment shows that the device or matter claimed is anticipated by former patents or publications, after which the applicant may either amend his application or demand a reconsideration of the decision. As a rule applications are amended; and as they may be amended as often as new reasons or references are given by the examiner, which by reason of the change in the claims often becomes necessary, it is not extravagant to say that the average actions, each of which amounts to a decision upon evidence, which the Examiner himself must find are not less than four to each application, so that upon the twenty-three thousand applications filed during the past year not less than ninety-two thousand decisions were made. With the force now provided by law the twenty-four Principal Examiners … are required to superintend and are held responsible for this large number of decisions, making for each [Principal] examiner about four thousand decisions during the year.[181]

[177] Report of the Commissioner of Patents for the Year 1858, available at https://babel.hathitrust.org/cgi/pt?id=uc1.b3361464&view=1up&seq=7, at p. viii.

[178] M. F. Bailey, *History of Classification of Patents*, 28 J. Pat. Off. Soc'y 463, 470 (1946) ("On March 1, 1872, a revised classification was adopted … This classification comprised 145 classes … ").

[179] M. F. Bailey, *History of Classifications*, at p. 468: "It was not until 1866 that printing of specifications of patents was begun in earnest." Around the same time, an effort was made to retroactively convert the old patent drawings to a standard format, for ease of searching.

[180] Report of the Commissioner of Patents for the Year 1880, available at https://catalog.hathitrust.org/Record/002138126, at p. v.

[181] Ibid., at p. v.

The private side of the legal system changed along with Patent Office practice. Beginning in the 1840s, shortly after examination was established in the 1836 Patent Act, patent agencies emerged.[182] These were private legal firms that promised inventors help in prosecuting patent applications in the Patent Office. Then as now many of those who held themselves out to inventors were former patent examiners. Then as now they made more money doing this than they had as examiners in the Patent Office. And then as now they switched sides with great fluidity, going from bureaucrats charged with weeding out weak patents to private agents hired to obtain patents for as many inventions as they could. As is true today, patent agents did not often enforce patents in court. The legal profession with respect to patents was split between those paid to obtain them ("prosecutors") and those paid to enforce them ("litigators").

3.3.5.1 The Birth of Modern Patent Political Economy

With the growth in patent volume, and the emergence of patent agencies, came a new political dynamic that established other patterns still evident today. Patent agents (and later, patent lawyers) are paid to get patents. But the Patent Office is supposed to grant patents only on worthwhile inventions. The entire rationale for the 1836 Act was to rein in the number of weak patents, and in turn reduce the incidence of nuisance or inefficient patent litigation.[183]

The result was a constant two-way pressure on the Patent Office. Patent examiners and other patent officials make their money on fees paid to the Office. And Office employees hear from and see patent agents every day. Immediate financial incentives and social proximity thus make the Office prone to seeing patent seekers as its primary constituency. It is a special instance of the general phenomenon known as "regulatory capture": A government agency charged with limiting and supervising

[182] Naomi R. Lamoreaux and Kenneth L. Sokoloff, *Long-Term Change in the Organization of Inventive Activity*, 93 Proc. Nat'l Acad. Sci. 12686 (1996).

[183] Kara W. Swanson, *The Emergence of the Professional Patent Practitioner*, 50 Tech. & Cult. 519, 526 (2009) (footnote omitted):

> In the first year that the Patent Act of 1836 was in place, [the first examiner] Keller rejected about 75 percent of all the applications he received. The rejection rate would continue to fluctuate between 25 and 67 percent throughout the antebellum period. Clearly, getting a patent had become a trickier business, and there was a much greater incentive to hire someone who could anticipate and prepare for the type of examination given to applications …

This changed quickly. See Kara W. Swanson, The Surprisingly Engrossing History of Patent Examiners, Slate.com, May 7, 2014, at p. 6.

> In the 1850s, Secretary of the Interior Robert McClelland, who held authority over the patent office, pushed a solution that neatly fit his own goals. In place of the best-trained scientific minds as examiners, he sought to hire political supporters, a common and legal approach in the 19-century civil service. By the end of the decade, these less scientific examiners were granting two-thirds of applications. The patent commissioner in 1858 urged examiners to welcome "the inventor as a friend" and fired those who were too "unsympathizing" when considering applications.

an aspect of commercial life is co-opted into seeing things from the point of view of the companies it is supposed to supervise.[184]

Simultaneously, Congress and federal courts oversee the functioning of the Patent Office. Courts are charged with ultimate responsibility in the legal administration of the patent system; they have the final say over the meaning of statutory requirements such as utility, novelty, and "invention." These are important policy instruments that calibrate the availability of patents, their scope, and ultimately their value. Meanwhile Congress is subject to lobbying by industries strongly affected by patents. Sometimes, lobbyists argue for less stringent patent requirements – by overturning a restrictive federal court case, for example. But lobbying in the opposite direction, at least at certain times, is also common. Companies and consumer groups have traditionally pushed hardest for Congressional solutions when there is a perception that the patent system is over-rewarding the "wrong type" of patent owner. The crucial indicator is patent litigation: When people and businesses are sued too frequently for their tastes, they resort to Congress.[185] Their pleas for "patent reform" are a response, in other words, to a sense that patent enforcement has gotten out of hand. Whatever the appropriate level of patent licensing and litigation – the "optimal enforcement rate" – lobbyists at times claim that it has been exceeded, and that as a result the patent system needs fixing.

Calls for patent reform have been around for as long as the federal patent system. The reason is simple: One person's positive incentive is another person's negative rent[186] – a wasteful "tax on innovation." Put another way, there is a thin line

[184] See Thomas W. Merrill, *Capture Theory and the Courts: 1967–1983*, 72 Chi.-Kent L. Rev. 1039 (1997). See generally Richard White, The Republic for Which It Stands: The United States during Reconstruction and the Gilded Age, 1865–1896 (Oxford: Oxford University Press, 2017) (society-wide story of capture and corruption in the post-Civil War and Gilded Age period). For an intriguing study of the effect of Patent Office funding pressures on the actions of individual patent examiners, see Michael D. Frakes and Melissa F. Wasserman, *Does Agency Funding Affect Decisionmaking?: An Empirical Assessment of the PTO*, 66 Vand. L. Rev. 65 (2013) (examiners issue more patents when Patent Office is under financial pressure).

[185] See the earlier discussion of railroad industry lobbying. See generally the masterful account of nineteenth-century patent litigation by Christopher Beauchamp, The First Patent Litigation Explosion (describing the high rate of litigation from 1850 to 1910, and industry and consumer group responses to it).

[186] Technically speaking, an economic rent is simply the value that is demanded by the owner of a thing to put that thing into use by employing it, selling it, allowing others to use it, etc. As mentioned in Chapter 1 "rent-seeking" denotes the pursuit of wealth by manipulation of government rules or regulations. This activity limits competition without adding real value. See Anne Krueger, *The Political Economy of the Rent-Seeking Society*, 64 Am. Econ. Rev. 291 (1974); Kevin Murphy, Andrei Shleifer, and Robert Vishny, *Why Is Rent-Seeking So Costly to Growth?*, 83 Am. Econ. Rev. (Pap. & Proceedings) 409 (1993). So, in a technical sense I use "rent" in this discussion as a shorthand for "the product or result of rent-seeking activities." In this case, the rent-seeking activities are pursuing and asserting low-value patents in order to extract high profits from people and companies than can be successfully sued for infringing the low-value patents. From a moral perspective, the wrong in rent-seeking litigation is that it transfers value from one who legitimately created it (and therefore deserves it) to one who did

(sometimes vanishingly thin) between (a) a valuable invention whose creator deserves compensation and (b) a cleverly drawn up legal right, covering nothing of intrinsic value, whose holder has a ticket to drag into federal courts various manufacturers, distributors, and consumers, for the purpose of extracting from them legal settlements that inure exclusively to the benefit of expert patent litigators and their financial backers.

The first defense against patents becoming a tax on innovation comes in patent examination. If all patents that emerge from examination cover valuable improvements, weak-patent, rent-seeking litigation by definition more or less disappears.[187] But given the vast volume of patent applications, ever since the 1850s or 1860s the goal of making every patent a gold-plated, high-quality grant has been elusive. The second defense comes at the enforcement stage, when myriad rules, doctrines, and statutory requirements can be tuned and tweaked to disfavor low value litigation and favor rewards for meritorious inventors. The line drawing exercise just described has, since the nineteenth century, been fought with the dueling narratives of valuable incentive versus socially wasteful rents.

3.3.5.2 Placing the Nineteenth-Century Patent Office in Context: Administrative Agency and Courts in the "Economic Development State"

The Patent Office predated the modern "administrative revolution" that began in the federal government. This revolution, dating from the 1870s, was a response to the accumulation of private power and the complex problems brought on by rapid industrialization. The powerful federal agencies created during this era – beginning with the Interstate Commerce Commission, continuing with the Food and Drug Administration, and then later the "alphabet soup" of agencies from the 1920s to the 1960s – had much to do with counterbalancing the emergent power of large, concentrated industries and very little to do with the original Patent Office mandate.[188]

But this dynamic post-dates the formative period of the Patent Office. The patent system was one of the earliest instruments of economic development put in place by the young United States. It represents a distinctly pre-twentieth century policy – one of the strands in the policy instruments sturdy rope that powered the early Republic

not earn it and therefore does not deserve it. See generally Robert P. Merges, Justifying Intellectual Property, at chapter 6.

[187] See, on this topic in the contemporary context of battles over patent "trolls," Robert P. Merges, *The Trouble with Trolls: Innovation, Rent-Seeking, and Patent Law Reform*, 24 Berkeley Tech. L.J. 1583, 1588–1589 (2009):

> [T]he fundamental purpose of patent law is to encourage true innovation ... [But] there is a difference between a reward for true innovation and a legal instrument which permits rent-seeking activities. Only if there is a gap between what is truly innovative and what is permissibly patented and asserted is there space for the concept of a patent troll.

[188] See generally Thomas McCaw, Prophets of Regulation (Cambridge, MA: Belknap Press, Harvard University, 1984).

forward into prosperity.[189] It is crucial to understand, however, that this system was the product of a much smaller and weaker state than the one we currently inhabit.[190]

Legal scholar Herb Hovenkamp has accurately described the situation:

> At the beginning of the 19th century the United States was severely underdeveloped. Government intervention in the economy took the form of monopoly grants to encourage economic development, as well as tax breaks and other subsidies dedicated to the creation of infrastructure. The early American state also took a much heavier role in fostering innovation through the patent system, encouraging the actual development and deployment of patented devices and processes. Under the leadership of Chief Justice Marshall the Supreme Court facilitated the use of monopoly grants. It also furthered a strongly national and pro-regulatory interpretation of the Commerce Clause, designed to facilitate national development and limit state free riding and other self-interest.[191]

The early history of the administrative patent function is a choppy one. As we saw in Chapter 2, the initial 1790 Act, with its heavyweight "examiner corps" of the Secretaries of State and War, and the Attorney General, quickly gave way to a pure registration system. From 1793 to 1836, inventors who sent the proper documents to the State Department received a patent. Fights between rival inventors as to who invented first were resolved by the District Courts. And patent validity was not reviewed until the patent owner tried to enforce the patent. The resulting system, whereby federal judges determine patent validity in the context of a defense to patent infringement, was and is a distinctive aspect of US patent practice.[192]

189 As described in Chapter 1, legal historian J. Willard Hurst described the entire nineteenth-century American legal tradition in these terms.

190 As far as I know, the earliest patent scholarship on the topic in this section is John F. Duffy, *The FCC and the Patent System: Progressive Ideals, Jacksonian Realism, and the Technology of Regulation*, 71 U. Colo. L. Rev. 1071, 1079–1080 (2000):

> [W]hile the Progressive-era regulatory agencies have gone from fashionable innovations to antiquated relics during the twentieth century, the patent system continues to thrive with much the same structure that it was given in 1836 ... [A]gencies created in the twentieth and later part of the nineteenth centuries were influenced by then-fashionable political and regulatory philosophies, which radically overestimated the abilities of public agencies. In contrast, the modern American patent bureaucracy was established during the Jacksonian era, which was nothing if not realistic about the abilities of government officers and institutions. [In addition,] the patent system provides further cause to check the enthusiasm of today's [regulatory agency] reformers. For agency abolitionists who seek to idealize the common law, the patent system provides a well-documented failure of the common law to regulate effectively without the assistance of an administrative agency.

191 Herbert Hovenkamp, *Appraising the Progressive State*, 102 Iowa L. Rev. 1063, 1068 (2017) (footnotes omitted).

192 In most other countries, validity (even post-patent issuance) continues to be the province of the national patent office, with courts typically limited to patent enforcement issues (infringement, remedies, etc.). See Robert P. Merges and Seagull Haiyan Song, Transnational Intellectual Property (London: Edward Elgar, 2018), at pp. 35–39 (introducing the European and Chinese patent systems).

With the advent of patent examination in 1836, the administrative side of US patent law began to take shape. But the early period continued to influence the post-1836 scene, particularly with respect to the important role of courts in the system.[193] A good example is that under the 1793 Patent Act, one who believed a patent had been obtained fraudulently could have the patent invalidated by applying to a local federal district court and initiating an invalidity proceeding.[194]

The use of courts as federal outposts was simply a function of the limited availability of federal institutions. The same is true of the copyright system. For instance, under the 1790 Copyright Act, works subject to copyright had to be deposited in the federal district court nearest the author's residence.[195] With so little federal power in toto, there was more concern with pulling together federal power than with the *separation* of powers. There was at this time what might be called a unitary conception of federal authority, with all three branches of the government engaged in the important business of national economic development.

In total, thousands of patents were issued under the 1790 and 1793 Patent Acts. As might be expected from a pure registration system, patent quality was a serious issue.[196] Indeed, as we have seen, concerns with quality were the driving force behind the 1836 Patent Act and the creation of an administrative examining corps. Even so, the important role of courts in determining patent validity during this period well illustrates the unitary government in action.[197] This tradition of court involvement left a lasting impression on the law as well.

[193] See Edward C. Walterscheid, *To Promote the Progress of Useful Arts: American Patent Law and Administration, 1787–1836 (Part I)*, 79 J. Pat. & Tm. Off. Soc'y (1997) ("The Patent Act of 1836 is generally acknowledged to be the foundation for the modern patent examination system in the United States. It created the Patent Office, a corps of examiners, modern interference practice, administrative appeal practice, and the modern patent numbering system. But what is frequently forgotten or ignored is that the patent system it created came into existence predicated on – and in no small measure in reaction to – decades of prior administrative practice under a detailed statutory scheme which had received rather extensive judicial interpretation. Almost ten thousand patents had been issued by 1836. There thus was a significant background, both legal and administrative, against which to view the Act of 1836." (footnote omitted)).

[194] Act of February 21, 1793, 1 Stat. 318, 323 §10 (1793).

[195] Act of May 31, 1790, 1 Stat. 124, 125 §3 (1790).

[196] See generally Edward C. Walterscheid, *The Winged Gudgeon: An Early Patent Controversy*, 79 J. Pat. & Trademark Off. Soc'y 533 (1997) (discussing early problems with the patent registration system, including the Patent Commissioner's published notice that registered patent was not innovative and was being used to extort licenses from "infringers").

[197] Jerry Mashaw, in his work on early administrative law, notes the presence of "mongrel" agencies and officers (including the original U.S. attorneys), noting that they were "outside of any departmental hierarchy." Mashaw, *Recovering American Administrative Law*, at 1291. He concludes:

> [E]arly Congresses created departments and officers, charged them with administrative tasks, and subjected them to political supervision in a variety of ways that exhibit modest concern for rigid or formal conceptions of the separation of powers. While one can find individual expressions of doctrinaire, or even extreme, opinions on separation of powers questions in the debates, when Congress acted, it acted in a spirit of pragmatic compromise.

Ibid., at 1291–1292.

* * * *

The history of the Patent Office shows the administrative response to the rapid economic development of the United States between 1820 and 1880. While there were other fundamental changes in the United States in these years – social, political, and cultural[198] – I have emphasized technological and economic development. The crucial change in technology was the coming of large-scale mechanization, first in textiles and wood working, and then in a wide range of industries, from papermaking to railways to the making of steel. Alongside these changes, reacting to them but also spurring them on, were changes in the dominant form of business enterprise. This period saw the end of the partnership era, and the advent of the corporation. Patents, so central to technology-based partnerships (especially the regional franchise), were becoming just another type of asset owned and controlled by the corporation. The changing place of patents in the business enterprise was a response to increased technical complexity. More complex machines made it harder to organize an enterprise around a single patent. Corporations were a more efficient ownership structure for groups of patents; the era of the patent portfolio began to take shape. A more complex, variegated technology landscape led to important developments in the legal and business features of patents. Patents were becoming far more numerous, and more often covered a component or feature of a larger system or product, rather than an entire product. Patents map ownership claims onto technological space; they divide up and place boundaries around discrete portions of new technologies. So, in response to a more sophisticated technology landscape, patent law brought forth new, sharper doctrinal tools. The invention test, announced by the Supreme Court in 1851, added a new requirement to patent law; it cut down on the issuance of patents for trivial variations on what was already known. Likewise, the refinement of legal rules surrounding patent claims helped better define and demarcate individual claims in a more crowded landscape.

In these and other ways, patent law participated in the great wave of mechanization, modernization, and maturation of nineteenth-century law and business. As things turned out, the emergence of the corporate form, and the nationwide (indeed, international) capital markets it engendered, were just the start of a revolution in business and commerce that would completely transform the economy, the political system, and society in the years between 1880 and 1920. As with so many other businesses, and the legal fields supporting them, the technology-intensive firms at the center of patent law experienced rapid and far-reaching changes in these years. The year 1880 marks roughly the beginning of this period of mass "corporatization," and that is the period we turn to next.

[198] I have said very little here about the most important developments in the nineteenth century: the Civil War, end of legalized slavery, Reconstruction, and its ultimate failure. For some insight into the deprivation of patent protection for the inventions of slaves, see Brian L. Frye, *Invention of a Slave*, 68 Syracuse Law Rev. 181 (2018).

4

Corporatization, 1880–1920

CHAPTER OUTLINE

Between 1880 and 1920 the US economy rode several transformative technologies into a new economic era.The transportation and communication revolutions that began earlier in the nineteenth century gained momentum: rail networks grew astronomically, and the telephone accelerated the communications revolution that the telegraph had begun. Meanwhile, although the corporate form as a legal entity was well established by 1880, it was in the years leading up to 1920 that very large, nation-spanning business enterprises came to dominate the economy. The cause was those famous Chandlerian twins, scale and scope.[1] Corporations as a legal category were well known by 1880; but large, vertically integrated corporations as the prime mover of a rapidly expanding economy took over after that. This is the story of the corporatization of the American economy.

Two major things happened in the patent world during this era. First, the primary locus of inventive work shifted from independent inventors and small shops to large corporate research and development (R&D) labs. Invention came in-house. Second, patent rules and doctrines adjusted accordingly. The conception of an individual patent shifted. No longer the nucleus around which a firm or business was formed, the individual patent became just one chip in a much larger game of corporate strategy. In-house R&D, together with patents acquired during mergers, produced large patent portfolios. Many of the patents in these portfolios lay dormant, waiting for technology to change course, or for a rival to infringe. Patents became corporate options that might or might not pay off. The legal system had to adjust to this, and it did, most notably in the *Continental Paper Bag* case of 1908 (see later in this chapter).

The second major adjustment in the law concerned patent ownership. Given the strong traditions of "shop culture," and the Founding era imprint favoring dispersed, small owners, patent law at first chafed against the logic of corporatization. Though post-grant ordering was common (as we saw in Chapters 2 and 3), initial ownership under patent rules went to the individual inventor. Yet the imperatives of corporatization pushed hard in the direction of centralized ownership and control: that is, toward corporate ownership. Slowly, over the period covered in this chapter, centralization won out.[2] A series of changes in patent law doctrine made corporate ownership the norm. While some saw in this the crushing of the individual inventor, from the Chandlerian point of view it all made sense.[3] Individualistic property claims, held by dispersed inventors, had the potential to undermine the smooth operation of the vertically integrated, multi-division firm. Some countries – notably Germany, and the Asian countries that borrowed from the German civil law tradition – initiated a parallel system of employee compensation, allowing for

[1] See Section 4.3.1.1.

[2] The best account of this process is in a book written by one of my Berkeley colleagues: Catherine L. Fisk, Working Knowledge: Employee Innovation and the Rise of Corporate Intellectual Property, 1800–1930 (Chapel Hill: University of North Carolina Press, 2009), discussed in this chapter.

[3] See Eric S. Hintz, American Independent Inventors in an Era of Corporate R&D (Boston: MIT Press, 2021) 4 ("[I]ndividual post-heroic [i.e., post-Morse, Edison, Bell] inventors were not supplanted by corporate R&D labs but instead persisted alongside them as an important, though less visible, source of inventions.").

centralized ownership with equitable employee compensation.[4] But the United States eschewed this path. As a consequence, one continuing legacy of the era of corporatization is the extreme pro-employer nature of invention ownership rules.

Along with these major changes came a host of smaller, incremental changes in the administration of patent law. The Patent Office fairly quickly acquiesced to the new dominance of the in-house R&D division. Though continuing to serve independent inventors and small firms, the Office was often caught between their interests and those of the large corporate world. The latter usually won out when the stakes were high. At the same time the Patent Office was adapting to corporate R&D, the work lives of the lawyers and patent agents who filed and prosecuted patents were changing too. They were undergoing what sociologists call the process of professionalization. Along with other engineering and technical specialties, the period 1880–1920 witnessed the emergence of numerous new professional organizations that cultivated norms and solidified professional identities in important ways. Many of these changes are reflected in the pages of the pre-eminent patent law professional journal, the Journal of the Patent Office Society, which was founded in 1917. Through its earliest years we can see the emergence of a more technocratic, bureaucratized Patent Office, patent bar, and patent practice generally.

4.1 ECONOMIC TRENDS, 1880–1920

The founding impulse in favor of practical new technologies gathered steam (so to speak) during the period economic historians refer to as "the long nineteenth century."[5] Patent law in the nineteenth century, as exemplified by the "paper patent" doctrine described in this chapter, is a perfect embodiment of J. Willard Hurst's idea that legal policy in this era was directed to a "release of creative energy."[6] Paper patents were those describing inventions that had not actually been implemented, and they were strongly disfavored. In this field Hurst's "active release" formulation meant that the law privileged technology immediately applied to industry, and yielding observable economic activity. When patents were placed on the

[4] Under these employee compensation regulations, a government board awards monetary payments for employees who make exemplary inventions. These awards do not disturb a large employer company's ownership of any resulting patents. See, e.g., Sebastian Wündisch, *Employee-Inventors Compensation In Germany: Burden or Incentive?*, 52 les Nouvelles – Journal of the Licensing Executive Society (No. 3, June 2017), earlier version available at https://papers.ssrn.com/sol3/papers.cfm?abstract_id=2961884; Stephen Yang, *Service Invention In China: Current Provisions & Proposed Changes*, 52 les Nouvelles – Journal of the Licensing Executive Society (No. 3, June 2017), earlier version available at https://papers.ssrn.com/sol3/papers.cfm?abstract_id=2961862.

[5] Meaning, roughly, 1790–1920. See, e.g., Zorina Khan, The Democratization of Invention: Patents and Copyrights in American Economic Development, 1790–1920 (Cambridge: Cambridge University Press, 2009).

[6] J. Willard Hurst, Law and the Conditions of Freedom in the Nineteenth-Century United States (1956), at p. 6.

shelf, contributing nothing to actual economic activity, or worse, slowing it down by providing an excuse for rent-seeking litigation, they were in many cases interpreted narrowly so as not to interfere with legitimate economic activity.

Figures 4.1–4.3 document the rise in corporate patent ownership and enforcement between 1810 and 1950. Notice the rapid "corporatization" between 1870 and 1910.

The graph in Figure 4.4 shows the percentage of all patent cases in which one or more parties were corporations, in ten-year intervals from 1810 to 1950. Data is from Westlaw.

Figure 4.5 shows the percentage of all patent-related cases in which the plaintiff was a corporation. In most such cases this means the patent owner is a corporation. But in some cases, for example, declaratory judgment actions, this may not be true.

Figure 4.6 takes all patent cases where one or more parties are corporations and shows the percentage of them in which the plaintiff (and presumptive patent owner) is a corporation. It shows that where corporate parties are involved in patent litigation, the patent owner is very likely to be a corporation.

So much for aggregate statistics. They show the rise of corporations as the predominant holders and enforcers of patents. But how exactly did businesspeople use patents in the age of corporatization? What role did they play in the new business organizations and corporate strategies of the 1880–1920 period? How

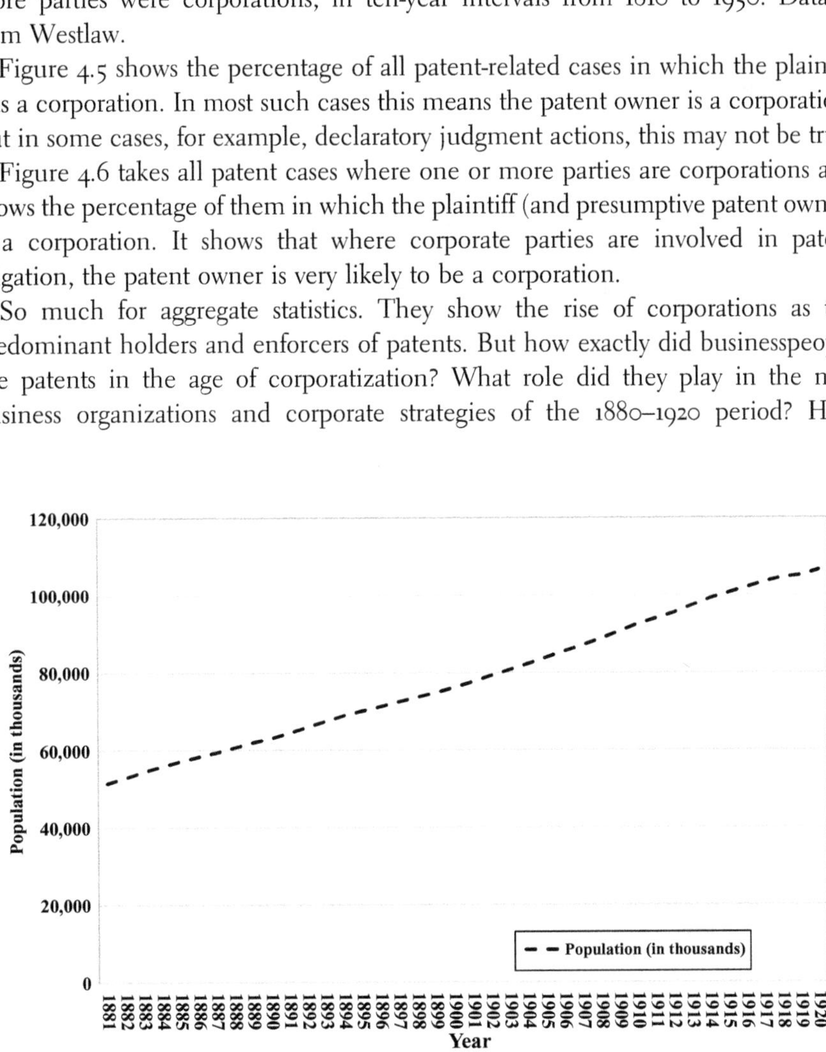

Data Source: Samuel H. Williamson, 'What Was the U.S. GDP Then?' MeasuringWorth, 2020. www.measuringworth.com/datasets/usgdp/result.php

FIGURE 4.1. US population, 1880–1920

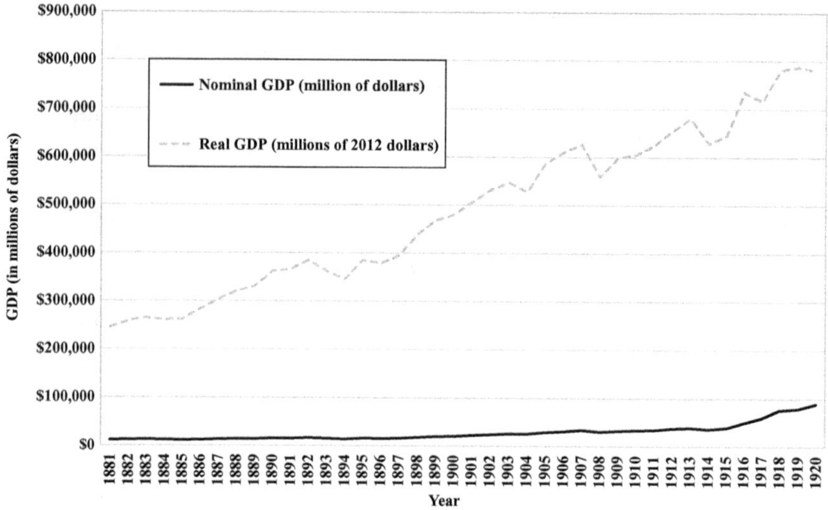

Data Source: Samuel H. Williamson, 'What Was the U.S. GDP Then?' MeasuringWorth, 2020. www.measuringworth.com/datasets/usgdp/result.php

FIGURE 4.2. Real GDP growth, 1880–1920

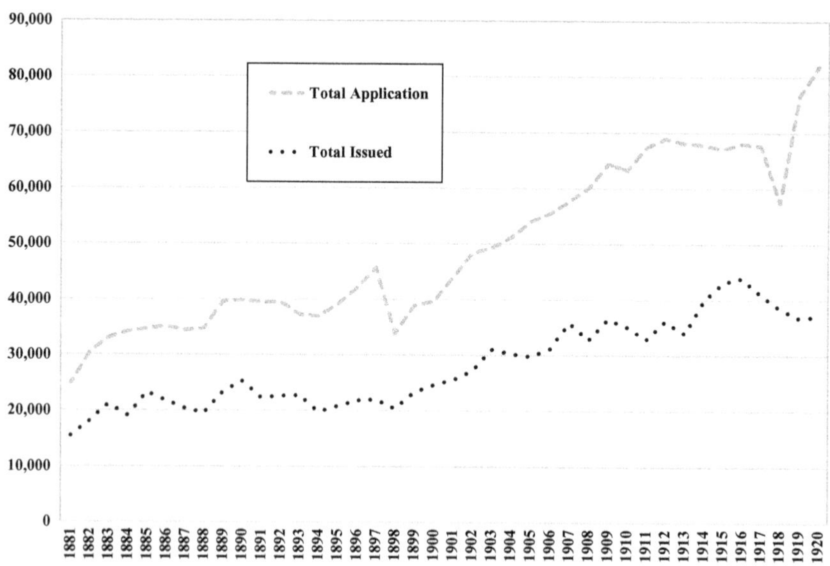

FIGURE 4.3. Patent applications and grants, 1881–1920

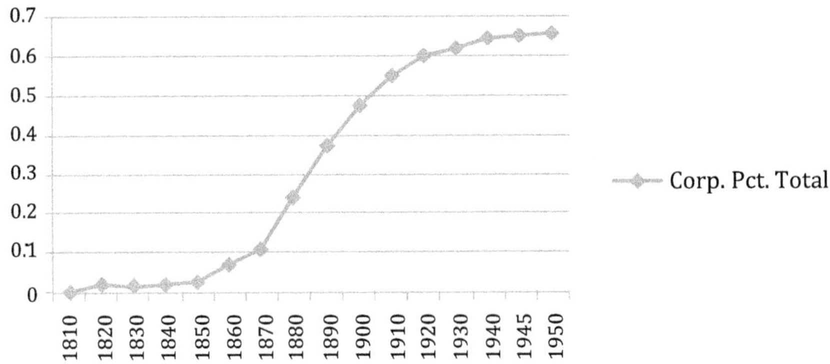

FIGURE 4.4. Corporate share of patent litigation

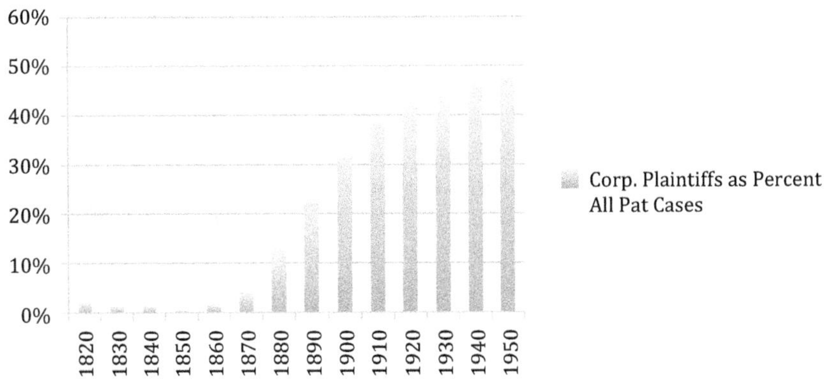

FIGURE 4.5. Corporate plaintiffs as a percentage of all cases

successfully did patents contribute to the goal Hurst identifies as central to nineteenth century American legal sensibilities – economic growth? That all comes next.

4.2 PATENTS IN BUSINESS ORGANIZATIONS, 1880–1920: FORMATIVE MOMENTS, CORPORATE R&D LABS, AND NEW FIRM ENTRY

The 1880–1920 period saw a fundamental transformation in the use of patents by business firms. Through about 1870, as we have seen, it was common for a single patent or small group of patents to form the nucleus around which a firm was built. Even with the trend away from single patents defining a discrete product market,

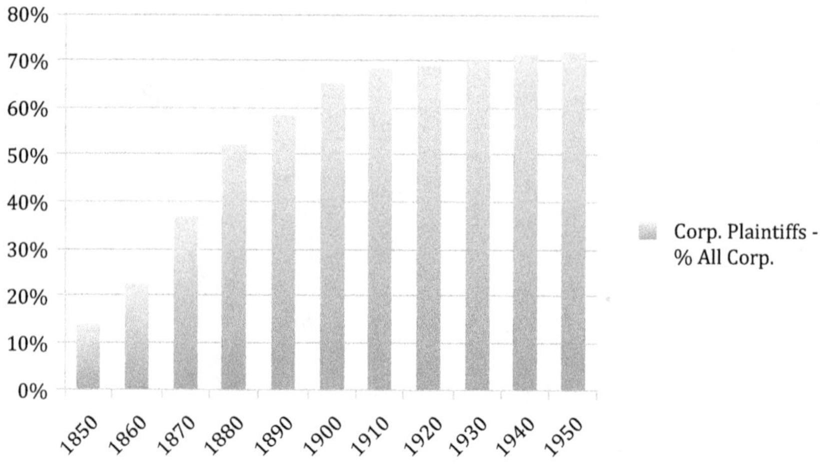

FIGURE 4.6. Percentage of corporate cases where patent owner is a corporation

patents over design variations and product features were considered core assets of many firms. Fairbanks Scales, discussed at length in Chapter 3, serve as a useful example. But with the rise of massive companies of unprecedented scale, this changed. The core of the new behemoth firms was their huge investments in capital assets, in service of vertical integration and the end of semi-regionalized production as practiced by Fairbanks Scale. In network industries, massive single-firm investments made possible integrated, "end to end" service.[7] In power generation and

[7] This was true outside of the electrical industries, but also outside them. John D. Rockefeller's Standard Oil integrated crude oil extraction, oil refining, gasoline distribution and marketing, and retail gasoline sales. See Ron Chernow, Titan: The Life of John D. Rockefeller, Sr. (New York: Vintage Press, 2nd ed., 2004), at p. 288 ("[John D.] Rockefeller created the model for the vertically-integrated oil giants that would straddle the globe in the twentieth century."). And as historian Christopher Beauchamp emphasizes in his masterful history of the Bell telephone patents,

> The success of companies such as the Singer sewing machine enterprise and Cyrus McCormick's harvester business rested heavily on their construction of marketing organizations, which eventually included branch offices and a salaried sales force. Like other companies formed to commercialize new inventions, these firms had begun by selling through licensed agents – a strategy that mitigated capital shortage and allowed rapid progress to market for what was, after all, a time-limited intellectual property asset. As the patent-holding companies gained their feet, however, they discovered the advantages of more integrated sales channels … By the 1880s, centralized sales organizations had become de rigeur for the leading suppliers of new business machines like cash registers and typewriters, as well as for the makers of producer goods like elevators and electrical equipment.

Christopher Beauchamp, Invented by Law: Alexander Graham Bell and the Patent That Changed America (Cambridge, MA: Harvard University Press, 2015), at p. 172.

telephony, it is plausible to imagine modular designs permitting competition among service segments. But both engineering imperatives and the rapidly emerging ethos of big business militated against modularity. What emerges instead was vertically integrated, centralized control by single corporations. In the new world of large "systems" companies, patents were by themselves no longer dominant assets.

But that does not mean they were not important. They were – as strategic tokens that could be deployed skillfully on the bigger game board. At crucial stages in the evolution of the new electrical industries, patents conferred decisive leverage. They protected against entry in various industry segments, or at any rate raised the cost of entry. They undermined the advantages of adversaries. And they created a tangled ownership picture, which provided a strong impetus to resolve the mess through the simple expedient of corporate mergers. This push toward resolution by consolidation was in the end the greatest contribution of patents to the new, much more complex, landscape of the American business enterprise.

4.2.1 *Patents and Large Enterprise Formation: AT&T and GE*

For American Telephone and Telegraph and General Electric, patents were instrumental at the formative stage as bargaining chips among the smaller constituent firms that merged to create the new behemoths. The patent holdings of the constituent firms played into bargaining over ownership shares in the new, integrated companies. In forming General Electric, two constituent companies, Thomson-Houston and Edison General Electric, were the main parties to the merger, with a few smaller companies thrown in. For AT&T, it was largely Bell Telephone, Western Union, and some smaller companies that pooled their assets to form what came to be known as "the Bell system," the new phone behemoth. In each case the patent holdings of the merging firms helped determine the ownership share each received at the formation of the integrated firm (GE or AT&T). A merging firm's patent portfolio served as a rough gauge of its relative contribution to the backbone technologies of the new industry. Portfolios thus translated, indirectly and only partly, into ownership shares in the integrated company formed by the merger.

4.2.1.1 AT&T

The predecessor to AT&T, Bell Telephone, began life with a corporate structure typical of nineteenth-century enterprise based on new technologies. It was organized around two basic patents, granted to Alexander Graham Bell in 1876 and 1877.[8] These patents served as the hub around which was built a complex web of regional

[8] US Patent 174,465, "Improvements in Telegraphy," filed February 14, 1876, issued March 7, 1876; and US Patent 186,787, "Improvements in Electric Telephony," filed January 15, 1877, issued January 30, 1877.

associates. These associates differed from the earlier nineteenth-century model, however. They were licensees under the patents, rather than exclusive regional assignees. And the central hub organization retained partial ownership interests in the associate firms, in the form of minority stockholdings. Thus, in its early years, Bell Telephone had some similarities to the regional-franchisee structure common in the early nineteenth century. But there were differences too – harbingers.

The regional affiliates were themselves corporations. The corporate form worked big changes compared to past practices. To grow a complex business with national scope, it was no longer enough to divide a single patent among separate regional owners. To operate a telephone network, regional affiliates needed access to large sources of capital, far beyond the scale familiar from the earlier era of simple patent co-ownership with perhaps a partnership structure. And in any event Bell Telephone would want to limit its liability for issues generated in the different regions, another reason to avoid partnerships. In place of the old regional assignment scheme, Bell licensed patents to its regional affiliated corporations.

The flexibility of the corporate form allowed Bell to duplicate useful aspects of the older arrangement. In place of management through partnerships, Bell made minority equity investments in its regional affiliates. This gave Bell a voice in governance of those affiliates, replacing the simpler but more rigid co-ownership/partnership arrangement. For other investors in the regional companies, the corporate form facilitated the wide sale (and re-sale) of equity to many dispersed investors. These investors obtained a portion of the total assets and value of a company, in an amount proportional to the size of their stock holdings, as opposed to a fractional share of a single co-owned patent asset. And the market for equity was much larger and "thicker" than the old market for patent shares and regional patent rights.

Using all the tools and tactics made possible by the new corporate form of organization, the centralized Bell company reached its full level of control over basic telephone technology in 1879. In that year Bell settled a complex tangle of patent litigation with Western Union. The core of this litigation was a patent priority fight celebrated in the annals of American patent law. Elisha Gray and Alexander Graham Bell each filed applications for a basic telephone within hours of each other on the same day – Valentine's Day (February 14) of 1876.[9] Gray, working under contract with Western Union, had been exploring a way to conduct multiple, simultaneous telegraph transmissions. (Thomas Edison had worked on the same problem). Bell's Boston backers pushed him to also tackle this "multiplex" telegraph problem, but he resisted. As a teacher of deaf students, Bell had an intrinsic interest in the transmission and reception of the human voice, as opposed to telegraphy. In

[9] Given the date, it is ironic that several interested parties insisted that Bell had obtained a sweetheart deal from the Patent Office. These charges included some serious allegations of corruption. See Christopher Beauchamp, Invented by Law, at pp. 88–99. The allegations are reviewed and dismissed in the *Dolbear* case, see 126 U.S. 1, at 567–571.

any event, this potentially titanic battle, in the form of a priority contest between Gray and Bell, went out with a whimper when it was settled by the parties.[10]

The background of the settlement has more to do with finance and Gilded Age stock manipulation than invention or patents. The driving force was Jay Gould – operating the pulleys and levers of Wall Street in one of his famous investment gambits. Gould's real quarry this time was Western Union, the dominant telegraph company.[11] He saw the Bell company as a source of potential competition for Western Union and began making a play for the stock of Bell franchises. As historian Leonard Reich recounts,

> If he could gain control of Bell, Gould would be able to subject Western Union to competition from a combined telegraph-telephone system. Gould's position would be further enhanced, of course, if the courts decided the patent suit between Bell and Gray in Bell's favor. At this point Western Union's directors decided that it best served their interests to strengthen the Bell company in order to keep it from Gould's hands, receiving as much for their beneficence as possible, then retreating to their reasonably secure market for telegraphy. After considerable negotiation … Western Union agreed to … transfer its telephone-related patent rights to Bell. In return, Bell would … give Western Union 20% of its revenues while the contract remained in force.[12]

[10] Some of the facts appear in the famous case of *Dolbear* v. *American Bell Telephone Co.*, 126 U. S. 1 (1888), the only patent case in US history that occupies an entire volume in the U.S. Reports. The report is lengthy because it consolidates several challenges to Bell's basic patents, US Patent 174,465, "Improvements in Telegraphy," filed February 14, 1876, issued March 7, 1876; and US Patent 186,787, "Improvements in Electric Telephony," filed January 15, 1877, issued January 30, 1877. Several competitive phone companies had formed on the basis of earlier inventions by Amos Emerson Dolbear (a professor at the University of Kentucky, and later, Tufts College (now University), see http://dl.tufts.edu/catalog/tei/tufts:UA069.005.DO .00001/chapter/D00047), Daniel Drawbaugh (an inventor from rural Pennsylvania), and others; the backers of these companies hoped to either establish their licensor/champions (Dolbear, Drawbaugh, etc.) as the true claimant of the basic telephone patent or at least invalidate Bell's two basic patents. Both hopes were dashed in the course of the definitive 576-page Supreme Court ruling. For the best and most thorough account of the Bell priority issues, see Christopher Beauchamp, Invented by Law, Alexander Graham Bell and the Patent That Changed America, supra. For another failed attempt to invalidate the Bell patents on the basis of earlier "public use" evidence, see *American Bell Telephone Co.* v. *American Cushman Telephone Co.*, 35 F. 734, 742–743 (C.C.N.D. Ill. 1888) ("[The evidence] falls far short of establishing beyond reasonable doubt the fact that Dr. [S.D.] Cushman in 1851 invented the telephone [in Racine, Wisconsin]; that [what] was done by him must and should be treated as, at best, only an abandoned experiment.").

[11] Federal Communications Commission, Investigation of the Telephone Industry in the United States, Pursuant to Public Resolution No. 8, 74th Congress (Washington, DC: Gov't Printing Office, 1939), available at www.archive.org (https://ia801608.us.archive.org/0/items/InvestigationOfTheTelephoneIndustry/Investigation_of_the_Telephone_Industry .pdf), at p. 125 (describing Gould's tactics).

[12] Leonard S. Reich, The Making of American Industrial Research: Science and Business at GE and Bell, 1876–1926 (Cambridge: Cambridge University Press, 1985), at p. 134.

The machinations of Gilded Age finance drove the deal. But Western Union's patent holdings drove the *terms* of the deal. This transaction established a pattern that was repeated in many forms throughout the late nineteenth and early twentieth century. Patent holdings served as bargaining chips in a bigger strategic game.

PATENTS AND PATENT STRATEGY AT AT&T The unified Bell structure that emerged from the Western Union settlement held steady during the early "monopoly period" of the industry, and then weakened considerably after expiration of the basic Bell patents in 1894. An effort to extend the dominant patent era failed when some late-issuing patents were construed narrowly by the courts.[13] So began the period of often intense competition between the original, centralized Bell entity and a host of smaller regional entrants, called independents. This period saw Bell's market share fall, and along with it, the price of phone equipment and service.

But Bell saw it coming. The company hatched a strategy that incorporated patents:

> One way in which Bell did prepare for this inevitable competition was to acquire patents on every possible improvement to telephony. In 1881, [Boston financier William H.] Forbes and the board of directors approved establishment of the Electrical and Patent Department [at Bell Telephone], which would conduct development work on telephone transmission and switching systems as well as evaluate the importance of outside inventions. In 1884 the Bell firm also put Thomas Edison on retainer and acquired an option on any telephone inventions he might make. During the monopoly period, inventors had no sure way to exploit their patents other than selling rights to Bell; in this way the company collected 900 telephone-related patents by 1894.[14]

For insight into this post-monopoly strategy, consider an invention by the inventor Hilborne Roosevelt (cousin to future Presidents Theodore and Franklin D.). Roosevelt the inventor was primarily interested in electric pipe organs; he founded one of the first electric-action organ manufacturers and helped build a number of the largest pipe organs ever constructed.[15] But as with so many inventors of the period, he was interested in telephony as well. In 1879 he was issued a patent on a

[13] Ibid., at p. 138.

[14] Ibid., at p. 137. Some inventive contributors to the development of e-commerce software may face a similar problem in the 2020s. Extreme concentration can create a monopsony market for patents and innovative technologies: with only one feasible buyer (Bell after 1890, companies such as Amazon.com in 2022) profits go down for "outside" inventors and contributors who must sell their ideas to the dominant firm. Research may tend to become overly concentrated in the dominant firm – cutting off the flow of fresh, outside ideas, potentially leading to stagnation. See Chapter 6.

[15] See Organ Historical Society, OHS Pipe Organ Database, entries for Hilborne Roosevelt and Roosevelt Organ Works [Hilborne Roosevelt Organs], available at www.pipeorgandatabase.org. See also US Patent 340,461, "Cabinet Pipe-Organ," issued to Hilborne Roosevelt and Charles S. Haskell, issued April 20, 1886.

"Telephone Switch," which was a mechanism that cut the phone connection when the caller was finished with the call. Roosevelt's design used the weight of the mouthpiece, hanging from the phone speaker cord, to pull down on a lever that broke the electrical connection used to transmit the call. Figure 4.7 shows the basic idea.

Roosevelt's patent was acquired by Western Electric, the exclusive manufacturing supplier to Bell Telephone, and later a division of AT&T. Bell asserted the patent against a company called Western Telephone Construction Company ("Western Construction," no relation to Western Electric), which was one of the earliest and largest suppliers of phone equipment to the independent Bell competitors. Western Construction was, at least as of 1898, using a design similar to Rooselvelt's for breaking a phone call connection: the familiar switch hook, a metal piece from which the phone mouthpiece was hung. As with the Western Electric Roosevelt device, the weight of the mouthpiece engaged a lever that cut the circuit. A typical

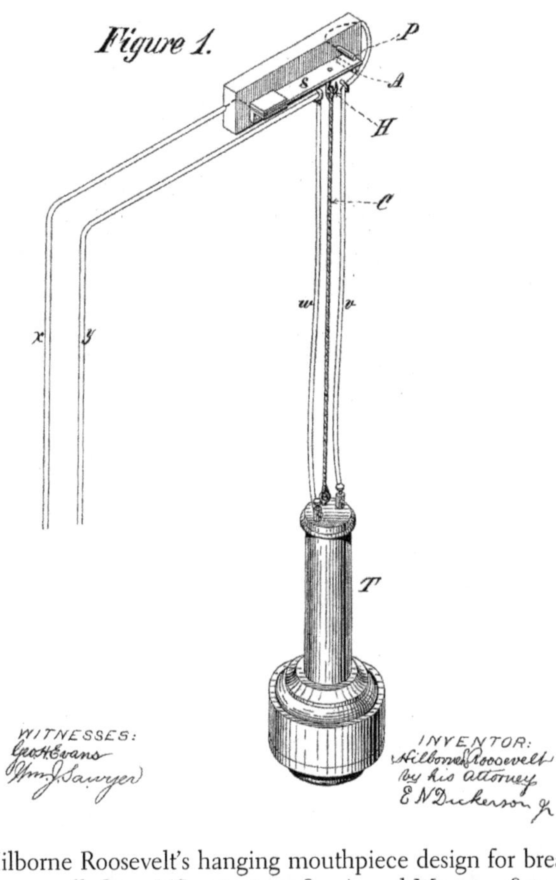

FIGURE 4.7. Hilborne Roosevelt's hanging mouthpiece design for breaking a circuit and ending a phone call, from US patent 215,837 issued May 27, 1879

FIGURE 4.8. Western Telephone Construction phone from 1898, switch hook holding hanging mouthpiece on the left

Western Construction phone from its 1898 catalogue shows the switch hook on the left side (Figure 4.8).

Western Electric lost the infringement suit against Western Construction. Judge Grosscup of the District Court in Chicago wrote:

> I feel myself compelled . . . to hold that his patent is self-limited to such mechanism as [described in the patent specification] . . . In the defendants' mechanism, when the connection is closed, the receiver must be hung upon a fork, – a prescribed manual act on the part of the operator; in complainant's, it is dropped on its cord, thus avoiding this otherwise definite manual act . . . I recognize that [Western Construction's] conception of changing back and forth the switches, by virtue of the resting and lifting of the telephone upon the forks, is a close copy of Roosevelt's conception, and that perhaps his claims, standing apart from his description, are broad enough to cover the incidental deviations. But, after all, the main purpose of the invention must control the scope of the claims, and such purposes certainly did not include the defendants' mechanism.[16]

The Seventh Circuit affirmed in a cursory opinion.[17]

16 *Western Electric Co.* v. *Western Telephone Construction Co.*, 79 F. 959, 961 (C.C.N.D. Ill. 1897), aff'd, 92 F. 181 (7th Cir. 1899). This opinion, incidentally, perfectly fits the prevailing interpretive style of its era. The emphasis on the inventive contribution, or technological context, of the subject invention, rather than on the linguistic context of the words of the claim (as is current practice), marks this as a quintessentially nineteenth century patent decision. See Robert P. Merges and John F. Duffy, Patent Law and Policy: Cases and Materials (Charlottesville, VA: Carolina Academic Press, 8th ed., 2021), at pp. 676–680 (comparing technological context approach, as seen especially in the patent law decisions of Judge Learned Hand, with present-day formalist, textualist approach).

17 *Western Elec. Co.* v. *Western Telephone Construction Co.*, 92 F. 181, 186 (7th Cir. 1899) ("No claim of the patent can fairly be given a construction which would include either form of apparatus manufactured by the appellees [Western Construction]. The decree below is therefore affirmed.").

Though this case was not a winner,[18] it helped fulfill the overall strategy of Western Electric and Bell. The basic idea was to use the Western/Bell patent portfolio to prevent the independents from becoming comfortable. The litigation itself was the primary object; winning lawsuits would be considered icing on the cake. This was spelled out in Bell's Annual Report for 1894. There Frederick Fish, chief Bell patent lawyer (and master player in the new era of big company patent strategy), explained things this way:

> The policy of bringing suit for infringement on apparatus patents is an excellent one because it keeps the concerns which attempt opposition [i.e., the independents] in a nervous and excited condition since they never know where the next attack may be made, and since it keeps them all the time changing their machines and causes them ultimately, in order that they may not be sued, to adopt inefficient forms of apparatus.[19]

The blatant deployment of patents as part of a pressure campaign may not be laudable. In later years it might have qualified as an antitrust violation.[20] But it certainly shows one of the many ways Bell/Western Electric put its extensive patent portfolio into action to serve its strategic goals.

The independent companies tried to fight back. They surely understood that one effect of the Bell patent assertions was to sew fear and doubt among the independents and their potential customers. Buying equipment from an independent supplier (such as Western Telephone Construction, as described earlier) might well put an

[18] Federal Communications Commission, Investigation of the Telephone Industry in the United States, Pursuant to Public Resolution No. 8, 74th Congress (Washington, DC: Gov't Printing Office, 1939), available at www.archive.org (https://ia801608.us.archive.org/0/items/InvestigationOfTheTelephoneIndustry/Investigation_of_the_Telephone_Industry.pdf), at p. 134:

> [T]he Bell System placed the burden of attempting to prolong its patent monopoly on the Western Electric Co. This latter company brought suits for infringement against companies using telephone appliances such as switches, signalling apparatus, call boxes, etc. These suits extended over the period 1894 to 1911. In all, 74 suits were brought upon such patents, of which 5 were instituted by the American Bell Co. and 69 by the Western Electric Co. All of these suits did not come to a final decision. The attempt of the Western Electric Co. to prolong the Bell System's monopoly by means of suits for patent infringement did not meet with complete success.

[19] Leonard S. Reich, The Making of American Industrial Research, at pp. 138, 282 n. 16, quoting Testimony of Theodore N. Vail, President of Bell Telephone, in Federal Communications Commission Investigation, Exhibit 2112 [Investigation Final Report of 1939, from this Investigation].

[20] Under antitrust law developed long after these suits, there is a presumption that acquiring and asserting intellectual property rights is a legitimate business practice, but this may be rebutted by evidence that IP assertion is a cover or "pretext" for anticompetitive motives. See *Image Technical Services, Inc.* v. *Eastman Kodak Co.*, 125 F.3d 1195, 1219 (9th Cir. 1997) (use of patents to control copy machine repair market: "Neither the aims of intellectual property law, nor the antitrust laws justify allowing a monopolist to rely upon a pretextual business justification to mask anticompetitive conduct.").

independent phone service company in the position of a patent infringer – and therefore within Bell's sights.

Independents tried to offer relief from this threat. They did this in two ways: (1) by assuring buyers that all equipment purchased form Independent phone companies was independently designed and thus did not infringe Bell's patents; and (2) by promising to pay for their customer's defense in any patent infringement suit brought by Bell/Western Electric (i.e., an indemnification clause – a form of privately contracted lawsuit insurance policy). The Western Telephone Construction Company product catalogue from 1898 spells this out:

> The Company [Western Telephone Construction] regularly employs its own patent attorneys and experts, who are men of unquestionable ability and standing in this line of work. They are employed for the sole purpose of steering the course of this company, so as to avoid the many legal rocks which lie hidden in the general sea of ignorance of the patent question.
>
> That a piece of apparatus is manufactured by the Western Telephone Construction Company is in itself a sufficient guarantee that it is safe for any person to purchase and use it. We have taken this stand from the start, and have maintained it with increasing vigor as time advances.
>
> This Company enters in to a written agreement with the purchasers of its apparatus to manage and defend at its own cost, all suits which may be brought against purchasers by virtue of the use of the same, and to assume all responsibility in connection with such suits, and to pay all damage and expense that may accrue.[21]

Patent assertion remained an important aspect of the Bell strategy. So much so that the President of Bell Telephone from 1901 to 1907 was Frederick Fish, the quintessential Gilded Age patent lawyer and strategist.[22] AT&T's independent competitors were successful in creating a "patent safe zone" for a time. But eventually, the independents were absorbed into the growing AT&T network. This engulfment strategy originated with another Gilded Age legend, J. P. Morgan. To finance its fight for market share with the regional entrants, and to skirt Massachusetts statutory limits on corporate capitalization, AT&T (which became the master parent company in 1885) issued a series of bonds. When growing competition made

[21] Western Telephone Construction Company, 1898 Catalogue, available at Hagley Museum Online Collection, https://digital.hagley.org/I20091118_059, at p. 10. Indemnification from patent risk as a customer service is still used as a strategic tactic. See "Why Microsoft offers uncapped indemnification for open source in Azure," November 8, 2017, available at https://azure.microsoft.com/en-us/blog/why-microsoft-offers-uncapped-indemnification-for-open-source-in-azure/ (Microsoft customer indemnification against patent infringement suits for users of its Azure open source cloud software program). It is worth pointing out that the Independents' promise that all their devices were developed themselves was not, and still is not, a defense to patent infringement.

[22] See David Noble, America by Design (Cambridge, MA: MIT Press, 1977), at p. 9 (Fish was "one of the country's leading patent attorneys" who became President of Bell "largely as a result of his prowess in handling that company's patent cases").

stockholders jittery, Morgan saw an opportunity. Amid the chaos of a declining share price and undersubscribed bond issues, Morgan snapped up a large share of the bonds. He had AT&T reincorporated under New York State's more liberal general incorporation law; converted the bonds into AT&T stock; and took over the newly recapitalized company. His first move after gaining control in 1907 was to install an old telephone pioneer and ally as President of AT&T, Theodore Vail. It was not too long before the newly constituted AT&T decisively ended the era of competition and initiated the long period that it always insisted was its "natural monopoly" destiny.

BIRTH OF AT&T CORPORATE R&D The post-monopoly Bell system, controlled now by a rejuvenated AT&T, achieved its monopoly through a long series of systematic maneuvers. Each remaining regional operator and independent phone company was slowly absorbed into the parent company, AT&T. In the end, Theodore Vail made good on his pet slogan, "One policy, one system, universal service." Once the challenge from parallel operating companies was removed, the only remaining threat was some as yet unknown technology wielded by some future competitor. To protect against that, Vail charged the Bell Research Lab with remaining at the forefront of research on telephony and related equipment. The birth of what became the famous Bell Labs was therefore rooted in a defensive motive: Keeping up with all things telephone-related would protect Vail's cherished monopoly from ever being outflanked by something unforeseen.

Even well before 1907, Bell executives thought in terms of protecting or defending the company's revenue streams and lines of business:

> The immediate objective of the Bell group [between 1875 and 1881] was to "occupy the field," an especially important objective in its competition with Western Union over dominance of the field of telephony, prior to the execution of the agreement late in 1879. After this objective was attained it was protected through the Bell Co.'s activities in attempting to buy or control important patents and, as [President Theodore] Vail stated it, of surrounding itself with everything that would afford protection, including knowledge of the business, as well as patent control of all the kinds of auxiliary apparatus necessary for development of the business.[23]

But after the Western Union settlement, and prior to 1907, much of the acquired knowledge related to engineering and optimization of existing equipment. A comprehensive government report on Bell/AT&T prepared later said:

> Prior to 1907 little attention had been given to what came to be known later as "fundamental research." Acquisitions of controlling patents were made through the patent department from sources external to the Bell System. The policy rather was

[23] Federal Communications Commission, Investigation of the Telephone Industry (1939), at p. 181.

> for technical activities to extend long-distance service and to aid in the fight against competition; to design and improve apparatus in its more minor details; and in general to attempt to meet all competitive offers of telephone service of improved quality, at lower cost and in greatly increased quantity.[24]

This began to change around 1910, with the christening of the Research Branch.[25] This Branch, a new corporate division, immediately began hiring more scientists with university graduate training,[26] and the term "fundamental research" began to creep into the AT&T lexicon. As the Chief Engineer in charge of the newly constituted Research Division put it in 1911,

> As soon as the research branch was established, work on the telephone-repeater problem [i.e., research on telephone line amplifiers, important for long distance voice transmission] was taken up on a comprehensive scale ... The research work in this case has been undertaken on the broadest possible lines ... During the last 10 or 15 years that branch of physics which forms a part of electrical science has made wonderful advances. In connection with many of these advances practical applications have from time to time been suggested by engineers and physicists ... Research work is being conducted covering the phenomena involved in the cases which seem most likely to have practical application to the repeater problem. It is yet too soon to report as to the commercial results of this study, but with reference to the proposition as a whole, it should be stated that here is a field of large possibility which will unquestionably pay liberally for whatever investigations may be made ... [27]

Research on a commercially useful repeater led to the first successful high-volume signal amplification device manufactured in bulk quantities. Proof of the concept came as part of the Panama-Pacific Exposition of 1915 (Figure 4.9).[28] During the Exposition, Alexander Graham Bell himself placed a trans-continental phone call

[24] Ibid., at pp. 184–185.

[25] Leonard S. Reich, The Making of American Industrial Research, at p. 159.

[26] Federal Communications Commission, Investigation of the Telephone Industry (1939), at p. 187 (quoting Report of Chief Engineer John J. Carty).

[27] Ibid., at p. 187 (quoting Report of Chief Engineer John J. Carty). The effort to develop a successful "repeater" melded the new science-based research with other established tactics. AT&T acquired the valuable "audion" (vacuum tube) patents from Professor Lee DeForest of Columbia University, which grew out of a research project on wireless communication that was a precursor to radio transmission. Leonard S. Reich, The Making of American Industrial Research, at p. 163. And members of the new Research Branch adapted a public domain filament developed in Germany as a crucial part of the signal repeater. See Ibid., at p. 163. All these tactics were combined to serve the basic purpose of the Research Branch: "research that would make sure Bell never had to tie in with other communications systems against its will and never lost its position of control in wired telephony." Ibid., at p. 165.

[28] This was a typical late nineteenth-, early twentieth-century culture and technology exposition, meant to showcase new technologies, commercial products, etc. This particular exposition had two additional purposes: to show the world that San Francisco was recovering from the devastating earthquake of 1906; and to highlight the relative ease of travel to the west coast of the United States by way of the recently opened Panama Canal.

FIGURE 4.9. The Palace of Fine Arts, San Francisco (architect: Bernard Maybeck), built for the Panama-Pacific Exposition, 1915, site of the first transcontinental phone call using AT&T's newly developed voice repeater circuits

from New York to San Francisco, where the Exposition was held (Figure 4.10). Reprising the legendary "first phone call" on his experimental apparatus in Boston in 1875 (when, after spilling acid, he said "Watson! Come here, I need you"), Bell placed the call to fellow phone pioneer and former assistant Thomas Watson. Watson's reply showed how far communication was ahead of transportation: "It will take me five days to get there this time!"

The phone call highlighted the success of the Research Branch. This success reverberated through not only AT&T but American industry generally. The advent of organized, centralized corporate R&D had pronounced effects on a number of areas – including patent strategy. In the old engineering departments, at AT&T and elsewhere, the search for technical solutions began with a known problem. One

FIGURE 4.10. Bell about to Call Watson, New York–San Francisco, January 24, 1915
Source: Scientific American. Copyright expired.

piece of equipment was experiencing problems in light of new demands on it; or a new way of performing a conventional task was needed in light of the demand for higher speeds or increased durability. Engineers tried different solutions, until the identified problem was solved. The AT&T research lab operated on a different principle. Here the idea was to conduct scientific research on basic phenomena with the understanding that this would periodically lead to "practical applications." Research *began* with an interesting phenomenon; applications were expected to emerge. No longer was technical search aimed at a specific target, with the end use already in mind.

This meant that, even where practical applications did emerge, they were not necessarily ready to be immediately fitted into current operational systems. They might be *potential* applications, useful perhaps later if overall system requirements made them feasible. In this setting, patents were not always acquired to cover operational aspects of the telephone system. Inventions developed in the Research Branch might or might not end up finding their way into actual AT&T systems. It is better to think of them as options: rights over technology that might later have value. Holding them kept open numerous future paths of technology development. As described in the government report cited earlier,

> [I]t is a definite company policy to carry research activities to the point where they will "support" patent applications on all the available and known alternative methods of accomplishing a specific result. Obviously, it is not a company policy to develop all these alternative forms to the point where they may be exploited commercially through standardization, manufacture, and introduction in large

> quantities into the extensive telephone plant. This aspect of patent policy affords a further method of distinguishing between these two fields of activity [i.e., research and engineering], for research activity is shown to have certain objectives which are served as soon as patents have been obtained on all alternative methods. It is at this point in the technical process that a selection must be made from among the several available forms evolved in the research laboratory, whereupon only the form thus selected is exploited commercially through engineering development and standardization.[29]

This states quite clearly the relationship between the in-house corporate research lab and the rise of the strategic patent portfolio. This passage emphasizes the importance of stockpiling multiple patented solutions, so the best one can be chosen and implemented.[30] In future years, researchers, lawyers, and executives would pioneer other patent-related strategies to capitalize even on un-implemented patents, i.e., those that do not cover company products. But widespread industry licensing campaigns, the sale of patents on the "secondary market," and other patent activation tactics were still many years away in this early era.

4.2.2 *GE: Origins with Thomas Edison*

General Electric proper was formed in 1891 out of a merger of two major electrical power and lighting companies, Edison General Electric (EGE) and the Thomson-Houston Electric Company (T-H). As for EGE, its origins run through Menlo Park, New Jersey, site of the now-legendary research lab of Thomas Edison. When in 1900 GE, by that time far beyond Edison's personal influence, started one of the world's first corporate research labs, it was in some ways returning to its roots in Menlo Park.

Edison had little formal schooling; his classroom was the early telegraph industry, and the questing, curious group of electrical researchers that grew up around it. Edison was one of many ambitious, technically curious young people who gravitated toward a career in the exciting new field of telegraphy. While working as a telegrapher in Cincinnati in 1867, twenty-year-old Thomas Edison filled a notebook with different telegraph repeater designs, predecessors to the DeForest telephone

29 Federal Communications Commission, Investigation of the Telephone Industry (1939), at p. 180. See also M. D. Fagen, ed., A History of Engineering and Science in the Bell System: The Early Years (1875–1925) (Murray Hill, NY: Bell Telephone Laboratories, 1975); Lillian Hoddeson, *The Emergence of Basic Research in the Bell Telephone System, 1875–1915*, 22 Tech. & Cult. 512 (1981); and Neil H. Wasserman, From Invention to Innovation: Long-Distance Telephone Transmission at the Turn of the Century (Baltimore: Johns Hopkins University Press, 1985). It should be noted that a concerted plan to acquire patents so as to systematically foreclose competition might today in some cases raise antitrust concerns.

30 Scholars have recognized the utility of an options-oriented view of patents, see Christopher A. Cotropia, *Describing Patents as Real Options*, 34 J. Corp. L. 1127 (2009). Some have tried to squeeze patents into formal real options pricing models used by financial economists, but it is an awkward fit. Patents are options in a non-technical sense: instruments that permit flexibility in future decision making, preserving multiple alternative paths as time goes by.

repeater vacuum tube mentioned earlier. He also published a literature review on the topic in a widely read trade journal called *The Telegrapher*.[31] Two years later, Edison moved to New York City where he promptly invented several important improvements in the telegraph industry: the duplex (two messages at once), quadraplex (four), and printing telegraph (which kept a printed record of the transmitted code).[32] Beginning what became a lifelong practice, Edison aimed his inventive talent precisely where it would make the most money. In these years wealthy risk-seekers from Wall Street jousted vigorously for dominance in the telegraph industry. They were willing to pay a premium to get ahead or stay ahead in the quickly evolving telegraphy market; Edison profited. With the proceeds from his telegraph inventions, Edison moved to the quiet town of Menlo Park where he set up his famous research facility.

The Menlo Park lab was not a pure "idea factory," at least not primarily. More in the way of an incubator, Edison did not pursue a licensing strategy for his inventions. His goal was to build entire businesses around the kernel of his new technological advances. This was at least in part because outside of his telegraph and telephone work, Edison's research projects were conducted in unplowed fields. The technologies were so new there were no incumbent firms out there to license and develop them. Thus, after Menlo Park hatched the incandescent light bulb, it helped form an integrated company – power generation, distribution, and lighting – to exploit it. The research lab needed to invent not only the final product (light bulb) but the entire end-to-end solution required to get that bulb to light up. Later, Edison and the lab created the phonograph and promptly founded the Edison Phonograph Company (1888). To have something to play on the phonograph, Edison Records – one of the first record "labels" ever founded – was formed. After the invention of the continuous film-roll motion picture camera and viewer (the Kinetoscope) in 1891, companies were formed to produce the viewers and to make films for them (the first film studio).[33]

Because each invention in effect created a new industry, after creating each new technology Edison had to solve all manner of practical problems. Mass production, distribution, and marketing of new ideas were as much the province of Edison's team as were the inventions themselves – at least until the viability of each new industry had been established. After that, aided by the massive movement toward corporate integration, Edison could combine his companies with others. The newly

[31] Paul Israel, From Machine Shop to Industrial Laboratory: Telegraphy and the Changing Context of American Invention, 1830–1920 (Baltimore: Johns Hopkins University Press, 1002), at pp. 69, 71.

[32] Leonard S. Reich, The Making of American Industrial Research, at p. 43.

[33] See Library of Congress, "Collection: Inventing Entertainment: Inventing Entertainment: The Early Motion Pictures and Sound Recordings of the Edison Companies," available at www.loc.gov/collections/edison-company-motion-pictures-and-sound-recordings/articles-and-essays/history-of-edison-motion-pictures/origins-of-motion-pictures/.

merged entities then typically chose specialized professional managers, and Edison would remain as an influential founder, board member, and stockholder.

This need to in effect invent an entire industry with each major invention posed some stiff challenges. In the case of the light bulb, Edison grew his team of expert electrical researchers at Menlo Park at a rapid pace to solve each emergent problem as it came up. Menlo Park engineering/research employment went from fifteen in August of 1878 to thirty-five in mid-1879. By February of 1880, after the successful test of the pioneering Pearl Street power generation/distribution plant in New York City, the work force rose to sixty-four.[34] By mid-1886, Edison had replicated the Pearl Street success fifty-five times around the country, illuminating a total of 150,000 lights. At the beginning of 1888, total power plants were 121, and total lights served were 325,000.[35]

Edison was first with his specific business model – central power generation, lighting up incandescent light bulbs. But he was far from the lone inventor of the light bulb, and his companies were far from unique in the lighting field. A primary competitive technology in the 1870s and 1880s was arc lighting: a form of illumination that sent power through carbon rods or "pencils," generating light from the jump of current between two or more of the rods. One early champion of this technology was a pair of professor/inventors from MIT, Elihu Thomson and Edwin Houston, founders of the Thomson-Houston Electric Company (T-H) of Lynn, Massachusetts. The ever-fecund George Westinghouse of Pittsburgh (more on him below) was also in the game; by 1886 he was proving the superiority of alternating-current (AC) as the chief source of power. Under license from one French and one British inventor, and later Nikola Tesla, Westinghouse began building the all-important AC power transformers that allowed current to be generated, transmitted long-distance, then stepped down in voltage at a point nearby customers.[36]

Once again, patents and patent strategy had a hand in the consolidation of an important technology-based industry. Edison's multiple companies based on different components of electrical systems had in 1889 been combined into one omnibus organization called Edison General Electric (EGE). EGE's combined patent portfolio was powerful, given the Edison Lab's early entry in the field. But T-H had a broad, impressive portfolio of its own. Through astute acquisition of third-party patent rights,[37] and some sophisticated patents from in-house

[34] Robert Friedel and Paul Israel, with Bernard S. Finn, Edison's Electric Light: Biography of an Invention (New Brunswick, NJ: Rutgers University Press, 1987), at p. 146.

[35] Leonard S. Reich, The Making of American Industrial Research, at p. 46.

[36] George Westinghouse's first important invention was an improved air brake for railroad cars. It was only after cashing in on his railway patents did Westinghouse move into the electric power field. See infra, section B.3.a.

[37] See W. Bernard Carlson, *The Coordination of Business Organization and Technological Innovation within the Firm: A Case Study of the Thomson-Houston Electric Company of the 1880s*, in Naomi R. Lamoreaux and Daniel M.G. Raff, eds., Coordination and Information:

research,[38] T-H amassed a portfolio that stood directly in the path of EGE's expansion plans:

> T-H gained such a strong patent position that EGE could not manufacture state-of-the-art traction [electric railway], lighting or power equipment without fear of infringement suits or injunctions. Of course, T-H faced the same threat from EGE ... With the exception of electric traction, the two rivals' capabilities and interests seemed to be complementary: EGE in DC [direct current power], T-H in AC; EGE in incandescent lamps, T-H in arcs; EGE with extensive manufacturing facilities, T-H with a strong sales organization and an aggressive, efficient management.[39]

The resulting merger to form GE in June of 1892 seems all but inevitable, coming as it did on the cusp of an era described as "the great merger movement."[40] But despite the scope of the new GE, it was eight more years before the research lab was established. And unlike at Bell/AT&T, senior executives at GE did not uniformly support the idea of corporate scientific research.

As was typical of the era, problem-solving in the newly merged firm took place where it always had: in production facilities and testing labs connected to the various operating divisions. The former T-H President who led GE after the merger,

Historical Perspectives on the Organization of Enterprise (Chicago: University of Chicago Press, 1995), at pp. 55, 81:

> To reduce the threat of patent litigation, [Elihu] Thomson helped the company [T-H] arrange a patent-sharing agreement with Westinghouse ... After several meetings, officials from Thomson-Houston and Westinghouse reached an agreement in August 1887. In return for a license to sell Thomson-Houston arc-lighting equipment, Westinghouse allowed Thomson-Houston to manufacture AC systems without fear of infringing the Westinghouse AC distribution patent. [Though the agreement terminated within 2 years because the relevant patents were declared invalid, it gave T-H time to improve its knowledge of AC equipment.]

38 Acquired strategically to work around Westinghouse's strong patent position:

> Knowing that a patent-sharing agreement [with Westinghouse] could be only a temporary expedient, Thomson next initiated a new strategy to bypass the Westinghouse patent. Because Westinghouse controlled the right to the broad principle of using transformers for distribution, Thomson filed patents in 1888 on the designs of the most efficient transformers. Thus, the Westinghouse company would be unable to use its rights to apply the broad principle, because all of the best transformer designs would be owned by Thomson-Houston. In pursuing that strategy, Thomson filed patents for transformers with laminated cores of different shapes, and he began using an oil insulation bath.

See W. Bernard Carlson, *The Coordination of Business Organization and Technological Innovation within the Firm*, at p. 81. This is a class instance of the pioneer-improver scenario much studied by students of patent law and economics. See, e.g., Suzanne Scotchmer, Innovation and Incentives (Cambridge, MA: MIT Press, 2006); Mark A. Lemley, *The Economics of Improvement in Intellectual Property Law*, 75 Tex. L. Rev. 989 (1997).

39 Ibid., at p. 47.

40 Naomi Lamoreaux, The Great Merger Movement in American Business, 1895–1904 (Cambridge: Cambridge University Press, 1985).

Charles Coffin, was not technically trained (unlike the early executives at AT&T),[41] but even so it became obvious by 1900 that some sort of centralized research facility would be a good idea. It was in that year that GE's ace electrical researcher Charles P. Steinmetz[42] hired Willis Whitney to head up the newly formed GE Research Laboratory. Whitney had more than a bit of the absent-minded professor in his demeanor, but he did assemble what is often recognized as the first corporate-based scientific research organization.[43] After a few fits and starts, GE research grew into one of the most prominent of the early industrial research labs.[44] In time, both Steinmetz and Whitney won awards from major scientific organizations, recognizing that corporation-employed scientists had the capability to make important contributions in their research fields.[45]

The scientific prowess of the GE Research Lab was well established by the 1930s, which saw the first-ever Nobel Prize awarded to an industrial researcher, chemist Irving Langmuir.[46] But the inventive work behind Langmuir's prize reveals more

[41] Leonard S. Reich, The Making of American Industrial Research, at p. 51. After noting that Coffin's background was in the shoe manufacturing industry, Reich writes of Coffin's conservative attitude toward electrical innovations:

> GE produced far fewer innovations between 1892 and 1900 than had EGE or T-H individually in the years before the merger; it was also less innovative than many of its smaller competitors. Even as the economy picked up [after a financial panic in 1893] and GE sales rose to $16 million in 1888, $20 million in 1889, and $29 million in 1900, with concomitant increase in profits, President Coffin maintained his strongly conservative outlook.

[42] Steinmetz devised a brilliant mathematical model of AC power generation that revolutionized the theoretical basis of power supply. See Thomas P. Hughes, American Genesis: A Century of Invention and Technological Enthusiasm: 1870–1970 (New York: Viking Press, 1989), at pp. 161–164. Steinmetz's tenure at GE began before establishment of the research lab; he was originally hired into what was called the Calculating Division. Ibid.

[43] See George Wise, Willis R. Whitney, General Electric and the Origins of US Industrial Research (New York: Columbia University Press, 1985), at p. 1 :

> Whitney did as much as or more than any other single person to shape the institution we know today as industrial research. In 1900, there were a few dozen laboratories in American industry that employed professional scientists. None of them fit the description implied today by the term "industrial research": a place where scientists can contribute to the advance of science while they put science to work. Whitney consciously created such a laboratory, deliberately blending the traditions of the academic laboratories that he had been trained in [at MIT and Leipzig, Germany] with the realities he observed at the GE Works in Schenectady.

[44] See Alfred D. Chandler, *Book Review*, 20 J. Econ. Hist. 101 (1960) (reviewing Kendall Birr, Pioneering in Industrial Research: The Story of the General Electric Research Laboratory (Washington, DC: Public Affairs Press, 1957), at p. 101 ("General Electric was the first large American corporation to set up an organization to concentrate on fundamental research.").

[45] George Wise, A *New Role for Professional Scientists in Industry: Industrial Research at Research General Electric, 1900–1916*, Tech. & Cult. 21 (1980).

[46] Leonard S. Reich, *Edison, Coolidge, and Langmuir: Evolving Approaches to American Industrial Research*, 47 J. Econ. Hist. 341, 349 (1987) ("In 1932 Irving Langmuir won the Nobel Prize in chemistry for his research on physical processes at the surface of incandescent

than just a talented researcher working solo. The Prize rewarded work done in the 1920s on an advanced light bulb filament to replace the crude bamboo and other earlier organic materials. The goal was to develop a hardened and very thin titanium filament. This required a team of chemists, metallurgists, and die-makers schooled in advanced metal molds.[47] It was just the kind of research that fulfilled the early dreams of the Lab's founders: a cross-disciplinary team, each member at the cutting edge of his (later, his or her) field,[48] each contributing to a novel and synergistic whole. Cross-disciplinary teams such as this helped push corporate research well beyond the days of the individual inventor, working autonomously, often on problems affecting a range of industries. It also explains why the rules of employee invention ownership changed during this period: Individual employee contributions were now joined in a collaborative whole, making it difficult (and usually inefficient) to allow each contributor to retain individual patent rights over their particular contribution.[49]

* * * *

For firms like GE and Bell, as well as non-electrical firms that grew organically into behemoths, such as DuPont Chemical, massive scale and scope meant massive revenue streams. Senior managers recognized almost immediately that revenue sources had to be protected for these new large corporations to maintain their dominant positions. Out of this motive to protect future revenue came the impetus to form large company-owned research labs. The labs were also a result of the greater sophistication of the electrical industries; as mentioned, the hands-on experience of machinists in the shop was no longer enough to generate new improvements

filaments, the first time that an American industrial scientist had achieved the honor. More important for GE, Langmuir acquired 63 U.S. patents over the course of his career, many of great commercial value.").

47 See Alfred D. Chandler, *Book Review of Kendall Birr*, at pp. 101–102:

> Work in one field [at the GE Research Lab] often led quite unexpectedly to the development of new products in other areas. Investigations in the incandescent lamp technology brought the development of the high vacuum electron tube and the x-ray tube. Research on filament-drawing dies resulted in cemented tungsten carbide, which helped revolutionize the machine tool industry and brought General Electric into still another line of business. The study of the arc in switches demonstrated new facts about welding arcs and in time had General Electric making acetylene. Projects to improve insulating materials led the company into the production of a variety of goods based on alkyd resins in the 1920's and silicone resins in the 1930's.

48 Leonard S. Reich, *Irving Langmuir and the Pursuit of Science and Technology in the Corporate Environment*, 24 Tech. & Cult. 199, 200 (1983):

> Irving Langmuir received a B.S. in metallurgical engineering before acquiring his Ph.D. in physical chemistry, and William Coolidge, his well-known contemporary at GE, began with a B.S. in electrical engineering, then went on to a physics Ph.D. Many other researchers with formal training in only one area assimilated the outlook of complementary disciplines.

49 This doctrinal change is discussed in Section 4.3.

and inventions. Formal scientific training came more and more to be required for the improvement and advancement of these technologies. This was as true in the newly emerging chemical industry (as exemplified by DuPont) as in the electrical industries: telegraph, telephone, and power generation/transmission. By 1920, the locus of inventive work related to industrial products had for the most part moved out of the traditional workshop and into the corporate-owned R&D lab. Although a steady stream of inventions flowed from these labs – some quite innovative – in this context patents were initially a defensive tool. At least at the outset companies did research and stockpiled patents not so much to blaze new trails as to prevent being locked out of their own fertile pastures. Unforeseen innovations did come, later. But these were not the primary goal of the early labs. They were instead mostly unintended results of a primarily defensive strategy, at least at Bell/AT&T and GE.

4.2.3 *Patents and New Firm Entry*

With large-scale industry taking root in the 1880s and 1890s, entry into an established industry became more difficult. A new or small company with some good new technical ideas had to position itself carefully so as not to be crushed by large incumbent firms. Here patents played a crucial role. Without them, new process technologies or product features could be easily copied by existing big players – leaving the startup with no way to survive. Creating a lower-cost or higher-quality alternative to an established product component, or perfecting a more efficient production process, were entry strategies that could be assisted by patents.[50] In several cases – most notably the Westinghouse family of companies – the origin story begins with successful invention and robust patent protection. With this as a

[50] Early attention to patent portfolio building makes sense for many small entrants, because small firms must rely more on patent protection than large firms. This is due to their inability to recoup research costs through non-patent corporate strategies – strategies available only to larger firms. See Jonathan M. Barnett, Innovators, Firms, and Markets: The Organizational Logic of Intellectual Property (Oxford: Oxford University Press, 2021). For empirical evidence on the importance of patents (and especially a patent "win" in the first few years after entry), see Alberto Galasso and Mark Schankerman, *Patent Rights, Innovation, and Firm Exit*, 49 RAND J. Econ. 64 (2018) (empirical study of Federal Circuit cases from 1982 to 2010 shows that for small companies, a patent invalidation reduces future patenting by 50 percent and may be associated with eventual firm failure (exit); no similar effects for litigation outcomes involving large firms). Of course, in some industries, and for some firms, patents may not be necessary for effective entry. For a good overview, see, e.g., Daniel Jacob Hemel and Lisa Larrimore Ouellette, *Innovation Policy Pluralism*, 128 Yale L.J. 544 (2019). For an early statement, see Richard C. Levin, Alvin K. Klevorick, Richard R. Nelson, and Sidney G. Winter, *Appropriating the Returns from Industrial Research and Development*, 3 Brookings Pap. Econ. Activity 783 (1987). In this chapter, and the book as a whole, I necessarily emphasize patent-centric strategies – this being a history of patent law, not of overall innovation. But my emphasis should not be mistaken for a normative claim that patents are a net positive for the economy and society, or even that they are necessary for economic development. That is, as they say, beyond the scope of the present study. (And probably beyond the scope of present knowledge as well.)

lever, some new entrants themselves grew into large firms. The point is, in the era of extensive large-firm patent portfolios, entry was still possible, sometimes with help from a good set of patents in the hands of the new entrant. In this way, patent strategy became a game not just for the big firms. It was also necessary for new entrants to play as well.

4.2.3.1 Westinghouse

George Westinghouse was a multi-talented inventor who took his start as one of many outside contributors to the railroad industry. Unlike many who added improvements to steam engines, rail cars, and associated technologies, when Westinghouse hit on a good idea, he did not simply sell it to the Pennsylvania Railroad or another established rail line. He started a company – a very successful one, and one of many he would go on to lead. Westinghouse's energies were directed to air brakes, the hydraulically operated braking systems that exerted massive force to help train engineers stop the ever-lengthening trains of the later nineteenth century. These were a revolutionary improvement over existing mechanical brakes, which were manually operated by a "brakeman" on each car, with the brakemen throwing a large lever that mechanically applied pressure to the wheels to slow them down. In contrast, the actuating power of the Westinghouse brake was a pressurized air supply line that ran the length of the train. In Westinghouse's earliest designs the air line constantly refreshed a pressurized reservoir in each rail car. When the engineer engaged the brake, the reservoir on each car was opened, and the pressurized air exerted hydraulic force on a mechanical brake attached to the train wheels.

Westinghouse's original air brake patent issued in April of 1869 – good timing, given the rapid post-War growth of American railroading. Immediately in the same year, he organized the Westinghouse Air Brake Company and installed himself as president. The success of the air brake provided the seed capital from which a rich and diversified corporate empire then grew. But Westinghouse and his team were not content to simply cash in on an original idea. They continued to improve on the original brake design, making a number of important refinements including an automatically-engaging brake and a redesigned valve system that allowed faster emergency stopping by drawing air both from each car's air reservoir and from the continuous line connecting all the cars. Figure 4.11 shows an illustration from Westinghouse's initial, breakthrough train brake.

Westinghouse eventually moved his air brake manufacturing out of Pittsburgh to nearby Wilmerding in 1889. By this time, the factory occupied over nine acres of buildings, and by 1905 it employed close to 3,000 people. It was estimated that in that year over 2,000 railway cars and 89,000 locomotives were equipped with the Westinghouse brake.[51]

The "triple-valve" at the heart of the advanced Westinghouse models was the subject of an important patent case in 1898, which serves as an excellent exemplar of

[51] Adventures in Power: A Fact History of Westinghouse (Pittsburgh, PA: Westinghouse Electric Corp., 1953), available at www.historicpittsburgh.org.

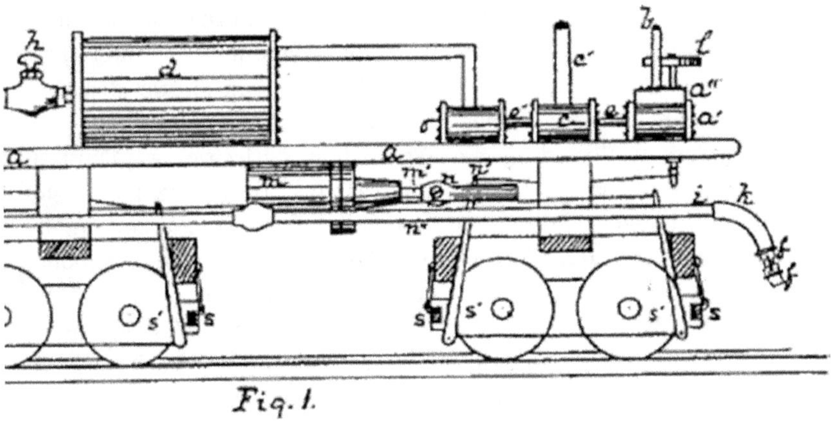

FIGURE 4.11. The Westinghouse Automatic Air Brake, from US patent RE5,504, July 29, 1873, reissued from original US patent 88,929, issued April 13, 1869

patent analysis in US courts in the late nineteenth and early twentieth century.[52] In addition to his wide-ranging inventive talents, and his superior team-building

[52] *Westinghouse* v. *Boyden Power Brake Co.*, 170 U.S. 537 (1898). This case held that a modified brake valve design, invented and patented by the rival Boyden Company, did not infringe one of Westinghouse's later patents on the triple valve. It was typical of an era when courts tried to identify the magnitude and significance of a patented invention when evaluating whether the patent was infringed:

> The Court noted that the literal wording of the Westinghouse patent could be read to cover Boyden's brake, since it included what could be described as a "triple valve." But it refused to find infringement on the ground that Boyden's was a significant contribution that took the invention outside the equitable bounds of the Westinghouse patent.

Robert P. Merges and Richard R. Nelson, *On the Complex Economics of Patent Scope*, 90 Colum. L. Rev. 839, 862–863 (1990). In the words of the Supreme Court opinion,

> We are induced to look with more favor upon th[e] [defendant's] device, not only because it is a novel one and a manifest departure from the principle of the Westinghouse patent, but because it solved at once in the simplest manner the problem of quick [braking] action, whereas the Westinghouse patent did not prove to be a success until certain additional members had been incorporated into it.

170 U.S. 537, at 572. The weighing of the merits of the patented invention and the item accused of infringement is a characteristic of patent infringement analysis in this era. (See supra this Chapter.) Note that Westinghouse's inventive genius was well recognized in other cases of the era; his *original* patent was widely lauded as a "pioneer patent," and so was given a very broad interpretation in infringement cases. See *Westinghouse* v. *Gardner, etc., Air Brake Co.*, 29 F. Cas. 798, 799 (C.C.N.D. Ohio 1875) (No. 17450):

> The organisms [sic] covered by the fourth and fifth claims of [Westinghouse's original] patent, reissue 5,504, seem to have been entirely new with him; and the incorporation of these elements, together with that of graduating the air pressure in the brake-cylinders – also shown to be new and of the highest importance and utility – in claims 1, 2, 3, and 6, with other substantial and material differences not necessary to enumerate, fully substantiate his pretensions as an original and meritorious inventor, and entitle him as such to the amplest protection of the law.

skills,[53] Westinghouse applied his knowledge of patents and knack for patent strategy in the other technology-based ventures he went on to found. The most significant clustered in the new electrical industries. We have seen already that the most important was in AC power generation and distribution.

AC generation was based in the Westinghouse Electric & Manufacturing Company, founded 1884. In addition to his own original inventions, Westinghouse licensed exclusive rights to some important patents covering the key generation technology of famed inventor Nikola Tesla. Once Westinghouse had rights to Tesla's polyphase alternating current techniques in 1888, Tesla himself went to work for Westinghouse. As mentioned earlier,[54] the Westinghouse patent portfolio helped create leverage with Thomson-Houston. The cross license between the firms allowed each to move forward with AC power generation. By the time Thomson-Houston was absorbed into General Electric, the diversified Westinghouse empire, which started with patent-protected train brakes, had grown too large and too profitable to fall prey to the widespread merger mania of the time. It went on to pioneer commercial radio broadcasting (in 1920), and was absorbed into CBS, and then later Viacom, where it continues as a division.

4.2.3.2 Leo Baekeland and Bakelite

The story of Leo Baekend is another example of patents assisting entry during the era of corporatization. Baekeland was a chemist, born and educated in Ghent, Belgium. As part of his university training, he became interested in light-sensitive chemical agents: applied to paper, these became the basis of photographic printing paper. In place of the very slow "sun exposure" method used by photographers such as Matthew Brady, Baekeland's print papers required only a short burst of light exposure to create the image on the paper. After moving to the United States, Baekeland set up a company called Nepera Chemical Co., backed by his partner Leonard Jacobi.[55] Baekeland worked intensively for several years to perfect a commercially viable photographic quick-print paper. He succeeded, and named the paper Velox. Because he had had some financial difficulties with Nepera, and wanted some solid return on the sweat and time invested, Baekeland was happy to sell the Velox

53 Westinghouse hired the first female mechanical engineer in the United States, Bertha Lamme Feicht, along with many other talented people. Bertha Lamme was listed, among other senior executives, as Assistant Chief Engineer, in a short item, "Westinghouse Changes," in the Railroad Gazette, February 7, 1902, p. 99. For a sampling of Lamme's technical contributions, see Bertha G. Lamme, "The Technical Story of the Frequencies," Am. Institute of Elec. Engineers Transactions, January 1918, at pp. 65–89.

54 See Section 4.2.2.

55 Charles F. Kettering, Biographical Memoir of Leo Hendrik Baekeland, 1863–1944, 24 National Academy of Sciences Biographical Memoirs, 8th Memoir, NAS Meeting 1946, at p. 284.

technology outright in 1899 to George Eastman of Eastman Kodak. Baekeland and Nepera Chemical received $750,000 for Velox, of which Baekeland himself netted $215,000.[56] This was during the period when Eastman was moving aggressively to turn Kodak into the vertically integrated Goliath of the camera-film-photo industry. For Eastman, Velox printing paper plugged a glaring gap in Eastman's end-to-end vision of industry dominance.[57]

Baekeland's Velox windfall served the same function in his career as Edison's profit from his early stock ticker and telegraph inventions. This was also the same function that the train brake served in Westinghouse's: it gave him autonomy to pursue what interested him. And what seized Baekeland in the period after he sold Velox to Eastman was synthetic materials. He began with an interest in trying to create a synthetic shellac, a hardened coating traditionally used as a sealant but after 1900 or so also used to make phonograph albums. (In this sense, Edison's phonograph and Baekeland's synthetic chemical experiments were intertwined.) Existing shellacs were derived from the secretions of the lac beetle. Working from prior research on synthetic dyes, which in some cases had yielded unworkable blobs of a soft, gooey mass, Baekeland reacted phenol and formaldehyde under stringent temperature and pressure conditions. What he ultimately derived (in 1907, patent granted in 1909)[58] was a hard manmade plastic suitable for a number of industrial applications (telephones, car parts, etc.) and consumer products (funnels, cigarette boxes, ashtrays, tape measures, and so on).[59] The eponymous new material was called Bakelite. It was the first workable synthetic plastic, a fairly simple chemical polymer, and as such the forerunner to rayon, nylon, polyethylene, polypropylene, etc.

56 See Wiebe E. Bijker, The Fourth Kingdom: The Social Construction of Bakelite, in of bicycles, Bakelites, and Bulbs: Toward a Theory of Sociotechnical Change (Cambridge, MA: MIT Press, 1997), at pp. 134–136. On the different assessments of Velox's value going into the negotiation, see Robert Merges, *Intellectual Property Rights and Bargaining Breakdown: The Case of Blocking Patents*, 62 Tenn. L. Rev. 75, 106 (1994). Note that Baekeland never obtained a patent on Velox, so that legally the technology was sold as a trade secret. Baekeland later explained that while he could have afforded the filing fees, he could not at that time have afforded patent litigation to defend any patent he might get. See U.S. Cong., House Comm. on Patents, Hearings on H.R. 5012 and H.R. 7010, July 9–30, 1919 (Washington, DC: Government Printing Office, 1919), at p. 85. See also Joris Mercelis, The Photographic Paper That Made Leo Baekeland's Reputation: Entrepreneurial Incentives for Not Patenting, in Stathis Arapostathis and Graham Dutfield, eds., Knowledge Management and Intellectual Property (Cheltehham, UK: Edward Elgar, 2013), at pp. 62 et seq.

57 See Reese V. Jenkins, Images and Enterprise: Technology and the American Photographic Industry 1839 to 1925 (Baltimore: Johns Hopkins University Press, 1975), at pp. 198–204, 204 (explaining Eastman's steps toward vertical integration, and the need to defend Kodak's market position in the photographic printing paper sector of the industry).

58 US Patent No. 942,699, December 7, 1909, "Method of Making Insoluble Products of Phenol and Formaldehyde," granted to Leo H. Baekeland.

59 See www.bakelitemuseum.de. It was useful for telephones and electrical insulation because it was a good insulator and had very low electricity conductivity.

Baekland thought that Bakelite, and plastics in general, had a bright future. So instead of offloading the technology to someone else, he decided to grow the Bakelite empire himself. He began with a solid patent portfolio, which he had begun building from his very first interest in the new material. It proved extremely valuable to investors, and helped him draw the capital he needed to start not just a research project but an actual operating company:

> On 9 December 1909 Baekeland had been granted five U.S. patents concerning various products and processes, including his so-called heat-and-pressure method for controlling the phenol-formaldehyde reaction. About two months earlier Baekeland had filed additional patent applications so as to prevent competitors from being able to "invent around" his IP. By the summer of 1910 he could clearly substantiate his claim to potential investors that "the patents are so arranged that it is almost impossible to carry out anything practical without infringing at least three or four patents at the same time." In his prospectus for forming a Bakelite company, Baekeland also explicitly referred to his international patents, claiming that his IP position was even more satisfactory due to "the fact that the same patents have been granted in other foreign countries where rigid preliminary examinations are involved."[60]

From this strong foundation, Baekeland continued to build a sturdy patent portfolio. Baekeland's strategy was very intentional, and this strong patent position helped. He planned to first partner, through patent licenses, with various "candidate" firms. These firms would invest much of the money required to scale up Bakelite, and to figure out how to make it in high quality at commercial scale. After these developmental projects were complete, Baekeland would choose the best performers among the licensee companies and propose a consolidation into an industry-spanning plastics concern:

> Baekeland purposefully introduced Bakelite only gradually. Rather than establishing a Bakelite company of his own, he collaborated with a limited number of firms with whom he proposed IP licensing arrangements regarding either broad (for example, as electrical insulator) or very specific (such as for grinding wheels) uses of the material. In doing so Baekeland effectively outsourced much of the development work, thereby allowing himself and his small laboratory staff in Yonkers to focus on preparing different grades of phenolic resin and providing technical support. During his stay in Berlin Baekeland had found some time to reflect on a future business plan ... [H]e had confided to [fellow inventor/entrepreneur Elmer] Sperry [profiled just infra this Chapter] "his idea of in the U.S. trying Bakelite with several then finding out by experience who are really the wide-awake firms, then afterwards grouping them all in one big Bakelite consolidated Co. thus proceeding

[60] Joris Mercelis, *Leo Baekeland's Transatlantic Struggle for Bakelite: Patenting Inside and Outside of America*, 53 Tech. & Cult. 366, 381 (2012) (footnotes omitted, citing to Baekeland journals, correspondence, etc.).

by natural selection, eliminating the non fit and non desirable and thus building up an enormous enterprise."[61]

This vision never quite came to pass. But Baekeland did successfully deploy his patent arsenal, which allowed General Bakelite and various of its corporate affiliates to either combine with other big players (as in Europe), or to fight off competitors, as in the United States. Both the merger strategy (an echo of the formative stage of GE and AT&T) and the enforcement strategy gave proof to the statement that "his patents had proved to be a major force in the industry."[62] The timing of Baekeland's ultimate sale of the Bakelite companies to Union Carbide, in 1939, probably was the result of Baekeland's decision to retire, rather than a sign of the company being outflanked in the young industry it had helped to shape.

In retrospect, Baekeland's career shows the continued relevance of patents in the era of corporatization.[63] With Velox, Baekeland took a page from other inventor-entrants, such as George Westinghouse. He concentrated on an important logjam in the development of a growing industry, solved a crucial problem, and (with the backing of patents) capitalized on his improved technology – in Baekland's case, by selling out to an established industry player. For his second act, Baekeland entered the pioneering stage of a new industry, synthetic chemicals. The chemistry behind Baekelite became the foundation of an entire company, from research to marketing to product distribution. Baekeland grew the firm's patent portfolio,[64] and with its help[65] nurtured his new family of chemical compounds into a full-fledged company that rode the rising tide of the innovative plastics industry until selling to Union Carbide a few years before Baekland retired. Along the way, he earned the title "father of plastics," and became the prototype of the twentieth-century scientist-entrepreneur.[66]

4.2.3.3 Elmer Sperry

Elmer Sperry's life had many parallels with that of George Westinghouse. Born in the dead center of New York State, 100 miles from Westinghouse's birthplace and sixteen years after Westinghouse, he showed an early interest in invention and was

[61] Mercelis, *Leo Baekeland's Transatlantic Struggle*, at p. 380 n. 53, quoting various Baekeland personal journal entries.

[62] Joris Mercelis, *Leo Baekeland's Transatlantic Struggle*, at p. 383.

[63] Baekeland as exemplar of a larger group of independent inventors active from 1880 to 1920, see Eric S. Hintz, American Independent Inventors in an Era of Corporate R&D, at pp. 111 et seq.

[64] A search on Google Patents for patents through 1939 assigned to a company with "Bakelite" in its name yields over 1,500. Search conducted April 22, 2021.

[65] Joris Mercelis, Leo Baekeland's Transatlantic Struggle, at p. 367 (description of Baekeland's powerful patent portfolio as a "glass wall" behind which he could work patiently on developing the technology).

[66] Joris Mercelis, Beyond Bakelite: Leo Baekland and the Business of Science and Invention (Cambridge, MA: MIT Press, 2020), at p. 2 ("father of plastics" title bestowed on Baekland at the New York World's Fair of 1939).

fascinated by electricity. His first serious efforts were directed to power generation and arc lights, which he worked on in a workshop near his hometown, in Cortland, New York. He next moved to arc lighting, founding a company to commercialize his inventions after moving to Chicago in 1880.[67] He successfully established power generation stations in downtown Chicago, Omaha, and various other cities and towns. But, as was typical of Sperry's career, once the difficult initial engineering problems were solved, he was eager to move on to the next frontier.[68] In designing some mining equipment he saw the need to provide electric power to miners working underground, which required heating the copper wires to prevent corrosion.[69] The superior power supply so increased productivity in the mines that there was a need to replace the old mule-hauled coal wagons with something better. So, he invented a special electric locomotive to haul coal out of the mines. Operational details were not for him, however, so he eventually sold his arc light and power generator patents to General Electric and moved on.[70]

The next stop was Cleveland, and its high-profile community of electrical-industry inventors and companies. According to economic historian Ken Sokoloff:

> Sperry had ... been enticed to Cleveland (and to Brush [Electric Company, founded by noted electrical inventor Charles F. Brush]) by ... major investors associated with National Carbon [Co., of Cleveland]. Collectively known as the Sperry Syndicate, this group contracted with Sperry in 1890 to develop a prototype for an electric streetcar, promising that, if the prototype proved workable, the syndicate would either form their own company to build the cars or sell or license the patents to another company that would. This arrangement was really early stage financing. Although Sperry already had some patents in the area, he had not yet developed a working model. Sperry developed his streetcar over the next couple of years and, in 1892, the syndicate arranged to exploit the invention in a joint venture with the Thomson-Houston Electric Company (which a few months later became General Electric). The resulting Sperry Electric Railway Company contracted to pay Sperry a lucrative salary as consultant in addition to a share in the company's profits.[71]

67 J. C. Hunsaker, Biographical Memoir of Elmer Ambrose Sperry (Washington, DC: National Academy of Sciences, 1954), available at www.nasonline.org/publications/biographical-memoirs/memoir-pdfs/sperry-elmer.pdf, at p. 224.

68 Thomas P. Hughes, Elmer Sperry: Inventor and Engineer (Baltimore: Johns Hopkins University Press, 1971), at p. xvi.

69 See The Electric Coal-Digger, 13 Science (No. 322: April 5, 1889), at pp. 250–251 (photo of "The Sperry Electric Coal-Digger"). This was developed for the Sperry Electric Mining Machine Company (incorporated in 1889). See Naomi R. Lamoreaux, Margaret Levenstein, and Kenneth L. Sokoloff, "Financing Invention during the Second Industrial Revolution: Cleveland, Ohio, 1870–1920," November 2004, National Bureau of Economic Research, Inc. NBER Working Paper No. 10923, at p. 25; Thomas P. Hughes, Elmer Sperry, at pp. 50–51.

70 J. C. Hunsaker, Biographical Memoir of Elmer Ambrose Sperry, at p. 225.

71 Naomi R. Lamoreaux, Margaret Levenstein, and Kenneth L. Sokoloff, "Financing Invention in Cleveland," at p. 25; Thomas P. Hughes, Elmer Sperry, at pp. 70–73.

The pattern continued, with Sperry striking out in numerous directions, including invention of an electric car, electric batteries (to power the car),[72] various chemical processes, and ultimately, the technology he is best remembered for: a non-magnetic, rotational compass – the Sperry gyroscope.

The gyroscope happened this way. After his work on the electric car, Sperry bounced his way through a rough sea passage across the Atlantic. During the crossing, Sperry began to think about how gyroscopes might help to stabilize a moving vehicle. Building on the work of the French Scientist Leon Foucault, Sperry began experimenting with small gyroscopes on model ships.[73] This led him to take up a suggestion by Foucault that it should be possible (in theory) to build a non-magnetic compass using a gyroscope. There was great need for this at the turn of the twentieth century as steel ocean liners and battleships were becoming common, but the metal hulls interfered with traditional magnetic compasses developed in the days of wooden sailing ships. Advances in electric motors made the Foucault theory a reality: with steady power to the gyroscope, it could be spun at a constant rate, at speeds sufficient to allow the compass to indicate true north based on the rotation of the earth.[74] To pursue his work on stabilizers and compasses, Sperry (who had moved to New York) founded the Sperry Gyroscope Company in 1910.[75] The first major customers were the US and British navies, and demand was brisk, especially after the outbreak of World War I. Figure 4.12 shows the primary features of Sperry's revolutionary gyroscopic compass, especially the floating gimbal that allows movement in three dimensions to maintain its true north indication even in rough seas.

From this beginning, Sperry and associates branched out. They rigged a compass to the steering mechanism of a ship, allowing the ship to maintain a consistent

[72] See, e.g., U.S. Patent 640,698, "Electric Vehicle," issued January 9, 1900, to Elmer A. Sperry. The Cleveland Machine Screw Company produced Sperry's electric car. Sperry assigned his patents and received company equity, also staying on as an electrical engineer. This car business, together with Sperry's patents, were ultimately sold to the American Bicycle Company in 1900, as part of that company's entry into the auto business. Richard Wager Golden Wheels: The Story of the Automobiles Made in Cleveland and Northeastern Ohio, 1892–1932 (2nd ed. (corrected), Cleveland, OH: John T. Zubal, Inc., Publishers, 1986), at pp. 221–223.

[73] J. C. Hunsaker, Biographical Memoir of Elmer Ambrose Sperry, at p. 232.

[74] Technically, the fast-spinning disc at the center of a gyrocompass will experience torque from the Earth's gravity, which causes it to orient or "precess" in the direction of true (earthly rotational) north, as opposed to the (slightly different) orientation of a magnetic compass toward earth's magnetic north. The same phenomenon makes a spinning disk stand upright when you spin it very fast and hang it from a string holding one side of a gimbal. The gimbal-disk assembly seems to be magically held up by an invisible string on the other end of the gimbal. The effect is created because the spin generates torque or force, which is translated to the side of the gimbal attached to the string. This torque pushes down on the end of the string and holds the disk upright though it seems intuitively it should fall down from lack of a string on the other side.

[75] Ibid., at pp. 232–233.

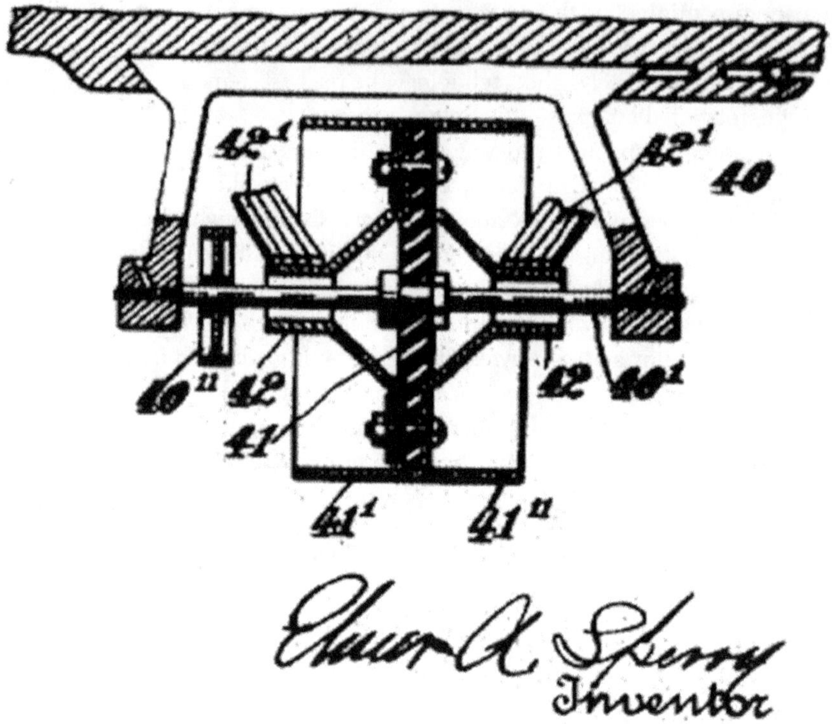

FIGURE 4.12. From US patent 1,279,471, "Gyroscopic Compass," issued to Elmer A. Sperry, September 17, 1918

bearing – an autopilot for battleships. Sperry and team designed instruments to help gunships aim their guns at a given target and coordinate firing along a battery of guns on different ships. The Sperry companies went on to design airplane stabilizers and autopilots, and flying instruments of other kinds as well. Diversification continued, with the company acquiring various divisions and becoming Sperry Rand Corporation in the 1950s. Sperry Rand's pioneering mainframe computer business (creator of the UNIVAC computer) started in the 1960s, and was sold to form part of Unisys Corporation. Numerous reorganizations and selloffs leave only the Sperry Marine Company (maker of nautical instruments) as the sole surviving unit tracing its provenance back to Elmer Sperry. But for its era, the Sperry corporate family was one of the most consistently innovative and forward-thinking forces in US business.

* * * *

Westinghouse, Baekeland, and Sperry all leveraged early patented technologies into establishment of technologically diverse and significant commercial enterprises. For them, the trend toward large scale, vertically integrated companies actually assisted their ability to enter new fields. Senior managers of firms such as GE and Eastman

Kodak wanted to form large industry-spanning companies. In their desire to lock up all new technologies that could threaten them, they licensed or purchased outright small innovative firms and the patents they owned. By licensing or selling early inventions, Westinghouse, Baekeland, and Sperry gained seed capital while they retained autonomy. Each used both well: Baekelad and Sperry went on to create important technologies, and to shape new companies to exploit them, after cashing in on an original success. There were many factors at work in this process. Patents were only one. Technological opportunities abounded in the rapid "take off" period when all three inventors were active. And the merger mania loose in the economy made it easy to find a market for small, innovative companies. But patents did enter in; they were one instrument supporting serial entrepreneurs between 1880 and 1920. In this way, the growth of the Chandlerian firms that dominated the era should be seen as a major part of the era's story – but not the entire story.[76] Though large companies came to dominate the corporate ecosystem, there were niches and entry points left where a small, nimble, and innovative firm could start with a promising technology and gain a foothold. The behemoths that grew during this period were surely quite important. But they were not just vacuum cleaners scooping up all in their paths. They also created a market – for small firms and new technologies. With the help of this market, in the shadow of the giant beasts, other innovative companies found a place. Westinghouse, Baekeland, and Sperry harnessed creativity and patent holdings to make room for new firms in an ecosystem dominated by giants.

4.3 DOCTRINE AND PATENT ADMINISTRATION

Patent doctrine adjusted to corporatization in a number of ways. We saw in Chapter 3 how patent law was beginning to adjust to more crowded patent landscapes – to the growing volume of patent holdings and the finer granularity of the typical individual invention. Greater attention to patent claims and the improvised doctrine of double patenting were two examples of such adjustments.

Established doctrines also bent with the times. First was the attitude of courts toward patent owners who sued on, but did not actually implement, inventions claimed in their patents. This issue was acute in cases where a patent owner sought an injunction to shut down a patent infringer. Corporate owners worked to convince courts that holding and asserting unused (or "paper") patents was not equivalent to rent seeking or misusing the patent system. In explaining that this was an appropriate strategic use of their patent portfolios, in furtherance of competition for productive activity, they were asking courts to recognize the new reality: Patents could be valuable as future options and strategic weapons, even if not every single patent in a portfolio was being "worked" or put in practice. In the era of large portfolios,

[76] The same point is made, and made convincingly, in Eric S. Hintz, American Independent Inventors in an Era of Corporate R&D.

companies argued that traditional skepticism toward "unworked" or "paper" patents was no longer warranted.

The second crucial doctrine to be reworked between 1880 and 1920 was patent ownership – who, as between inventor and employer, takes title to a new invention? Corporatization, in an era of growing technical complexity, and the growth of formalized team R&D, led to rules favoring concentration of ownership in corporate hands. Although centralized ownership and control makes sense for practical reasons, the new rules seemed to dispossess technical workers of a certain nobility that went along with holding title to their patented inventions. The working out of professional norms, and the resettling of expectations around patent ownership, were also part of the story of this doctrinal change.

4.3.1 *"Paper Patents" and the* Continental Paper Bag *Case*

Legal historian J. Willard Hurst was one of the foremost students of nineteenth-century legal doctrine and economic development.[77] Hurst famously summarized a century of court opinions and legal developments in saying that courts favored "a release of entrepreneurial energy."[78]

Solicitude for the release of energy, or active use of assets, found clear expression in patent law and nowhere was it as prominent as in the notion of "paper patents."[79]

[77] Another is Morton Horowitz. See especially his The Transformation of American Law, 1780–1860 (Cambridge, MA: Harvard University Press, 1977). With respect specifically to innovation and the evolution of industry structure the standard is Herbert Hovenkamp, Enterprise and American Law, 1836–1937 (Cambridge, MA: Harvard University Press, 1991).

[78] J. Willard Hurst, Law and the Conditions of Freedom in the Nineteenth-Century United States (1956), at p. 6. Hurst elaborates this theme in his monumental book Law and Economic Growth: The Legal History of the Lumber Industry in Wisconsin, 1836–1915 (Cambridge, MA: Harvard University Press, 1964), at 358 ("Nineteenth century public policy in the United States generally favored action and the venture of capital in production.") Hurst reported the Wisconsin courts' consistent solicitude for what he calls the "active operator," i.e., an entrepreneur who works hard to put resources into productive use. See e.g., ibid., at 358–359 (describing cases friendly to lumbermen who mistakenly felled and sold timber that they did not in fact have legal title to). On Hurst, see Harry Scheiber, *At the Borderland of Law and Economic History: The Contributions of Willard Hurst*, 75 Am. Hist. Rev. 744 (1970).

[79] Other manifestations include cases holding that an inventor who first reduces an invention to practice should have priority over another inventor who merely theorized about an invention, see e.g., *Bedford* v. *Hunt*, 3 F. Cas. 37, 38 (No. 1217) (C.C. D. Mass. 1817) (Story, J.) ("If it were the mere speculation of a philosopher or a mechanician, which had never been tried by the test of experience, and never put into actual operation by him, the law would not deprive a subsequent inventor, who had employed his labor and his talents in putting it into practice, of the reward due to his ingenuity and enterprise."); and opinions barring enforcement when patentees had acquiesced for considerable periods in a third party's use of the invention, see e. g. *American Middlings Purifier Co.* v. *Christian*, 1 F.Cas. 683, 687 (No. 307) (C.C. Minn. 1877) (Miller, J., riding circuit; dictum):

> [T]he argument of the defendants is that the plaintiff, having procured his patent in 1863, laid by and took no steps to enforce it against anybody until 1874 or 1875. That argument struck me at first as having a good deal of force in it, and it is founded, if it were true, and there is no excuse for it, in very strong principles; because if a man has a patent of that

This referred to inventive concepts that were captured in patent documents, but never found their way into active technological or commercial use. Paper patents were disfavored under nineteenth-century case law in two distinct situations. A dormant paper patent, whose subject was never actually implemented, was considered suspect. Many courts presumed it to be inoperative or ineffective – what the courts called "a failed experiment."[80] This meant that a paper patent in the prior art was unlikely to preempt a later inventor's patent application. The thought was that if the prior patent had in fact described a workable invention, it would naturally have been put into practice. The preference for productive action was so strong, in other words, it was expressed as a presumption. Surely any invention worth its salt would be put into effect, as soon as practicable. Thus, a negative inference was warranted when an invention was *not* implemented, when an idea remained only on paper, never having been made into a concrete, useful thing.[81] When an idea was described and claimed in a patent document, but never put to actual work, it was either not practical or it simply did not work at all. The result was that courts discounted or discarded mere "paper patents" when examining the prior art. An inventor whose patent was being challenged as invalid was presumed by the court to be an active entrepreneur. As between this presumably productive agent, and a dormant inventive concept lying fallow in the prior art, the active force usually won out.

> kind and he sees the world at large using it for eight or ten years, takes no steps to arrest it, sues nobody, sets up no claim, gives no warning, it is a very natural and strong reason why, under these circumstances, he should not be permitted to come subsequently and arrest everybody by process of injunction. In each and in every case that question depends upon its own facts.

80 See, e.g., *New York Belting & Packing Co.* v. *Sibley*, 15 F. 386 (C.C. Mass. 1883) ("[T]he plaintiffs contend the Nichols, Livesey & Wroughton patent was a paper patent merely, and that the machine described in it would do no useful work."); *Taylor* v. *Sawyer Spindle Co.*, 75 F. 301, 308 (3d Cir. 1896) (dismissing prior art as non-anticipatory: "The Cramer patent is only 'a paper patent,' and has never been put into practical use, and may be considered as an abandoned experiment."). This rule was always subject to a caveat: that even an inoperative invention had some prior art effect, so long as its disclosure was easily supplemented by the knowledge of one skilled in the art. See, e.g., *Pickering* v. *McCullough*, 104 U.S. 310, 319 (1881):

> It is objected, however, that the machines described in these patents are mere paper machines, not capable of successful practical working. But on examination it sufficiently appears, we think, that the objections can be sustained only as to minor matters of detail in construction, not affecting the substance of the invention claimed, and could be removed by mere mechanical skill, without the exercise of the faculty of invention. In this view, the Wise and Smith patents are not rendered inefficient as defences in this suit, by reason of the alleged imperfections of the machines described in them.

In time, this caveat came in a sense to swallow the rule. By the 1940s an unpracticed invention was given the same potentially patent-defeating effect as any other type of prior art. See, e.g., *De Cew* v. *Union Bag & Paper Corp.*, 57 F.Supp. 388, 395 (D.C.N.J. 1944) ("It is well settled that a paper patent may negative otherwise patentable novelty where, as here, it sufficiently discloses the principles of the alleged invention, and the objections to impracticability can be obviated by mere mechanical skill.")

81 See John F. Duffy, *Reviving the Paper Patent Doctrine*, 98 Cornell L. Rev. 1359 (2013).

Paper patents also came into play in the law of infringement. A defendant who had been accused of infringing a patent could point out that the patentee had never commercialized the claimed technology.[82] Courts responded in different ways. Sometimes a restrictive remedy would be applied: damages, but no injunction.[83] At other times, the absence of commercialization would trigger a defense of patent misuse or an outright antitrust violation. Most frequently, however, paper patent status was invoked in support of a narrow or restrictive reading of the claims of a patent. It was in effect an interpretive doctrine. In a significant number of cases, a patent covering an invention that had not been put into practice was "strictly construed," or "limited to its own terms." It was excluded from that class of patents for which a broad and liberal construction was thought to be appropriate.[84] The attitude of the courts was plain. Paper patents were technically valid but narrowly enforced.

As with so many longstanding patent doctrines, the description and application of the paper patent doctrine tends to bleed from one substantive issue to another. It, as with other nineteenth-century doctrines, might almost be described more accurately as a motif or trope than a fixed and finite doctrine. So, for example, in a number of cases concerning preliminary injunctions, the paper patent concept is mentioned along with the generally accepted principle that an injunction is available only for well-established patent rights – those supported by an injunction in an earlier case, or those long acquiesced in by the industry. Or consider cases in which the "paper" qualities of the prior art are compared to the widespread adoption of a patented invention. Evidence of practical superiority was powerfully persuasive in nineteenth-century patent cases. A case on chick-hatching incubators captures this well. There the court remarked that although prior art designs for keeping incubators warm seem similar to the patented invention at issue, the simple fact was that farmers strongly preferred the new design:

82 *Long* v. *Pope Mfg. Co.*, 75 F. 835, 840 (1st Cir. 1896):

> If this invention had been put in early use, and so continued with a long public acquiescence, it might, perhaps, have safely received therefrom a practical construction more favorable to the complainants. But, in view of the rapidity with which mechanical improvements advance in this age, it would establish a very dangerous precedent to give to a mere paper patent, which has lain dormant for years, a breadth not contemplated on its face . . .

83 See, e.g., *New York Paper-Bag Mach. & Mfg. Co.* v. *Hollingsworth & Whitney Co.*, 56 F. 224, 231 (1st Cir. 1893) ("[A]s the patentees have never made any use of their alleged invention, nor attempted to do so, nor permitted its use by others, nor given an explanation of the nonuser, or any reason for it, I doubt whether the case submitted is not one of a mere legal right, and whether the complainant should not be left to its remedy at common law [i.e., damages], if entitled to any relief at all.").

84 See, e.g., ibid.

> It is contended in support of the validity of the patent in suit that the prior patents hereinbefore considered and claimed as anticipations were mere paper patents, and that it does not appear that any of them were capable of practical successful operation ... That the device of the patent in suit marked an advance beyond all previous devices is evident. Its utility is established by undisputed testimony. The sales of complainant's incubators, since the adoption of the improvement herein claimed, have increased from 300 to 10,000 or 12,000 per annum. It is claimed that the number of incubators containing this heater is greater than that of all the other makes combined. I am inclined to give greater weight to the evidence of utility, because it is not open to the objection [that success is not the result of technical features of the invention]. The class of persons who use incubators are not likely to be induced to buy by reason of an alluring trade-mark, attractive finish, or the energy of the traveling salesman. The rival incubators are operated side by side at the country fair, and the practical farmer may count the eggs and hatching chickens, and reduce the question of comparative utility to a mere mathematical exercise.
>
> [T]he complainant [patentee], responding to the public demand for the better results accomplished by the device of the patent in suit, is forced to discard the [ineffective features of the prior art], and the defendant has not seen fit to imitate them in his device. This patent seems to fall within the settled rule that where a number of persons have all been engaged in repeated, but unsuccessful, efforts to accomplish a certain result, and one of them finally succeeds in devising the necessary means, and secures a patent therefor, the courts will not be inclined to adopt such a narrow construction as would be fatal to the validity of such patent.[85]

The case of *New Departure Bell Co.* v. *Bevin Bros. Mfg. Co.*[86] provides another good example. There, the court considered the validity of a patent issued to Rockwell on the simple yet ingenious thumb-operated bicycle bell, still in use today (see Figure 4.13). The district court had upheld the validity of the Rockwell patent over a large number of potentially anticipating references (produced, no doubt, in response to the "bicycle craze" of the 1890s.) One piece of prior art was a British patent, issued to one Bennett, for a bell striking mechanism used as a doorbell or the like. The district court dismissed the Bennett design as irrelevant, but on appeal the Second Circuit (via Judge Lacombe) reversed. Lacombe begins by noting the obscurity of the Bennett reference, saying that "[t]here is no reason to suppose that Bennett or his bell was ever heard of by any bell manufacturer in this country until his patent was unearthed by a search for anticipating devices."[87] Even so, because of

[85] *Stahl* v. *Wiliams*, 64 F. 121, 123–124 (C.C. Conn. 1894). The type of evidence the court found persuasive here is still relevant in modern cases, though the doctrine has undergone a number of subtle changes over the years. See Robert P. Merges, *Economic Perspectives on Innovation: Commercial Success and Patent Standards*, 76 Cal. L. Rev. 803, 866 et seq. (1988) (section on "Failure of Others: The Legacy of Learned Hand").

[86] 73 F. 469 (2d Cir. 1896).

[87] 73 F. 469, 475.

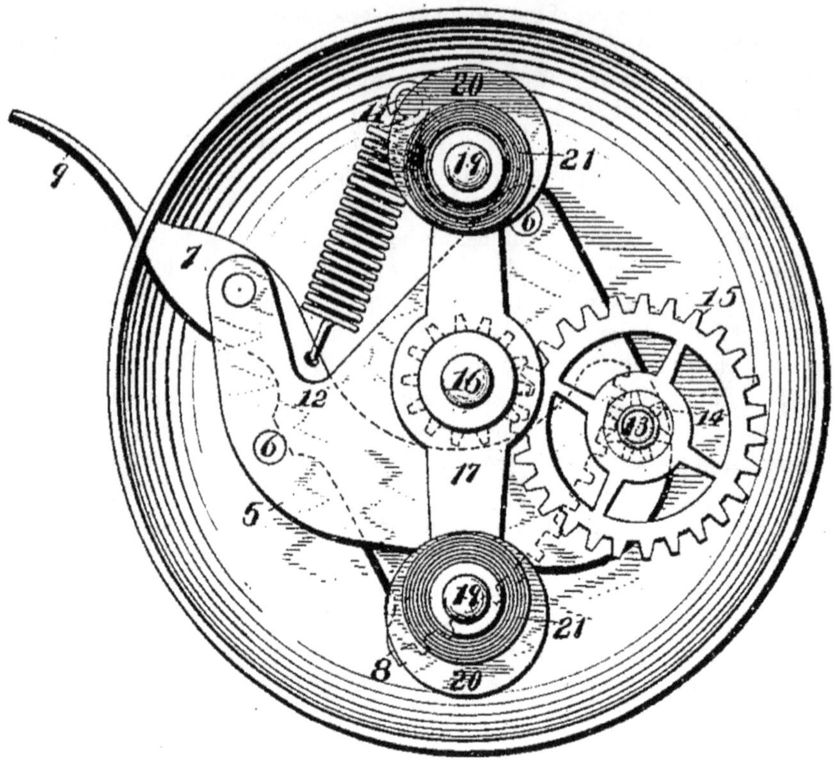

FIGURE 4.13. E. D. Rockwell, US patent 471,982, "Bicycle Bell," issued March 29, 1892. Assigned to New Departure Bell Co.

what the court perceived as the similarity of designs, Bennett was found to anticipate Rockwell's bicycle bell patent. This is standard fare in the patent world; it follows from the principle that ideas in the public domain must be fiercely guarded. What is noteworthy is the almost apologetic tone of the court's treatment of the obscure Bennett reference:

> No doubt, Rockwell devised the striking mechanism set out in his patent independently, and with no knowledge of what Bennett had done; and, since that mechanism was better adapted to meet the requirements of a bicycle bell than anything which rival manufacturers had succeeded in producing, it may be accepted as the fruit of an inventive conception, but its novelty is negatived by the British patent . . . It may be a hardship to meritorious inventors, who, at the expenditure of much time and thought, have hit upon some ingenious combination of mechanical devices, which, for aught they know, is entirely novel, to find that, in some remote time and place, some one else, of whom they never heard, has published to the world, in a patent or a printed publication, a full description of the very combination over

> which they have been puzzling; but in such cases the act, none the less, refuses them a patent.[88]

Even in an opinion invalidating a patent, the court felt it necessary to contrast the "inventive conception" of a "meritorious" inventor with the technical prior art "unearthed" only in response to litigation that prompted a search for anticipating devices. Activity and energy are acknowledged, then, even in a case where they are overcome in importance by relatively technical legal principles.

A late nineteenth-century case from the printing press industry well illustrates the favorable judicial bias in favor of active enterprise.[89] The Campbell Printing Press & Manufacturing Company (Campbell Printing) acquired two printing press patents in 1892, the first an invention by Wellington Kidder from Boston, and the second by John H. Stonemetz of Erie, PA. Both were independent inventors not formerly associated with Campbell Printing. The month after the acquisitions were complete, Campbell Printing sued a Boston-area manufacturer of printing presses. After that suit settled, Campbell Printing sued the Duplex Printing-Press Company of Michigan. The opinion in *Campbell Printing Co.* v. *Duplex Printing-Press Co.* is instructive not for its holding – that the defendant Duplex did not infringe either of Campbell Printing's patents – but for its strong bias in favor of the active use of technology. The patentee lost the case, not because its patents were held to be invalid, but because they were restricted to a very narrow scope. This was appropriate, the court thought, because while Campbell Printing's patented inventions accounted for essentially no practical, commercial activity, the accused infringer, Duplex, used its own proprietary designs as the foundation of a thriving business making and selling printing presses.

As is often true of patent cases, the important policy point is hidden inside of technical details, in this case, the respective design features of the patented and infringing printing presses. The specification for the patented Kidder press shows a vertical bed to hold the metal type for printing. Vertical rolling cylinders press the type onto a moving, continuous sheet of paper, called a web. Duplex, the accused infringer, made a press that worked differently: in it, the rolling cylinders as well as the paper web are oriented horizontally. Figures 4.14 and 4.15 will give you a bit of the flavor of the two inventions and how they worked. The first figure (Figure 4.14) is from the accused infringer, Duplex; the second figure is from the Kidder patent.

The outcome of the case turned on the meaning of the term "stationary bed" in claim 1 of the Kidder patent. In a literal sense, the horizontal beds of the Duplex press remain stationary; so, they would appear to infringe. But the court interpreted the claim very narrowly, relying in part on drawings showing that the Kidder type bed was oriented vertically. In the context of the patent, in other words, the court held that "stationary" implicitly meant "vertically stationary." In the game of patent

[88] 73 F. 469, 476.

[89] *Campbell Printing Co.* v. *Duplex Printing-Press Co.*, 86 F. 315 (E.D. Mich. 1898).

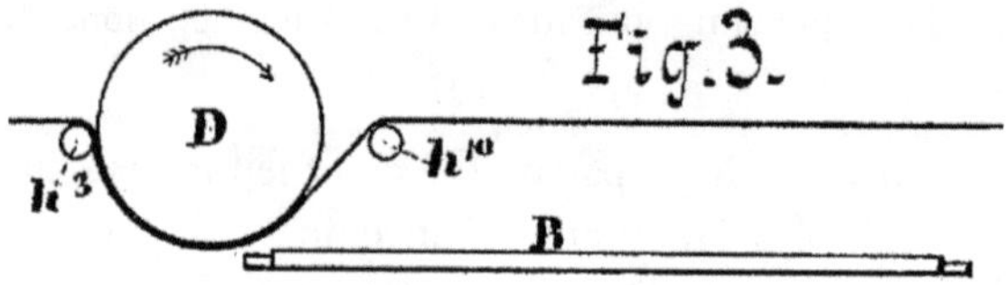

FIGURE 4.14. Duplex printing press design

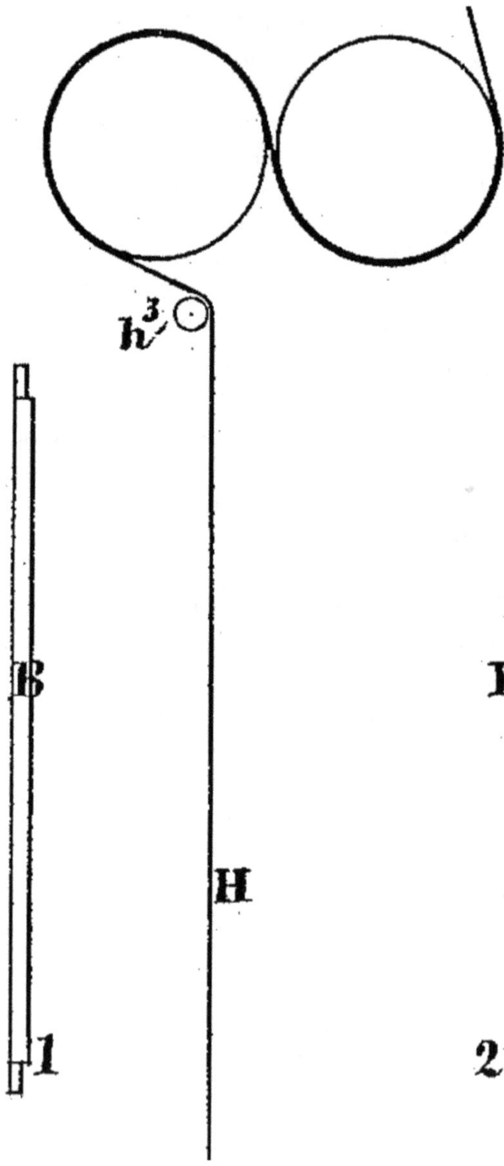

FIGURE 4.15. Kidder patented printing press

claim interpretation, this is a common enough move. What is interesting is the animating force behind it. The *real* issues driving the decision were (1) the fact that the patentee's device was not much more than a "mere disembodied idea," having been implemented only once, and that in a feeble prototype; and (2) the accused device was a whopping success story, showing printing speeds three times faster than the Kidder prototype, and resulting in a highly successful business:

> [I]n view of the state of the art, and the fact that [the patented Kidder] machine is scarcely an improvement in the art, and certainly not a commercial success, that its capacity did not exceed that of presses then in use, and it failed to meet the demands of the trade for expedition and cheapness, while the defendant's machine has met with a large sale, and prints more than three times as rapidly as Kidder's, while but one of the latter has been put in use since the issue of the patent in 1884, a radical difference in operation and mechanism between the Kidder machine and that of defendant is strongly, if not conclusively, suggested.[90]

The ultimate technical question – whether the accused product infringed patentee's claim 1 – was thus resolved by asking which of the parties had shown greater activity and success in the practical world of commerce. Sounding the "paper versus practice" theme, the court concluded:

> Three years of effort have been spent [by the patentee] upon the production of a single press without result, although supposed improvements were added to it; but neither the patented construction nor its additions have yet seen the light. Whether styled an abandoned patented experiment, or an inoperative conception, there is no evidence which establishes its utility except the issue of the patent, the prima facie effect of which is overcome by the proofs. The later patent to Cox [assigned to Duplex], which has demonstrated its utility, ought not to be held an infringement of a mere paper design.[91]

The fact that the accused infringer, Duplex, had received its own patent (to Cox, in 1892) also impressed the court. Its thinking was that a separate patent gave some proof that the design of the infringer must differ in some material way from that of the patentee:

> The presumption from the granting of Cox's 1892 patent, in view of the issue of the Kidder patent, is that there is a substantial difference between the inventions and that the latter is not an infringement of the earlier patent ... That presumption is fortified by the success of the defendant's machine, and the fact that Kidder's has not met the requirements of the trade, nor justified the manufacture, and has remained moribund for nearly three-fourths of its term.[92]

[90] 86 F. 315, at 320.

[91] 86 F. 315, at 331.

[92] 86 F. 315, 326-327.

The same bias in favor of active use shines through when the court turns to a second patent in the case, issued to an inventor named Stonemetz. This too was acquired by Campbell Printing and asserted against Duplex. Again, the court emphasizes the absence of any practical benefit, given that not even a single instance of the Stonemetz design had ever been successfully built. Once again, the court found no infringement. But its treatment of Stonemetz is even more dismissive. "Thus far [the Stonemetz design] has proved utterly sterile," the court said; "an unproductive conception rather than an invention."[93] The court went on to say:

> [B]ecause of these considerations – notably the neglect of Stonemetz and his assigns for 10 years to reduce his invention to practice, or even to put his conception into a tangible form – the Stonemetz press, though covered by a patent, seems to me a mere disembodied idea, which, whatever its merit, is not here entitled to equitable aid, nor within the spirit of the patent system, which requires diligence in giving to the public the benefit of his improvement.[94]

A number of doctrinal issues in *Campbell Printing* are quite straightforward – common then as now. For instance, the effect of a separate patent issued to the accused infringer was and is a common factor in infringement cases. What is more unusual, to the contemporary eye, is the explicit comparison of the merits of the patented design as compared to the infringer's products. With regard to the Stonemetz patent, the court says: "During the 10 years of inactivity of the owners of the Stonemetz patent the defendant has been making and selling as many as 60 of Cox's presses per annum."[95] Likewise, the court probes extensively into the technical performance and market success of the Kidder and Cox presses – and finds the former quite inferior to the latter. This is an unusual move by the standards of twenty-first-century patent litigation, in which such explicit product-to-product comparisons are very rare. Today, courts hone in on the precise language of the patentee's claims, and compare that specific language, in a careful and highly technical way, to the products sold by the accused infringer. The merits of the accused infringer's products are not much discussed, and they are almost never compared with the merits of the patentee's commercial product or business. Indeed, from 1982 to 2006, it was actually irrelevant whether the patentee was making or selling any actual products under its patents. The *eBay* case changed that, of course.[96] But it only decided that district court judges can consider the non-practice of a patent among other factors when deciding whether to issue an injunction. In that sense the result in nineteenth-century cases such as *Campbell Printing* went much further. By starting infringement analysis with a review of the patent's merits and the business of the patentee, and more specifically on a comparison of the

93 86 F. 315, 328.
94 86 F. 315, 331.
95 86 F. 315, 328.
96 *eBay v. Mercexchange*, 547 U.S. 388 (2006).

relative "activity level" and industry impact of the patentee with the infringer, judges in the nineteenth century went far beyond an *eBay*-style adjustment in patent remedies. Non-practiced patents might be invalidated or found not infringed, outcomes that reach far beyond remedial matters and go instead to the heart of the patent grant.

The opinion in *Campbell Printing* reveals just how aptly J. Willard Hurst's release of energy (i.e., favor activity) principle captures the spirit behind many patent law opinions of the nineteenth century.[97] The judge repeatedly employs the language of inactivity, rest, and sleepiness when describing the patentee. The Kidder patent is "scarcely an improvement"; with "no evidence to establish its utility"; it "remained moribund" and "failed to meet the demands of the trade." The second patent acquired by Campbell Printing, the Stonemetz patent, is "utterly sterile," a "mere disembodied idea," or "paper design," which was "not within the spirit of the patent system." Meanwhile the accused infringer is uniformly described with the language of vigor, activity, and success. The Cox device of Duplex, the accused infringer, is noted for "its successful working and its favor with the craft"; it "has demonstrated its utility"; it has sold well, viz., defendant sells "as many as 60 of Cox's presses per annum"; and Cox himself is described as "a press builder, inventor, and operator of printing presses of many years' experience."[98] In addition, many of Cox's prior patents are cited at various points in the opinion, and some of the innovations attributable to Cox are highlighted.[99] There is no doubt which of the parties the court sees as embodying the true "spirit of the patent system." So the defendant, the active and efficacious entrepreneur, wins the day over the patent owner who by comparison merely sits in repose.

4.3.1.1 The Fruits of Rapid Industrialization and "Corporatization": *The Paper Bag Case* as Exemplar

Even as the paper patent doctrine was being routinely invoked, however, the pace of industrialization was quickening. With this came a more complex generation of machinery and network technologies, and ultimately centralized research and development (R&D) labs. Corporate officials, including leading researchers and

[97] See J. Willard Hurst, Law and the Conditions of Freedom in the Nineteenth Century (Madison: University of Wisconsin Press, 1967), at p. 6. Hurst said that nineteenth-century American citizens believed "[t]he legal order should protect and promote the release of individual creative energy to the greatest extent compatible with the broad sharing of opportunity . . ."

[98] 86 F. 315, 331.

[99] 86 F. 315, 326 (noting the novelty of Cox's feed mechanism); ibid., at 323–324 (citing testimony from plaintiff's expert that the idea of using double horizontal type beds in a fixed position originated with Cox, and not Kidder: "[Campbell Printing] sought to expand its claims to cover a construction which complainant's own expert, Wood, admits was unknown to the art before Cox devised it.").

their newly emergent agents, professional patent lawyers, began to see problems with the paper patent doctrine. There were now good, strategic reasons why an innovative company might keep a fair number of its patents "on the shelf." As we saw in the case of the Bell system, advancements in complex technologies often called for multiple potential approaches to technical problems. Technology changed so rapidly that new directions had to be explored and staked out before they were known to be commercially viable. Out of this backdrop there emerged a new, sophisticated understanding of patents: the option model. Under this model a patent was not just a simple property right over a single existing marketable product. A patent could represent one of several ways of performing one of several component functions related to an actual product, potential future product, or product variant. Thus, a patented invention that was not currently in use might nevertheless play a useful role in the strategy of an innovative, forward-looking company. The paper patent doctrine was, as a consequence, becoming obsolete.

Here then I turn to the story of how the paper patent doctrine came to be reined in and limited. This is a very salient way that industrialization left its imprint on US patent law. While no single legal dispute can do this comprehensively, sometimes an individual case comes close. One example is what came to be known as *The Paper Bag Case*.

A REPRESENTATIVE CASE: THE PAPER INDUSTRY Paper bag manufacturing, as with papermaking generally, was one of many industries that moved from an artisanal trade to large-scale industrial production over the course of the nineteenth century. The American colonists brought with them traditional techniques for making paper, largely by hand. The initial steps toward mechanization took place in Europe. The Fourdrinier machine for making paper was developed in France and patented there in 1799. Named for the family that provided the lion's share of financing to develop it, the original Fourdrinier design was picked up and refined by a number of other papermakers, in particular a British mechanic named Brian Donkin.[100] From Britain the Fourdrinier machine travelled to the United States, where a growing population and burgeoning publishing industry stimulated significant demand for paper. As in other countries, local mechanics set to work immediately to improve each discrete component of the Fourdrinier machine. While no single incremental invention was crucial, many were important enough to merit a patent grant, and in the aggregate these efforts contributed to a rapid increase in the speed and volume of paper production.[101]

[100] Judith McGaw, Most Wonderful Machine, at p. 96.

[101] To take one example, paper production on the typical Fourdrinier machine doubled from 100 feet of paper produced per minute in 1867 to 200 feet per minute in 1880. McGaw, Most Wonderful Machine, at 100: "[I]nventors quickly patented individual improvements that remedied defects in the Fourdrinier process."

The Fourdrinier machine worked in large part by recreating some of the physical motions required to make paper by hand. It converted the batch production of hand techniques into an automated process, by using a continuous wire screen in the shape of a belt, in place of the old flat screens on which the wet paper mixture was placed to dry. Part of the machine, called the vatman, imitated the shaking motion traditionally performed by the worker with that name.[102] Scraping and drying processes took place further downstream, after the paper mixture had settled. The continuous operation increased production dramatically. Even so, a good deal of skill was required to operate the machine. In addition, there was never a truly "standard model" Fourdrinier machine. The barebones version sold by suppliers was adapted in each locale for specific conditions, and a host of substantial modifications were typically made to keep it running and to increase efficiency.[103]

A very detailed study of the period by Judith McGaw, who concentrates on the Berkshire Mountain region, tells the story well.[104] According to McGaw,

> Like Berkshire County, the nation in 1800 supplied an extraordinary array of natural advantages, ranging from rapidly flowing rivers and pure water that proved crucial to Berkshire County's development as a paper-making region to the mineral, forest, and agricultural riches that contributed to paper industry development and provided the raw materials processed by most nineteenth-century American industry. As in Berkshire County, the nation's population … shared a Calvinist heritage that accorded respect to the craftsman who had learned technical skills, saved his wages, and became a proprietor. Likewise, most of the nation experienced the [religious] revivalism that swept through Berkshire towns, promoting disciplined, intensified work by employer and employee; encouraging continued reinvestment; contributing to increased faith in human ability to change; and laying a foundation on which middle-class businessmen constructed networks of trust and exchange. Finally, much of the northeast shared with Berkshire County its growing access through improved transportation to a major commercial center, enabling rural entrepreneurs to take fuller advantage of natural resources and waterpower, if only they could find an alternative to reliance upon the few skilled craftsmen, whose long training precluded their rapid multiplication. In sum, early nineteenth century Americans were uncommonly well prepared to adopt machines.[105]

Many paper-related products were subject to intense mechanization during the nineteenth century. One in particular, paper bag making, gave rise to a highly significant patent case. We use this as the focal point for understanding this chapter in the history of corporatization.

[102] McGaw, Most Wonderful Machine, at p. 97.

[103] Ibid., at p. 97 n. 4.

[104] Ibid.

[105] Ibid., at p. 378.

MARGARET KNIGHT AND THE ORIGINS OF PAPER BAG MANUFACTURING Paper was used for packaging almost as soon as it was produced in quantity. But until the nineteenth century, most packages were handcrafted at the point of sale (the classic "brown paper packages tied with a string"). The spirit of the age, however, did not seem to tolerate this sort of inefficient, one-off production; it was only a matter of time before packaging became more standardized.

The person who stepped forward to meet the need is typical of nineteenth-century inventors in many ways. She was Margaret E. Knight, a New England native who became a major inventive force in a number of nineteenth-century industries. Knight went to work – again, typically – in a textile mill at an early age. There she showed the first glimmerings of inventive talent when, at the age of twelve, she designed a mechanism to prevent the shuttle on a loom from flying off and injuring the loom operator.[106] As with so many nineteenth-century inventors, Knight became something of a professional freelance problem-solver. Aside from her pioneering paper bag machine (about which, more in a moment), she contributed other patented inventions in papermaking as well as other industries, including the shoe industry and the automotive field. Knight is representative of a breed of lone inventors who contributed important, usable technologies to a number of nineteenth-century industries; she ended up with fourteen patents to her name.[107] A highly developed social network connected these inventors to the large companies rising up across the industrial landscape. This represents an important transitional stage in the movement from an early nineteenth-century model of the inventor-entrepreneur to the fully integrated, corporate-owned R&D labs of the early twentieth century.[108]

[106] See Henry Petroski, *The Evolution of the Grocery Bag*, 72 Am. Schol. 99, 101 (2003).

[107] See Zorina Khan, *"Not for Ornament": Patenting Activity by Nineteenth Century Women Inventors*, 31 J. Interdisc. Hist. 159, 184 (2000).

[108] See Naomi R. Lamoreaux and Kenneth L. Sokoloff, *Long Term Change in the Organization of Inventive Activity*, 93 Proc. Nat'l Acad. Sci. 12686, 12686 (1996) (During the late nineteenth and early twentieth centuries, "[a] self-reinforcing process whereby high rates of inventive activity encouraged the evolution of a market for technology, which in turn encouraged greater specialization and productivity at invention as individuals found it increasingly feasible to sell and license their discoveries, appears to have been operating."). For a description of how patents, specifically, promote specialized "idea factories," see Robert P. Merges, *A Transactional View of Property Rights*, 20 Berkeley Tech. L.J. 1477 (2005). During this transitional era, another important institution developed: the machine shop or workshop. See, e.g., Paul Israel, From Machine Shop to Industrial Laboratory: Telegraphy and the Changing Context of American Invention, 1830–1920 (Baltimore: Johns Hopkins University Press, 1992). The interplay of collective sharing of techniques, together with proprietary treatment for important inventions, is described in another context in Robert P. Merges, From Medieval Guilds to Open Source Software: Informal Norms, Appropriability Institutions, and Innovation (November 13, 2004), available at http://papers.ssrn.com/sol3/papers.cfm?abstract_id=661543 (Arguing that guilds and modern institutions share three features: (1) an "appropriability structure" that makes it profitable for individual entities to develop new technologies and sometimes share them; (2) reliance on group norms, as opposed to formal legal enactments, as an enforcement mechanism; and (3) a balance of competition and cooperation that determines

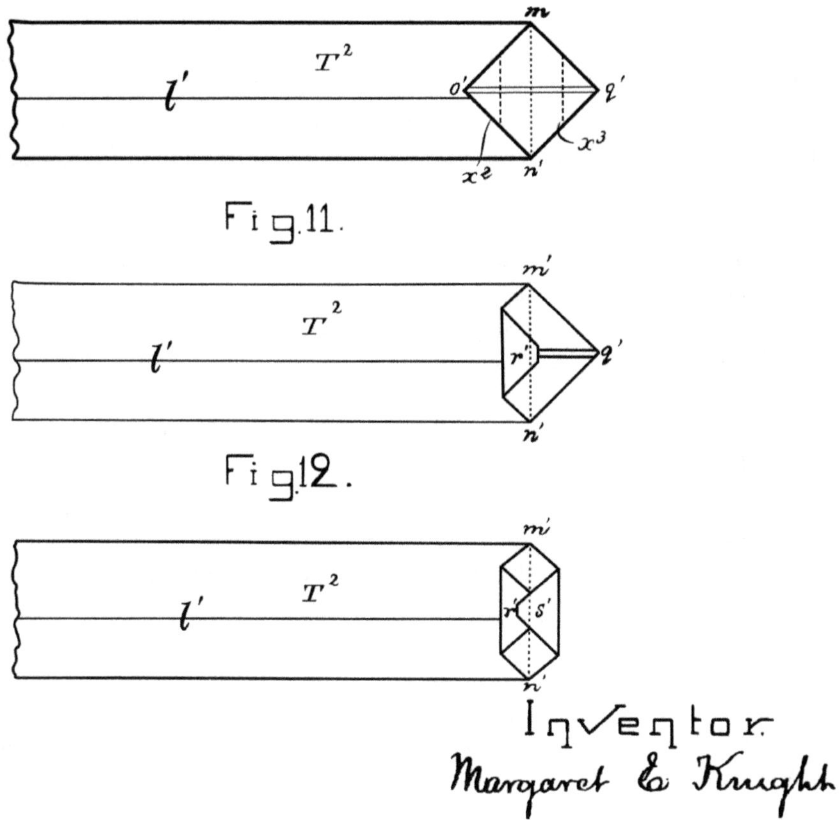

FIGURE 4.16. Bags from Margaret Knight's revolutionary paper bag making machine

Knight is generally credited with inventing the first functional paper bag-making machine in 1871. The Knight design employed a series of grabbers and fingers that took a flat piece of paper, rolled it upwards, then folded it in a diamond pattern and which was glued in the folds place to form the bottom of the bag. Hers was the first paper bag that could stand upright on its own; prior bags had been formed of two flat pieces of paper, making them in effect not much more than oversized envelopes. For the first time, with the Knight bags, cashiers could place a bag on a flat surface and use two hands to load it with items. Knight's invention surely fit the spirit of the age, which was rapidly moving toward standardization and efficiency in all aspects of the retail consumer experience. The key to Knight's design was the way her machine created the diamond-shaped fold on the bottom of the bag, which shown looked as in Figure 4.16.

Knight assigned the key patent, and some related patents, to the Eastern Paper Bag company of Hartford, which she co-founded. Knight's arrangement with

what information is to be shared with the group, and what (if any) individual-proprietary information is not.).

Eastern included a licensing deal that brought her $2,500 up front and a stream of continuing royalties on the use of her machine (capped at $25,000).[109] Though Knight was a founder and principal, in many ways her arrangement with Eastern was typical of those from the late nineteenth century transitional era. She was not an employee, but an independent agent who sold her inventive output to the company. As with many other serial inventors, Knight's affiliations were fairly fluid. After a period of exclusivity with Eastern, she moved on to make other inventions that were sold or assigned to companies in various industries. Inventive talent was scarce enough, and inventive work was generic enough, that a skilled inventor was not forced into an employee relationship. For a number of reasons, employment soon became the norm. By the 1920s, a career like Knight's was much less common. But Knight lived before the era of intense specialization and centralized in-house R&D labs – a sort of golden era for independents, as described earlier in this Chapter.

Knight's Eastern Paper Bag Company operated as a regional paper company until 1899, but then was swept up in the most systematic consolidation in the history of the American economy: "the great turn-of-the-century merger wave."[110] Between 1897 and 1904, according to economic historian Tom Nicholas, "200 industrial consolidations were formed, which changed the entire landscape of American business."[111] The paper and paper bag industries were part of this movement.[112] Eastern became part of one of these "industrial consolidations," the Union Paper Bag Company – which was referred to by people in the paper industry simply as "the Paper Bag Trust."[113] When Union Paper absorbed (!) its six rivals, including Eastern, according to one industry executive, bag prices immediately increased by 25 percent.[114]

This was, of course, precisely the type of rapid and radical concentration that ushered in the trust-busting era. Indeed, to show the power of this wave of consolidation, Eastern's counterparty Continental was in later years acquired by an even

[109] Petroski, *Evolution of the Grocery Bag*, at 104.

[110] Tom Nicholas, *Why Schumpeter Was Right: Innovation, Market Power, and Creative Destruction in 1920s America*, 63 J. Econ. Hist. 1023, 1025 (2003).

[111] Ibid., at 1025.

[112] Gary Bryan Magee, Productivity and Performance in the Paper Industry: Labour, Capital, and Technology in Britain and America, 1860–1914 (Cambridge: Cambridge University Press, 1997), at pp. 216–217:

> This movement towards combination … started to reach fever pitch between 1890 and 1914. Reasons for the movement lay in the significant economies of scale available to those who could expand production, the vast amounts of capital investment needed to modernize and attain this scale, and the ever-present desire of manufacturers to maintain prices and profits through the exercise of market power. Beneath all this, however, lay the rapidly growing demand for paper in America, without which it would not have even been possible for paper manufacturers to plan such bold expansions.

[113] Trial Transcript, *Eastern Paper Bag Co. v. Continental Paper Bag Co.*, vol. 2, at 438 (testimony of Herman Elsas, General Manager of the Continental Paper Bag Company).

[114] Elsas Testimony, at 415, 438.

larger combine – the International Paper Company.[115] Yet despite such an obvious movement toward oligopoly, some economists claim that the efficiencies created by the massive scale of these consolidations actually produced a net gain for the US economy.[116]

Studies of the paper industry bear this out. Average firm size in the paper industry grew by 200 percent between 1895 and 1905, with the average mill increasing in size by 121 percent.[117] Concentration through these "combinations," as they were known, surely affected prices, as theory would predict. But they also influenced "the rate of technological accumulation," permitting the new, larger firms "to attain the long runs and continuous production that were most susceptible to the economies of practice."[118] The story in paper, then, closely mirrors the larger story told so well by the business historian Alfred Chandler.[119] Through the "visible hand" of managerial capitalism, enabled and supported by well-organized equity markets, American industry raced down the learning curve made possible by massive increases in scale and scope. Concentration and anticompetitive practices ensued; but so did unprecedented increases in productivity.[120]

[115] Elsas Testimony, at 415, 420, 422 (International Paper is the largest stockholder in Continental; Continental has a requirements contract with its parent International for all the paper bags International might need). See Thomas Heinrich, *Product Diversification in the U.S. Pulp and Paper Industry: The Case of International Paper, 1898–1941*, 75 Bus. Hist. Rev. 467, 484 (2001) (describing International Paper's backward integration strategy in the 1910s). International itself was formed in 1898, out of a merger of seventeen independent pulp and paper mills. International Paper Company, Generations of Pride: A Centennial History of International Paper, 1898–1998 (Purchase, NY: International Paper, 1998), at 112. It was vertically integrated from the beginning: "Holdings also included 1.7 million acres of timberland in the Northeastern states and Canada." Ibid. This gave International a commanding market share in important industry segments: "During its early years, IP was the nation's largest producer of newsprint, supplying 60 percent of all newsprint sold in the U.S . . . " Which, not surprisingly, led to "several highly publicized Congressional hearings" around the so-called newsprint trust. Ibid., at 164.

[116] Tom Nicholas, *Why Schumpeter Was Right* (After the great merger wave, "firms with high levels of market power appear to have been disproportionately innovative.").

[117] Magee, Productivity and Performance in Paper, at 217.

[118] Ibid., at 216.

[119] Alfred D. Chandler, The Visible Hand: The Managerial Revolution in American Business (Cambridge, MA: Harvard University Press, 1993); Alfred D. Chandler, Scale and Scope: The Dynamics of Industrial Capitalism (Cambridge, MA: Harvard University Press, 1994).

[120] In addition, there is evidence of robust entry in the paper industry during this period. See, e.g., "Construction News," Paper, March 9, 1921 ("Elite Paper Box Co." incorporated in Brooklyn to manufacture paper bags; Cooper Paper Box Company incorporated in Buffalo with $300,000 in capital, to make paper bags; other news of burned-down plants being immediately rebuilt; news of contracts for sale of output from factories, including paper bag factories; etc.). As a theoretical matter, this is always of interest, because it suggests price discipline for existing companies, despite seemingly high industrial concentration ratios. See William Baumol, Microtheory (Cambridge, MA: MIT Press, 1986), at chapter 1, "The Theory of Contestable Markets," pp. 1–54.

Whatever the macro effects of consolidations such as the one that formed Union Paper Bag, the remaining competitors on the ground often fought back. In the paper bag field, some long-time industry participants organized a large competitor, the Continental Paper Bag Company. One aspect of the Continental strategy was to evade the extensive patent portfolio that Union Paper had assembled in the process of acquiring the many independent paper bag companies that comprised it. This evasion strategy led Continental to base its bag-making machinery on a series of patents issued to an inventor named Claussen. When Union Paper Bag – through its proxy, Eastern – fought this move, the forces were joined for a crucial case testing how the patent system was going to respond to the economic and technological changes sweeping through the industry, and indeed the economy as a whole.

Then as now, sophisticated businesspeople well understood the strategic value of patents. All the major companies not only filed many patents on their own internal inventions but also stayed active in the market for patents developed by third parties. It was one of these patents, acquired by Eastern (and hence, ultimately, the Union Paper Bag Company) that formed the centerpiece of the Eastern-Continental litigation.

William Liddell was a Scottish machinist who had emigrated to the United States in 1888.[121] At the time of the Continental litigation, Liddell had eight patents to his name, all on various aspects of papermaking. Like so many other inventors of his era, he was more or less of an independent engineer. Though three of his patents from the 1890s had been assigned to Eastern, he was not a permanent employee. He moved around various engineering firms, working throughout the industry for various paper companies and in various capacities. As a result, he had access to all manner of useful information about what was going on in the field, and what various companies were up to from a business and technical point of view. This was not lost on those in the industry: Charles F. Coburn, General Manager of Eastern, hired Liddell as a sort of roving scout for several years around the turn of the century; the Liddell-Coburn contract instructed Liddell to "keep your eyes & ears open & find out all you can, that [sic] going on in Bag Machines and report to me [Coburn]." Liddell, however, appears to have become disgruntled with Eastern.[122] At any rate, he ended up consulting for Eastern's rival, Continental; testifying for Continental against Eastern; and even attacking the validity and importance of his own patent, asserted by Eastern in its patent infringement suit against Continental.[123] It

[121] The information here comes from the Liddell deposition in vol. 1 of the Continental Paper Bag case file, pp. 527 ff.

[122] It may not be coincidental that Liddell buddied up to Continental only after Coburn apparently tried to reduce his compensation under the annual "scouting" contract from $200 per year to $175. See Liddell Testimony, Continental Transcript, vol. 2, at 772.

[123] Liddell testified that the patent lawyer who prepared his application added material that made the invention unworkable, and that differed from Liddell's plans for the technology. Transcript, vol. 1 at 495–555, Liddell affadavit, Transcript at 770. See *Minerva Surgical, Inc.* v. *Hologic, Inc.*, 141 S. Ct. 2298 (2021) (doctrine of assignor prohibits assignor from attacking the validity of an assigned patent or application, but only if the patent claims have not been broadened or modified post-assignment).

was just this sort of situation, incidentally, which tested the limits of when an inventor-assignor such as Liddell is permitted to later attack the validity of the very patent he or she has assigned.[124] Liddell's behavior also illustrates some of the problems employers encountered with an engineering workforce comprising independent agents who moved freely from firm to firm – a little-noticed additional reason, perhaps, for the rapid emergence of the fully integrated, dedicated R&D division that employs primarily full-time, permanent employees.[125]

[124] This is the doctrine of assignor estoppel. See *Westinghouse Electric & Mfg. Co.* v. *Formica Insulation Co.*, 266 U.S. 342, 349 (1924) ("[A]n assignor of a patent right is estopped to attack the utility, novelty or validity of a patented invention which he has assigned or granted as against anyone claiming the right under his assignment or grant."). But see *Scott Paper Co.* v. *Marcalus Mfg. Co.*, 326 U.S. 249, 254 (1945):

> [I]n the circumstances of this case we find it unnecessary to ... determine whether, as respondent asks, the doctrine of estoppel by patent assignment as stated by the *Formica* case should be rejected. To whatever extent that doctrine may be deemed to have survived the Formica decision or to be restricted by it, we think that case is not controlling here. For other considerations are dispositive of this case, in which, unlike Formica, the accused machine is precisely that of an expired patent. Neither in that case nor in any other, so far as we are advised, was the doctrine of estoppel applied so as to penalize the use of the invention of an expired patent. That we think is foreclosed by the patent laws themselves.

The Federal Circuit limited *Scott Paper* to its facts, saving the doctrine of assignor estoppel from oblivion, in *Diamond Scientific Co.* v. *Ambico, Inc.*, 848 F.2d 1220 (Fed. Cir. 1988) , cert. dismissed, 487 U.S. 1265 (1988). The *Diamond Scientific* case was somewhat controversial because many had argued that continued viability for assignor estoppel was inconsistent with the spirit of the Supreme Court decision eliminating the related doctrine of licensor estoppel, in *Lear, Inc.* v. *Adkins*, 395 U.S. 653 (1969) (emphasizing the important public interest in eliminating invalid patents, which outweighs the encouragement of good faith bargaining by a patent owner who licenses its patent based at least implicitly on the premise that the patent is valid). See generally, Rochelle Dreyfuss, *Dethroning Lear: Licensee Estoppel and the Incentive to Innovate*, 72 Va. L. Rev. 677, 680 (1986) ("Provisions requiring licensees to pay royalties even after patent lapse and agreements requiring licensees to waive the right to contest patent validity allocate to the licensee a portion of the risk that the patent will be denied or subsequently held invalid and therefore enhance the value of discoveries to their inventors." (Footnote omitted)).

[125] See generally, Robert P. Merges, *The Law and Economics of Employed Inventors*, 13 Harv. J. L. & Tech. 1 (1999) (explaining rules favoring employers in assignment of employee inventions in terms of transaction costs, including employee opportunism). See also Dan L. Burk and Brett H. McDonnell, *The Goldilocks Hypothesis: Balancing Intellectual Property Rights at the Boundary of the Firm*, 2007 U. Ill. L. Rev. 575, 624 (mentioning employee opportunism as a factor in the appropriate IP-mediated boundaries of a firm). Note that this functionalist explanation contrasts somewhat with the interpretation put forward in the excellent study of the rise of corporate R&D employment during this period, Catherine L. Fisk, Working Knowledge: Employee Innovation and the Rise of Corporate Intellectual Property (Chapel Hill: University of North Carolina Press, 2009). Fisk emphasizes the effects of corporatization on employees who were technically skilled engineers, describing them as a "new middle class," which moved from a tradition of "free labor" (on the model of roaming inventors such as Knight and Liddell) to the more bureaucratized form of employment in which labor was rapidly "commodified," a process facilitated by judges' perceptions and ultimately the self-image of R&D workers themselves. See ibid., at 245–249.

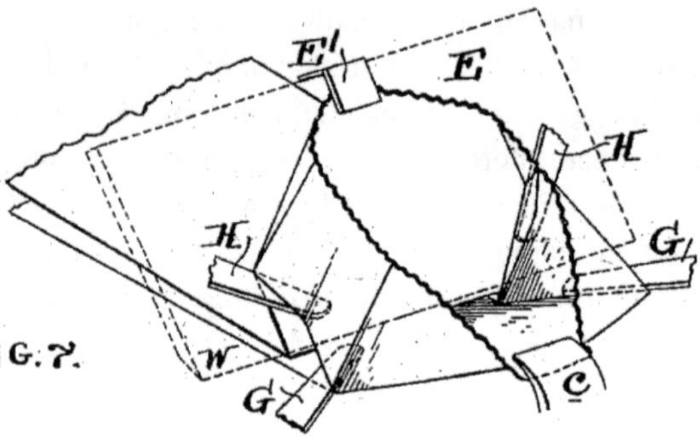

FIGURE 4.17. Liddell paper bag folding patent

The specific patent Liddell assigned and later attacked was US patent 558,969, issued in 1896. Liddell's patent was entitled "Paper Bag Machine," but it actually covered only one small (but crucial) step in the process of making the familiar brown paper grocery bag: the folding and gluing of the bottom of the bag into a square shape. This gives the bag the handy feature – still in evidence today – of both lying flat during transport and opening to form a flat-bottomed surface to receive the items placed into the bag. (It also provides the occasion for the artful "snap," made when an expert bagger whips out a flat paper bag and puts it into working shape to receive the groceries.) The trick to making the flat-bottomed bag is the folding of the paper during manufacture. And it was this fold, or rather the machinery to execute it, that was the subject of Liddell's patent.

Liddell's machinery picks up at the stage where the bag is still in the shape of a tube. It then performs what might be described as a form of industrial origami. The machine grasps one end of the tube with a series of metal fingers, opens it out, and then simultaneously folds it and smushes it down, forming a flat surface. Figure 4.17 from the Liddell patent shows the critical step. One remaining fold, not shown, is required to close the bottom of the bag with the two end flaps. The result is what is called in the bag trade, for reasons obvious when you look at it, the diamond-fold.[126]

As clever as the Liddell design is, the precise feature that made his invention patentable was the use of a rotating cylinder to advance each tube-shaped bag to the folding stage of the operation. Prior art designs used an oscillating plate to grasp and advance each bag. All the other features described by Liddell aside from the cylinder were old in the art; as the district court noted, some twenty prior patents had been issued on various components of machines for making diamond-fold bags.[127] Yet even so the lower circuit court held that Liddell was entitled to claim the full range

[126] Another term is "self-opening square" bags, or "S.O.S. bags." See *Eastern Paper Bag Co.* v. *Continental Paper Bag Co.*, 142 F. 517, 520 (C.C. Me. 1905) (accounting phase of *Continental Paper Bag* suit).

[127] *Eastern Paper Bag Co.* v. *Continental Paper Bag Co.*, 142 F. 479, 487–488 (C.C. D. Me. 1905).

of techniques for implementing his rotating-cylinder idea.[128] In addition, though the substitution of a cylinder for an oscillating plate was far from revolutionary (so to speak), it did reflect the requisite degree of "invention" to deserve a patent. Indeed, as the lower court said, the plaintiff Eastern, after acquiring the Liddell patent, chose not to implement the Liddell design in its own machinery: "[T]his invention did not constitute an advance in the state of the art in such a sense that the complainant [Eastern] deemed it advisable to discard its old machinery and use Liddell's. Invention may clearly exist, notwithstanding it does not accomplish so fundamental a result."[129]

But while Eastern's bag making equipment continued to use the old oscillating plate, the defendant Continental had switched over to a bag feeder that employed a cylinder. This cylinder, while differing in some respects from the detailed drawings of the Liddell patent, operated on much the same principle. The upshot was that although the patent owner, Eastern, held a patent on a technique that it did not itself use, defendant Continental *was* using it – and so was found to infringe. The lower circuit court seemed reluctant to issue an injunction on these facts. But, acknowledging the weight of clear precedent in favor of this remedy, the court felt it had no choice:

> [I]t is maintained that, under the circumstances, equity will not take jurisdiction for an injunction. We have stated that no machine for practical manufacturing purposes was ever constructed under the Liddell patent. The record also shows that the complainant, so to speak, locked up its patent. It has never attempted to make any practical use of it, either itself or through licenses, and apparently its proposed policy has been to avoid this. In this respect, it has not the common excuse of a lack of means, as it is unquestioned that the complainant is a powerful and wealthy corporation. We have no doubt that the complainant stands in the common class of manufacturers who accumulate patents merely for the purpose of protecting their

[128] 142 F. 479, at 493, 497:

> From what appears as to the state of the art, it must be held that the invention in issue lies in the peculiar suggestion of oscillating the forming-plate on its rear edge, and that … Liddell having pointed out how that suggestion could be practically worked out, his invention, his patent, and his claims, and his rights against infringers are as broad as that suggestion. This is a broad application of the laws of mechanical forces and all the rest is detail, which detail can be worked out in the manner pointed out by the specification, or in any other method …
>
> If there are any such differences whatever with reference to the forming-plate and its method of operation, they are obviously of the same mechanical character which we have already described, of no importance in this case, because the claims in issue require only that the forming-plate shall oscillate about its rear edge on the surface of the cylinder. As we have said, the application of the mechanical laws by virtue of which a forming-plate, oscillating about its rear edge, so that necessarily, as the cylinder advances, the plate turns the ends of the paper-bag blank back upon its body, form the essence of this element in the claims, and neither the invention nor the claims involve any particular method or mechanism by which the oscillating about the rear edge is accomplished.

[129] 142 F. 479, 488.

> general industries and shutting out competitors. According to the view of the court as now constituted ... a case like this at bar exhibits no interest involved as to which a complainant can suffer legal detriment pending litigation in the courts of common law. Nevertheless, in some way the practice seems to have crystallized otherwise, and the court sees no relief for the respondent in this direction, unless in some way obtained from the Supreme Court.[130]

In a fairly perfunctory opinion, a panel of the First Circuit affirmed.[131] It deferred to the lower court on the many complex factual issues in the case. And on the crucial question of whether Continental should be enjoined, Judge Lowell, writing for the court, held clearly if not emphatically in favor of an injunction:

> The machine of the patent in suit is mechanically operative, as was shown experimentally for the purposes of this suit, but it has not been put into commercial use. No reason for the nonuser appears in the evidence, so far as we can discover. The defendant's machine has been an assured commercial success for some years. It was suggested at the oral argument that an unused patent is not entitled to the protection given by the extraordinary remedy of an injunction ... While this question has not been directly passed upon, so far as we are informed, in any considered decision of the Supreme Court, yet the weight of authority is in favor of the complainant ... As we find the claims in suit to be valid and to have been infringed by the defendant, the complainant is entitled to an injunction ...[132]

District Judge Aldrich, sitting by designation, took issue. In a very lengthy, comprehensive opinion, Aldrich ranged from the constitutional foundations of patent law to the detailed record in the case to the sweep of Supreme Court case law, finding support in every instance for the idea that equity should not aid the owner of a "paper patent" in a scheme of nonuse:

> I contend that injunctive relief should not be granted because it is an infringement of a paper patent deliberately held in nonuse for a wrongful purpose ... The injunction is not asked against the use of a machine which infringes one which the plain-tiff below is making and vending under a patent, but against the use of a machine which infringes a patent under which the plaintiff is not making and vending, and one which the plaintiff intends to withhold from the public ... The primary purpose of the framers of the Constitution was not unconscionable private pecuniary gain, but to encourage invention in the interests of general business and of the public, and the act of Congress which followed soon after was to protect the right to make, use, and vend, under a given patent, thus stimulating invention in the public interest, and there was no thought of giving countenance to the idea of acquiring and locking up inventions, and improvements upon inventions, to the end that the general benefits of invention should be turned back; and the idea that a

[130] 142 F. 479, 487.

[131] *Continental Paper Bag Co.* v. *Eastern Paper Bag Co.*, 150 F. 741 (1st Cir. 1906).

[132] 150 F. 741, 743–744.

> court of equity should help to accomplish such a result is contrary to the spirit of equity, and offends public policy . . .[133]

Toward the end of his dissent, Aldrich connected the paper patent issue to the rising tide of combinations then rushing through the American economy:

> The supposition would seem to be logical that if a party may acquire and hold a single competing patent in deliberate and intentional nonuse for the purpose of overthrowing competitive conditions, and may have [an] equitable injunction to that end, he may acquire and suppress all competing inventions and have equitable aid; and it would seem not to have been authoritatively decided that individuals or corporations may acquire all useful inventions relating to a particular industry . . . and force into . . . the various industries of the country a single appliance or a particular machine through an artificial necessity and demand created in its behalf through a monopoly of patent statutory and competing rights intentionally held in nonuse for such a purpose, and that they may have the monopoly influenced in behalf of such a scheme through injuncti[ve] relief in equity.[134]

The dissent was long enough, detailed enough, and forceful enough that it placed the issue of "nonuse" squarely on center stage in the case. And this was the issue that ultimately brought the greatest attention from the Supreme Court.[135] Because the plaintiff-patent owner (Eastern-Union Bag) had never implemented the Liddell design, Continental argued, based in part on cases deriving from the "paper patent" era described earlier, the Supreme Court should definitively deny injunctive relief. The ultimate court of equity was being asked to punish a patent owner that "had, so to speak, locked up its patent."[136]

THE SUPREME COURT OPINION In a closely watched opinion said to be one of the most important in many years, the Supreme Court upheld the injunction. Nonuse was discussed at length but ended up a non-factor. The Court's opinion rang with what a later generation would call "property talk": a patent was a property right; its owner could do what it pleased as long as it stayed away from blatantly illegal conduct; the decision not to deploy a patent was a lesser included privilege, safely inside the broader circle defined by the impregnable "right to exclude."

[133] 150 F. 741, 744, 744 (Aldrich, J., dissenting).

[134] 150 F. 741, 744, 749–750 (Aldrich, J., dissenting).

[135] Indeed, it was identified in the Petitioner's cert. petition, for Continental, as the original and novel question of law at issue in the case. See Brief for Petitioner Continental in support of a Grant of Certiorari, *Continental Paper Bag Co.* v. *Eastern Paper Bag Co.*, at p. 2 (electronic file at p. 2) ("Does equity have jurisdiction of a bill of complaint which is based on alleged infringement of a paper patent, the invention covered by which has long and always and unreasonably been held in non-use . . . ?").

[136] 142 F. 479, 487.

For these reasons it is easy to see why many scholars characterize *Continental Paper Bag* as a classic exemplar of *Lochner*-era formalism.[137] Yet as we will see, *Continental Paper Bag* also fits a newer, revisionist narrative concerning the nature of gilded age jurisprudence. Although the subject matter is literally a machine, the opinion itself is far from the parody of mechanical jurisprudence that lit the fires of the legal realists. It is, instead, an opinion that does not rely strictly on an absolutist vision of property rights to reach its conclusions. While property talk enters in, to be sure, the Court also shows a serious concern with the facts of the case and the economic forces behind it.

This is evident from the outset of the opinion, where Justice McKenna, writing for an 8–1 majority, first considers the question of infringement. Under early twentieth-century doctrine, the first step in deciding infringement was to assess the merits of the claimed invention as compared to the prior art. This step graded the invention along a spectrum, ranging from (1) pioneering to (2) basic to (3) fair or moderate contribution to (4) a bare minor improvement. Pioneering inventions were given the broadest protection under patent law. They were subject to a very wide scope of "equivalents," meaning that the patent covered a wide range of devices that might vary substantially from the inventor's claimed invention. So long as the accused infringer made or operated something embodying the key principle of the invention, the patent would cover it.[138] Basic inventions, those of a "high rank," were not as significant as pioneering ones, but were nonetheless deserving of substantial protection – a substantial range of equivalents. Moderate inventions were those entitled to a reasonable level of protection, which usually meant that protection extended to the mechanism described in the patentee's specification plus "obvious mechanical equivalents." For bare minor improvements, patent coverage was limited strictly to the precise embodiment of the invention described in the inventor's specification; essentially no range of equivalents was extended in such a case.[139]

[137] See, e.g., Lior Jacob Strahilevetz, *The Right to Destroy*, 114 Yale L.J. 781, 810 (2005) ("In a fascinating opinion called *Continental Paper Bag* … [t]he Court used Blackstonian, formalist rhetoric … [and] invoked the notion of an absolute right to exclude …").

[138] Though my purpose here is historical, it is worth noting that this approach has some advantages over the highly technical yet somewhat arbitrary approach of contemporary courts. On this, see Dan L. Burk and Mark A. Lemley, *Quantum Patent Mechanics*, 9 Lew. & Clark L. Rev. 29, 30 (2005):

> [W]e might instead start with the patentee's invention itself, construing patent claims narrowly and in light of the actual invention when the claim terms are ambiguous. Courts could then supplement this narrower claim construction with a doctrine of equivalents analysis, which would permit them to decide how broadly to apply the principle of the invention. But for this approach to work, courts must apply the doctrine of equivalents with an eye towards proper protection, rather than cabining it with formal rules.

[139] See, e.g., *Hoe v. Miehle Printing Press & Mfg Co*, 149 F. 213, 216 (2d Cir. 1906) ("Concurring as we do in the conclusion of the Circuit Court that Read's is not a pioneer patent, we cannot expand its claims sufficiently to cover defendant's structure.").

The Court characterized the Liddell invention at issue in *Continental Bag* as "one of high rank and entitled to a broad range of equivalents."[140] Although the lower courts had used different terminology in categorizing the invention, they both agreed that there was merit to the claimed invention, and therefore that it would not be limited to the precise form described in the Liddell specification. Liddell's invention, on the spectrum described earlier, was basic, if not pioneering.

With this settled, the analysis turned to the differences between the Liddell machine and the ones that Continental was actually using to make paper bags. Although there were some differences, they were minor. Therefore, because the Liddell patent was entitled to some range of equivalents, and because the Continental machines differed only slightly, a clear case of infringement had been made out. "The lower courts, therefore, found that the invention was a broad one, and that the machine used by the Continental Company was an infringement,"[141] and because of the factual nature of these findings, the Court would not disturb them on appeal.[142]

Before moving on, the Court paused to consider what Liddell claimed and disclosed, and precisely how these compared to Continental's machines. The question turned on a phrase or limitation in the Liddell patent claims, as follows: "Operating means for the forming plate, adapted to cause the said plate to oscillate about its rear edge upon the surface of the cylinder during the rotary movement of said cylinder."[143] The "operating means" in the Liddell drawing was not the same as the one used by Continental on its machines. Did Liddell's patent cover all means that could be used to make the forming plate oscillate; only the specific one disclosed in the Liddell specification and drawings; or something in between? Following precedent, which was later codified in § 112 of the 1952 Patent Act, the Court in effect chose "something in between," by affirming the lower courts' rulings that the Continental machine "was within the doctrine of equivalents" despite the fact that it varied in some details from Liddell's specification.[144] The phrase in

[140] *Continental Paper Bag Co.* v. *Eastern Paper Bag Co.*, 210 U.S. 405, 414 (1908). 210 U.S. 405, 28 S. Ct. 748, 52 L. Ed. 1122 (1908)

[141] 210 U.S. 405, 416.

[142] "And these were questions of fact upon which, both of the courts concurring, their findings will not be disturbed, unless clearly wrong." 210 U.S. 405, 416.

[143] The phrase comes from claims 1, 2, and 7 of the Liddell patent, US Patent 558,969, quoted at 210 U.S. 405, 420.

[144] 210 U.S. 405, 421. Liddell's invention involved an interface between a cylinder, which carried the tubular paper, and the forming plate, which grabbed one side of the tube, folded it backward, and then executed the series of folds that produced the diamond-shaped bottom as well as the two lengthwise folds that permitted the finished bags to lie flat. The cylinder cannot simply transfer the paper tube to the forming plate; to work properly, it must carry the tube forward for some distance while the forming plate makes the folds in the tube. Liddell's patent shows the forming plate hinging on an axis, which keeps it in contact with the cylinder for some distance. Continental's machines took a different approach: in them, the cylinder itself moves down and away from the forming plate. The Court held in effect that the

question, which the Court paraphrased as "mechanical means to bring into working relation the folding plate and the cylinder," was, it said, "the very essence of the invention, and marks the advance upon the prior art."[145] In contemporary lingo we might say that the feature in question was the "point of novelty" in the Liddell invention, and therefore that the Court was loathe to interpret it too narrowly.

With infringement out of the way, the Court got down to the crux of the case, the injunction. The discussion was couched in terms of jurisdiction, the idea being that a court of equity could hear the case only if an injunction were the proper remedy. The majority, per McKenna, starts out by noting that Continental's argument is not about mere nonuse, but turns instead on "*unreasonable* nonuse."[146] And reasonability in this context means quite simply this: whether "the derelict patentee" has acted in a way that "contraven[es] the supposed public policy of the law."[147] Rather than dive right into the remedy, however, the Court starts with the nature of the right at issue. And in doing so, it looks to the words of the statute, and "not [to] matters outside of it – not to circumstances of expediency ..."[148] The statute is simple, of course; "the language of complete monopoly has been employed."[149] Moreover, the Court says, patent law does not really give the inventor anything he or she did not already have. The exclusive rights granted under the statute merely extend the inherent right of the inventor over an invention to a wider scope. They give the inventor a general right, but only because the inventor chooses to publicly disclose the nature of the invention. The Court's review of prior cases shows just how familiar these tropes are in the discussion of patents. Its conclusion is unremarkable: "[W]henever this court has had occasion to speak, it has decided that an inventor receives from a patent the right to exclude others from its use for the time prescribed in the statute ... [P]atents are property, and entitled to the same rights and sanctions as other property."[150] Period.

So far, so formal. But the Court does not stop there. Justice McKenna reviews the cases Continental cites in favor of the no-injunction rule. He reiterates the underwhelming enthusiasm felt by both lower courts in reaching their holdings. And he rehearses Judge Aldrich's dissent in the First Circuit, specifically repeating Aldrich's claim that, prior cases notwithstanding, the nature of the nonuse by Eastern –

Continental machines did employ "operating means [causing the] plate to oscillate upon the surface of the cylinder," as that phrase was used in the Liddell patent: so, infringement.

145 210 U.S. 405, 421.

146 210 U.S. 405, 422 (my emphasis).

147 Ibid.

148 210 U.S. 405, 423.

149 Ibid. The specific "language" the Court refers to is the "exclusive right to inventors to make, use, and vend their inventions." Ibid. This is a paraphrase of section 22 of the 1870 Act which defines the patent grant as: "[T]he exclusive right to make, use and vend the said invention or discovery throughout the United States." Patent Act of 1870, Ch. 230, 16 Stat. 198–217 (July 8, 1870), at § 22.

150 210 U.S. 405, 425.

nonuse in service of a new-fangled industrial combination, the Union Paper Bag Company – rendered Union-Eastern's nonuse far less benign than the innocent nonuser of the prior cases.[151] In response to these arguments, McKenna quotes from Eastern's brief, which explains the nonuse as a matter of simple economics: It would be expensive to replace the existing bag-making machines in its Rumsford mill with machines designed in accordance with the Liddell patent. Though Liddell's design is workable, and in some ways superior, the sunk costs are too great. So, it chooses to stand pat. Therefore, we come to see that Eastern's assertion of the patent is not motivated by a desire to exclude others from any technique the company is currently using.[152] It is motivated instead by strategic considerations: the simple desire to exclude a key competitor, Continental, from using an Eastern-patented technique.

The opinion then takes dead aim at the idea animating Continental's argument: that Eastern's strategy here is inconsistent with the public policy behind patent law:

> But, granting all this, it is certainly disputable that the nonuse was unreasonable, or that the rights of the public were involved. There was no question of a diminished supply or of increase of prices, and can it be said, as a matter of law, that a nonuse was unreasonable which had for its motive the saving of the expense that would have been involved by changing the equipment of a factory from one set of machines to another? And even if the old machines could have been altered, the expense would have been considerable. As to the suggestion that competitors were excluded from the use of the new patent, we answer that such exclusion may be said to have been of the very essence of the right conferred by the patent, as it is the privilege of any owner of property to use or not use it, without question of motive.[153]

[151] 210 U.S. 405, 427–428.

[152] 210 U.S. 405, 428–429 (quoting from respondent Eastern's brief):

> [T]he circuit court inferred the motive of the respondents from the unexplained nonuse of the patent. But petitioner has given its explanation of the purpose of respondent. Quoting Judge Aldrich, that the patent in suit has been 'deliberately held in nonuse for a wrongful purpose,' petitioner asks, 'What was that wrongful purpose? It was the purpose to make more money with the existing old reciprocating ... machines and the existing old complicated ... machines than could be made with new Liddell machines, when the cost of building the latter was taken into account. And this purpose was effective to cause the long and invariable nonuse of the Liddell invention, notwithstanding that new Liddell machines might have produced better paper bags than the old ... machines were producing.'

[153] 410 U.S. 405, 429. The absoluteness of common law entitlements such as property is taken for granted. This certainly looks to be consistent with the thinking of a Justice who joined the majority in *Lochner* v. *New York*. I would remind the reader, however, that one can see patents as property rights without going all the way to *Lochner*. There are more flexible ways to view the common law baselines, and their interaction with the general welfare. See, e.g., Cass R. Sunstein, Lochner's *Legacy*, 87 Colum. L. Rev. 873 (1987). Putting aside property theory, there is an additional dimension to the opinion in *Continental Paper Bag* – something that reaches beyond property talk and touches on important facts concerning the industrial context from which the case arose.

The property talk at the end of this paragraph might easily obscure the point made at the beginning. The Court notes the absence of evidence that the Liddell patent contributed to a "diminished supply" or an "increase of prices" with respect to paper bags. Consumer harm, which drove Judge Aldrich's dissent, is simply an unproven assertion as far as the Court is concerned. But would the outcome change if Continental could show affirmative consumer harm? Quite possibly; as the concluding sentence in the opinion says, "Whether, however, a case cannot arise where, regarding the situation of the parties in view of the public interest, a court of equity might be justified in withholding relief by injunction, we do not decide."[154] Once again, the Court implies that in the right case, a patent might have to give way to other public policy concerns.[155] This is just not that case.[156]

Why not? Because although Eastern kept its patent on the shelf, the underlying invention had merit – enough, in fact, that the defendant Continental was practicing it. Also, Eastern was an active manufacturer. Patent nonuse, in other words, was not a corporate policy. It was simply dictated *in this instance* by two sets of costs: the sunk costs in current machinery, and the switching costs of implementing the Liddell design. Behind the property talk, then, was an awareness of the industrial context that gave rise to the Liddell patent, and that influenced whether and how Eastern used it. The Court ratified Eastern's strategic use of the patent in this case, without, it is true, commenting on whether such a strategy writ large would promote innovation. Yet it does mention that Congress had acquiesced in patent nonuse by failing to amend the Patent Act. Also, the Court implied that robust enforcement of

[154] 410 U.S. 405, 429.

[155] This might be read as support for the revisionist idea that gilded age formalism and "mechanical jurisprudence" might be oversimplified shibboleths that belie the fact that judges in this era often reasoned in ways that are usually associated with the later legal realists. See Brian Z. Tamanaha, Beyond the Formalist-Realist Divide: The Role of Politics in Judging, 71–89 (Princeton, NJ: Princeton University Press, 2009) (collecting instances of this phenomenon). It is easy to overstate both aspects of this, however. Formalists earned their reputation for a reason, and McKenna's extensive property talk in *Continental* is certainly a difference in style, and I would argue in substance, with the way a realist judge would be likely to handle the same issue. See generally, Barbara H. Fried, The Progressive Assault on Laissez Faire: Robert Hale and the First Law and Economics Movement (Cambridge, MA: Harvard University Press, 1998) (detailing the many ways in which the writings of Robert Lee Hale quite substantially deviated from the conventional formalist thinking of the gilded age and *Lochner* era); Frederick Schauer, *Legal Realism Untamed*, 91 Tex. L. Rev. 749, 754 (2013) (arguing that reliance on non-legal sources is legal realism's most important contribution). To the extent McKenna makes mention of data beyond the case law – such as the lack of proof of consumer harm, and the legitimate rationale for Eastern's nonuse – his opinion might be described as a version of "formalism plus."

[156] Justice Harlan, the lone dissenter, disagreed; he thought this was precisely that case. Here is the full text of his dissent:

> Mr. Justice Harlan thinks that the original bill should have been dismissed. He thinks the facts are such that the court should have declined, upon grounds of public policy, to give any relief to the plaintiff by injunction, and he dissents from the opinion and judgment.

210 U.S. 405, 430 (Harlan, J., dissenting).

rights would often lead to productive outcomes that would vindicate the basic policy behind granting rights in the first place.

AFTER *CONTINENTAL BAG* Policymakers concerned with new industrial combinations reacted quickly to the decision. Part of the Oldfield Bill, drafted to respond to the wave of industrial concentration, was a provision punishing patent nonuse. The hearings on the Bill rehearsed the concern voiced by Judge Aldrich in dissent in the First Circuit, over the use of patents to reinforce monopoly power. Commentators, however, were split: The *Harvard Law Review* reacted immediately with a call to overturn the decision by legislation; the author wanted to insert into US law a European-style "working requirement" that would do just that.[157] An article in the *Yale Law Journal* took the opposite view, arguing that the Court was undoubtedly correct in declining to impose its own policy views in place of the business strategy employed by the patent owner.[158]

For their part, R&D managers and patent professionals saw immediately that *Continental Paper Bag* had given an important boost to the new patent strategies that were being worked out at the time. Almost immediately, the decision was seen to support a major shift in understanding about what patents were all about. Unlike the early nineteenth-century view, the individual patent was no longer seen as giving legal protection over a single, discrete technology, sold in the market as a standalone product. The lone patent was now thought of as covering a single feature or component, rather than an entire product. And a given patent might never be implemented. It might represent a future possibility, or one among several potential ways to construct a component of a larger product. In this sense, *Continental Paper Bag* helped to usher in the era when patents were understood as *options*, and partial options at that. It also reflected the understanding that the proper unit of analysis was not the single, freestanding patent, but rather the patent *portfolio*. Going forward, participants in the patent system were to judge the efficacy of patents not simply by reference to individual patents over individual components but as part of a larger set of practices and strategies in which multiple patents were accumulated and deployed in various ways that served the interests of patent owners.

Implicit in the Court's reasoning in *Continental Paper Bag* was this idea: Eastern was a large, active manufacturer. It used one patent, the Liddell patent, not to protect a manufacturing technique, but to sue a rival. Indirectly, this strategy supported Eastern's manufacturing operations. It did not need to actually practice the Liddell patent to benefit from it. And as long as it was benefitting, and not directly and immediately harming consumers, that was enough for the Court.

Both parts of the Court's thinking were important. In court cases and legislation, they were expanded and modified over time. The consumer harm idea was

[157] Note, *Rights of the Owner of an Idle Patent in Equity*, 20 Harv. L. Rev. 638 (1908).
[158] Note, *The Effect of Nonuse on a Patentee's Remedy against Infringement*, 18 Yale L.J. 52 (1908).

developed in depth with subsequent opinions that probed into patent-related practices. Many of these practices were found to have far less benign effects on consumer welfare than Eastern's simple nonuse; the large body of law on patent-antitrust and patent misuse attests to this. At the same time, there was a much more positive reception for the other aspect of the decision. The notion gained currency that corporate patent portfolios could stimulate innovation just as individual patents had in earlier times. The case was therefore an important step in adapting the patent system to the era of large industrial scale, highly concentrated production, complex, multi-component technologies, and the carefully constructed patent portfolio.

After *Continental Paper Bag*, and until very recently, patent nonuse was a non-factor. Only with the rise of "patent trolls" was the basic logic of the *Continental* case called into serious doubt. And just as larger pressures were at work in forging the *Continental* rule, so the recent *eBay*[159] case limiting the reach *of Continental* owes much to the pressure built up by the changing dynamics of patent litigation.

* * * *

Taking the long view, the movement from "paper patents" to the *Paper Bag Case* looks like a straightforward Hurstian story, or maybe even an "efficiency of the common law" story. Changing times, changing technology, led to a responsive change in legal doctrine. Yet we ought to be just aware enough of ideas in legal history to be wary of these Whiggish instincts. As Morton Horwitz has shown so well,[160] legal rules affecting economic development inevitably have winners and losers; it may not be as simple as saying that we are all winners when dynamic innovators are rewarded. Someone pays for these rewards as well, and if there are systematic patterns in the list of winners and losers, that has to count as an important (though yet largely unwritten) aspect of the legal history of this branch of law.

4.3.2 *Employee Inventions*

Corporations grew dramatically in size and impact between 1880 and 1920. Industrial R&D was more and more concentrated in corporate research labs. We have seen how the growth of corporate patent portfolios initiated an adjustment in judicial attitudes toward patents: active use was not always required, or even favored after the *Continental Paper Bag* case. The next set of legal developments gathered around the law of patent ownership. As between individual inventor and corporate sponsor or employer, who should receive ownership of patents stemming from inventive research? The answer changed drastically in the years leading up to 1920.

From 1790, patents rested initially with the inventor or inventors. As we saw in Chapter 2, ownership transfers to an assignee (usually an early investor) were

[159] *eBay Inc.* v. *MercExchange, L.L.C.*, 547 U.S. 388 (2006).
[160] Morton Horwitz, The Transformation of American Law, 1780–1860.

common in the Founding Era. And Chapter 3 showed that, post-1836, the Patent Office was empowered to issue a patent jointly to an inventor and assignee – when the inventor had assigned the patent application, and the assignee/partner thus had an ownership interest at the date of patent grant.

The important point is this: ownership rested (and still rests) *initially* with the inventor. For a non-inventor to become an owner, the inventor had to act: By contract or instrument of assignment (technically, a property grant), the inventor was required to take legally cognizable action. An inventor had to move affirmatively move from the initial vesting of title at the time of patent grant. Without a legal instrument – assignment, license, or the like – the inventor remains the owner. This was true in 1880 and it remains true today.

The tradition of inventor as the default patent owner came into conflict with corporate agendas in the late nineteenth century. After 1880, corporate managers and executives felt a strong imperative to concentrate invention ownership in the hands of the corporation. Many of the various strategies we have reviewed in this chapter require ownership (or at least effective control) over a large patent portfolio. In patent law, inventors were (and are) always natural persons: real people. It was true in 1790, and 1880, and remains true today, that corporations are not inventors. It follows that General Electric, per se, cannot be listed as the inventor of anything. The same with AT&T, Westinghouse, etc. And what this means is that, if corporations were to come to own all the patents stemming from their investments in R&D, they would have to do so by means of patent *transfers*: From employee inventor to corporate owner. If corporations could never be inventors, it was essential that it become trivially easy for them to become *owners*. Thus, the law of patent ownership in the corporatization era would have to be realized through the instrument of contract law. The systematic corporatization of patent ownership, then, would depend on a smooth and almost invisible conduit to channel legal rights from inventor to corporate employer.

But the goal of frictionless rights-transfers ran up against long-established norms.[161] There was a long tradition under which skilled machinists were treated with the dignity befitting skilled artisans. This included solicitude for their work as inventors – which meant machinists, even in the employ of a partnership or corporation, were often deemed the owner of many inventions they made while on the job. There was an exception, stating that inventions made at the express direction of a superior, or in direct pursuit of the machinist's particular duties, would belong to the employer. But this was narrow. A representative case is *Whiting* v. *Graves*,[162] which centered on the activities of machinist Elijah L. Howard. Howard was employed by

[161] The essential account of the sociology and power relations behind these norms – and of the changes wrought by growing corporate interests – is Catherine L. Fisk, Working Knowledge: Employee Innovation and the Rise of Corporate Intellectual Property.

[162] 29 F. Cas. 1059 (C.C.D. Mass. 1878) (No. 17,577).

Whiting as a machinist, in Whiting's factory, which produced "fancy dry goods" – fancy dresses, bonnets, etc. Howard's duties were "the making and keeping in order of ruffling [bunching or pleating fabric], ruching [i.e., making pleated ribbons], and fluting [creating wavy accents on fabrics] machines, and all attachments or machinery required for the manufacturing of any goods which might be necessary to be made."[163] In adapting and maintaining Whiting's textile machinery, Howard made some "little additions to sewing and other machines as were necessary to adapt them to the making of flutings, ruffles and ruchings";[164] these inventions were assigned to Whiting, and Whiting patented them. But Howard also made two more significant and general inventions, which the court described as "contrivances applicable to sewing-machines generally, being for improved mechanisms for operating such machines."[165] Whiting – Howard's employer – also patented these two, and Howard objected. Employee Howard was apparently not too greedy; all he sought was "an equitable interest in one-half of the rights under these two patents."[166] He claimed this based on an oral agreement with Whiting, under which Whiting was to pay the expenses for obtaining the patents, giving Howard a one-half interest in them (a common arrangement, as we have seen in Chapters 2 and 3). The court ruled for employee Howard, in an opinion that conveys a respect for Howard's work, along with an intuitive sense that unless subject to a contract or exceptional circumstances, Howard's inventions rightfully belong to Howard:

> [T]here would seem to be no good reason why Howard should not receive some benefit from the use of his inventions in other factories than Whiting's, and from the sale of his inventions to others. It was no part of the original employment of Howard, according to Whiting's statement of his understanding of it, to invent machinery for general use, but only in the factory of Whiting.[167]

This is a good example of general attitudes at the time. According to legal scholar Catherine L. Fisk, the preeminent expert on employee-created works in the nineteenth century: "[J]udges and lawyers, skilled workers and those who hired them, acted as if they believed that workplace knowledge was a valuable possession, or more likely an attribute, of the individual worker."[168]

But this began to change. At first, a number of cases simply expanded the implied contractual rights of the employer. A New Jersey equity case from 1893 shows the turn toward contract:[169]

[163] 29 F. Cas. 1059, 1060.
[164] Ibid.
[165] Ibid.
[166] Ibid.
[167] Ibid.
[168] Catherine L. Fisk, Working Knowledge: Employee Innovation and the Rise of Corporate Intellectual Property, at p. 22.
[169] *Eustis Mfg. Co.* v. *Eustis*, 51 N.J. Eq. 565, 570, 27 A. 439, 441 (Ch. 1893).

> The question then presents itself whether the complainants are entitled to an irrevocable exclusive license to use the patents, and to relief to that extent, and an injunction to protect them in its enjoyment. The mere fact that Eustis made these inventions while in the service and pay of the company, and in the line of his employment, in the absence of an agreement to that effect, gives the company no right to the ownership of the patents ... But the right to an exclusive license to use the patent may be given by agreement, or inferred from circumstances.

Such a case presents a compromise, or midway point (perhaps appropriate for an equity court): The inventor retains what is sometimes called "dignity of title," the claim to ownership; but the (corporate) employer receives an implied exclusive license to use the invention. The end result is that while the inventor may technically claim ownership, the benefit of exclusive use goes to the employer.

A common application of implied contract rules during this period produced what became known as the "shop right." Unlike the outcome in the *Eustis* case just discussed, a shop right gives the employer a *nonexclusive* right to use the invention. The employee-inventor retains not only technical title but also the right to assert the patent against anyone except the employer. The rationale is familiar to students of restitution or unjust enrichment: A shop right arises when an inventor avails him or herself of the assets of the employer in the course of the work leading up to the invention. Having used these corporate inputs, the thinking goes, the employer deserves some use right to the resulting invention. Without it, the inventor could turn around and sue the very employer whose machines, tools, facilities, and other employees contributed to the invention. The manifest unfairness of this leads to what might be seen as a split entitlement: The employee-inventor receives title, but the employer receives a right to use the resulting invention in the same workplace where the employee-inventor created it.[170]

The legal category of implied contract provided the rationale for cases such as *Eustis*, as well as the shop right. As legal tools go, this one is fairly flexible in application, and has proven malleable over time. With implied contract, legal outcomes depend largely on what a judge or jury believes would be a reasonable expectation on the part of the two parties involved. (A classic implied contract is formed when you go to a restaurant, look over the menu, and order some food: you

[170] See *Solomons* v. *United States*, 137 U.S. 342, 346 (1890):

> [W]hen one is in the employ of another in a certain line of work, and devises an improved method or instrument for doing that work, and uses the property of his employer and the services of other employes [sic]to develop and put in practicable form his invention, and explicitly assents to the use by his employer of such invention, a jury, or a court, trying the facts, is warranted in finding that he has so far recognized the obligations of service flowing from his employment and the benefits resulting from his use of the property, and the assistance of the co-employes, of his employer, as to have given to such employer an irrevocable license to use such invention.

See also *McClurg* v. *Kingsland*, 42 U.S. 202, 204 (1843) ("[T]he facts [showing invention in the defendant's shop] justified the presumption of a license or grant to use the invention, and that defendants were protected thereby ...").

have agreed to pay for the meal, and the restaurant has agreed to supply the food represented on the menu.) An implied contract, under which an employee implicitly agrees to assign title to company-related inventions made during employment, and the company implicitly agrees to pay the employee's salary for work performed, serves the purpose of low-friction title transfer needed to centralize patent ownership in the hands of a corporate employer.

As norms change, so does the sense of what is reasonable. This is evident from another lines of cases concerning employees who were "employed to invent." Starting about 1925,[171] the rule became: If the very purpose and goal of employing someone is to have him or her work on a specific invention, by implication title to that invention goes to the employer.[172] To vest title in the employee would be unfair.[173] As older contracts cases say, this would deprive the employer of "the benefit of the bargain." But what does it mean to be employed to invent? How specific do the employer's instructions have to be to have the employee's efforts treated as the precise purpose and subject of the employment? These are questions whose answers changed subtly over time.

The change is evident in a Supreme Court case from 1924, *Standard Parts* v. *Peck*. In a gesture that seems within the rule from prior cases, employee Peck had offered

171 As late as 1895, even where the facts establish without doubt that a mechanic was employed specifically to make an improvement in known designs, the employee retained ownership of a patent on the new design. See, e.g., *Withington-Cooley Mfg. Co.* v. *Kinney*, 68 F. 500, 505 (6th Cir. 1895) (Employee Kinney employed specifically to design a new type of power press, which he later patented; "[Employed inventor Kinney] must be presumed to have granted to Babcock a personal license to make and sell power presses embodying the improvements covered by his patent."). Compare *Gill* v. *United States*, 160 U.S. 426, 435 (1896) (holding that patentee Gill was estopped from asserting a claim against the government for use of his patents, having encouraged and acquiesced in government use for an extended period without mentioning his patents; in dictum, "[I]f the patentee be employed to invent or devise such improvements, his patents obtained therefor belong to his employer, since in making such improvements he is merely doing what he was hired to do.").

172 *Pressed Steel Car Co* v. *Hansen*, 137 F. 403, 416 (3d Cir. 1905) (Acheson, J., dissenting) ("The proofs, I think, bring this case squarely within the just principle enunciated by the Supreme Court in three recent cases- that, where a person is employed and paid to devise improvements, his inventions and patents obtained therefor belong to his employer.").

173 See *Houghton* v. *United States*, 23 F.2d 386, 388–89 (4th Cir. 1928), where a patent was granted to government employee Houghton on a fumigant gas for disinfecting vessels visiting US ports:

> [T]he case here presented is that of an employee to conduct experiments for the purpose of making [an invention] … All that [employee Houghton] did was to … conduct experiments under [his Department's] direction, for the purpose of determining how best to produce and combine the gases … For this he was relieved of other work and sent to the Edgewood Arsenal to make the experiments. His regular salary was paid to him while he was thus engaged, and, when he deducted [deduced] from the experiments the method to be followed in producing and combining the gases, he did merely that which he was being paid his salary to do. Under such circumstances, we think there can be no doubt that his invention is the property of his employer, the United States.

his employer a shop right to Peck's patented invention, made while employed by Standard Parts. The Court found that, under the facts, this was not enough:

> [Peck] yields to Standard Parts] a shop right only, free from the payment of royalty, but personal and temporary – not one that could be assigned or transferred. Peck therefore virtually asserts, though stimulated to services by [his employer] and paid for them, doing nothing more than he was engaged to do and paid for doing, that the product of the services was so entirely his property that he might give as great a right to any member of the mechanical world as to the one who engaged him and paid him – a right to be used in competition with the one who engaged him and paid him. We cannot assent to this . . .[174]

To be sure, this did not mark an end to solicitude for the employee inventor. Courts, including the Supreme Court, continued in some cases to give the benefit of the doubt to the employee when it came to patent ownership.[175] But overall, the cases more and more found that employees who were steered toward research projects were creating inventions that would be owned by the corporate employer, and not themselves.[176]

4.3.2.1 Engineering a Solution: The Employee Assignment Contract

It is crucial to understand that the cases reviewed so far all involved inventive employees who *had not signed an express contract* of assignment with their

[174] *Standard Parts Co.* v. *Peck*, 264 U.S. 52, 60 (1924).

[175] See *United States* v. *Dubilier Condenser Corp.*, 289 U.S. 178, 188, amended 289 U.S. 706 (1933):

> The reluctance of courts to imply or infer an agreement by the employee to assign his patent is due to a recognition of the peculiar nature of the act of invention, which consists neither in finding out the laws of nature, nor in fruitful research as to the operation of natural laws, but in discovering how those laws may be utilized or applied for some beneficial purpose, by a process, a device, or a machine. It is the result of an inventive act, the birth of an idea and its reduction to practice; the product of original thought; a concept demonstrated to be true by practical application or embodiment in tangible form . . .

[176] See, e.g., *United States* v. *Dubilier Condenser Corp.*, 289 U.S. 178, 215–216, amended 289 U.S. 706 (1933) (Stone, J., dissenting, joined by Hughes, J., and Cardozo, J.):

> [A]s the patent is the fruit of the very work which the employee is hired to do, and for which he is paid, it should no more be withheld from the employer, in equity and good conscience, than the product of any other service which the employee engages to render. This result has been reached where the contract was to devise a means for solving a defined problem, *Standard Parts Co.* v. *Peck*, supra, and the decision has been thought to establish the employer's right wherever the employee is hired or assigned to evolve a process or mechanism for meeting a specific need.

Note that, in contrast to the majority opinion highlighting the special (semi- mystical) act of invention, the dissenters in *Dubilier Condenser* treat inventions as just another work product of an employee – no different from "the product of any other service" the employee is paid to provide. It is this "routinization," or professionalization, of invention that came to prevail. See Catherine L. Fisk, Working Knowledge: Employee Innovation and the Rise of Corporate Intellectual Property.

employer.[177] The best way for a corporate employer to avoid the morass of shop rights and "employed to invent" cases was to require research-oriented employees (or any employee who might conceivably make an invention) to sign an assignment contract at the start of employment. With an express contract, implied contact cases were (and are) irrelevant. The law provides that the corporate employer owns the employee's inventions from the moment of invention. The assignment contract, in other words, pre-assigns rights in inventions not yet made. When they are made, ownership flows instantly and automatically to the employer.[178]

The benefits of insuring corporate ownership through employee contracting were described by an early patent strategist, Edwin Prindle, one of the founders of the Patent Office Society and author of an influential series of practical patent advice articles for the technical community:

> [I]t is evident that it is desirable to have a contract with every employee who is at all likely to make inventions which relate to the business of the employer, and as the courts will sustain such contracts, even though they contain no further provision for return for the inventions than the payment of the ordinary salary, the employer should have such a contract with every such employee. There are manufacturing concerns where every man in the drafting room and in the sales department, and every skilled employee, is under such a contract. The difficulty of inducing the employees to sign such a contract will be reduced if the officers of the company will set the example by signing such a contract. This is often a mere matter of form, as the officer is frequently a man who is either not inventive, or one who is glad to take his returns in the form of dividends from the stock.[179]

[177] See *Dalzell* v. *Dueber Watch-Case Mfg. Co.*, 149 U.S. 315, 320 (1893) (equity suit to specifically enforce alleged oral contract of assignment; Court held the evidence was too contradictory to establish an oral contract; thus, under the facts, defendant company, plaintiff's former employer, "is not entitled to a conveyance of patents obtained for inventions made by him while so employed, *in the absence of express agreement to that effect.*" (emphasis added)). *Schmitt* v. *Nelson Valve Co*, 125 F. 754, 757 (3d Cir. 1903) (refusing to enforce an alleged parol (oral) additional promise, for a ten-year employment term at escalating salary levels, made to an employee at the time of patent assignment).

[178] In technical terms: The present assignment of a future invention immediately conveys "equitable title" over the future invention to the assignee. See *Littlefield* v. *Perry*, 88 U.S. 205, 226–227 (1874) ("An assignment of an imperfect invention, with all improvements upon it that the inventor may make, is equivalent in equity to an assignment of the perfected results. The assignment in this case being such a one, the assignees became in equity the owners of the patent granted upon the perfected invention [i.e., the improvement patent] ... [The inventor of the improvement, the assignor] took the legal title in trust for them, and should convey. Courts of equity in proper cases consider that as done which should be. If there exists an obligation to convey at once, such courts will oftentimes proceed as if it had actually been made."). As mentioned, this equitable title automatically converts to the more secure "legal title" when an invention is made and a patent application filed. See *FilmTec Corp.* v. *Allied Signal, Inc.*, 939 F.2d 1568, 1572 (Fed. Cir. 1991).

[179] Edwin J. Prindle, *Patents as a Factor in a Manufacturing Business: Part 4, The Patent Relations of Employer and Employee*, 32 Engineering Magazine 407, 415–416 (1907).

When written contracts like these were first coming into widespread use, there were some arguments against enforcing them. When invention rights were added to the basic bargain of showing up to work in exchange for wages, it was said, there was no additional benefit offered the employee – a failure of contractual "consideration" for the extra element, the patent rights. Agreements to assign patent rights were against public policy, it was argued, on the ground that this restrained trade in the patented invention; presumably, this was because the inventor himself was precluded from leaving employment and competing against the employer. Both these arguments were shot down, and an express assignment upheld, in one case from 1895.[180] The court noted that, prior to the invention in question, several former employees had patented inventions made while working for the company.[181] It struck the court as manifestly unfair for these former employees to obtain patents and sue the very company where they learned about the relevant technology:

> Is this contract unreasonable or unconscionable? The Bonsack Machine Company owned valuable patented machines, employed in the manufacture of cigarettes. Comparatively the invention was in its infancy, and the machinery was known to be difficult of operation, and open to improvement. Any one entering into the employment of the company had full opportunity of learning the merits of the

[180] *Hulse* v. *Bonsack Mach. Co.*, 65 F. 864, 867 (4th Cir. 1895) (consideration):

> [I]t cannot be said that this agreement, or any part of it, is without consideration. In the absence of fraud [etc.], courts cannot inquire into the inadequacy of the consideration of a contract, or set up their own opinions respecting that which parties in good faith on both sides have agreed upon ... Some consideration is requisite to support a contract, but the sufficiency of the consideration cannot be inquired into.

Ibid., 65 F. 864, 869 (restraint of trade):

> In [a prior case], the court refused to extend the doctrine of restraint of trade to a covenant in an assignment of a patent by an inventor 'to use his best efforts to invent improvements in the process, and to transfer them to the buyer; to do no act which may injure the buyer or the business; and at no time to aid, assist, or encourage in any manner any competition against the same.' Speaking of this doctrine, the court says: 'It has never been extended to a business protected by a patent. Nor does it extend to a business which is a secret, and not known to the public, because the public has no right in the secret.' This is not literally an agreement in restraint of trade ... There is no presumption that such a contract is void. The presumption is in favor of the competency of the parties to make the contract, and the burden is upon the party who alleges that it is unreasonable or against public policy.

[181] *Hulse* v. *Bonsack Mach. Co.*, 65 F. 864, 864 (4th Cir. 1895):

> In several instances persons ... employed [by defendant Bonsack Machine Co.] discovered improvements in working [the Bonsack machines, which revolutionized the cigarette industry as the first automatic cigarette rolling machine, see U.S. Patent 237,640, issued March 8, 1881], and, without disclosing the discovery, took out patents, which they used or sold in competition with the company. To avoid this in the future, the company adopted a rule by which it required all persons entering its employment to agree to give the company the benefit of any improvement made while in the employment of the company, or at any time afterwards.

> machines, and, by constant and daily use, could see where the machine was defective, and where improvement was needed. If any improvement suggested itself to his mind, he could, by using the machine and the time and material of the company, experiment upon it, and ascertain its value ... [Any such improvement would] owe ... its suggestion and origin, its progressive development and perfection, to the business, the practical working, the opportunity afforded by the company. When, therefore, the company, taught by costly experience, determined to protect itself from the discovery of improvements by its own servants, it did a natural and reasonable thing; and, when it protected itself by a covenant in advance of any employment with those seeking its service, it did a fair thing.[182]

Certainly by 1900 the advice given by Edwin Prindle, just quoted, had been widely followed.[183] So by written agreement, or as a fallback, implied contract, most research-oriented employees parted ways with the ownership of their patent-worthy inventive output from their first day on the job.[184]

There are several ways to look at, or explain, the change in employer ownership rules: the greater tendency of courts to imply an obligation to assign invention ownership, and the willingness to enforce assignment contracts with little hesitation. Inventive employees were seen as just another "cog in the wheel" of the emerging

[182] *Hulse* v. *Bonsack Mach. Co.*, 65 F. 864, 867–868 (4th Cir. 1895).

[183] True as to trade secrets as well as future inventions:

> [B]efore the employment began, and before the defendant was permitted to enter the complainant's glass works, he signed and affixed his seal to a written contract bearing date September 4, 1901, which contains the following provisions:
>
> First. The employer is engaged in the manufacture of glass, glassware, and mechanical devices in connection therewith, and that such manufacture is carried on by means of certain secret formulas, methods, processes, tools, machinery, patterns, and appliances, and the same are the property of the employer, and intended to be kept and guarded by the employer as secrets; and that all knowledge and information which the employe now possesses, or shall hereafter acquire, respecting such secrets, and all inventions and discoveries made by said employe during the term of his employment, shall at all times, and for all purposes, be regarded as acquired, and held by the employe in a fiduciary capacity, and solely for the benefit of the employer.'
>
> "Fourth. That the employe will, when required, make and execute any and all assignments in writing which may be deemed by the employer proper and necessary to transfer and vest in the employer the entire right, title, and interest in all inventions and discoveries made by the employe during the term of his employment."

Mississippi Glass Co v. *Franzen*, 143 F. 501, 501–502 (3d Cir. 1906).

[184] Some limitations on an employer's claim to ownership did emerge over time, including: (1) limits on the ability of an employer to claim ownership of work-related inventions after an employee left the employer company (so-called trailer clauses); see, e.g., *Aspinwall Mfg. Co.* v. *Gill*, 32 F. 697 (C.C.D. N.J. 1887) (invalidating agreement to assign all future inventions, whether made during or after employment); *Dorr-Oliver, Inc.* v. *United States*, 432 F.2d 447, 452 (Ct. Cl. 1970) (to be enforceable, trailer clause must be limited in both time and scope, i.e., limited to technology related to the former employer's product lines); and (2) so-called right to invent laws, enacted by eight states, limiting a former employer's claims, see Robert P. Merges, *The Law and Economics of Employee Inventions*, at p. 9 ("between 1977 and 1989, eight states passed legislation limiting employers' ownership claims over employee inventions").

large corporation. The bureaucratization and professionalization of the work force penetrated through the ideology of independence and autonomy that had surrounded the skilled crafts person. The culture of the workshop, or free labor, was giving way to the "organization man [sic]." From this perspective, individual ownership was inconsistent with the general trend toward the flattening and regularizing of the labor force that attended corporatization.[185]

Aside from the changing culture of employment, there were more functional reasons for the increased emphasis on corporate ownership of inventions. The technology of production was becoming more complex. Researchers specialized more in single product components, which then had to be integrated into machinery, systems, and consumer products. In this setting, individual ownership claims on the part of employees could create serious problems.[186] The promise of patent royalties might encourage inefficient behavior: putting more effort into creating patentable designs, and less into overall product integration; ignoring aspects of the job that are unrelated to invention; and in general acting out of self-interest rather than the best interests of the research team and the company.[187] Though sometimes

185 For evidence of this, see Catherine L. Fisk, Working Knowledge, at p. 240:

> The growth of corporations and the rapid spread of office and factory work significantly changed the application of legal rules regarding intellectual property ownership. As is always the case with law, the changing applications ultimately changed the rules themselves.
>
> The acceptance of corporations as legal 'persons' with all the rights and privileges of personhood provided a new legal framework to reconcile the traditionally individualistic presumptions of patent and copyright law, which focus on *the* author or *the* inventor, with the new social reality of collective innovation.
>
> [The legal system] naturalized the[se] radical developments and made a revolution seem normal, inevitable, and uncontroversial.

186 Inventions created by teams sometimes result in multiple inventors; co-invention, as a form of collective ownership, could ameliorate some of the transaction costs of many dispersed owners of patents on multiple product components. The available evidence, however, suggests that at least on average, most patents continued to list only slightly more than one inventor until fairly recently. See Tom Nicholas, *The Role of Independent Invention in U.S. Technological Development, 1880–1930*, 70 J. Econ. Hist. 57, 63 (2010) (random sample of patents shows average inventor per patent increased only slightly between 1880 and 1930, from 1.09 in 1880, 1.12 in 1930); Dennis Crouch, Person(s) Skilled in the Art: Should the Now Established Model of Team-Based Inventing Impact the Obviousness Analysis?, www.Patently-O.com (patent law blog), May 17, 2011, available at www.patentlyo.com/patent/2011/05/persons-skilled-in-the-art-should-the-now-established-model-of-team-based-inventing-impact-the-obviousness-analysis.html ("In [1952], 82% of patents listed only one inventor and a mere 3% listed three or more inventors. By 2011, the statistics had inverted. Less than one-third (32%) of patents issued so far [in 2011] list just a single inventor and 43% identify three or more inventors. During this 60-year period, the average number of inventors per patent has more than doubled."). See also Dennis Crouch, Continued growth in the number of inventors per patent, Patently-O Blog, March 11, 2021, available at https://patentlyo.com/patent/2021/03/continued-growth-inventors.html ("The average (and median) patent application publication now lists three or more inventors.").

187 These issues are discussed in Robert P. Merges, *The Law and Economics of Employee Inventions*.

seen as a naked corporate power grab,[188] the concentration of patent ownership via employee assignment agreements certainly had its practical appeal.

4.3.3 *Progressive Era Antitrust*

In time, especially in the late 1930s and 1940s, it became hardly possible to talk about patents in some circles except in connection with antitrust law. If this later period represents perhaps an overcommitment to policing anticompetitive behavior predicated on patent-related contracts, we can see the roots of the movement in the period from 1880 to 1920. Though for some courts, patent rights were something like a "get out of jail free" card with respect to antitrust issues, there were also cases that pushed back against the aggressive use of patents to restrict consumers in various ways. Before the 1910s, a business arrangement that bound patent licensees in highly restrictive licensing arrangements might well be excused if patent rights were at the bottom of it. But when it came to restrictive patent licenses, strong countercurrents were at work by 1917; these turned out to be the headwaters of what became, by the late 1930s, a roaring river.

An Ngram graph will give some idea of how Progressive Era antitrust policy began to affect policy discussions of patents. This shows the occurrence of the phrase "patent monopoly" – typically associated with an antitrust-oriented view of patent law – in published books from the early nineteenth century until roughly 1930 (Figure 4.18).

We will return to patent licenses. Before that, it is worth a brief look at patents and corporate mergers – another setting that conjoined patents with concerns about monopolization. Here the courts proved far more wary about reining in patent-related activity than in the area of patent licensing. As we have seen at numerous points in this chapter, patents were often one impetus for the wave of industry consolidation after 1880. Thomson-Houston was formed to make peace with Brush; GE to make peace with Thomson-Houston; Bell and Western Union partially consolidated (and split up their respective markets as well); even Westinghouse and Eastman Kodak made numerous strategic patent acquisitions to dampen product competition and maintain end-to-end control of their primary products. Yet even after the Sherman Act in 1890, vertical integration per se was rarely targeted by the newly formed antitrust authorities (particularly the Department of Justice). When vertical acquisitions were challenged, such as when a steel company bought up a coal mine, deep structural remedies to prevent further integration were rarely

188 See David Noble, America by Design, at p. 85 ("Within a half century [of 1860] ... the American patent system had undergone a dramatic change; rather than promoting invention through protection of the inventor, the patent system had come to protect and reward the monopolizer of inventors, the science-based industrial corporations."); Jay Dratler, Jr., *Note, Incentives for People: The Forgotten Purpose of the Patent System*, 16 Harv. J. Legis. 129 (1979).

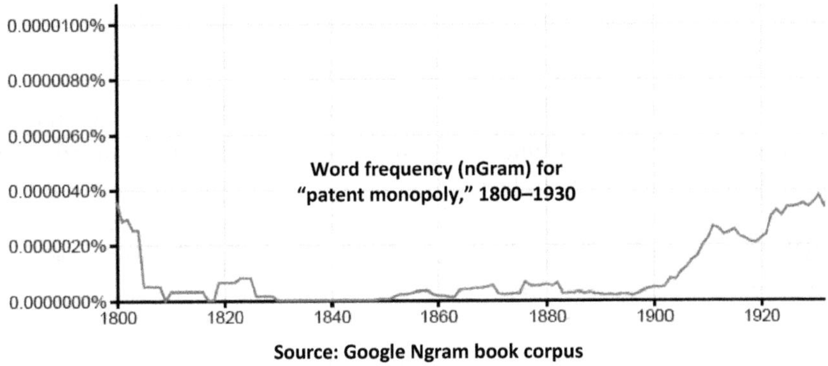

FIGURE 4.18. Word frequency (nGram) for "patent monopoly," 1800–1930

obtained. Some observers (notably Alfred Chandler) credit Gilded Age antitrust law as a perhaps unintentional paragon in the annals of industrial policy: Successful attacks on horizontal (competitior-competitor) arrangements prevented competitors from carving up markets through horizontal arrangements, while a laissez faire approach to vertical integration encouraged the building of corporate behemoths well positioned to reap the advantages of enterprises with massive scale and scope. To the extent antitrust law encouraged formation of the Chandlerian firm, and to the extent this variety of firm unlocked new levels of economic growth, the Sherman Act and related legislation can be seen as a great success.

We return to patents and corporate mergers in Chapter 5. For now, keeping attention on the years between 1880 and 1920, we look at how some companies tried to harness the power of patents to plow forward with an aggressive business model. The chief strategies involved patent-related contracts. Where consumers or distributors wanted the use of a patented item, the patent owner would add conditions to the contract of use, in aid of the owner's overall business aims. So users of then-new mimeograph machines – the blurry but effective predecessor to the Xerox machine – had to agree to buy mimeo ink only from the owner of the patent on the machine.[189] Likewise, early movie theater operators wanted to show films on the Edison Company's patented film projector, so Edison added a condition, saying that use of the projector was permissible only with films authorized and sold by Edison's film studio.[190] The mimeo business contract was upheld, while the film studio contract was struck down as an illegal "tie-in," an impermissible leveraging of the projector patent to exert power over the film industry. Not much separates the two situations. The Edison case is perhaps explainable by the audacity of the business ploy: using a

[189] *Henry* v. *A.B. Dick Co.*, 224 U.S. 1 (1912).
[190] *Motion Picture Patents Co.* v. *Universal Film Mfg. Co.*, 243 U.S. 502 (1917).

patent on the feeder mechanism for film projectors to try to dominate the nascent movie business.[191]

In addition to these cases, classified as patent-related "tie-ins," other disputes arose from contracts under which a patent owner sold to distributors on the condition that products incorporating the patented invention must not be sold to consumers for less than a certain price. Distributor licenses including these "resale price maintenance" terms were condemned out of hand in 1911.[192] A very similar arrangement, however, was upheld as reasonable fifteen years later.[193] The distinction between the cases rests on the thin premise that in the later case, distributors and salespeople were not licensees but *agents* of the patent owner, General Electric. This agency relationship meant that GE was merely directing its agents regarding corporate pricing, rather than attaching a price fixing commitment to an arm's-length transfer of the patented item (light bulbs). Because the agents were alter egos of GE, somewhat akin to employees, it was not wrong for GE to set a minimum price.[194] By analogy, if a company owns both a factory and retail outlets, that company can set the retail price however it wishes. The Court said in effect that GE's agency arrangement was no different.

These cases are consistent with many of the early antitrust cases under the Sherman Act (passed in 1890), and later the Clayton Act (1914). Under the case law there were a few situations where antitrust violations were self-evident ("per se"), but for the most part outcomes were fact-dependent. Only *unreasonable* restraints of trade were condemned – and the "rule of reason" left wide room for judicial

[191] Peter S. Menell, *Envisioning Copyright Law's Digital Future*, 46 N.Y.L. Sch. L. Rev. 63, 170 n. 372 (2003) (after the *Motion Picture Patents* case "the Edison Company's film division rapidly declined as others entered the industry," citing Eileen Bowser, The Transformation of Cinema, 1907–1915. History of the American Cinema, Vol. 2 (Berkeley: University of California Press, 1990); Charles Musser, Before the Nickelodeon: Edwin S. Porter and the Edison Manufacturing Company (Berkeley: University of California Press, 1991); History of Edison Motion Pictures: Decline of the Edison Company (1908–18) [U.S. Library of Congress, available at www.loc.gov/collections/edison-company-motion-pictures-and-sound-recordings/articles-and-essays/history-of-edison-motion-pictures/decline-of-the-edison-company/]).

[192] See *Dr. Miles Med. Co.* v. *John D. Park & Sons Co.*, 220 U.S. 373 (1911) (technically a trade secret license, because the "folk remedies" or so-called patent medicines at issue were not actually patented), overruled much later by *Leegin Creative Leather Prod., Inc.* v. *PSKS, Inc.*, 551 U.S. 877 (2007).

[193] *United States* v. *General Electric Co.*, 272 U.S. 476 (1926) (GE license to Westinghouse, to manufacture light bulb elements, upheld despite including a resale price maintenance provision).

[194] *United States* v. *Gen. Elec. Co.*, 272 U.S. 476, 488, 47 S. Ct. 192, 196, 71 L. Ed. 362 (1926) (Taft, J.):

> [T]here is nothing as a matter of principle or in the authorities which requires us to hold that genuine contracts of agency like those before us, however comprehensive as a mass or whole in their effect, are violations of the Anti-Trust Act. The owner of an article patented or otherwise is not violating the common law or the Anti-Trust Act by seeking to dispose of his articles directly to the consumer and fixing the price by which his agents transfer the title from him directly to such consumer.

discretion.[195] As mentioned, patent owners came away from these Progressive Era cases with some wins and some losses. But despite optimism in some quarters that patents would serve as a shield against antitrust liability, there were plenty of indications that courts would continue to scrutinize patent licenses carefully. If there had ever been a pure and simple era when patents, as property, served as a firewall against antitrust scrutiny, that era was surely ended by 1915.[196] As historian Steven Wilf writes,

> With rapid industrialization from the 1880s onwards, more Americans lost control of their productive lives and became dependent upon those who controlled the means of production for wages and the conditions of their workplaces. Progressives recognized that industrial liberty meant both freedom from oppressive government regulation and freedom from the mastery of private entities within markets. The definition of market power was not always rigorously parsed. It was often identified with the negative effects of the rise of an industrial economy of scale, including the emergence of impersonal corporate relationships, the decline of a self-employed quasi-autonomous middle class, and the willingness of corporate entities to exercise power without regard to personal or social costs.
>
> Progressive Era jurists saw intellectual property through the optic of antitrust. As one court stated, "Patents, copyrights, and trade-marks excite two deeply seated feelings. One is the feeling of anyone who has originated anything of his right to claim an exclusive property in it and to the trade growing out of it. The other is a hatred of monopoly."[197]

This sentiment found even fuller expression in the 1930s and 1940s, as we will see in Chapter 5.

[195] See *Nash* v. *United States*, 229 U.S. 373, 377 (1913):

> [The early antitrust] cases may be taken to have established that only such contracts and combinations are within the act as, by reason of intent or the inherent nature of the contemplated acts, prejudice the public interests by unduly restricting competition or unduly obstructing the course of trade.

Citing *Standard Oil Co. of New Jersey* v. United States, 221 U.S. 1, 32 (1911) (breaking up John D. Rockefeller's Standard Oil trust, through which he quite thoroughly monopolized the oil industry); *Northern Securities Co.* v. *United States*, 193 U.S. 197, 360 (1904) (creation of stock holding company to monopolize entire region's railway system a clear violation of the Sherman Act: "[I]t is manifest that if the antitrust act is held not to embrace a case such as is now before us, the plain intention of the legislative branch of the government will be defeated. If Congress has not, by the words used in the act, described this and like cases, it would, we apprehend, be impossible to find words that would describe them.").

[196] A more mature understanding of patent license restrictions developed over time. See, e.g., Herbert Hovenkamp, *Antitrust and the Design of Production*, 103 Cornell L. Rev. 1155, 1180–1183 (2018) (tracing the development of cases on "tie-ins", and arguing that courts and antitrust enforcement authorities have come to see that many tie-ins are benign features of various business models; thus the prevailing requirement that an antitrust plaintiff prove "market power" in the "tying" product market in order to establish liability for an illegal tie-in).

[197] Steven Wilf, *The Making of the Post-War Paradigm in American Intellectual Property Law*, 31 Colum. J.L. & Arts 139, 149–150 (2008), citing *Loughran* v. *Quaker City Chocolate & Confectionary Co.*, 286 F. 694, 697 (3d Cir. 1924).

4.3.4 *Patent Office Administration*

The story of patent administration at the turn of the twentieth century is the story of professionalization. People directly in charge of filing, pursuing, examining, and granting patents came to see themselves as a distinct professional group – a group defined by shared knowledge, which in turn gave them a shared identity. The emergence of patent-related experts, as a distinct group, precisely paralleled the trajectory followed by professional engineers. In the years between 1852, when civil engineers pioneered the idea, and 1908, when the American Institute of Chemical Engineers held its first annual meeting, each group of engineering specialists founded organizations, held conferences, and began publishing proceedings.[198] One important component of professionalization is authority over some body of knowledge: the power to both define and disseminate information (and often, a set of values) that must be learned in order to claim membership in the professional group. Engineering societies were often intertwined with the new schools of engineering that started to appear in American universities in the late nineteenth century. Course requirements in these schools defined who would be considered a professional engineer.[199] Throughout the twentieth century, professionalization continued in various forms with respect to a wide number of occupations.

Patent examiners, Patent Office officials, and the lawyers who regularly dealt with them enthusiastically joined in this movement.[200] Within the Patent Office, professionalization proceeded slowly. The work of representing inventors at the Patent Office was performed, often by former patent examiners, without the need for formal credentials throughout much of the nineteenth century. The first restriction

[198] See David Noble, America by Design, at chapter 3, "The Wedding of Science and the Useful Arts," at pp. 33 et seq.

[199] See David Noble, America by Design, at p. 44 ("The engineers who undertook to regulate the historical process of modern technology in order to consolidate their professional position were drawn inescapably toward engineering education."); ibid., at pp. 45–49 (describing rise of engineering-oriented universities such as the Massachusetts Institute of Technology (MIT) and their interaction with professional engineering societies).

[200] Professionalization is closely associated with bureaucratization, so it is no surprise that patent practice was professionalized at a time when the volume for patent applications had reached far beyond the levels of the mid-nineteenth century. See Bernard Barber, *Some Problems in the Sociology of the Professions*, 92 Daedelus 669, 678–679 (1963):

> Modern society is characterized by a multiplicity of specialized goals and specialized, formal organizations, or "bureaucracies," devoted to the realization of such goals. It is this aspect of modem society that [sociologist Max] Weber had in mind when he spoke of "the bureaucratization of the world." In all kinds of bureaucratically stuctured organizations (government, business, etc.) professionals of many different kinds (lawyers, doctors, scientists, etc.) are now indispensable. The sociology of the professions has, therefore, been much interested in the relationships between professional roles and organizational requirements, or necessities.

was introduced in 1861, when Congress authorized the Patent Commissioner to exclude inventor representatives who commit "gross misconduct."[201]

Though no one was aware of it, this regulation established the Patent Office as the official gatekeeper to the profession of patent lawyer and patent agent.[202] Ever since, the office of the Commissioner of Patents had fulfilled this role. Requirements shifted slowly over time, from an early emphasis on character and honesty (a response to unscrupulous patent agents) to a primary emphasis on knowledge and competence.[203] Enforced through informal requirements for many years, registry was formalized with creation of a written patent bar exam in 1938.[204] Authority over the specialized bar exam was the final step in the process by which the Patent Office came to control the patent law profession.

An important milestone for patent professionals was the founding of the Patent Office Society in 1918. The Society was (and is) open to patent professionals both within the Patent Office and outside it, that is, practicing patent lawyers (and agents). In keeping with the basic goals of most professional associations, the Society immediately established a professional journal whose purpose was to promote knowledge about patent practice and related issues among the membership:[205]

> It is hoped to make the journal [of the Patent Office Society] a forum for the presentation and discussion of legal and technical subjects relating to the useful arts: and further, a medium through which a wider knowledge of the workings and advantages of the patent system may be gained by inventors and manufacturers, and

[201] *Sperry* v. *State of Fla. ex rel. Fla. Bar*, 373 U.S. 379, 388–389 (1963).

[202] Patent agents, as we have seen, were originally just ex-patent examiners who set up shop to help inventors prosecute patents. In the era of professionalization, the requirements to become an agent were tightened. Today a patent agent is one trained as a scientist or engineer, but not as a lawyer, who has passed the Patent Bar exam. Agents can prosecute patents but are not licensed to litigate cases in federal courts or otherwise practice law. This is a unique two-part structure. It unites lawyers and agents (both take the Patent Bar exam), while segregating them by job function and status.

[203] There is still today provision for excluding unscrupulous practitioners, as indicated by the name of the Patent Office division responsible: the Office of Enrollment and Discipline.

[204] Dale L. Carlson, Robert A. Migliorini, and Carolyn J. Vacchiano, *Re-Thinking Patent Bar Admission: Which Bag of Tools Rules?*, 87 J. Pat. & Trademark Off. Soc'y 113, 115 (2005) ("It was not until 1938 that both lawyers and non-lawyers were required to pass a rigorous examination, which became known as the patent bar examination, before being permitted to practice before the PTO." (footnote omitted)).

[205] See Robert K. Merton, *The Functions of the Professional Association*, 58 Am. J. Nursing 50, 52 (1958):

> The [professional] association works ... to help prepare the practitioner for the more effective discharge of his professional roles. It acts on the philosophy that professional education is a lifelong process; establishes institutes to advance the education of the practitioner; protects both him and the public by working toward legally enforced standards of professional competence; and helps motivate practitioners to develop their skills and to extend their knowledge.

through which all interested in the improvement of the patent system may work to the common end.[206]

Along these lines, the Journal published copies of the tests used by the Patent Office to promote examiners.[207] It also published detailed analyses of Patent Office rules of practice.

At least some sociologists see an additional function for professional societies: inculcating a sense of community or solidarity.[208] There is abundant evidence that the Patent Office Society served this function as well. Numerous articles in the Journal of the Patent Office Society commiserate with examiners about the need for higher salaries, for improved organizational structure, and for moving the Patent Office out of the Interior Department and into a separate, independent agency home.[209] Throughout, the implicit message of a shared culture and values – particularly, the oft-neglected but essential work of patent examiners, and the economic importance of the patent system generally – was repeated and passed along for the Society's members.

One reason for this communal spirit was to resist and counteract a rising anti-patent sentiment among some politicians and members of the public. Farmers in some parts of the United States had become victims of voracious patent "sharks" – akin to modern-day patent trolls. The sharks bought up patents on simple farm implements, then sued general stores and farmers looking for quick settlements. The Granger movement – a potent political force uniting farmers and others in the rural economy – took up patent reform in its economic agenda.[210] Members of the US House of Representatives were listening. In 1912, in the wake of the apparently unpopular *A.B. Dick* decision, the House Committee on Patents held hearings on a proposed patent reform bill. The bill and the hearings were named after the Committee's Chairman, Rep. William A. Oldfield. Oldfield was a second-term Democratic Representative from a rural part of Arkansas.[211] Throughout what came

[206] Editorial, 1 J. Pat. Off. Soc'y 1 (1918).

[207] See, e.g., promotion exam questions for junior, associate and assistant examiner promotion exams, 7 J. Pat. Off. Soc'y 599–601 (1925).

[208] See Malcolm Waters, *Collegiality, Bureaucratization, and Professionalization: A Weberian Analysis*, 94 Am. J. Soc. 945, 946–948 (1989) (comparing views on professional groups in the classic and contemporary sociological literature; comparing Emile Durkheim's optimistic view of professional organizations as repositories of community and ethical standards, with one strain of Max Weber's writings, which emphasize these groups as limiting new entrants and thereby gaining an economic advantage (i.e., "occupational closure")).

[209] See *The Patent Office as an Independent Bureau*, 1 J. Pat. Off. Soc'y 315 (1919).

[210] See Solon Justus Buck, The Granger Movement: A Study of Agricultural Organization and Its Political, Economic, and Social Manifestations (Cambridge, MA: Harvard University Press, 1913), available at https://babel.hathitrust.org/cgi/pt?id=hvd.hwww24&view=1up&seq=7. See also Christopher Beauchamp, *The First Patent Litigation Explosion*, 125 Yale L.J. 848, 925 (2016) (recounting the role of the Granger movement and the concern over "patent sharks").

[211] See United States. 70th Cong., 2d sess., 1928–1929. House. Memorial services held in the House of Representatives of the United States, together with remarks presented in eulogy of

to be widely known as the "Oldfield Hearings," Rep. Oldfield repeatedly emphasized two themes: the aggregation of power in the hands of large, patent-holding companies; and the consumer impact of patent-related sales and marketing practices:

> The Chairman [Rep. Oldfield] "I want to know what you think about this proposition. Of course, the patent is a monopoly. Do you think it is a good thing for the public to permit what is known as a 'monopoly of monopolies?' In other words, take the General Electric Co., for example, and that field – the electrical field. Do you think the General Electric or any other electrical manufacturing concern ought to be permitted to buy up all the competing patents and suppress all but some particular kind?"[212]
>
> * * * *
>
> Chairman [Oldfield:] "There is the consumer, you know, as well as the retailer, that ought to be looked after. We have got to look after the consumer as well as the retailer."[213]

Oldfield took specific aim at tie-ins, called into prominence by the *A.B. Dick* case, as well as retail price maintenance. He opposed both practices, and included detailed limitations on them in his proposed patent reform bill.[214]

Subsequent versions of the Oldfield Bill went further, however. One from 1914 included a section that would have fundamentally altered the trajectory of US patent law. It permitted anyone to petition a district court to prove that a patent

William A. Oldfield, late a Representative from Arkansas. Washington: Government Printing Office, 1929 (memorial service for Oldfield includes biography for the ten-term (twenty-year) Representative).

[212] Hearing before the Committee on Patents, H.R. [resolution] 23417, Oldfield Revisions and Codification of Patent Statutes, 62d Cong., 2d Sess., April 19, 1912, available at https://babel.hathitrust.org/cgi/pt?id=nyp.33433019377419&view=1up&seq=9, at p. 12.

[213] Oldfield Hearings, April 19, 1912, at p. 12.

[214] See Oldfield Hearings, April 19, 1912, at p. 27 (discussing draft bill section 32, specifically overruling *A.B. Dick* and prohibiting conditions on purchase of a patented item unless the buyer also purchases unpatented items. On resale price maintenance, see Oldfield Heaings, April 19, 1912, at p. 12:

> The Chairman: [Rep. Oldfield, discussing resale price term applied to "$1 watches", which a discounter wishes to sell for 50 cents:] "I think you ought not to have any remedy under an infringement suit on that."

When informed that most manufacturers agreed to buy back unsold goods such as Gillette Safety Razors at the wholesale price paid by the retailer, as a way of preventing discounting, Rep. Oldfield replied:

> Recently I received a letter from a friend in Michigan, who bought phonographs and phonograph records from the Edison Co., who offered to take back at 5 and 10 cents each record which they had sold to him at 21 and 30 and 50 cents. What do you think of that?

See Oldfield Hearings, April 19, 1912, at p. 10.

was being "withheld or suppressed by the owner of the patent," and, if proven, required the court to order that the patent owner issue a license to the petitioning party.[215] This section took dead aim at the *Continental Paper Bag* decision; it reflected the view that patent accumulation and suppression were evils associated with big companies, eliminating competition and raising prices for the consumer.[216]

The large structural reforms of the Oldfield Bill were opposed by all the major companies, of course. But they were also condemned by the representatives of the newly professionalizing patent profession.[217] Indeed, the voices opposing the Oldfield Bill were often those of cross-overs: lawyers who had worked at the Patent Office, but who had gone on to private patent law practice.[218] The growing volume of lawyers employed in industry who were hired after being examiners at the Patent Office was noted by one witness.[219] And the ubiquitous Edwin J. Prindle, co-founder

[215] Oldfield Reform Bill, section 3, quoted in Hearing Before the Committee on Patents, 63rd Cong., 2d sess., May 27, 1914 (Part 1), Statement of Mr. William A. Redding, Representing the Merchants Association, New York City, at p. 4.

[216] This section 3 exempted patents held by their original inventors. Oldfield Reform Bill Hearings, May 27, 1914, quoting section 3. It applied only to patents that had been *assigned* – i.e., company-owned patents.

[217] Opposition started with the Commissioner of Patents. See Letter from Commissioner of Patents to Rep. William A. Oldfield, April 17, 1912, Oldfield Hearings at p. 3: "It is urged by some that the different industrial conditions which exist at the present time, especially in respect to the power of large corporations which is based upon patents, seem to necessitate a revision of the existing laws." He strongly disagreed. See ibid.

[218] Gilbert H. Montague, *The Proposed Patent Law Revision*, 26 Harv. L. Rev. 128 (1912) ("[O]ut of the sixty persons whose testimony and communications were reported in these [Oldfield Bill] hearings, less than half a dozen favored the proposals which have been embodied in the bill recommended."). The author goes on to list opponents of the Bill at p. 128 n. 5:

> H. Ward Leonard, Dr. L. H. Baekeland, Benjamin M. Des Jardins, F. L. O. Wadsworth, Cortlandt F. Carrier, Jr., Spencer Miller, and Thomas A. Edison; eminent patent lawyers and publicists, such as Frederick P. Fish, Livingston Gifford, Louis D. Brandeis, E. J. Prindle,. Samuel Owen Edmonds, Horace Pettit, Frank L. Dyer, Walter F. Rogers, and William W. Dodge; manufacturers representing concerns such as Thomas A. Edison, Inc., U. S. Mail Chute System, Bissell Carpet Sweeper Co., Gillette Safety Razor Co., Columbia Phonograph Co., Brown & Sharpe Co., C. B. Cottrell & Sons Co., R. H. Ingersoll & Bro., and the Lidgerwood Mfg. Co.; representatives of scientific societies and associations, such as the Inventors' Guild, the American Institute of Chemical Engineers, the Association of Registered Patent Attorneys, the Merchants' Association of New York City, the National Association of Stationers and Manufacturers, the Pennsylvania Retail Jewellers' Association, the Chambers of Commerce of Rochester, and of Cleveland, and the Patent Law Association of Washington, D. C.

Many of these figures had extensive experience and background at the Patent Office and then in private practice or as inventors. On the author of the Harvard Law Review article, see Wyatt Wells, *Counterpoint to Reform: Gilbert H. Montague and the Business of Regulation*, 78 Bus. Hist. Rev. 423 (2004) (detailing career of lawyer/lobbyist Montague, primarily with respect to antitrust issues). For another highly critical view of the Oldfield Bill, see Otto Raymond Barnett, *The Oldfield Bill (H. R. 23417.)*, 22 Yale L.J. 383 (1913).

[219] May 25, 1912, letter from earlier witness inventor Robert Lundell, reprinted in Oldfield Hearings, May 27, 1912, at p. 109 ("[O]ver ninety percent of the members of the General

of the Patent Office Society, even intervened in the overall debate with an article aimed directly at one of the key reform constituencies, farmers.[220] Prominent inventors of the era weighed in as well.[221]

In the end, given this extensive opposition from patent professionals, and their veto power in the legislative process, the Oldfield Bill died. The only patent reforms that came out of these hearings, and out of the Progressive Era generally, were technocratic ones – written by and for the patent professionals themselves. One such reform quite self-consciously formalized the profession when the Commissioner of Patents called for the "creation of a patent bar," so as "to require a higher standard of qualifications for registry."[222]

This is as clear an expression of the wave of professionalization as can be found. The Commissioner's power to regulate entry into the patent bar was established in legislation in 1912 and has continued since.[223]

Electric patent department have ben recruited from the Patent Office."). Lundell was involved in an interference (on an "Electric Railway Motor") with an inventor named C. J. Van DePoele, who had assigned to GE, Interference no. 16751, cited in 1912 Hearings at p. 42.

220 Recall that Prindle was a former patent examiner, representative of General Electric, early patent strategist, and co-founder of the Patent Office Society. Prindle sounded the alarm for all who shared his experience and values, which included a deep respect for patents and the patent system as it had evolved in the era of corporatization. Prindle's defense of the patent system acknowledged that "patent sharks" had preyed on farmers but stated that the net effect of the system was still positive. See Edwin J. Prindle, *The Farmer and the Patent System*, 3 J. Pat. Off. Soc'y 113, 113 (1920) ("It will be interesting to review some of the benefits that the farmer has derived from the patent system and which much more than overbalance the losses it may have brought him.").

221 See Leo Baekeland, *Legalized Blackmail: A Sample of Ignorant Patent Legislation*, 62 Electrical World 1146, 1147 (December 6, 1913) (Commenting on a recently enacted provision tying US patent terms to those of foreign countries where patent protection had been obtained: "[T]he legislation just passed is not much worse than some of the provisions of the pending Oldfield bill and similar patent laws which have been proposed of late. It shows how dangerous it is for congressmen or senators who have neither experience nor proper knowledge of our patent laws to tinker with patent legislation . . . [S]hall we have a competent patent commission [to revise patent law], or shall we go on 'monkeying with a buzz-saw'?"

222 *Sperry* v. *State of Fla. ex rel. Fla. Bar*, 373 U.S. 379, 388–389 (1963) (citing Oldfield Hearings). The Supreme Court in a 1963 case explained the earlier history of patent bar regulation in these terms:

> The power of the Commissioner of Patents to regulate practice before the Patent Office dates back to 1861, when Congress first provided that "for gross misconduct he may refuse to recognize any person as a patent agent, either generally or in any particular case * * *." The 'Rules and Directions' issued by the Commissioner in 1869 provided that '(a)ny person of intelligence and good moral character may appear as the attorney in fact or agent of an applicant upon filing proper power of attorney.'10 From the outset, a substantial number of those appearing in this capacity were engineers or chemists familiar with the technical subjects to which the patent application related.

373 U.S. 379, 388–389.

223 Current standards may be found at: 37 C.F.R. § 11.7 Requirements for [patent practice] registration.

Perhaps the final step in the emergence of a distinctive profession of patent expert was when the Patent Office was moved from the Department of the Interior to the Commerce Department, headed by the noted technocrat Herbert Hoover. When Hoover was appointed to the relatively new Department of Commerce in 1920,[224] he made it a point to associate the Department with the exciting new technologies and industries of the day, particularly wireless (radio) and air travel. It was thus a natural that the Patent Office was moved from Interior to Commerce by executive order in 1925.[225] Members of the newly formalized Patent Bar expressed high hopes that Commerce would be a good fit for the rapidly modernizing field of patent law.[226]

Whatever the bureaucratic rationale, the move symbolized the end of an era. It severed the historic association between property rights for new inventions and the Interior Department, grantor and guardian of federal lands. Henceforth, land patents and invention patents would go their separate ways. The move was not as momentous as the closing of the physical American frontier, because so many significant inventions lay just over the horizon. But the move re-assigned the Patent Office from the domain of the small grant, the original home of the "democratic property" policy, to the official government agency charged with promoting the fast-industrializing, globe-straddling behemoth that was the US economy in the twentieth century.[227] The move announced a new identity, and a new orientation: patent law was now seen as one of the aids to established industries, and a link that would help government officials manage the transition to whatever new industries lay ahead.

But the association between patents and commerce, with its strong hints of big business and world trade, was to prove much more challenging than the optimists imagined in 1925. By 1935, at the height of the Depression, the concerns of the Oldfield Hearings would return with a vengeance. By then there was even more concern about the patent system, and its basic viability, as we shall see in Chapter 5.

[224] See Kenneth White, Hoover: An Extraordinary Life in Extraordinary Times (New York: Knopf, 2017), at p. 270 (early in his tenure at Commerce, Hoover declared "a new era in the organization of industry and commerce . . . ").

[225] See Notes, 7 J. Pat. Off. Soc'y 599–604 (1925).

[226] See Notes, 7 J. Pat. Off. Soc'y.

[227] The Commerce Department was founded in 1903 to "facilitate industrial development and promote commerce at home and abroad . . . We will look to this Department to give direction to the energetic campaign that has for its object the conquest of the markets of the world by American merchants and manufacturers." Congressman Charles F. Cochiran, Congressional Record, January 15, 1903. Quoted at www.commerce.gov/about/history.

5

1921–1982: Patents In and Out of the Headlines

CHAPTER OUTLINE

The Progressive Era antitrust movement left its imprint on the patent system, as we saw in the last chapter. But as we also saw, the imprint was light. The patent system was not much changed by virtue of the Oldfield Hearings of 1912 and related congressional inquiries. Nevertheless, a precedent was set. While patent specialists followed the professionalizing path, pro-consumer voices in Congress and advocates of the evolving antitrust laws had both established that patent-related activity was likely to cause economic harm. Little came of this in the 1920s, but after the onset of the Depression big business skeptics aimed their fire at patents with a force rarely seen in this corner of economic policy. The Oldfield Hearings turned out to be a mere dress rehearsal for the main event. The Temporary National Economic Committee Hearings of 1935 made the earlier Oldfield initiative look like a patent fan club. For the first time in the United States,[1] serious voices were calling for the abolition of the patent system, or, at minimum, a radical overhaul of some of its primary features.

Two aspects of patent law were common targets from the 1930s to the 1950s: the "invention test," a key requirement of patentability; and contracts along a product

[1] The anti-patent outcry in nineteenth-century Europe never had much of a following in the United States. The European movement is well described in Fritz Machlup, *The Anti-Patent Controversy in the Nineteenth Century*, 10 J. Econ. Hist. 1 (1950). The movement's peak may have come in 1869 with this statement: "It is probable enough that the patent laws will be abolished ere long ... " Editorial, The Economist, June 5, 1869, p. 656. The patent abolition movement did succeed, for a brief interval. For example, Switzerland and the Netherlands abolished patents in this era, only to reinstate them later. See Erich Schiff, Industrialization Without National Patents: The Netherlands, 1869–1912; Switzerland, 1850–1907 (Princeton, NJ: Princeton University Press, 1971). This movement seems to have been connected with the liberalization that was general on the continent in these years. Patent reform was pushed by many of the same reformist economists and politicians who also championed the interests of the new manufacturing class, such as free trade. See e.g., Kevin H. O'Rourke, *British Trade Policy in the 19th Century: A Review Article*, 16 Euro. J. Pol. Econ. 829 (2000). No such spirit pervaded the United States. Instead, future President Lincoln lectured civic groups on the strong vigor of "young America," as compared to the "old fogy," Europe. See Abraham Lincoln, "Lecture on Inventions and Discoveries," as delivered at various towns in Illinois in 1958 and 1859, available at www.abrahamlincolnonline.org/lincoln/speeches/discoveries.htm ("The great difference between Young America and Old Fogy, is the result of Discoveries, Inventions, and Improvements."). Lincoln himself held a (never commercialized) patent. US patent No. 6,469 for "Buoying Vessels Over Shoals," issued to Abraham Lincoln on May 22, 1849.

supply chain restricting how patented items could be used, sold, or re-sold. With respect to these contracts (which antitrust experts call "vertical agreements" or vertical restraints), enforcement targeting continued well into the 1970s. For much of the period under study in this chapter, large patent-holding and patent-producing US companies often assumed a dual strategy: in public, a defensive crouch, intoning the traditional virtues of patents but always in low-key ways. More quietly, large stakeholders plied the levers of power, hemming in anti-patent initiatives while planning countermoves. In many federal courts, in the rising academic field of antitrust law, and among a fair number of politicians, there was a relentless association of patents with monopolization and disregard for consumer interests. The very early years of law and economics as an academic discipline, and the (related) political shift associated with President Reagan's election in 1980 marked a change of direction, but those forces were just coalescing by the end of the era under study, 1982. For most of the years between 1920 and 1980, headlines brought bad news for supporters of patents.

Outside the headlines, below the tempestuous surface, things were quite different. Innovation by some measures increased after 1920, and many new firms were founded to capitalize on new technologies. In industries such as wireless (radio), chemicals (especially plastic polymers), pharmaceuticals, consumer electronics, and later, computer hardware, new technology-based companies continued to enter the scene. Some of them (particularly in chemicals and pharmaceuticals) embraced the patent system with gusto. Other companies, including the already-established but fast-growing auto manufacturers, were less patent-dependent, but often managed to employ patents in at least some aspects of business strategy. As these twentieth-century industries emerged and grew, they reshaped patent law in important ways – particularly in the chemical and pharmaceutical industries, where a fast-growing sub-specialty called forth many significant adjustments to patent doctrine and administrative practices. These new developments occurred largely outside the direct gaze of antitrust-oriented patent skeptics. So even though the validity and deployment of big company patents were often under fire in the headlines, smaller companies and newer entrants acquired and deployed patents, in some cases quite effectively.

5.1 MACRO TRENDS

In the period after 1920, the US economy reaped what had been sown at the turn of the twentieth century. The Great Inventions of electrical power transmission, mass illumination, mass market automobiles, etc., matured, diffused, and seeded secondary economic growth. As the economic historian Robert J. Gordon put it:

> The Great Inventions of the late nineteenth century created an utter transformation in both the rural and urban standard of living that could happen only once, though

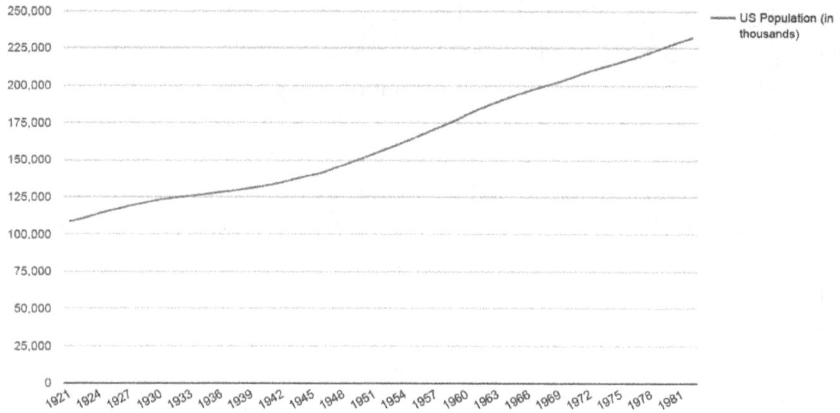

FIGURE 5.1. US population, 1921–1982
Source: measuringworth.com

the transition after each of the Great Inventions was not instantaneous but rather spread out over many years.[2]

The follow-on technologies fueled a growing economy that needed labor power, first and foremost. Immigration declined in the period around 1920, as compared with the peak years of the late nineteenth century. Yet fully half the American population in 1920 was the product of immigration since the nation's founding; the natural projected increase of the original 1790 population accounted for roughly 52 million of the total 106 million Americans in 1920.[3] Figure 5.1 shows population growth throughout the 1920–1982 period of interest to us.

The growing population, powered by the newly harnessed productive forces, powered a noteworthy boost in GDP over these years. Growth was steady until the Depression, then dipped precipitously, only to recover with vigor during the years of World War II. Figure 5.2 tells the tale.

For the Depression years, the patent data tell a different story. Perhaps counter-intuitively, patent applications and grants continued to grow through the Depression years. In part, small companies learned from the big ones. Aggregate data on research activity during the period show strong evidence of "diffusion of research laboratories from larger to smaller firms within manufacturing."[4] In fact, the data show that ever-smaller companies engaged in active research activities as the years

2 Robert J. Gordon, The Rise and Fall of American Growth: The U.S. Standard of Living since the Civil War (Princeton, NJ: Princeton University Press, 2016), at p. 129.

3 Robert J. Gordon, The Rise and Fall of American Growth, at p. 35.

4 David C. Mowery, *Industrial Research and Firm Size, Survival, and Growth in American Manufacturing, 1921–1946: An Assessment*, 43 J. Econ. Hist. 953 (1983), at p. 964. The author continues: "Such imitative adoption of a new organizational form is consistent with [Alfred] Chandler's analysis of the development of modern corporate structure, in which a few early adopters became very large firms." For more on Chandler, see Chapter 4.

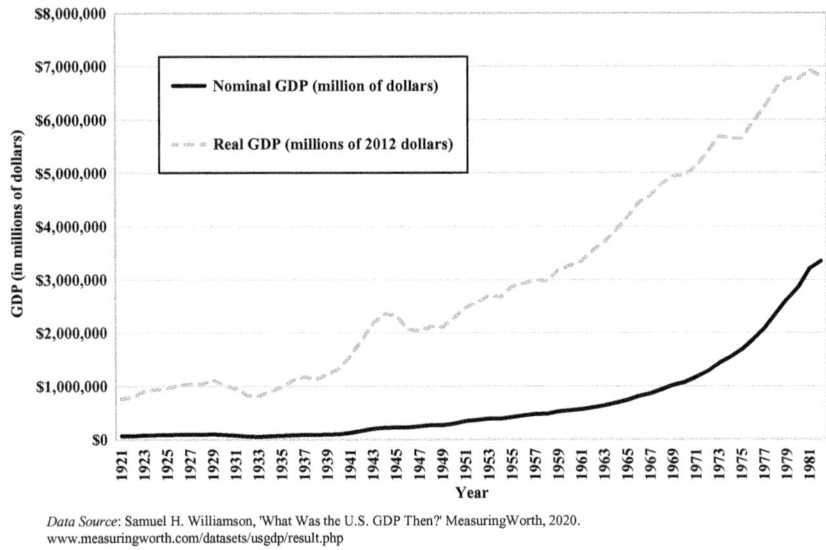

FIGURE 5.2. Real and nominal GDP, 1920–1982

went by.[5] In some industries, small, established firms, as well as new entrants, saw the need to conduct research (Figure 5.3). All of this research paid off in a burst of productivity growth in the post-War years, which propelled the US economy to a dominant position.[6]

Though patenting held surprisingly steady during the Depression, there was a mild dip in patent activity during the post-War period, roughly 1947–1960.[7] The cause is not entirely apparent. Economic growth was robust in the post-War years. Federal spending on scientific research, taken to new heights during the War effort,

5 David C. Mowery, *Industrial Research and Firm Size, 1921–1946*, at pp. 962–963 (footnotes omitted):

> [Data show] a steady decline throughout 1921-1946 in the minimum or threshold firm size associated with positive levels of research employment. In constant 1926 dollars … this threshold size for firms not in the chemicals or primary metals industries declines from $256 million in 1921 to $94 million in 1933, and zero in 1946 [i..e, a startup company]. For chemicals firms, the threshold is much lower in 1921 and 1933, and is essentially constant during 1921–1933, changing from $49 million in 1921 to $50 million in 1933 in constant dollars.

6 David C. Mowery, *Industrial Research and Firm Size, 1921–1946*, at p. 977: "Research activity thus appears to have had a substantial impact on the growth of firms during the 1933–1946 period, an impact that was roughly similar for large and small firms."

7 There was a more noticeable dip in patents in force, but that simply the cumulative effect of the multiple years of reduced applications and issued patents during the Depression years.

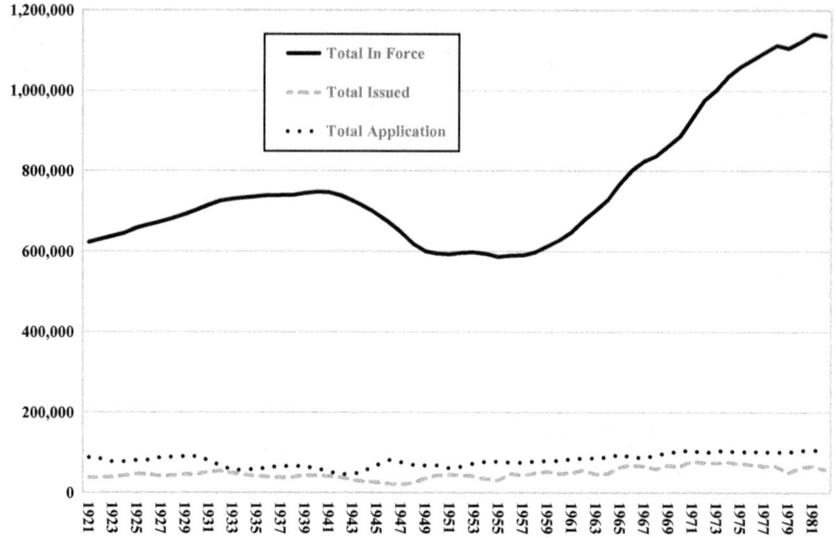

FIGURE 5.3. Patents applied for, issued, and in force, 1921–1982

continued and even increased after the War.[8] Despite these positive developments, there were some significant headwinds in the patent world that perhaps show up in these data. First, US industry was highly concentrated, suggesting that entry had perhaps become more difficult. To the extent entrants drive innovation (and hence patenting), this may partly explain the drop in patent activity.[9] Second, robust antitrust enforcement has been identified as one causative factor in the decline in concentration after the 1950s. But, to the extent this enforcement included increased scrutiny of patent-related transactions and activities, it may have had a dampening effect on patent activity. When patents were swept into the antitrust movement, the association of patents with anticompetitive behavior may have suppressed participation in the patent system. This might have been a result of declining economic value; a patent has lower value if there are more restrictions on what an owner can do with it. In a more general sense, interest in the patent system may simply have declined in tandem with the rise in headlines associating patents with economically

[8] See Steven W. Usselman, *Research and Development (R&D)*, in Hugh R. Slotten, ed., The Oxford Encyclopedia of the History of American Science, Medicine, and Technology (Oxford: Oxford University Press, 2014), at pp. 369–387.

[9] See William G. Shepherd, *Causes of Increased Competition in the U.S. Economy, 1939–1980*, 64 Rev. Econ. & Stats. 613 (1982), at p. 613 ("There was a substantial rise of aggregate and market concentration in the manufacturing sector during 1909–70."). A later study supported Shepherd's analysis that competition increased (i.e., concentration decreased) in the 1960s and 1970s, but then dropped later, after 1980. See Frederic L. Pryor, *New Trends in U.S. Industrial Concentration*, 18 Rev. Ind. Org. 301 (2001) (increased concentration between 1980 and 2001).

questionable and socially harmful practices of big companies. Whatever the cause, the data are clear enough: There was a patent slump in the post-War years, which ended roughly around the end of the Eisenhower administration and the election of John F. Kennedy in 1960.

5.2 PATENTS AND THE TWO-TIERED STRUCTURE OF ENTERPRISE

For some scholars, and much of the public, big companies, patents, and anticompetitive behavior were linked together after 1920. This led to intensive concentration on the patent activities of big companies. In practice, this took the form of intensive antitrust scrutiny of patent quality (where the "invention" test was a key focal point) as well as patent licensing and its attendant restrictions on licensee activities (i.e., vertical restraints under antitrust). But below the radar screen of policy and public attention, innovation and new technologies were emerging during this era. And patents performed useful functions still, for big and small companies alike. We return to the story of big companies and patent skepticism later in this chapter. We turn now to some case studies in the less visible ways patents continued to affect economic activity after 1920.

5.2.1 *Dynamic Entry and Growth: Patents Outside the Headlines*

We will see later in this chapter that most of the patent-related headlines were fairly negative between 1920 and 1982. Especially in the peak years of antitrust enforcement, roughly 1930–1980, patents were typically seen primarily as tools of big business – and harmful tools, at that. But outside the front-page news, it was a dynamic, innovative century. Technology in many ways built on the gains from the Corporatization period (Chapter 4): The auto industry grew and prospered into the largest industrial ecosystem in the United States. The chemical industries saw initial takeoff conditions, and then sustained growth. And other nineteenth-century stalwarts such as GE and Westinghouse, in electrical equipment, and AT&T in telephony, grew in step with the overall economy. Later in this chapter we consider the continuing role of patents in these large-scale industrial enterprises.

But first, it is important not to overlook the many smaller innovative companies that have their origins in this period. Though not typically front-page news, in many ways they carried forward the legacy of patents as an important strategic instrument in the rise of young technology-based companies. Many were the byproducts of nineteenth-century innovations, particularly in the electrical field. As electric power became ubiquitous, and after the initial network-building phase,[10] a host of follow-

[10] On which, see the masterful Thomas P. Hughes, Networks of Power: Electrification in Western Society (Baltimore, MD: Johns Hopkins University Press, 1983) (a techno-social history of electrification around the world).

on innovations tapped the new-strung grid to power all sorts of products. With the growth of leisure time and disposable income, markets opened up for entertainment technologies especially. Thus, companies such as RCA, the radio industry pioneer; Philco and Magnavox, early TV companies; and later Dolby and Ampex, with their advanced sound technologies, came to life in these years. As did W. L. Gore and Associates, makers of Gore-Tex. Partly because the large incumbents such as GE were so capable of expanding into these markets, newer entrants often relied on patents to establish a foothold.[11] Once launched, they often used patents to defend revenue streams and, in the case of Dolby, directly generate substantial revenue by assisting entry in competitive submarkets. Several plowed revenue back into R&D, establishing a virtuous cycle of research, invention, and product innovation. Outside the front-page headlines, in other words, patents were acquired and deployed by at least some smaller companies in service of new technologies and industries, much as they had been in the nineteenth century.

There are many examples.[12] I will choose just the three already mentioned: Ampex, Dolby Sound, and W.L. Gore.

[11] There is indirect evidence that patents help the earnings of at least some inventors involved in startups. See Otto Toivanen and Lotta Väänänen, *Returns to Inventors*, 94 Rev. Econ. & Stats. 1173, 1174 (2012) (study of a sample of named inventors on US patents, between 1991 and 1998):

> We find that inventors who initially own their patents [an indicator of startup activity] first forgo some of their earnings but eventually earn substantially higher rewards than inventors who do not have the intellectual property rights over their invention [i.e., employed inventors who assign title form the commencement of employment]. The returns to inventors who initially own their patents is of the order of a 15% to 30% premium in gross earnings in the fifth to sixth year after patent grant (in contrast to the 4% to 5% average premium for those who do not).

The same research is relevant to the discussion in Chapter 4 of the law of patent ownership for employee inventions. The authors find that even inventors who make a blanket assignment to their employers nevertheless enjoy some profit from inventive activity and patenting:

> We find that inventors get a temporary reward of about 3% of their gross annual earnings in the year of the patent grant, presumably corresponding to a one-time bonus for being awarded a patent. In addition, patent grants result in a 4% to 5% average premium in annual earnings three to four years after the patent grant. This premium remains for at least the following two years, possibly representing a permanent wage increase.
>
> When we include the quality of patent output as a categorical variable depending on the expected lifetime citations received, we find that patents with twenty to thirty citations generate a premium of about 20% in annual earnings in the sixth year and patents with over thirty citations generate a premium of over 30% from the fourth year onward. In contrast, patents with fewer than twenty citations seem to generate no returns. Returns to inventors are thus very heterogeneous and tied to observable signals of the quality of the patent.

Otto Toivanen and Lotta Väänänen, *Returns to Inventors*, at p. 1174.

[12] See Eric Hintz, American Independent Inventors in an Era of Corporate R&D (Cambridge, MA: MIT Press, 2021).

5.2.1.1 Ampex

Alexander M. Poniatoff was an American electrical engineer originally from Russia. He learned about electrical technology in the power generation industry in Shanghai, China. After he came to the United States, he first worked for an electrical technology company (Dalmo-Victor), then in 1944 founded Ampex.[13] Ampex first worked on small electric motors for military applications. But with the war over, Poniatoff was sure that larger electric motor manufacturers would soon enter and take over the Ampex niche. So Ampex decided to pivot into sound engineering.[14] Poniatoff hired an engineer named Harold Lindsay, who was a music fan as well as an engineer. (Lindsay's "concerts" in Tilden Park in Berkeley, where he blasted classical music recordings powered by his state-of-the art stereo player and speakers, were said to be famous in the area.)[15] Lindsay was hired to lead an engineering team at Ampex, tasked with the development of a studio-quality sound recording machine. One impetus for the project was a series of demonstrations of the German magnetophone, a high-quality magnetic tape recording system developed by the Germans during World War II.[16]

The Ampex team built a prototype of the new Model 400A. They demonstrated it to radio star Bing Crosby, and when he heard the sound quality he instantly agreed to buy several, so he could record his radio programs at leisure and have them played for broadcast at the appointed times. (Sound quality was too poor prior to the Ampex 400A to make this work.) Large-scale production of these studio audio recorders began in 1948, and they quickly became industry standard equipment for audio broadcasters all over the United States. The income from the 400A was put partly back into R&D. A team, again led by Lindsay (and including several young engineers from UC Berkeley), was assembled to work on a video tape recorder, or VTR. The breakthrough came when the idea occurred to re-set the record/play heads and lay down the video signal transversely, staggered diagonally down the length of the recording tape. Many other problems were solved with respect to the

[13] History of The Early Days of Ampex Corporation, as told by John Leslie and Ross Snyder, available at Audio Engineering Society website, www.aes.org/aeshc/docs/company.histories/ampex/leslie_snyder_early-days-of-ampex.pdf (last visited April 3, 2020).

[14] This was in keeping with the enthusiasm for high-fidelity or "hi-fi" sound in the post-War years. See John M. Conly, "Hi-Fi for All," Atlantic Monthly 194 (September 1954).

[15] History of The Early Days of Ampex Corporation, at p. 2.

[16] David L. Morton, *The Rusty Ribbon, John Herbert Orr and the Making of the Magnetic Recording Industry*, 1945–1960, 67 Bus. Hist. 589 (1993), at p. 600: "[After the War] the Commerce Department released [German] technical reports, captured documents, and patents related to the Magnetophone, allowing any other interested manufacturers access to information relating to tape recording technology." The Magnetophone was created by the German companies AEG (which made the recorder) and IG Farben (the chemical company, which developed the chemistry behind magnetic tape). See British Patent GB 466,023, "Improvement in the Manufacture and Production of Sound Record Carrier," issued November 18, 1936 (basic magnetic tape patent to IG Farben).

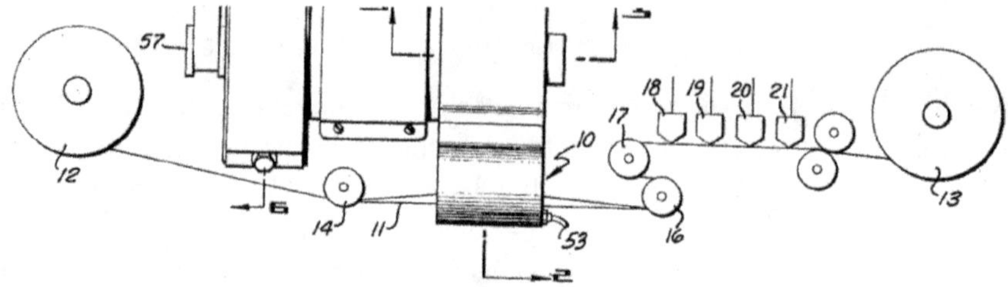

FIGURE 5.4. Ginsburg-Henderson design for the original Ampex video tape recorder, the VTR-1000. From US patent 2,866,012, issued December 23, 1958, to Charles P. Ginsburg and Shelby Henderson. Note the four tape heads on the right (elements 18, 19, 20, and 21), which gave the unit the name "Quadraplex"

tape reels, reading heads, and audio signal processing. Ultimately, a working VTR, dubbed the VTR-1000, was unveiled at a broadcast event in 1956, and Ampex was immediately swamped with orders.[17] The era of delayed broadcasts, video editing, spliced-in commercial advertising, and so on, had begun. Figure 5.4 shows the design of the reel and recording head portion of the VTR-1000, invented by two Ampex engineers, Charles P. Ginsburg and Shelby Henderson.

Ampex's advance made immediate inroads on the leading firm in broadcast technology, RCA. Since its founding in 1919, with a push from the US government, RCA had dominated radio broadcast technology.[18] But the introduction of the

[17] See Arch Luther, Many Threads: The Saga of an Electronics Engineer (Morrisville, NC: Lulu.com Publishers, 2008) (biography of RCA engineer), at p. 83: "Ampex developed the first successful video recorder, the four-head system known as quadraplex. The Ampex VR-1000 had 80 orders from the day it was announced."

[18] RCA's formation will be familiar from the founding stories of GE, Westinghouse, etc.: it was motivated in part by a desire to break patent-related deadlocks. The famous Italian inventor Guglielmo Marconi held a diode patent (on the vacuum tube) that was found to dominate the patented triode tube invented by Columbia University Professor Lee DeForest and licensed to RCA. Marconi Wireless Tel. Co. of Am. v. De Forest Radio Tel. & Tel. Co., 236 F. 942, 955 (S. D.N.Y. 1916), aff'd, 243 F. 560, 566-67 (2d Cir. 1917). Despite the standard "blocking patent" posture, neither party would license the other. See Federal Trade Comm'n, Report of the Federal Trade Commission on the Radio Industry in Response to House Resolution 548, 67th Cong., 4th Sess., December 1, 1923, at p. 26 (1924). See generally Robert Merges, *Intellectual Property Rights and Bargaining Breakdown: The Case of Blocking Patents*, 62 Tenn. L. Rev. 75 (1994). As a consequence, no one used the admittedly revolutionary DeForest triode for a time. The various pioneers formed RCA to break the deadlock; the new company promptly acquired the American rights to the Marconi patents. The companies that owned most of the major radio patents became RCA shareholders. See Report of the Federal Trade Commission on the Radio Industry, at pp. 20–21. With all the constituent radio technologies under one roof, RCA established itself as the technical leader in radio and dominated radio-related research for many years. See Margaret Graham, RCA and the VideoDisc: The Business of Research 41 (Cambridge: Cambridge University Press, 1986) (describing RCA's use of package licensing to broadcasters; the end-to-end packaging of broadcast technology allowed RCA to dominate the radio industry from the 1920s until an antitrust enforcement action in 1958 loosened its control). See generally Robert P. Merges and Richard R. Nelson, *On the Complex Economics of Patent Scope*, 90 Colum. L. Rev. 839, 892–893 (1990).

Ampex VTR-1000 revealed to RCA engineers how far the company had fallen behind in the cutting-edge field of broadcast tape recording.[19] The Ampex quadraplex recording technology was almost instantly adopted as the industry standard video format.[20] RCA scrambled to catch up: It offered to partner with Ampex. RCA would bring Ampex in on RCA's new color broadcast technology, at that time an experimental field, so Ampex could adapt its VTR for color broadcasts. Ampex accepted, and in the process made itself a leader in second-generation, color broadcast, recording.[21]

Ampex also sold precision recording equipment for the oil industry (where geologic data from exploration needed to be recorded accurately) and for specialized applications such as the "black boxes" that airline flight data in airplanes. It never successfully expanded into the consumer market, however, and like most other vacuum-tube-dependent companies it did not see the transistor revolution coming in the 1960s. An attempt to gain access to transistor technology led to a licensing agreement with Sony that eventually opened the door to the Sony BetaMax, which revolutionized home video recording. Ampex survives to the present time, repurposed as a data security and specialty recording company.[22]

5.2.1.2 Dolby Labs[23]

One of the engineers who worked at Ampex was Ray Dolby, who left in 1957. After a Ph.D. at Cambridge University, Dolby founded Dolby Labs in London in 1965. His goal was to work on sound engineering projects. His noise reduction technology,

[19] Arch Luther, Many Threads: The Saga of an Electronics Engineer, at p. 85 ("RCA was at least a year behind [Ampex].").

[20] Andrew F. Inglis Behind the Tube: A History of Broadcasting Technology and Business (Stoneham, MA: Focal Press, 1990), at p. 91.

[21] Arch Luther, Many Threads: The Saga of an Electronics Engineer, at p. 85 (detailing signing of RCA-Ampex cross-license agreement).

[22] See S. J. Liebowitz and Stephen E. Margolis, *Path Dependence, Lock-in, and History*, 11 J. L. Econ. & Org. 205 (1995), at p. 219. In the license with Sony, Ampex gave up the right to recording technology for the consumer market, which Sony famously leveraged into its product-defining consumer VCR, the Sony Betamax. Ampex also licensed the Japanese professional/studio market, in a contract with Toshiba. In later years these deals would be seen as ceding the future of the electronics industry to Japanese firms, but in the late 1960s they made some sense. See Richard S. Rosenbloom and Karen J. Freeze, *Ampex Corporation and Video Innovation*, in Richard S. Rosenbloom ed., Research on Technological Innovation, Management & Policy (1985), Bingley, U. K.: JAI Press, at pp. 113, 126 (noting that some participants recalled an ambiguous letter from U.S.-based Ampex Corp. to Sony which seemed to inadvertently gave away a license over basic video recorder technology – giving rise to an "implied license" to key Ampex patents). See generally Richard S. Rosenbloom and Michael A. Cusumano, *Technological Pioneering and Competitive Advantage: The Birth of the VCR Industry*, 29 Cal. Mgt. Rev. 51 (1987) (recalling the Betamax vs. VHS video tape format competition between Sony, Matsushita, and other firms).

[23] Note: The author of this book has been a consultant to both Dolby Labs and its subsidiary, Via Licensing.

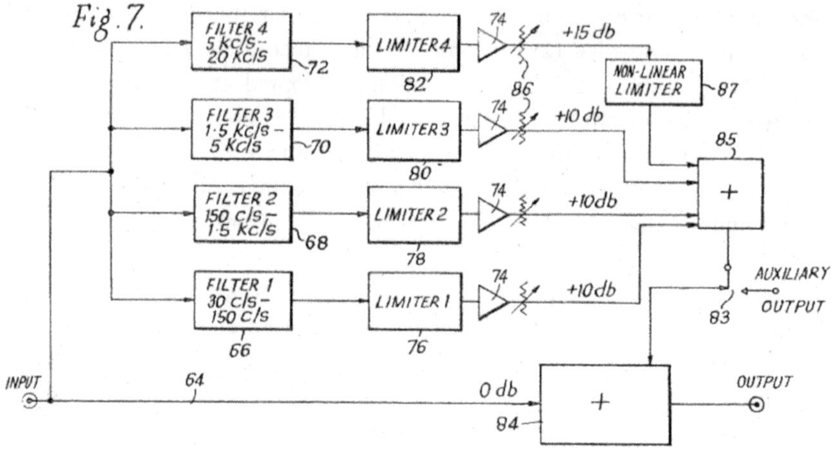

FIGURE 5.5. From Ray Dolby, US patent 3,846,719 "noise reduction systems," issued November 5, 1974, assigned to Dolby Laboratories, Inc.: One of the basic noise reduction patents. This diagram shows the signal "compression" stage, where filters (66, 68, 70, and 72) split the input signal into four frequency bands, each of which is passed through a "limiter" that reduces signals in ranges near the top of each band; when the compressed signal is expanded in the second part of the system (outside the diagram, to the right), the resulting signal is almost completely free of residual "noise" (such as "hiss")

invented soon after, was rapidly adopted in recording studios in London and then the United States.[24] Dolby moved its headquarters to San Francisco in 1976, after the company's noise reduction and sound quality innovations were applied to the cinema movie industry. When the "Star Wars" films debuted in 1977, Dolby sound processing gained worldwide exposure.

Dolby filed basic patents on noise reduction beginning in 1969. Figure 5.5 is from his 1974 patent on Noise Reduction Systems.

The early work with industry-leading recording and movie studios led Dolby to focus on manufacturing for these markets only. But noise reduction (and later sound technologies) can also be embedded in consumer products, where they can increase the quality of sound for mass market music players such as cassette decks (in the 1970s), CD and DVD players, and later, music streaming on computers, TVs, and mobile devices. From the company's inception, a two-part strategy was employed: manufacture for the high end, license for the low (consumer) end.[25] This has led to

[24] See "Ray Dolby," MIT Jerome Lemelson Center, available at https://lemelson.mit.edu/resources/ray-dolby.

[25] "Early on, Dolby decided that the company would manufacture professional products only and would license technologies that were appropriate for consumer applications." Dolby: History, available at www.dolby.com/us/en/about/history.html.

a stable and profitable company. With over 500 licensees worldwide,[26] revenues were $1.2 billion in 2019, with net income of $255 million.[27]

At Dolby revenue from professional product manufacturing and consumer product licensing has consistently been reinvested into R&D, which has kept Dolby on the leading edge of sound technology since its inception.[28] Dolby pioneered "surround sound," first in movie theaters and then for the home market. And the company has progressed through numerous consumer noise reduction technologies over the years. In recent years, specially equipped movie theaters have debuted an innovative "sound scape" for film viewing, which features hundreds of small precision speakers coordinated by sophisticated software, to create complex and unprecedented ambient sound effects.

The licensing program is based on the Dolby patent portfolio, which contained 11,400 total patents and 4,100 patent applications, and was spread across 100 countries worldwide, as of 2019.[29] From the outset, the company was founded on the belief that patents were an essential component of its business model. Dolby himself said in 1986: "I have a general principle that I follow ... I don't go into any area that I can't get a patent on ... [If you deviate from this] you quickly find yourself manufacturing commodities."[30] The combination of continuous innovation and an active licensing program make Dolby a good example of a specialized "idea factory," a latter-day Edison Lab for sound. (Though Dolby does continue to manufacture products for high end music and post-production in film studios.) In 2019, Dolby earned 11 percent of its annual revenue from manufacturing, and 89 percent from various licensing programs.[31] While Dolby is not a huge company, it represents a successful, specialized company that maintains its independence and innovative corporate culture, built on a foundation of IP licensing.[32] In fact, Dolby's licensing experience is so broad that it founded a special subsidiary, Via Licensing,

[26] See "Licensed Dolby Manufacturers," www.Dolby.com, available at www.dolby.com/us/en/professional/licensing/licensed-dolby-manufacturers.aspx.

[27] See Dolby Laboratories, Inc., 2019 SEC Form 10-Q, at p. 28 (financials), available at www.sec.gov/ix?doc=/Archives/edgar/data/1308547/000162828019014472/a10-kfy19q4.htm.

[28] Dolby spends over $235 million on R&D each year. See Dolby Laboratories, Inc., 2019 SEC Form 10-Q, at p. 8, available at www.sec.gov/ix?doc=/Archives/edgar/data/1308547/000162828019014472/a10-kfy19q4.htm. This, on revenues of $1.2 billion, represents roughly 20 percent of revenue that is spent on R&D.

[29] Dolby Laboratories, Inc., 2019 SEC Form 10-Q, at p. 6, available at www.sec.gov/ix?doc=/Archives/edgar/data/1308547/000162828019014472/a10-kfy19q4.htm.

[30] Richard Halstead, Silence Golden for SF-Based Dolby, S.F. Bus. J., June 23, 1986, at 1 (interview with Ray Dolby), quoted in Robert P. Merges, *Uncertainty and the Standard of Patentability*, 7 [Berkeley] High Tech. L.J. 1, 5 n.11 (1992).

[31] Dolby Laboratories, Inc., 2019 SEC Form 10-Q, at p. 2, available at www.sec.gov/ix?doc=/Archives/edgar/data/1308547/000162828019014472/a10-kfy19q4.htm.

[32] See Pamela Hawkins Williams, Dotcy Isom III, and Tini D. Smith-Peaches, A *Profile of Dolby Laboratories: An Effective Model for Leveraging Intellectual Property*, 2 Nw. J. Tech. & Intell. Prop. 81 (2003), available at https://scholarlycommons.law.northwestern.edu/njtip/vol2/iss1/4. IP protection is crucial for a company that depends on licensing a series of innovative

which helps companies form and administer patent pools.[33] This grew out of Dolby's extensive internal experience as a member and founder of several pools.

5.2.1.3 W. L. Gore and Gore-Tex

Corporate spinoffs have powered specialization, entry, and innovation in a number of industries. A good example from the chemical industry is W. L. Gore and Associates, a firm that had its origins in DuPont's famous polymer research program from the 1930s onward. One of the interesting polymers synthesized during this time was polytetrafluoroethylene, or PTFE as it came to be known. This is the plastic film used to make Teflon, a non-stick coating for kitchen pots and pans. PTFE was originally synthesized in 1938 and had its first large-scale application in the Manhattan Project for the creation of the first atomic weapons. PTFE could withstand the highly corrosive atmosphere of the uranium enrichment or separation process, where uranium 235 isotopes are separated from uranium 238; the uranium 235 isotopes, in sufficient concentration, are capable of chain reaction nuclear fission.[34]

PTFE is an unusual polymeric molecule. It is produced from a Freon base, using an expensive process that results in a polymer which is high in fluorine – a relatively expensive chemical element. The resulting polymer is famously extremely slippery, making it ideal for applications such as gaskets and other parts where friction and corrosion are common, and where resistance to bonding with other materials (such as lubricants or contaminants) is highly desirable. DuPont acquired the basic product (molecule) patents, including this original patent (Figure 5.6) issued to DuPont polymer scientist Roy Plunkett in 1941.

There was a small but profitable market for PTFE in Teflon form. By 1960, sales were up to $28 million per year on total production volume of 10 million pounds. According to the leading historian of DuPont research, "DuPont's proprietary

technologies. See Robert P. Merges, A *Transactional View of Property Rights*, 20 Berkeley Tech. L.J. 1477 (2005).

33 As of 2020, Via administers nine separate patent pools and is actively organizing others. See www.via-corp.com/licensing/.

34 See David A. Hounshell and John Kenly Smith, Jr., Science and Corporate Strategy: DuPont R&D, 1902–1980 (Cambridge: Cambridge University Press, 1988), at pp. 482–483. The gaseous separation process was pioneered in Britain and was folded into the Manhattan Project as part of the coordinated wartime research effort that produced innovations such as synthetic rubber. See Edward R. Weidlein, *Industrial Research and the Patent System*, 28 J. Pat. Off. Soc'y 79 (1946), at p. 80:

> The paramount importance of inventions during the mechanized war just completed was emphasized by the Federal Government. Our Government literally called upon the inventors of America through such agencies as the National Inventors Council, the National Advisory Committee for Aeronautics, the Office of Scientific Research and Development and the various research laboratories of the executive departments, as well as all research laboratories and universities throughout the country, to invent against this type of warfare.

Patented Feb. 4, 1941 **2,230,654**

UNITED STATES PATENT OFFICE

2,230,654

TETRAFLUOROETHYLENE POLYMERS

Roy J. Plunkett, Wilmington, Del., assignor to Kinetic Chemicals, Inc., Wilmington, Del., a corporation of Delaware

No Drawing. Application July 1, 1939, Serial No. 282,437

3 Claims. (Cl. 260—94)

A. This invention relates to new compositions of matter, being polymers of exceptional properties.

B. At the present time there are no totally satisfactory materials for handling certain corrosive agents, such as hydrofluoric acid, or for protecting workers against the fumes which arise from such reagents. Goggles having glass disks are attacked by the fumes, and shortly become unserviceable

time the unpolymerized tetrafluoroethylene was removed, leaving a residue of 0.6 part of white solid polymer. The yield was 7.1% or a polymerization rate of 0.71% per day.

Example II

Tetrafluoroethylene (7.8 parts) was placed in a container under pressure at 20° C. The yield of polymer after 21 days was 0.05 part or 0.64%.

FIGURE 5.6. Original PTFE patent, issued to Roy Plunkett and assigned to Kinetic Chemicals, Inc. (a DuPont subsidiary) in 1941. This is the material behind Teflon and, later, Gore-Tex fabric

position accounted for some of the success of Teflon; it gave the company the incentive to invest the considerable resources necessary to transform this chemical curiosity into a useful product."[35] DuPont developed a number of applications for PTFE, including insulation for electrical wires. This and other applications required solutions to difficult problems in polymer fabrication. One of the DuPont engineers assigned to these problems was Wilbert L. Gore of the Research Division. It was while Wilbert was working at home that son Robert Gore (then an engineering student) suggested placing wires inside two strips of PTFE film, to form a wire "ribbon." When Wilbert's boss at DuPont told Wilbert DuPont had no interest in pursuing this PTFE market, Wilbert left to form his own company, with the blessings of DuPont.[36]

A classic stroke of serendipity led Robert Gore to stretch heated Teflon at a much quicker rate than had been tried before. The result was an unexpected breakthrough: the high-temperature stretch created sheets of material with millions of tiny pores per inch. These are too small to admit water droplets, but large enough to

[35] David A. Hounshell and John Kenly Smith, Jr., Science and Corporate Strategy: DuPont R&D, at pp. 484–485.

[36] Ibid., at p. 485.

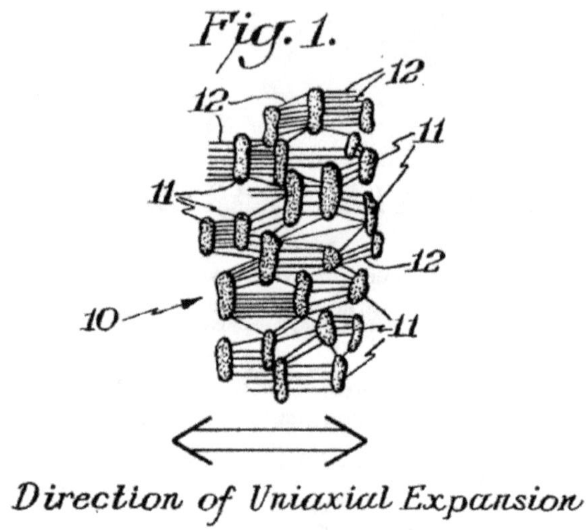

FIGURE 5.7. Making Gore-Tex by ultra-fast stretching of PTFE rods under high temperatures (over 300 degrees Centigrade). US patent 3,953,566, "Process for Producing Porous Products," issued to Robert W. Gore on April 27, 1976, assigned to W. L. Gore and Associates[37]

permit water evaporation: a breathable yet waterproof combination. The stretching of Teflon rods is depicted in Figure 5.7 from the key Gore patent.

The applications for this material number in the dozens. It can be used for computer cabling, outdoor wear, guitar strings, sealants, filtration, venting, and even medical grafts.[38] W. L. Gore manufactures products in many forms useful to industry (rods, sheets, tubes, etc.) but also offers its technologies to more specialized manufacturing partners.[39] Gore has a patent portfolio of over 2,000 patents, which helps to support its $3 billion per year in revenues.[40] Gore provides manufacturing inputs to many of its customers (material in raw form that is incorporated as a component in a final product – fabric covering, gasket material, etc.). Patents may be especially important for this business model because of the detailed information sharing that often must take place with customers and their engineers.[41]

[37] Claims 1 and 17 of this patent were invalidated in a patent infringement suit in 1983. See *W. L. Gore & Assocs., Inc.* v. Garlock, Inc., 721 F.2d 1540 (Fed. Cir. 1983) (remaining claims not invalid).

[38] MarketLine, Company Profile, W. L. Gore and Assocs., Inc., December 13, 2019 (Ebsco Accession Number 141337024), available at www.connect.Ebsco.com (Ebsco Connect database), at p. 3. On one of the original medical applications, see A. McL. Jenkins, A *New Prosthesis for Vascular Access*, 2 Brit. Med. J. 280 (1976) (GoreTex fabric successfully used as vascular graft in five patients).

[39] MarketLine, Company Profile, W. L. Gore 2019, at p. 5 ("[Gore] collaborates with various partners to … enhance its product portfolio.").

[40] MarketLine, Company Profile, W. L. Gore 2019, at p. 3.

[41] Ashish Arora and Robert P. Merges, *Specialized Supply Firms, Property Rights and Firm Boundaries*, 13 Indus. & Corp. Change 451 (2004).

Trade secrets are important too, as they are with any process-intensive technology.[42]

To match its innovative materials technology, W. L. Gore from the beginning adopted a novel organizational structure. Wilbert Gore and his wife Vieve decided to forego a normal hierarchical corporate structure in favor of a completely "flat" group of co-equals. This so-called lattice organization works by interconnecting each "associate" (not employee) with all others on a project-by-project basis.[43] This "task force" oriented structure brings together specific teams for specific tasks, and then just as rapidly disbands them.[44] It is one example of the autonomy that comes with independence, and the value of diversity of thought that accompanies multiple small units of R&D activity, rather than just a few huge research labs. When Gore spun off from DuPont, it formed a separate, independent organization with a distinctive culture. Patents help Gore remain an independent and autonomous source of innovative ideas.

5.2.2 *The Rise of the Chemical Industry*

Gore-Tex has many uses, but the chemical industry goes far beyond synthetic material for clothing and the like. Indeed, David S. Landes, a noted historian of technology, has called the business of chemical manufacture "the most miscellaneous of industries."[45] These industries cover everything from fertilizers and pesticides to pharmaceuticals, from synthetic chemicals to cement. Taken together, the many sectors of the industry represent one of the most explosive sources of economic growth after 1920. To make sense of this diverse industry, historians and economists

42 See, e.g., *W. L. Gore & Assocs., Inc. v. Wu*, No. CIV.A. 263-N, 2006 WL 2692584, at *2 (Del. Ch. September 15, 2006), aff'd, 918 A.2d 1171 (Del. 2007) (footnotes omitted):

> Gore spends substantial time, effort and money developing and maintaining the confidentiality of its trade secrets. Accordingly, Gore only discloses its trade secrets and confidential information on a need to know basis, requires employees to sign confidentiality agreements and trains all its associates on the importance of keeping such information confidential. Further, all associates that have access to Gore's confidential fluoropolymer processing information must sign additional confidentiality agreements and undertake additional obligations to Gore.

43 Debra R. France, *Fostering Connections in a Lattice Organization*, 42 People & Strategy 16 (Spring, 2019):

> Bill Gore and his wife, Vieve, designed a nearly flat, lattice-style organization to drive innovation. Just as the company has learned to create unique value in the pores of the polymer it evolved, W. L. Gore & Associates has also refined practices for collaboration and innovation in the spaces created by its lattice organization.

44 See Michael J. Milne, *The Gorey Details*, 74 Mgt. Rev. 16 (March, 1985), at p. 16 (referring to the "task force concept" of research organization).

45 David S. Landes, The Unbound Prometheus: Technological Change and Industrial Development in Western Europe from 1750 to the Present (Cambridge: Cambridge University Press, 2nd ed., 2003), at p. 269. Much of the material in this part of Chapter 5 is drawn from Robert P. Merges and Richard R. Nelson, *On the Complex Economics of Patent Scope*, 90 Colum. L. Rev. 839 (1990).

divide it into three parts: bulk or industrial chemicals, such as ammonia and petrochemicals; specialty or fine chemicals, such as synthetic materials or pesticides; and pharmaceuticals. Accordingly, I will follow this three-part division in my analysis.

A preliminary word is in order regarding why these industries are sufficiently similar to be grouped together. The justification centers on the research process and the perceived importance of patents. Although research techniques may vary, research is very expensive in all three. In the chemical industries, researchers traditionally use primarily laborious empirical techniques to screen a large pool of candidate compounds. Research proceeds by varying small elements of a promising molecule or single steps of a potentially useful process in an attempt to obtain improved results. After the expense of homing in on the most useful member of a chemical family of interest, however, chemical entities are easy to copy once their structure is known. (Efficient production, however, may not be so easy to duplicate.) As some researchers say, the first copy of a new compound costs tens of millions to make, but the next 10 million copies cost very little. Patents are thus seen as crucial to appropriating the benefits of research in the chemical industries.[46] As a consequence, these industries are comparable to biotechnology in this important respect: Patents are critical to securing the financial returns needed to propel the industry forward.

In the chemical industries, research-intensity and patent-intensity go hand in hand. Historical data show conclusively that chemical companies spend more on R&D than other companies. This holds for all companies, big and small. As economist David Mowery has written:

> By 1933 … larger firms within chemicals are significantly more research-intensive than larger firms in other manufacturing industries, while the minimum firm size associated with a research laboratory in chemicals has declined relative to that observed in other industries. Certainly the [data] … suggest[] that larger chemicals firms were increasing their research intensity more rapidly during 1921–1933 than

[46] The essentiality of patent protection for the chemical and pharmaceutical industries is perhaps the most robust and oft-verified finding in the large body of research studying the importance of patents for various industries. See, e.g., Richard C. Levin, Alvin K. Klevorick, Richard R. Nelson, and S.idney G. Winter, *Appropriating the Returns from Industrial R&D*, 1987 Brookings Papers on Economic Activity 783 (1987); William M. Cohen, Richard R. Nelson, and John P. Walsh, "Protecting their Intellectual Assets: Appropriability Conditions and why U.S.Manufacturing Firms Patent (or not)," Nat'l Bur. Econ. Res., NBER Working Paper 7522 (revised, 2004); Stuart Graham, Robert Merges, Pamela Samuelson, and Ted Sichelman, *High Technology Entrepreneurs and the Patent System: Results of the 2008 Berkeley Patent Survey*, 24 Berkeley Tech. L.J. 255 (2009) (importance of patents in biotechnology industry). Research costs may drive chemical industries to embrace patent protection, but it's also true that chemical structures provide relatively clear boundaries around a claimed chemical invention, and they are also relatively easy to search when looking for chemical prior art. See Christina Mulligan and Timothy B. Lee, *Scaling the Patent System*, 68 N.Y.U. Ann. Surv. Am. L. 289 (2012) (compatibility of chemical structure patents and increased patent volumes).

were larger firms in other industries within this population. By 1946, chemicals firms no longer display a significantly lower minimum size associated with research employment, but larger firms within this industry remain more research intensive than is true of larger firms in other manufacturing industries. The behavior of the firm size-research employment relationship during 1921–1946 within this small-firm population is consistent with a delayed emergence of larger firms within the chemicals industry as major research performers . . . The chemicals industry thus appears to have emerged as a "leading sector" in the growth of industrial research intensity within this small-firm population, as was observed within the large-firm population . . . [47]

5.2.2.1 Bulk Chemicals

Bulk chemicals are used almost exclusively to make a vast range of secondary or specialty chemicals. Examples include sulfuric acid, ammonia, the olefins, such as ethylene and propylene (used to make synthetic materials), and the aromatics, such as benzene. Bulk chemicals are almost exclusively produced in huge plants; minimum efficient scale for a given chemical is often measured in the hundreds of thousands of tons per year.

Almost all the products of the bulk chemical industry have been well known for many years. For example, acids have long been used for tanning, curing, and other industrial purposes; bleaching agents and dyes have been used in the textile industry for centuries. The same is true for the other major bulk chemicals. Taylor and Silberston, in their study of patents in the chemical industries, state:

> The range of products has not widened very much over half a century, although naturally their relative importance has greatly changed. Most research efforts are directed towards the reduction of unit costs and improvements in the purity and consistency of standard products. There is relatively little work on new products . . . [48]

Thus, process improvements are often the important inventions in bulk chemicals.[49] We will therefore focus on the scope of process patents in this industry. The growth of the high-volume bulk chemical industry can be traced to the late nineteenth

47 David C. Mowery, *Industrial Research and Firm Size, Survival, and Growth in American Manufacturing, 1921–1946*, at p. 973.

48 C. T. Taylor and Z. A. Silberston, The Economic Impact of the Patent System (Cambridge: Cambridge University Press, 1973), at p. 268.

49 See, e.g., Manuel Bauer and Jens Leker, *Exploration and Exploitation in Product and Process Innovation in the Chemical Industry*, 43 R&D Mgt. 196 (2013), at p. 199:

> For instance, the global market dominance of the German chemical company Merck KGaA in the field of liquid crystals is mainly due to its unmet product purity resulting from its innovation of a unique production process. The same holds true in the case of Wacker Chemie AG. Their knowledge about high-purity production processes from their silicon wafers subsidiary can be transferred to their polysilicon business (the primary material in photo voltaic panels) where Wacker competes successfully against low-cost competitors based on their production purity competence.

century.[50] A good example of a process invention from this era, and indirectly of the role of patents, is the Solvay process for producing alkali. In 1861 a Belgian named Ernest Solvay had patented a process for alkali manufacturing using ammonia.[51] It was a major advance over the traditional "LeBlanc" method.[52] In 1880 he licensed an American firm to use both the original patent and an improved process patented in 1873.[53] This licensee was the sole American firm in the industry until a series of patent cases in the 1890s opened up the industry for competition. One case held the Solvay improvement patents to a narrow scope. According to the historian David Noble, "[i]n that year, as a result, two new companies appeared, the Michigan Alkali Company and the Mathieson Alkali Company."[54] A second case in 1898, brought by Michigan Alkali, invalidated an improvement patent on the Solvay process.

The impression left by the Solvay process cases is that patents with broad scope had the potential to hold up progress in the bulk chemical industry. This is misleading, however, for a number of reasons. First, firms around the world continued to invent new processes for producing alkalis. L. F. Haber and David Noble have noted the growth of the electrolytic process of caustic soda production beginning in the early 1900s,[55] which Noble says was "the biggest boon to the alkali industry" in the nineteenth century.[56] Second, even when Solvay held his broad original patent he chose to license a number of foreign firms, including the Solvay Process Corporation of America.[57] This is quite typical in bulk chemicals. Taylor and Silberston have explained that firms in the industry are often dependent on cross-licensing, which they find mutually advantageous partly because alternative process technologies are constantly being developed. Freeman has described how licensing aided the development of an independent industry for chemical plant construction firms, which depends on the licensing of process technology:

[50] Christopher Freeman, The Economics of Industrial Innovation (Cambridge, MA: The MIT Press, 2nd ed., 1982), at p. 31; Ludwig F. Haber, The Chemical Industry during the Nineteenth Century: A Study of the Economic Aspect of Applied Chemistry in Europe and North America (Oxford: Clarendon Press, 1st ed., 1958).

[51] John Jewkes, David Sawers, and Richard Stillerman, The Sources of Invention 50 (New York: Macmillan, 2nd ed., 1969).

[52] Christopher Freeman, The Economics of Industrial Innovation, at pp. 28–29.

[53] On the improvement patent of 1873, see Jewkes et al., The Sources of Invention, at p. 50; *Solvay Process Co.* v. *Michigan Alkali Co.*, 90 F. 818 (6th Cir. 1898). On the American licensee, see David Noble, America by Design: Science, Technology, and the Rise of Corporate Capitalism (Oxford: Oxford University Press, 1977), at p. 14.

[54] David Noble, America by Design, at p. 14. The original patent to Solvay of 1861 had, of course, expired by this time.

[55] Ludwig F. Haber, The Chemical Industry during the Nineteenth Century, at p. 177; David Noble, America by Design, at p. 14.

[56] David Noble, America by Design, at p. 14.

[57] Christopher Freeman, The Economics of Industrial Innovation, at p. 29. The primary foreign licensee was Brenner, Mond and Co. of Britain and Germany. Ludwig F. Haber, The Chemical Industry during the Nineteenth Century, at p. 177.

> Technological progress in established basic industrial chemicals is so rapid and so internationalised that more is generally to be gained for both the firm and the country if each national process innovation is exploited by licensing the contracting industry and selling know-how ... [58]

Likewise, competition in the oil refinery construction industry depends more on process technologies and engineering expertise than exclusion of competitors with product patents.[59] This highly international sub-industry is characterized by intense competition among highly specialized firms.[60] Typical of innovation in this sector was the work of Union Oil Products (UOP), a leading firm specializing in design and construction of oil refineries all around the world. In the late 1940s, a UOP researcher named Vladimir Haensal pioneered an advanced platinum-silica catalyst for "cracking" crude oil that revolutionized oil refining just as automobile travel was picking up in the post-War years.[61]

5.2.2.2 Fine or Specialty Chemicals: The Case of Synthetic Materials

Specialty chemicals are sold in their final chemical form, unlike most bulk chemicals. They are then used to make a very wide variety of end products. This is a very broad category of chemicals, which includes synthetic materials (polyethylene, polypropylene, etc.), agricultural chemicals (pesticides, fertilizers, etc.), and a host of others (soaps, paint, dyestuffs, etc.).[62]

The story of specialty chemicals is coextensive with the growth of analytical chemistry. After 1880 or so the nature of chemical research changed. If the main line of development before 1880 had been an increasing awareness of the wide capabilities of chemical science in creating commercial products, the emphasis after 1880 was on the importance of precise investigations of chemical structure. The methods of the German school of analytical chemistry swept the western world

[58] Christopher Freeman, *Chemical Process Plant: Innovation and the World Market*, 1968 Nat'l Institutes Econ. Rev. 29 (No. 45, 1968), at p. 50.

[59] These process-intensive parts of the industry often depend on patent licensing in their business model. See Ashish Arora, *Patents, Licensing, and Market Structure in the Chemical Industry*, 26 Res. Pol'y 391 (1997), at p. 392: "[I]ncreased licensing of process technologies [in the chemical industries after 1945] played a major role in enabling new firms to enter, and in turn, entry induced existing producers to increase licensing."

[60] See Ashish Arora and Alfonso Gambardella, *Domestic Markets and International Competitiveness: Generic and Product-Specific Competencies in the Engineering Sector*, 18 Strat. Mgt. J. 53 (1998).

[61] See US patent 2,479,110, "Process of Reforming a Gasoline with an Aluminum-Platinum-Halogen Catalyst," issued to Vladimir Haensal on August 16, 1949, assigned to UOP. See generally Charles Remsberg and Hal Higdon, Ideas for Rent: The UOP Story (Des Plains, IL: UOP Press, 1994).

[62] On these segments of the specialty chemicals business, see Basil Achilladelis, Albert Schwarzkopf, and Martin Cines, A *Study of Innovation in the Pesticide Industry: Analysis of the Innovation Record of an Industrial Sector*, 16 Res. Pol'y 175 (1987) (agricultural chemicals).

during this period. And inevitably this approach led to the increasing specialization of the field that continues today.

The important trends are all reflected in the early history of synthetic dyestuffs.[63] From very early times, a considerable range of vegetable dyes has been used to add color to textiles. A discovery in 1856, however, revolutionized the dyestuffs trade. This discovery was that of mauve, made by W. H. Perkin in 1856. Although the story properly begins some ten years earlier with the work of the distinguished German chemist, August Wilhelm von Hofmann, who first realized that the accumulation of benzene as a byproduct of the expanding gas industry provided a valuable "feed-stock" for producing useful organic chemicals, it was von Hofmann's student Perkin who first realized the full potential of benzene-derived organic chemical products. Perkins noticed a resemblance between the formula of allyl-toluidine, a derivative of the aniline von Hofmann synthesized from benzene, and the very important anti-malarial drug quinine. Perkin tried but failed to use allyl-toluidine to make quinine. So, he next tried the same experiment with aniline: from the black sludge resulting from his experiment, he obtained some purple crystals. To his great surprise, he found that his "mystery crystal" would dye silk a brilliant mauve that did not fade in sunlight and could not be washed out. When he received an enthusiastic response from a silk company, Perkins immediately patented his dye, and with the help of his father and elder brother built the first large-scale "synthetic" dye plant in 1857.

Perkin's success led other organic chemists to investigate the possibility of making other synthetic dyes from aniline and its chemical derivatives. In 1859 magenta was discovered, then a whole series of violet dyes. Then came rosaniline blue, aniline black, and a host of others. At about the same time a German chemist named Peter Griess discovered the diazo compounds, which spawned another series of important dyestuffs. But even more important was the development of synthetic versions of dyes previously available only from natural sources, which demonstrated with finality the superiority of the new analytic techniques.

This was possible because of the rapid progress being made in theoretical organic chemistry. In 1869 two German chemists, K. Graebe and K. Liebermann, synthesized alizarin. Their discovery was refined and made practical by Heinrich Caro, working for the Badische Anilin-und-Soda Fabrik (BASF), who incidentally filed his patent in Britain the day before Perkin lodged one for the same process. The discovery spelled ruin for the European growers of the plant (named madder) that had previously supplied the raw material for the dye, but clothing was cheaper, and the chemical industry was given a critical impetus. In 1897 synthetic indigo was

[63] The account here is taken from Fred Aftalion, A History of the International Chemical Industry (Otto Theodor Benfey trans.) (Philadelphia: University of Pennsylvania Press, 1991), at pp. 35 ff. For a more detailed study, emphasizing business strategy, patenting, and national institutions, see Johann Peter Murmann, Knowledge and Competitive Advantage: The Coevolution of Firms, Technology, and National Institutions (Cambridge: Cambridge University Press, 2003).

developed, again by a German chemist; there followed a huge outpouring of new synthetic dyestuffs that became available before the end of the nineteenth century.

German firms dominated the industry. As one history maintains,

> The number of patents relating to dyes filed in Britain each five-year period was 20 in 1860 and 52 in 1900: the figures for Germany, for the same years, were 8 and 427 respectively. For this, various reasons have been advanced: important factors were certainly the greater availability of raw materials in Germany; a better system of technical education, with strong financial support from the state; and a readiness to use technically qualified men in all branches of the business. A measure of the grip that Germany had established is given by the fact that, when war broke out in 1914, only 20 per cent. of the dyes used in Britain were of domestic manufacture, a grave strategic disadvantage, even the dyeing of military uniforms presented a serious problem.[64]

Improved understanding of chemical dyes was just the beginning. Synthetic materials are another important branch of the specialty chemicals industry, and their development has been well described. We will therefore consider them as a case study that may shed light on the development of this sector in the period from 1920 to 1982.

One of the earliest synthetic materials was Bakelite, a phenol-formaldehyde compound invented by Leo Baekeland in 1907 (described in detail in Chapter 4). It was used as an electrical insulator and in the early manufacture of radio sets and electrical accessories for cars. As mentioned earlier, Baekeland obtained two broad patents on Bakelite, one over the process and one over the product.[65] Reported patent infringement suits indicate that Baekeland enforced his patents and suggest that their scope was sufficient to have an effect on the development of the nascent synthetics industry.[66]

64 Thomas K. Derry and Trevor Iltyd Williams, A Short History of Technology: From the Earliest Times to A. D. 1900 (Oxford: Clarendon Press, 1960), at p. 546.

65 Ludwig F. Haber, The Chemical Industry during the Nineteenth Century, at p. 6; Christopher Freeman The Economics of Industrial Innovation (Cambridge, MA: MIT Press, 3rd. ed., 1997), at p. 88. See *General Bakelite Co.* v. *Nikolas*, 225 F. 539 (E.D.N.Y. 1915) (upholding Bakelite patents over challenge by manufacturer of synthetic rubber).

66 Congressional testimony by Baekeland's son George, President of the company in the 1930s, suggests that the patents were in fact broad enough to deter entry by others. When asked if competitors had entered the field after expiration of the broad, early patents, he responded:

> A number of competitors or new companies came into the field and some of our larger customers were tempted to go into the manufacture of plastics on their own for their own uses. So that we have lively competition today and the patents under which we [General Bakelite] are now operating are not basic patents; they are just improvement patents.

Testimony of George Baekeland before the Temporary National Economic Committee (T.N. E.C.), quoted in G. Folk, Patents and Industrial Progress 190 (1942). Compare *Frischer & Co.* v. *Bakelite Corp.*, 39 F.2d 247 (C.C.P.A. 1930) (upholding exclusion order against foreign infringers of improvement patents on Bakelite).

But here as in bulk chemicals the scope of these early patents was more limited than this story implies. We know, for instance, that a German firm independently developed a phenol-formaldehyde compound that was very similar to Bakelite.[67] Litigation ensued, and the foreign defendants apparently became licensees or somehow settled, because they continued to produce their substitute product.[68] In any event, it was not too long after the introduction of Bakelite that the first of the modern hydrocarbon polymer plastics were introduced. General Bakelite lived on into the era of modern plastics, finally merging with Union Carbide in 1939 (see Chapter 4).

Of the post-Bakelite synthetic materials, nylon and polyethylene were most important. DuPont researchers first synthesized nylon in the late 1930s. The company obtained a series of broad product patents, culminating with the "Nylon 66" patent covering a commercially valuable form of the fiber.[69] Polyethylene was discovered in 1935–1936 by scientists from Imperial Chemical Industries of Great Britain (ICI), which held the early product patents.[70] As part of a general cross-licensing and market-sharing arrangement, ICI and DuPont licensed these valuable patents to one another for production in their respective home markets.[71]

This arrangement was challenged by US antitrust authorities in the late 1940s and early 1950s.[72] The resulting consent decree ordered DuPont and Imperial to license all patents covered by their agreements, including those remaining on nylon and polyethylene.[73] A follow-up study in Congress concluded that

> the judgement appears to have made it possible for a substantial number of companies to enter this field. There appears to be substantially more competition in the manufacture and sale of polythene [i.e., polyethylene] products than there was before the judgment was entered.[74]

67 Ludwig F. Haber, The Chemical Industry during the Nineteenth Century, at pp. 6, 113.

68 Ibid., at p. 113: "[T]he chemical factory of H. Albert . . . independently of Baekeland patented a phenol-formaldehyde resin in 1910, which, under the name of 'Albertol', became popular after [World War I]."

69 C. T. Taylor and Z. A. Silberston, The Economic Impact of the Patent System, at p. 342.

70 2 William J. Reader, Imperial Chemical Industries: A History 351–354 (Oxford: Oxford Univ. Press, 1975); James A. Allen, Studies in Innovation in the Steel and Chemical Industries (Manchester: Manchester University Press, 1967), at p. 47 (citing Imperial's 1937 British patent); John Jewkes, David Sawers, and Richard Stillerman, The Sources of Invention, at p. 280; 2 William J. Reader , Imperial Chemical Industries: A History, at p. 357 ("In the USA, the most important market, ICI held a 'composition of matter' patent which protected polythene [i. e., polyethylene] itself, regardless of the process by which it was made.").

71 William J. Reader, Imperial Chemical Industries: A History, at pp. 52–53.

72 Ibid., at pp. 428–444.

73 See *United States* v. *Imperial Chemical Industries, Ltd.*, 105 F. Supp. 215 (S.D.N.Y. 1952). The compulsory licensing of polyethylene is ordered at 223.

74 Staff of the Subcommittee on Patents, Trademarks, and Copyrights of the Senate Comm. on the Judiciary, 86th Cong., 2nd Sess., Compulsory Licensing of Antitrust Judgments, 13 (Staff Report 1960) (Written by Marcus A. Hollabaugh and Robert L. Wright).

Indeed by 1954 at least eight companies were said to be competing in the market for manufactured polyethylene on the strength of licenses under the decree.[75] Without the forced licensing mandated by the antitrust decree these competitors would not have been able to enter the field. As in the bulk chemical industry, these key early patents appear to have had a good deal of blocking power. But as in bulk chemicals, the appearance is misleading. Even these broad, early patents would probably not have prevented the introduction of competitive products.

Just as in the alkali trades discussed earlier, synthetic materials competitors were at work on improved processes. In the early 1950s researchers at Phillips, DuPont, and the Max Planck Institute in Germany began exploring alternative methods of producing polyethylene. Their research explored new metal catalysts that made it possible to produce a polymer of higher density at lower pressures and temperatures.[76] Because the original patent contained limitations relating to temperature, pressure and oxygen concentration, the new process – and the product it yielded – did not infringe Imperial's patent. In fact, one historian of the industry suggests that the search for high-density polyethylene may have been motivated in part by a desire to skirt the Imperial patent.[77]

Just after Zeigler at Max Planck and his American counterparts made their first discoveries, an Italian chemist named Guilio Natta of the Polytechnic Institute in Milan began exploring improvements in the Zeigler catalytic process.[78] Parallel work was done in the United States.[79] These researchers invented more than an improved process for making polyethylene, however. They discovered catalytic principles that made it possible to cheaply produce another important polymer: polypropylene. Polypropylene has emerged as a substitute for polyethylene in several key applications.[80] Product patents on polypropylene were filed by five companies from a broad swath of the chemical industries, based on invention dates between 1953 and 1955. A four-company interference (priority dispute) commenced in 1958 and was finally completed in 1980 – a classic example of the high costs of

[75] The Polyethylene Gamble, Fortune, February 1954, 134, 136. See also Staff Report on Licensing at 13 (showing that Imperial had issued nine licenses on polyethylene by 1955; DuPont had issued seventeen for polyethylene and forty for nylon).

[76] John Jewkes, David Sawers, and Richard Stillerman, The Sources of Invention, at p. 280.

[77] James A. Allen, Studies in Innovation in the Steel and Chemical Industries, at p. 47: "Many of the early would-be Zeigler licensees ... were, however, probably seeking a route free from the I.C.I. patents, either because they wished to be free, or could not get the know-how as well as the patents."

[78] Christopher Freeman, The Economics of Industrial Innovation, at p. 67.

[79] See *Standard Oil Co.* v. *Montedison*, 494 F.Supp. 370, 374 (D.Del. 1980), aff'd 664 F.2d 356 (3d Cir. 1981) (patent interference between four firms).

[80] See Modern Plastics, February, 1988, at 98–100 (discussing strong market for "polyolefin foam," including both polyethylene and polypropylene, in applications relating to packaging); Textile World, May 1987, at 12 (describing interchangeability of polyethylene and polypropylene in uses such as specialty papers, films, and disposables, all in the general category of nonwoven polymers).

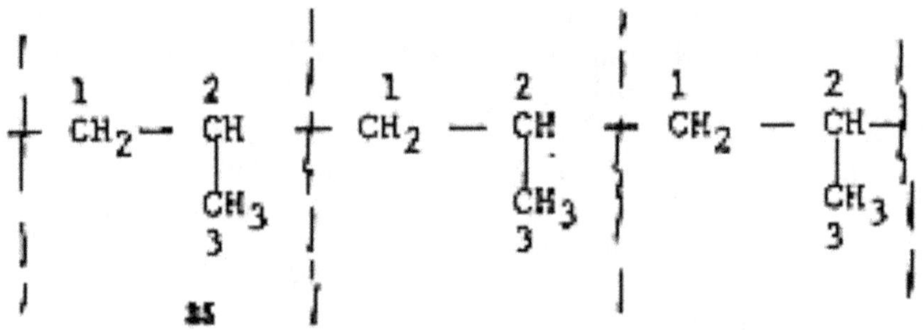

FIGURE 5.8. Basic structure of polypropylene. From *Standard Oil Co. (Indiana) v. Montedison, S.p.A.*, 494 F. Supp. 370, 376 (polypropylene interference)

the old (pre-2011) "first to invent" system. Figure 5.8 shows the basic structure of polypropylene.

Phillips Petroleum of Oklahoma ended up as the winning party in the interference. Phillips, like many oil companies, entered the plastics industry as an offshoot of its oil business. The basic inputs to plastic manufacture are often drawn from the waste products that result when oil is refined into gasoline. What is interesting about the interference is how much it reveals about the sophistication of industrial research, at least in the synthetics field. Zeigler and Natta, the pioneering academic chemists, were well known leaders in the field. But unbeknownst to them, or to most others in the field, two applied chemists working for Phillips at their research lab in Bartlesville, Oklahoma were in the thick of polymer research at the same time. Only the subsequent patent, filed on March 26, 1956, and issued in 1958,[81] informed the research world that Phillips had been in the game all along (Figure 5.9).

There is no doubt that the research of Zeigler and Natta broke new ground; the two scientists shared the 1963 Nobel Prize for their efforts.[82] Even so several factors limited the scope of their patents. The first was (and is) inherent in chemical inventing: the problem of being unable to predict how a new principle will work in a specific context. One infringement case involving two Zeigler catalyst patents provides an excellent example. In holding that the defendant's process did not infringe Zeigler's patents, the court pointed out that the defendant's process used slightly different catalytic ingredients and reaction conditions than the ones claimed

[81] The court actually found that Phillips had produced, and recognized, crystalline polypropylene by late January of 1953. See *Standard Oil Co. (Indiana) v. Montedison, S.p.A.*, 494 F. Supp. 370, 418 (D. Del. 1980), aff'd, 664 F.2d 356 (3d Cir. 1981). Though the pioneering work on metallic polymer catalysts had already been underway in the labs of Zeigler and Natta, Natta, did not create commercially viable polypropylene until "Natta's priority date of June 8, 1954." See *Standard Oil Co. (Indiana) v. Montedison, S.p.A.*, 494 F. Supp. 370, 392 (D. Del. 1980), aff'd, 664 F.2d 356 (3d Cir. 1981). See also Mike Sutton, Paving the way to polythene, Chemistry World, October 10, 2013, available at www.chemistryworld.com/features/paving-the-way-to-polythene-/6675.article (Natta had produced polypropylene by March 1954).

[82] *Studiengesellschaft Kohle mbH v. Eastman Kodak Co.*, 616 F.2d 1315, 1322 (5th Cir. 1980).

The terminal vinyl type of unsaturation is characterized by the structure —CH=CH$_2$. The vinyl group may be attached to the molecule either internally or terminally as represented, for example, by such formulas as:

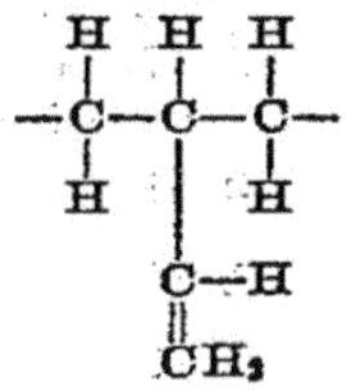

and

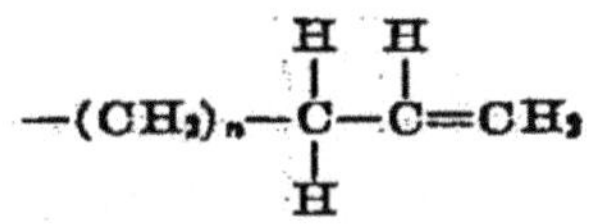

(terminal vinyl)

These structures are definitely different types of structures from those predominating in the polymers of the prior art, which have been found and are known in the literature to have the major portion of their unsaturation of the branched vinyl type, which may be illustrated, for example, by the structure

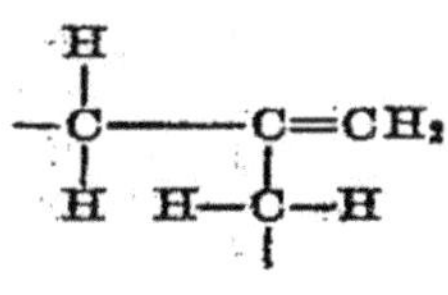

FIGURE 5.9. Excerpt from US patent 2,825,721, March 4, 1958, "polymers and production thereof," issued to John Paul Hogan and Robert L. Banks, assigned to Phillips Petroleum, Inc. A five-way interference finally ending in 1980 determined that Hogan and Banks were the first to make commercially useable Polypropylene

in the Zeigler patents.[83] Because of the unpredictability of catalyst inventions the court was unwilling to interpret the Zeigler claims as covering the accused catalytic process:

> [I]n catalytic chemistry, minor changes in components, their ratio, or the external condition of the reaction may produce major changes in the reaction itself. A catalyst which works well at one temperature and pressure, for example, may be totally ineffective at another. Similarly, a small change in the oxidation state of

[83] 616 F.2d 1315, 1341–1342.

> one element of a compound may produce an entirely new catalytic process. Each component of the process – the precise compounds, the ratio of their combination, the external condition of the reaction – may be critical.[84]

The second reason extremely broad patents never issued was that there were many competitors in the game. The four-party interference mentioned earlier is one example of this.[85] Many more can be found in accounts of research in related patent infringement decisions; these show very close parallel research efforts by many teams.[86] As a consequence, no one team had the luxury of exploring all the applications of each of its small advances. Also, this resulted in a constant stream of competing patent applications and scientific articles, some of which became prior art further limiting the scope of future claims.[87]

Because Zeigler was an academic scientist, if he wanted to profit from his research he would have to form a company or license his catalyst patents.[88] In fact, licensing was important throughout the industry. Even a huge chemical company like Imperial Chemical found it beneficial to grant licenses to several competing producers of polyethylene before the 1952 antitrust consent decree. The reason is probably the same as for bulk chemicals: No one producer could cover all the markets for applications of the products. There was also an incentive to cross-license; here as elsewhere competing firms embarked on a series of important process improvements. Even the holder of a basic product patent, such as Imperial with

[84] 616 F.2d at 1341. A practice guide for chemical patent lawyers suggests the same applies to product patents in the polymer field: "Given that [the] basic formula of the polymer is already known, it is still possible to obtain new and patentable polymers by various kinds of modification, provided they give useful and nonobvious results." Phillip W. Grubb, Patents for Chemists 155 (Oxford: Oxford University Press, 1st ed., 1982), at p. 155. See also E. *I DuPont de Nemours Co.* v. *Phillips Petroleum Co.*, 849 F.2d 1430, 1432 (Fed. Cir. 1988) (plaintiff's polyethylene copolymer claims include limitation of "density in the range of 0.9 to 0.95," suggesting higher-density copolymer would escape infringement; since defendants' researchers may have anticipated invention of claimed product anyway, case remanded).

[85] *Standard Oil Co.* v. *Montedison*, 494 F.Supp. 370, 374-375 (D.Del. 1980).

[86] See, e.g., *Phillips Petroleum Co.* v. *United States Steel Corp.*, 673 F.Supp. 1278, 1338, 6 U.S.P.Q.2d 1065 (D.Del. 1987) (describing Phillips scientists' close tracking of Natta results and subsequent attempts to apply them to the production of polypropylene); *Studiengesellschaft Kohle mbH* v. *Eastman Kodak Co.*, 616 F.2d 1315, 1321 (5th Cir. 1980) ("The news of Zeigler's success with polyethylene prompted vigorous research by scientists around the world, as they and Zeigler worked on ways to improve the effectiveness of the catalysts and to polymerize higher members of the [olefin] series [of compounds].").

[87] See, e.g., *E. I. dupont de Nemours & Co.* v. *Phillips Petroleum Co.*, 849 F.2d 1430, 1434 n.3 (Fed. Cir. 1988) (invalidating certain claims in a DuPont patent on polyethylene copolymers due to prior work of two Phillips employees); *Phillips Petroleum Co.* v. *United States Steel Corp.*, 673 F.Supp. 1278, 1338, 6 U.S.P.Q.2d 1065 (D.Del. 1987) (describing Natta's published article on his original work).

[88] *United States* v. *Studiengesellschaft Kohle m.b.H.*, 670 F.2d 1122, 1124 (D.C.Cir. 1981) (describing Zeigler's exclusive license to make and sell catalysts to Hercules Incorporated, as well as his licensing of several others to use those catalysts in in-house production).

polyethylene, could probably not afford to ignore an economical improvement, even if that meant licensing the product patent to get it.[89]

As a consequence of these factors, even broad basic patents on synthetic polymers failed to severely drag down the industry. True, in the case of polyethylene and nylon, forced licensing of the product patents speeded the diffusion and application of these polymers. But as we have seen, even here, as with the other synthetics and the bulk chemicals examined earlier, competition from new products and from process innovations limited the blocking effect of these early patents. The structure of chemical patent law actually helped in this regard. The inherent unpredictability of chemical compounds led the law to take a conservative view of the scope of even an early, basic invention. The result was that no single patent blocked progress for long in these branches of the chemical industries.

5.2.2.3 Pharmaceuticals

The modern pharmaceutical industry is the successor to both traditional medicine and the "patent medicines" of the nineteenth century. The former offered typically plant-based therapies based on centuries of received knowledge. The latter was the province of traveling salesmen and newly emerging newspaper and magazine ad campaigns. In both sectors, effective (though sometimes limited) medicines vied with harmless but overhyped "cures" for the attentions of hopeful patients.

When chemistry attained a more scientific foundation in the latter half of the nineteenth century, the new learning launched the modern pharmaceutical industry. As with other parts of the chemical industries, the geographic center was Germany. One of the earliest firms established on this basis was Merck. In 1827, Heinrich Emanuel Merck, inheritor of a family pharmacy in Darmstadt, Germany (near Frankfurt), set up a factory to produce alkaloids. Together with other pioneers, Merck introduced a number of important innovations to the craft-based traditions of the pharmacy industry. The most important was a reliance on the emerging sciences of chemistry and pharmacology. The primary contribution of the German firms

[89] Thus, it is possible that Imperial would have continued to license Union Carbide in exchange for Carbide's new process. Carbide had begun operating under an interim product license during World War II, and without the antitrust action Imperial would have had the right to terminate this license after the War. See William J. Reader, Imperial Chemical Industries: A History, at p. 357 (Imperial was fortunate to have a US product patent "because in Union Carbide, unknown to ICI, work was going on to develop a process entirely independent of ICI's, and it succeeded"). See also ibid. at 433, describing DuPont's strategy of pursuing process-oriented research to lower the royalty Imperial could charge on polyethylene: DuPont, according to an Imperial official, "claim, as I expected, that they have done much on the process side and that we only invented the product and a half-baked way of making it." (Citation omitted.) ibid. at 358–359 (discussing Imperial's close decision on whether to license the Germans in polyethylene just before the War).

came from their close connections to German universities and their preeminence in the chemical sciences.

German universities set the standard for intellectual rigor and disciplinary excellence in the latter part of the nineteenth century.[90] They pioneered greater disciplinary specialization, more organized instructional sequences,[91] and (most importantly) graduate school and postdoctoral study as a training ground for research.[92] Historians have shown that, as the German university system gained strength in the field of chemistry, the national chemical industry also grew in prominence and worldwide market share.[93] According to the leading account by Peter Murmann:

> [German] [a]cademics formed more extensive commercial ties with industry and engaged in joint lobbying efforts to increase funding to organic chemistry and protect the synthetic dye industry. The higher number of organic chemistry graduates from German universities gave Germany a larger number of potential entrepreneurs ... Germany indeed had a larger number of [chemical] start-ups in the period 1857–1913 than all other countries. This led to keen competition among German firms but also to the largest number of firm failures in any of the five countries. The German firms that emerged successful from this competition fought over access to the leading academic chemists because in the first 20 years blockbuster innovations came out of university laboratories.[94]

[90] Lenore O'Boyle, *Learning for Its Own Sake: The German University as Nineteenth-Century Model*, 25 Comp. Stud. Soc. & Hist. 3 (1983).

[91] A nineteenth century American student in Germany commented:

> When a young man [sic] attends [a German] university, he is supposed to have some definite object in view; he wishes to fit himself to become a theologian, or a lawyer, or a ... chemist ... But this of itself implies the pursuance of a certain routine or order in study ... So in chemistry a knowledge of general organic and inorganic chemistry is required before passing to analysis ... [T]his is something altogether different from a curriculum in which mathematics, classics, mataphysics, history, and the natural sciences are pursued simultaneously [i.e., the traditional American and British curriculum of the time].

J. M. Hart, German Universities: A Narrative (New York: J.M. Putnam's Sons, 1874), at p. 46. See generally Konrad H. Jarausch, *American Students in Germany, 1815–1914: The Structure of German and U.S. Matriculants at Gottingen University*, in Henry Geitz, Jurgen Heideking, and Jurgen Herbst, eds., German Influences on Education in the United States to 1917 (Cambridge: Cambridge University Press, 1995), at pp. 195–211.

[92] See Walter Rüegg, ed., A History of the University in Europe. Vol. III: Universities in the Nineteenth and Early Twentieth Centuries (1800–1945) (Cambridge: Cambridge University Press, 2004).

[93] Peter Murmann, *The Co-Development of Industrial Sectors and Academic Disciplines*, 40 Sci. & Pub. Pol'y, 229 (2013) (study of German and Swiss synthetic dye industries and national scientific research communities after 1850).

[94] Peter Murmann, *The Co-Development of Industrial Sectors and Academic Disciplines*, at pp. 237–238.

A number of long-lived firms originated in Germany in this era, including BASF, Hoeschst, Bayer, and Merck.[95] These were "crossover" firms: Based on analytical chemistry techniques developed in the dye industry, they moved laterally into production of pharmaceuticals on an industrial scale. As with the dye industry, the key to successful innovation was an extensive network of university and industry chemical experts.[96] Together they brought the science of analytical chemistry to bear on production of chemical and pharmaceutical products. Many of the earliest pharmaceuticals were alkaloids: a very broad class of chemicals, originally isolated from plants, that includes opioids, quinine, ephedrine, etc. Merck's papavarine, an opium isolate (used as a painkiller) is a good example.[97] At Merck and throughout the German industry, new pharmaceutical and chemical products were introduced in large numbers between the late 1890s and roughly 1905.[98] A contributing factor in the success of the German firms, some have said, was the fact that German patent law protected only processes until 1877, which permitted free entry and encouraged efficiency. After the industry had weeded out production inefficiency, product patents – which encourage research into new chemical compounds – then supported a shift to a more innovative industry orientation.[99]

Despite this head start, it was not long before other countries – particularly the United States – caught up, on both the research and industrial fronts.[100] Typical of the rapid maturation of the pharmaceutical industry in the United States was the Eli Lilly Company. From its origins as a small-town pharmacy business in the nineteenth century[101] (much like Merck), Lilly combined the advancing waves of

95 See Carsten Burhop, *Pharmaceutical Research in Wilhelmine Germany: The Case of E. Merck*, 83 Bus. Hist. Rev. 475 (2009).

96 Ibid., at p. 476.

97 Miles Weatherhall, In Search of a Cure: A History of Pharmaceutical Discovery (Oxford: Oxford University Press, 1990), at p. 36. See generally, vols. 1–8, R. H. F. Manske. The Alkaloids: Chemistry and Physiology (New York: Academic Press, 1965).

98 Carsten Burhop, *Pharmaceutical Research in Wilhelmine Germany*.

99 See Johann Peter Murmann, Knowledge and Competitive Advantage, at p. 29: "The most important institution in the early success of the German dye industry was the university system, but patent laws were a second key factor that allowed the German firms to capture a dominant position."). On the handoff of leadership in the dye industry from Britain to Germany in the late nineteenth century, see David Landes, The Unbound Prometheus, at p. 275.

100 The rising and important field of physical chemistry serves as an example. See John W. Servos, Physical Chemistry from Ostwald to Pauling: The Making of a Science in America (Princeton, NJ: Princeton University Press, 1996), at p. 73:

> Prior to 1908, more than one third of the American chemists writing five or more articles in physical chemistry received their doctoral degrees in Germany. An additional thirty percent (19 of 65) went to Germany just before or after receiving doctorates at American universities. The number receiving doctorates in 1908 and after, however, was negligible; nondegree and postdoctoral study in Germany likewise disappeared almost completely.

101 See Gene E. McCormick, *Henry C. Lawrence, 1820–1862: Mentor of Eli Lilly*, 16 Pharmacy in Hist. 89, 93 (1974) (describing craft techniques such as hand dipping of medicines in gelatin to make pills, taught to the young Eli Lilly by a local pharmacist).

increasing scientific sophistication and industrialization to build one of the first nationwide pharmaceutical companies. Eli Lilly himself attended the Philadelphia College of Pharmacy (PCP), the same school his father went to before founding the pharmacy in Indianapolis. But the younger Lilly benefitted from the greater scientific rigor of pharmacy training after the turn of the twentieth century.[102] Upon his return to Indianapolis, Lilly set out to incorporate much of the new learning he had absorbed into the pharmacy's business model. The result was the first systematic integration in the U.S. of university-level scientific knowledge into pharmaceutical research and production.[103] This included the hiring of university-trained scientists and the equipping of a state-of-the-art research lab. Almost from its inception, the Eli Lilly firm yoked its business prospects to the efficacy of science-based corporate research.

Several other firms employed higher scientific standards as part of their entry into the pharmaceutical field. The firm of H. K. Mulford, founded in the 1880s by Henry Kendall Mulford, is a good example. Mulford graduated from the Philadelphia College of Pharmacy, some years prior to Eli Lilly.[104] Mulford and his colleague Milton Campbell decided to focus the company's energies on vaccines – a new and fast-growing sector of the pharmaceutical field at the end of the nineteenth century. Their "entrepreneurial instincts" led them, in 1895, to the introduction of the first successful diphtheria antitoxin made in a United States factory. Like Eli Lilly, the Mulford firm hired well-trained scientists and outfitted modern laboratories, becoming one of the leading sources of first-generation biologics, including the isolation of purified adrenalin.[105] Mulford became an industry leader in the sale of vaccines and

[102] James H. Madison, *"Oh, Mama, I Smell the Business!": The Growing Up Years of Eli Lilly, 1885–1907*, 31 Pharm. Hist. 160 (1989), at p. 162. (The title refers to the young Eli Lilly's excitement as a boy when getting close to the site of the family business: Cooking patent medicines sometimes created strong smells).

[103] See James H. Madison, Eli Lilly: A Life, 1885–1977 (Indianapolis: Indiana Historical Society, 1989).

[104] See Louis Galambos with Jane Eliot Sewell, Networks of Innovation: Vaccine Development at Merck, Sharp & Dohme, and Mulford, 1895–1995 (Cambridge: Cambridge University Press, 1995), at p. 9.

[105] More tightly controlled pharmacological research led to isolation of a number of hormones and related biological agents in the 1910s and 1920s. The most famous was the isolation of purified, clinically usable insulin to treat diabetes. See, Michael Bliss, The Discovery of Insulin (Toronto: University of Toronto Press, 3rd ed., 1982) (describing research by Frederick Banting and Charles A. Best, and colleagues, which led to the awarding of the Nobel Prize in 1923). The adrenaline isolation work was performed by the noted Japanese chemist Jokichi Takamine, under contract with a rival to Mulford, Parke-Davis. Mulford's attack on the resulting patent led to a famous patent case, with the definitive opinion penned by Judge Learned Hand, which upheld the patentability of the isolated adrenaline over the objection that it was merely a "product of nature." *Parke-Davis & Co. v. H. K. Mulford Co.*, 189 F. 95, 103 (C.C.S.D.N.Y. 1911) (L. Hand, J.) ("Takamine was the first to make it available for any use by removing it from the other gland-tissue in which it was found, and, while it is of course possible logically to call this a purification of the principle, it became for every practical purpose a new thing commercially and therapeutically. That was a good ground for a patent."), aff'd in part,

antitoxins around the turn of the century. As its founders faded into the background, however, Mulford lost its leading position and was eventually acquired (in 1929) by rival pharmaceutical firm Sharp & Dohme – which was itself acquired by Merck in the 1950s.[106]

SULFA DRUGS AND AFTER Right around the time Mulford was acquired, another research path in pharmaceuticals was just opening up. In late 1932, Bayer Laboratories, part of the large German chemical combine I.G. Farben, filed a patent application for a new antibacterial drug called Prontosil.[107] It was the first of a family of drugs called sulfonomides, which came to revolutionize medicine. Prontosil had its origins much earlier, as part of the systematic chemical research on textile dyes (azo dyes) funded by Bayer. The idea of a targeted drug to arrest the effects of bacteria first occurred to a medical researcher named Paul Ehrlich, originator of the "germ theory" of human infection.[108] A Bayer researcher named Gerhard Domagk, interested in finding chemicals to fight bacterial infections, was aware that a dye compound invented by I.G. Farben researcher Henrich Horlein was known to bind strongly with proteins in wool and silk. Domagk reasoned that this binding action might carry over to human body tissues, and thus might be a good candidate to target bacterial growth.[109] His theory was correct; the use of the sulfonamide compounds created what came to be known as chemotherapy. Bayer persisted in research along these lines throughout the 1920s despite early failures, and Prontosil was the result. Figure 5.10 shows the basic structure of the sulfonamide family of antibacterial drugs.

The specific sulfa compounds produced as part of the Bayer research were covered by US patent 2,085,037, "Azo Compounds and Their Production," issued to Fritz Mietzsch and Josef Klarer (colleagues of Damagk), on June 29, 1937.[110]

rev'd in part sub nom. *Parke-Davis & Co* v. *H. K. Mulford & Co*, 196 F. 496 (2d Cir. 1912). On the history of the *Parke-Davis* case, see Jon M. Harkness, *Dicta on Adrenalin(e): Myriad Problems with Learned Hand's Product-of-Nature Pronouncements in Parke-Davis v. Mulford*, 93 J. Pat. & Trademark Off. Soc'y 363, 369 (2011). On Takamine's eventful life, see Tetsumori Yamashima, *Jokichi Takamine (1854–1922), the Samurai Chemist, and His Work on Adrenalin*, 11 J. Med. Biography 95 (2003).

[106] Louis Galambos with Jane Eliot Sewell, Networks of Innovation.

[107] John E. Lesch, The First Miracle Drugs: How the Sulfa Drugs Transformed Medicine (Oxford: Oxford University Press, 2007), at p. 3.

[108] Ibid., at pp. 8–45.

[109] Ronald P. Rubin, *Gerhard Domagk (1895–1964) and the Origin of Anti-Bacterial Therapy*, 3 Internal Med. Res. Open J. 1, 3(2018).

[110] This patent was assigned to Winthrop Chemical Company of New York (subsidiary of I.G. Farben). This was the US counterpart to the German application filed December 24, 1932, the original sulfa drag patent application. Winthrop was a US pharmaceutical firm that had purchased the US business of Bayer, the I.G. Farben subsidiary, whose assets were auctioned off as part of the wartime sale of seized enemy property during World War I. See John P. Swann, *The 1941 Sulfathiazole Disaster and the Birth of Good Manufacturing Practices*, 41 Pharm. Hist. 16 (1999), at p. 16.

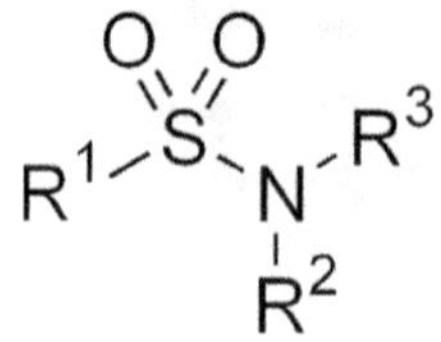

FIGURE 5.10. Chemical structure of the sulfonomide family of antibacterial drugs. The "Rs" represent variable components of the structure; they can be entire carbon rings, NH2 groups, etc.; so, a typical sulfonomide (sulfamethoxazole) has the chemical formula $C_{10}H_{11}N_3O_3S$

These drugs played a major role in reducing death from bacterial infection during World War II. Because German patents and company assets were seized by the US government during World War I, the sulfa compounds later came into the hands of US pharmaceutical firms.[111]

Sulfa drugs were soon eclipsed in the pharmacopeia by another, more successful, family of "miracle drugs": penicillin and its offspring. Developed through a famous bit of serendipity (mold growing in a petri dish where bacteria were being cultured), penicillin was first identified by Alexander Fleming of London in 1928. It was only later cultured and refined into a useable therapeutic, coming into widespread use in the early 1940s.[112] Partly because it was ignored for a time, and partly because the researchers working on it were ambivalent about patents, penicillin was never effectively patented. Other antibacterials in the same family were soon developed, however, and several of these were covered by patents that proved lucrative. Chief among these rapid follow-on drugs was streptomycin, developed in 1948 at Rutgers University by Dr. Selman Waksman and his graduate assistant, Albert Schatz.[113]

Pharmaceutical research branched in many directions as research funding grew between 1950 and 1980. Most research at this time followed one of several standard paths. One was to pursue chemical analogs of compounds that had been proven effective for some therapeutic purpose. The hope was that small structural

[111] See generally Dale Cooper, *The Licensing of German Drug Patents Confiscated during World War I: Federal and Private Efforts to Maintain Control, Promote Production, and Protect Public Health*, 54 Pharm. Hist. 3 (2012); Dale Cooper, *The Trading with the Enemy Act of 1917 and Synthetic Drugs*, 47 Pharm. Hist. 47 (2005).

[112] See American Chemical Society, Discovery and Development of Penicillin: International Historic Chemical Landmark, n.d., available at www.acs.org/content/acs/en/education/whatischemistry/landmarks/flemingpenicillin.html.

[113] See A. Schatz et al., *Streptomycin, a Substance Exhibiting Antibiotic Activity against Gram-positive and Gram-negative Bacteria*, 55 Proc. Exp. Biol. Med. 66 (1944) (first publication); US patent 2,449,866, "Streptomycin and Process of Preparation," filed February 9, 1945, issued September 21, 1948, to Selman Waksman and Albert Schatz, assigned to Rutgers Research and Endowment Foundation. The patent was licensed to Merck and the royalties split (after an acrimonious negotiation between the two co-inventors) among Waksman, Schatz, and Rutgers. See H. Boyd Woodruff, *Selman A. Waksman, Winner of the 1952 Nobel Prize for Physiology or Medicine*, 80 Appl. & Environ. Microbiol. 2 (2014).

differences might lead to enhanced effectiveness; pharmacological activity was known to be unpredictable, and sometimes even slight changes led to significant results. (This influenced the emerging specialty of chemical/pharmaceutical patent law, see later in this chapter.)

Another standard path was to work backward from a physiological discovery, looking for compounds that would mimic the natural outcome (if it was beneficial), or inhibit it (if it was detrimental). A good example of the former was described earlier in this chapter: the work of Jokichi Takamine in isolating purified adrenaline. This was part of a broad program of research into human hormones and various hormone-related treatments – that is, the field of endocrinology. Isolation and, later, lab-based synthesis of hormones such as cortisone and thyroxine led to significant therapeutic benefits in the twentieth century.[114] One example is the development of norethindrone, a pregnancy inhibitor that formed one of the first successful contraceptive pills.[115]

The second research path seeks to block the deleterious effects of the endocrine system. A good example is the research leading up to the important high blood pressure compounds known as angiotensin converting enzyme (ACE) inhibitors. Professor John Vane of the Royal College of Surgeons discovered that an enzyme called angiotensin was responsible for the constriction of blood vessels that often leads to high blood pressure (hypertension) (Figure 5.11).[116] Vane's Nobel Prize-winning work led some researchers to look for chemical compounds to inhibit angiotensin activation, reducing constriction, and thus treating hypertension. Two researchers at the pharmaceutical company E. R. Squibb, David Cushman and Miguel Ondetti, tested over 2,000 candidate compounds before settling on one structure that showed promise.[117] (Because compounds were frequently tested by spraying them one by one on a lab sample of the substance sought to be treated, this technique was sometimes called spray and pray.). This they then refined into sixty

[114] See Jamshed R. Tata, *One Hundred Years of Hormones*, 6 EMBO Rep. 490 (2005). See generally Clarence D. Turner and Joseph T. Bagnara, General Endocrinology (Philadelphia: Saunders Publishing, 5th ed., 1971).

[115] See Planned Parenthood, The Birth Control Pill: A History, available at www.plannedparenthood.org/files/1514/3518/7100/Pill_History_FactSheet.pdf (describing early funding of birth control research by pioneering feminist Margaret Sanger and colleagues). On the derivation of norethindrone from a species of Mexican yam, see Lara V. Marks, Sexual Chemistry: A History of the Contraceptive Pill (New Haven, CT, Yale University Press, 2001); Carl Djerassi, This Man's Pill: Reflections on the 50th Birthday of the Pill (Oxford: Oxford University Press, 2001). See also US patent 2,744,122, "Δ-4-NOR17- α-Ethinylandrosten-17β-OL3-One and Process," issued to Carl Djerassi and George Rosenkranz, issued May 1, 1956, assigned to Syntex, Inc. (patent on the synthesized hormone-inhibiting compound).

[116] See Jenny Bryan, From snake venom to ACE inhibitor: The discovery and rise of captopril, The Pharm. J., April 17, 2009, available at www.pharmaceutical-journal.com/news-and-analysis/news/from-snake-venom-to-ace-inhibitor-the-discovery-and-rise-of-captopril/10884359.

[117] See David W. Cushman and Migeul Ondetti, *History of the Design of Captopril and Related Inhibitors of Angiotensin Converting Enzyme*, 17 Hypertension 589 (1991).

FIGURE 5.11. Brazilian viper, *Bothrops jararaca,* whose venom was the chemical source of the first ACE inhibitor anti-high blood pressure drug, captopril. Photo credit: Felipe Sussekind, c. 2002. Used under Creative Commons Attribution 2.0 Generic License. See https://commons.wikimedia.org/wiki/File:Bothrops_jararaca_1.jpg

specific candidates before hitting on the best one for the task, which was named captotril. Squibb's patent on this compound[118] opened the door to a number of follow-on research projects at Squibb and elsewhere, which resulted in an entire family of ACE inhibitor drugs.[119]

PHARMA RESEARCH UP TO 1982 The unpredictability of chemical compounds is nowhere more evident than in the pharmaceutical industry. One student of pharmaceutical research described the invention process in these terms:

> Drug discovery is an intricate and complex process, differing in important ways from many other forms of scientific research. Since new drugs cannot be designed by logical deductions from valid general principles, drug research is a trial-and-error process organized on the basis of a series of provisional hypotheses systematically refined by feedback from empirical tests. In retrospect, the discovery of a drug will be seen to have rested on a few critical findings during the discovery process, although many other observations and false starts will have been made which turn out in the end not to be useful. These cannot be avoided; that they eventually will prove to be of no use can be ascertained only in retrospect. Because of this, the process of discovery of a new drug is long, tedious, and expensive.[120]

[118] US patent 4,046,889, "Azetidine-2-Carboxylic Acid Derivatives," issued September 6, 1977, to Miguel Angel Ondetti and David W. Cushman, assigned to E. R Squibb & Sons, Inc. (patent on the commercial product captopril).

[119] A similar research path led to the development of a family of calcium channel blockers, also used to treat high blood pressure. See N. Dawson et al., *Hypertension: Calcium Channel Blockers*, 35 Med. 599 (2007).

[120] D. Schwartzman, Innovation in the Pharmaceutical Industry (Baltimore: Johns Hopkins University Press, 1976), at p. 48. See also David Fishlock, Deep roots of a drug's development, Financial Times, July 26, 1990, sec. I, p. 16 (detailing drug development process at Glaxo, a British pharmaceutical company, which lasts on average more than eight years; includes

Although the details of this procedure have changed considerably since the early days of the pharmaceutical industry in the late nineteenth century, it has retained its basically empirical nature.[121] The number of commercially significant patents in the early days of the pharmaceutical industry is too great to recount here in any detail. Nevertheless, a brief review of one pharmaceutical research program – development of Tagamet, an important ulcer drug developed by Smithkline Beckman – may serve to ground the discussion.

Like many related drugs, Tagamet is an "antagonist" designed to interfere with a deleterious natural reaction inside the body. In this particular case, the reaction involves the excessive production of hydrochloric acid in the stomach, which is stimulated by the release of histamine. The drugs work by inhibiting the release of the histamine. Less acid is produced as a result, making for an effective treatment of stomach ulcers.

Tagamet's development followed a fairly standard pattern. It was, first of all, modelled on other drugs that had proved successful at blocking other natural reactions. Sir James Black developed the drug while working for Smithkline in Britain. After working on development of a related series of drugs, called beta blockers, he became interested in the effects of histamine. At the time, the effects of histamine could be only partly blocked by antihistamines and none of the drugs then available could block histamine's ability to stimulate the secretion of acid in the stomach. In his research, Sir James focused on developing a drug against a histamine receptor on stomach cells called the H2 receptor. The goal was to develop a drug that would allow peptic ulcers in the stomach and duodenum to heal quickly and painlessly. The research that led to the development of the drug cimetidine (tradename, Tagamet) took fourteen years, in part because for a long time Sir James's team misled itself in testing 700 compounds by using too small an amount of histamine to have the intended effect. This is also characteristic of drug development in two respects: the large number of compounds screened and the long time required to reach the final goal.[122] For his contribution to science, he shared the

description of one drug that was in development for almost twenty years before regulatory approval was applied for).

[121] Artificial intelligence may be changing this. See, e.g., John Jumper, et al., *Highly accurate protein structure prediction with AlphaFold*, 596 Nature 583 (2021) (describing AlphaFold AI software from Deepmind, a subsidiary of Google (Alphabet), which radically improved the ability of scientists to predict how a given amino acid chain (i.e., protein) will fold after it is synthesized – a crucial capability given that protein shape is essential to its interaction and effect on other biomolecules).

[122] See generally Yuan Hao, The Rise of Centaur Inventors: How Patent Law Should Adapt to the Challenge to Inventorship Doctrine by Human-AI Inventing Synergies, Aug. 10, 2022, avail. at SSRN: https://ssrn.com/abstract=4186684 (analyzing challenges of AI-human inventions; proposing "constructive conception" doctrine when a human researcher frames a question and a powerful AI tool reaches a distinct solution). In recent years, the pharmaceutical industry has spent approximately $90 billion per year. See www.phrma.org/en/Advocacy/Research-Development. By comparison, the federal government spent a total of $127 billion on R&D. Of this, the National Institutes of Health spends roughly $34billion. See U.S. National Science

1988 Nobel Prize in Physiology and Medicine, a rare award of the prize to an industrial researcher. His contribution to the pharmaceutical industry was to inspire the invention covered by US patent 3,950,333, "Pharmacologically Active Guanidine Compounds," which included cimetidine.[123]

Thus, we see from this one example two themes common across many cases of pharmaceutical invention: (1) the economic significance of patents in the field, due to (2) the expense of drug research, occasioned by its primarily empirical character. Later in this chapter we will see how the Patent Office, courts, and patent bar adapted to the special needs of pharmaceutical and chemical firms. From the unique, specialized chemical-pharmaceutical complex there emerged unique, specialized doctrines and practices: another example of the patent system's flexibility and adaptability in the face of changing conditions.

5.2.3 *The Auto Industry: Big, but Not Threatening*

With a few notable exceptions, patents have not factored much into corporate strategy in the auto industry. This is primarily because the basic technologies were each developed over a long period of time, and the first successful car models included little in the way of innovative technical features. The first great corporate success, Ford Motor Company, was far more a story about efficient manufacturing technique – the famous assembly line – than about a novel combination of old features or an innovative design. Though the automobile seemed an entirely new product at the turn of the twentieth century, it was in fact built from well-known and well-developed components. Many metal components benefitted from knowhow developed during the bicycle craze of the late nineteenth century – particularly metal stamping, a decided improvement over the old forging techniques.[124] The internal combustion engine, in its early two-stroke embodiment, had undergone considerable evolution by the time Ford's Model T was introduced in 1908. And long experience in the horse-drawn wagon industry meant that many refinements in wheelmaking, axles, suspension, and the like were ready to be incorporated into gas-powered vehicles.

The innovative element was rapid, uniform manufacturing. Though it, too, had antecedents, most historians believe the continuous-flow auto assembly line was

Foundation, Survey of Federal Funds for Research and Development, Fiscal Years 2018–19, available at https://ncsesdata.nsf.gov/fedfunds/2018/html/ffs18-dt-tab004.html.

[123] Another aspect of the Tagamet story is representative: It was both protected by a strong patent and yet subject to significant competition from other related drug compounds, most notably Glaxo Pharmaceutical's ranitidine, which sells under the tradename Zantac. This was originally patented in 1978 under US patent No. 4,128,658. In 1985, Glaxo was awarded a second patent, US patent No. 4,521,431 covering "Form 2" of the compound, which is a somewhat different crystalline form of the same compound. Such "new dosage forms" or slight variations on an original broad compound are one example of how firms seek to extend their exclusive market position with a successful drug by patenting minor variations on it, called evergreening.

[124] David A. Hounshell, From the American System to Mass Production, 1800–1932 (Baltimore: Johns Hopkins Press, 1984), at p. 209.

Ford's true contribution to US industrial development.[125] As the authoritative historian David Hounshell put it:[126]

> [We must not underestimate] the singular importance of the changes made at the Ford Factory in 1913 and 1914 (as well as how they came about) and the way these changes were rapidly diffused throughout the Western world. Both the *act* of mass-producing the Model T Ford and the rapid *diffusion of the techniques* by which it was mass-produced had a profound impact on the twentieth century. Fordism, a word coined to identify the Ford production system and its concomitant labor system, changed the world.

The auto industry saw massive new firm entry in its early days. Though most of the early car makers are long since forgotten, there was an almost manic rush into the field by aspiring firms: over 500 entered between 1890 and 1920.[127] No one had the time or inclination to use patents to restrict entry during this formative period. The diversity of auto technology also might have played a part. There were viable electric vehicles in the early days of autos, as well as steam-powered cars and a variety of internal combustion engines. No single, dominant patent on auto technology ever emerged, so patent strategy was less important as compared to electrical equipment, telephony, and the like.

The one exception to this rule was the famous Selden patent. Awarded to patent lawyer/inventor George Selden, this was a basic patent on the concept of the automobile. This has proven to be a controversial patent in the eyes of historians. Though Selden did build a workshop, and did truly make some contributions to development of an engine first invented by an engineer named George Brayton, it is also true that Selden kept his original 1879 patent application in the Patent Office until 1895 – with the result that the patent conveniently issued just at the dawn of the commercial auto industry. Figure 5.12 shows an auto diagram from the famous/ infamous Selden patent.

The engine in the Selden design was located over the front wheels, so the crankshaft was very short – just long enough to transmit power from the two-stroke engine to the front axle. The engine itself was based on the simple one-piston design of the engineer George Brayton, itself patented in 1872 (Figure 5.13).

The Brayton engine uses an expander cylinder (on the left in Figure 5.13), which pre-heats an air-fuel mixture (entering from the left, outside the diagram). This mixture is ignited as it is fed into the compression cylinder on the right, with the

[125] The impact was monumental. See Robert J. Gordon, The Rise and Fall of American Growth, at p. 130. "But nothing in the millennia of human history, at least until the 1950–55 spread of television sets into the American home, rivals the speed with which automobile ownership spread in a mere two decades between 1910 and 1930 to the majority of American households."

[126] David A. Hounshell, From the American System to Mass Production, at p. 218 (emphasis in original).

[127] Steven Klepper, *The Capabilities of New firms and the Evolution of the US Automobile Industry*, 11 Indust. & Corp. Change 645, 646 (2002).

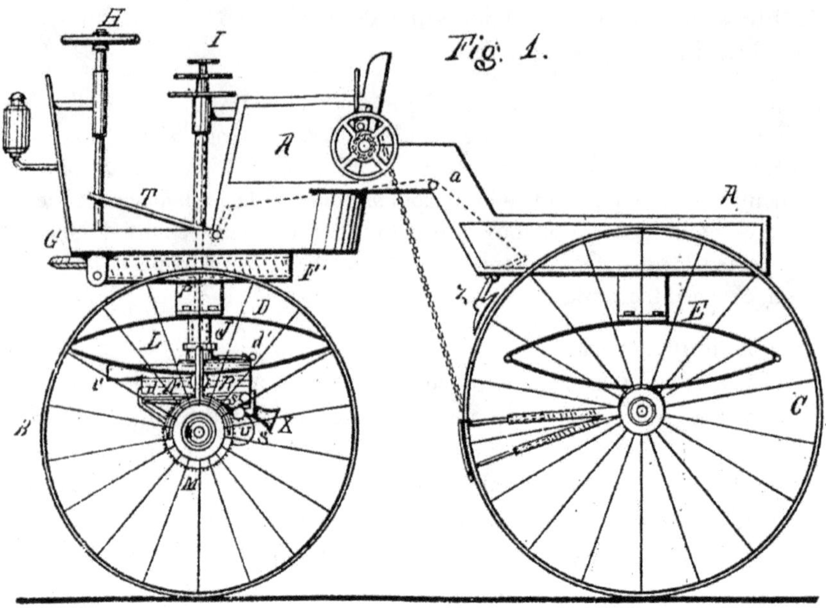

FIGURE 5.12. Diagram from the famous Selden "road engine" (automobile) patent, US patent 549,160, issued November 5, 1895

resultant slow expansion creating the power stroke. There is no instant "explosion," just a slow combustion causing the air-fuel mixture to expand. Selden's engine was a variation on this design.

Selden tried yet failed to go into commercial production on his auto. But his patent was the basis of a royalty campaign that resulted in the creation of the Association of Licensed Auto Manufacturers (ALAM). John Seymour, the Commissioner of Patents, dubbed it "the pioneer invention in the application of the compression gas engine to road or horseless carriage use."[128]

As part of his industry-wide enforcement campaign, Selden's company asserted the Selden 549,160 patent against Ford Motor Company in 1903. Ford, famously stubborn and proud of his company's product, refused to sign a license. Ford Motor fought the Selden patent through a trial and an appeal. Ford and others tried to invalidate the Selden patent on several occasions but with no success. Apart from

[128] See William Greenleaf, Monopoly on Wheels: Henry Ford and the Selden Automobile Patent 38, 49–50 (Detroit, MI: Wayne State University Press, 1961). See ibid. at 106–111 (detailing Selden's efforts to assert his rights against Ford and others). Others see Selden as a pioneer of a different sort. He "pioneered" a new type of "legal blackmail," according to economists Michele Boldrin and David K. Levine in their book, Against Intellectual Monopoly (Cambridge: Cambridge University Press, 2008). See ibid., at p. 84 ("Once Selden's patent, no. 549,160, was awarded, it commanded royalties of 1.25 percent on the sale value of every automobile sold in the United States.").

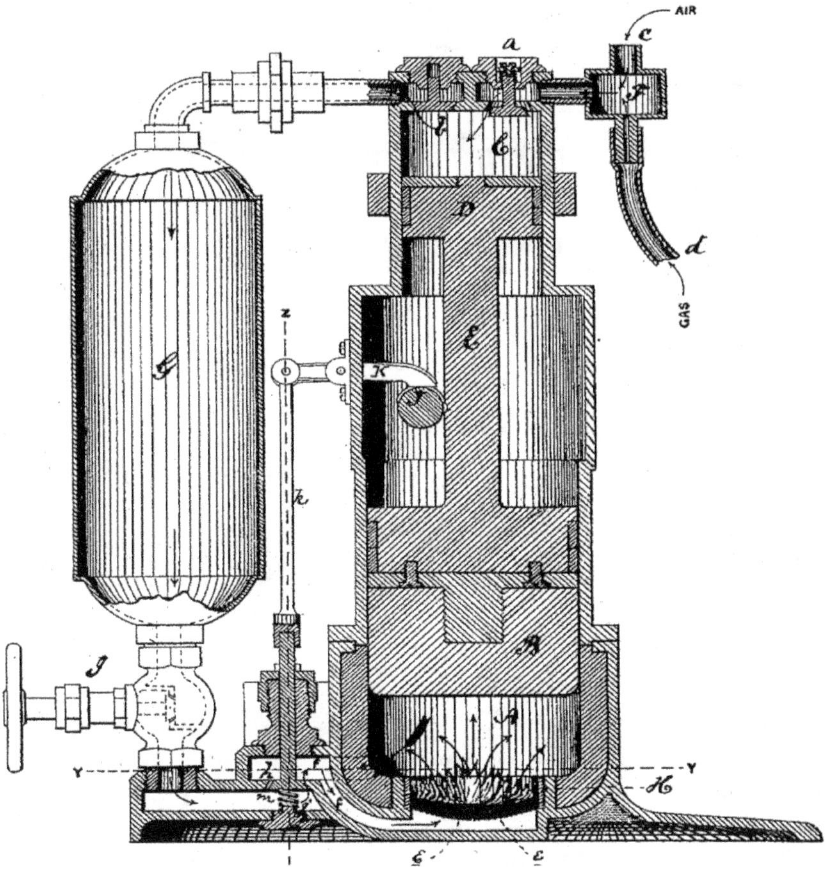

FIGURE 5.13. Two-stroke engine of George Brayton; US patent 125,166, "improvement in gas engines," issued April 2, 1872

trying to invalidate Selden's patent, Ford argued that its car engines were based on a fundamentally different design – the internal combustion principle of Otto's engine. The Otto engine was the first to use the now-standard four stroke compression cycle, illustrated in Figure 5.14 from an 1896 engineering publication.

In the Otto engine, high compression and electric spark ignition cause a forceful explosion in the third cycle, the power stroke ("firing" stroke in Figure 5.14). The air-fuel mixture, channeled through the two left-most valves ("gas valve" and "air valve" in the diagram), is supplied from an external carburetor (not shown).

Ford's first attempt to invalidate Selden's patent failed as premature. The second attempt came in the context of a full trial. It also failed, but it produced an interesting opinion from Judge Hough of the Southern District of New York. Hough was undoubtedly aware of the charge that Selden was not a "true inventor," and that the sixteen-year pendency of the Selden patent undermined its legitimacy.

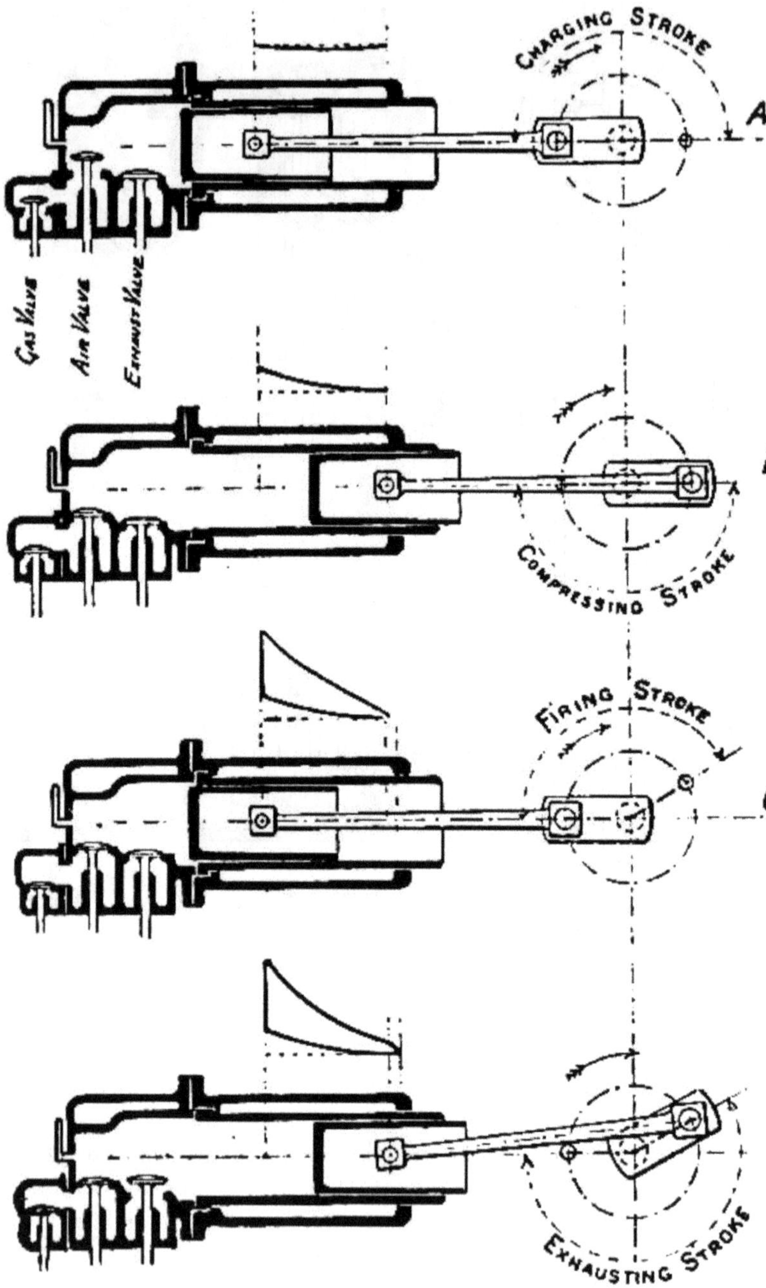

FIGURE 5.14. Four-stroke gasoline-powered internal-combustion engine designed by Nicolaus A. Otto

Source: U.S. Library of Congress, image available at www.loc.gov/resource/cph.3c10412/ (from William Norris, "A practical treatise on the 'Otto' cycle gas engine" (London: Longmans, Green, 1896) (copyright expired)

The court defended Selden as a true inventive type, and implicitly rejected the idea that his patent was designed to capture the inventions of others:

> The record shows [Selden was] always interested in mechanical pursuits, receiving an appropriate education for the theoretical side thereof, but not himself a skilled practical mechanician. His application for a patent on a rubber tire wheel, made in 1869, is significant and interesting, and in view of quite recent litigation in this circuit instructive. Taking his evidence in connection with his letters and notes, he is shown especially attentive to traction problems from his early manhood. I am persuaded that he carefully studied Brayton's engine and understood it practically; but his knowledge of the theory of thermodynamics seems fairly illustrated by a remark to his workman ... when his original engine turned over: 'We have struck a new power.' There is no satisfactory evidence that before [the] application [was] filed he knew thoroughly anything of Otto's compression engine. All this was not a very complete equipment; but he had the true inventor's enthusiasm, and for more than five years, as the Chief Justice said of [telegraph inventor Samuel F.B.] Morse, in [*O'Reilly* v. *Morse*, 56 U.S. 62, 109 (1853)], "he pursued these investigations with unremitting ardor and industry, interrupted occasionally by pecuniary embarrassments."[129]

Despite praise for Selden, Ford and his allies won a famous victory when the case was appealed in 1911. The Second Circuit held that, though the Selden patent was valid, Ford cars did not infringe it. The key to the decision was the existing state of engine design in 1879, when the patent was filed, and the specific engine used in Ford cars by the time of the lawsuit. The court began by acknowledging the perceived importance of the Selden patent, but trained attention on Selden's contribution to the auto field:

> [W]hen we see that 30 years ago an application for a patent was filed which even pointed the way to the modern automobile, we can hardly fail to receive the impression that an idea of great importance must have been embodied in it. But, as we shall later see, the development of the automobile was not so sudden as we have thought. It developed step by step at the beginning; the startling activity has come at the end. Moreover, a great idea may be embodied in a patent, and yet the patentee take nothing of value by it. That which he takes is that which he describes and claims. His discovery may be of importance, but he may limit it by his claim, and his claim may proceed in the wrong direction.[130]

The court later added: "[A]ny contention that a motor vehicle constructed by the patentee according to the teachings of the patent operated so successfully as to

[129] *Elec. Vehicle Co.* v. *C.A. Duerr & Co.*, 172 F. 923, 930–31 (C.C.S.D.N.Y. 1909) (Hough, J.), rev'd sub nom. *Columbia Motor Car Co.* v. *C.A. Duerr & Co.*, 184 F. 893 (2d Cir. 1911).

[130] *Columbia Motor Car Co.* v. *C.A. Duerr & Co.*, 184 F. 893, 895 (2d Cir. 1911).

demonstrate that Selden had solved a great problem and is entitled to the status of a pioneer inventor is, we think, without foundation."[131]

In keeping with the style of the day – a style some have found appealing, and superior in some ways to twenty-first century US practice[132] – the opinion used this general assessment as an aid in interpreting Selden's broad claim. As is common, the court said, Selden "claimed broadly the combination of a 'liquid hydrocarbon gas engine of the compression type' with the other elements" of a functioning car (drive train, steering, etc.).[133] Selden also added conventional language of non-limitation: "Any form of liquid hydrocarbon engine of the compression type may be employed in my improved locomotive."[134]

This made an effective claim, quite broad; but it ran into the problem broad claims always face – the prior art. A broad patent claim embraces many alternatives, which is helpful for the patentee in the future; but the same breadth often covers many old teachings as well. This subjects it to invalidation, for a claim that covers the prior art is an invalid claim; it fails the test of novelty or "invention" (non-obviousness). It is this backward-looking breadth that spelled trouble for Selden. After reviewing a number of pre-1879 engine designs, for boats, streetcars, and the like, the court concluded that "we can reach no other conclusion than that with [these pre-existing engines] in the prior art the claim in question must be held invalid for want of invention if it be given the broad construction the language apparently calls for."[135] But, as noted, the court felt that Selden had made a non-trivial (if also non-pioneering) contribution to the field. So, the only way out was – again in keeping with the style of the time – to construe Selden's claim quite narrowly. Practically, this meant that the phrase "liquid hydrocarbon gas engine of the compression type" must be interpreted narrowly. The court held that the quoted phrase covered only the Brayton-type engines:

> The claim is held to be valid as covering a combination in a road locomotive of the different elements with a liquid hydrocarbon compression engine of the Brayton type; the limitation to this type being read into the claim by the specification to save it from invalidity.[136]

[131] *Columbia Motor Car Co.* v. *C.A. Duerr & Co.*, 184 F. 893, 909 (2d Cir. 1911).

[132] John F. Duffy, *Counterproductive Notice in Literalistic Versus Peripheral Claiming*, 96 B.U. L. Rev. 1197, 1200 (2016) ("[T]he traditional approach to 'peripheral claiming' – an approach that worked well for nearly a century prior to the creation of the Federal Circuit – was nothing like the more literalistic approach applied by the Federal Circuit."); ibid., at 1211: "In a series of [nineteenth and early twentieth century] decisions, the Supreme Court articulated rules of patent claim construction that demand an assessment of the true merits of the invention as disclosed in the specification.").

[133] 184 F. 893, 900 (2d Cir. 1911).

[134] 184 F. 893, 901 (quoting from Selden's patent).

[135] 184 F. 893, 901.

[136] 184 F. 893, 907–908. This is a good example of the old interpretive canon in patent law to the effect that patent claims should be read wherever possible in a way that preserves their validity.

Ford was off the hook. Its use of Otto engines meant that Ford vehicles did not infringe claim 1 of Selden's patent. The end result was paradoxical: a legal victory hailed as a boon to consumers, with the end of industry-wide royalty payments, but a victory for the leading member of the quickly-emerging industry oligopoly – the famed "big 3."[137]

This established a pattern for Ford: Patents were rarely central to its corporate strategy. Outside of some early efforts in the control of vertical dealer relations, using then-standard dealer agreements that included licenses to Ford patents in exchange for resale price maintenance (rejected by a federal court)[138] and strict territorial limits (enforced in a state court),[139] Ford rarely asserted the patents it did acquire. It was much more frequently a defendant in patent infringement suits. Because of its advanced vertical integration approach, Ford brought a great deal of component manufacture in-house. This subjected it to infringement suits by the makers of all sorts of car parts – from side windows[140] to door

See, e.g., Bragg-Kliesrath Corporation v. Walter S. Vogel & Co., 67 F.2d 531, 533 (2d Cir. 1933) (L. Hand., J.) ("Patent claims are peculiar in that in a proper case courts will save them by limiting their expressed extent to so much of the field as the prior art leaves open. . . ."). This old canon rarely fires a shot in the modern era, however. It survives as a minor, narrow "tiebreker" rule applied in rare cases. See Peter S. Menell et. al., *Patent Claim Construction: A Modern Synthesis and Structured Framework*, 25 Berkeley Tech. L.J. 711, 719 (2010) (only in cases where the Patent Office issued a claim knowing one interpretation of it would be invalid can it be inferred that the alternative, narrower interpretation, was intended).

137 See William Greenleaf, Monopoly on Wheels: Henry Ford and the Selden Automobile Patent (1961) (describing Ford's celebrated victory as a strong blow against monopoly in the auto industry, and an invaluable public relations coup that launched Ford Motors into wide public consciousness).

138 *Ford Motor Co.* v. *Union Motor Sales Co.*, 225 F. 373, 383 (S.D. Ohio 1914), aff'd, 244 F. 156 (6th Cir. 1917) (holding that post-sale dealer restrictions were unenforceable, because Ford's patent rights were exhausted after sale of vehicles to dealers).

139 *Coleman* v. *Ford Motor Co.*, 193 S.W. 866, 866 (1917), upholding the following provision in a dealer contract:

> If the dealer–licensee shall sell or deliver or cause to be sold or delivered any of the manufacturer–licensor's automobiles to any person or persons residing outside the territory licensed in this agreement, the manufacturer–licensor shall have the right and privilege to immediately terminate this agreement and the dealer–licensee agrees to forfeit to the manufacturer–licensor the contract deposit made with this agreement. * * * It being agreed and understood that such sales shall be construed as a violation of the spirit of this license agreement and an infringement of the Ford patents and the rights granted to other dealer–licensees and subdealer licensees who are thus affected by dealer–licensees selling or disposing of Ford automobiles in outside territory licensed to other dealer–licensees or subdealer–licensees.

The court said a patent is "a reward for inventive genius and intended as a stimulation thereof; [and] the right extends not only to that of making, but also to the right of selling," so the contract restriction should be enforced. 193 S.W. 866, 868.

140 *Ford Motor Co.* v. *Ohio Stamping & Eng'g Co.*, 56 F.2d 807, 808 (6th Cir. 1932) (Invalidating side "curtain" patent asserted against Ford: "We think that Towers' [patented] smoothly stretched side curtain, although an improvement upon [the prior art] Pearson [design], sprang from an obvious application of simple mechanical principles, generally known rather than from inventive thought . . . ").

locks,[141] and from gear design[142] to radiator caps[143] to windshields.[144] Ford racked up a remarkable string of victories in these cases, losing only the occasional infringement suit in the 1920s and 1930s.[145] Because of its almost insatiable demand, and to insure against disruptions in its supply chain, Ford adopted the practice of always having at least two sources for each important car component.[146] This "second

[141] *Blackmore* v. *Ford Motor Co.*, 56 F.2d 806 (6th Cir. 1932) (Blackmore patent No. 1,437,390, claims 1–10, 22–29, for automobile door lock, asserted against Ford; held invalid for lack of invention).

[142] *Seymour* v. *Ford Motor Co.*, 44 F.2d 306, 307 (6th Cir. 1930) (invention was for beveling the teeth on interlocking gears at different angles, so that when first engaged, before the two gear sets were aligned, the gear teeth would more easily slide into full engagement. Held: patent invalid for lack of invention: "[W]e are of the opinion that the court below was right in holding that that which is of truly trivial effect in the art, solves no real problem, and answers no recognized need, cannot be said to rise to the dignity of invention. It lies, rather, within the domain of the right of selection open to all.").

[143] *Bridgeport Brass Co* v. *Ford Motor Co*, 278 F. 881 (6th Cir. 1922) (Webster patent, No. 1,125,229, for filler tube cap for automobile radiators, held void for lack of invention, as being merely the making of prior art caps formerly made by casting with the newer technique of sheet brass stamping).

[144] See *Stahlbrodt Co* v. *Ford Motor Co*, 238 F. 365, 366 (2d Cir. 1916) (invalidating windscreen patent):

> The motor car industry has developed so enormously during the last 15 years that we are apt to regard the completed car of to-day as something akin to the miraculous. The truth is that the perfected structure is due to the evolution of the art by which changes were made and improvements added as the necessity therefor developed. As speed increased, the demand for protection from the wind, rain and dust became urgent. It required no inventive genius to accomplish this result, at least in a primitive manner.

See also *Banker* v. *Ford Motor Co*, 3 F. Supp. 737 (W.D. Pa. 1933), aff'd 69 F.2d 665 (3d Cir. 1934) (delay of over sixteen years before bringing action at law for damages for infringement of patent relating to improvement in automobile windshields held to prevent recovery on grounds of laches and estoppel). The laches defense in patent cases such as *Banker* was eliminated by a much later case, *SCA Hygiene Products Aktiebolag* v. *First Quality Baby Products, LLC* 137 S. Ct. 954 (2017).

[145] Two reasons might explain this success. Ford was a "repeat player," i.e., a frequent litigation party – proven to give an advantage in the litigation game. Marc Galanter, *Why the "Haves" Come Out Ahead: Speculation on the Limits of Legal Change*, 9 Law. & Soc. Inquiry 165 (1994). And most of the cases were contested in the Eastern District of Michigan, Southern Division – i.e., Detroit. It was in the 1920s and 1930s that this court established its reputation as the US District Court for the Big 3 District.

[146] *Ford Motor Co.* v. *K.W. Ignition Co.*, 278 F. 373, 375 (7th Cir. 1921) (infringement suit by Ford supplier K.W., owner of a patent on electrical coils for auto starters; judgment for Ford, on the basis that by its past actions in acquiescing to supply by a competitor, the supplier is estopped from claiming past infringement by Ford in use of the competitor's coils):

> It was understood at the time of the adoption of this coil as a part of its standard equipment that appellant should, on account of its extensive business, have two sources of supply. To avoid the delays and damage resulting from fires, strikes, etc., appellant insists on two sources of supply for all of its standard equipment. It was therefore understood and agreed that appellant should install a department for the manufacture of these coils. It was equipped by appellant, but Williams assisted in the selection and arrangement of machinery. Thereafter the enormous demand for these coils was supplied by both parties.

sourcing" policy seems to have had an important spillover effect on suppliers of parts and components. They appear to have competed vigorously for patents on new designs and features. Compared to the large auto manufacturers (the Big 3) parts suppliers obtained fifteen times more patents per dollar of R&D, according to one study.[147] While the prevalence of second sourcing might have undermined the ability of a parts supplier to litigate against competitors,[148] suppliers had a separate reason for patenting: to fend off competition from the auto manufacturers themselves, who relentlessly integrated backward into parts and components over time.[149] In such a context, patents were very helpful for smaller parts companies that wanted to remain independent of the Big 3.[150]

When Ford did lose an infringement suit in its early years, the loss tended to occur in cases involving process technologies, such as iron rustproofing.[151] So, while

[147] Kim B. Clark, W. Bruce Chew, Takahiro Fujimoto, John Meyer, and F. M. Scherer, *Product Development in the World Auto Industry*, 1987 Brookings Papers on Economic Activity 729 (1987), at pp. 778–779:

> In automobile assembly, 0.28 invention patents were obtained per $1 million of 1974 R&D; in auto parts, 4.35 patents were obtained. Clearly, the partsmakers' work is more inventive in the conventional sense. Could this mean that relatively more weight should be given to work that is contracted out? . . . [This] higher outside invention rate per unit of input demonstrate [es] greater partsmaker efficiency [as compared to auto manufacturers].

On the general topic of what makes some firms seek more patents than others, see F. M. Scherer, *The Propensity to Patent*, 1 Int'l J. Ind. Org. 107 (1983).

[148] In some cases at least, a strong patent is said to have provided an exception to the ubiquity of "second sourcing." See Lane Kenworthy, Stewart Macaulay, and Joel Rogers, *"The More Things Change . . .": Business Litigation and Governance in the American Automobile Industry*, 21 Law & Soc. Inquiry 631 (1996), at p. 646 n.32 ("[A] supplier firm will occasionally hold a key patent on an item. If this is an optional item for car buyers, the companies may tolerate a single supplier situation."). See also Lawrence J. White, The Automobile Industry since 1945 (Cambridge: Harvard University Press, 1971), at pp. 84–85.

[149] Steven Klepper, The Capabilities of New Firms and the Evolution of the US Automobile Industry, at pp. 651, 652 (by 1930, the Big 3 structure had emerged, with 80 percent market share for GM-Ford-Chrysler; "The initial producers were largely assemblers, but over time firms integrated backwards into producing their own parts.").

[150] On the economics of supplier viability, see Robert P. Merges, A Transactional View of Property Rights; Robert P. Merges, *Specialized Supply Firms, Property Rights, and Firm Boundaries*, 13 Indus. & Corp. Change 451 (2004).

[151] *Parker Rust Proof Co.* v. *Ford Motor Co.*, 6 F.2d 649, 657–658 (E.D. Mich. 1925). The patent was issued to inventor Coslett on a technique for rust proofing of iron. The invention enabled an iron phosphate coating for iron, achieved by immersing the iron item in a hot bath of phosphoric acid. The court found it an important advance:

> I have no doubt whatever but what this patent is valid and is a pioneer patent . . . This is a valuable patent, it is a basic patent, and a number of manufacturers have been licensed under it. Those licensed under the other patents owned by the plaintiff are also licensed under this patent, and all use the principles taught by Coslett.

Patent owner Parker Rust Proof Co. proved the patent valid and infringed by Ford. On the damages phase of the case see 23 F.2d 502 (E.D. Mich. 1928). But Ford did not lose all cases involving patented manufacturing techniques. See *Thomson Spot Welder Co.* v. *Ford Motor*

Ford might swat away lawsuits based on minor car part patents, its "core competency" was in fast adoption of advanced manufacturing techniques, which sometimes exposed it to infringement liability at the hands of pioneering manufacturing process firms.

The same pattern, roughly speaking, held for other automakers. Weak component patents were fended off,[152] partly because there was so much entry[153] that autos became a "crowded field."[154] Even so, auto companies did indeed acquire patents, sometimes fighting hard to obtain them.[155] General Motors, for example, occasionally licensed auto suppliers under patents developed by GM.[156] These agreements,

Co., 268 F. 836 (E.D. Mich. 1920), aff'd, 281 F. 680 (6th Cir. 1922), decree aff'd, 265 U.S. 445 (1924) (patent on spot-welding technique, held by company affiliated with Thomson-Houston Company (see Chapter 4), invalidated by Ford for proven prior public use by others in Ohio and Massachusetts).

[152] See, e.g., *Kessler* v. *Buick Motor Co.*, 64 F.2d 599, 600 (5th Cir. 1933) (Patent on rocker arms in engine valves, held invalid as anticipated); *General Motors Corp.* v. *Deppe*, 21 F.2d 44, 46 (3d Cir. 1927) (Pre-mixing and heating of liquid fuel and air, claim interpreted to include mechanical mixing element, held, not infringed by Chevrolet's engine design, which lacked a mechanical pre-mixer); *Wolfe* v. *Bedford-Chevrolet Sales Corp.*, 31 F.2d 124, 128 (E.D.N.Y. 1929) ("The patent in suit [on a convertible auto top] is invalid for anticipation and lack of patentable novelty."); *Irvin* v. *Buick Motor Co.*, 88 F.2d 947, 952 (8th Cir. 1937) (engine valve patent, limited to one claim at trial by stipulation, held not infringed); *Densmore* v. *Noyes Buick Co.*, 18 F. Supp. 978, 980 (D. Mass. 1937) (no infringement of automatic transmission device where patent covered only one forward and one backward speed, while auto transmissions provided three forward speeds); *Utah Radio Prod. Co* v. *Gen. Motors Corp*, 106 F.2d 5, 8 (2d Cir. 1939) (Patent for electrical device in cars for converting battery power into voltage and frequency required for car radios; "[W]e are of the opinion that all the claims in suit are invalid [for lack of invention]"); *Suczek* v. *Gen. Motors Corp.*, 132 F.2d 371 (6th Cir. 1942) (another appeal from an Eastern District of Michigan decision in favor of the Big 3; patent to inventor Suzcek on improved car suspension invalid in light of earlier patent).

[153] Ioannis Ioannou, *When Do Spinouts Enhance Parent Firm Performance? Evidence from the U. S. Automobile Industry, 1890–1986*, 25 Org. Sci. 529 (2014) at p. 535 (The early auto industry was characterized by "a large entry wave – peaking at 208 firms in 1910 – followed by a rapid industry shakeout. By 1986, only twelve firms remained alive, forming an oligopolistic market structure in which only three firms – General Motors, Ford, and Chrysler – were the dominant players. Thus, 1,587 firms (or 57 percent) in the sample [beginning in 1890] survived for less than a year without ever proceeding to commercial production. Of those, 433 (or 15 percent) were at least able to build a car at the prototype stage."). See also Steven Klepper, *Disagreements, Spinouts, and the Evolution of Detroit as the Capital of the U.S. Automobile Industry*, 53 Mgt. Sci. 616 (2007).

[154] See, e.g., *Ross* v. *Chevrolet Motor Co.*, 7 F. Supp. 745, 747 (D. Colo. 1934) (No impulse to find infringement: In this case, infringement "calls for a liberality of construction that the law does not favor, especially in a situation where, as here, the invention constitutes only a slight advance in a crowded field. If the inventor was a pioneer in the art, or the patent 'basic,' the argument might be more persuasive.").

[155] See, e.g., *General Motors Corp.* v. *Coe*, 120 F.2d 736, 736 (D.C. Cir. 1941) (Unsuccessful appeal of a final rejection of GM patent on muffler component).

[156] See, e.g., *General Motors Corp.* v. *Leer Auto Supply Co.*, 60 F.2d 902 (2d Cir. 1932) (GM licensed to supplier as in the *Apollo Magneto* case, infra; co-plaintiff in this case, Laminated Shim Company, Inc., had an exclusive license; in suit against a rival supplier of soft metal-faced bearing shims (used to maintain a tight seal between the main engine bearing and the crankshaft the bearing surrounds), GM's narrow shim patent upheld as valid over a dissent from

or rather litigation over them, provide some insight into the early days of auto industry supply line management.

One such case, *General Motors Corporation* v. *Apollo Magneto Corporation*, found GM and one of its parts suppliers, Safety Steering Control Corporation, suing another auto supplier (defendant Apollo) for infringing two patents on anti-shimmying components for cars.[157] One patent was developed by GM, the other by an employee of its supplier Safety Steering.[158] Shimmying is the term for vibration or wobble in the front suspension and steering mechanism of a car. The GM solution was simple: a brace that pushed up on the front axle of the car thereby preventing the axle from moving too much. This is described in a patent issued to inventor Samuel A. Stranahan, apparently a GM employee (Figure 5.15).

The simple GM solution is illustrated in Figure 5.16.

In the lawsuit, GM first won on the patent developed at Safety Steering but lost on its own patent when the Second Circuit Court of Appeals found it invalid. The great judge Learned Hand – respected across legal disciplines, including patent law – dissented. This led to a rare rehearing, and a reversal of course by the court: The GM patent was found valid. As Judge Hand wrote in his dissent (which effectively became the majority opinion after rehearing):[159]

Judge Augustus Hand, see infra). GM also licensed-in some patents from third parties. See, e.g., *Swan Carburetor Co.* v. *General Motors Corp.*, 42 F.2d 452, 453 (N.D. Ohio 1927), aff'd sub nom. *General Motors Co.* v. *Swan Carburetor Co.*, 44 F.2d 24 (6th Cir. 1930) ("[Patent license from Swan Carburator to GM] included the right to make, use, and sell, not merely the form specifically disclosed, but any form covered by any patent that might be issued on the original or any divisional or continuation application."); *Universal Rim Co.* v. *General Motors Corp.*, 31 F.2d 969, 970 (6th Cir. 1929) (licensing agreement dispute may result in compensation for patentee-licensor, but case must be brought at law, not equity); *Ottinger* v. *General Motors Corp.*, 27 F. Supp. 508, 509 (S.D.N.Y. 1939) (Possibility of waiver and estoppel on the part of the plaintiff/inventor, who claimed against GM but whose former licensee was acquired earlier by GM, raises fact issues that cannot be resolved at this preliminary stage).

[157] 101 F.2d 53 (2d Cir.), decree modified, 102 F.2d 455 (2d Cir. 1939).

[158] The Safety Steering-owned patent was US patent 1,846,694, applied for by inventor Stephen Seth in January 1932 and issued to Safety Steering in February of 1932 (the Depression having apparently suppressed patent volume, the pendency for the application was quite short). At the time of the litigation, Safety Steering was no longer a partner and supplier with GM, but because GM had licensed its anti-shimmying patent to Safety Steering. GM participated in the lawsuit against Apollo Magneto. See *General Motors Corp.* v. *Apollo Magneto Corp.*, 101 F.2d 53, 53 (2d Cir.), decree modified, 102 F.2d 455 (2d Cir. 1939):

> On December 7, 1928, before the issuance of the patents, appellant arranged with Seth [and safety Steering] to manufacture his device upon a royalty basis. Because the sales were unsuccessful, after a large expenditure for advertising, the contract was cancelled in 1930 and a release given to appellant [GM] of its obligations in April, 1931. April 24, 1933, a license under the Stranahan patent, was granted by General Motors to Seth [and Safety Steering].

[159] *General Motors Corp.* v. *Apollo Magneto Corp.*, 102 F.2d 455, 456 (2d Cir. 1939) ("Stranahan disclosed an authentic invention in his specifications for the reasons stated in the dissenting opinion upon the original hearing.").

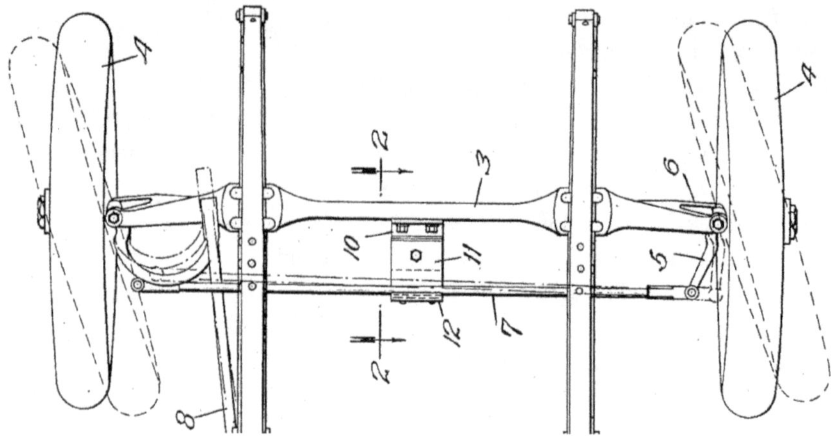

FIGURE 5.15. Diagram in GM patent (US 1,713,242 to Samuel A. Stranahan in 1929) illustrating front axle "shimmying"; invention relates to a device attached to bracket "11" in the diagram

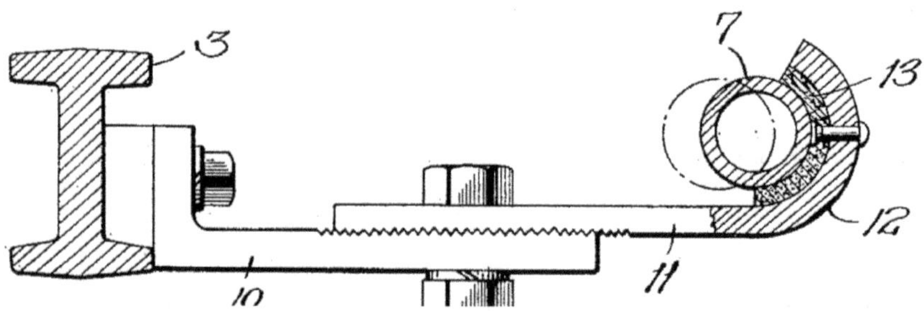

FIGURE 5.16. Anti-shimmying device from US patent 1,713,242 to Stranahan, "steering gear check," May 14, 1929; car front axle is element "7," bracket that holds down axle is "11"

> [T]here were six earlier efforts to meet the same defect [of shimmying]; none of them were simple; all were apparently unsatisfactory; they were pretty evenly distributed throughout the [eighteen year] period [when the problem was being worked on]. In their place Stranahan substituted merely a two piece bracket, which dispensed with the springs that had been usual heretofore, was easy to adjust, and went out of action as soon as the wheels were turned to either side. It seems to me that there could be no better evidence of invention than such a history. As I have said, the disclosure has not gone into very wide use; and that is true, though a million [units sold], even in the automobile industry, is not a quantity to be ignored; but I conceive that that is not an important consideration here. The defendant assures us that the need has now been superseded [by use of a superior design, since

> widely adopted] but it very clearly existed for a long time, and success is of moment only as it is evidence of the right answer. Here we do not need that evidence, for obviously Stranahan did find the right answer.[160]

Besides being a good example of Learned Hand's "contextual" approach to the presence or absence of invention (nonobviousness),[161] the opinion illustrates an important point at the intersection of patents and the auto industry. Even an invention found noteworthy by Judge Hand covered a narrow slice of ground. The suspension system in the patent found valid followed on from six less successful solutions to the problem. Though the early efforts were less successful, this shows that at least seven different inventors or teams were focused on the single, limited problem of preventing shimmying. Note too that the patent in the case was itself superseded fairly rapidly. This helps explain two things. First is the crowded nature of most auto-related technologies. As we have seen, component designs and product features were only occasionally the subject of a powerful patent or group of patents. Most individual auto patents were narrow, and many that were asserted against auto manufacturers were found invalid.

This leads to the second point: In a setting like this, we would expect companies to think and act, when it came to patents, in terms of numbers and volume. Patent portfolios were important, in part because individual patents were not. The major auto companies adapted to life among this proliferation of patents. One important response is the one we cover next – the emergence of the auto industry patent pool. The auto industry pool was one of the largest and most effective patent pools of the twentieth century. Along with the airplane pool, it set the standard for large-scale industry patent peace in the era of burgeoning patent portfolios.

5.2.3.1 Patent Pools: Solution to the Transactional Challenges of High-Volume Patenting

Cars are complex. They include thousands of components, many of which (including engine parts and electronics) are themselves far from simple. Yet there has also been, at times at least, extensive competition among numerous companies to develop superior components and features. This is a recipe for very extensive patent litigation. But the volume of auto patent litigation never seems to have grown

[160] *General Motors Corp.* v. *Apollo Magneto Corp.*, 101 F.2d 53, 56 (2d Cir.), decree modified, 102 F.2d 455 (2d Cir. 1939) (L. Hand, J., dissenting). Judge Learned Hand's view of the case having been adopted, his brother Judge Augustus Hand – who had voted in the majority in the original opinion – then dissented to the decision as modified..

[161] See John F. Duffy, A *Timing Approach to Patentability*, 12 Lewis & Clark L. Rev. 343, 369 (2008) (footnotes omitted) ("The great Judge Learned Hand was one of most ardent champions of [the "history of the art" as a key to patent validity cases] ... Learned Hand continued to endorse using 'the history of the art' as a primary and more reliable test throughout his career ... ").

beyond a manageable level. We have seen two reasons for this so far: extensive vertical integration and a high risk of patent invalidation, the latter a result of above-average litigation talent capable of finding and exploiting a wide range of prior art in this quickly crowded field. But one final factor must be mentioned. It is perhaps the most important one: the Automobile Manufacturers Association (AMA), one of the first successful, industry-wide patent pools.

The AMA was founded in 1914 and grew to become "one of the most significant patent licensing collectives in industrial history."[162] As mentioned, at the time the AMA was formed there were dozens of car manufacturers and many small- and medium-sized parts makers. Entry was robust. In addition, the industry-wide chokehold of the Selden patent had only recently been loosened by Henry Ford. But it had become apparent to auto companies that some solution to potential patent bottlenecks had to be found. As we saw in Chapter 4, similar patent-related logjams had formed in the development of the telephone and electrical power industries. In those industries, the solution took the form of mergers. But autos are not a networked product. Person A has little stake in the auto used by person B; they are not interconnected in such a way that a single system architecture benefits all, as is true for power and telephone systems. And, especially in the early stages of the auto industry, capital formation sufficient to achieve an efficient scale was quite possible. This encouraged competition, and discouraged consolidation by merger.

With multiple, dispersed innovators, what was needed for autos was a solution to the transaction costs of multiple, dispersed patent holders – but not necessarily in the form of merger into a single dominant firm. The solution was an industry-wide, royalty-free patent sharing arrangement that encouraged "patent peace" among auto manufacturers and parts makers alike. The pool made it possible for auto companies

[162] Michael Mattioli, *Power and Governance in Patent Pools*, 27 Harv. J.L. & Tech. 421, 451 (2014). See also *Manufacturers Aircraft Association: Antitrust Laws*, 31 Op. Att'y Gen. 166, 169 (1917); Pooling of Patents: Hearings on H.R. 4523 Before the House Comm. on Patents, 74th Cong., 1st Sess. at p. 775 (1935) (statement of Frank H. Russell, President of the Manufacturers Aircraft Association (MAA)):

> Any member company, to become a member [of the aircraft pool, MAA], after he has bought a share of stock has to agree to exchange all patents which he may have either for nothing, or, if he feels that the patent has cost him a lot of money or is of great advantage to the art, or is bringing something to the development in the process which did not previously exist, he has the right to ask for a special royalty, and that reference is then sent to a board of arbitration which is made up of a member representing him or himself, a member of the association, and a third member who is selected by the other two. [I]n the airplane cross-licensing agreement, after completely abolishing the monopoly of the individual inventor and opening every patent to every member of the association, it provides that a board of arbitrators may decide in any case what reward should be paid to individual patent owners and this is based not upon the official determination of patentability by the Patent Office, but upon the unofficial determination of the importance of the invention by a board of arbitrators.

to operate with standard, modular technologies, without fear of patent litigation.[163] Unlike the contemporaneous pool in airframe manufacturing,[164] the AMA did not allocate royalties among patent owners who joined the pool. Instead, the pool administrators excluded "revolutionary" (pioneering) patents from the pool. These exclusions arguably segregated high-value (or potentially high-value) patents from mere "commodity" patents. Only the latter were included in the royalty-free structure. This arrangement reduced transaction costs for most patents, while preserving incentives to perform pioneering R&D.

Complex, multi-component products can be covered by hundreds of patents, sometimes more. While few patent owners can afford to enforce their patents against all potential and actual infringers, it would still be prohibitively costly for each of several hundred patent owners to license its patents to a significant proportion of the many infringing companies. And where licensing negotiations are involved, some fraction predictably lead to litigation – adding to the transaction costs of extensive patent licensing. Pools solve these transactional problems. They combine an up-front agreement among patent owners, covering whether and how to allocate pool royalty income, with (typically) a single, uniform patent license, offered on fixed terms to all comers, covering the entire bundle of pooled patents. In the auto pool, the structure was made simpler by the fact that the pooled patents were available royalty-free. Pools such as this, as industry representatives said, substituted an industry-generated licensing system in place of the potentially high cost of widely dispersed and strongly enforced patent rights.

The question naturally arises: If the auto industry had to negotiate a substitute exchange mechanism to work around the high costs that would otherwise accompany industry patenting, why not champion a legal policy to eliminate patents for the industry as a whole? And why not do the same for other industries facing similar problems?

The answer is that the patent pool mitigated burdensome transaction costs, while retaining some residual benefits for patent owners. The pool created an "inner circle" of pool members. Inside that circle, patent litigation was eliminated in exchange for access to all member patents. Among other things, this recognized that companies within the circle had all contributed in various ways to the basic technology incorporated in a modern automobile. It also removed patents from the battlefield of intercompany strategic competition. But it is important to remember two points: (1) the pool did not include new technologies, obtained through

[163] This fit into an auto industry pattern; the industry was said to in general be averse to litigation. See Lane Kenworthy, Stewart Macaulay, and Joel Rogers, "The More Things Change . . .," at p. 644 ("The major automobile manufacturers seldom sue each other.").

[164] On this, see Robert P. Merges, *Contracting into Liability Rules: Intellectual Property Rights and Collective Rights Organizations*, 84 Cal. L. Rev. 1293, 1342–1347 (1996).

acquisition or developed in-house[165] and (2) it did not apply to non-members. So, for new developments, patent strategy remained relevant.

Meanwhile as to those not within the inside circle – established firms holding out from the pool, or outsider companies from other industries – patents retained their value as a strategic weapon. A patent pool forms a sort of patent "waiver" zone. Within it, enforcement rights are surrendered in exchange for various benefits.

But acquiring and enforcing patents may still make sense, because those patents can be against those "outside the circle." This arrangement shows as well as any the nature of patents (and other property rights, including other IP rights): They are options, which may be enforced if and when the owner chooses. But they can also be waived when that makes sense. Critics of the patent system who point to pools as evidence that patents are not necessary, or are more costly than they are worth, usually miss this point.[166] The auto companies understood it, though. This explains why these companies both promoted the auto patent pool and continued to acquire patents during the pool's existence. Patents may have their problems, but the fact they are occasionally bundled into pools does not prove that they are a fundamentally flawed idea.[167]

Though there were plainly observable benefits from this arrangement,[168] the auto pool (AMA) was questioned (along with the air frame pool) both in the late 1930s and then, more successfully, during the period of high antitrust enforcement in the 1960s. It was eventually abandoned – a victim of overzealous concern with the market power conferred by patents. Ironically, it ran out of gas (so to speak) just when a fresh burst of engineering and production innovations were about to hit the auto industry from overseas in the 1970s. US auto technology stagnated in that era – part of the general economic doldrums that led to the revitalization of patent law in the early 1980s (Chapter 6).

[165] See, e.g., *Gen. Motors Corp.* v. *Apollo Magneto Corp.*, 101 F.2d 53, 56 (2d Cir.), decree modified, 102 F.2d 455 (2d Cir. 1939), discussed supra (GM patent enforcement action against a parts company); *General Motors Corp.* v. *Leer Auto Supply Co.*, 60 F.2d 902 (2d Cir. 1932) (GM joins licensee and partner in suit against a third party).

[166] See, e.g., Walton Hamilton, Patents and Free Enterprise, U.S. Senate, Temporary National Economic Committee, Sen. Comm. Print, Monograph No. 31, 76th Cong. 3d Sess., March 14, 1941, at p. 122. Walton Hamilton, a Yale Professor who wrote this 1941 report, which was highly critical of the patent system, spoke of the success of the automobile pool as proof of the creaky substructure of the patent system. "A heterodox chapter," he concluded, "challenges the whole theology of the patent system."

[167] Pools were also praised by the noted economist Alfred Kahn. See Alfred E. Kahn, *Fundamental Deficiencies of the American Patent Law*, 30 Am. Econ. Rev. 475, 491 (1940) ("All things considered, it must be concluded that the pool is a distinct improvement over the patent law as originally contemplated in effecting technological advance under modern conditions.").

[168] Measurably true of most patent pools formed since the 1920s. See Robert P. Merges and Michael Mattioli, *Measuring the Costs and Benefits of Patent Pools*, 78 Ohio St. L.J. 281 (2017).

5.3 PATENT DOCTRINE AND ADMINISTRATION

The first part of this chapter was titled "Patents Outside the Headlines." It detailed the many dynamic entrants, some reliant on patents, in various industries between 1920 and 1982. But if this topic was not in general the subject of patent-related headlines, what topics were? The answer largely revolves around antitrust. High-level patent policy in these years was dominated by what came to be called the "patent-antitrust interface." Rarely were patents mentioned in discussions of important federal policy without being linked to antitrust and competition concerns generally. The auto and chemical industries described in Section 5.2 were not immune from antitrust scrutiny, as we will see. But the concern with patents as tools of anticompetitive corporate behavior spanned all important industries.

5.3.1 *The Anti-patent Movement: Attack from All Sides*

Beginning in the 1930s, antitrust experts orchestrated a concerted attack on the overall value of the US patent system. Hearings by the 1935 Temporary National Economic Committee (TNEC) set the high-water mark, perhaps. But there were plenty of other forums where the dangers and evils of patents were laid out. The target was almost always the deployment of patents by big business. When these officials spoke of "small business," they were more likely to invoke localized producers and retail outlets – the "mom and pop" shops often celebrated as repositories of American virtue. At this time, entry into new industries and small, specialized production companies were not much in evidence in the writings of antitrust scholars. Nor was the development of new technologies in general. Overall, they adopted a highly static view of industry and the economy.[169] Pictured within this frame, patents posed a menacing image: they kept prices above the competitive level at best, and helped big businesses in their relentless efforts to raise consumer prices and restrict consumer choice.

A common refrain among antitrust lawyers and scholars was that the patent system had outlived its usefulness – or had failed to adapt to modern conditions, at least. Yale Professor Walton Hamilton led the charge here, but he had plenty of company. The primary count in the indictment was this: The patent system, once of noble purpose, had not been changed in line with changes in the economy. The reward to

[169] The static view of production technology in mid-twentieth century antitrust thinking is hinted at in some comments by Herbert Hovenkamp, who writes:

> In the 1940s and 1950s, neoclassical industrial-organization economists, such as Joe Bain, the leading protagonist of the Harvard School of industrial economics, tended to view the competitive rationales for vertical integration as driven purely by [existing] technology – justified where a physical step could be eliminated between two processes, but not otherwise.

Herbert Hovenkamp, *The Law of Vertical Integration and the Business Firm: 1880–1960*, 95 Iowa L. Rev. 863, 872 (2010) (footnotes omitted).

inventors of the eighteenth century had transformed into a tool of corporate control in the twentieth. It was time to bring the patent system up to date with the realities of the twentieth-century economy:[170]

> As an instrument passes from any one group to another, its adopted habitat imposes upon it a new role. It should accordingly occasion not even mild surprise that as, by act of assignment, a patent passes from the inventor to the corporation, it undergoes a profound change in character. The dominant concern of the business unit is to make money, not to promote the useful arts. It contributes to their advance, if the pursuit of gain lies that way. But if the purpose of the grant is antithetical – or even irrelevant – there is little place for public purpose in the formulas through which the corporation carries on ... [A] situation has blundered into being which calls for drastic amendment ... The grant of a patent is intended to protect an invention; in practice it repeatedly operates to block off a whole technology.

Professor Hamilton simplified the message in a more popular article published in *The American Scholar* in 1948. There Hamilton put the matter succinctly:

> The conditions of invention have changed [since the eighteenth century]; the "sole, true and only inventor" has been superseded by a corps of technicians, working for a corporation in a laboratory. Research has become a cooperative task. The inventor, wearing the livery of his corporate master, works on a salary. The crafts and trades of old have been succeeded by industries with far-flung organizations. Our culture has been transformed by a technical revolution grounded in mechanics. It is now being played upon by a second industrial revolution springing from progress in the chemistries, metallurgy, electronics. The tempo of technical change today is to that of 1787 as the motor car is to the horse and buggy. It would be strange if a late eighteenth-century policy should fit mid-twentieth century conditions.[171]

In this article and elsewhere, Hamilton identifies the two patent-related practices needing the greatest attention from regulators: assignments (the transfer of patents from individuals to corporate ownership); and licensing contracts. For reasons described in Chapter 4, proposals such as Hamilton's that would permit inventors

170 Walton Hamilton, Patents and Free Enterprise, U.S. Senate, Temporary National Economic Committee, Sen. Comm. Print, Monograph No. 31, 76th Cong. 3d Sess., March 14, 1941, at pp. 159–160.

171 Walton Hamilton, *Is Our Patent System Obsolete? Yes*, 17 Am. Scholar 470, 471 (1948). See also S. Colum Gilfillan, The Sociology of Invention (Chicago: Follett Publishing, 1935; reissued Boston: MIT Press, 1970) (strong claim that almost all inventions are attributable to social forces and group effort, and not individual inventors). Letters in response to the Hamilton's American Scholar article went even further than he did in condemning patents. One, by the young sociologist Robert Lynd, suggested that the patent system was part of a systematic takeover of the technocratic levers of power by big business. See [Robert Lynd, *"You Can't Skin a Live Tiger ...", Letter to the Editor*, 18 Am. Scholar 109 (1948), at pp. 109–110 ("The problem we face today is that, in an era that increasingly lives by science and technology, business control over science and its application to human needs, gives to private business effective control over all the institutions of democracy, including the state itself.").

to retain patent ownership never made much sense once transaction costs were introduced to the analysis. But Hamilton's attack on licensing practices was more effective. It might be inevitable that corporations would own many patents, but reformers set out to limit the degree of effective corporate control that could be exerted under patent licensing agreements. The basic problem was once again spelled out by Hamilton:

> The pattern of permission [in licensing agreements] according to use is a rich fabric. The license may – and usually does – state the amount which may be manufactured, the territory within which sales may be made, the minimum prices which must be charged. Thus the patent-owner determines who is to enter the industry and the rules under which he [the entrant] can carry on. If a licensee trespasses upon a use not granted him, or if he exceeds the quota assigned, sells in another man's territory, or cuts prices, he by doing so becomes a chiseler, and at law an "infringer." Thus the public courts may be invoked to police a system of private government.[172]

In this antitrust-oriented view of the world, there is one variety of patent evil and two primary vehicles for delivering it. The evil is lessened competition – or, in the Chicago school era (roughly post-1970), a loss in consumer welfare. The two vehicles by which patents cause harm are, first, competitor-to-competitor mergers, contracts, and tacit agreements – horizontal arrangements, in other words. The second way patents cause harm is from vertical arrangements: a merger, contract, or tacit agreement between a seller and a supplier, a seller and a distributor, a seller and a retailer, etc.

There was no shortage of antitrust activity on the horizontal level. Mergers were famously targeted, including a merger that would have produced a merged firm with a mere 7.5 percent market share in the highly competitive Southern California consumer grocery market.[173] In the realm of patents, cross-licensing and patent pools were both thought to be suspect during this period of high antitrust enforcement.[174] The oldest and most successful patent pools, in the auto and aircraft industries, were

[172] Walton Hamilton, *Is Our Patent System Obsolete? Yes*, at p. 472.

[173] United States v. Von's Grocery Co., 384 U.S. 270 (1966) (affirming decision blocking a merger between the third and fifth largest grocery store chains in Southern California).

[174] See generally Steven Wilf, *The Making of the Post-War Paradigm in American Intellectual Property Law*, 31 Colum. J. L. Ent. & Arts, 139 (2008), at p. 191 (footnotes omitted):

> New Deal courts continued the Progressive Era courts' tradition of hostility to patents, often invalidating them on such grounds as prior anticipation, lack of invention, or failure to comply with various formal statutory requirements. Patents were seen as a form of corporate property granted as monopoly. Patent pools and patent tying mechanisms raised concerns as potential violations of antitrust law. Courts spoke of "a tension between a strong public policy against monopoly and a desire to encourage inventions which will benefit the public."

both targeted and more or less shut down during this period, based on what now appear to be faulty theories and quite limited data.[175]

Even so, the increase in horizontal level policing was mild compared to the scrutiny reserved for vertical business relationships. Since patent licensing is a classic vertical contract, much antitrust scrutiny was centered on the provisions and "restraints" in these agreements, as we will see.

5.3.1.1 Vertical Restraints and the Battle of Goliath vs. David

Economic theory in the 1930s and 1940s taught that "vertical restraints" could lessen competition in a number of ways.[176] Given the theory, it made sense to target patents, because patent protection provided a convenient cover to disguise the deleterious effects of contractual restrictions. The idea was that anticompetitive restraints such as price fixing, territorial restrictions, and tie-ins could be dressed up as practical adjuncts to a patent license. Hamilton and his peers wanted to pierce through the cover story of patents to reveal the ugly anticompetitive power play underneath these restrictive contracts. The historian and antitrust scholar Herbert Hovenkamp traces the origin of restrictive doctrine to the patent exhaustion cases reviewed at length in Chapters 3 and 4. The anti-restriction cases of the 1930s and 1940s proceeded on a simple (perhaps simplistic) analogy: just as those who bought a patented item from an authorized dealer in one territory were free to carry it, use it, resell it, etc., in any territory, so should a manufacturer buying an input, a wholesaler distributing a good, or a retailer selling it be free to act as he or she pleased.[177] This line of thought culminated in a ruling that vertical restraints were illegal in and of themselves. No defense based on business necessity or efficiency was to be heard.[178]

[175] See Robert P. Merges and Michael Mattioli, Measuring the Costs and Benefits of Patent Pools (reviewing antitrust-based objections to patent pools, and showing that only rarely would these outweigh the measurable benefits of patent pools as a transaction cost-saving institution). See Section 5.2.3.1 for a discussion of the formation and operation of the auto industry patent pool.

[176] This was part of a general attack on the anticompetitive effects of vertical dealing in general. See Herbert Hovenkamp, The Law of Vertical Integration and the Business Firm: 1880–1960, at p. 876 ("U.S. antitrust policy was about to undertake a thirty-year war against the evils of vertical integration.").

[177] See *Carbice Corporation of America* v. *American Patents Development Corp.*, 283 U.S. 27, 31–32 (1931) (citing older Supreme Court exhaustion cases). Justice Brandeis in that case refused to enforce a contract saying if a buyer wanted to buy defendant's patented ice box, that buyer had to agree to also buy (unpatented) dry ice exclusively from the patentee/defendant. The holding was based on the notion that the defendant was trying to extract an extra or excessive royalty through sale of "the unpatented supplies" used with its patented ice box, which would tend to "monopolize the commerce in a large part of the unpatented materials used in its manufacture." The borrowing of exhaustion doctrine is described in Herbert Hovenkamp, *Robert Bork and Vertical Integration: Leverage, Foreclosure, and Efficiency*, 79 Antitrust L.J. 983, 993 (2014).

[178] *United States* v. *Arnold, Schwinn & Co.*, 388 U.S. 365 (1967) (vertical restraints per se illegal), later overruled by *Continental T. V., Inc.* v. *GTE Sylvania Inc.*, 433 U.S. 36 (1977) (antitrust

The language of antitrust is abstract: vertical and horizontal, per se and rule of reason; pro-competition and anti-competitive. To see what all this theory and doctrine meant on the ground, consider an actual patent in an actual industry, an actual contract involving that patent, and an actual antitrust ruling against the patent owner who licensed the patent. Consider the small canning industry company called G. S. Suppiger Company of southern Illinois.

Gerhart S. Suppiger had a canning company in Belleville, Illinois. A subsidiary was devoted to a sideline business, sale of a patented salt-adding machine, used to add salt during the canning of produce, such as tomatoes. As one court put it,

> Plaintiff [Suppiger] is a canning company which owns and operates a wholly owned subsidiary devoted to making and leasing a patented tablet depositing machine and to making and selling salt tablets of a particular design and configuration. This last-named business is much smaller than plaintiff's main business, which is canning.[179]

According to a definitive history of the ketchup industry (a phrase I did not imagine ever writing), Suppiger's canning company had at least one regionally famous brand, Brooks Brand Catsup.[180] Suppiger in later years moved to nearby Collinsville, Illinois, and then was acquired and folded into a ketchup company from Philadelphia, named Ritter's.[181] Suppiger and Collinsville loom large not in the annals of canning industry domination, but for the fact that the custom water tower at Suppiger's cannery was and is known as "the World's Largest Ketchup Bottle."[182]

Suppiger's machinery subsidiary was known in the early years as the Scientific Tablet Company. The patent in the case covered a Tablet Depositing Machine, and was issued to joint inventors Clyde Alexander and Gerhart Suppiger himself.[183] According to at least one court that considered Suppinger's patent, his company was "a pioneer" and a success in the automated dispensing of salt during canning operations.[184] Suppiger had earlier patented some related machines for injecting

"rule of reason" – which permits defense of contract terms as required for efficiency – applies to vertical restraints).

179 G. S. *Suppiger Co.* v. *Morton Salt Co.*, 117 F.2d 968, 969 (7th Cir. 1941), rev'd, 314 U.S. 488 (1942).

180 See Andrew F. Smith, Pure Ketchup: A History of America's National Condiment, with Recipes (Columbia, SC: University of South Carolina Press, 1996), at p. 42: Ritter Catsup, made by the P. J. Ritter Company, was sold in Philadelphia.

181 See www.catsupbottle.com/archive/1946/index.html (Suppiger company was located in Collinsville, IL, and its factory drew water from a public water tower shaped like a Ketchup bottle, known as "The World's Largest Ketchup Bottle").

182 Ibid.

183 See U.S. Patent 2,060,645, issued November 10, 1936, assigned to Scientific Tablet Company of Belleville, Illinois.

184 G. S. *Suppiger Co.* v. *Morton Salt Co.*, 117 F.2d 968, 970 (7th Cir. 1941):

> Plaintiff and its predecessor pioneered in the salt tablet industry (placing salt of predetermined quantity in a definite amount of canned vegetables, through the use of salt tablets deposited by a machine) as applied to the canning industry and developed it to its present success.

flavoring into canned products during the canning process,[185] which it commercialized using the same business model as for the salt tablet machine.[186] In the main, however, most of the income from the subsidiary came as the result of the sale of salt tablets that were specially designed for use with the tablet dispenser.[187]

The tablet income was driven at least in part by a tie-in clause in the contract under which Suppiger licensed/leased its tablet-dispensing patent. The tie-in clause appeared in contracts Suppiger signed with canneries, permitting the canneries to use Suppiger's tablet dispensers. According to the Seventh Circuit Court of Appeals,

> [Suppiger] did not sell but leased said [tablet] machines made under the patent in suit and their other patents to commercial canners of vegetables, as tomatoes, and the like, in the many states wherein such canners are located. The leases were in writing and included a license to use the patented machine, upon the condition and agreement by the lessee that plaintiff's and its predecessor's salt tablets be used exclusively in said patented, leased machines.[188]

The other party to the case was the old, established industry player Morton Salt. Morton was founded in 1895, and seems to have grown steadily over the years, particularly via acquisition of smaller salt companies.[189] Morton sold salt in all its various forms, including rock salts, consumer kitchen salt, and salt tablets for

[185] See US patent 1,887,073, "method of flavoring in canning, preserving, and operations," issued to Gerhart S. Suppiger, November 8, 1932; US patent 1,887,073, also issued November 8, 1932, "apparatus for dispensing flavoring materials," to inventors Clyde Alexander and Gerhart Suppiger. Both were assigned to Scientific Tablet.

[186] *G. S. Suppiger Co.* v. *Morton Salt Co.*, 117 F.2d 968, 969 (7th Cir. 1941) ("They [Suppiger] also manufactured or had manufactured for them machines under the patent in suit and also other machines under patents owned by them for depositing salt tablets.").

[187] See *G. S. Suppiger Co.* v. *Morton Salt Co.*, 117 F.2d 968, 969 (7th Cir. 1941), rev'd, 314 U.S. 488 (1942):

> The manufacture and sale of the salt tablets is and was the main business of plaintiff's predecessor [i.e., Scientific Tablet] and of plaintiff [the parent company, Suppiger] after it acquired that business in June, 1928, and which it has since carried on as a subsidiary company. The end and aim of the business was and is the sale of the salt tablets in which its profits lie. The patented depositing machine of the patent in suit and of other patents is a mere secondary adjunct.

[188] *G. S. Suppiger Co.* v. *Morton Salt Co.*, 117 F.2d 968, 969 (7th Cir. 1941).

[189] See Carol D. Litchfield, "Carol Litchfield Collection on the History of Salt," University of Pennsylvania – Hagley Museum and Library, available at http://dla.library.upenn.edu/cocoon/dla/pacscl/ead.pdf?sort=date_added_sort%20desc&fq=top_repository_facet%3A%22Hagley%20Museum%20and%20Library%22&id=PACSCL_HML_2012219&, last updated on August 21, 2018, at p. 5:

> Morton Salt began in Chicago in 1880 when Joy Morton (1855–1934) became a partner in the salt making company E.I. Wheeler & Co. Morton took over the company after Wheeler's death in 1895, and the company was incorporated as the Morton Salt Company in 1910. Morton acquired a number of smaller companies such as Bevis Rock Salt Company in 1919, The Worcester Salt Company in 1943, and the Canadian Salt Company in 1954.

industrial dispensers such as Suppiger's.[190] But Morton also competed in the machinery end of the industry,[191] and, according to Suppiger, Morton's tablet-dispensing machines infringed the Suppiger patent. Figure 5.17 will you give you an idea of what the tablet dispensing machines looked like.

The case began, then, as a case of the niche machinery maker (Suppiger) going up against the large, vertically integrated industry incumbent (Morton). The original posture was David v. Goliath, with Suppiger yielding the slingshot against the company (Morton) that might as well have been called "Big Salt." In the event, Morton's lawyers, eager as all lawyers are to control the narrative of a lawsuit, plucked from their own heads the black hat of legal offender and promptly put it on Suppiger's. The switch was possible because Suppiger chose to license its patents to canning companies, and the licenses included a specific paragraph restricting the canners' freedom of action: a vertical restraint. Morton went from an infringer of Suppiger's hard-won patent rights to the champion of canners wriggling under Suppiger's blatant abuse of a patent right.

Note well: Morton itself did not suffer from Suppiger's dreaded tie-in clause – Morton was not a licensee/lessee of Suppiger. The law allowed Morton to seize on Suppiger licenses to others as a defense for Morton – a complete stranger to those Suppiger-canning company licenses. In fact (irony!) Morton actually included the same tie-in clause in its own leases/licenses with Morton customers – so Morton was guilty of precisely the same wrong it accused Suppiger of,[192] but that did not matter.

[190] Morton's consumer salt product became popular because it was formulated in a way to prevent clumping or clogging in damp weather. (Technically, it included a small amount of magnesium carbonate.) Promoting this feature gave rise in 1911 to the famous Morton logo, a little girl with an umbrella against the rain, letting some Morton salt pour freely behind her as she walks, with the tag line "When it Rains, it Pours." See www.mortonsalt.com/heritage-era/littlegirl-grew-upto-icon/.

[191] See *G. S. Suppiger Co.* v. *Morton Salt Co.*, 117 F.2d 968, 969 (7th Cir. 1941):

> The defendant [Morton] is in the business of mining, processing and selling salt for commercial canning and for other purposes. It also makes and sells salt tablets such as those made and sold by plaintiff for use in the canning industry. It also makes and leases salt tablet depositing machines to canners, and in particular the salt depositing machines charged to infringe the patent in suit. Defendant's salt tablet depositing machine is not patented.

[192] *G. S. Suppiger Co.* v. *Morton Salt Co.*, 117 F.2d 968, 970 (7th Cir. 1941):

> Defendant [Morton] also makes and licenses a tablet depositing machine. It has continuously operated its business since 1927. Its machine is allegedly an infringement of plaintiff's patent. It also leases its machine to the trade and provides in its lease that the lessee shall use only salt tablets made by it.

The one difference was that Morton's machine was not patented. But in the absence of market power conferred by Suppiger's patent, this should not matter. And note that Morton's (possibly non-infringing) presence in the market, as well as the availability of a distinct and apparently non-infringing alternative design (the International Salt patent – see infra) suggests the strong possibility that there were viable competing technologies and thus that Suppiger did not have market power.

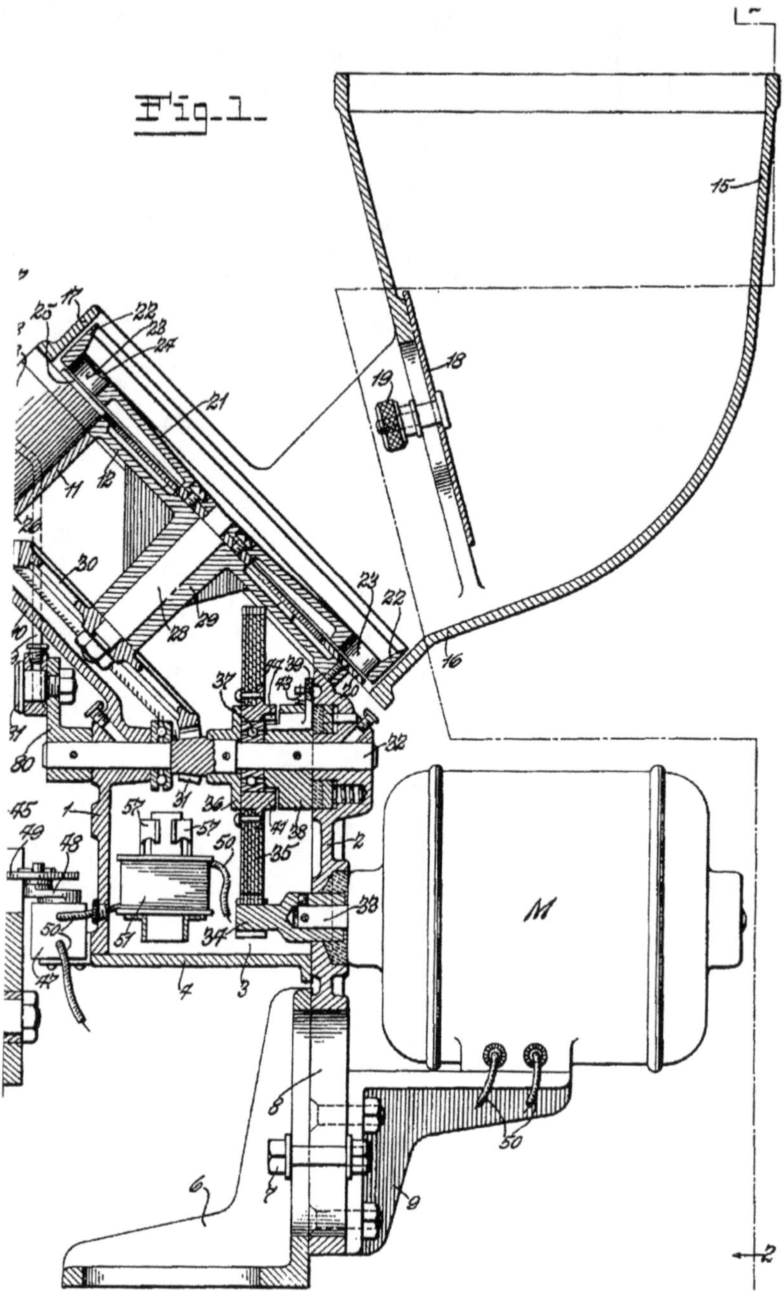

FIGURE 5.17. From US patent 2,060,645 (1936), to G. S. Suppiger: Basic design of salt tablet feeder

First because it was Suppiger's patent that was at issue, so Morton's licensing practices were irrelevant. And second, because Morton had no patent to license, Morton's tie-in clause in its customer contracts was probably legal anyway.

To sum up: Morton argued it was not the existence of Suppiger's patent that caused the problem, it was the restrictive terms under which the patent was deployed: the exclusive salt-purchase provision, a vertical restraint on canners. Through the Clayton Act defense that Morton deployed,[193] Suppiger went from aggrieved victim of Morton's piracy (as patent owner lawyers are wont to say) to the virtuous discoverer of third-party patent licenses that went too far, and that harmed competition. Such was the jiu-jitsu-like role reversal that was available to infringement defendants at the height of the no-vertical-restraints era.

This is not to say that a patent licensor may never legitimately run afoul of antitrust law. If Suppiger had market power in the canning machine industry – if it had a very large chunk of a not very competitive market, for example – a tie-in might be suspect. The increased cost to customers represented by a predatory tie-in (the extra amount they paid for salt over the competitive price, for example) in effect represents a price increase. And the very definition of market power is the ability to raise prices beyond the competitive level while suffering few customer defections.

Despite this possibility, there is little evidence that Suppiger had market power. There were a number of alternative canning technologies that were not covered by Suppiger's patent. One was of course whatever technology preceded the Suppiger machine; canning was going on long before his patent's issue date of 1938. Another was the Morton tablet dispenser. If Suppiger's patent infringement suit had proceeded, Morton's design might have been found non-infringing. In addition, a related antitrust enforcement action brought by the US government against a Suppiger competitor, International Salt,[194] revealed an alternative tablet dispensing design that does not appear to have infringed Suppiger's claims.

The International Salt dispenser was at the center of a separate lawsuit (not involving Suppiger or Morton) by the US government against the patent owner,

[193] G. S. *Suppiger Co.* v. *Morton Salt Co.*, 117 F.2d 968, 971 (7th Cir. 1941):

> Section 3 of the Clayton Act, 15 U.S.C.A. § 14, upon which defendant-appellee particularly relies, makes unlawful the lease of machinery (either patented or unpatented) on condition that the lessee shall not use the supplies or other commodities of a competitor. However, unlawfulness is made to depend upon a provision which is here important, – where the effect of such lease or such condition may be substantially to lessen competition or tend to create a monopoly in any line of commerce.

The Seventh Circuit did not believe that Suppiger's patent tended to lessen competition or create a monopoly, but the Supreme Court did.

[194] *Int'l Salt Co.* v. *United States*, 332 U.S. 392, 396, (1947). The patent in this case is discussed in the main text. The Court held: "[T]he tendency of the [exclusive salt purchase] arrangement [in the International Salt lease/license] to accomplishment of monopoly seems obvious.").

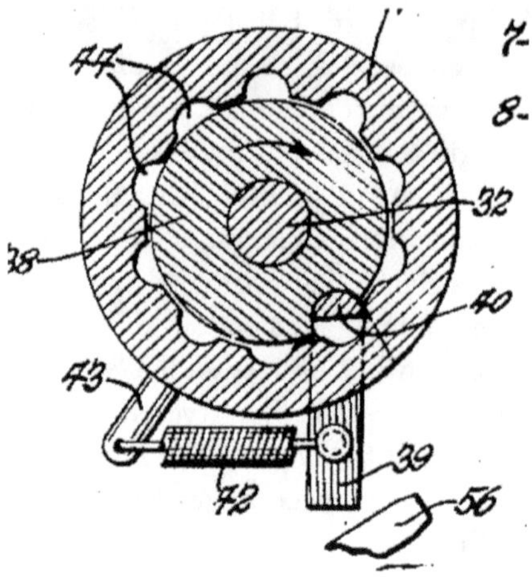

FIGURE 5.18. From US patent 2,060,645 (1936), to G. S. Suppiger: Rotating multi-tablet plate for tablet feeding

International.[195] The design patented by International in 1943[196] does not appear to infringe the claims of the Suppiger patent at issue in *Suppiger* v. *Morton Salt*. The Suppiger design, as claimed, had a rotating plate with multiple tablet-sized holes to dispense tablets to the chute leading out of the hopper, as shown in Figure 5.18.

The International Salt design worked on a different principle. It used a rotating semi-circular scoop to feed individual salt tablets into the chute leading to the tablet container, as shown in Figure 5.19.

The International Salt machine would not have met at least some of the claims of the Suppiger patent; claim 1, for instance, requires "a rotating plate having means for separating unit articles from the bulk of articles … "[197]

Regardless of how many non-infringing substitutes there were for Suppiger's patented machines, the point remains: this looks like a competitive industry, with Suppiger, Morton and International all investing funds to design and license proprietary canning technologies. There is no real evidence that Suppiger had

[195] *Int'l Salt Co.* v. *United States*, 332 U.S. 392, 393 (1947): "The Government brought this civil action to enjoin the International Salt Company, appellant here, from carrying out provisions of the leases of its patented machines to the effect that lessees would use therein only International's salt products." Between the patent owner in this case, International, and the plaintiff and defendant in the *Suppiger* case, it appears the "purchase my salt only" provision was a standard term in dispenser machinery lease agreements.

[196] US patent 2,308,188, "Tablet Dispensing Machine," issued to Louis J. Madden, January 12, 1943, assigned to International Salt.

[197] US patent 2,060,645, to Suppiger, at p. 4, col. 1, claim 1; and several other claims (2, 3, etc.) require a "revoluble plate" [sic]. Some of the claims focus on the bottom part of the machine, where tablets are discharged into single cans of canned goods – possibly one or more of these claims might be infringed by the International Salt machine. Note that Suppiger never sued International, so we do not know for sure.

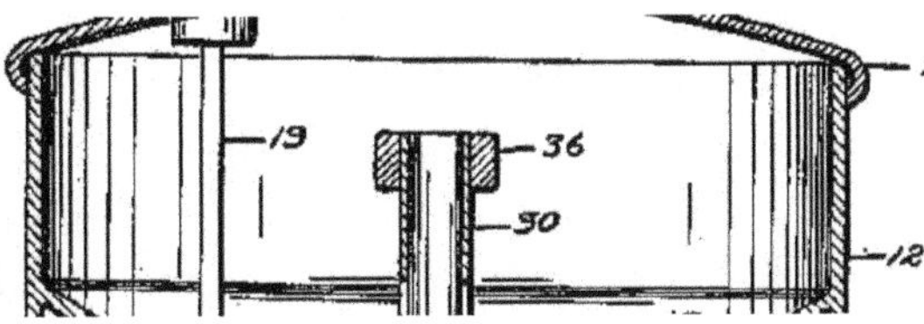

FIGURE 5.19. From US 2,308,188 patent (1943) assigned to competing firm, International Salt. Tablet intake mechanism, showing rotating tube (30) inside salt tablet hopper (12); tube has opening (36), which pulls in one tablet at a time for the rotating tube; this design would not infringe the Suppiger claims, implying there were viable substitutes for the Suppiger design and that Suppiger had little market power

market power, or that its lease/license terms improperly leveraged the power conferred by its patent. In fact, that patent had helped Suppiger make some money from its investment in machinery. And it may have protected a niche in the tablet dispensing market. But it hardly seems like a monopoly-creating government franchise allowing Suppiger Co. to bestride canneries like a Colossus.

This is all the truer when you recall the scale of the two companies involved in the Suppinger-Morton lawsuit. Morton was very well-established, an iconic American consumer product company. But Suppiger after 1948 seems to have pulled in its wings to concentrate on canning; it never pushed boldly back into machinery. Today all that's left of the David (Suppiger) who was taken down by the salty Goliath (Morton) is this: The World's Largest Ketchup Bottle, a local landmark in Collinsville, Illinois. On the other hand, the aggressive law of vertical restraints at work in *Suppiger* is also long gone: And it didn't even leave a ketchup bottle to remember it by.

The movement to rethink and reform antitrust law was building beginning in the 1960s, and the strongest anti-patent push from antitrust was over by the late 1970s.[198] But the real change in scholarship and policy began in 1980 with the election of President Reagan, which we take up in Chapter 6.

[198] Two more legacies from the pre-1980 period are (1) a series of cases ordering mandatory licenses to all industry competitors who ask for them, as a remedy for antitrust violations ("compulsory licensing"), see *Besser Mfg. Co. v. United States*, 343 U.S. 444, 449 (1952) ("We can see no abuse of discretion here. Compulsory licensing and sale of patented devices are recognized remedies."), and (2) the "Nine No-Nos," a list of prohibited or suspect patent licensing terms as announced by an official from the Department of Justice in 1969. See Bruce B. Wilson, *Remarks to Michigan State Bar Antitrust Law Section and Patent Trademark and Copyright Law Section*, reprinted in [1969–1983 Current Comment Transfer Binder] Trade Reg. Rep. (CCH) ¶ 50,146, at 50,146. (September 21, 1972). One of the no-nos was anticompetitive patent pooling, a topic addressed at length in Chapter 4. See generally, Daniel P. Homiller, *Patent Misuse in Patent Pool Licensing: From National Harrow to "The Nine No-Nos" to Not Likely*, Duke L. & Tech. Rev., March 3 2006, at 7; Robert J. Hoerner, *The Decline (and Fall?) of the Patent Misuse Doctrine in the Federal Circuit*, 69 Antitrust L.J. 669, 670 (2001) (description of "patent misuse" doctrine, a patent law non-statutory defense to patent infringement modeled on the lines of patent-related antitrust violations.

5.3.1.2 The Invention Test as Anti-Patent Policy Lever

Patent validity, along with anti competitive licensing practices, was another branch of the law that was used at times to reduce the economic clout wielded by patent owners. The story of mid-twentieth-century patent standards in the Supreme Court is captured well by a case involving costume jewelry. Fine jewelry is usually hand crafted, one piece at a time, with at least a certain degree of uniqueness. Costume jewelry aims to imitate fine jewelry as closely as possible, at a very much lower price. In 1938, an inventor named Thoger Jungerson applied a variation on an ancient molding technique to the copying of fine jewelry pieces. The Jungerson approach worked well enough for a number of jewelry companies to employ it on their own. Jungerson set out to enforce the patent on his method, and met with success in federal courts in Maryland and Pennsylvania.[199] But when he brought a case in New York, his luck changed. Over the objections of Learned Hand, a recognized expert in intellectual property cases, the Second Circuit Court of Appeals invalidated the Jungerson patent. Typical for the era, the newspaper headline said the Supreme Court agreed with the Second Circuit.[200] (The stinging dissent from Justice Robert Jackson did not make the papers). The Court applied a very stringent version of the requirement known as the invention test, invalidating a patent on a technique that seems to have acquired sime lustre in the eyes of the jewelry trade. What began as a patent cobering a new way to cast jewelry instead stood among a handful of mid-twentieth century cases that recast the "invention" test in a decidedly anti-patent mold.

In Jungerson's method, a hand-crafted original piece of jewelry could be copied using a high-quality mold. The specific technique was the age-old "lost wax" procedure, with a twist. In the lost wax procedure, the original piece is covered with a casting material such as rubber or silicone. The rubber mold is removed from the piece, then filled with a small amount of wax, which is spread around the inside of the mold to form a hollow wax copy of the inside of the mold. The hollow wax copy is reinforced with stucco or similar material, at which point this stucco-reinforced hollow copy is filled with hot liquid metal. The metal melts the wax while taking on the shape of the hollow stucco mold (thus, "lost wax"). When the metal has cooled, the stucco material is chipped away. What remains is a metal cast copy of the original jewelry piece.

[199] *Jungersen* v. *Jenkins*, 30 F. Supp. 615, 616 (D. Md. 1939) ("The patent relates to the jewelry art and shows a new combination, process or method of casting articles of jewelry of intricate design, at a cost very greatly less than by methods previously in vogue in the jewelry trade.").

[200] "Court Rejects Plea on Jewelry Patent," New York Times, October 18, 1955, at p. 32 (In a "patent infringement suit against a number of manufacturers of costume jewelry," the Court ruled against the inventor because "several other inventors held patents on virtually the same system.").

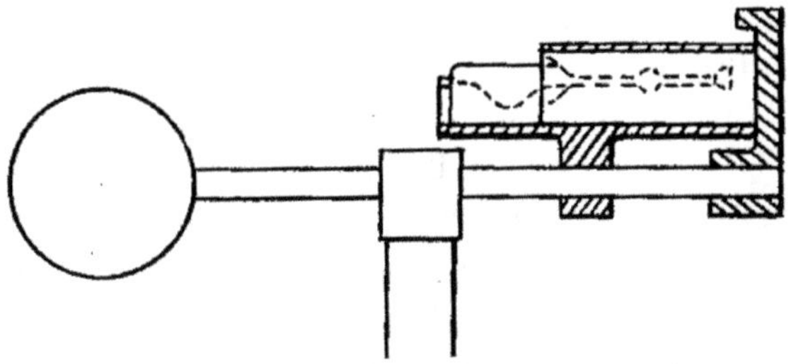

FIGURE 5.20. Jungerson "lost wax" casting technique for fine jewelry pieces. The structure on the right contains the mold for the jewelry piece; the mold is rotated rapidly around the axis (with the heavy ball on the left providing a counterweight); liquid metal is injected into the mold during rotation, and centrifugal force pushes the liquid metal into all the nooks and crannies of the mold. From US patent 2,118,468, issued May 24, 1938, to Thoger G. Jungerson

The twist that Jungerson added was to make the wax mold of the jewelry piece with the assistance of centrifugal force. The rubber or silicone copy of the original piece is rotated quickly while wax is injected into it. This fills the tiny spaces in the rubber mold, providing a very detailed wax copy of it. When this detailed wax copy is covered with material such as stucco, it is then easy to inject liquid metal into it. Thus Jungerson created a process for accurately and cheaply casting small, intricate objects such as fine metal jewelry. The basic design looks as in Figure 5.20.

The invention was a success. According to a legal filing in the case,

> Jungerson "took out patents in Canada, the United States, Great Britain, and many other countries. He eventually sold the Canadian patent for $5,000 . . . and went on with the exploitation of his patents in other countries, selling licenses in the United States, England, Sweden, Norway, Finland, Germany, France, Belgium, Australia, India, Brazil, Argentina, Java, etc. He issued somewhere between sixty and seventy licenses in the United States . . . From 1938 to October 16, 1945 "approximately $120,000" in royalties were collected [approximately $2.2 million in 2020 dollars] of which $10,250 [approximately $188,000 in 2020] was from foreign licenses.[201]

Not everyone who used the Jungerson technique paid up, however. So he asserted his patent – he sued some costume jewelry makers. Jungerson was successful in a suit against a Maryland company. The judge in the case noted that using Jungerson's method, jewelry could be copied at "a cost very greatly less than by methods previously in vogue in the jewelry trade."[202] The defendant in the case, who presumably knew something about the prior art of jewelry fabrication, even stipulated that the patent was valid, choosing to contest only whether its particular

[201] Brief for Petitioner Jungerson, in *Jungersen* v. *Ostby and Barton Co.*, 1948 WL 47126 (U.S.), at pp. 8–9 (U.S., 2006).

[202] *Jungersen* v. *Jenkins*, 30 F. Supp. 615, 616 (D. Md. 1939).

manufacturing technique infringed the patent. Jungerson then sued another company, this one in Pennsylvania. Again, the judge found the patent was both valid (that it embodied "invention"), and that it was infringed.[203] After an extensive review of the prior art, the judge concluded that Jungerson's combination of the old lost wax technique with centrifugal force at the wax-mold stage was inventive enough to merit a patent. And the judge added: "Even were there any doubt in my mind concerning novelty or patentability, the attested and conceded commercial success of the process would turn the scales in favor of patentability."[204]

A third judge, this one in New Jersey, concurred as well. He too said "in the view of the Court, the Jungersen patent discloses that 'flash of creative genius' sufficient to provide the basis of patentability,"[205] a statement that referenced (without citing) the 1944 Supreme Court *Cuno Engineering* case.[206] And in rebuttal to an argument that the "lost wax" technique was known as far back as ancient Egypt and the Renaissance, the judge added: "[I]t is no argument for invalidity to assert that the use of centrifugal force is the mere substitution of equivalents which do substantially the same thing [as the older, gravity-dependent, techniques]."[207]

Despite these accolades, one judge in the Southern District of New York disagreed, finding that Jungerson's technique lacked "invention" as required by the law.[208] The Second Circuit Court of Appeals affirmed. The majority, per Judge Clark, said Jungerson's patented design lacked invention and so was invalid: "[P]laintiff's patent can be sustained only if the use of force to cast the wax and the metal is such a change of a known method as to amount to invention. We think it is not."[209] The court emphasized that "the use of applied force to cast metal was shown in several patents prior to the plaintiff's."[210]

The most patent-savvy judge on the Circuit, however, was the well-respected Judge Learned Hand. With the majority and its views, he registered more than disagreement; the sentiment in his dissenting opinion was closer to dismay. He wrote:

203 *Jungersen* v. *Morris Kaysen Co.*, 31 F. Supp. 703 (E.D. Pa. 1940).

204 31 F. Supp. 703, 707 (E.D. Pa. 1940).

205 *Ostby & Barton Co.* v. *Jungersen*, 65 F. Supp. 652, 656 (D.N.J. 1946).

206 *Cuno Engineerg Corp.* v. *Automatic Devices Corp.*, 314 U.S. 84, 91 (1941) (Douglas, J.) (opinion invalidating patent for a dashboard-mounted cigar lighter for cars) ("[T]he new device, however useful it may be, must reveal the flash of creative genius not merely the skill of the calling. If it fails, it has not established its right to a private grant on the public domain.").

207 65 F. Supp. 652, 656 (D.N.J. 1946), aff'd, 163 F.2d 312 (3d Cir. 1947).

208 *Jungersen* v. *Baden*, 69 F. Supp. 922, 922 (S.D.N.Y. 1947), aff'd, 166 F.2d 807 (2d Cir. 1948), aff'd sub nom. *Jungersen* v. *Ostby & Barton Co.*, 335 U.S. 560 (1949). Later proceedings, see *Jungersen* v. *Axel Bros.*, 121 F. Supp. 712, 716–717 (S.D.N.Y.), aff'd sub nom. *Jungersen* v. *Axel Bros.*, 217 F.2d 646 (2d Cir. 1954).

209 *Jungersen* v. *Baden*, 166 F.2d 807, 809 (2d Cir. 1948), aff'd sub nom. *Jungersen* v. *Ostby & Barton Co.*, 335 U.S. 560 (1949).

210 166 F.2d 807, 809.

> [As to patentability,] the answer must therefore depend upon how we shall appraise the departure from what had gone before in terms of creative imagination; indeed, I do not understand what other test could be relevant. If that be the test, I submit that Jungersen's process meets it …
>
> If all the information was at hand, why was the new combination so long delayed? What better test of invention can one ask than the detection of that which others had all along had a strong incentive to discover, but had failed to see, though all the while it lay beneath their eyes?[211]

After this strong assertion, couched partly as rhetorical questioning, Judge Hand addressed with characteristic frankness the deep background that really drove the case. Hand recognized that a "shift" had taken place on the subject of patents; and that it was an "authoritative" shift. By this he surely meant the widely understood hostility to patents evidenced in Supreme Court "invention" cases such as *Cuno Engineering*.[212] But he might well have intended to embrace the entire gamut of Supreme Court jurisprudence on patents, and perhaps most prominently the patent-antitrust cases from the years prior to 1948. In this passage, Judge Hand expresses agnosticism concerning the overall project of the patent system, but states the embarrassing truth that the Supreme Court cases, despite paying "lip service," had made it nearly impossible to "apply the system as it is":

> True, the whole approach to the subject has suffered a shift within the last decade or so, which I recognize that we should accept as authoritative. Moreover, I am not of the slightest bias in favor of the present system; I should accept with equanimity a new system or no system. However, I confess myself baffled to know how to proceed, if we are at once to profess to apply the system as it is, and yet in every concrete instance we are to decide as though it did not exist as it is. In the case at bar, I can only say that, so far as I have been able to comprehend those factors which have been held to determine invention, and to which at least lip service continues to be paid, *the combination in suit has every hall-mark of a valid patent*.[213]

Strong words. Hand says in effect that to follow the "authoritative" guidance laid down by the Supreme Court in recent years, he has to decide as if "the system," meaning the patent system, does "not exist as it is." He stops short of saying the Supreme Court has, *sotto voce*, repealed the patent system. But he implies it, he strongly implies it.

The justices of the Supreme Court held true to form after this provocative jab from Judge Hand. They ignored it. The Court agreed with the Second Circuit

[211] *Jungersen* v. *Baden*, 166 F.2d 807, 812 (2d Cir. 1948) (L. Hand, J., dissenting), majority op. aff'd sub nom. *Jungersen* v. *Ostby & Barton Co.*, 335 U.S. 560 (1949).

[212] *Cuno Engineerg Corp.* v. *Automatic Devices Corp.*, 314 U.S. 84, 91 (1941) (Douglas, J.) (opinion invalidating patent for a dashboard-mounted cigar lighter for cars) ("[T]he new device, however useful it may be, must reveal the flash of creative genius not merely the skill of the calling. If it fails, it has not established its right to a private grant on the public domain.").

[213] 166 F.2d 807, 812 (2d Cir. 1948) (L. Hand, J., dissenting) (emphasis added).

majority and found Jungerson's patent invalid. This despite the fact that thirteen costume jewelry companies and partnerships had intervened in the appeal on behalf of the infringer – a strong indication that the patent had made a distinct impression throughout the costume jewelry field.[214] Justice Reed and a majority on the Supreme Court were unimpressed: "Long before the issuance of this patent ... those skilled in the art recognized and disclosed the necessity for the application of force in order to make molten materials fit snugly the intricate details of the mould," he wrote.[215] In this, the final appeal for inventor Jungerson, with the exception of two notable dissents,[216] there would be no attention to Jungerson's subtle adaptation of the prior art: his use of centrifugal force not to force hot liquid into a final mold during casting, but how to force wax into a mold shell as an intermediate step in casting. Lost wax was old; centrifugal force in casting was old; Jungerson's invention was not significant. One imagines the costume jewelry industry celebrating the elimination of this "insignificant" patent and returning right away to their extensive use of the Jungerson technique.

Justice Jackson, in the second of two forceful dissents, sounded the final, sour, note on the proceedings:

> I think this patent meets the patent statute's every requirement. And confronted by this record an industry heretofore galled by futility and frustration may well be amazed at the Court's dismissal of Jungersen's ingenious and successful efforts. Of course, commercial success will not fill any void in an invalid patent. But it may fill the void in our understanding of what the invention has meant to those whose

[214] Brief for Petitioner Jungerson, *Jungersen* v. *Ostby and Barton Co.*, 1948 WL 47126 (U.S.), at p. 3:

> After issue was joined, seven corporations and fifteen individuals comprising six partnerships were allowed to intervene ... The intervenors are jewelry manufacturers and the stated justification for the intervention was that "by mutual agreement among themselves and with defendants, intervenors have openly participated in and contributed to the defense of this suit, to the knowledge of plaintiff."

[215] 335 U.S. 560, 564.

[216] Justice Frankfurter, joined by Justice Burton, simply reproduced the Learned Hand dissent from the Second Circuit opinion – a remarkable nod in the direction of the greater craftsman of patent doctrine. Frankfurter added a brief prologue, notable in part for a probably unintended slight of the costume jewelry business. Nevertheless, Frankfurter showed interest in, if not support for, Hand's strongly implied view that the Supreme Court had come close to abrogating the patent system:

> This is not one of those patent controversies that carry serious consequences for an important industry and thereby for the general public. The case does, however, raise basic issues regarding the judiciary's role in our existing patent system. These issues were stated by Judge Learned Hand when the litigation was before the Court of Appeals for the Second Circuit. Since this Court's opinion has not, to my mind, met the questions which he raised, and since I cannot improve upon what Judge Learned Hand wrote, I adopt his opinion as mine.

Jungersen v. *Ostby & Barton Co.*, 335 U.S. 560, 568 (1949) (Frankfurter, J., dissenting). The second dissent was by Justice Jackson, see infra.

> livelihood, unlike our own, depends upon their knowledge of the art . . . Jungersen's success was grounded . . . in the hard-headed judgment of a highly competitive and critical if not hostile industry. Knowing well its need for and its failure to achieve improvements on available processes, that industry discarded them, adopted this outsider's invention, and made it a commercial success . . .
>
> It would not be difficult to cite many instances of patents that have been granted, improperly I think, and without adequate tests of invention by the Patent Office. *But I doubt that the remedy for such Patent Office passion for granting patents is an equally strong passion in this Court for striking them* down *so that the only patent that is valid is one which this Court has not been able to get its hands on.*
>
> I agree with the opinion of Judge Learned Hand.[217]

The dissent's statement about "the only valid patent" has become a classic. But besides the blunt language, what is noteworthy here is the admission that there may well be a problem with the quality of patents issued by the Patent Office. There is an echo here of Judge Hand's agnostic attitude toward the value of the patent system. But Jackson shares a tacit understanding with Hand: Invalidating every patent reaching the courts is not an effective solution to the patent quality problem. As a policy, it has to fail: very few issued patents reach the courts generally, let alone the Second Circuit or Supreme Court. More importantly, to strike down patents that seem valid, and that arguably embody the benefits of granting patents, deprives the Patent Office and lower courts of valuable guidance. As long as Congress has not eliminated patents, Hand and Jackson are saying, patent institutions must sort good from bad. A blanket policy of calling all patents bad (invalid) cannot substitute for Congressional judgment, and it only causes uncertainty. As we will see, Hand and Jackson may have been dissenters in the *Jungerson* case, but other actors – in particular, the professional patent bar – were paying close attention. The dissenters' views found full expression in the soon-to-be-drafted 1952 Patent Act.

5.3.2 *Adaptive Patent Doctrine: Structure, Function, and Timing in the Chemical Arts*

Patent law adapted admirably to the emergence of modern chemical research. Some important adjustments were needed, because this research is quite different from the pursuit of inventions in the mechanical and electrical fields – the primary domain of patent law prior to the twentieth century. In these fields, researchers set out to achieve a desired end. They begin with at least a loose idea of what the final structure should look like, based on what they want it to do. Thus Edison, developing the light bulb, knew he needed an evacuated globe, a power source, and an

[217] 335 U.S. 560, 572 (Jackson, J., dissenting) (emphasis added). Jackson referred to Jungerson as an "outsider" because he was originally from Denmark and made his invention in Canada before becoming a naturalized US citizen. See Brief for Petitioner Jungerson, *Jungersen* v. *Ostby and Barton Co.*, 1948 WL 47126 (U.S.), at p. 1.

incandescing element. Inventors in the shoemaking, textile, papermaking, and auto industries – typical mechanical fields – work in much the same way. In general, the structure of any eventual invention is envisioned, at least vaguely, because structure is shaped by the desired function.

Chemical invention is different. Things are often the other way around: A search for a desired function or property does not usually begin with any specific idea of the required chemical structure. In most cases, a large number of candidate structures are screened for some low-level evidence of workability.[218] If some candidates show promise, they, and variants on them, are tested further. With luck and a good deal of persistence, a handful of candidates may stand out. These will usually share some structural similarities; only when these structures are identified will there be a chance of linking these structures to the desired function. But even this is not essential: A fair number of effective pharmaceuticals were deployed long before their chemical structure was known, and obviously therefore without knowing why their structure made them effective.

5.3.2.1 The Utility Requirement for Chemical Inventions

Put simply, much chemical experimentation is a search through known structures to find one that achieves the desired purpose. Function follows form. This other-way-around feature of the chemical arts puts pressure on several doctrines in patent law. The first is the law of utility. For an invention to be patentably useful, it simply has to be operable – to perform its intended purpose. It need not be outstanding, superior, or commercially viable when a patent application is filed. It just has to work. Mechanical and electrical inventions almost never fail to meet this requirement because they are built from the beginning with an end or purpose in mind.[219] But utility poses problems for chemical inventions. Chemical structures are known at

[218] In the chemical field, structures are often synthesized and described because of their inherent interest. Chemical synthesis may be of interest to show that a certain structure is possible, or to show that a former structural principle can be extended or modified, etc. Cf. In re Stemniski, 444 F.2d 581, 585 (C.C.P.A. 1971) ("Considering only the structure of the involved compounds as an academic matter or in the abstract – as perhaps would a chemist who has little interest or concern in what the compounds ultimately are useful for as a practical matter . . . "); Larry S. Gangnes, *Patents Patentability of Chemical Compounds-Chemical Compounds Are Patentable Over Structurally Obvious Prior Art Compounds Even in the Absence of Proof That the Claimed Compounds Exhibit Properties Not Actually Possessed by the Prior Art Compounds*, 50 Tex. L. Rev. 566, 571 (1972) (discussing chemical patent case where "the prior art compounds were not known to possess any significant property or utility.").

[219] See *Process Control Corp.* v. *HydReclaim Corp.*, 190 F.3d 1350, 1358 (Fed. Cir. 1999) (basic operability is all that is required). They might lack utility if they have only insidious uses, e.g., a torture machine. See Robert P. Merges, *Intellectual Property in Higher Life Forms: The Patent System and Controversial Technologies*, 47 Md. L. Rev. 1051, 1062–1068 (1988). Scientifically preposterous inventions also lack utility. See *Newman* v. *Quigg*, 681 F. Supp. 16, 17–18 (D.D.C. 1988), aff'd 877 F.2d 1575 (Fed. Cir. 1989) (perpetual motion machine); In re Swartz, 232 F.3d 862 (Fed. Cir. 2000) ("cold fusion").

the outset in many cases,[220] so the difficult issue concerns evidence of utility. In particular, how much evidence of usefulness must be proven as of the patent filing date to make for a valid patent?

The salience of this question arises from the pressure on inventors to file a patent application as early as possible. We have seen already that the chemical field is highly competitive. So virtually all chemical researchers know that other would-be inventors are simultaneously pursuing the same quarry they are. Even before the United States adopted a "first to file" priority rule, there was a premium on early patent filing.[221] With this in mind, chemists had strong incentives to file patent applications at the first hint or whiff of utility. Or even before then.

But this raises a problem. If the patent system permits very early filing, too many resources may be diverted toward filing numerous speculative patent applications covering chemical structures. If the utility standard is too lax, applicants will file patents on all manner of chemical structures that *may* in the future turn out to have utility. The result would be a proliferation of speculative patents. These patents on unproven structures would undermine legitimate chemical research. A chemist who discovers an effective compound, for example a promising therapeutic drug, might find that one or more earlier-granted patents already covers the results of her work. Indeed, the hope of covering someone else's later-discovered high-value invention is one of the reasons an earlier applicant might file speculative applications in the first place.

One important case from the 1960s includes some details that should clarify how this principle applied.[222] An inventor named Manson filed a patent application with the intent to contest priority with an already-issued patent.[223] To initiate the priority contest, Manson needed to show that his patent application met the requirements of patentability, including the utility requirement. The patent examiner rejected Manson's application on the ground that it lacked utility. The Court of Customs

[220] And it is relatively easy to find them with specialized tools designed to search for chemical structures. See Christina Mulligan and Timothy B. Lee, Scaling the Patent System ("Chemical formulas allow efficient retrieval of chemical patents, just as geographic coordinates allow efficient retrieval of real estate records. In other words, chemical patents are indexable. That means that finding a patent based on its chemical formula is [relatively easy] . . . just as it is for real property records.").

[221] So as to preserve patent rights outside the United States, where the "first to file" priority rule has long been in effect; and, in the pre-AIA days, so as to gain the upper hand in a patent interference in the United States, in which the first filer (or "senior party") enjoyed several procedural advantages.

[222] *Brenner* v. *Manson*, 383 U.S. 519 (1966).

[223] The process invention Manson claimed related to endocrinal-active compounds and, by coincidence, the applicant Manson was seeking a priority determination (in a patent interference) against two of the Syntex researchers (Ringold and Rosenkranz) whose patent on a birth control pill was cited earlier in this chapter. See US patent 2,908,693 "Process for the production of 2-MethylDihydrotestoserones," issued to Howard J. Ringold and George Rosenkranz, October 13, 1959, assigned to Syntex, Inc. (cited as prior art against the Manson patent application, which claimed the same process).

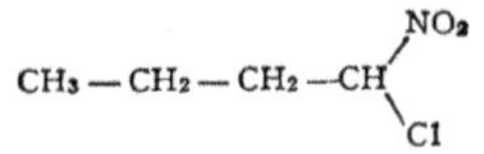

FIGURE 5.21. Lower homologue

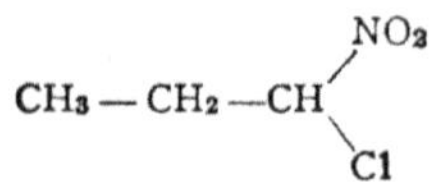

FIGURE 5.22. Higher homologue. This molecule adds an additional methylene (CH_2) group between the initial CH (methylidyne) and the CH_3 (methyl) group on the left. From In re Hass, 141 F.2d 130, 131 (C.C.P.A. 1944)

and Patent Appeals (which heard Patent Office in this pre-Federal Circuit era) reversed this rejection in an extreme opinion which held that any process that successfully produces a known compound has utility, even if the compound that it produces itself has no known use.[224] Manson made a number of arguments to the Supreme Court when it granted review of the Appeals Court decision. The most important of Manson's points related to a prior scientific article that disclosed chemicals very similar to the ones made by his claimed process. The similarity was that the prior art compound was an "adjacent homologue" of the compound produced by Manson's process.

A homologue is a close chemical cousin, another member of a finite series of structurally related compounds. The chemical structures shown in Figures 5.21 and 5.22 (which are not from the *Manson* case) are adjacent homologues, with the "lower" member shown first.

This was enough, Manson said, to make his patent valid. His thought was that a disclosed structure that is very similar to a structure with proven utility has enough proof of usefulness to deserve a patent. The Supreme Court disagreed:

> [The prior art reference from] 1956 ... reveal[s] that an adjacent homologue of the steroid yielded by [Manson's] process has been demonstrated to have tumor-inhibiting effects in mice, and that this discloses the requisite utility. We do not accept ... [this] theor[y] as an adequate basis for overriding the determination of the Patent Office that the "utility" requirement has not been met.[225]

Put simply, Manson filed too soon – before adequate proof of utility. The adjacent homologue in the prior art might be useful, but that did not render the claimed homologue useful. Something more was required for that: more than Manson had on hand, or was able to prove, as of his patent filing date. Manson may have made a nontrivial scientific contribution in creating his process for making the compound

[224] In re Manson, 333 F.2d 234, 235 (C.C.P.A. 1964).

[225] *Brenner* v. *Manson*, 383 U.S. 519, 531 (1966).

that was similar to the ones in the prior art. But this contribution was, nevertheless, unpatentable unless and until Manson proved a practical utility for it:[226]

> This is not to say that we mean to disparage the importance of contributions to the fund of scientific information short of the invention of something "useful," or that we are blind to the prospect that what now seems without "use" may tomorrow command the grateful attention of the public. But a patent is not a hunting license. It is not a reward for the search, but compensation for its successful conclusion. "(A) patent system must be related to the world of commerce rather than to the realm of philosophy" . . . [227]

The Court's oft-cited statement that "a patent is not a hunting license" aptly summarizes the idea that patents should not be awarded too early in the research process.

On the other hand, patent courts recognize that it is also unwise to require too much proof of utility. Many cases, for example, state that patentable utility is far below the standard required to prove that a drug candidate is "safe and effective" to the satisfaction of the Food and Drug Administration (FDA). The rationale again derives from the competitive nature of chemical research. If multiple research teams are vying for a common goal, and if FDA-worthy proof of utility is required to obtain a valid patent, some researchers may be scared away. As one important case framed the issue,

> FDA approval . . . is not a prerequisite for finding a compound useful within the meaning of the patent laws. Usefulness in patent law, and in particular in the context of pharmaceutical inventions, necessarily includes the expectation of further research and development. The stage at which an invention in this field becomes useful is well before it is ready to be administered to humans. Were we to require Phase II testing [i.e., extensive human subject testing under FDA rules] in order to prove utility, the associated costs would prevent many companies from obtaining patent protection on promising new inventions, thereby eliminating an incentive to pursue, through research and development, potential cures in many crucial areas such as the treatment of cancer.[228]

[226] The Patent Board opinion was reversed in In re Manson, 333 F.2d 234 (C.C.P.A. 1964) (an outcome that was itself later reversed (reinstating the Board opinion) in *Brenner* v. *Manson*, 383 U.S. 519 (1966)). The *In re Manson* CCPA opinion said:

> [T]he [patent appeals] board would require that before an applicant may have his claims to a new process placed in interference to determine the issue of priority of invention . . . he must show that a utility for the compound produced by the process was known at the time he invented the process. This requirement cannot be justified . . .

333 F. 2d 234, 235.

[227] *Brenner* v. *Manson*, 383 U.S. 519, 535–36 (1966) (citation omitted).

[228] In re Brana, 51 F.3d 1560, 1568 (Fed. Cir. 1995) (citing older cases in the opinion).

The worry is that one's research team might spend tens or even hundreds of millions of dollars in pursuit of an effective drug compound, only to find that just prior to assembling the requisite proof, another team has won the race. This would make chemical research very risky: in our example, the firm spends millions and comes away with no patent. Risk on this scale might force one or more teams to forego the race altogether; and in the extreme, maybe no team at all will pursue the goal.

The law of chemical patenting responded by crafting a utility doctrine designed to get this balance just right. Chemical utility doctrine seeks to require (1) some proof of "practical utility," enough to prevent purely speculative patenting; while (2) awarding a patent early enough in the process to make for a manageable degree of financial risk. The losing teams in the race might lose out, but they don't lose so much that they are driven away at the outset. The winning team – the research group that is able to prove "practical utility" first – gains the knowledge that the remainder of their expensive research will take place under the protective umbrella of a patent.[229] No other team can take away the winner's exclusive right to the end result. This encourages the winning team to finish out the remainder of the research, secure in the knowledge that if the promise of utility ultimately leads to a viable pharmaceutical treatment, the patent on that treatment will belong to them.

In setting the utility standard, courts intuited a practical solution to the balancing problem.[230] It has much in common with the rules that evolved with respect to mining claims. The problem there is the same: how to encourage early investment in effort while not rewarding unproductive speculation. This preference for early-stage effort over immediate investment takes many forms. In purely economic terms, early-stage effort may be preferred because it reveals valuable information.

[229] This feature is captured in economic models of "patent races," in which all other entrants drop out of the race as soon as someone wins. See Glenn C. Loury, *Market Structure and Innovation: A Reformulation*, 94 Q.J. Econ. 395 (1979). Partha Dasgupta and Joseph Stiglitz, *Uncertainty, Industrial Structure and the Speed of R&D*, 11 Bell J. Econ. 1 (1980). For a more sophisticated version of the racing concept, see Drew Fudenberg, Richard Gilbert, Joseph Stiglitz, and Jean Tirole, *Preemption, Leapfrogging and Competition in Patent Races*, 22 Euro. Econ. Rev. 3 (1983).

[230] For elaboration, see See Robert P. Merges and John F. Duffy, Patent Law and Policy (Charlottesville, VA: LexisNexis Publishing, 4th ed., 2007), at pp. 253–256, section on "Note on the Economics of the Utility Requirement: Races, Rent Dissipation, and Anticommons Problems." See generally, Dean Lueck, *The Rule of First Possession and the Design of the Law*, 38 J. L. & Econ. 393, 417–418 (1995). See generally, Dotan Oliar and James Y. Stern, *Right on Time: First Possession in Property and Intellectual Property*, 99 B.U. L. Rev. 395, 395 (2019); Matthew Erramouspe, Comment, *Staking Patent Claims on the Human Blueprint: Rewards and Rent-Dissipating Races*, 43 UCLA L. Rev. 961 (1996).

In the United States, the General Mining Act of 1872,[231] for example, requires some minimum exploratory activity before a miner can "perfect" his or her claim. Historically, mining claims of limited scope could be staked by initial locators for $5.00 per claim (with limits on the number allowable per miner at any one time). To perfect title, however, miners had to do something more: They had to invest at least $100 per year in mining-related improvements on a claim.[232] This level of investment required a showing of real effort to develop the claim – while falling considerably short of a requirement that a miner show actual mineral deposits of any kind.[233] Note that preliminary development activity reveals valuable information about the nature and extent of mineral deposits on the claimed site and, often enough, on contiguous sites as well – akin in many ways to the value of learning that a chemical compound has some practical utility.[234]

One additional reason that this stake- and- develop system might be preferred is to reward hard work – to demonstrate a societal preference for effort over access to capital. (A Hurstian perspective, as explained in Chapter 4.) Social and moral attitudes reflect some ambivalence about speculation, and society might well decide there is long-term value in rules that strive to prevent excessive rewards for speculators.[235] There is also concern that an early speculator may end up capturing value that is attributable to the efforts of others. A clever early-stage property claim over a resource may rise in value when another person expends effort to develop that resource. In chemical research, this would take the form of a broad, early patent on a large family of chemical structures. If one or more of the structures were later

[231] 30 U.S.C. §§ 22–42.

[232] See Gordon Morris Bakken, The Mining Law of 1872: Past, Politics and Prospects 55 (Albuquerque: University of New Mexico Press, 2008) (citing General Mining Act, section 5). The $ 100 per year expenditure and mining patent perfection requirements are spelled out in United States v. Shumway, 199 F. 3d 1093, 1099 (9th Cir. 1999).

[233] While there are no dollar thresholds in the law of chemical patent utility, the current standard requires investment in preliminary screening of a pharmaceutical compound, with the lab-based screening test showing some level of effectiveness or success. See In re Brana, 51 F.3d 1560 (Fed. Cir. 1995) (So-called in vitro, or lab-based test, whereby claimed compound was found to kill an appreciable number of cancer cells in a standard lab cancer cell line, held sufficient to establish utility. FDA approval or human testing – which is far more expensive – is not required.)

[234] See generally, Edmund Kitch, *The Nature and Function of the Patent System*, 20 J. L. & Econ. 265 (1977) (drawing on 1872 federal mining law to support arguments about how patent law is structured). For mining claims as well as patents, the requirement of some tangible early effort prevents pure speculation. Society benefits as a result. Pure speculation tends to drive bids so high that most or all of the latent value in the resource being claimed is "dissipated" in the bidding process. So much is expended to acquire title that the economy as a whole gains nothing; the bidding represents a simple exchange of dollars today for future investment returns. See generally, Mark F. Grady and Jay I. Alexander, *Patent Law and Rent Dissipation*, 78 Va. L. Rev. 305 (1991).

[235] See, e.g., David D. Haddock, *First Possession versus Optimal Timing: Limiting the Dissipation of Economic Value*, 64 Wash. U. L.Q. 775 (1986); Dean Lueck, The Rule of First Possession and the Design of the Law.

laboriously explored by another person, and shown to be valuable, the early claimant would in effect "reap where they had not sown."[236] The utility requirement as applied to chemical research is just one of many legal doctrines that embody this principle.

5.3.2.2 Chemical Nonobviousness

Chemical structures by themselves have some value. But ultimately, in the eyes of patent law, what matters most is what a structure does. Utility, as we have seen, requires some minimal proof that a chemical structure does something. The next requirement for a patent is novelty – only inventions that are new are eligible. Newness for a chemical invention depends on exactly how the invention is covered by the written patent claims. A claim to a chemical structure – a molecule, for example – requires that the structure not be present in the prior art earlier than the patent's filing date. Even a structure present in the prior art, but with no known use, knocks out a claim to the same structure.[237] In such a case, however, it is possible to obtain a process patent for a new *use* of that chemical structure. This is an example of a process patent; its format would be "the use of [old] chemical structure X for [the newly discovered use]." This and similar formats[238] can be used where the old chemical structure was known for one use and turns out to have an additional use – for example, when a chemical structure being tested for use against high blood pressure turns out to facilitate male hair growth.[239]

So, to recap: structures are valuable, but you have to have evidence of utility, And an old structure can be claimed for a new use. What about a new structure that is very similar to an old one? Can it be patented?

[236] The legal and moral dimensions of property rights as they relate to the efforts of others are explored in Robert P. Merges, Justifying Intellectual Property (Cambridge, MA: Harvard University Press, 2011), at chapter 6 ("The Proportionality Principle"), pp. 159 ff. On the "reap where one has not sown" principle and IP law, see Wendy J. Gordon, *On Owning Information: Intellectual Property and the Restitutionary Impulse*, 78 Va. L. Rev. 149, 156 (1992); Robert P. Merges, *Restitution, Property and the Right of Publicity: A Tribute to Professor Wendy Gordon*, 99 B.U. L. Rev. 2415 (2019).

[237] In re Hafner, 410 F.2d 1403, 1405 (C.C.P.A. 1969) (holding that an application for a chemical patent can be rejected where the chemical itself, but no use for the chemical, was in the prior art).

[238] E.g., "the combination of old compound X with a carrier [or substrate or delivery method etc.] made from Y." See Ex Parte Skuballa, 12 U.S.P.Q.2d 1570, 1989 WL 274384 (B.P.A.I. 1989).

[239] *Upjohn Co.* v. *Medtron Lab.*, 751 F. Supp. 416, 418 (S.D.N.Y. 1990) (inventor set out to "study minoxidil as an anti-hypertensive agent in humans," and it was then claimed in a process patent for treating male baldness. See US patent 4596812, "Methods and solutions for treating male pattern alopecia [baldness]," issued June 24, 1986, to Charles A. Chidsey and Guinter Kahn, assigned to Upjohn Co. (patent on treatment for male baldness, one of two patents at issue in the *Upjohn* case).

The answer changed over time, showing how patent law adapted to the proliferation of chemical inventions and the importance of chemical research. In the earlier cases, particularly in the 1940s, a very similar structure spelled the death of a product claim.[240] Doctrinally, this was a question of "invention" (or later, nonobviousness). It is not a question of novelty: that only bars a patent when a claimed structure is identical to a structure in the prior art. Adjacent homologs and isomers[241] are typical examples of close structural similarity. Over time, the law of chemical patenting recognized that this "mechanical" rule of nonobviousness was a mistake. In a number of important cases, a minor structural variant on a prior art structure turned out to have significant benefits. Particularly in pharmaceuticals, the vagaries of human physiology dictate that a small change can lead to big differences in efficacy. Because of this, the early cases were later overruled. Judges deciding whether a claimed structure was nonobvious began to look at the combination of structure plus function.[242] A minor structural change that leads to an unexpected result, or a surprisingly high level of effectiveness for a predicted result, no longer bars the award of a patent. This specialized branch of patent law came to appreciate the unique structure-function relationships that hold true in the world of chemistry.[243]

[240] "[T]he nature of homologues and the close relationship the physical and chemical properties of one member of a series bears to adjacent members is such that a presumption of unpatentability arises against a claim directed to a composition of matter, the adjacent homologue of which is old in the art." In re Henze, 181 F.2d 196, 201 (C.C.P.A. 1950), overruled by In re Stemniski, 444 F.2d 581 (C.C.P.A. 1971). This case was often cited along with a similar case, In re Hass, 141 F.2d 122 (C.C.P.A. 1944), to form what was called the "*Hass-Henze* doctrine." See Bruce M. Collins, *The Forgotten Chemistry of the* Hass-Henze *Doctrine*, 44 J. Pat. Off. Soc'y 284 (1962); Alvin Guttag, *The* Hass-Henze *Doctrine*, 43 J. Pat. Off. Soc'y 808 (1961).

[241] Two molecules are isomers if they have the identical structure, but different geometries. One common type is a stereoisomer, where two molecules are mirror-images of each other (enantiomers). A number of molecules have this property, where they can be "flipped" along an axis and result in stable but mirror-image versions of each other. See www.chemguide.co.uk/basicorg/isomerism/structural.html.

[242] See In re Papesch, 315 F.2d 381, 387 (C.C.P.A. 1963); In re Stemniski, 444 F.2d 581 (C.C.P.A. 1971). See generally, Larry S. Gangnes, Patents Patentability of Chemical Compounds-Chemical Compounds:

> Hinting at the fundamental rationale of the decision, the court suggested [in *Stemniski*] that structural similarity should not determine obviousness when the prior art lacks any suggestion of utility or beneficial properties that would motivate a person skilled in the art to modify the reference compound. Citing *Papesch* ... for the proposition that structural obviousness does not necessarily indicate obviousness of the subject matter as a whole, the court delivered the coup de grace to the *Hass-Henze* doctrine.

[243] One way to view this is to say that structural similarity does not predict the success of particularly high-functioning structures. From this perspective, chemical cases follow the same principle as all cases under 35 U.S.C. § 103, the nonobviousness requirement. See *KSR Int'l Co. v. Teleflex Inc.*, 550 U.S. 398, 401 (2007) ("[A] combination of familiar elements according to known methods is likely to be obvious when it does no more than yield predictable results."); Robert P. Merges, Uncertainty and the Standard of Patentability.

5.3.2.3 Enablement and Claim Scope

To judge from the cases and commentary, one of the greatest challenges created by the analytic/structuralist trend in chemical research was to traditional notions of claim scope. In particular, greater theoretical understanding of the relationship between different members of the same structural "family" caused patent applicants to seek claims covering a large number of embodiments. At the same time, since these techniques were diffusing rapidly across the international chemical industry, competitive pressure was pushing applicants to draft claims broad enough to thwart the efforts of skilled chemists to devise non-infringing compounds that were functionally identical to those of the applicant.

A prime example of the pressures for claim expansion is the special form of genus claim, termed a "Markush expression," that was created around this time.[244] Such claims take the form of an expression such as "An X selected from the group consisting of A, B, and C," where X describes the functional class to which A, B, and C belong. These claims are often, but certainly not always, used in patents to chemical compositions.[245]

[244] So named from Ex parte Markush, 1925 Dec. Comm'r Pats. 126, 340 Off. Gazz. Pat. Off. 839 (Comm'r Pat. 1924). See 2 D. Chisum, Patents § 8.06[2] (1978 & Supp. 2019); Ronald B. Hildreth, Preparation of Patent Claims: Review of the Basics, in Advanced Claim Drafting and Amendment Writing Workshop 7, 12–13 (Practicing Law Institute, Patents, Copyrights, Trademarks and Literary Property Course Handbook Series, No. 327, 1991). Hildreth gives the following example:

1. A composition comprising
   (a) a solid selected from the group consisting of
      (1) sodium chloride,
      (2) potassium chloride and
      (3) lithium chloride;
   (b) a liquid selected from the group consisting of
      (1) sulfuric acid,
      (2) nitric acid . . . .

Another example would be:

1. A compound of the formula
   R_1-CH_2-COOH

wherein R_1 is phenyl, naphthyl or anthracyl.

The "family" of variations encompassed by a Markush group must share a common principle. As stated in In re Schechter, 205 F.2d 185, 189 (C.C.P.A. 1953), such a claim will be allowed "where the substances grouped have a community of chemical and physical characteristics which justify their inclusion in a common group, and such inclusion is not repugnant to the principles of scientific classification." See generally, In re Harnisch, 631 F.2d 716, 719–720 (C. C.P.A. 1980) (summarizing *Markush* case and claim format).

[245] See, e.g., a rather whimsical patent claiming a cigarette filter made of cheese, whose claim 2 reads: "A cigarette filter according to claim 1, in which the cheese comprises grated particles of cheese selected from the group consisting of Parmesan, Romano, Swiss and cheddar cheeses." US patent 3,234,948, "Cheese filter cigaret," issued to Stuart M. Stebbings, on February 15, 1966.

Expanding claims drew a predictable judicial response: elaboration of the doctrine on claim breadth, under what is termed today the enablement requirement. An important early case was *Bracewell* v. *Passaic Paint Works*.[246] Here the patentee had claimed a textile dying method for imprinting colored patterns on a background of aniline-black. The claim recited the use of any "zinc compound" as the resist factor in the dying that prevented the oxidation of the black-dyed background. The court commented as follows:

> The essential feature of the process is the use of a zinc compound as the active element in the resist. The oxide of zinc when used in the process performs the double function of acting as a resist for the aniline black and as a base of the fixing agent which fixes the color to the cloth. Oxide, hydrate or carbonate of zinc seem to be regarded by the complainant as indispensable to the patented process. In this connection it must be remembered that [the inventor], neither in the description nor in the claim, confines himself to zinc oxide or any particular form of zinc solution. He prefers oxide but distinctly asserts that he is not restricted to the same and that any zinc compound may be used, and that he is not confined to the exact quantity of zinc specified ... It is proved beyond contradiction that there is a large number of zinc compounds, that few of them are capable of acting as a resist against aniline black and that whether they will so act or not can only be determined by experiment and cannot be known in advance ... The expert witnesses, all chemists of wide experience, agree that an untried zinc compound could not be used in the Whitehead process with any certainty that it would operate successfully as a resist against prussiate aniline black. For instance, neither zinc sulphide, which chemically resembles zinc oxide, nor zinc chloride will operate successfully while zinc acetate will do so. How is a calico printer to know what zinc compound will operate and what will not? ... [The inventor] has claimed all zinc compounds as broadly as possible in the claim ... He stretched his net to catch as infringers all users of zinc compounds and if he has stretched it to the breaking point he has only himself to blame. The courts should be liberal in construing patents, but they cannot rewrite the description and claims, they cannot construct an entirely new patent even to save a meritorious invention. *If the complainant's contention be correct a patentee can claim blindly an entire group of compounds relying on the court, after subsequent investigation and experiment, to limit the claim to the one which gives the best results. This will not do.*[247]

A contemporary case, *Matheson* v. *Campbell*,[248] makes a similar point on the way to a holding that the claims in the patent at issue were too broad in light of the specification's disclosure:

> The evidence shows conclusively that the statement that they had discovered that "any sulpho acid of any radical" treated according to their process would give the

[246] 107 F. 467 (C.C.S.D.N.Y. 1901).
[247] 107 F. 467, at 472–473 (emphasis added).
[248] 78 Fed. 910, 921, 923 (2d Cir. 1897).

> product they said it would was untrue. Briefly stated, the "discovery" which the inventors profess to disclose is that all mono sulpho acids, and all di sulpho acids treated in a prescribed way, will give a specific result, while the fact is that, so far as appears no mono sulpho acid thus treated will give such result, and when they professed thus to disclose their "discovery" they either knew that the mono sulpho acids will not give such result, or else knew nothing about the reaction of mono sulpho acids under such process. In either case the "discovery" which they disclosed is not the "discovery" which they made, and it is for the discovery or invention which the patentee makes and discloses that patent issues.

In the early twentieth century the patent practice literature was full of analysis of the expanding doctrine on "breadth and scope of chemical claims."[249] There is praise in at least one source for an early case holding that claims to a broad genus ought to be construed as limited to those species that later turn out to be operative – an example of the now-outmoded style of claim construction that focused on the inventor's actual contribution.[250]

The enablement standard from these early cases has been considerably liberalized over the years. Broad chemical claims are routinely upheld. The conventional defense of such broad claims is that it is possible to adequately enable them because the level of skill in the chemical field has risen dramatically over the years.[251] Thus chemists are now adept at making routine substitutions, and the legal standard does not require that an applicant actually construct each instance of the set of things encompassed by her patent claim. Thus, in one case, a patent application was filed in 1968 for "Organometallic Complexes As Alkylaromatic Oxidation Catalysts."[252] The key contribution of the claimed invention was that organometallic chemical complexes could be reacted so as to form "hydroperoxides," which were discovered to have excellent catalyzing effects in the refining of crude oil:[253]

[249] See, for example, the article with that title in 2 J. Pat. Off. Soc'y 598 (1919).

[250] In re Ellis, 167 O.G. 981 (1899).

[251] The more highly educated the average chemical inventor becomes, the more routine substitutions in chemical formulae are assumed to be straightforward. This pushes in favor of permitting broadened claims, because "routine" (but not "undue") experimentation is permitted to extrapolate from a patent specification's disclosure to the actual synthesis of all or most members of the claimed genus. See In re Wands, 858 F.2d 731, 737 (Fed. Cir. 1988) (emphasis added):

> Factors to be considered in determining whether a disclosure would require undue experimentation ... include (1) the quantity of experimentation necessary, (2) the amount of direction or guidance presented, (3) the presence or absence of working examples, (4) the nature of the invention, (5) the state of the prior art, (6) *the relative skill of those in the art*, (7) the predictability or unpredictability of the art, and (8) the breadth of the claims.

[252] In re Angstadt, 537 F.2d 498, 499 (C.C.P.A. 1976).

[253] See generally, Christian R. Mercilly, *Present Status and Future Trends in Catalysis for Refining and Petrochemicals*, 216 J. Catalysis 47 (2003) (includes discussion of organometallics in context of oil refining catalysts). Angstadt was a chemist at Sun Oil Company, later Sunoco. See related US patent 3,836,589, filed September 24, 1969, issued September 17, 1974, to Howard P. Angstadt, assigned to Sun Oil Co.

> [T]he oxidation products of the instant process are generally, alcohols, aldehydes, ketones, hydroperoxides, or mixtures thereof. Of these various products, maximization of the formation of the hydroperoxides is generally preferred . . . Accordingly, as a preferred embodiment of this invention, it has been discovered that certain of the various metals . . . are particularly effective as catalysts in the preparation of hydroperoxides from secondary and tertiary alkylaromatic compounds . . . [254]

The patent examiner rejected the resulting Markush claims as too broad, noting that although the applicants (Angstadt and Griffin) had synthesized forty working examples of their catalysts, the claims encompassed far more than forty species, and the specification gave no guidance about which of the many claimed species would actually work. The Board of Appeals supported the examiner, but the Court of Appeals reversed:

> Appellants [i.e., the inventors] have apparently not disclosed every catalyst which will work; they have apparently not disclosed every catalyst which will not work. The question, then, is whether in an unpredictable art, [the] section [35 U.S.C.] 112 [enablement provision] requires disclosure of a test with every species covered by a claim. To require such a complete disclosure would apparently necessitate a patent application or applications with "thousands" of examples or the disclosure of "thousands" of catalysts along with information as to whether each exhibits catalytic behavior resulting in the production of hydroperoxides. More importantly, such a requirement would force an inventor seeking adequate patent protection to carry out a prohibitive number of actual experiments. This would tend to discourage inventors from filing patent applications in an unpredictable area since the patent claims would have to be limited to those embodiments which are expressly disclosed. A potential infringer could readily avoid "literal" infringement of such claims by merely finding another analogous catalyst complex which could be used in "forming hydroperoxides."[255]

Knowledgeable commentators have come to criticize the distinct strand of enablement when it comes to "inventions in chemistry and the experimental sciences, which courts have deemed the 'unpredictable' arts."[256] Skilled practitioners

> in these fields often cannot predict if a reaction protocol that works for one embodiment will work for others. Thus, the applicant typically must enable multiple embodiments with a specific and detailed teaching because there is a danger that embodiments not so described either cannot be made or may require unduly extensive experimentation.[257]

[254] Patent application specification, quoted in In re Angstadt, 537 F.2d 498, 500 (C.C.P.A. 1976).

[255] In re Angstadt, 537 F.2d 498, 502–503 (C.C.P.A. 1976).

[256] Sean B. Seymore, *The Enablement Pendulum Swings Back*, 6 Nw. J. Tech. & Intell. Prop. 278, 282 (2008).

[257] Sean B. Seymore, *The Enablement Pendulum*, at p. 282. See generally Dmitry Karshtedt, Mark A. Lemley & Sean B. Seymore, *The Death of the Genus Claim*, 35 Harv. J.L. & Tech. 1 (2021).

Even so, this "multiple embodiments" rule has not restrained chemical patent lawyers from claiming very broadly. This has been criticized as an inefficient system that over-rewards chemical inventors.[258] Because structural formulas can be claimed in a general way, with multiple Markush-type structural variables (each of which can take on many different specific forms), it has been estimated that "a single generic [chemical] claim can easily encompass millions, billions, or novemdecillions of compounds."[259]

5.3.2.4 The Patent Law/FDA Complex

After numerous scandals involving tainted or adulterated drugs, the Food and Drug Act of 1906 empowered the Bureau of Chemistry to regulate food and drug products. (The Bureau later became the Food and Drug Administration (FDA).)[260] Regulations were tightened later in the century, under the Food Drug and Cosmetic Act of 1938 (FDCA).[261] Standards of drug approval became even more stringent in 1962, again in response to side effects from a dangerous pharmaceutical, thalidomide. The 1962 amendment to the FDCA established contemporary standards for clinical drug trials, required drugs to be proven "safe and effective," and established the obligation to track and report drug side effects.[262]

As mentioned earlier in this chapter, in the discussion of the utility requirement for pharmaceutical patents, drug approval research is extremely expensive, roughly $1.3 billion on average (as of 2016) for the full development path from test compound to market-approved drug.[263] This costly research has become a separate barrier to entry in pharmaceutical research, distinct from patent protection.

[258] Sean B. Seymore, *Heightened Enablement in the Unpredictable Arts*, 56 UCLA L. Rev. 127, 130 (2008) ("[T]he current patent examination framework [for chemical patents] allows a patentee to obtain a broad claim encompassing millions of compounds enabled by a trivial amount of supporting disclosure … ") (footnote omitted); ibid., at 144 ("[An] array of chemical compounds which are structurally similar may differ radically in their properties … ").

[259] Sean B. Seymore, Heightened Enablement in the Unpredictable Arts, at p. 146 (2008) (footnotes omitted). A novemdecillion is 10, followed by 60 zeros. Ibid., at 146 n. 104: One extreme example is a European Patent entitled

> Bis-Benzo or Benzopyrido Cyclo Hepta Piperidene, Piperidylidene & Piperazine Compounds & Compositions, European Patent No. 0,535,152 (filed June 21, 1991) Patent No. 0,535,152 (filed June 21, 1991). One commentator conservatively calculates that the number of compounds covered by the patent is at least one novemdecillion (which is 10 followed by 60 zeroes). See Mario Franzosi, *Markush Claims in Europe*, 25 Eur. Intell. Prop. L. Rev. 200, 200 (2003).

[260] Pure Food and Drug Act, P.L. 59-384, 34 Stat. 768, 59th Cong. 2d Sess., January 1, 1906.

[261] On this early FDA history, see Katherine A. Helm, *Protecting Public Health from Outside the Physician's Office: A Century of FDA Regulation from Drug Safety Labeling to Off-Label Drug Promotion*, 18 Fordham Intell. Prop. Media & Ent. L.J. 117, 125–127 (2007).

[262] Kefauver-Harris Amendment, P.L. 87-781, 76 Stat. 780, 87th Cong. 2d Sess., October 10, 1962.

[263] Joseph A. DiMasi, Henry G. Grabowski, and Ronald W Hansen, *Innovation in the Pharmaceutical Industry: New Estimates of R&D Costs*, 47 J. Health Econ. 20 (2016).

Because test data submitted by a drug research firm is kept confidential, follow-on researchers who want to start selling the drug must conduct their own duplicate studies to prove safety and efficacy. At the same time, the lengthy FDA review period uses up the first seven or eight years of the patent coverage on a new drug. This means that when the drug is finally approved, it may be protected by a patent for only twelve years – the first eight years of the patent term having been consumed by FDA testing.

Congress addressed both problems in the Hatch-Waxman Amendments in 1984. This Act tried to strike a balance between the two ever-contentious cohorts in the pharmaceutical industry: the pioneer firms, discoverers of new compounds and therapies; and the generic drug makers, whose forte is copying existing medications and selling them as cheaply as possible.[264] Hatch Waxman gave pioneers a long patent term, by creating a system of patent term extensions to partly offset the lost patent term due to FDA review. The 1984 Act also gave generics something: limits on the length of time generic firms are excluded from access to the pioneer's drug-related data.[265] During what is known as the "data exclusivity period," generics cannot free ride on the pioneer's clinical data, a significant limitation.[266] But the Hatch-Waxman Act ends the exclusivity period well before the pioneer's patent expires, and it allows generics to rely on the pioneer's clinical data in seeking FDA approval of their own generic versions of the pioneer drug.

Hatch-Waxman adds to pioneers' profits through longer patent terms. Yet given the complexity of some diseases, even the liberalized patent extensions the Act provides may not give enough time to earn enough profit to make some research cost-effective.[267] The highly specialized and complex intertwining of FDA approval

[264] See Henry Grabowski and John Vernon, *Longer Patents for Lower Imitation Barriers: The 1984 Drug Act*, 76 Am. Econ. Rev 195 (1986).

[265] See, e.g., 21 U.S.C. § 355(j)(5)(F)(ii) (providing that generic drug approval applications cannot be submitted until five years after approval of a new drug with a new active ingredient, or four years in the case of a patent challenge).

[266] The data include records of every version of an experimental drug, every dose to every clinical patient, every record of drug efficacy, and every side effect observed. This is all very expensive to generate, but essential to obtaining FDA approval. Hatch-Waxman allows generics to re-use (or piggyback on) the pioneer's valuable clinical data. The data exclusivity period has been recognized as a separate and distinct form of intellectual property. See Rebecca S. Eisenberg, *The Role of the FDA in Innovation Policy*, 13 Mich. Telecomm. & Tech. L. Rev. 345, 360 (2007) (calling exclusivity "FDA-administered proprietary rights in regulatory data, awarded to encourage particular kinds of innovation"). On new initiatives to assemble large collections of drug performance data, by freeing data from their restricted-access "silos," see Arti K. Rai, *Risk Regulation and Innovation: The Case of Rights-Encumbered Biomedical Data Silos*, 92 Notre Dame L. Rev. 1641, 1642 (2017).

[267] See Erika Lietzan and Kristina M. L. Acri nee Lybecker, "Distorted Drug Patents, 95" Forth. Wash. L. Rev. (1317); U. Missouri School of Law, Legal Studies Res. Pap. No. 2019-20, available at SSRN: https://ssrn.com/abstract=3458588 (collecting data on biases caused by the FDA and patent term extension regime; in particular, finding that drug research has lagged regarding treatments for diseases that take a long time to study prior to clinical approval).

and patent coverage has brought into being one of the most profitable, and most contested, legislative influence operations in the pantheon of federal lobbying.[268] Because the highly specialized "pharma industry" lobbying wars only heated up after Hatch-Waxman, we take this up again in Chapter 6.

5.3.3 *Patent Professionals Rise Up: The 1952 Patent Act*

The Patent Act of 1952 came with a story that concealed and drew attention away from what was in fact its deeper agenda. The cover story was the need to update the Patent Act. The 1870 Act, barnacled with various amendments, was badly out of date, and in some ways out of touch with contemporary trends. The absence of a statutory codification of the invention test, which dated from 1851, is a prime example. Infringement law was also far different from what it had been in 1870. As were a number of other requirements and defenses in patent law.

The overall impetus, to judge from official documents, was a simple desire to codify, restate, and tidy up patent law. Major substantive changes to the law were intentionally put off for the future. The emphasis was on a crisp and contemporary restatement of existing patent law. First comes the neatening up, the thinking went, then maybe the big changes. The House Report accompanying the proposed revision put the matter this way:

> [I]t was decided not to include most of the proposed [major] changes in a bill but to defer them for later consideration and to limit the bill to the main purpose of codification … with only some minor procedural and other changes deemed substantially noncontroversial and desirable.[269]

But there was a deeper motivation for the 1952 Act, only rarely discussed overtly in polite company, and more often spoken of only among patent insiders. This was the felt need to counteract certain Supreme Court cases from the 1930s and 1940s. The Court's cases on the invention test were intolerable to most patent lawyers and to officials in the Patent Office as well. Justice Douglas's notorious "flash of genius" dictum felt like a direct assault on the established and accepted contours of patent law. Routine, incremental innovation – the lifeblood of corporate R&D, and the bread and butter of Patent Office work – appeared to be devalued. An entire professional infrastructure of inventors, patent lawyers, and patent examiners rebelled at the thought that patents would henceforth be available only for the rare,

[268] See Rebecca S. Eisenberg and Daniel A. Crane, *Patent Punting: How FDA and Antitrust Courts Undermine the Hatch-Waxman Act to Avoid Dealing with Patents*, 21 Mich. Telecomm. & Tech. L. Rev. 197 (2015) ("[The] FDA has sought to avoid any responsibility for reading patents, insisting that its role in administering the patent provisions of the Hatch-Waxman Act is purely ministerial. This gap in regulatory oversight has allowed innovators to use irrelevant patents to defer generic competition.").

[269] House Report 1923, Revision of Title 35 United States Code, "Patents," Comm. on the Judic., U.S. House of Rep., H.R. 7794, 82d Cong., 2d Sess., May 12, 1952, at p. 3.

edge-shattering invention. So, a quintessential insider's committee was assembled to put things right. Under the rubric of restating and tidying up patent law, the real goal was to push back, subtly but effectively, against the Supreme Court's recent apostasies.

The composition of the primary drafting committee is revealing. Drawn from a committee of the New York Patent Law Association – a typical professional practitioner group from mid-century patent practice – it underscored the degree of specialization that characterized patent policy. A young second-generation patent lawyer, Giles Rich, was one of the prime movers. A second heavy contributor was P. J. "Pat" Federico, a highly respected career Patent Office official whose depth of knowledge and interest was widely appreciated.[270] A third practitioner joined the initial drafting committee for a model bill. Many of the provisions of what became the 1952 Patent Act were drawn up by these consummate "insiders", And despite the deflective and mild-mannered public posturing, there were substantive changes and slanted restatements aplenty in the new Act. The two most important revisions were aimed directly at reversing or heavily tempering some recent trends in the cases coming from the Supreme Court, starting with the "flash of genius".

5.3.3.1 Section 103 of the 1952 Act: Invention to Nonobviousness

The House Report accompanying the 1952 Patent Act plays down the significance of the new section 103, titled "Requirements for Patentability; Nonobviousness." According to the Report: "This paragraph is added with the view that an explicit statement in the statute [of the "invention" test] may have some stabilizing effect, and also to serve as a basis for the addition at a later time of some criteria which may be worked out."[271] The choice of the "stabilizing" metaphor is interesting: It betrays a sense that the recent case law was unstable, shaky, unreliable, and that some sense of order and balance needed to be restored. This is true as far as it went; there was more than a little confusion about how to apply cases such as the *Jungerson* decision (described earlier this chapter), or what to do with the *Cuno Engineering* case.[272] Judge Learned Hand, in a series of decisions made after enactment of the 1952 Act, described quite well the conundrum judges felt in applying the "invention" test in the 1940s, in the wake of the Supreme Court's *Jungerson* and *Cuno Engineering*

[270] For a small sampling of Federico's published works, see P. J. Federico, *Commentary on the New Patent Act*, 75 J. Pat. & Trademark Off. Soc'y 161 (1975 reprint; original 1954); P. J. Federico, *Intervening Rights in Patent Reissues*, 30 Geo. Wash. L. Rev. 603 (1962).

[271] House Report 1923, Revision of Title 35 United States Code, at p. 18.

[272] *Cuno Engineerg Corp.* v. *Automatic Devices Corp.*, 314 U.S. 84, 91 (1941) (Douglas, J.) (opinion invalidating patent for a dashboard-mounted cigar lighter for cars) ("[T]he new device, however useful it may be, must reveal the flash of creative genius not merely the skill of the calling. If it fails, it has not established its right to a private grant on the public domain.").

decisions. Writing of the old "invention" test only three years after the new Act became law, Judge Hand wrote:

> The variants were numberless; and "invention" became perhaps the most baffling concept in the whole catalogue of judicial efforts to provide postulates for indefinitely varying occasions. However, the [Supreme] Court never formally abjured it; nor has it ever substituted any other definite test ... [A]lthough it may have ceased in practice to be followed, and had come to enjoy no more than lip service, there never has been the slightest intimation of any definite substitute; nothing more than an unexpressed and unacknowledged misgiving about the increased facility with which patents were being granted.[273]

Judge Hand is here arguing that the 1952 Act was much more than a "stabilizing" restatement. As he had in his dissent in the Second Circuit opinion in *Jungerson*,[274] Hand is saying in effect that the law had become a complete cipher. The Supreme Court had not *said* that the old standard of invention was superseded by a much stricter standard; but their decisions indicated that this was so. Judge Hand's 1960 opinion in *Reiner* v. *I. Leon Company* further describes the confusing state of the law – and in the process explains why the 1952 Act can only reasonably be seen as Congress's *sub silentio* return to the earlier, pre-1940s, standard:[275]

> There can be no doubt that the Act of 1952 meant to change the slow but steady drift of judicial decision that had been hostile to patents which made it possible for Mr. Justice Jackson in dissent [in *Jungerson*] to speak of the "strong passion in this Court for striking them" (patents) "down so that the only patent that is valid is one which this Court has not been able to get its hands on." That was in 1945, while the test laid down in *Hotchkiss v. Greenwood*, 11 How. 248, 266 [(1851)] ... still had a nominal authority, of which little remained in actual application. We still cannot escape the conclusion – as we could not when Lyon v. Bausch & Lomb Optical Co. [224 F. 2d 530 (2d Cir. 1955)] supra, was decided in 1955 – that Congress deliberately meant to restore the old definition, and to raise it from a judicial gloss to a statutory command. It is not for us to decide what "discoveries" shall "promote the progress of science and the useful arts" sufficiently to grant any "exclusive right" of inventors (U.S. Constitution, Article 1, § 8). Nor may we approach the interpretation of § 103 of the Title 35 with a predetermined bias.

Giles Rich, key architect of the 1952 Act,[276] wrote later in terms that showed just how much he sympathized with Judge Hand's views, and therefore just how much more than "stabilization" was intended for the new Section 103:

[273] *Lyon* v. *Bausch & Lomb Optical Co.*, 224 F.2d 530, 536–37 (2d Cir. 1955) (L. Hand, J.), on reh'g in part, Case No. 216, 1955 WL 71945 (2d Cir. July 29, 1955).

[274] See this chapter.

[275] *Reiner* v. *I. Leon Co.*, 285 F.2d 501, 503 (2d Cir. 1960) (L. Hand, J.). For the Jackson dissent, quoted by Hand, see this chapter.

[276] Giles S. Rich, *Laying the Ghost of the "Invention" Requirement*, 14 Fed. Circuit B.J. 163, 168 (2005):

> Then in 1955 came Judge Learned Hand's *Lyon v. Bausch & Lomb* opinion (106 USPQ 1) and in 1960 his *Reiner v. I. Leon* opinion (128 USPQ 25), both of which realistically appraised and appreciated what section 103 had done, namely, to restore the law to what it had been 20 or 30 years earlier ... While saying "The test laid down [in 103] is indeed misty enough," he was able, with the evidence provided, to follow it. Certiorari was denied in both of those cases.[277]

In a speech in later years, Giles Rich (by then a judge on the Court of Customs and Patent Appeals, or CCPA) spoke of Congress's intention to substitute a more definite "yardstick" for the "invention" test. The notion that Congress settled on a specific standard, he said "clears up the 'codification' question. Whatever you call it, the purpose was to substitute Section 103 for the requirement of 'invention' and for all prior case law ... even though some cases contained the same principles. It was to be statutory, not case law in the future."[278]

The substantive thrust of the new § 103 is nowhere more evident than in the second sentence of the paragraph laying out the new requirement of nonobviousness. The second sentence, as drafted in 1952, read: "Patentability shall not be negatived by the manner in which the invention was made." As the House Report says:

> The second sentence [of § 103] states that patentability as to this requirement is not to be negatived by the manner in which the invention was made, that is, *it is immaterial whether it resulted from long toil and experimentation or from a flash of genius.*[279]

The reference to Justice Douglas's recent (1944) *Cuno Engineering* opinion could not be more apparent. Douglas, you recall, had invalidated the patent at issue in the *Cuno Engineering* case (a deluxe cigar lighter for installation in a car).[280] Justice Douglas wrote: "[T]he new device, however useful it may be, must reveal the flash of creative genius not merely the skill of the calling."[281] Eight years later, the Douglas standard – and thus the Supreme Court itself – was overruled as

> In the depression and post-depression thirties and forties we were going through one of the strict [anti-patent] periods. Pressure began to build up to curb the courts by statute. Some bills were introduced. Just at that time the Congressional committee in charge of codifying the various titles of the U.S. Code decided it would be a good idea to codify Title 35, the patent law. That enterprise got under way through what was called the Coordinating Committee, a group of about 30 lawyers from private, corporate, and government practice, which worked with the House subcommittee. I was a member of the Coordinating Committee and of its small Drafting Committee.

[277] Giles S. Rich, *The Vague Concept of "Invention" as Replaced by § 103 of the 1952 Patent Act*, 14 Fed. Circuit B.J. 147, 159–160 (2005) (reprinted; originally published in 1 A.I.P.L.A.Q.J. 26 (1972)).

[278] Giles S. Rich, *Laying the Ghost of the "Invention" Requirement*, at p. 172.

[279] House Report 1923, Revision of Title 35 United States Code, at p. 18 (emphasis added).

[280] *Cuno Engineerg Corp.* v. *Automatic Devices Corp.*, 314 U.S. 84, 91 (1941) (Douglas, J.).

[281] 314 U.S. 84, 91.

"immaterial." A bit of heavy lifting from an Act intended merely to "codify" and "stabilize" the law.

Judge Rich, in later comments, once again dispels any doubt:

> On the point of Section 103 being "codification" it is interesting to consider the last sentence of the section which said "Patentability shall not be negatived by the manner in which the invention was made." The specific intent of that sentence, which courts universally accepted without question, was to overrule the *Cuno* case dictum that a "flash of genius" was necessary. One cannot call that "codification."[282]

In another speech, Judge Rich said: "[P]rior to 1948 when I began this enterprise [of patent law], there were two things that were bothering the Patent Bar."[283] The first was the "invention" test and cases such as *Jungerson* and *Cuno Engineering*. "The other," according to Judge Rich, "was contributory infringement, which we in the Bar thought, at least in New York, had been abolished as a practical matter by the Supreme Court's *Mercoid* decision in 1944." That decision, and the harsh treatment of patent rights at the hands of antitrust law, was the next target of the mild-mannered 1952 "codification" project.

5.3.3.2 Contributory Infringement

Typical (or "direct") patent infringement is simple: If you make, use or sell something that meets the terms of a patent claim, you are an infringer. But sometimes, a person or company does something that doesn't quite fall precisely within a patent claim. Example: A patent on a chair might include the terms "chair back," "seat," and "four legs." What about a company, call it Three Legged Chair, Inc., which sells a "chair kit," featuring a chair back and seat, but only *three* legs? The law of contributory infringement unfolded over time to address just this type of situation. In our example, especially if Three Legged Chair sells its eponymous product with instructions about how to acquire and attach a fourth leg, a judge might well find Three Legged liable as an infringer. The reasoning in the early cases extended patent infringement doctrine to do what the judges felt was fair. If it seemed as though the company selling the three-legged chairs knew about the patentee's chair patent, and was intentionally trying to skirt that patent, a court was likely to hold the company liable. Though technically it is the three-legged chair *buyer* who becomes an infringer the moment the fourth chair leg is acquired and attached, the logical

[282] Giles S. Rich, *Laying the Ghost of the "Invention" Requirement*, at p. 172. The clunky verb "negatived" was changed to the more euphonious "negated" in 2011. See America Invents Act, Pub. L. 112–129, September 16, 2011, § 3, 125 Stat. 287–288.

[283] Giles S. Rich, *Address to American Inn of Court, May 20, 1992*, 76 J. Pat. & Trademark Off. Soc'y 320, 320–321 (1994).

patent enforcement target is Three Legged Chair.[284] Contributory infringement is the doctrinal bridge developed to span the gap between technical (direct) infringement and the wrong committed by a clever but ill-willed infringement-skirter. It is a doctrine designed to pull the support from under Three Legged Chair, Inc.

As an equitable extension of conventional doctrine, contributory infringement makes sense. But in the 1930s and 1940s, any rule that "extended" a patent raised red flags in the antitrust community. A tie-in seems to stretch the reach of a patent to embrace items not covered by the patent grant. Following the same principle, contributory infringement seemed to stretch the reach of a patent to components or sub-assemblies that do not by themselves technically infringe a patent. The unifying concept runs under the rubric of "leverage," and it was applied repeatedly during the high antitrust enforcement era. Whenever the economic power of a patent was brought to bear on an item or practice that did fall fully within the patent's claims, the inference was that the patent was being used improperly. Put differently, the concept was that the claim scope and legal reach of a patent ought to be coextensive.

When applied robustly, the idea of illicit leverage would seem to seriously restrict contributory infringement – at the limit, to eviscerate it. To see why consider the Supreme Court cases mentioned by Judge Rich in his retrospective account of the 1952 Act. That case, *Mercoid Corporation* v. *Mid-Continent Investment Company*,[285] featured a patent on a temperature-controlled furnace, for home heating. A patent was issued in 1930 to Walter M. Cross, who assigned it to his company, Cross Coal-O-Matic.[286] Cross-Coal-O-Matic was succeeded by a company called Mid-Continent Investment Company. So, it was Mid-Continent that brought suit, first against an individual homeowner (to establish direct infringer) and then against the company that sold the homeowner the core component of his temperature-controlled home heating system, called a combustion stoker switch. Mid-Continent Investment was joined as a plaintiff by the company that had taken a license to the Cross patent, the large heating and thermostat company Minneapolis-Honeywell Regulator Company (Honeywell). Of note, the licensing agreement from Mid-Continent to Honeywell pegged Mid-Continent's royalties to the number

[284] For the simple reason that it takes 300 lawsuits to directly enforce a patent against 300 buyers but only one lawsuit to enforce a patent against a company with sales of 300 units. To set up the contributory infringement suit, Mid-Continent originally sued an individual homeowner who installed a Mercoid stoker switch sold by defendant Mercoid in his home heating system. *Mid-Continent Inv. Co.* v. *Mercoid Corp.*, 43 F. Supp. 692, 693 (N.D. Ill.), aff'd in part, rev'd in part, 133 F.2d 803 (7th Cir. 1942), rev'd, 320 U.S. 661, 64 S. Ct. 268, 88 L. Ed. 376 (1944) ("Plaintiff Mid-Continent Investment Company, during August 1935, brought suit against E. O. Smith of Carthage, Missouri, for infringement of the domestic heating system patent of Cross No. 1,758,146 by installing in his home a heating system including controls manufactured by the defendant [Mercoid].").

[285] 320 U.S. 661 (1944).

[286] US patent 1,758,146, issued May, 1930, to Walter M. Cross.

of combustion stoker switches sold by Honeywell.[287] Mid-Continent and Honeywell said the license was structured this way because the stoker switch was the crucial component of the Cross/Mid-Continent invention.[288]

The Cross heating system combines an automated coal feeder device with a thermostat. The coal feeder pushes a fresh pile of coal into the furnace when it is activated. It can be activated manually by the homeowner. But the innovative feature of the Cross system was the thermostat-controlled stoker switch. In warm weather a homeowner typically doesn't turn on the furnace. But to keep the furnace burning at a low level, to be ready next time heat is needed, a constant low flame is maintained. The stoker switch activated the automatic coal feed, to keep the fire going, when the temperature inside the furnace dropped below a certain level. So basically, when the furnace fire was dying, coal was fed to the furnace to keep the fire burning. The coal feeder mechanism is shown in Figure 5.23, and Figure 5.24 illustrates the design of the stoker switch.

To reiterate: the switch was integral to the furnace system, but the patent claimed the overall *system*, not just the switch.[289] The district court had held that selling the switch by itself could not infringe the Cross patent. The Seventh Circuit disagreed. It found that Mercoid's stoker switch was specifically made for use in the heating system as claimed by Cross, and that there was "no other use" for such a

[287] *Mid-Continent Inv. Co.* v. *Mercoid Corp.*, 43 F. Supp. 692, 694 (N.D. Ill.), aff'd in part, rev'd in part, 133 F.2d 803 (7th Cir. 1942), rev'd, 320 U.S. 661 (1944):

> [I]t was agreed [by Honeywell] that the royalty payments to be made [under the license from Mid-Continent] shall be made or based only upon what are known to the parties as a combustion stoker switch, specifically defined as a combustion stoker control unit including an automatic electric switch responsive directly to temperatures of combustion gases or boiler water produced by an automatic coal fed stoker. Minneapolis-Honeywell Regulator Company agreed to pay a royalty for each licensed combustion stoker switch made and sold by it and by its sub-licensees.

[288] Brief for Respondent Mid-Continental Investment Co., *Mercoid Corp.* v. *Mid-Continent Inv. Co.*, 1943 WL 54372 (U.S.), 5–6 (U.S., 2006):

> While the other elements of the combination [claimed in the Cross patent] may have had other uses, it was conceded that the main use, and perhaps the only use, for the holdfire [i.e., stoker] switch would be in the Cross system . . . It followed that each sale of a holdfire switch together with distribution of wiring diagrams showing the switch mounted in the [hopper and feeder mechanism] and connected in parallel with the room thermostat would establish the existence of a heating system covered by the Cross patent. For this reason, royalty payments were based on what were known to the parties as "combustion stoker switches."

[289] Claim 1 of the Cross patent is representative:

> A heating system comprising a combustion pot, means for feeding fuel thereto, a combustion space above the combustion pot, means controlled by the temperature of the rooms to be heated for· automatically regulating the fuel feeding means, and a separate thermostatic ·control actuated by predetermined minimum temperatures in said combustion space for preventing extinguishment of the fire when operating under low heat requirement conditions.

US patent 1,758,146, at p. 3.

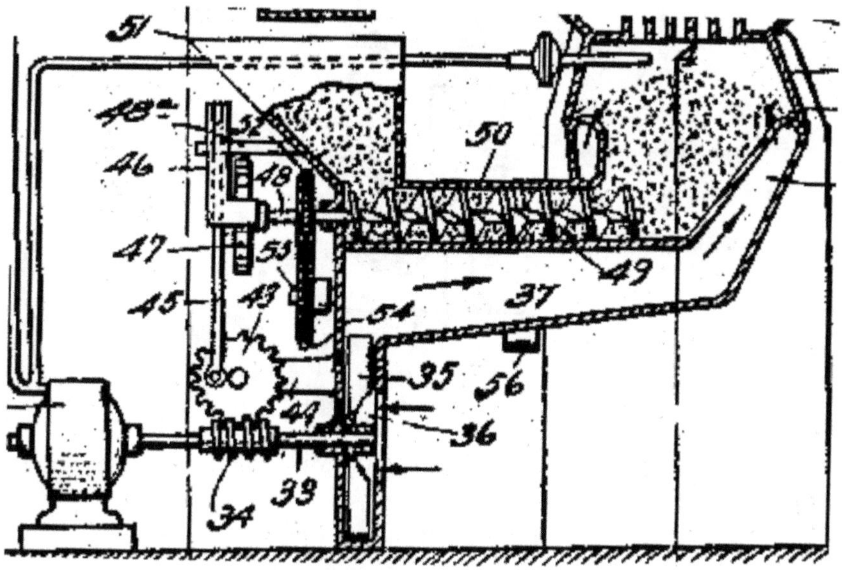

FIGURE 5.23. Mid-Continent automatic coal feeder device, from US patent 1,758,146, issued May 1930, to Walter M. Cross, licensed to Honeywell. The screw drive pushed coal into the combustion area (on the right), in response to a signal from the combustion stoker switch

switch.[290] The Seventh Circuit then rejected the district court holding that simply pleading contributory infringement under these circumstances was itself a per se antitrust violation, because it was an illicit attempt to in effect expand the scope of the patent.[291]

The Supreme Court reinstated the district court opinion: The Mid-Continent/Honeywell license violated the antitrust laws. The rationale matched that of the tie-in cases: Mid-Continent was using the power of its heating system patent to earn extra profit in a separate market, the market for standalone stoker switches. Because this market was not coextensive with the scope of the Cross patent, and because

[290] *Mid-Continent Inv. Co. v. Mercoid Corp.*, 133 F.2d 803, 810 (7th Cir. 1942), rev'd, 320 U.S. 661 (1944):

> [District Court] Conclusion of law 4 states that [Mercoid's stoker switch] was no[t] built for the express purpose of providing purchasers with means to perform the Cross heating system. It is not denied that it is one element thereof. The record discloses no other use, and Mercoid suggests none. We think this finding has no factual support.

[291] *Mid-Continent Inv. Co. v. Mercoid Corp.*, 133 F.2d 803, 810 (7th Cir. 1942), rev'd, 320 U.S. 661 (1944):

> [A]nti-trust laws do not forbid contracts between the owners of patents and their licensees which are legitimate and within the scope of the patent . . . A patent owner, in the legitimate exercise of his rights, may restrain contributory infringement of his patent by the sale of the "advance of the art," if such sale is made with the knowledge and intention that the subject matter thus sold is to be used for the purpose of contributing to infringement of the patent.

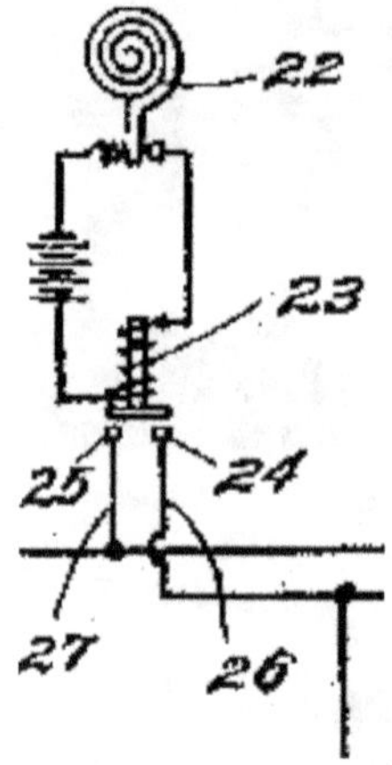

FIGURE 5.24. The combustion stoker switch in the Mid-Continent automated furnace

Mid-Continent's contributory infringement action would give it effective control of this market, that action constituted misuse of the patent.

> There was ample evidence to sustain the findings of the District Court that respondents endeavored to use the license agreement so as to prevent the sale or use of combustion stoker switches in these heating systems unless they were the switches made by Minneapolis-Honeywell and purchased from it or its sub-licensees.[292]

The rationale was, again, extension of the patent grant – and why this is prohibited. "[T]he limits of the patent are narrowly and strictly confined to the precise terms of the grant," the Court said. "The method by which the monopoly is sought to be extended is immaterial." This applies "[w]hen the patentee ties something else to his invention," which is how the Court saw the contributory infringement issue in this case. The contributory infringement action was not strictly speaking a tie-in; Mercoid was not bound to the Mid-Continent license with Honeywell. But the effect of a contributory infringement action, the Court said, was the same: It was an effort by the patent owner to apply the power granted by the patent in a market separate from the one strictly defined by the patent grant.[293] The Supreme Court opinion implied what other courts made explicit. Henceforth, simply pleading contributory infringement would be enough to constitute an antitrust violation.[294]

[292] *Mercoid Corp.* v. *Mid-Continent Inv. Co.*, 320 U.S. 661, 663 (1944).

[293] The court picked up on the formal Answer filed by the accused infringer, Mercoid: "Mercoid in its answer denied contributory infringement and alleged that Mid-Continent should be barred from relief because it was seeking to extend the grant of the patent to unpatented devices." *Mercoid Corp.* v. *Mid-Continent Inv. Co.*, 320 U.S. 661, 662 (1944).

[294] See *Stroco Products, Inc.* v. *Mullenbach*, 67 U.S.P.Q. 168, 170 (S.D. Cal. 1944) ("Plaintiff is, by its action against defendants for contributory infringement, attempting to use its patent to secure a monopoly on unpatented portions of the complete combination covered by the claims of its patent.").

Contributory infringement doctrine had developed over time, in the usual common law pattern.[295] As explained earlier, it is a doctrine rooted in fairness to the inventor or patent owner. Infringement rules are "stretched" to capture one who cleverly evades the technical details of a patent claim, but who nevertheless profits from the heart or key insight of the patented invention.[296] With the *Mercoid* decision, patent insiders felt they were experiencing the de facto abolition of this venerable doctrine. As Judge Rich explained,

> [W]e in the Bar thought, at least in New York, [contributory infringement] had been abolished as a practical matter by the Supreme Court's *Mercoid* decision in 1944 ... [A] Committee went to work to perfect a bill to survive [sic] contributory infringement ... [297]

Contributory infringement was thus added to the substantive "wish list" put together by the patent bar. Even before a liberalized contributory infringement provision found expression in the 1952 Act, it was the subject of several special bills introduced in 1948 and 1949.[298] The version found in the 1952 Act was the culmination of these efforts to restore contributory infringement to its traditional parameters, and – again – to sub silentio overrule an unfavorable Supreme Court case (*Mercoid*).

In the end, the 1952 Act returned contributory infringement to its pre-*Mercoid* shape. The new provision, 35 U.S.C. § 271(d), reinstates contributory infringement while listing factors that closely track the facts in *Mercoid*. It said:[299]

> (d) No patent owner otherwise entitled to relief for infringement or contributory infringement of a patent shall be denied relief or deemed guilty of misuse or illegal extension of the patent right by reason of his having done one or more of the following: (1) derived revenue from acts which if performed by another without his

[295] See, e.g., *Leeds & Catlin Co.* v. *Victor Talking Mach Co*, 213 U.S. 325, 337 (1909) (upholding infringement, and subsequent contempt, findings, of record player combination patent – stylus plus record disc – for sale of discs alone).

[296] Contributory infringement is kin, in this respect, to the doctrine of equivalents, which also evolved from equitable impulses. See Robert P. Merges and John F. Duffy, Patent Law and Policy: Cases and Materials (7th ed., 2017), at chapter 8.

[297] Giles S. Rich, Address to American Inn of Court, at pp. 320–321 (1994).

[298] P. J. Federico, Commentary on the New Patent Act, at pp. 212–213 (1975 reprint; original 1954). The 1948 Congressional Hearings on this issue, and especially Giles Rich's Congressional testimony, are recounted in the post-1952 Act contributory infringement case of *Dawson Chem. Co.* v. *Rohm & Haas Co.*, 448 U.S. 176, 205 (1980).

[299] 35 U.S.C. § 271(d) (1952 Act). Several additional subsections were added in 1988; these are discussed in Chapter 6. See

> [Or] (4) refused to license or use any rights to the patent; or (5) conditioned the license of any rights to the patent or the sale of the patented product on the acquisition of a license to rights in another patent or purchase of a separate product, unless, in view of the circumstances, the patent owner has market power in the relevant market for the patent or patented product on which the license or sale is conditioned.

PL 100–703, November 19, 1988, 102 Stat 4674, 100th Cong., 2d Sess., November 19, 1988.

consent would constitute contributory infringement of the patent; (2) licensed or authorized another to perform acts which if performed without his consent would constitute contributory infringement of the patent; (3) sought to enforce his patent rights against infringement or contributory infringement.

Subsection (3) directly overrules the suggestion in *Mercoid* that simply pleading contributory infringement can be an illicit extension of a patent. Subsections (1) and (2) in effect remove the per se illegality of agreements such as the one negotiated by Mid-Continent and Honeywell. That agreement says, in effect "Mid-Continent authorizes Honeywell to sell stoker switches notwithstanding that these sales constitute contributory infringement of the Cross patent." After the 1952 Act, a contract authorizing conduct that might well constitute contributory infringement will not be considered an illicit extension of the patent monopoly. The provision does not make these agreements per se legal; it only says that they are permitted where a patent owner is "otherwise entitled to relief for contributory infringement." Permissible license scope is once again tied to infringement liability. A contract that *recognizes* this does not by its terms extend a patent. It simply permits licensing within the proper scope of the patent, which includes acts of contributory as well as direct infringement.

The new statute exposed a logical gap in the *Mercoid* rule. The Supreme Court had not purported to outlaw contributory infringement actions by patent owners. Instead, the Court prohibited *contracts allowing* contributory infringement (in exchange for royalties). The antitrust violation was the contract, as opposed to a lawsuit asserting contributory infringement by some third party. So, one reading of *Mercoid* is this: A patentee has fewer rights vis-à-vis a licensee than as against a perfect stranger. The Court in effect shrunk the patent entitlement when it was the subject of a voluntary license, while maintaining the patentee's full set of rights in actions against non-contractual infringers.[300]

To the extent this is accurate, the 1952 Act takes on a slightly different complexion. Patent lawyers were not just seizing back turf in 1952, turf won through the professionalization movement at the turn of the century. They were also perhaps trying to sustain and cultivate the deep roots of patent grants in the body of law governing individual contracting and transactions. They attended to patent law's *private law* roots. This shows up throughout the 1952 Act, in provisions on patent assignments, co-ownership default rules, and the rights of conflicting licensees to the

[300] Of course, it is also true that an extension of a patent right by contract only triggers antitrust concern when the extension exceeds the bounds of the legal right. So arguably, Mercoid did do away with contributory infringement; after all, a contract can't be condemned unless it operates to extend a patent right beyond that patent's proper limits. Those limits are defined by the law of infringement. Thus, if all contracts permitting use of a component or subassembly are illicit, it must follow this is because a contributory infringement action against the contract-permitted activity would be an illicit contract extension.

same patent. The amendments to § 271 were from this point of view congruent with an important aspect of the 1952 Act. The new Act neatened up the patent statute. And it added the indispensable "codification" of the invention test in § 103. But in a fair number of less-noticed sections, the Act preserved and updated the transactional framework within which patent-related private ordering takes shape. In this sense, *Mercoid* had to go; not so much to preserve contributory infringement, as to preserve a broad possible canvas for patent-related contracting.

5.3.4 *Patent Office Administration*

The Patent Office between 1920 and 1982 grew more fully into its place as a highly professional and specialized bureaucracy, with close ties to private patent practitioners. Though nominally adversarial, the relationship of patent office personnel and the private lawyers trying to obtain patents for their clients was more than civil. First of all, the boundaries between them were quite fluid. Many patent examiners went to law school at night to obtain the law degree that would open doors in private practice.[301] Patent Commissioners came from the ranks of practicing lawyers, typically.[302] Camaraderie was also high because patent "insiders," whether from the PTO or practice, had more in common with each other than with outsiders, especially critics of the patent system.

The specialized nature of the patent bar, and the foreignness of its folkways to mainstream judges, were commonplace facts by 1930. This became increasingly true in the period up until 1982. An after-dinner speech to the Patent Bar by Justice Hughes in 1930 might as well have been made in 1965 or 1975:

> You are the priests of the inner mysteries of the temple of justice. Even in your gladsome moments you have the air of being on familiar terms with the doctrine of relativity, and that puts companionship to a severe test ... You have not only your own Bar and your own Association, but your own language.[303]

The sense of specialization, and perhaps isolation, was symbolized by the relocation of the Patent Office from the seat of government in Washington to a suburban office park setting in Virginia. This was a long way from the days when the Patent Office Building was thought important enough to be saved from destruction at the hands of marauding British in the War of 1812, or when wounded Union soldiers lying in the patent model room inspired sympathy from Walt Whitman.

301 See, e.g., as one of hundreds, N.a., *Necrology: Merrell E. Clark*, 23 J. Pat. Off. Soc'y 780, 783 (1941) (was simultaneously an examiner and a night student at George Washington Law School).

302 See, e.g., *John A. Marzall Appointed Commissioner of Patents*, 32 J. Pat. Off. Soc'y 5 (1950) (Chicago patent practitioner with twenty years of experience appointed Commissioner of Patents by President Truman).

303 Justice Charles Evans Hughes, *The Patent Bar*, 12 J. Pat. Off. Soc'y 292 (1930).

On the less symbolic level, the large and ever-growing bureaucracy[304] simply needed more space. (Even before 1920, patent people began to refer to the "examining corps," in recognition that this was a large body of specialized professionals.)[305] The move to Virginia took place between 1967 and 1969. The PTO took up a number of scattered buildings in Arlington, Virginia, until an integrated complex was finally built in nearby Alexandria in 2005.[306] In some ways this was the culmination of several centuries of plans to give the Patent Office adequate space to do its work. The other constant refrain of Commissioners past and present was still in evidence, however: The Patent Office was a net revenue center for the government (running a profit most years), but Commissioners were constantly asking Congress to permit the Office to keep more of their own revenues to invest in patent quality and the like.[307]

On the substantive level, the Patent Office became more specialized in response to the high volume of patent applications. In keeping with the trends described earlier this chapter, beginning in the early twentieth century the Office geared up for the complex issues raised by chemical patent practice.[308] The rapidly evolving doctrine on issues such as chemical nonobviousness found its way quickly into

[304] The bureaucracy has grown at variable annual rates. There were 610 patent examiners in 1930. See Jo Bailey Brown and Richard Spencer, *Interference Revision*, 12 J. Pat. Off. Soc'y 5, 7 (1930) (610 examiners in 1930). This increased slowly. See US Patent Office, *Patent Office Annual Report Fiscal Year* 1954, 36 J. Pat. Off. Soc'y 763, 766 (1954) (650 examiners in 1954). There was then steady growth from the 1950s until around 2005: from 650 examiners in 1954 to 4,200 in 2005. See U.S. General Accountability Office, Report to Cong. Committees, "USPTO Has Made Progress in Hiring Examiners, but Challenges to Retention Remain," June 2005, available at https://patentlyo.com/media/docs/2005/06/d05720.pdf. (But since 2005 there has been a burst of rapid growth. In keeping with calls for better initial examination, in an environment of ever-rising patent applications, the examining corps expanded to over 8,000 examiners in 2020. See USPTO, Performance and Accountability Report, Fiscal Year 2020, available at www.uspto.gov/sites/default/files/documents/USPTOFY20PAR_2.pdf, Table 8, p. 231.

[305] N.a., *Notes*, 1 J. Pat. Off. Soc'y 41, 41 (1918) (speaking of "Additions to the Examining Corps"); N.a., *New Primary Examiners*, 18 J. Pat. Off. Soc'y 735, 735 (1936). ("Joseph A. Kurz Principal Examiner, Division 18 … On May 23, 1916, he entered the examining corps of the Patent Office as a Fourth Assistant Examiner, serving in Division 41 … "). The examining corps has been unionized since 1964, and is represented by the Patent Office Professional Association (POPA). See, U.S. General Accountability Office, Report to Cong. Committees, "USPTO Has Made Progress," at p. 3.

[306] n.a., *The Patent Office to Leave Washington*, 24 J. Pat. Off. Soc'y 66 (1942) (wartime partial removal of Patent Office to Richmond, VA, presages later outright move to Arlington, VA, where the Patent Office relocated between 1967 and 1969). The scattered PTO operations in Virginia were consolidated into a single complex in 2005. See Nate Smith, The Peripatetic U. S. Patent Office: Locations 1790 to Present, Inside Adams: Science, Tech. & Bus. Blog, U.S. Library of Congress, July 13, 2020, available at https://blogs.loc.gov/inside_adams/2020/07/the-patent-office/.

[307] See, e.g., Jerry Cohen, *Functions, Costs and Fees of the U.S. Patent Office*, 54 J. Pat. Off. Soc'y 462 (1972).

[308] Charles W. Rivise, *Inventions in the Chemical Field*, 32 J. Pat. & Trademark Off. Soc'y 439 (1950).

patent examination procedures, adding to their complexity and highlighting the need for chemical specialists in the Patent Office: "Examination and prosecution of chemical product applications are the subject of the most complex problems of United States patent practice. There appears to be more jurisprudence on certain aspects of this subject in our country than many other topics of patent law."[309] One particularly important area of attention was the searching of chemical prior art. This differs from other searching in that structural formulae must be searched as well as documents and patents that use particular chemical terminology. Early efforts to design structural search tools date back at least to 1957.[310]

By the 1970s, the list of new technologies posing difficult challenges for the PTO had expanded to include computer technology (hardware and software) and biotechnology. The PTO had been entertaining computer-related applications since the 1950s at least, but the new wave of patents related to computer software posed serious problems because much software code is not published and was of questionable patentability until the 1980s. There were also problems adjusting traditional doctrines such as enablement to the world of software technology.[311]

The PTO was generally receptive to biotechnology-related patents, but again the new technology demanded some rapid adjustments. For inventions dependent on specific living organisms, full enablement came to mean that samples of the organisms had to be deposited with a certified open-access scientific repository.[312] In general, there was extensive interchange among the patent lawyers shaping the new biotechnology industry in the 1970s and the PTO, charged with applying traditional patent standards to this new, fast-moving branch of technology.[313]

On the procedural front, it was only at the very end of the period under study that fundamental change started to creep into the patent system. Patent quality had been one chief topic in the "outsider" review of patent law commissioned by President

[309] Irving Marcus, *Chemical Product Patent Practice in the United States*, 52 J. Pat. & Trademark Off. Soc'y 543 (1970).

[310] Julius W. Frome, et al., Recent Advances in Patent Office Searching: Steroid Compounds, Patent Office Research and Development Office, Report No. 8, 1957, available at https://ipmall.law.unh.edu/sites/default/files/hosted_resources/patent-R&D-reports/Report_No_08.pdf. In light of the importance of steroidal chemistry, described earlier in this chapter, it is no surprise that this early effort to organize computer record-based structural searches was aimed at structures relevant to the steroid field.

[311] See, e.g., Kenneth W. Dobyns and Marc A. Block, *Adequate Disclosure of Computers and Programs for Computers in Patent Specifications*, 56 J. Pat. Off. Soc'y 574 (1974).

[312] See In re Argoudelis, 434 F.2d 666 (CCPA 1970).

[313] See Thomas D. Kiley, *Common Sense and the Uncommon Bacterium: Is Life Patentable*, 60 J. Pat. Off. Soc'y 468 (1978) (article by first Genentech General Counsel, Thomas Kiley). See generally, Oral History of Thomas Kiley, University of California Program in the History of the Biological Sciences and Biotechnology, Genentech Legal Counsel and Vice President, 1976–1988, and Entrepreneur, Thomas D. Kiley, with Introductions by Rebecca S. Eisenberg and James W. Geriak, An Interview Conducted by Sally Smith Hughes, Ph.D. in 2000 and 2001 at http://texts.cdlib.org/view?docId=kt9g5015sn&doc.view=entire_text.

Johnson in 1966.[314] One result of the Johnson Commission Report was the call for a post-patent-grant review of issued patents by the Patent Office – the first serious proposal for administrative patent validity trials. The idea was roundly criticized at first,[315] but with the backing of Patent Commissioner C. Marshall Dann it became law shortly thereafter.[316] The creation of the Patent Reexamination procedure in 1980 started a movement that culminated with the full-bore PTO validity trials authorized by the 2011 America Invents Act, a topic we take up in Chapter 6.

* * * * *

As we have seen, despite the "headlines" featuring patents as a rogue challenge to healthy competition, there was plenty of technology-driven entry in US industry between 1920 and 1982. For this the patent system received some credit, at least implicitly. It was considered a part of the constellation of practices and policies that both embodied and reflected the fundamental technological optimism of the American people. When, in yet another comprehensive study of the patent system, economist Fritz Machlup in 1958 gave his famous lukewarm verdict on the merit of the patent system,[317] this probably captured the median sensibility about patents at the time among policymakers and perhaps the population at large. It was an old institution; it had its apparent benefits; and there was not enough evidence to scrap it. It was an old reliable policy instrument. Not yet obsolete, but hardly at the leading edge of economic policy.

That changed in the years leading up to 1982. The 1970s (with a few exceptions)[318] were not a friendly era for large-scale technologies (apart from space exploration). The traditional idealism about technological solutions, and economic progress in

[314] See To Promote the Progress of Useful Arts, Report on the President's Commission on the Patent System, U.S. Senate, Comm. on the Judiciary, Subcomm. On Patents, Trademarks and Copyrights (Washington, DC: Gov't Printing Off., February 2, 1967), available at https://digitalcommons.law.scu.edu/cgi/viewcontent.cgi?article=1010&context=historical. See also Gerald D. O'Brien, *An Appraisal of the Report of the President's Commission on the Patent System*, 49 J. Pat. Off. Soc'y 139 (1967).

[315] See, e.g., Arthur R. Whale, *Patent Law Revision: A Dark Look at S. 2255*, 59 J. Pat. Off. Soc'y 153, 160 (1977) (proposed reexamination, later passed in 1980, "resembles an opposition proceeding. Both are unnecessarily burdensome, complex and costly.").

[316] C. Marshall Dann, *What Lies Ahead for Patents*, 59 J. Pat. Off. Soc'y 600, 604 (1977) ("It still seems to me that some changes in the law should be made. In particular I would like to see legislation to provide a general opportunity for reexamination throughout the life of a patent.").

[317] Fritz Machlup, An Economic Review of the Patent System, Study No. 15, Sen Res. 236 (Committee Print), A Study of the Subcommittee on Patents, Trademarks and Copyrights, Comm. on the Judiciary, U.S. Senate, 85th Cong., 2d Sess., n.d., at p. 80:

> If we did not have a patent system, it would be irresponsible, on the basis of our present knowledge of its economic consequences, to recommend instituting one. But since we have had a patent system for a long time, it would be irresponsible, on the basis of our present knowledge, to recommend abolishing it.

[318] On the large industrial scale, the Apollo Moon missions come to mind. On a smaller, more personal level, the counter-cultural origins of the do-it-yourself computer-building culture of the 1970s is a counterexample: a new technology that garnered attention and inspired passionate interest, at least among a small group of enthusiasts. More on these topics in Chapter 6.

general, ran aground amidst the storm and swirl of the "first" environmental movement. A focus on the distribution of income raised questions not about the pace of economic growth (which was taken for granted), but about who in American society benefitted most from the fruits of innovation and market profit. And the hugely unpopular Vietnam War brought attention to defense-oriented research projects (napalm, for example) and companies that cast a dark, depressing shadow over much of the research enterprise. Maybe it was inevitable that the country would turn back to its tradition of embracing new technologies. In any event, the prolonged economic stagnation of the late 1960s and 1970s, combined with the rising economic profile of Japanese industry in the 1970s and 1980s, opened the door to policies meant to resuscitate and rejuvenate the American research enterprise. Then came the election of President Ronald Reagan in 1980 on a platform of renewed economic dynamism. The creation of the Federal Circuit in 1982 was one of many Reagan-era policies, but in the world of patents, it was by far the most important. As with the 1952 Act, the superficial rationale for the new court was a bland one: efficiency and uniformity were the primary themes. But the not-so-hidden-agenda underlying the public posturing soon became apparent. The Federal Circuit came to praise patents, not to bury them. How the new court succeeded, and what happened as a result, is a topic for Chapter 6.

6

The Federal Circuit Era

CHAPTER OUTLINE

6.1 MACRO TRENDS: "STAGFLATION," "JAPAN AS NUMBER ONE," AND TECHNOLOGICAL PESSIMISM

6.1.1 *The Economy Comes Back to Earth*

In many ways, the United States did not enter the 1980s on a winning streak. Although the post–World War II economic boost continued through most of the 1960s, the 1970s were a series of setbacks, course corrections, and downright embarrassments for the US economy. Ever since 1945, when most of the developed world outside the

United States lay in various states of ruination, and much of the rest was in one or another stage of emerging from colonialism, Americans had enjoyed the sense of being alone at the top of the world economy. Rapid growth, and relatively fair distribution of its benefits, opened the way not only to prosperity but to a strong sense that people were on an upward-ascending escalator whose top was as yet far ahead.

To put that into numbers: according to economic historian Robert J. Gordon,

> The epochal rise in the U.S. standard of living that occurred from 1870 to 1940, with continued benefits to 1970, represent the fruits of the Second Industrial Revolution [i.e., nineteenth-century industrialization, see Chapters 4 and 5] ... Many of the benefits of this unprecedented tidal wave of inventions show up in measured GDP and hence in output per person, output per hour, and total factor productivity (TFP), which ... grew more rapidly in the half century 1920–1970 than before or since.[1]

Things changed after 1970. When the oil-producing nations of the Arab world cut off oil supplies to the United States in 1973 (the first "oil shock"), it halted the growth curve and broke the spell of post-War impegnability.[2] This first oil shock, coupled with the War in Vietnam, punctured the sense of post-War complacency.[3] The political turmoil of the Watergate scandal also contributed to an attitude of loss and decline. A second oil shock in 1979 boosted the already-high inflation rate to unprecedented levels: core inflation reached an annual rate of 13 percent in 1979,[4] and it took heroic

1 Robert J. Gordon, The Rise and Fall of American Growth: The U.S. Standard of Living since the Civil War (Princeton, NJ: Princeton University Press, 2016), at p. 566.

2 See generally, Nuno Luis Madureira, *Waiting for the Energy Crisis: Europe and the United States on the Eve of the first Oil Shock*, 39 Hist. Soc. Res. 70 (2014).

3 See Natasha Zaretsky, *In the Name of Austerity: Middle-Class Consumption and the OPEC Oil Embargo of 1973–1974*, in Van Gosse and Richard Moser, eds., The World Sixties Made: Politics and Culture in Recent America (Philadelphia: Temple University Press, 2008), at p. 139: "The [OPEC Oil] embargo [of 1973] raised a host of questions about the future of the American middle class in an age of diminishing resources and economic dislocation." And, at p. 138: "[O]pinion polls suggested that, even as the public remained skeptical and divided over the causes of the embargo, they agreed that it constituted evidence of national decline in the immediate wake of the Vietnam War and as revelations about the Watergate scandal moved higher and higher up the chain of command." From a global perspective, Giuliano Garavini, *Completing Decolonization: The 1973 "Oil Shock" and the Struggle for Economic Rights*, 33 Int'l Hist. Rev. 473, 474 (2011), at p. 474: Anti-colonial aspects: "the co-operation between oil-producing countries and the rest of the developing countries of the Third World, without which both the cohesion and boldness of oil producers as well the weakness and fears in the industrial countries cannot be explained."

4 One aspect of the inflation cycle was psychological: Once inflation was established, the expectation that it would continue became entrenched. See, e.g., Robert J. Gordon, *Can the Inflation of the 1970s Be Explained?*, 1 Brookings Pap. Econ. Act. 253 (1977), at p. 277:

> The outlook for inflation is rather grim. Despite the continuing output gap, the statistical evidence ... indicates that any further deceleration in inflation is highly unlikely. On the contrary, it points to the probability of some acceleration as the economy continues its recovery. While the extent of that acceleration will depend on the speed of the recovery, inflation rates of 6 or 7 percent seem likely for the next several years, compared with the 5 percent rate during 1976.

(and economically devastating) inflation fighting tactics such as a 21 percent prime lending rate to bring inflation under control.[5] By the time President Jimmy Carter ran for reelection against Ronald Reagan in 1980, the bumps and jolts of the 1970s had left people hungering for a return to "normalcy" – prosperity, American autonomy, hope for the future.[6]

Enter Ronald Reagan: stage right, in more ways than one. Reagan's 1980 campaign was aimed directly at assuaging American indignity over the rude treatment at the hands of the 1970s. The 1980s, the new administration promised, would be very different. Under the rubric of "smaller government," the Reaganites promised deregulation and a return to pro-business policies designed to restore prosperity and return the United States to preeminence. Behind the campaign lay an elaborate network of foundations, think tanks, political operatives, and like-minded individuals (many wealthy). Some, such as the Olin Foundation, had been building intellectual momentum since the 1960s. Others such as the Federalist Society were organized and launched during the 1980s. Together with a commitment to appointing young, Republican-approved officials throughout the government, these institutions helped reshape policy almost as drastically as the New Deal had in the 1930s. Innovation policy, including patent law, revision, was high on the Reagan agenda, as we see in Section 6.3 when examining the gestation, delivery, and infancy of the new Federal Circuit court in 1982.

6.1.1.1 Japan and the Era of "Competitiveness" Policies

Part of 1970s angst was based strictly on domestic concerns: poverty, environmental degradation, and various forms of corruption. But there were also grave concerns over the future of US economic leadership in the early 1980s. These mostly centered around the rise of Japan as an economic powerhouse. The Japanese economy was damaged and depleted in 1945. Only forty years later the rapid rise in economic performance, powered by manufacturing exports, became known far and wide as the "Japanese Miracle."[7] Japan became the focal point of American

5 See Robert D. Hershey, Jr., Volcker Out After Eight Years as Federal Reserve Chief; Reagan Chooses Greenspan, New York Times, June 3, 1987, at p. A1, col. 6; Joseph B. Treaster and Paul Volcker, The Making of a Financial Legend (New York: John Wiley Publishing, 2005), at pp. 3–5 (recounting peak 21 percent interest rate in 1980, followed by a 16 percent rate the next few years).

6 The well-loved author and essayist E. B. White – he of the iconic and uplifting children's book "Charlotte's Web" – even wrote in 1975 of "so much that is disturbing our lives and clouding our future ... extending ... to our unhappy land and our plundered planet ... " E. B. White, Letter from the East, February 8, 1975, reprinted in Essays of E. B. White 71 (New York: Harper and Row Publishing, 1977), at p. 79. See also Eric Hobsbawm, The Age of Extremes (New York: Vintage Books, 1994), at p. 403: "The history of the twenty years after 1973 is that of a world which has lost its bearings and slid into instability and crisis."

7 See, e.g., Chalmers Johnson, MITI and the Japanese Miracle: The Growth of Industrial Policy, 1925–1975 (Stanford, CA: Stanford University Press, 1982). The great economic US-Japan rivalry was short-lived, however. The fast growth in Japan had been achieved using a great

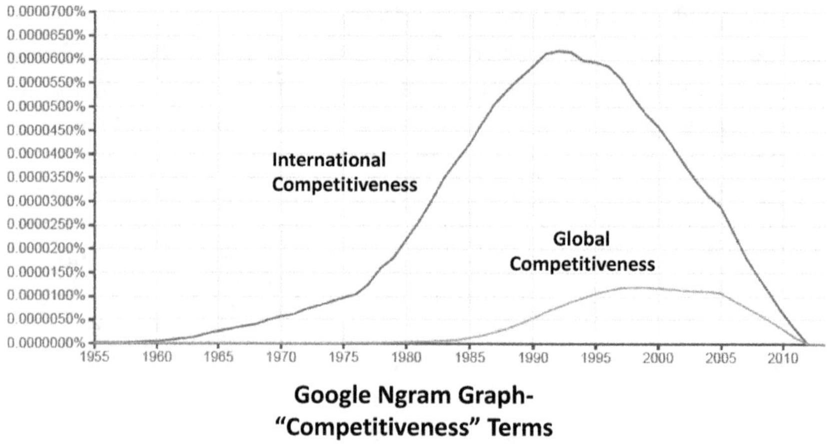

FIGURE 6.1. Google ngram graph: "Competitiveness" terms

policy[8] as the Reagan-era US government committed to fully engaging the machinery of the state to empower the private sector, and thus to restore growth and retain a leading position in world economic affairs. The short-hand term for this newfound concern was "competitiveness," or "international competitiveness." The shown here graph (Figure 6.1) displays just how common this term became in the 1980s and 1990s.

deal of debt. A financial crisis in 1990–1991 began a great unraveling of asset prices, and the result was a "lost decade" after the collapse of Japan's "bubble economy." Jennifer Amyx, Japan's Financial Crisis: Institutional Rigidity and Reluctant Change (Princeton, NJ: Princeton University Press, 2004), at p. 147 ff.

8 The auto industry was a focal point of American concern. Many features of modern auto manufacturing had been developed in the United States (see Chapter 5), but the consolidation of the industry in the "Big Three" (Ford, GM, Chrysler) led to a period of stagnation. See David Halberstam, The Reckoning (New York: Wm. Morrow, 1986). Japanese producers introduced small, inexpensive, yet reliable vehicles, based on production parceled out to a far-flung constellation of parts makers. See Michael A. Cusumano, The Japanese Automobile Industry: Technology and Management at Nissan and Toyota (Cambridge, MA: Council on East Asian Studies, Harvard University Press, 1985), at p. 377 (dis-integration of production (outsourcing) of components and subcomponents was one of the "most 'revolutionary' changes the Japanese made" in the auto industry). See also ibid., at p. 374–375:

> By the end of the 1960s, Nissan and Toyota had surpassed American productivity levels as well as learned how to produce small cars that compared favorably in quality, performance, and price with European vehicles. By the end of the 1970s, [375] Americans and Europeans had become painfully aware of just how much the Japanese had improved their ability to compete in the automobile industry … [due to] a unique mixture of technology transfer [both direct, through joint ventures, or "tie-ups", and indirectly, by copying successful designs] and process innovation.

The people who spoke of "competitiveness" were worried about the decline in (relative) US economic performance, and motivated to find ways to reverse it. Typical of this large genre was a study of what had happened to various US manufacturing industries since the 1960s.[9] Just such a study listed three primary reasons why television manufacturing, to take one example, had shifted from the United States to Japan during the 1970s:[10]

> Capital costs were higher in the U.S., and the difference [with Japan] increased sharply in the period in which the [television] industry was being abandoned (the prime interest rate in the U.S. passed 20 percent in the 1970s) ... The Japanese emphasis on teamwork and quality gave them advantages over American firms. In the U.S., poorer teamwork between product-development and manufacturing activities often contributed to delays in bringing new products to market ... American technology and patents were initially licensed by foreign competitors, but as U.S. firms cut back on research and development and as overseas companies increased theirs, the patent advantage turned heavily to the Japanese.

All three of the factors listed were addressed by Reagan-era economic policies. But it is the final one that concerns us. An uptick in attention to R&D[11] will almost always spark interest in the patent system. The early 1980s was no exception.

9 Policies to improve economic performance vis-à-vis Japan often ran under the rubric of "industrial policy." The worrisome topic of the US "balance of trade" also came up frequently, because Japan in the 1960s–1980s pioneered many of the export-driven growth and technological "catch-up" strategies of China after the 1980s:

> MITI ... had various policies intended to exclude foreign enterprises from the Japanese domestic market – informal rules such as not allowing foreigners to own more than 50 percent share in a joint venture, restricting the number and voting rights of foreigners on the Boards of Directors of Japanese firms, [etc.] ... ultimately, excluding all foreign participation in the Japanese economy without MITI's position.

Chalmers Johnson, MITI and the Japanese Miracle: The Growth of Industrial Policy 1925–1975, at p. 246.

10 Michael L. Dertouzos, Richard K. Lester, and Robert M. Solow, eds., Made in America: Regaining the Productive Edge (MIT Commission on Industrial Productivity) (Cambridge, MA: MIT Press, 1989), at p. 219.

11 Historians say the "competitiveness" agenda was a novel rationale for R&D spending, supplementing the older rationale of military-defense preparedness. See Sheila Slaughter and Gary Rhoades, *The Emergence of a Competitiveness Research and Development Policy Coalition and the Commercialization of Academic Science and Technology*, 21 Sci. Tech. & Hum. Values 303, 304 (1996):

> Even before the standard justifications used to defend government spending on science and technology came into question, a new rationale for R&D policy began to emerge. The "competitiveness" agenda was proposed as a basis for science and technology policy in the 1980s, during the Reagan and Bush administrations, and found an articulate and ardent champion in President Clinton ... Science and technology policy directed toward competitiveness uses government funds to commercialize science and technology via corporations and R&D agencies. The aim is to increase U.S. shares of global markets and to increase the numbers of high-technology, high-salaried jobs in the domestic economy.

6.1.2 *Technology: The Post-1970s Restoration*

The 1970s also continued a trend originating in the 1960s – a largely unprecedented (for Americans) questioning of the value of new technologies. It would be too much to say that this era was anti-technology,[12] though critiques of specific innovations, and even sweeping condemnation of technology in general, were certainly in the air.[13] One reason for the loss of faith in the benefits of new technologies was the creeping realization that the growth-inducing technologies of the early twentieth century, particularly the automobile and electric power generation, were major sources of industrial pollution.[14] The environmental movement gathered

[12] Space exploration, capped off by the moon landing in 1969, showed that the American public still found in some technical feats a source of awe and wonder. See David E. Nye, American Technological Sublime (Cambridge, MA: MIT Press, 1996), at p. 240 (observing that a visit to a space launch or landing is a contemporary, secular "pilgrimage," undertaken "to renew [the viewers'] belief in the powers of American technology and to reinforce their patriotism."). On a more prosaic level, innovations in consumer goods – such as faster, lighter snow skis and tennis rackets, and higher quality stereophonic equipment – stimulated aficionado subcultures and fed into large and lucrative markets. See John T. McQuiston, (Obituary) Howard Head, 76; Designed Metal Skis and a Tennis Racket, New York Times, March 4, 1991, at p. 55, col. 1 (inventor of metal skis and aluminum tennis rackets); Daniel Shannon, Sales of Stereos are Less Sound as Audio Industry's Markets Slip, New York Times, May 23, 1982, at sec. 3, p. 4, cols. 3–6 ("As surely as the needle tracks the groove, the stereo component industry followed a path of ever-rising sales and profits during the 1970's boom decade."). See also Lynn Olson, A Tiny History of High Fidelity, Part 2, Nutshell HiFidelity (website/blog, http://nutshellhifi.com), available at http://nutshellhifi.com/library/tinyhistory2.html (describing origins of 1970s high-end high fidelity subculture, organized around a hand-drawn magazine called Stereophile: "[H]ere and there, in little workshops all around the land, folks were building strange new products … vacuum-tube electronics, electrostatic speakers, making direct-to-disc recordings, all kinds of zany items.").

[13] See, e.g., Donald S. Chisum, *Napalm, Proxy Proposals and the SEC*, 12 Ariz. L. Rev. 463 (1970). See generally Langdon Winner, The Whale and the Reactor: A Search for Limits in an Age of High Technology (Chicago: University of Chicago Press, 1986). Winner called for "a critical philosophy of technology," ibid., at p. 6. He critiqued the nature of and need for nuclear power (ibid., at p. 19), calling it "authoritarian"; while solar power is "democratic" – an example of his maxim that "technical things have political qualities" (ibid.). And he said (ibid., at p. 29): "The fundamental choice about an antiballistic missile or supersonic transport is whether or not the thing is going to join society as a piece of operating equipment."

[14] Two infamous ecological emergencies trace their origins to the steel and electric power industries, and in particular, to two companies that were stalwart contributors to nineteenth-century American industrialization. The first was the Lake Erie (actually Cuyahoga River) fire of 1969 in Cleveland, when accumulated industrial pollution, produced in part by steel maker Jones and Laughlin, caused Lake Erie (one of the "Great Lakes") to catch fire and burn. This was a major stimulus to the Clean Water Act amendments of 1972, United States. Federal Water Pollution Control Act Amendments of 1972, Pub.L. 92-500, 86 Stat. 816, 92nd Cong., 2d Sess., October 18, 1972. See David Stradling and Richard Stradling, *Perceptions of the Burning River: Deindustrialization and Cleveland's Cuyahoga River*, 13 Env. Hist. 515, 529 (2008) (describing large Jones and Laughlin presence on the banks of the river in Cleveland). The second ecological emergency was the discovery of millions of pounds of polychlorinated biphenyls (PCBs) in New York State's Hudson River, the product of decades of waste discharge from General Electric plants making capacitors and transformers. The PCBs were used as

momentum in the 1960s, and burst into full public awareness with the first Earth Day in 1970.[15] Overall, what was called the "appropriate technology" movement probably captures the 1970s zeitgeist best: not that technology was inherently bad, but that its modern incarnation was the root cause of widespread social dislocation and individual alienation.[16] Though energy conservation, solar power, and "clean" (pro-environment) technology all trace their origins to this early environmental movement, at its inception it had little good to say about the then-dominant technologies of production, transportation, and contemporary life in the 1970s. New technologies were not exactly suspect; some (such as the "personal" computer, see later in this chapter) even contributed to greater freedom and autonomy. But new technologies did not receive a free pass either. At a minimum, the populace thought it best to keep an eye on them.

You can see this clearly through the history of the Office of Technology Assessment (OTA), a quintessential manifestation of the 1970s *zeitgeist*. Congress formed the OTA with the Technology Assessment Act of 1972, which in section Two explains the rationale for the Act and the movement it came out of:

> (a) As technology continues to change and expand rapidly, its applications are
> (1) large and growing in scale; and
> (2) increasingly extensive, pervasive, and ***critical in their impact, beneficial and adverse***, on the natural and social environment.
>
> (b) Therefore, it is essential that, to the fullest extent possible, the consequences of technological applications be anticipated, understood, and considered in determination of public policy on existing and emerging national problems ...[17]

And in § 3(c), the new Congressional agency received its mandate:[18]

> The basic function of the Office shall be to provide ***early indications of the probable beneficial and adverse impacts of the applications of technology*** and to develop other coordinate information which may assist the Congress.

fireproof insulators in these power generation components. But their discharge into the Hudson poisoned over 300 miles of the river ecosystem, which became one of the first "Superfund" environmental cleanup sites in the United States. See U.S. Environmental Protection Agency (EPA), Hudson River PCBs Superfund Site, "Hudson River Cleanup," last updated April 19, 2022, available at www3.epa.gov/hudson/cleanup.html#quest1.

15 See, e.g., Ernst Friedrich Schumacher, Small Is Beautiful: Economics as If People Really Mattered (London: Blond & Briggs, 1973).

16 Barrett Hazeltine and Christopher Bull, Appropriate Technology: Tools, Choices, and Implications (New York: Academic Press, 1999).

17 Technology Assessment Act of 1972, P.L. 92-484, October 13, 1972, 86 Stat. 797 et seq., 92d Cong., 2d Sess., section 2(a) (emphasis added).

18 Technology Assessment Act of 1972, § 3(c), 86 Stat. at 797 (emphasis added).

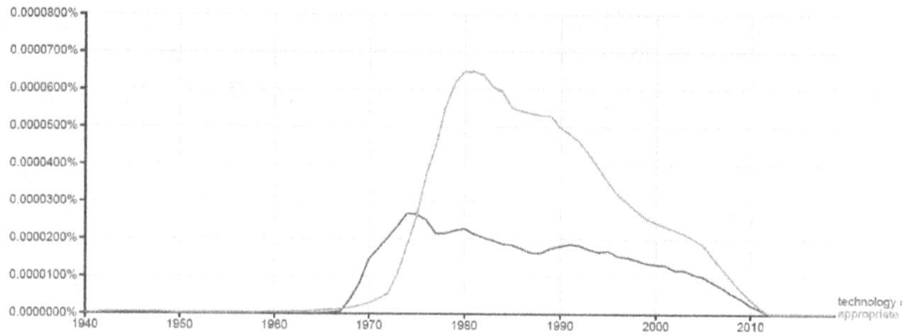

Google Ngram: Technology Assesment, Appropriate Technology, 1940-2015

FIGURE 6.2. Google ngram graph: Appropriate technology

The OTA's chief output was the 750 reports and white papers it published between 1972 and the closing of the office in 1995. These reports described new fields and technologies – copyright and home copying, genetic engineering, space exploration and weaponry, and many more. The typical Report briefly explains the technology; explores its potential payoffs, benefits, costs, and threats; and proposes legislation and other policy solutions.[19] The following nGram shows the rise in popularity of technology assessment and appropriate technology. It peaked around 1980, when interest shifted back to promoting new technologies for economic gain, as seen in Figure 6.2.[20]

6.1.3 *The First Nudge: The Bayh-Dole Act of 1980*

In the same way most boundary lines on a map are not completely straight, the demarcations between historical periods are rarely neat and clean.[21] So one of the signature policies of the "Reagan Era" was the result of legislation conceived and advanced by a moderate Democratic Congressman, Robert Kastenmeier, and signed

[19] See, e.g., U.S. Congress Office of Technology Assessment, Copyright and Home Copying: Technology Challenges and the Law, Report No. OTA-CIT-422 (Washington, DC: U.S. Government Printing Office, October 1989), available at https://ota.fas.org/reports/8910.pdf; U.S. Congress, Office of Technology Assessment, Intellectual Property Rights in an Age of Electronics and Information, Report No. OTA-CIT-302 (Washington, DC: U.S. Government Printing office, April 1986), available at https://ota.fas.org/reports/8610.pdf.

[20] The rubric of technology assessment slipped out of fashion in policy circles. But the basic idea of weighing the costs and benefits of technologies, and of being more aware of the effects of technologies on individuals and human communities, lives on in many ways. Attention to claimate change, oOrganic farming, vegan diets, carbon footprint awareness, concern with online personal privacy, and so on, are all expressions of the impulse to think closely about production technologies and the ways they affect people and the environment.

[21] See Steven F. Hayward, The Age of Reagan: The Fall of the Old Liberal Order: 1964–1980 (Roseville, CA: Prima Publishing, 2001).

into law by President Jimmie Carter. The Bayh-Dole Act passed in December of 1980, a month before Reagan took office. The Act made important practical changes to the handling of scientific research conducted with federal money. But it was also the first in a string of initiatives to reinvigorate federal innovation policy.[22] With the threat of international competition hanging in the air, and the stirring of interest in delegating government functions to the private sector – what came to be known as privatization – Bayh-Dole bears the very clear imprint of the early 1980s.[23]

The central idea was to devolve patent ownership downward, away from centralized federal ownership to more localized ownership in the hands of research institutes and universities. Bayh-Dole replaced a patchwork of different patent ownership practices with a single unified policy: wherever possible, patents should be owned by the institutions whose employees made the invention. After Bayh-Dole, the federal agency that provided money for research – the National Institutes of Health, for example, or the National Science Foundation – would normally not retain title to patents. And, equally importantly, the patent royalties should be shared between a university or research institute and the scientists who performed the research and made the patented invention. University ownership, and mandated shared royalties, were the two pillars around which Bayh-Dole was built.

[22] Many Reagan-era policies owed their intellectual origins to the years when Republicans were fighting against the New Deal, beginning in the 1930s. See Kim Philips-Fein, Invisible Hands: The Businessmen's Crusade against the New Deal (New York: W.W. Norton, 2010). An especially potent manifestation of conservative ideas was the founding and cultivation of free market research shops located in Washington – "think tanks," as they came to be called. See Kim Philips-Fein, Invisible Hands, at pp. 168–172 (describing the early founding of the American Enterprise Institute, and the 1973 founding of the more aggressively free-market Heritage Foundation in 1973). The blueprint for free-market-oriented policy advocacy was written by Lewis Powell, Jr., later appointed by President Nixon to the Supreme Court in 1971. See Jane Mayer, Dark Money: The Hidden History of the Billionaires Behind the Rise of the Radical Right (New York: Anchor Publishing, 2016), at pp. 89–94. Just prior to his nomination, Powell wrote a confidential memo to the U.S. Chamber of Commerce entitled "Attack on American Free Enterprise System." It outlined the need for vigorous research and advocacy to protect the United States against the incursion of radical attacks on the free market system. Ibid. In US law schools, this advocacy was furthered, beginning in the 1980s, by the largesse of a conservative foundation formed by a wealthy businessman named John M. Olin. The Olin-Mathieson Chemical Company was punished in the 1970s for its history of environmentally destructive production practices, and the push for deregulation funded by the Olin Foundation may have been a reaction to this. In any event the Olin Foundation chose to aim its resources at American law school programs in the field of Law and Economics. Its quiet but effective strategy was to establish a "beachhead" at elite universities to promote business-oriented ways of looking at legal issues. Olin gave away $68 million to various law schools, with the free-market-oriented University of Chicago receiving $7 million. See Jane Mayer, Dark Money, at pp. 130–132. (Disclosure: UC Berkeley Law School received some Olin money in the period after 1995 and I, the author here, might have benefitted indirectly, though I did not receive direct Olin funding.)

[23] If stimulating private initiative in areas like innovation was one earmark of the Reagan years, activating social conservatives was another. See, e.g., Robert O. Self, All in the Family: The Realignment of American Democracy since the 1960s (New York: Farrar, Strauss, 2012).

From the very beginning, Bayh-Dole struck some as a terrible idea.[24] The first objection was based on common sense: Shouldn't the one who paid for something get to own it? The federal government paid scientists to do research. Federal grant money is spent on lab equipment, salaries, supplies, scientific subscriptions, attendance at conferences, and so on: all the basic inputs that go into advanced work in chemistry, biology, physics, and engineering. A federal agency that paid for research was only acting within its rights to insist on owning title to patents. The agency was, as the name suggests, acting as an agent for all taxpayers. So, title to patents, by logic and basic fairness, ought to reside in the taxpayers who paid for it – by vesting in the funding agency. Anything else was illogical and unfair. Patents held by universities, and licensed to for-profit firms, would inevitably result in exclusive fields of technology being exploited for private gain. Whatever commercial products were derived from federal research money would be covered by patents – with the well-known effect of raising prices for those commercial products.

What it all amounted to, some said, was an elaborate scam on the public. Consumers would "pay twice" for the fruits of federally funded research. Once in taxes, to pay the researchers. Then a second time, in the form of patent-protected (and thus inflated) consumer prices for research-derived commercial products. Any product sold on the market by private companies licensing patents from universities would be subject to a patent tax, that is, the extra cost attributable to the higher profit margins associated with patent-protected products.

Competitiveness concerns and the privatization movement converged to challenge this common sense. The key to their arguments was to recognize that something was malfunctioning in the "common sense" regime of federal patent ownership, or more accurately, diversified and agency-driven patent ownership rules. The malfunction can be described in one word: *under-utilization*. The basic point was that the commonsense federal ownership regime completely ignored the matter of incentives. In the status quo pre-Bayh-Dole, federal agencies often had no good reason to push for the commercialization of patented technologies. Would-be licensees faced twenty-six different patent ownership policies spread across all federal agencies that financed scientific research. Empirical evidence supported the under-utilization thesis: Only 5 percent of government-owned patents were commercialized prior to Bayh-Dole.[25] Bayh-Dole as it took form, was designed to address under-utilization by devolving ownership downward. The simple theory was, put patents in the hands of people who have an incentive to commercialize them. That this represented movement in ownership from the (newly suspect) federal

[24] For a sense of the 1980s era debate on Bayh-Dole, including the objections mentioned in this paragraph, see Martin Kenney, Biotechnology: The University-Industrial Complex (New Haven, CT: Yale University Press, rev. ed., 1988).

[25] See Congressional Research Service, "The Bayh-Dole Act: Selected Issues in Patent Policy and the Commercialization of Technology" (CRS Report No. RL32076, December 3, 2012), at p. 2.

TABLE 6.1. *Bayh-Dole in action (2007–2017). Source: National Science Board of the National Science Foundation, Science and Engineering Indicators, Invention, Knowledge Transfer and Innovation, available at https://ncses.nsf.gov/pubs/nsb20204/knowledge-transfer#tableCtr1895*

Technology transfer activity	2007	2012	2017
Invention disclosures and patenting			
Inventions disclosed	14,398	19,827	24,998
Patent applications	11,797	14,192	15,335
Patents issued	3,622	5,153	7,459
Licensing			
All licenses, total active in the year	30,351	40,006	45,657
Licenses issued	4,354	5,130	6,283
Startup companies			
Startup companies formed	555	705	1080
Operational startups	3,388	4,002	6,050

bureaucracy to private (or at least non-federal) actors was a plus, given the emerging ideology of the times.

In 1983, the Reagan Administration quietly modified Bayh–Dole so it applied to federally funded research activities in private companies as well as universities and research institutes. Some evidence shows that Bayh-Dole replaced internal company R&D spending with federal funds – not the hoped-for increase in total R&D, but a "displacement" effect instead.[26] In one respect, however Bayh–Dole achieved its goal of stimulating licensing of patents based on research performed with federal funds. University licensing officials noted that licensing activity picked up just after the Act was signed,[27] and more recent data show that the trend toward more licensing has continued, as Table 6.1 demonstrates.

As hoped, these licenses have produced income for recipients of federal grant funding. Figure 6.3 shows licensing income from 2001–2005 and 2012 to 2015, for all the research entities surveyed (the "n" for each year is shown in parentheses next to the year).

But lost in the high theory was something more important. The under-utilization problem was actually the result of a faulty understanding of research-based

[26] Evidence shows that when a large company is given ownership of patents from government-funded R&D, this squeezes out company-internal R&D. From this, it could be argued that Bayh-Dole simply offloads corporate R&D costs onto government agencies – not the Act's advertised result, and certainly not its original purpose. See Yun Hou and Ivan P.L. Png, Government R&D and Private Innovation: Empirical Evidence from the Bayh-Dole Act, 1 Acad. Mgt. Proc. 11747 (December 5, 2020). Available at SSRN: https://ssrn.com/abstract=3498899 or http://dx.doi.org/10.2139/ssrn.3498899.

[27] See Congressional Research Service, "The Bayh-Dole Act: Selected Issues in Patent Policy and the Commercialization of Technology" (CRS Report No. RL32076, December 3, 2012), at p. 9 (interviews with university technology transfer professionals and some economists, all reporting that Bayh-Dole has been a success beginning in 1980).

Academic patenting and licensing activities: 2001–15

(Millions of current dollars and number)

Activity indicator	2001 (139)	2002 (156)	2003 (165)	2004 (164)	2005 (159)
Net royalties[a]	753.8	868.9	866.8	924.9	1,588.1
Gross royalties[a]	868.3	997.8	1,033.6	1,088.5	1,775.0
Royalties paid to others	41.0	38.8	65.5	54.4	67.8
Unreimbursed legal fees expended	73.5	90.1	101.3	109.2	119.1

(Millions of current dollars and number)

Activity indicator	2012 (155)	2013 (162)	2014 (155)	2015 (165)
Net royalties[a]	1,708.4	1,816.1	2,038.4	1,760.0
Gross royalties[a]	1,955.3	2,089.9	2,223.4	1,946.0
Royalties paid to others	87.6	92.2	103.0	143.5
Unreimbursed legal fees expended	159.3	181.6	185.0	186.0

FIGURE 6.3. Licensing income from Bayh–Doyle Act 2001–2015
Source: National Science Foundation, National Science Board, Science and Engineering Indicators 2018, Appendix Table 8-26, available at www.nsf.gov/statistics/2018/nsb20181/assets/1178/tables/at08-26.pdf.

inventions. Unlike most products of corporate R&D departments, university research is typically directed by faculty interest – often pure intellectual curiosity, or an interest in getting to the root of how something works. So, university research rarely produces a market-ready consumer product. It often reveals a basic mechanism or phenomenon that has commercial potential – but is far from market-ready at birth. According to some research on the matter,

> Although it was not a part of the rationale for Bayh–Dole, a share of license revenue for the inventor was among the requirements of the Act. It was only later that survey evidence indicated the importance of inventor effort for commercial development of many inventions. A 1996 survey of US universities indicated that 45% of the inventions they licensed were only a proof-of-concept when they were licensed, with another 37% no more than a laboratory-scale prototype. The view of the technology transfer personnel executing the licenses was that three-fourths of these would need inventor effort for commercial application ... This is consistent with survey evidence from business executives involved in licensing US university inventions. In their estimation, three-fourths of the inventions they licensed were no more than a laboratory-scale prototype at the time of license, and for 55% of these licenses, they engaged the inventor in the development process. They engaged the

inventor much less for inventions ready for the market, but these inventions represented only 7% of their licenses from universities ... [28]

Prior to Bayh–Dole, the nub of a good idea was likely to sit on the shelf. This was, in a sense, a failure to properly locate patent ownership. Federal ownership inefficiently separated patent title from the actual inventors – the skilled people who had performed the research in the first place. They were the best situated to commercialize it. This was a useful policy change, but not because it was a sterling example of privatization. Relocating ownership from the federal government to research institutions was effective not because nimble private sector heroes outperformed those federal bureaucratic sluggards.[29] It was because pre-1980, centralized federal ownership cut the connection between patented *invention* and the actual *inventors*. What Bayh-Dole did was move ownership closer to the inventors, the research scientists themselves.[30] After 1980 the owner of patented research often issued licenses to companies formed by the same academic scientists who did the patented research. So, in effect Bayh-Dole made it easier for university researchers to form a startup company based on their own federally funded, and patented, scientific research.

6.1.3.1 The Upstream Research Problem

At first, some opposed Bayh-Dole because it might divert research and make consumers pay twice for taxpayer-funded research discoveries. Over time, observers started to see another potential issue: Bayh-Dole might be pushing universities to aggressively patent more "upstream" scientific discoveries.[31] In scientific research, for example, isolating a cellular mechanism might open the way to various medical therapies. In the past, scientists published these upstream results all the time, but universities and institutes eschewed patents. This changed. Increasingly, when researchers discovered a door-opening mechanism, a versatile new technique, or

[28] Erika Farmstrand Damsgaard and Marie Thursby, *University Entrepreneurship and Professor Privilege*, 22 Indus. Corp. Change 183 (2013).

[29] One comprehensive review of Bayh-Dole found it a "mixed" success overall. See Richard Nelson, Bhaven N. Sampat, and Arvids Ziedonis, Ivory Tower and Industrial Innovation: University-Industry Technology Transfer Before and After the Bayh-Dole Act (Stanford, CA: Stanford University Press, 2015), at p. 95 ("[C]urrent research ... provides mixed support for the argument that patenting and licensing are necessary for the transfer and commercial development of university inventions.").

[30] Peter Lee, *Transcending the Tacit Dimension: Patents, Relationships, and Organizational Integration in Technology Transfer*, 100 Cal. L. Rev. 1503 (2012).

[31] See, e.g., Michael A. Heller and Rebecca S. Eisenberg, *Can Patents Deter Innovation? The Anticommons in Biomedical Research*, 280 Sci. 698 (1998), at p. 698 ("[T]his article identifies an unintended and paradoxical consequence of biomedical privatization: A proliferation of intellectual property rights upstream may be stifling life-saving innovations further downstream in the course of research and product development.").

the like, publication was accompanied by a patent.[32] The new practice disrupted old patterns and upset expectations. What had been a foundational finding or tool, free for commercial researchers to use, now becomes a research institution bearing an aggressive claim to some of the "downstream" profits earned from use of the discovery. What had been free inputs into the research enterprise now come with a price tag – potentially a big one. While the courts seem to have rebuffed the most aggressive instances, institutional incentives and clever patent claiming both suggest that this will be a continuing problem under Bayh-Dole.[33] It might be seen, in fact, as a subset of the larger problem of royalty-hungry universities, armed with sizeable patent portfolios, turned loose on the world of applied industrial research.[34]

[32] Richard R Nelson, Bhaven N. Sampat, and Arvids A Ziedonis, Ivory Tower and Industrial Innovation, at pp. 116–118 (empirical research shows patenting is positively associated with high-quality scientific publications, so no evidence of a diversion effect away from publication toward long-term secrecy). But see Jerry G. Thursby and Marie C. Thursby, *University Licensing and the Bayh-Dole Act*, 301 Sci. 1052 (2002), at p. 1052, where empirical data are reported showing that Bayh-Dole delays publication of research results (references omitted):

> Does licensing restrict dissemination of academic research? A survey of industry licensing executives shows 27% of their university licenses include clauses that allow deletion of information from papers before submission, and 44% ask for publication delay (3.9 months on average) ... Life science faculty involved in commercial activity often deny requests by other scientists for research results, although multiple factors are involved ... This problem is more likely related to research that is company sponsored rather than federally funded, because companies can protect IP with secrecy, whereas Bayh-Dole requires eventual disclosure through patents.

For a discussion of sharing norms among research labs, and the relationship to formal IP protection, see Robert P. Merges, *Property Rights Theory and the Commons: The Case of Scientific Research,* 13 Soc. Phil. & Pol'y 145 (1996). Some worried that scientists after Bayh-Dole would refrain from incorporating into their own work new research from other labs, but empirical research shows that research scientists routinely just ignore patent rights. See Wesley Cohen, *Patents and Appropriation: Concerns and Evidence,* 30 J. Tech. Transfer 57 (2005) at p. 64 (noting "pervasive infringement of patents in the course of laboratory research at [the] pre-product stage ... [which is] common in both public research institutions, notably universities, and in [the basic research acitivities of] firms."). On the prevalence of, and rationale for, this form of widespread, informal waiver of rights, see Robert P. Merges, Justifying Intellectual Property (Cambridge, MA: Harvard University Press, 2011), at pp. 84–85.

[33] More aggressive patenting is partly a function of the interest group that Bayh-Dole created: those who staff university technology transfer offices. See generally, David Mowery, Bhaven N. Sampat, and Arvids Ziedonis, *Learning to Patent: Institutional Experience, Learning, and the Characteristics of U.S. University Patents after the Bayh-Dole Act, 1981–1992,* 48 Mgt. Sci. 73 (2002). For an example of an unsuccessful try at patenting and profiting from a basic research discovery, see *Ariad Pharmaceuticals, Inc.* v. *Eli Lilly & Co.*, 598 F.3d 1336 (Fed. Cir. 2010) (invalidating patent issued to Massachusetts Institute of Technology, Harvard University, and the Whitehead Institute, which built on research identifying the structure of an important gene expression inhibitor, NF-KB; the claims in the patent (U.S. Patent 6,410,516) tried to cover a "method of using" NF-KB to inhibit gene expression, which would have covered all applied uses of the inhibitor, even though the uses were not themselves identified by the researchers).

[34] On this, see Derek Bok, Universities in the Marketplace: The Commercialization of Higher Education (Princeton, NJ: Princeton University Press, 2003). See generally Robert Kuttner, Everything for Sale: The Virtues and Limits of Markets (Chicago: University of Chicago Press, 1999).

6.1.3.2 University Licensing: Bayh-Dole Effect, or Biotech Effect?

Bayh-Dole came along at almost exactly the same time as the modern biotechnology industry. The Cohen-Boyer patent on genetic engineering issued to inventors from the University of California and Stanford in 1980 and was the first blockbuster patent widely licensed in the first years of the new Bayh-Dole regime.[35] Biotechnology is an example of a "science-based" industry, one where "technical advance is driven by developments in science outside the industry."[36] Many of the earliest prominent biotechnology companies were founded by university scientists. This includes Genentech (founded by Herb Boyer of the University of California), Cetus (co-founded by Donald Glaser of UC Berkeley, and later part of Hoffmann-LaRoche), and Biogen (co-founded by Phillip Sharp of MIT and Walter Gilbert of Harvard), among many others.[37]

With the exciting research coming from universities, and given the importance of private capital in turning basic research into commercial products, university-based entrepreneurship was likely to emerge even without Bayh-Dole.[38] The potential gains from applying these breakthrough technologies were so large that it probably would have made sense for venture capitalists and company founders to navigate a more complex licensing pathway, such as those common in the years before Bayh-Dole. The location of patent ownership may not have mattered as much with such glowing opportunities on the horizon. In a number of instances, both universities and private firms acted similarly with respect to patent licensing.[39] They both pursued certain licensing practices, for example, such as the widespread and

[35] Stanley Cohen and Herbert Boyer, US patent No. 4,237,224, "Process for producing biologically functional molecular chimeras," issued December 2, 1980, assigned to Stanford University under a royalty-sharing agreement with the University of California (where Boyer was on the faculty). On the wide licensing of the patent and the early days of biotechnology research, see Katherine Ku, Licensing DNA Cloning Technology, LES Nouvelles, June 1983, at 14. See also Kenneth Sutherlin Dueker, *Biobusiness on Campus: Commercialization of University-Developed Biomedical Technologies*, 52 Food & Drug L.J. 453, 496 (1997) (showing licensing revenue generated by the Cohen-Boyer patents and two later, related patents).

[36] Robert P. Merges and Richard R. Nelson, *On the Complex Economics of Patent Scope*, 90 Colum. L. Rev. 839, 880 (1990).

[37] See Martin Kenney, *Schumpeterian Innovation and Entrepreneurs in Capitalism: A Case Study of the U.S. Biotechnology Industry*, 15 Res. Pol'y 21 (1986) (describing the role of scientists, as well as entrepreneurs and capitalists, in forming early biotech cmpanies).

[38] Another impetus, in the same year Bayh-Dole passed, was the Supreme Court case of *Diamond v. Chakrabarty*, 447 U.S. 303 (1980). This case validated a patent on the proto-biotech invention of placing multiple bacterial plasmids (short, naturally occurring rings of DNA) in a single cell to produce bulk amounts of useful proteins. It was taken as a "full speed ahead" signal from the Supreme Court to the nascent biotechnology industry.

[39] For the Cohen-Boyer patents, lifetime royalties under licenses to 340 companies (nonprofits were exempt) totaled over $250 million in revenue. See Maryann Feldman, Alessandra Colaianni, and C. Liu, *Lessons from the Commercialization of the Cohen-Boyer Patents: The Stanford University Licensing Program*, in Anatole Krattiger, R. T. Mahoney, and Lita Nelsen et al., eds., Intellectual Property Management, in Health and Agricultural Innovation: A Handbook of Best Practices (Oxford: MIHR and Davis, US: PIPRA, 2007), available online

moderately priced licensing of foundational techniques in the biotechnology field. It is quite apparent that even aside from Bayh-Dole, the emerging biotechnology industry was different enough from other industries that novel patent licensing arrangements were likely to emerge. With the source of basic ideas separated from the companies that knew how to develop industry products, extensive contractual coordination was always likely to play a large part in the industry.

Despite all this, there are reasons to think that Bayh-Dole is more than a biotech story. There is extensive Bayh-Dole licensing activity *outside* of biotechnology. Although roughly 80 percent of high-impact (i.e., very profitable) licenses under Bayh-Dole are to life sciences companies, that still leaves 20 percent of licensing to non-health-related companies.[40] This may be because more and more industries resemble biotechnology in that they rely on recent scientific research to spark innovations.[41] Or it may be, at least in part, that technology licensing offices inside universities are directing effort at diversifying their patent portfolios. And finally, it may be a consequence of biotechnology as a highly visible success story, which leads researchers in other fields to emulate the entrepreneurial activities of their life sciences colleagues. Whatever the various ingredients in the causative stew, Bayh-Dole and the patent-related practices it inspired now reach outside of biotechnology

at www.ipHandbook.org. A second major technique patent, on the Polymerase Chain Reaction and Taq polymerase rapid gene sequence duplication method, was issued to private company Cetus, which also licensed it very widely on a non-exclusive basis. See Joe Fore, Jr., Ilse R. Wiechers, and Robert Cook-Deegan, *The Effects of Business Practices, Licensing, and Intellectual Property on Development and Dissemination of the Polymerase Chain Reaction: Case Study*, 1 J. Biomed. Discovery & Collab. Article number 7 (2006), at p. 1 (PCR and related technologies earned over $2 billion under a very extensive licensing program run first by Cetus then by Roche Molecular, to which Cetus sold the PCR business).

40 See Lori Pressman et al., The Economic Contribution of University/Nonprofit Inventions in the United States: 1996–2017, Report to the Biotechnology Innovation Organization (BIO) and the Association of University Technology Managers (AUTM), June 5, 2019, available at https://autm.net/AUTM/media/About-AUTM/Documents/Economic_Contribution_Report_BIO_AUTM_JUN2019.pdf, at p. 7. For a list of industries besides biotechnology that have used university-licensed technology, see ibid., at p. 35 (listing plastics, machinery, motor vehicles, processing, computer systems, etc.).

41 Sheila Slaughter and Gary Rhoades, The Emergence of a Competitiveness Research and Development Policy Coalition and the Commercialization of Academic Science and Technology, at p. 329:

> Across all fields, the number of articles co-authored by academic and industrial scientists rose from 22 percent of all articles written by scientists in industry in 1981 to 35 percent in 1991 … This increase may reflect the success of legislation designed to stimulate collaboration between universities and industry in an effort to make the United States more competitive in global markets.

These results are consistent with an increase in the "science content" of industrially relevant research. But they are also consistent with Bayh-Dole and related changes as a way to outsource the funding of research from private companies to federal research agencies.

and related fields.[42] Not everyone is convinced that widespread university patenting outside the life science industries is a good thing, but good or bad this seems to be a lasting legacy of Bayh-Dole and related policies.[43]

6.1.3.3 Slow, Mostly Steady Economic Growth after 1980

New technologies are not essential to economic growth, though they can contribute mightily to it. In the American tradition, however, since the Founding Era, innovation has been both an instrument of progress and evidence that the instrument is working. It is difficult enough, however, to identify how innovation contributes to growth. So, it is even harder to hazard a guess whether *attitudes* toward innovation play any part at all. All we can say for sure is that a number of new technologies leaped into the lives of many Americans after 1980 (especially microcomputers, biotechnology, and the Internet, see later), and though not without controversy, they seem to have recaptured some of the flavor of the technological sublime so common between 1870 and 1965 or so.

Regardless of what caused it, the data below show a steady rise in GNP beginning in the early 1980s.

As for patent-related data, the steady (sometimes rapid) increase after 1982 was, in the 1970s, far from a sure thing. As we will see in Section 6.3, a sizeable wave of federal policies and reforms may have contributed to growth in patenting – the Bayh-Dole Act of 1980, and of course creation of the Federal Circuit in 1982. Note the drop in patents and applications around the time of the 2008 financial collapse, and another dip after the record setting years around 2015 (Figure 6.4).

[42] B. Graham, "Patent Bill Seeks Shift to Bolster Innovation," The Washington Post, April 8, 1978; Stevens, "The Role of Public Sector Research," 536. www.everycrsreport.com/files/20121203_RL32076_836129be0e45a4049a32a64c143ec94df38236be.pdf.

Sheila Slaughter and Gary Rhoades, The Emergence of a Competitiveness Research and Development Policy Coalition and the Commercialization of Academic Science and Technology, 21 Sci. Tech. & Hum. Values 303 (1996).

Louis G. Tornatzky and Elaine C. Rideout, Innovation U. 2.0: Reinventing University Roles in a Knowledge Economy, Report of the State Science and Technology Institute, available at https://ssti.org/report-archive/innovationu20.pdf

Some of the more controversial university patent litigation success stories involve non-life sciences industries. See, e.g., *Carnegie Mellon Univ.* v. *Marvell Tech. Grp., Ltd.*, 986 F. Supp. 2d 574, 633 (W.D. Pa. 2013) (upholding jury award of $1.169 billion for infringing university patent on high-density disk drive data retrieval technique), aff'd in part, vacated in part, rev'd in part, 807 F.3d 1283 (Fed. Cir. 2015). The award in this case was reduced on appeal, leading to a settlement. Jonathan Stempel, "Marvell Technology to pay Carnegie Mellon $750 million over patents," Reuters New Service, February 2015, available at www.reuters.com/article/us-marvell-technlgy-carnegiemellon/marvell-technology-to-pay-carnegie-mellon-750-million-over-patents-idUSKCN0VQ2YE.

[43] See, e.g., Mark A. Lemley, *Are Universities Patent Trolls?*, 18 Fordham Intell. Prop. Media & Ent. L.J. 611 (2008). (Bayh-Dole and the incentives it creates are likely to produce negative effects in the software industry).

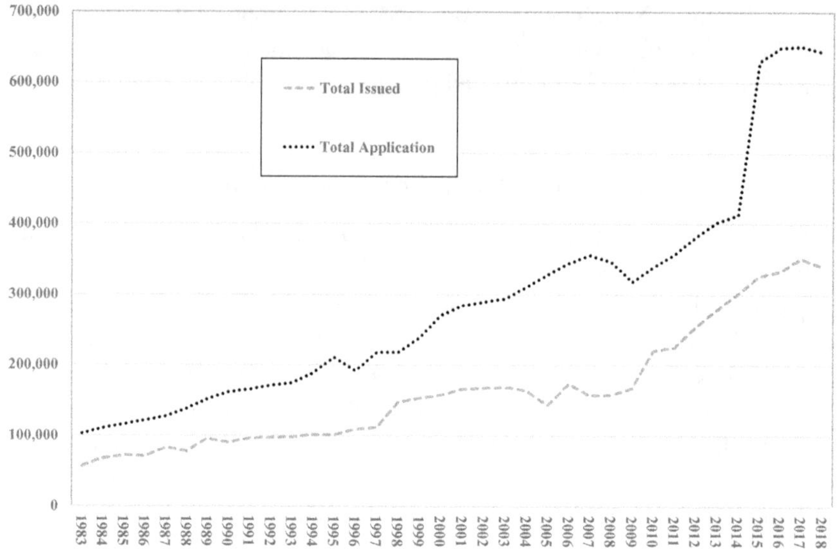

FIGURE 6.4. Total number of issued patents and patent applications per year 1983–2018

The sections ahead review what kinds of businesses were receiving these patents, and what they hoped to do with them.

6.2 PATENTS IN BUSINESS; PATENTS AS A BUSINESS

6.2.1 *Technology Trends: Microelectronics, Software, and Biotechnology*

As with the period covered in Chapter 5, the headlines do not tell the entire story. There was, as said, a good deal of vocal concern about technology in the years just ahead of 1982. Yet quietly, and in a minor key, revolutionary technologies were taking shape in the 1970s. When combined with the policy initiatives of the early Reagan Administration (1980–1984), these became major forces shaping the innovation landscape after 1982. The most important were computer hardware and software (i.e., information technology or IT), and biotechnology. Though on the surface the 1970s were largely a dry, or at least mixed, period for technological enthusiasm, the subterranean flow of new technologies continued as it had for the past hundred years. Future industries – ecommerce, mobile phones, and gene therapy, for example – were taking shape, out of the sight of the headlines. They would begin to make headlines of their own before the 1980s were over.

6.2.1.1 Microelectronics

Microelectronics came of age in the 1970s and 1980s, but the computer industry itself began much earlier. Specialized mathematical computing machines originated in the nineteenth century, but only reached a commercial market in the

1950s.[44] The IBM 360 mainframe computer, launched in 1965, was the culmination in some ways of the industry's earliest product lines, many of which originated in work for agencies of the US government.[45] The System/360, as it was known, replaced the earlier vacuum tube components with individual hardware transistor circuitry connected to other components on a ceramic plate or "board" – an interim step on the way to the true integrated circuit. These early mainframe computers were large and expensive, but very efficient for routine calculation jobs such as for actuarial tables and financial record-keeping.

Beginning in the 1960s, computers got smaller, faster, and cheaper every year, and they have ever since engineer Gordon Moore declared what came to be known as Moore's Law: the number of transistors on a computer chip will double every two years.[46] The invention of semiconductors and transistors, made possible through advances in electronics and material science/physical chemistry,[47] was the key that unlocked this historic exponential growth. The rapid increase in circuit density then invited more and more sophisticated computer instruction and coding – that is, the development of modern computer software. When telecommunication networks were then adapted for computer communication – again, initially by the Defense Department – the Internet was launched. This forms the basic infrastructure for e-commerce, content distribution, and (as of 2020) thousands of other applications. And Moore's Law marches on: A typical mobile phone in 2018 had over 1,000 times the processing power of the computers on board the Apollo 11 spacecraft that landed on the moon in 1969. The same phone has over 7 million times more storage space for software code (ROM), and over 4 million times as much memory as the Apollo computer (Figure 6.5).[48] As Robert J. Gordon wrote: "The improvement in the performance of computers has been continuous and exponential since 1960, and *the rate of improvement dwarfs any precedent in the history of technology*."[49]

Semiconductors can manipulate and store tiny electrical charges. They can be constructed in the form of a tiny electrical gate called a transistor, with the most useful form being a metal oxide semiconductor field effect transistor (or MOSFET). These transistors are formed by chemically etching silicon wafers, with the etching

[44] See Kenneth Flamm, Creating the Computer: Government, Industry and High Technology (Washington, DC: Brookings Institution Press, 1988), at pp. 1–15.

[45] See James W. Cortada, IBM: The Rise and Fall and Reinvention of a Global Icon (Cambridge, MA: MIT Press, 2019), at chapter 8, "System 360: One of the Greatest Products in History?," pp. 203–232.

[46] See J. A. N. Lee, Computer Pioneers: Gordon Moore, IEEE Computer Society, updated 2019, available at https://history.computer.org/pioneers/moore.html.

[47] Largely funded in the early stages by direct military grants and procurement policies. See Richard Levin, The Semiconductor Industry, in Government and Technical Progress: A Cross-Industry Analysis (Richard R. Nelson, ed.) (New York: Pergamon Press, 1982), at pp. 68 et seq.

[48] Graham Kendall, Would your mobile phone be powerful enough to get you to the moon?, The Conversation, July 1, 2019, available at https://theconversation.com/would-your-mobile-phone-be-powerful-enough-to-get-you-to-the-moon-115933.

[49] Robert J. Gordon, The Rise and Fall of American Growth, at p. 441. See also ibid., at p. 444 (documenting a 44 percent *annual* growth rate in computing power since 1976).

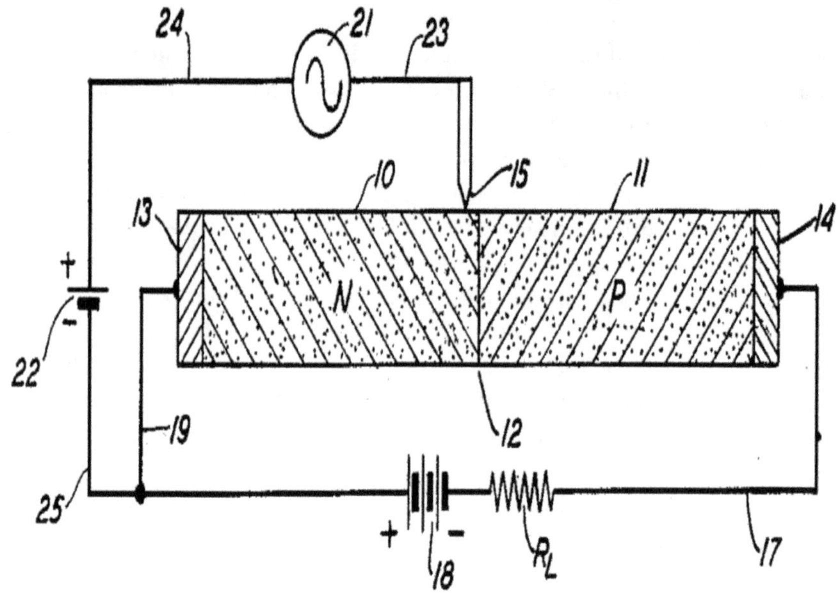

Patented Apr. 4, 1950 **2,502,488**

UNITED STATES PATENT OFFICE

2,502,488

SEMICONDUCTOR AMPLIFIER

William Shockley, Madison, N. J., assignor to Bell Telephone Laboratories, Incorporated, New York, N. Y., a corporation of New York

Application September 24, 1948, Serial No. 50,895

9 Claims. (Cl. 179—171)

1

This invention relates to means for and methods of translating or controlling electrical signals and more particularly to circuit elements utilizing semiconductors and to systems including such elements.

One general object of this invention is to provide new and improved means for and methods of translating and controlling, for example amplifying, generating, modulating, etc., electric signals.

2

Other objects and features of this invention will appear more fully and clearly from the following description of illustrative embodiments thereof taken in connection with the appended drawings in which:

The single figure shows in section a device suitable for practicing the invention, in connection with an appropriate circuit.

The device of this invention is in some respects like devices illustrated and described in the ap-

FIGURE 6.5. Bell Labs semiconductor patent, US patent 2,502,488, "semiconductor amplifier," issued to William Shockley, April 4, 1950
William Shockley, John Bardeen, and William Brittain shared the 1956 Nobel Prize in Physics for their discovery. See www.nobelprize.org/prizes/physics/1956/summary/

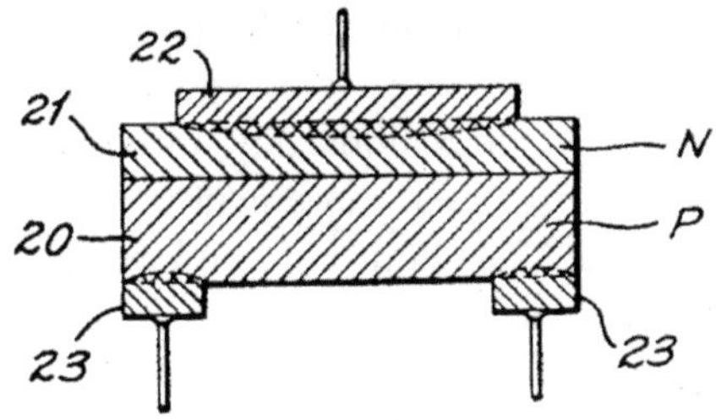

FIGURE 6.6. Basic circuit element in US patent 3,138,743, "miniaturized electronic circuits," issued June 23, 1964, to Jack Kilby, assigned to Texas Instruments, Inc.

guided by minute, amazingly detailed patterns called masks. This series of technologies, developed and perfected from the 1940s to the 1980s, forms the backbone of modern microprocessors and memory chips – integrated circuits. The first patent on the electronic elements of the integrated circuit was granted in 1964 to Texas Instruments inventor Jack Kilby. It showed the classic three-terminal transistor design that is repeated over and over in the structure of an integrated circuit (Figure 6.6).

A very similar patent was issued to Robert N. Noyce, co-founder (with Gordon Moore) of Intel Corporation.[50]

The integrated circuit, formed by silicon etching, proved to be an enormously fruitful design. Mainframe computers became more and more powerful, while the emergence of "mini"-computers such as the Digital Equipment Corporation's VAX brought brute force computing power to more and more applications in the 1980s. It is a testament to the cost of computing that when the VAX 11/780 was introduced in 1978, it was considered a thrifty alternative to mainframe computers, though priced from $120,000 to $180,000 depending on configuration.[51]

Around the same time, a completely different group of innovators was forming, with the goal of building computers at home from individual components. The pioneers of this emergent do-it-yourself culture had roots in shortwave radio clubs and home stereo equipment enthusiasts.[52] Though other hobbyist cultures pushed

[50] See US patent 2,981,877, "semiconductor device and lead structure," issued April 25, 1961 to Robert N. Noyce, assigned to Intel Corporation.

[51] See Exhibition – Mainframe Computers – What Became of Mainframes: DEC VAX 11/780, Computer History Museum website, Mountain View, CA, available at www.computerhistory.org/revolution/mainframe-computers/7/182/736. The VAX used a 32-bit instruction set and architecture and was the successor to DEC's smaller but versatile 16-bit pioneer, the PDP-11 computer. See Edgar H. Schein et al., DEC Is Dead, Long Live DEC: The Lasting Legacy of Digital Equipment Corporation (Oakland, CA: Berrett-Koehler Publishers, 2004).

[52] Kevin Driscoll, *Professional Work for Nothing: Software Commercialization and "An Open Letter to Hobbyists,"* 50 Info. & Cult. 257 (2015), at p. 279 n. 7 (recounting the role of a magazine called "73" in the hobbyist culture):

> 73 magazine represents a particularly important crossroads between amateur radio and hobby computing. The founding editor of 73, Wayne Green, would later start Byte, one of the first widely circulated personal-computing magazines. Green also published an

forward other technologies,[53] the computer hobbyists were an early example of the mix of technically intensive knowledge with countercultural values that came together in the Silicon Valley innovation community beginning in the 1970s.[54] One active branch of the do-it-yourself movement was the Homebrew Computer Club, which popularized the Altair build-yourself computer kit and similar early hardware. But smaller computers outgrew the Homebrew Club in a hurry. The Apple I computer, designed by Steve Wozniak and Steve Jobs, was first demonstrated to the Homebrew group, and the first Microsoft software product was a version of the BASIC programming language co-written by Paul Allen and Bill Gates and marketed to Club members.[55]

These milestones and advances were not isolated; they exerted a mutual influence on each other. Thus, for example, more powerful computers made it possible to better simulate and thus optimize integrated circuit design, by emulating the operation of a proposed design and tweaking it for better results.[56] The co-evolution

edited collection of computer-related material from 73 to encourage amateur radio enthusiasts to participate in the nascent hobby-computing scene.

[53] See, e.g., Robert C. Post, High Performance: The Culture and Technology of Drag Racing, 1950–1990 (vol. 16, Johns Hopkins Studies in the History of Technology) (Baltimore, MD: 1994).

[54] See Kevin Driscoll, Professional Work for Nothing: Software Commercialization and “An Open Letter to Hobbyists,” at p. 257:

> Popular accounts of 1970s computing conventionally portray the technical culture of microcomputing as a populist movement aimed at wresting computing away from large, entrenched institutions and making it affordable and accessible for the everyday user.

A popular “underground” style book from this era tried to both demystify the “priesthood” of mainframe computers and advocate “people-centered” design principles for bringing computer power to everyday people. Theodor H. Nelson, Computer Lib/Dream Machines (self-published, 1974). For an appreciation, see Daniele C. Struppa and Douglas R. Dechow, eds., Intertwingled: The Work and Influence of Ted Nelson (New York: Springer International Publishing, 2015).

[55] Computer History Museum, Mountain View, CA, Exhibition: Personal Computers – The Homebrew Computer Club, available at www.computerhistory.org/revolution/personal-computers/17/312. A famous “Open Letter” from Bill Gates to the members of the Club in 1976 complained about the copying of Microsoft’s BASIC language program, marking for some the transition from a close-knit sharing culture to more of a commercial relationship between software companies and customers. See Kevin Driscoll, Professional Work for Nothing: Software Commercialization and “An Open Letter to Hobbyists.” For a description of research on other sharing-oriented communities, and their relationship to formal IP rights, see Robert P. Merges, *Economics of Intellectual Property Law*, in Franceso Parisi, ed., The Oxford Handbook of Law and Economics: Private and Commercial Law (Oxford: Oxford University Press, 2017), at pp. 4–6.

[56] The first computer-based circuit simulation software (called SPICE) was developed at UC Berkeley as a class project in 1969–1970. See L. W. Nagel and D. O. Pederson, “Simulation Program with Integrated Circuit Emphasis (SPICE),” presented at 16th Midwest Symp. on Circuit Theory, Ontario, Canada, April 12, 1973 and available as Memorandum No ERL-M382, Electronics Research Laboratory, College of Engineering, University of California, Berkeley, CA, www.eecs.berkeley.edu/Pubs/TechRpts/1973/ERL-382.pdf. The technique was adopted rapidly and employed in many variations. See, e.g., Robert P. Merges and others (uncredited),

of circuit density, hardware design, and the emergence of a free-standing software industry all culminated in the two pillars of corporate computing in the 1980s and 1990s: the Microsoft Windows and Intel 8086 de facto computing standard, often abbreviated "Wintel."[57] And it was the Wintel skeleton on which much of the computer industry ecosystem of this era was built – which explains why it was this era that popularized the notion of a technological platform, or basic constellation of building-block technologies.[58]

Microelectronic innovations are also behind some of the other signature technologies of the post-1982 period, including mobile telephony, digital switching, and e-commerce (via the Internet). The years after 1970 truly were the era of Moore's Law.

By the 2010s, two somewhat opposing patent-related forces were at work. The economic logic of network markets dictates that the more people who use a certain system, the more valuable that system becomes. So we get dominant platforms such as Amazon (a retail sales system), Google (search), and Facebook (social media). At the same time, many products in the information technology industries (mobile phones, computers, etc.) are made up of thousands of specialized components. These are designed and manufactured all around the world, with major parts and final products assembled in and distributed from various manufacturing centers. Outsourcing and complex value chain arrangements are possible because most of these components are *modular*: They can be produced separately, by different companies in different countries, then interconnected into a final product. Mobile phone companies assemble standards-compliant phones by following explicit descriptions regarding dimensions, materials, tolerances, rules regarding exchange of data, etc.

Despite the amazingly rapid progress in modular, standardized, networked markets, however, some say the economic impact falls short of that from electrical power generation and the internal combustion engine. Robert J. Gordon for example writes:

> The slower growth rate of measured productivity since 1970 constitutes an important piece of evidence that the Third Industrial Revolution … associated with

ICE 88 In-Circuit Emulator Operating Instructions for ISIS II Users, Intel Corporation User Manual, Manual Order Number 9800949-01 (Santa Clara, CA: Intel Corporation, 1979), available at http://bitsavers.trailing-edge.com/pdf/intel/ISIS_II/9800949-01_ICE-88_Operating_Instructions_Aug79.pdf (user manual for early version of circuit emulation, with portions written by early version of the author of this book).

57 See Stanley Mazor, *Intel's 8086*, 32 IEEE Ann. Hist. Computing 75 (2010). On Microsoft's emergence, see Michael A. Cusumano and Richard W. Selby, Microsoft Secrets: How the World's Most Powerful Software Company Creates Technology, Shapes Markets and Manages People (New York: Free Press, 1998).

58 See Geoffrey G. Parker, Marshall Van Alstine, and Sangreet Paul Choudary, Platform Revolution: How Networked Markets Are Transforming the Economy – and How to Make Them Work for You (New York: W.W. Norton, 2016).

computers and digitalization has been less important than [the Second Industrial Revolution from 1870 to 1940].[59]

Maybe so, but the patent system has had to adjust to the microelectronics revolution in many significant ways. Patent troll litigation is very common in the industries based on computer technology, partly because the dispersed nature of ownership together with the high volume of relevant patents (the anticommons problem) provides many opportunities for patent troll litigation. Standard-essential patents are also a byproduct of complex, modular technologies. Both these topics are addressed later in this chapter.

6.2.1.2 Biotechnology

Modern biotechnology began with the discovery of the double helix structure of cellular DNA by James Watson, Francis Crick, and Rosalind Franklin.[60] The next major step was the 1976 discovery of a way to take DNA from one species, transfect a bacterial cell so as to integrate the "foreign" DNA into the bacteria genome, and get the bacteria to express the protein that the DNA codes for. This is the famed Cohen-Boyer "gene splicing" process.[61]

Recombinant DNA technology has produced many commercial products in the years since 1976. The first was a recombinant form of insulin, the human protein needed as a supplement by diabetes patients. Eli Lilly Corporation, the large US pharmaceutical company,[62] set up a "horse race" between three competing labs: the first to produce human insulin by recombinant methods would partner with Lilly in commercializing what was sure to be a blockbuster drug. One of the Lilly competitors, the then-young Genentech Corporation, won the race.[63] With this success, Genentech was catapulted into the headlines and (soon enough) onto the New York Stock Exchange. And the modern biotechnology industry was born.[64]

59 Robert J. Gordon, The Rise and Fall of American Growth, at p. 566.

60 See Francis Crick, What Mad Pursuit? : A Personal View of Scientific Discovery (New York: Basic Books, 1988); Brenda Maddox, Rosalind Franklin: The Dark Lady of DNA (New York: Harper Perennial, 2003).

61 On Cohen, Boyer, and their patent, see Section 6.1.3 (Bayh-Dole).

62 On Eli Lilly and other early pharma companies, see Chapter 5. On the public concerns that led to a temporary moratorium on gene cloning, and how Genentech designed an experimental procedure to comply, see Sally Smith Hughes, Genentech: The Beginnings of Biotech (Chicago: University of Chicago Press, 2011), at pp. 22–24.

63 See David V. Goeddel et al., *Expression in* Escherichia Coli *of Chemically Synthesized Genes for Human Insulin*, 76 Proc. Nat. Acad. Sci. 106 (1979); Scott Stern, *Incentives and Focus in University and Industrial Research: The Case of Synthetic Insulin*, in Nathan Rosenberg, Annetine C. Gelijns, and Holly Dawkins, eds., Sources of Medical Technology: Universities and Industry (Washington, DC: National Academies Press, 1995), at p. 157 (describing parallel research efforts at Harvard, UCSF, and the new startup, Genentech, to develop recombinant insulin; Genentech, in partnership with Eli Lilly, won).

64 Sally Smith Hughes, Genentech: The Beginnings of Biotech, at pp. 158–161 (recounting Genentech Initial Public Offering, or IPO).

Goeddel and others proceeded with a simple heuristic in this early phase of genetic engineering: identify a natural protein needed for an essential biological function, one that would be valuable in bulk quantities to address a human disease or condition. Locate the gene that codes for the protein; splice it into a producing organism; harvest, purify, sell. This approach – simple to say, devilishly hard to pull off from end to end – led to one of Genentech's early successes: Tissue Plasminogen Activator protein, used to break up harmful blood clots, caused for example by a stroke.[65] Next came an even bigger success, human growth hormone, or HGH,[66] and then Factor VIII, a blood clotting protein.[67] By this time Genentech was far from alone; a host of startups[68] employed recombinant technology to induce bacteria to pump out a number of naturally occurring proteins as medical therapies: the anemia treatment erythropoietin, developed by Amgen in the 1980s;[69] various monoclonal antibody-based therapies;[70] and biologic products (i.e., therapeutic

[65] See David V. Goeddel, William J. Kohr, Diane Pennica, and Gordon A. Vehar, US patent 4,766,075, "human tissue plasminogen activator," issued August 3, 1988, assigned to Genentech, Inc. See generally, D. Collen and H. R. Lijnen, *The Tissue-Type Plasminogen Activator Story*, 29 Arterioscler. Thromb. Vasc. Biol 1151 (2009).

[66] David V. Goeddel and Herbert L. Heyneker, US patent 5,424,199, "human growth hormone," issued June 13, 1995, assigned to Genentech, Inc.

[67] Genentech faced an interesting challenge with respect to Factor VIII. After Genentech cloned the Factor VIII gene, a competitor, Scripps Institute developed a better technique for isolating factor VIII from human blood plasma. This set up a patent infringement action by Scripps against Genentech, for infringement of the Scripps Factor VIII product patent. See *Clinic & Research Found.* v. *Genentech, Inc.*, 927 F.2d 1565, 1581 (Fed. Cir. 1991) (remanding the case for consideration whether Genentech avoids infringement because its recombinant product was so fundamentally different that it ought to in all equity be found not to infringe the Scripps patent – an argument under the "reverse doctrine of equivalents."). The original Federal Circuit opinion was later clarified in an opinion denying rehearing, No. 89-1541, 1991 WL 523489 (Fed. Cir. April 30, 1991). And one aspect was later overruled by *Abbott Labs.* v. *Sandoz, Inc.*, 566 F.3d 1282 (Fed. Cir. 2009) (announcing a stricter reading of so-called product-by-process claims such as the ones at issue in the *Scripps* case). For more on the details and policy issues here, see Robert P. Merges, *A Brief Note on Blocking Patents and Reverse Equivalents: Biotechnology as an Example*, 73 J. Pat. & Trademark Off. Soc'y 878 (1991).

[68] Though big pharmaceutical companies often acquire biotechnology companies, arm's-length contracting for research and product discovery is also very common. This is a distinctive feature of the biotechnology industry. See Josh Lerner and Robert P. Merges, *The Control of Technology Alliances: An Empirical Analysis of the Biotechnology Industry*, 46 J. Ind. Econ. 125 (1998); Gary P. Pisano, *The R&D Boundaries of the Firm: An Empirical Analysis*, 35 Admin. Sci. Q. 153 (1990).

[69] See Fu Kuen Lin, US patent 4,703,008, "DNA sequences encoding erythropoetin," issued October 27, 1983, assigned to Kirin-Amgen, Inc. (later simply Amgen); discussed and partly upheld in what the Federal Circuit called a "landmark decision" in *Amgen, Inc.* v. *Chugai Pharm. Co.*, 927 F.2d 1200 (Fed. Cir. 1991) (holding that prior art knowledge of DNA sequence did not render obvious a claim to the recombinant version of the protein that this sequence codes for; i.e., protein not obvious despite prior knowledge of DNA sequence coding for it).

[70] Monoclonal antibodies serve the same purpose as natural antibodies: to neutralize malignant substances in the body (antigens). But monoclonals are human-made, with scientists selecting ideal antibody-binding properties, inducing a super-producer cell to express large quantities of the antibodies, and harvesting them for therapeutic use. There have been some notable patent

substances produced by living systems, such as vaccines produced by bacteria). An example of a biologic is Infliximab, which treats inflammation in the bowels and is sold by Johnson & Johnson (a large pharmaceutical company).[71] The human genome project, aided by rapid DNA replication techniques described earlier in the section on university licensing and Bayh-Dole, opened the way for a new and lucrative market not in treatment, but diagnosis. So diagnostic kits are now one of the industry's reliable sources of income.

So far, the basic science underlying biotechnology continues to flourish. New gene therapies;[72] products based on synthetic biology; new recombinant products made possible by the breakthrough CRISPR gene "editing" technique;[73] big data-enabled optimization of therapies and dosages – these and many other technologies are just forming on the horizon. With a steady source of research funding,[74] the industry – in keeping with past practice – is likely soon to explore each of these for commercial potential.

But the technology itself is not the entire story. University licensing under Bayh-Dole, venture capital funding, and industry-specific research and drug development alliances are also interwoven in the modern biotechnology industry. The overall U.S. pharmaceutical industry has grown significantly since the 1980s, in absolute size and in relation to new drug innovation worldwide. In the 1980s, less than 10% of

suits based on this technology. See, e.g., *Centocor Ortho Biotech, Inc.* v. *Abbott Labs.*, 636 F.3d 1341, 1347 (Fed. Cir. 2011) (patent infringement suit by Centocor, based on a monoclonal antibody product for blocking the harmful Tumor Necrosis Factor-A (TNF-a), useful against conditions such as arthritis).

71 www.accessdata.fda.gov/scripts/cder/daf/index.cfm?event=overview.process&ApplNo=103772 (product information on remicade).

72 See Gary P. Pisano, Science Business: The Promise, the Reality, and the Future of Biotech (Boston, MA: Harvard Business School Press, 2006), at p. 6; Expert Essays on the Future of Biotech, World Economic Forum Agenda, January 23, 2020, available at www.weforum.org/agenda/2020/01/6-expert-views-on-the-future-of-biotech/.

73 This research resulted in a Nobel Prize for Jennifer Doudna, Professor of Chemistry at U.C. Berkeley, and Emmanuelle Charpentier, Professor at the Max Planck Institute in Berlin. Katherine Wu, Nobel Prize in Chemistry Awarded to 2 Scientists for Work on Genome Editing, *The New York Times*, October 7, 2020. What will be probably the last classic patent interference (due to the passage of the AIA), pitting the Nobel winners against a team from the Broad Institute in Boston, will resolve priority (and thus patent ownership) for the foundational CRISPR patents. See Major CRISPR Patent Decision Won't End Tangled Dispute, *Nature*, March 9, 2022.

74 The profitability of the industry is at least to some extent a function of structural features of the US health care industry, which for various reasons tends to favor innovation over equal access. Pricing of biotechnology-derived drugs is likely to be a flash point in health policy. These drugs are at once an example of innovative success, and (due to their high, sometimes exorbitant, prices) of life-supporting therapies that are, for a substantial number of patients, simply too expensive. In re Humira (Adalimumab) Antitrust Litig., No. 19 CV 1873, 2020 WL 3051309, at *2 (N.D. Ill. June 8, 2020) ($20 billion in worldwide sales in 2018 for inflammation-control drug adalimumab; market described in antitrust action brought by drug purchasers, arguing that patent owner AbbVie (spun off from Abbott Labs) had monopolized the market for the drug, in part by acquiring over 100 patents on different aspects and features of the drug).

all new drugs (i.e., "new chemical entities" or NCEs) originated with U.S. firms. By 2018 that figure was close to 70%.[75]

6.3 ANOTHER INNOVATION IN CIRCUITS: THE FEDERAL CIRCUIT

In earlier chapters, for each era I have moved from macro trends to the private law aspects of patents – the business use of patents. Then, for each period, comes doctrinal and legislative changes, followed by developments in patent administration.

Here I diverge. In my mind, many of the business-related developments after 1982 are tied up with the Federal Circuit, and more generally with the 1980s policy push that thrust the Federal Circuit onto the scene. So, it makes sense to turn first to the founding of this specialized court in 1982. Then we can circle back to the way businesses adapted to the reinvigoration of patent law. A new era was at hand, to be sure. But it began with, and was partially orchestrated by, the early-1980s startup known as the Federal Circuit.

The idea of a special patent court was very old. It was first floated at various times in the nineteenth century. Across the many variants of the idea there was a through-line: technical complexity demanded specialization.[76] Because patent law deals with products of science and technology, the argument went, it has a unique quality. So, patent institutions should be unique, including the courts handling patent cases. "Generalist" judges, such as Learned Hand, lent support at times. In the course of a long and complex opinion, wrist-deep in some abstruse technology, a judge would decry the twisted path that brought him (always a "he" in those days) to this state of affairs.

[75] See Khushboo Sharma, U.S. Food and Drug Agency (FDA), Office of New Drugs, Center for Drug Evaluation and Research (CDER), CDER New Drugs Program: 2018 Update, December 11, 2018, available at www.fda.gov/media/119700/download, at p. 11. One critique of the pharma industry may be reflected in these numbers: me-too and "lifestyle" drugs (baldness, etc.) are common. A different concern is that pharma companies in countries outside the United States have in effect delegated new drug development to the US industry. At the same time, the Chinese pharma industry is still young, and it may hold innovative potential that has yet to manifest.

[76] Learned Hand, among a number of federal judges over the years, said in 1911 that he felt unqualified in a case about purified adrenalin:

> I cannot stop without calling attention to the extraordinary condition of the law which makes it possible for a man without any knowledge of even the rudiments of chemistry to pass upon such questions as these … How long we shall continue to blunder along without the aid of unpartisan and authoritative scientific assistance in the administration of justice, no one knows; but all fair persons not conventionalized by provincial legal habits of mind ought, I should think, unite to effect some such advance.

Parke-Davis & Co. v. *H.K. Mulford Co.*, 189 F. 95, 115 (S.D.N.Y. 1911), rev'd in part 196 F. 496 (2d. Cir. 1912) As discussed in this chapter, Judge Hand's opinion was relevant to later biotechnology patents in the 1970s and beyond. Its logic was questioned in *Assoc. Molecular Pathology* v. *Myriad Genetics, Inc.*, 569 U.S. 576 (2013).

So, the urge to reform the handling of patent cases was an old and persistent itch. But why, after a century and more of tossing around the notion of a Federal Circuit or something like it, was 1982 the year that scratched the itch? Three reasons seem apt: a general interest in studying and adjusting caseloads in federal courts; increasing consensus on the need for government action to stimulate innovation, spurred in part by the "competitiveness" movement (described earlier); and the formation of a solid coalition of manufacturing companies to back specific legislative proposals. Together, these forces turned the tide.

There was a good deal of interest in federal court realignment and reform prior to formation of the Federal Circuit.[77] One eyewitness talks of

> [T]he growing concerns about the federal appellate system in the early 1970s, manifested in the work and reports of the Freund Committee, the Hruska Commission, and the Advisory Council on Appellate Justice, the efforts of the latter culminating in the National Conference on Appellate Justice in 1975.[78]

There was also an internal reorganization working group created by the Justice Department. A contemporaneous account describes it:

> In 1977, the Justice Department took a further step toward judicial reform. Attorney General [Griffin] Bell [in the administration of President Carter] created the Office for the Improvements in the Administration of Justice (OIAJ), headed by Assistant Attorney General Daniel J. Meador, for the purpose of looking into various proposals and making recommendations for reform. A two year plan for the improvement of the judicial system was issued by OIAJ in May of 1977. The plan consisted generally of long term goals for improving the administration of justice and did not contain a specific proposal for the creation of a new specialized court;

[77] See generally, Michael J. Remington, *Circuit Council Reform: A Boat Hook for Judges and Court Administrators*, 1981 B.Y.U. L. Rev. 695 (1981).

[78] Daniel J. Meador, *Origin of the Federal Circuit: A Personal Account*, 41 Am. U. L. Rev. 581, 581–582 (1992) (footnotes omitted). For the Hruska Report, see Senator Roman L. Hruska, Chairman et. al., Commission on Revision of the Federal Court Appellate System Structure and Internal Procedures: Recommendations for Change, 67 F.R.D. 195, 220 (1975). The "Freund" group was headed by constitutional law scholar Paul Freund of Harvard Law School. For its report, see Paul Freund et al., Federal Judicial Center Report of the Study Group on the Case Load of the Supreme Court (1972). The Freund Committee was appointed in the fall of 1971 by Justice Burger under the auspices of the Federal Judicial Center and issued its report in December of 1972. The study group concluded that the Supreme Court was unable to carry out its job of resolving issues of conflict between the circuits due to the increase in workload; it proposed a new national court of appeals (never enacted), situated just below the Supreme Court, to resolve circuit conflicts. The Hruska Commission was headed by Senator Roman Hruska of Nebraska, who served in the Senate from 1954 to 1976. See William H. Honan (Obituary) Roman L. Hruska Dies at 94; Leading Senate Conservative, New York Times, April 27, 1999, sec. B, p. 8.

however, the plan did include developing proposals "for rationalizing and increasing the appellate capacity of the federal judiciary" . . . [79]

Some of these commission reports and studies touted the advantages of a specialized patent court; others did not.[80] But the general concern with court reform helped make creation of the Federal Circuit if not inevitable, then at least quite within the mainstream of thinking about the structure of federal courts.

The Federal Circuit gained momentum when this court reorganization movement met the unification wing of the patent bar.[81] Reading the many reports and Congressional hearings from the time, it is apparent there was a consensus in that wing that unification would in and of itself make patents more valuable. Under the surface, for some at least, was a bigger hope: that the Federal Circuit would unify patent law around principles more favorable to patent owners than the status quo. Put simply, an unstated goal for some was to not just unify patent law but to strengthen patents in the bargain.

A single specialized appeals court was not a goal shared by the entire patent bar.[82] Established patent litigators, for example, tended to oppose it. The Seventh Circuit Bar Association, for example, commissioned an extremely detailed study of patent cases in the Seventh Circuit between 1974 and 1981.[83] The purpose was to refute one

79 Jack Q. Lever, *The New Court of Appeals for the Federal Circuit (Part I)*, 64 J. Pat. Off. Soc'y 178 (1982), at p. 191 (references omitted).

80 Ibid., at pp. 189–190 (Hruska Commission feared "tunnel vision" and low-quality judges if a specialized patent court were formed).

81 An active and knowledgeable subject expert, Representative Robert Kastenmeier (Democrat from Wisconsin), also helped push for creation of the Federal Circuit. This was one of many policy initiatives in the IP field championed by Rep. Kastenmeier:

> In the intellectual property area we processed, in 1980, a series of amendments to the law providing for reexamination of patents, a uniform patent policy for small business and universities, and mandated a system of maintenance fees to provide a sound, long term method of financing a quality Patent Office. In the current Congress the full Judiciary Committee has reported legislation which will expand the resources available to the Patent and Trademark Office even further. In addition we are considering legislation to extent patent term for pharmaceuticals and chemicals which experience extraordinary pre-market regulation and testing. All of these activities – those already completed and those in process – represent bipartisan efforts to meet the needs of our nation's court and patent system. I would like to take this opportunity in closing to thank Senator [Robert] Dole [Republican from Kansas] for his leadership in the area and Congressman Tom Railsback [of Illinois], the senior Republican Member of my own subcommittee.

The Ninth Annual Judicial Conference of the United States Court of Customs and Patent Appeals, 94 F.R.D. 347, 359–360 (1982) (Statement of Rep. Robert Kastenmeier, D.-WI).

82 They had support from academics and some judges, who worried about the narrowing effect of specialized courts. These views are summarized in Hugh Scott and Dennis Unkovic, *Patent Law Reform: A Legislative Perspective of Extended Gestation*, 16 Wm. & Mary L. Rev. 16, 937, 968 (1975).

83 Position Paper of the Bar Association of the Seventh Federal Circuit On S-677 and S-678 Providing for Courts Having Exclusive Appellate Jurisdiction in Patent, Trademark and Tax Cases, June 5, 1979, reprinted in Hearings Before the Subcommittee on Improvements in

of the most common talking points of the pro-Federal Circuit crowd: the wild variations among circuits in their decisions on nonobviousness.[84] On page 695 of its report, the Bar Association presented this table of case outcomes, by circuit:

The point of the exercise was to show that the Seventh Circuit was no outlier, and that at a very general level the regional courts were operating with similar rules and obtaining similar results. The overall validity rate is 26 percent (36 valid out

Judicial Machinery of the Committee on the Judiciary, U.S. Senate, 96th Cong., 1st Sess., on S. 677 and 678, March 20, May 7, 9, 10, and June 18, 1979 (Washngton, DC: U.S. General Printing Office, 1979), at p. 660.

[84] Another frequent argument in favor of the new court was the need to rein in forum shopping among different Circuits, with patent owners and accused infringers both seeking to file cases and have them heard in regional circuits favorable to their side of the dispute. See, e.g., Judge Henry J. Friendly, Federal Jurisdiction: A General View (James S. Carpentier Lectures) (New York: Columbia University Press, 1973), at p. 155 (speaking of the "mad and undignified races between a patentee who wishes to sue for infringement in one circuit believed to be benign toward patents, and a user who wants to obtain a declaration of invalidity or non-infringement in one believed to be hostile to them."). Some have argued that this was overblown. See Cecil D. Quillen, Jr., *Innovation and the U.S. Patent System*, 1 Va. L. & Bus. Rev. 207, 228 (2006):

> Another claim by the proponents of the new court was that circuit-to-circuit variations led to forum shopping, which resulted in "unseemly" races to the courthouse, that would be eliminated by creation of a single appellate court for patent cases. This assertion was untrue; forum shopping was not a problem.

Quillen cites data from Gloria K. Koenig, Patent Invalidity: A Statistical and Substantive Analysis 4-32, tbl.15 (rev. ed. 1980). Quillen argues that

> [T]he 10th Circuit was the most favorable to patentees with a 59.6% validity rate and the 8th Circuit was the most favorable to alleged infringers with an 88.8% invalidity rate. Had forum shopping been a problem, these two circuits would have been swamped with patent litigation initiated by patentees and alleged infringers seeking the most favorable jurisdictions for their cases. But these two courts had fewer patent validity-invalidity decisions over the 1953–1977 time span than any other court except the Circuit Court for the District of Columbia. Together the 8th Circuit and 10th Circuit had only 8% of the validity decisions. (8th Circuit, 4.1%, 10th Circuit, 3.9%).

Quillen, *Innovation and the U.S. Patent System*, at p. 228 n. 62. Other evidence from the time suggests that regional court variations might have influenced business decisions other than where to locate an infringement suit. A patent infringement suit from 1983 shows as much. The Federal Circuit opinion in the case, *Central Soya Co.* v. *George A. Hormel & Co.*, 723 F.2d 1573, 1581 (Fed. Cir. 1983) (Rich, J.), includes part of a patent lawyer opinion letter that had been commissioned by the defendant Hormel, which had worried it might infringe Central Soya's patent on a food process patent:

> The [noninfringement opinion letter commissioned by defendant Hormel in 1970] closes with the cynical advice, which has caused so much amusement among readers for whom it was obviously not written, that if Hormel chose to go ahead and produce the questioned product, "as an added safety precaution," it should do so in the jurisdiction of the Eighth Circuit Court of Appeals. The writer says: "the Eighth Circuit has not held a patent either valid or infringed within recent history." He goes on to explain in detail where Hormel could operate and be within the Eighth Circuit's domain. Hormel did not take this advice either: it operated, alas for it, in the Tenth Circuit.

of 101 patent cases counted). And the Seventh Circuit validity rate is also 26 percent (6/23). Right at the national average, so no outlier.

Overlooked in this analysis is the fact that a 26 percent validity rate is perhaps nothing to be proud of. More to the current point, however, is that the patent litigators on the Committee no doubt had extensive experience (and probably good contacts) with the local courts – including of course the judges on the Seventh Circuit. It may have been a case of an embattled and defensive patent bar preferring the devil it knew to the devil it did not know, a new court.[85] However the alignment came about, the broader patent community included anti- and pro-Federal Circuit factions. According to Assistant Attorney General Meador, of the Justice Department:

> Objections were still being voiced from some segments of the patent bar, but these seemed to be outweighed by the support that had been manifested. During the previous fall of 1978, a clear split in the patent bar had become evident. [A staff member] reported that he had divided the letters OIAJ was receiving from patent lawyers into two stacks. The favorable pile consisted almost entirely of corporate letterheads; the unfavorable pile consisted almost entirely of trial lawyer letterheads. Taking advantage of the situation ... [one of] the OIAJ staff had organized the corporate patent counsel into an effective support group for the Federal Circuit.[86]

This support group rode the reorganization wave until it crested with the Federal Courts Improvement Act (FCIA), passed in April of 1982.[87] The primary purpose of the FCIA was to combine the Court of Customs and Patent Appeals (the CCPA) and the appellate Court of Claims into a single new court, the Federal Circuit.[88] But the Federal Circuit was much more than a consolidated form of something old. It was instead something quite new. It unified all patent-related appeals (and a

[85] A letter in the same Hearings volume lends support: "The Subcommittee may well find that one reason for the footdragging reluctance from the Patent Bar to sanction any change is the 'What are they trying to do to us now' syndrome." Letter from patent lawyer Phillip H. Mayer of the Chicago patent firm Leydig, Voit, Osann, Mayer and Holt, reprinted in Hearings Before the Subcommittee on Improvements in Judicial Machinery of the Committee on the Judiciary, U.S. Senate, 96th Cong., 1st Sess., at p. 531.

[86] Daniel J. Meador, Origin of the Federal Circuit: A Personal Account.

[87] Federal Courts Improvement Act of 1982, P.L. 97-164, 96 Stat. 25, April 2, 1982, codified at Chapters 28 and 35 U.S.C. and other sections.

[88] The CCPA already had expertise in patent law, because it heard appeals of administrative decisions made by the Patent Office. Beginning in 1956, patent lawyers had backed an initiative to increase the patent expertise of the CCPA. At least one study showed the new patent-oriented judges turned the CCPA in a more pro-patent direction. Lawrence Baum, *Judicial Specialization, Litigant Influence and Substantive Policy: The Court of Customs and Patent Appeals*, 11 L. Soc'y Rev. 824, 845 (1977):

> The change in the pattern of appointments to the CCPA beginning in 1956 brought about a fundamental change in the court's policies. The patent specialists on the court, appointed through the efforts of the patent bar, have led the CCPA to adopt a line of policy significantly different from the patent policies that prevail in most of the federal judiciary ...

number of other issues) into a single court.[89] The Federal Circuit took the administrative Patent Office appeals that had been going to the CCPA and added appeals from district court patent cases. Most of the talk leading up to the FCIA was about the novelty of moving patent cases out of the regional courts of appeals (the 1st, 2nd, 3rd Circuits, etc.) and into a single national court. But subtly, the FCIA worked a double revolution. In addition to centralizing appeals from patent infringement cases, the Federal Circuit also put administrative appeals under the roof of the same central court.[90] For the first time, appellate patent jurisdiction was defined not in terms of the initial legal forum – Patent Office or private enforcement action in a

[89] The Federal Circuit hears appeals of administrative trademark decisions; International Trade Commission decisions; appeals regarding patent issues in cases against the US government (from trials in the new Court of Claims); veteran's claim appeals; and various government contract claims (e.g., the Armed Services Board of Contract Appeals). See FCIA; see also Craig Allen Nard and John F. Duffy, *Rethinking Patent Law's Uniformity Principle*, 101 Nw. U. L. Rev. 1619, 1642 (2007) ("[T]he history shows that in an attempt to avoid creating an overly specialized court, Congress included within the jurisdiction of the Federal Circuit appeals involving other areas of the law, including takings cases, government contract cases, trade appeals from the Court of International Trade and the International Trade Commission, and personnel appeals from the Merit Systems Protection Board . . . " (footnote omitted); Charles W. Adams, *The Court of Appeals for the Federal Circuit: More Than a National Patent Court*, 49 Mo. L. Rev. 43, 62 (1984). See generally,

United States Judicial Conference Committee on the Bicentennial of the Constitution of the United States, A History of the Federal Circuit, 1982–1990 (Washington, DC: Committee on the Bicentennial of the U.S. Constitution, 1991), available at https://babel.hathitrust.org/cgi/pt?id=mdp.39015024778881&view=1up&seq=5, at p. iii (listing cases in all areas of the Federal Circuit's jurisdiction). See also ibid., at p. xii:

> The Federal Circuit, while unique among the circuits, has never been specialized in the sense of concentrating on only a single jurisdictional base which thereby may become separated from the mainstream of the law. The judges must be generalists in the tradition of our judicial system. From its inception, the court has had jurisdiction over widely diverse legal fields.

[90] One objection to the Federal Circuit was that deciding Patent Office appeals would make the new court biased against a conflicting decision on validity by a district court. So, for example, if the Federal Circuit upheld patent validity after an appeal from a Patent Office rejection, it might not be pleased if a district court invalidated the same patent as part of a patent infringement case brought by the patent owner:

> [T]he question of whether the very same court which ordered the issuance of a patent should be permitted to review a decision of a district court which disagrees with the propriety of that issuance. Under the present system, an appeal to the Seventh Circuit Court of Appeals has good prospects of affirmance. Are the winning party's chances in an implicitly biased court just as good? Certainly not when it is considered that the judges and their technical advisors on review of the evidence decide that their evaluation of the technical subject matter is superior to that the expert witness relied on by the district court.

Position Paper of the Bar Association of the Seventh Federal Circuit On S-677 and S-678 Providing for Courts Having Exclusive Appellate Jurisdiction in Patent, Trademark and Tax Cases, June 5, 1979, reprinted in Hearings Before the Subcommittee on Improvements in Judicial Machinery of the Committee on the Judiciary, U.S. Senate, 96th Cong., 1st Sess., on S. 677 and 678, March 20, May 7, 9, 10, and June 18, 1979 (Washington, DC: U.S. General Printing Office, 1979), at pp. 660, 689–690.

district court. The line was drawn instead strictly according to subject matter. What matters post-FCIA is that both types are cases about *patents*.

6.3.1 *The Early Days of the Federal Circuit*

With the court's subject matter focus, American patent law changed for good. The new court instantly fulfilled its mandate, providing a single national rule in each corner of patent doctrine. There was nothing remarkable in this. The Federal Circuit by its nature was destined to be a unifying force. But what was remarkable, or at least, what had escaped mention in the run-up to 1982, was that the new court would not just unify the formerly discordant sources of patent law. It would strengthen patents in various ways, especially in its early years.

Immediately, in its first opinions the Federal Circuit signaled the change. It was apparent quite soon that the court intended to spin the great wheel, hoist fresh canvas, and put the good ship Patents on a brisk new course. Its early decisions announced that unity and stability were surely part of the new regime. But so was this: a new and different attitude toward patents. The young court was in some ways pro-patent, particularly with respect to nonobviousness and patent remedies. But beyond the adjustment in particular doctrinal areas, there was a new general attitude. This new court was going to take patents *seriously*. And it quickly signaled that American business needed to follow suit. Over time, the new court succeeded perhaps too well: already by the late 1980s, patent-based rent-seeking (patent trolls) began to appear. This bred a countermovement, patent reform, pushing back against the rent-seeking forces the Federal Circuit unleashed (see this chapter).

Returning to the early days, part of the reason the new court had so much leeway to set a course was that the received precedent it inherited came only from its immediate predecessors: the CCPA and the Court of Claims.[91] CCPA precedent

[91] This principle was announced in the first written opinion ever issued by the Federal Circuit, on October 28, 1982:

> As a foundation for decision in this and subsequent cases in this court, we deem it fitting, necessary, and proper to adopt an established body of law as precedent. That body of law represented by the holdings of the Court of Claims and the Court of Customs and Patent Appeals announced before the close of business on September 30, 1982 is most applicable to the areas of law within the substantive jurisdiction of this new court. It is also most familiar to members of the bar. Accordingly, that body of law is herewith adopted by this court sitting in banc ...
>
> Other than that created by our predecessor courts, no body of law established by any other court or set of courts would appear a suitable candidate for adoption. No other such body would include all or as many of the areas of law with which this court will be dealing. In those areas new to this court, selection of one from many available bodies of law would require an immediate rush to resolution of numerous conflicts existing among them; yet resolution of conflict, a major element in this court's mission, requires not a one-shot selection but a careful, considered, cautious, and contemplative approach.
>
> As a court of nationwide geographic jurisdiction, created and chartered with the hope and intent that stability and uniformity would be achieved in all fields of law within its substantive jurisdiction, we begin by adopting as a basic foundation the jurisprudence of

only touched on patent validity; as the appellate court for the Patent Office, the CCPA never touched on enforcement-related doctrines such as claim interpretation, infringement, remedies, or defenses. And the Court of Claims, though it did handle infringement suits against the government, generated a narrow body of precedent specific to these government-defendant cases.[92] This gave the Federal Circuit wide latitude in shaping the law related to patent enforcement (i.e., patent infringement actions). Claim interpretation, the doctrine of equivalents, infringing acts, and defenses – the new court had few constraints with respect to these and related issues. The court seized the opportunity to shape, and in some cases reshape, the American law of patents.

Two sets of cases from the early years show what went on. The first concerned nonobviousness, a key validity doctrine. The second was about remedies, that is, injunctions and damages.

We saw in Chapter 5 that in 1966 the Supreme Court laid out its views on the nonobviousness requirement under § 103 of the 1952 Act. In *Graham* v. *John Deere*,[93] the Court devised a three-part test rooted in the statute:

> Under § 103, the scope and content of the prior art are to be determined; differences between the prior art and the claims at issue are to be ascertained; and the level of ordinary skill in the pertinent art resolved. Against this background, the obviousness or nonobviousness of the subject matter is determined.[94]

The Court then continued:

> Such secondary considerations as commercial success, long felt but unsolved needs, failure of others, etc., *might* be utilized to give light to the circumstances surrounding the origin of the subject matter sought to be patented. As indicia of obviousness or nonobviousness, these inquiries *may have relevancy*.[95]

> the two national courts which served not only as our predecessors, but as outstanding contributors to the administration of justice for a combined total of 199 years, the Court of Claims and the Court of Customs and Patent Appeals.

South Corp. v. *United States*, 690 F.2d 1368, 1370–1371 (Fed. Cir. 1982).

92 See Douglas A. Strawbridge et al., *Patent Law Developments in the United States Court of Appeals for the Federal Circuit During* 1986, 36 Am. U. L. Rev. 861, 879 (1987):

> The [Federal Circuit] court has few judges, however, who have extensive prior experience in the areas of substantive patent law that were previously within the domain of the regional federal circuit courts, such as infringement and certain defenses to liability.

See also Rochelle Cooper Dreyfuss, *The Federal Circuit: A Case Study in Specialized Courts*, 64 N.Y.U. L. Rev. 1, 13 (1989) ("[T]he CAFC has had greater success on the patentability issues because at least some of its members already had substantial experience in this area ... [S]ince the PTO does not handle defenses or damages issues, these judges had not previously grappled with enforcement and damages questions.").

93 383 U.S. 1 (1966).

94 383 U.S. 1, at 17.

95 383 U.S. 1, 17–18 (emphasis added).

These "secondary considerations" are circumstantial evidence of a significant invention. As such, they can be helpful to courts. They focus on easily comprehended signals or signs that there was an important invention.[96] They can also be misleading, because some of them (especially commercial success) have a number of causes besides the presence of a technically significant invention.[97] Whatever their merits, the Federal Circuit elevated these evidentiary factors to coequal status with the three mandated factors from *Graham*. In place of the Supreme Court's three-part test, with optional (secondary) factors, the Federal Circuit substituted a mandatory four-part test: the main *Graham* triad plus the secondary considerations.[98] The secondary considerations – which the Federal Circuit rebranded as "objective indicia"[99] – were no longer secondary.

At least one inexperienced commentator at the time connected the subtle modification of post-Graham doctrine with a favorable attitude toward patents:

> [T]he Federal Circuit appears to be a "pro-patent" court. Between 1982 and 1985, the court invalidated only forty-four percent of the patents it adjudicated on appeal from trial courts, a marked contrast to the old invalidation rate of approximately sixty-six percent. Perhaps more importantly, patent lawyers believe the court favors patentees – and presumably advise their clients accordingly. These changing perceptions indicate that at a practical level, respect for patents is probably growing.[100]

Though a bit premature, there were numbers to bear this out.[101] Eventually, the proclivity of the Federal Circuit to modify established Supreme Court doctrine caught up to it. In the law of nonobviousness, after the Federal Circuit developed an

96 See Rochelle Cooper Dreyfuss, The Federal Circuit: A Case Study in Specialized Courts (notes omitted):

> It is now [after Federal Circuit cases emphasizing the value of secondary consideration evidence] less probable that a lower court will declare invalid the patent on an invention that, because of the insight of its inventor, met long felt need, enjoyed commercial success, or displayed other objective indicia of having made an important social contribution. Since it is likely that the inconsistent treatment of such inventions was the most destablizing element of the system, the CAFC has, in this area, made strides in achieving the appearance of precision.

97 This unremarkable point is made in Robert P. Merges, *Commercial Success and Patent Standards: Economic Perspectives on Innovation*, 76 Cal. L. Rev. 803 (1988).

98 See *Bausch & Lomb, Inc.* v. *Barnes-Hind/Hydrocurve, Inc.*, 796 F.2d 443, 446–447 (Fed. Cir. 1986) (Secondary considerations are one of the "four inquiries mandated by [the] *Graham* [decision]"), cert denied, 108 S. Ct. 85 (1987); see also *Cable Elec. Prods., Inc.* v. *Genmark, Inc.*, 770 F.2d 1015, 1026 (Fed. Cir. 1985) (evidence on secondary factors must be considered even when the three *Graham* indicia point clearly to one conclusion); *Stratoflex, Inc.* v. *Aeroquip Corp.*, 713 F.2d 1530, 1539 (Fed. Cir. 1983) (under *Graham*, obviousness inquiry must include secondary factor evidence, with each given "its appropriate weight").

99 See, e.g., *Hodosh* v. *Block Drug Co.*, 786 F.2d 1136, 1144 (Fed. Cir. 1986) (Rich, J.) ("These considerations are objective criteria of obviousness that help illuminate the subjective determination involved in the hypothesis used to draw the legal conclusion of obviousness based upon the first three factual inquiries delineated in Graham.") (emphasis in original).

100 Robert P. Merges, *Commercial Success and Patent Standards*, at pp. 822–823.

101 See ibid., at p. 822 n. 71 (citing sources on which the calculations were based).

idiosyncratic approach called the teaching-suggestion-motivation test, the Supreme Court intervened in 2007 to restore its 1966 ruling in *Graham* v. *John Deere* as the centerpiece of § 103 decisions.[102]

Besides nonobviousness, the young Federal Circuit quickly placed its stamp on the law of patent remedies. Whether from inexperience with remedies or from a concerted desire to enhance respect for patent rights, the court one year after its founding announced a categorical rule:[103]

> [S]ome courts will not find irreparable harm to exist without a showing of financial irresponsibility. In this case, no such showing exists. However, none of the cases we have reviewed in which injunctions were denied for lack of irreparable harm involved such a strong showing of validity and infringement as exists in the instant case. Courts faced with strong showings of validity and infringement, on the other hand, have found irreparable harm from continued infringement of a valid patent ... We agree with the reasoning in these cases. The very nature of the patent right is the right to exclude others. Once the patentee's patents have been held to be valid and infringed, he should be entitled to the full enjoyment and protection of his patent rights. The infringer should not be allowed to continue his infringement in the face of such a holding. A court should not be reluctant to use its equity powers once a party has so clearly established his patent rights. We hold that where validity and continuing infringement have been clearly established, as in this case, immediate irreparable harm is presumed. To hold otherwise would be contrary to the public policy underlying the patent laws.

This set a template for what became known as the "automatic injunction rule," a highly pro-patent-owner standard that stayed in place until 2006, when the Supreme Court eliminated it in the landmark *eBay* decision.[104]

In cases on infringement damages, the Federal Circuit was less bold. It showed a willingness to affirm damages found by the district courts, and in the process upheld some damages assessments for over $ 1 million.[105] In its earliest years it also affirmed some modest damage awards[106] It was not until the pathbreaking instant

[102] See *KSR Int'l Co.* v. *Teleflex Inc.*, 550 U.S. 398 (2007).

[103] *Smith International, Inc.* v. *Hughes Tool Co.*, 718 F.2d 1573, 1580–1581 (Fed. Cir. 1983).

[104] *eBay* v. *MercExchange, LLC*, 547 U.S. 388 (2006).

[105] See, e.g., *Lam, Inc.* v. *Johns-Manville Corp.*, 718 F.2d 1056, 1069 (Fed. Cir. 1983) (affirming total damages of $1,639,824.21).

[106] See, e.g., *Hanson* v. *Alpine Valley Ski Area, Inc.*, 718 F.2d 1075, 1076, 1077 (Fed. Cir. 1983) (patent on what seemed to be a significant invention in snow making):

> The magistrate found that "[w]ithin the short span of twelve years, the airless snowmaking process has developed substantially and presently accounts for almost one half of all artificially produced snow." The Hanson patent expired in 1978 ... After a trial, the magistrate recommended that Hanson be awarded damages of $12,250 for the infringement.

See also *Stickle* v. *Heublein, Inc.*, 716 F.2d 1550, 1563 (Fed. Cir. 1983) (approving damages "greater than a reasonable royalty" so that the award adequately compensates the patent owner; "Such an increase, which may be stated by the trial court either as a reasonable royalty for an infringer ... or as an increase in the reasonable royalty determined by the court, is left to its sound discretion.").

photography case *Polaroid* v. *Kodak*[107] that the developing picture came into clear focus (so to speak). This case actually combined an unstinting adherence to the automatic injunction rule with an eye-popping damages award quite close to $1 billion.[108] The *Polaroid* decision was one of a number from the mid-1980s that immediately shoved patent law back into a place of prominence it had not occupied in the legal profession since the heyday of patent-antitrust cases in the 1940s and 1950s. The massive price tag on the *Kodak* case was enough to bump patent law from the province of corporate R&D and patent departments into the rarified strata of CEOs and Chief Financial Officers (CFOs). When patents moved from the realm of "millions," and suddenly was a topic necessitating talk of "billions," corporations noticed. It became common knowledge that the upstart court had done more than "stabilize" patent law. It had in fact strengthened patent rights along several crucial dimensions. And businesspeople had begun to notice.

An article in the Business section of the New York Times in 1986 captures the moment. Commenting on the *Polaroid* case, it said: "The Kodak-Polaroid patent dispute is the most prominent example of a pro-patent sentiment in American courts, patent attorneys agree."[109] Quoting a New York patent lawyer, it continued: "There's a real trend in this country toward upholding patents." This was a stark contrast to the recent past, the same article said: "The overemphasis of antitrust feeling prevalent in the 1970s is abating."[110] And the change in sentiment was traced to the FCIA: "The greatest impetus to the pro-patent shift occurred in October 1982, when at the urging of business leaders and bar associations, the twelve member United States Court of Appeals for the Federal Circuit was formed."[111] Looking back from later years, others agreed that the early- to mid-1980s was the key moment when the 1980s patent revival hit critical velocity.[112] The Federal Circuit was never a

107 *Polaroid Corp.* v. *Eastman Kodak Co.*, 228 U.S.P.Q. (BNA) 305, 343–344 (D. Mass. 1985) (acknowledging that an injunction against Kodak will shut down its instant camera division, causing the loss of 800 full-time and 3,700 part-time jobs; but granting the injunction, because "the public policy at issue in patent cases is the 'protection of rights secured by valid patents' . . . " (quoting *Smith International*, 718 F.2d at 1581)).

108 See *Polaroid Corp.* v. *Eastman Kodak Co.*, 16 U.S.P.Q.2d (BNA) 1481 (D. Mass. 1990), modified, 17 U.S.P.Q.2d (BNA) 1711 (D. Mass. 1991) (total damage award of $909 million). Analysts and observers had expected an even higher award, given the possibility of enhanced damages based on evidence of "willful infringement." L.A. Times Staff, Polaroid Wins $909 Million From Kodak: The firms have been involved in a patent-infringement suit for years. Analysts had expected the award to be much larger, L.A. Times, Finance Section, October 13, 1990, available at www.latimes.com/archives/la-xpm-1990-10-13-fi-1997-story.html.

109 Eric Schmitt, Business in the Law: Judicial Shift in Patent Cases, New York Times, January 21, 1986, p. D2, cols. 1–3.

110 Ibid., at col. 2, quoting Michael W. Blommer, Executive Director of the American Intellectual Property Law Association.

111 Ibid.

112 See, e.g., Ronald K. Fierstein, *Polaroid* v. *Kodak*: Still the Champ, IP Watchdog Blog, April 12, 2015, available at www.ipwatchdog.com/2015/04/12/polaroid-v-kodak-still-the-champ/id=56654/: "[I]t was clear that a new era took hold in the mid-1980s, and many looked on the result in the Polaroid v. Kodak case as the turning point." The objective data show that overall, the early Federal Circuit did raise the validity rate of litigated patents. But findings of infringement, and

"patentee always wins" court, and it has in its history at times moved quite far from this extreme. Even so, it has only rarely been accused of rabid anti-patent sentiment. It is not, for example, typically categorized along the lines of some of the courts and cases reviewed in Chapter 5, in which even noteworthy inventions were sometimes treated dismissively. In the Federal Circuit a patent is treated as a serious – though not sacrosanct – instrument: the embodiment of a policy favoring invention and innovation.

To recap: in 1982 Congress threw the switch, the new court went live, and the country witnessed the activation of the Federal Circuit. The ensuing jolt to the patent system was a surprise for some, but it was also just what many backers had hoped for. It is not true that in its earliest period, the Federal Circuit erected a large neon sign on the roof of its courthouse: "Open for business. Patents welcome." But 1982 did mark a major step-up in the visibility and impact of U.S. patents.

6.3.2 *The Changing Nature of the Patent Litigation Bar*

The change in patent court jurisdiction caused changes in the patent bar. Patent law was moving off the margins and back into the center of American law. This was, some said, more a restoration than a revolution. According to patent expert John F. Duffy,

> The [Supreme] Court [in the nineteenth century] had jurisdiction over all patent appeals from the nation's regional trial courts, much like the modern Federal Circuit has today. The Court's jurisdiction was mandatory, and it would regularly hear several patent cases each term. These cases defined the forefront of federal industrial policy and they attracted some of the best legal minds of the day, including Daniel Webster, Justice Benjamin Curtis, and Chief Justice Salmon Chase – all of whom represented private litigants in Supreme Court patent litigation. The practicing patent bar could even claim as its own Abraham Lincoln, who served briefly as counsel in a patent litigation against Cyrus McCormick (the inventor of the mechanical reaper), authored a famous speech on patent policy, and received a patent on a method he invented for lifting river boats over shoals.[113]

overall damages awards, were not as consistently pro-patent owner. See, e.g., Paul M. Janicke, *To Be or Not to Be: The Long Gestation of the U.S. Court of Appeals for the Federal Circuit*, 69 Antitrust L.J. 645, 653–654 (2002) ("The validity results have been somewhat to the advantage of patent owners, as compared with regional circuit results in the decades from the 1940s through the 1970s," but not so with respect to findings of infringement). But see the overenthusiastic assessment in Robert P. Merges, Commercial Success and Patent Standards: Economic Perspectives on Innovation, at pp. 805, 821 (Federal Circuit "appears to be a 'pro-patent' court").

[113] John F. Duffy, *The* Festo *Decision and the Return of the Supreme Court to the Bar of Patents*, 2002 Sup. Ct. Rev. 273, 274 (2002). On Lincoln's role in the McCormick reaper patent case, see Doris Kearns Goodwin, Team of Rivals: The Political Genius of Abraham Lincoln (New York: Simon and Schuster, 2005), at pp. 173–179 (describing the key role of the McCormick case in propelling Stanton into the highest echelons of the Supreme Court bar). The patent policy

By 1975, however, this heyday was long in the past. Constitutional law scholar Philip Kurland observed that although "[t]he subjects of the [Supreme] Court's historical opinions in this field [patent law] cover a very wide range," since the early twentieth century "[t]he [Supreme] Court has, for the most part, relegated the resolution of patent controversies to the lower levels of the federal judiciary."[114] As discussed in Chapter 5, in a fair number of Supreme Court cases after 1930, when the Court did touch on patents it was often in the negative context of antitrust law or patent misuse.

During this era, patent practice was concentrated in a specialized patent bar. There were, in the parlance, law firms (meaning general law firms) and patent firms. General firms typically referred all patent-related work to patent firms: prosecution, Patent Office appeals, licensing and other patent deal-making, and patent enforcement, that is, litigation. General firms touched on patents mostly in the context of their lucrative antitrust work, which had a much higher profile than patent work from 1920 to 1982 or so.[115] This specialized patent bar developed some distinctive features, particularly when it came to litigation. Virtually all patent cases were tried to a judge, rather than a jury, despite prior history of jury involvement in the patent system.[116] Educating the judge about the facts of a case became an important predicate to success, so lucid presentation of technical details was a prized skill among patent firm litigators. As District Judge Frank J. Coleman explained in the

speech Duffy refers to is a speech Abraham Lincoln gave several times on the spirit of "Young America" and its vibrant, dynamic contrast with the "Old Fogy" spirit of Europe. See Abraham Lincoln, Second Lecture on Discoveries and Inventions, February 11, 1859, 3 Collected Works of Abraham Lincoln (Reprint ed., Cabin John, MD: Wildside Press, 2008), available at https://quod.lib.umich.edu/l/lincoln/lincoln3/1:87?rgn=div1;view=fulltext. Lincoln's patent is US patent 6,469, "buoying vessels over shoals," issued May 22, 1849, to Abraham Lincoln. The McCormick case is *McCormick* v. *Manny*, 15 F. Cas. 1314 (C.C.N.D. Ill. 1856) (Cas. No. 8,724), aff'd sub nom. *McCormick* v. *Talcott*, 61 U.S. 402, 15 L. Ed. 930 (1857). Webster represented numerous patent owners, including Charles Goodyear, inventor of vulcanized rubber. See *Goodyear* v. *Day*, 10 F. Cas. 678 (C.C.D.N.J. 1852) (Cas. No. 5,569).

114 Philip B. Kurland, The Supreme Court and Patents and Monopolies (Chicago: University of Chicago Press, 1975), at pp. xi–xii.

115 Philip B. Kurland, The Supreme Court and Patents and Monopolies, at p. ix ("Since the passage of the Sherman law in 1890, antitrust cases have been treated by the [Supreme] Court as almost on a par in importance with the major constitutional controversies that come before it for resolution.").

116 See Mark A. Lemley, *Why Do Juries Decide If Patents Are Valid?*, 99 Va. L. Rev. 1673 (2013), 3; William C. Robinson, The Law of Patents for Useful Inventions §932 n.5 (1890) (noting that almost all patent cases were tried in equity after the 1870 Act, which permitted an equity judge to award both injunctions and damages); Gary M. Ropski, *Constitutional and Procedural Aspects of the Use of Juries in Patent Litigation (Part I)*, 58 J. Pat. Off. Soc'y 609, 610 (1976) (by 1940, only 2.5 percent of patent cases were tried to a jury; and fron 1940 to 1959, 3.4 percent of cases were tried to juries).

1930s,[117] in patent cases, the judge has the "difficult task of drawing factual conclusions in a field with which he may be unfamiliar. Unquestionably a new judge has a harder job on the facts in patent cases than in any other special branch with which he may be equally unfamiliar."[118] Patent lawyers were even said to have a fear of juries – perhaps because juries might not understand an invention, or had become hostile to patents, or just because trials to a judge had become conventional.[119]

Patent litigation was indeed treated as a "special branch" of the law during this era. In this, it had much in common with litigation in the field of admiralty (or maritime) law. Both fields have their specialized vocabularies, traditions, and institutions, and have been at times dominated by a specialized bar or group of law firms. Indeed, Judge Coleman, speaking to an audience of patent lawyers, said in 1933 that "[t]he admiralty bar is frequently coupled with you ... "[120]

The typical patent case during this era (roughly, 1950 to 1981) pitted litigators from two patent-specialty law firms against each other. The case was tried, by stipulation (and an unspoken "insider" norm), to a judge and not a jury. Validity was a tough sell in many courts. And when a patent owner won on validity and infringement, damages were often unexceptional.

But patent lawsuits, after 1982, began to outgrow the patent specialists. Judge Roger Andewelt explained why in 1993:

> The large money judgments that have resulted from decisions of the Federal Circuit have encouraged investment in technology and have encouraged investment in lawyers to maintain the value of your technology. There's now a lot of money at stake ... [121]

[117] Frank J. Coleman, *How to Try a Patent Case before a Judge Who Knows No Patent Law*, 15 J. Pat. Off. Soc'y 681 (1933). Judge Coleman served on the District Court for the Southern District of New York from 1927 to 1934. See www.fjc.gov/history/judges/coleman-frank-joseph.

[118] Frank J. Coleman, *How to Try a Patent Case*, at pp. 682–683.

[119] See Don W. Martens, *Remarks at the Tenth Annual Judicial Conference of the United States Court of Appeals for the Federal Circuit*, 146 F.R.D. 205, 375 (1993):

> [A]long came the Federal Circuit and I thought that jury trials would take a nosedive after that because there would no longer be the need for it. What instead happened is first of all, patent lawyers got used to trying cases before a jury and got a little bit more comfortable with it. They used to always have a fear of juries.

See The Tenth Annual Judicial Conference of the United States Court of Appeals for the Federal Circuit, 146 F.R.D. 205, 374 (1993) (statement of Judge Roger Andewelt, U.S. Claims Court). Judge Andewelt was on the Claims Court from 1987 to 2001. See www.fjc.gov/history/courts/u.s.-court-federal-claims-andewelt-roger-barry.

[120] Frank J. Coleman, *How to Try a Patent Case*, at p. 685.

[121] The Tenth Annual Judicial Conference of the United States Court of Appeals for the Federal Circuit, 146 F.R.D. 205, 374 (1993) (statement of Judge Roger Andewelt, U.S. Claims Court). Lawyer Martens agreed: "Plaintiffs' patent lawyers particularly got comfortable with [jury trial practice] and got to like it. Then, at the same time, along came, as [Judge Roger Andewelt] said [in his remarks at the same judicial conference], larger damages. With larger damages, you're

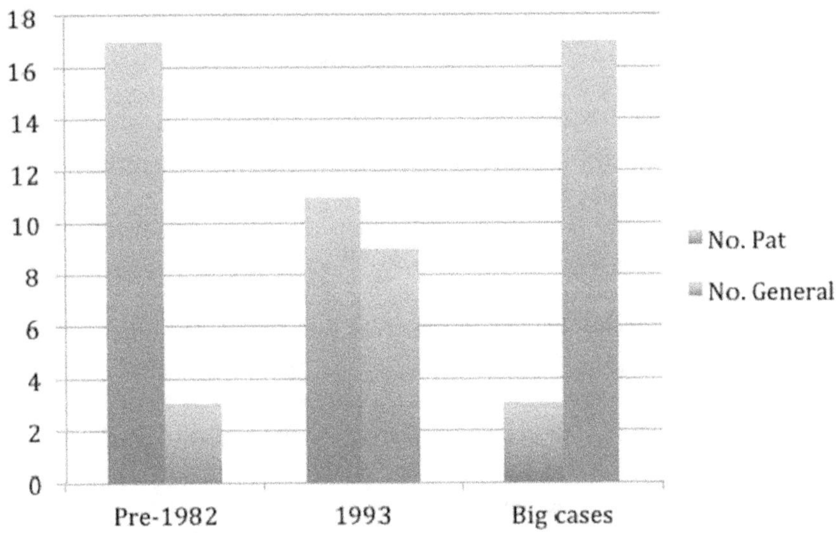

FIGURE 6.7. Patent litigation by patent specialist and general practice law firms in three time periods

Figure 6.7 tells the story of patent litigation in transition. A semi-random group of ten cases from before 1982 (1978–1981) are compared with ten notable cases from 1993, the year of the tenth Federal Circuit anniversary. (The final bars on the chart represent ten cases from 2003 to 2012 involving large damage awards and are discussed later).

General law firms were not the only ones to rediscover patents. The Supreme Court got in on the act too, re-entering the field with a vengeance circa 1996. Professor John Duffy, writing in 2002, celebrated the Supreme Court's "return to the bar of patents" in the Federal Circuit era. Though quite significant in its own right, this was in some ways merely the culmination of a trend that began soon after 1982. Ever since the Federal Circuit was formed, patent law had been climbing back into its historical place among the fields that demanded the attention of influential federal circuit courts and legal scholars. As we have seen, patent practice claimed the attention of large national law firms, which had mostly ignored patent law in the twentieth century. The cause again was stronger patents. Nothing quite quickens the pulse of the competitive trial lawyer like the prospect of a sleepy, insular field in which legal damages are poised to take a precipitous jump. The eye-popping $900 million damage award in the 1986–1990 case of *Polaroid* v. *Kodak* provided just such

going to find plaintiffs asking for a jury ... " Don W. Martens, *Remarks at the Tenth Annual Judicial Conference of the United States Court of Appeals for the Federal Circuit*, at p. 375.

a stimulus.[122] *Polaroid* joined a stream of other high-profile pro-patent cases that sent out an unmistakable signal: Patents were once again Serious Business. This in turn drew sophisticated general litigation talent back into the patent fray. Sensing the need to correct the Federal Circuit – and perhaps influenced by the newfound cachet surrounding patents – the Supreme Court also reprised its long, but also long forgotten, centerstage position in the patent drama.

After its early years, the new court presided over a patent system that had earned newfound respect in legal and business circles. But then something happened that the Federal Circuit founders did not expect: the great wheel turned, and the now-strengthened patent rights held such potential value that new business models sprang up to take advantage. Some of these business models were grouped together, more or less accurately, and referred to with a phrase that came to be the modern shorthand for the rent-seeking behavior we saw at work in certain other eras of US patent history. They were called patent trolls. The trolls in turn stimulated an aggressive patent reform movement that coalesced around a number of changes – first judicial (via the Supreme Court), and later legislative (in the America Invents Act of 2011). We return to the reform movement a bit later. Now, we need to review some of the ways business developed around and in response to the new Federal Circuit.

6.4 FROM PATENTS IN BUSINESS TO PATENTS AS A *BUSINESS*

Large technology companies hold tens of thousands of patents worldwide. They acquire thousands more every year.[123] The sheer magnitude of worldwide patents in force poses a challenge to everyone involved in invention and innovation. Particularly in complex information technology products such as mobile phones, semiconductors, and cloud services, and software generally, the huge numbers of

[122] *Polaroid Corp.* v. *Eastman Kodak Co.*, No. 76-1634-MA, 1990 WL 324105, at *84 (D. Mass. October 12, 1990) ("The total award is $909,457,567.00."), later reduced, see amended, No. CIV.A. 76-1634-MA, 1991 WL 4087 (D. Mass. January 11, 1991) ("[T]he corrected final judgment is $873,158,971."). One can imagine mixed feelings at the Kodak headquarters when this reduction was announced. It's nice to save $26 million dollars or so. But then again it was only a 3 percent reduction in the total. Along the way, the Federal Circuit had upheld findings that most of the Polaroid patents in the case were valid and had been infringed by Kodak. See *Eastman Kodak Co.* v. *Polaroid Corp.*, 89 F.2d 1556 (Fed.Cir.), cert. denied 479 U.S. 850 (1986). For the story of this epic lawsuit, as told by the Polaroid side, see Ronald K. Fierstein, A Triumph of Genius: Edwin Land, Polaroid, and the Kodak Patent War (Chicago: American Bar Association Press, 2015).

[123] One patent services firm estimated that when it comes to worldwide patents in thir corporate portfolio: "Samsung Electronics [is] in the top slot with 76,638 active patent families, followed by IBM at #2 with 37,304, Canon at #3 with 35,724, GE [General Electric] at #4, and Microsoft at #5." See IFI CLAIMS Patent Service, Press Release: Annual U.S. Patent Grants at All-Time High, January 14, 2020, available at www.businesswire.com/news/home/20200114005211/en/IFI-CLAIMS-Announces-2019-Top-Global-Patent.

patents in force make it very difficult to predict infringement or even keep track of relevant patents. Even in industries where there are on average fewer patents covering each commercial product, creative patent claim drafting and aggressive patent strategies mean that numerous patents may lie in wait for any successful product.

Big numbers lead to big changes. Today, the basic unit of analysis in corporate patenting is not the individual patent but the *patent portfolio*. One article describes two chief advantages of portfolios over individual patents: (1) "scale" and (2) diversity:[124]

> [A] well-conceived patent portfolio is in many ways a form of "super-patent," sharing many of the marketplace advantages conventionally attributed to individual patents (paradigmatically, rights to exclude others from the marketplace), only on a larger, broader scale. By aggregating the individualized value of a number of closely related patents, the scale-features of patent portfolios enable holders to realize true patent-like power in the modern marketplace to a degree which is impossible using individual patents alone.

What do all these patents do all day? Many sit in silence, awaiting their chance in the corporate tournament. They are markers, chips in the pile. They serve as bulk or ballast when sheer patent volume is needed, such as when two large companies cross license their patents, or to add to corporate valuation in a merger or acquisition. They also serve as options, as we saw way back in the *Continental Paper Bag* era from Chapter 4. So, a company might obtain a series of patents that cover different future possible ways a current technology might evolve. Some of these will be valuable: the ones that cover the actually-implemented technology. All the others will have little to no value, but that will be revealed only over time. Meantime, all the patents on each possible development path can be thought of as options. Most will "lapse," and not come into play.[125] A few will be "exercised" – the patents will be used as threats against other companies, or licensed to one or many others, or asserted in patent litigation.

Corporate patent licensing serves a number of goals and comes in several variations. IBM, for example, actively seeks out licensees for its vast patent portfolio. The average income of $1.2 billion each year defrays about 15 percent of the company's roughly $8 billion in annual R&D spending.[126] Cross-licensing is also

[124] See generally Gideon Parchomovsky and R. Polk Wagner, *Patent Portfolios*, 154 U. Pa. L. Rev. 1, 31–32 (2005) (outlining a theory of patent value in which the worth of a patent portfolio is greater than the sum of its individual parts). [At the same time,] "the inherent diversity created by the aggregation of many different patents offers holders a range of benefits – such as the ability to address the risk and uncertainty fundamental to innovation – that cannot be easily achieved absent the creation of such structures." See also Michael Risch, *Patent Portfolios as Securities*, 63 Duke L.J. 89 (2013).

[125] Early lapse is promoted by the maintenance fee structure. To remain in force, a patent owner must renew its patent (and pay a fee) at 3 years, 7 years, and 11 years after patent issuance. See 35 U.S.C. § 41.

[126] See "Patents Add to IBM Revenue," IPCenter [Law firm] website, available at https://theipcenter.com/2018/08/patents-add-to-ibm-revenue/. See generally, Robert P. Merges and

part of the IBM strategy: It licenses companies under some or all of its patents, in exchange for access to the licensee's patents. This allows IBM to stay abreast of all manner of new technologies being developed by small and large companies alike. Sometimes, a company will use its patents to help get through a period of bad financial losses. Texas Instruments Corporation used its valuable foundational patents on transistors and semiconductors for just such a purpose. When it found itself behind in the competition with its peer companies, and losing money on outdated products, it licensed patents to generate enough revenue to fund development of a new generation of products. When these new products gained traction, TI returned to industry relevance and once again counted on product sales for the bulk of its revenue.[127]

Patents serve a number of other purposes as well. They can be attractive to investors – especially for startup companies. They can be used as collateral against a loan. They can be sold outright on the "secondary market" (see this chapter). They can be waived or pledged in service of strategic corporate goals (as discussed next). As has been true throughout the history of patent law, private actors have integrated patents into all sorts of business models, corporate strategies, and private transactions. The uses listed here are just the latest in the long series of ways that businesses have found to put patents to work in pursuit of their goals.

6.4.1 *Modular Technologies and Patent Challenges*

As always, business use of patents is dictated in part by trends in technology. The franchise model of the early nineteenth century (Chapters 2 and 3) worked when an entire enterprise could be founded around a single patent and exploited by different agents in different locales. Industrialization, in the form of large, integrated national companies, concentrated patents into large, centralized firms, particularly after the establishment of internal corporate R&D departments. Post-1982, there is certainly no shortage of very large companies – by some measures the American economy is more concentrated in 2020 than it has been since the early twentieth century. Yet even so, many products on the market today must work together (or "inter-operate") with the products of other firms. And each product is itself often a composite of multiple components produced by multiple firms, often in different countries around the world. There is a design feature that enables all these complex pieces to fit together, and that is the idea of modularity.

Helen (Fang) Liu, IP Strategy for Business (Beijing: China Legal Publishing House, 2020) (text in English and Chinese), at p. 300 et seq.

127 For an overview of the TI "licensing bridge" strategy, see United Nations Organization for Economic Cooperation and Development, OECD Science, Technology and Industry Outlook 2006 (Paris: OECD Press, 2006), at p. 154. This has been described as a "patent bridge" strategy: leveraging patent income to successfully traverse an extended dip in corporate earnings. See Robert P. Merges and Helen (Fang) Liu, IP Strategy for Business, at pp. 299–301.

A concrete example may help. A mobile phone includes a data processing chip that itself embodies both physical components and numerous chunks of software code. The code must run on the chip it's designed for, the chip must receive instructions from other components about what is needed, and then must send its output through a channel to yet another component, and so on.

Interconnection like this is the rule today. It is a growing feature of consumer electronics, transportation (particularly with autonomous vehicles), appliances, the home environment (especially heating, air conditioning, and energy use), entertainment, and more. Even for conventional products, apart from data interconnection, manufacturing is often spread across many companies, frequently in many countries as well. These "value chains" require modular components that can be made separately and then integrated into a final product. This is how cars, mobile phones, and many other items are now made.

Putting aside pharmaceuticals and biotechnology for a moment, the basic characteristics of much manufacturing are: (1) patent intensity, plus (2) dispersed companies contributing to complex, composite products. These two elements combine in a number of corporate patent strategies that depend at least in part on the use of patents.

6.4.1.1 Waive for Friends, Enforce against Direct Competitors

A variant on the concept of corporate patents as options is a strategy of extensive waiver, accompanied by highly selective enforcement. This can be used to encourage consumer adoption of a "backbone" technology whose widespread use will benefit the patent owner.[128] The benefit usually comes in the form of sales of

[128] I choose the term "backbone" here despite the fact that such a technology could also be called a "platform." The word "platform" has taken on a constellation of meanings, which often vary depending on the subject matter specialty of the speaker. In business strategy, a common set of components that form the core of a machine, software system, or the like may be called a platform; an example would be Microsoft Windows. See Carliss Y. Baldwin and C. Jason Woodard, The Architecture of Platforms: A Unified View, in Platforms, Markets and Innovation (Annabelle Gawer, ed., 2009). Many computer programs, sold by many different companies, can "plug into" the Windows operating system, making Windows a frequently referenced "software platform." More recently, engineers and economists have reserved the word "platform" to refer to any physical or virtual thing, place or system that brings together multiple sellers and multiple buyers of products and/or services. These are often (and more properly) referred to as "two-sided platforms." Thus, a shopping mall (a building with multiple separate units for lease) brings together sellers and buyers of retail goods. Today, virtual platforms such as Amazon.com, Uber, and YouTube are much in the news because of their growing size and power. Amazon brings together buyers and sellers of a huge range of goods and services. Uber brings together (or "intermediates" between) independent drivers and riders. YouTube (along with Spotify and the like) brings together producers and consumers of content (video, audio, etc.). In a more general sense, all-purpose search engines such as Google also serve as two-sided platforms, bringing together advertisers and consumers, though in this and

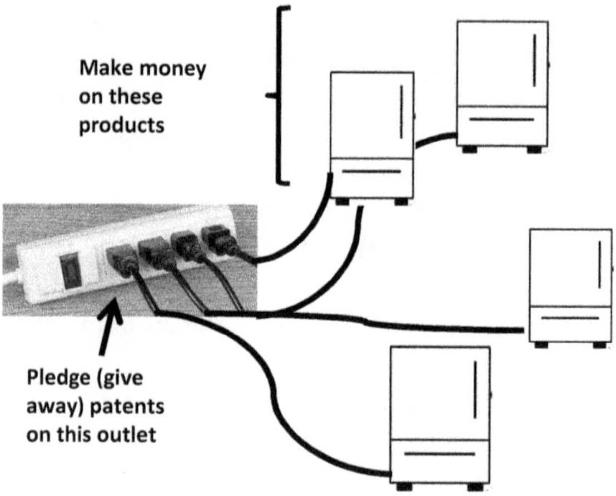

FIGURE 6.8. Incentives to pledge (or cheaply license) standard plug patents

products that "plug in" to the backbone technology.[129] As against the many consumers who want access to the backbone, and whose adoption makes it more valuable, property owners are most welcoming. They choose not to exercise their property rights; in legal terms, owners waive their rights on a massive scale.[130] An example: The owner of patents on the electrical outlet (plug) might want to encourage adoption of a standard outlet design. Waiving patents on the design might help with adoption. Promoting the standard design can increase sales of its profitable electrical appliances, which are made to fit the standard outlet. Figure 6.8 illustrates.

An example in the software industry is the "PDF" format created and distributed by Adobe Company. Adobe figured out a long time ago there was much money to be made in championing and then essentially giving away a document viewing format that is simple to use and appealing to many people. The gamble – which has

other cases of "ad-supported" content, ads are often an extraneous intrusion into the content or information sought by the consumer. These platforms might be said to bring together producers and consumers of information, in a format subsidized by advertisers. The advertisers use the platform to attract customers, even though the customers are (usually) not on the platform for the express purpose of looking at ads. In any event, to maintain clarity, I reserve the term "platform" for these two-sided platform companies. For me, by contrast, a "backbone technology" is a software system such as Microsoft Windows or the Adobe Corporation's PDF file format (referred to in the text).

[129] The example is drawn from Robert P. Merges, IP Rights and Technological Platforms (Working Paper, December 1, 2008), available at https://ssrn.com/abstract=1315522 or http://dx.doi.org/10.2139/ssrn.1315522.

[130] Waiver is sometimes an underappreciated feature of property. And giving away information and technologies can be a good strategy if it stimulates the market for profitable complementary products. On these issues, see Robert P. Merges, *To Waive and Waive Not: Property and Flexibility in the Digital Era*, 34 Colum. J.L. & Arts 113 (2011); Robert P. Merges, *A New Dynamism in the Public Domain*, 71 Chi. L. Rev. 183 (2004).

paid off handsomely – was that widespread adoption of the PDF format as a technological platform or standard would lead to robust sales of Adobe's proprietary Acrobat line of software, useful in composing and editing documents in the PDF standard.

What then is the value of property rights for such a backbone technology? The value is in excluding competitors, of course. For as surely as Adobe wants to encourage users to adopt its PDF format, it wants to prevent competitors as much as possible from exploiting the popularity of the PDF format. If it could not keep competitors from copying all aspects of the PDF standard, or duplicating all Adobe products that work with it, its strategy would be an abject failure. You can get a sense of how important this is every time you open a PDF document, and a long list of Adobe patents scrolls by in the opening screen. These patents are obviously irrelevant to the average user; they are part of the bundle of rights that Adobe implicitly waives when it gives away the PDF format, saying "please use this!"

Adobe's patents are aimed instead at competitors who might want to copy the functionality of Adobe's complementary products. Adobe is careful not to waive its rights against these direct competitors. And patents permit this; enforcement – whether, when, against whom – is strictly up to the patent owner. Which facilitates the drawing of a conceptual circle: friends inside, direct competitors outside.[131] Inside the circle, where the friends are, patents are irrelevant. But for those outside the circle, the threat of patent enforcement remains. Various legal limits may apply to prevent patents on a plug design from conferring too much market power in related markets (such as those for appliances).[132] But patents on all or part of the plug at least enable a company to attempt a "friendly circle" strategy.

6.4.1.2 Patent Pledges

Pledges make public, and in greater or lesser degree binding, a company's intention to permit others to use its patents for free.[133] They are an open and public declaration of the circumference of the free-use circle just described. They are meant to encourage adoption and development of a technology. A company may pledge to

[131] What is there to prevent a patent owner from drawing in "friends" and then demanding royalties? See Robert P. Merges and Jeffrey M. Kuhn, *An Estoppel Doctrine for Patented Standards*, 97 Cal. L. Rev. 41 (2009). On the idea of a property waiver for "insiders" and (at least potential) property enforcement against others, see Robert P. Merges, Property Rights Theory and the Commons: The Case of Scientific Research.

[132] The patent-antitrust "tie-in" cases, originating around the turn of the twentieth century (and reviewed in Chapter 3), set some of these limits. For an overview of the importance of device "interoperability" as a policy goal, see Peter S. Menell, *Rise of the API* [Application Program Interface] *Dead?: An Updated Epitaph for Copyright Protection of Network and Functional Features of Computer Software*, 31 Harv. J. L. & Tech. 305 (2018).

[133] See Jorge L. Contreras, *Patent Pledges: Between the Public Domain and Market Exclusivity*, 2015 Mich. St. L. Rev. 787 (2015).

make their patents available to anyone who will promote a certain technology. The US electric vehicle company Tesla made such a pledge in 2015. A Tesla's strategy was to widely promote the development of electric vehicles. The idea was that the more electric vehicles were sold by all companies – not just Tesla – the more money Tesla would make. Large numbers of vehicles would lead to more vehicle charging stations, faster development of battery technologies, and more widespread acceptance of electric vehicles generally.

Another reason companies make patent pledges is to make money on products that connect to those technologies covered by the patented interface. For example, imagine a company that sells electric appliances. It operates in the time before standard electrical outlets (or electrical "plugs") have been agreed upon. If such a company holds patents on a particular electrical outlet design or format, it might pledge those patents to the public.

If this pledge leads other companies to adopt and use the patented outlet design, this design may become the most common one. It may become a de facto "standard." In this way, the company that made the pledge will profit. The availability of common, standard plug design will make customers more willing to buy electrical appliances. The customers will know that they can use their appliances anywhere; that is what it means for the common plug to be a "standard."

This is a common strategy today in the software industry. It explains why for-profit companies sometimes spend a good deal of money on technologies and then waive the relevant patent rights.[134]

6.4.1.3 Patents and Technical Standards

The interoperability of product components has been an issue in many industries over time. But it has never been more important than today – thanks to the two factors emphasized earlier: many patents, and highly interdependent technical components. One solution was pioneered by engineers: a technical specification describing how a certain component fits into or connects with other components in a system. These specifications are like blueprints: Any company that builds its components in compliance with the agreed-upon design can sell in the market. Every buyer who sees a component complies with a certain agreed-upon standard can be confident it will effectively "plug into" a larger system. The blueprint for a working interface is agreed upon by those who participate in its design. After that, companies compete in the usual way in the market for the "standards-compliant" products. Using the jargon common in the standards community, these standards-using companies are called implementors.

[134] See, e.g., IBM Pledges 500 U. S. Patents to Open Source in Support of Innovation and Open Standards, IBM (January 11, 2005), available at www-03.ibm.com/press/us/en/pressrelease/7473.wss. For a general description of this and related strategies, see Jorge L. Contreras, *Patent Pledges*, 47 Ariz. St. L.J. 543 (2015).

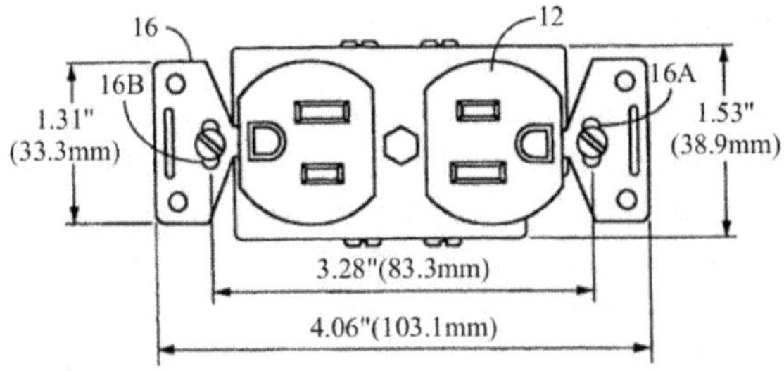

FIGURE 6.9. Standard electric plug

An early and simple example is the standard (American) electrical outlet or plug. Years ago, companies selling electrical appliances gathered together to agree on a common size and dimensions for an outlet. Figure 6.9 shows the standard plug design the various companies agreed on.

This simple example is meant to be a stand-in for the thousands of technical standards that govern all sorts of products and components. One large standard-setting organization (SSO), the American National Standards Institute (ANSI), administers 11,500 standards.[135] And there are roughly 240 other SSOs in the United States alone. Behind each standard is a group of organizations – manufacturing companies, researchers, product users, etc. Standards ensure that it makes no difference which company a buyer buys from: Any "standards compliant" company will make products that interface using the agreed-upon specification. In this way, standardization promotes modularity and makes possible product interdependence.

Each company with an interest in a standard dedicates one or more representative to the standard setting process (often engineers). Standards are set by negotiation – many companies have interests and opinions they want to express while the standard is under active consideration. Standard-setting brings together many different economic interests and corporate strategies. A number of variants and alternatives are usually discussed before agreement is reached on a final specification. SSOs stipulate sometimes detailed internal procedures (committees, subcommittees, votes, etc.) to govern these negotiations.[136] Big money may be at stake for some of the companies participating; one company may have investments that will pay off if one variant standard design is chosen, while another may stand to lose money unless an alternative variant is chosen. There are often several ways to perform a given function within a standard, so arguments about technical superiority (speed, efficiency, simplicity, backward compatibility) may become intertwined with more self-interested motives.

[135] See Introduction, American National Standards Institute website, available at www.ansi.org/about_ansi/introduction/introduction.

[136] See Benjamin Chiao, Josh Lerner, and Jean Tirole, *The Rules of Standard-Setting Organizations: An Empirical Analysis*, 38 RAND J. Econ. 4 (2007).

One complicating factor that affects the self-interest in standard-setting is the presence of patents. There are usually one or more patents that cover part of a standard design: a component, subcomponent, assembly, procedure, etc. that forms part of a product or procedure covered by a technical standard. Patents of this type are called Standard Essential Patents (SEPs). Every standards organization (SSO) has to deal with patents, because (a) patent-owning companies may argue for variants of the technical specification that fall under one or more of their patents and (b) companies that plan to build products under a standard may have an incentive to avoid a patent-covered variant, even if that variant would (absent the patent) be the top choice on strictly technical criteria.

SSOs have patent policies designed to push these issues to the side, so standard negotiators can concentrate only on technical feasibility and superiority. The most common policy requires all participants to identify (or "declare") any known standards-related patents, and then push all patent licensing issues into the future. This "kick the can down the road" approach takes the form of a general agreement to license standard essential patents (SEPs) to all those who will use (or "implement") a standard design. But the terms of the license are left open. The only restriction agreed to is that any future license under an SEP owned by any company participating in the standard setting will be licensed on Fair Reasonable and Nondiscriminatory terms: so-called FRAND licensing. A FRAND license commitment is a pledge by a participating company that if it has patents covering any part of the standard design, it will license those patents on FRAND terms when the time comes.

There are thousands of standards, and some include thousands of patents. In a large sense, FRAND licensing works fairly well. It certainly saves time and money in negotiations for the many standards that come to pass, and for standards that cover technologies that ever make headway in the market. Even for standards on successful products or components, FRAND saves time. In the delay that would inevitably result from a highly complex, multi-company patent valuation process (which might well be required in the absence of FRAND), the standard under review might be "scooped" by another, competing standard. And in any event, there is a good deal to be said in favor of waiting to negotiate until after the standard is adopted and diffused. There is much more information about the product and product market later in the game.

But FRAND has costs too. First, of course, is the cost of negotiating a license. This can be delayed, but (if a patent owner wants to make money) not put off forever. Even with more information, there can be big differences of opinion over the value of a specific subpart or component of a standard-defined product. Many standardized products carry the dual features described in the introduction to this section: (1) patent intensity, plus (2) dispersed companies contributing to complex, composite products. SEPs usually embody the challenges of valuing a small part of a larger whole, when only the larger whole (i.e., an assembled product, complete with all components) is sold on the market. There is no easy way to use "market value" for an individual component if that component is never sold on any market by itself. Putting a dollar value on a small part under these circumstances is never easy.

As if this were not challenge enough, standards and SEPs raise an additional problem in valuation. Standard-defined technologies are valuable in part precisely *because* they have been agreed to as standards. Once there is agreement on a technical specification, the inputs to the specified design (components, parts, etc.) take on additional value by virtue of being included in the agreed-upon standard. After it is included, there is a super-additive or synergistic value to each part of the standardized design. But this incremental value comes from the fact of agreement by an SSO; it is not intrinsic to the features of the chosen component. Of course, there is a limit to the extra value added by inclusion in a standardized design. Every standard design has a value ultimately set by consumers of end products. For a technical feature that is of limited utility to end users, a standardized design might add little to the economic value of the feature. And it follows that the parts, components, and assemblies that constitute that feature (and any patents on them) would accordingly be of limited value – despite being included in a standard design.[137] The very common scenario of multiple SEPs that read on or cover various aspects of a standardized design is shown in Figure 6.10, which pictures a standard electrical plug.

Patent cases over SEPs raise unique issues. This is partly the nature of the issues – as mentioned, SEP cases involve (a) modular technologies, composites of many separately-made components, which are (b) covered by multiple, dispersed patent rights. But there is another feature of these cases that makes them particularly unique and challenging: many are filed by non-practicing patent holders, some of which qualify as patent trolls (see later in the chapter). The maximum patent leverage sought by trolls makes these highly contentious cases. Companies accused of infringement – standards "implementers," that is, manufacturers of products covered by a standard – often place a miniscule value on any particular SEP patent. Manufacturers know that most standards include hundreds of patents. They also know there are many separate standards that apply to the large number of interoperable components in a final manufactured product. And finally, many SEPs are held by manufacturer/implementers who have a natural incentive to keep costs down (by holding down FRAND royalty rates). In some cases, standards cover "backbone" system elements. As we saw earlier in Section 6.4.1.2, some manufacturers benefit by wide adoption of backbone technologies. When in wide use, they may open markets for backbone-compatible products sold by a manufacturer. (The PDF document is an example.) Figure 6.10 shows a situation where manufacturers are eager to make

[137] See Norman V. Siebrasse and Thomas F. Cotter, *The Value of the Standard*, 101 Minn. L. Rev. 1159, 1164–1165 (2017).

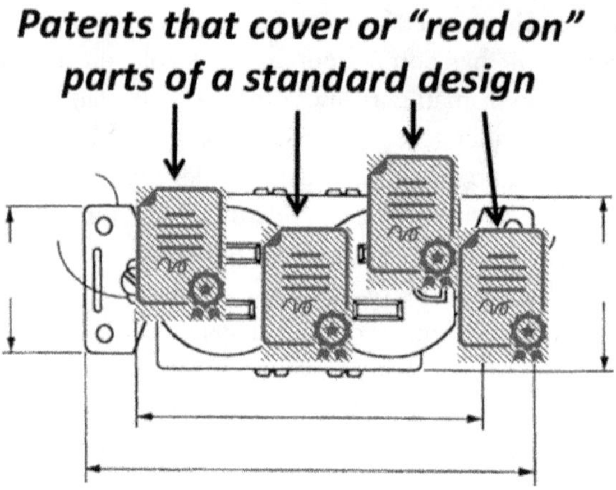

FIGURE 6.10. SEPs covering various components of a standard electrical plug

electrical plugs widely available, because it enhances sales of plug-compatible appliances.

But patent owners who file SEP infringement cases may own as few as one SEP patent. So, owners want to maximize the value of each patent they litigate. One could forgive the judges in these cases if they treated some SEP owners like toddlers at a birthday party: "Now American Ingenuity and Progress, Inc. (typical name for a Troll company: trying to sound like a real bona fide inventive hero) what would happen if everyone tried to take half the cake for themselves?"

In the event, these hard-fought cases have raised a number of difficult issues. The first concerns the remedies available to a holder of one or a few SEPs – in particular, the availability of an injunction. Should one or a few patents necessary to a single standardized component confer the power to shut down the market for the entire product? No, according to the US Supreme Court in the *eBay* case from 2006.The Court recited as its rationale the well-known problem of a bargaining "holdup": use of an ownership claim on a tiny portion of a composite asset to extract far more from the asset's owner than the single claim intrinsically merits.[138] Beyond this, SEP cases always present thorny variations on the problem of appropriately valuing a small part of a larger whole.

To top it all off, the most contentious SEP cases overlap with the thorny problem of patent suits brought by Non-Practicing Entities (NPEs), some of which are accurately classified as patent trolls. Companies whose business is patent

[138] The locus classicus for patent-related holdup theory is Mark A. Lemley and Carl Shapiro, *Patent Holdup and Royalty Stacking*, 85 Tex. L. Rev. 1991 (2007). Buried inside the rhetoric of "holdup" is a morality tale: legal systems have ways of adjusting government-granted entitlements when necessary. An adjustment like this helps stop an entitlement holder from extracting excessive value that is rightly attributable to the contributions of other stakeholders.

enforcement (usually backed by litigation) have every reason to push beyond a FRAND-level royalty. Sometimes these litigation firms acquire SEPs from other companies[139] – as explained later. Other times, a player in the patent litigation game develops a patent that is not covered by the FRAND obligation yet is nonetheless necessary for implementation of a standardized design. Non-FRAND yet essential patents are most likely to challenge the limits of component valuation: They are necessary in the composite product, they are the vehicle by which litigation firms make their money, and they are ideal candidates for a holdup strategy.

But just as there are two sides to every patent dispute, there is another strategy game in the SEP field – one that favors implementers (manufacturing companies). The basic idea is to use litigation to delay and wear down one or more SEP owner. The longer a company can keep from paying royalties, the more likely the relevant patents will expire, be invalidated, or become outdated. Even if that never happens, it can pay to string along a firm whose business model is litigation-dependent. A good number of tactics are available to implement a strategy of delay: bring an antitrust lawsuit against the patent owner; support a government antitrust investigation or lawsuit (a popular tactic in China); or simply stretch out a patent infringement suit (or suits: many are brought in Germany and China) as long as possible.[140] Collectively, these tactics are said to be part of a strategy called holdout. Succinctly, holdout is the counterpart to holdup. Patent owners try to maximize patent leverage; implementers try to string along patent owners.

Holdup versus holdout produces complex and contentious litigation. Parties bargaining in "the shadow of" FRAND commitments must move with delicacy. A licensing offer by an SEP owner must not be so high as to fail utterly to look "fair." A prospective licensee must make some sort of good faith effort to respond to a bona fide FRAND offer; ignoring a reasonable offer could easily be seen as a form of holdout. And once negotiations are under way, they must be conducted with some palpable effort to reach agreement. Yet although the SEP licensing "dance" is an

[139] Some litigation-oriented firms are the remnant of a former manufacturing firm, one that at one time made and sold products, but has been beaten in the product market. These former manufacturing companies hug the line between producer companies and patent trolls; see later in the chapter. An example is the company called Unwired Planet, which has brought a number of highly visible patent infringement suits against mobile phone handset makers such as Apple and Samsung. Unwired Planet evolved out of an early, successful mobile phone software company that pioneered software for pulling data off the Internet and onto individual mobile phones (e.g., for mobile phone email and messaging applications). See Kit Chellens, The 'Inventor' of the Mobile Internet Takes on Google, Samsung, Bloomberg News Service, October 1, 2015, available at www.bloomberg.com/news/articles/2015-10-02/nevada-patent-troll-takes-on-google-samsung-in-london-court.

[140] German courts favor the grant of injunctions, and resolve injunction requests quickly see Robert P. Merges and Seagull (Haiyan) Song, Transnational Intellectual Property (Cheltenham: Edward Elgar, 2018), at p. 206. In China, damages are low but injunctions are issued readily. On the other hand SEP cases can get caught up in courts' concern with promoting Chnese domestic interests; see id., at p. 226 (China).

anthropologist's dream – full of threat, display, misdirection, and efforts to impress – it is an act repeated over and over again in the high-volume world of SEP licensing. Because of this complexity, and the desire to funnel disputes out of the courts and into private negotiations, some court-decided SEP cases try to proscribe a preferred negotiating procedure.[141] In a way reminiscent of the drug industry's pioneer-generic company patent challenge protocol, laid down in the Hatch-Waxman Act, these SEP cases attempt to impose a regulatory negotiating framework. This framework governs a specific type of firm-to-firm interaction in a specialized industry.

6.4.1.4 Patent Pools

An alternative to a loose SSO is to form a patent pool. A pool bundles together related patents held by its members.[142] It then offers to other companies a single license that includes all the bundled patents. (The members of the patent pool typically receive a license as well.)[143] Many pools in the contemporary economy form around building-block components of complex technologies. Two examples are data compression protocols for transmitting video, graphics, and other high-density digital content, and data transmission rules that allow computers, tablets, and mobile phones to communicate with local area networks (i.e., WiFi standards).[144] Pools are more formal than FRAND commitments in that they set and charge a single price for use of the pooled patents; unlike FRAND commitments, they do not simply put off for another day the question of whether and how much a user must pay for a patent.

Patent pools are important to their members and to their licensees.[145] The benefit for licensees is easy to appreciate: "one stop shopping" for many patents at once.

[141] See, e.g., *Unwired Planet Int'l Ltd.* v. *Huawei Technologies Co. Ltd.*, [2017] EWHC 1304, EWHC (Pat) (UK), No. HP-2014-000005, 6/7/17, 2017 WL 01233380, reprinted in part in Robert P. Merges and Seagull Haiyan Song, Transnational Intellectual Property (Cheltenham: Edward Elgar Press, 2018), at pp. 214 et seq.

[142] See generally, Robert P. Merges and Michael Mattioli, *Measuring the Costs and Benefits of Patent Pools*, 78 Ohio St. L.J. 281, 297 (2017) (from which part of this section was drawn); Robert P. Merges, *Contracting into Liability Rules: Intellectual Property Rights and Collective Rights Organizations*, 84 Cal. Rev. 1293 (1996); Robert P. Merges, Institutions for Intellectual Property Transactions: The Case of Patent Pools, in Expanding the Boundaries of Intellectual Property: Innovation Policy for the Knowledge Society 123, 129–130, 132, 144 (Rochelle Cooper Dreyfuss et al. eds., 2000), available at www.law.berkeley.edu/files/pools.pdf [hereinafter Merges, Patent Pools] (last accessed January 29, 2016); Michael Mattioli, *Power and Governance in Patent Pools*, 27 Harv. J. Law & Tech. 421 (2014).

[143] Ibid.

[144] Two patent pool administrators, MPEG LA and Via Licensing Corporation oversee the licensing of patents covering the MPEG audio and video standards, 802.11 WiFi, and other protocols widely used in the consumer electronics industry. See "Current Programs" at www.mpegla.com/ (click on "Current Programs") (last visited January 29, 2016); "Licensing Programs" at www.vialicensing.com/ (click on "Licensing Programs").

[145] See Brad Biddle, Andrew White, and Sean Woods, "How Many Standards in a Laptop? (And Other Empirical Questions)," 2010 Int'l Telcomm. Union Sec. Telecomm. Standardization Kaleidoscope Acad. Conf. Prof. 123 (2010), available at http://papers.ssrn.com/sol3/papers.cfm?

This conserves on the cost of licensing numerous patents from dispersed patent holders by, in a sense, compressing that process into a single event. This yields a secondary benefit: Patent pools reduce the odds that any patent holder, aware that its permission is necessary to a licensee, will strategically hold out for exorbitant licensing fees.[146] For their members, meanwhile, pools provide compensation for the use of patented technologies while obviating the need to engage in multiple negotiations with licensees. Members of patent pools who are *also* licensees – a common scenario – benefit from both sides of the deal.

Sometimes, patent holders choose to forego pools and give away platform technologies for free. Or they may, as described, encourage the diffusion of platforms by putting off for the future any royalty demands, by making FRAND pledges for standard-essential patents. Indeed, pools are relatively rare compared to FRAND commitments.[147] These strategies require that companies have some other way to make money besides the sale of the platform itself, however. Usually, they sell software or other products that "plug into" the platform.[148] Encouraging adoption of the platform furthers sales of related products, as just described.

Many standards contributors do not have the option of profiting via complementary products. Universities, for example, sponsor research but do not generally sell products that plug into platforms.[149] For them, pools may often be the only way to obtain compensation for platform-related patents. Giveaways and pledges to forego enforcing their patent rights will not help them. More generally, allowing

abstract_id=1619440 (of 251 standards embodied in a laptop computer, only 3 percent are associated with patent pools).

146 See Thomas F. Cotter, *Patent Holdup, Patent Remedies, and Antitrust Responses*, 34 J. Corp. L. 1151, 1160 (2009) (describing this phenomenon).

147 Josh Lerner and Jean Tirole, Standard-Essential Patents 2 (Toulouse Sch. of Econ., Working Paper No. IDEI-803, 2013) ("[M]ost [standard- setting organizations (SSOs)] require the owners of patents covered by the standard to grant licenses on fair, reasonable and nondiscriminatory (FRAND) terms."); Jorge L. Contreras, *Fixing FRAND: A Pseudo-Pool Approach to Standards-Based Patent Licensing*, 79 Antitrust L.J. 47, 50–51 (2013) (asserting that FRAND licensing commitments are the "most prevalent" mechanism used in standard-setting to lower holdout risks).

148 A notable example is Sun Microsystems, Inc., which in the early 2000s – years before it was acquired by Oracle Corporation – licensed its Java software platform in hopes of encouraging software developers to adopt it. See Press Release, Sun Microsystems, Sun Opens Java (November 13, 2006), available at https://web.archive.org/web/20070124154133/http://www.sun.com/2006-1113/feature/story.jsp (last visited February 1, 2006).

149 See, e.g., Robin Feldman and W. Nicholson Price II, *Patent Trolling: Why Bio & Pharmaceuticals Are at Risk*, 17 Stan. Tech. L. Rev. 773, 784 (2014) ("Universities are in the business of scientific research and education, and they generally do not engage in the production of products from their inventors."); Liza Vertinsky, *Universities as Guardians of Their Inventions*, 2012 Utah L. Rev. 1949, 1960–1961 (2012) ("With some exceptions, U.S. research universities, particularly private research universities, have historically viewed their mission as one that excludes product-development activities . . . ").

direct compensation for specific technologies encourages specialization.[150] Without direct compensation, a platform specialist has to diversify into related products, which may not be its strength. The point is that patent pools provide some of the transaction cost savings of free patent giveaways and FRAND pledges but also provide higher monetary returns. This can be a good thing.

Patent pools, like all collaborations among competitors, pose a risk to consumers. They can serve as covers for anticompetitive arrangements that raise prices beyond what the competitive level. Antitrust regulators and courts are charged with assessing these potential costs along with the advantages that patent pools offer. To date, most proposed pools have been approved under the US Department of Justice "Business Review Letter" procedure. That does not stop potential licensee companies from challenging pools on antitrust grounds; some of the patent-antitrust cases from the 1940s and 1950s (reviewed in Chapter 5) are still on the books, available to justify challenges to pools. This despite the fact that evidence shows mostly net benefits for patent pooling – in part due to limitations on pools put in place by DOJ guidance.[151]

6.4.2 *Patent Litigation Post-1982: Rise of the Patent Trolls*

Earlier, in the section on the founding of the Federal Circuit, we saw that the new court sent a (probably intentional) shock through the patent system. A few lucky patent owners who had already been ramping up patent holdings (and enforcement litigation) received a windfall: the high-risk business of patent enforcement they entered in earlier days suddenly paid off like an overdue jackpot. The most prominent recipient of the post-1982 windfall was inveterate inventor Jerome Lemelson, who had been filing patents on all manner of things since the 1950s, from toys to quality control systems using real-time video monitoring. Lemelson made a career out of being an inventor, replicating in the 1970s the careers of some of the independent inventors from the late nineteenth century, who invented and patented across multiple fields, for example, shoe manufacturing and railroads.

Despite later hagiography (some self-funded), Lemelson was not as well-known as Thomas Edison or George Westinghouse, partly because his business was not in founding companies or industries, but in suing established manufacturers under his

[150] See Robert P. Merges, *A Transactional View of Property Rights*, 20 Berkeley Tech. L.J. 1477 (2005); Ashish Arora and Robert P. Merges, *Specialized Supply Firms, Property Rights, and Firm Boundaries*, 13 Indus. & Corp. Change 451 (2004) (explaining how intellectual property rights can promote technological advances in specialized firms). See generally, Alfred D. Chandler, Jr., The Visible Hand 15–36 (1977) (arguing that, to some extent, firm specialization spurs economic growth); Oliver E. Williamson, Markets and Hierarchies: Analysis and Antitrust Implications 197–205 (1975) (discussing economist George Stigler's views on research, economic growth, and firm specialization).

[151] See Robert P. Merges and Michael Mattioli, *Measuring the Costs and Benefits of Patent Pools*, at pp. 298–299 (describing Business Review Letters and the 1995 DOJ Licensing Guidelines they are based on).

many patents. But after 1982, Lemelson was sailing his patent-based enterprise in decidedly favorable winds. Before the Federal Circuit, he had made somewhere close to $7 million from licensing his inventions – not chicken feed. But with the advent of the new court, Lemelson boosted both his patenting and his enforcement efforts. Benefitting especially from the in terrorem effect of the almost $1 billion Polaroid-Kodak case (see earlier), and perhaps Japanese company fears of anti-Japanese sentiment from "competitiveness" concerns (see earlier also), he licensed major Japanese car companies for $100 million.[152] This gave him a war chest, which he immediately dipped into. He mounted a series of parallel campaigns with the same strategic objective: get as much in patent royalties from as many companies as possible. And when the smoke cleared on the various fields of battle, he was roughly $1.5 billion to the good. He received over 600 patents, many filed long before the 1980s, forming a portfolio that paid off late, but big. And crucially for the immediate future of patent law, he inspired a cohort of dozens to copy his patent-centric business model. Congress may have sent a jolt with creation of the Federal Circuit, but Lemelson showed how to tap into this fresh source of power to make real money. The resulting surge of patent litigation, and litigation-backed licensing demands, defined the start of the era of patents *as a business*. Lemelson may well have laughed all the way to the bank at those who doubted him. But the song he sang was destined to be the real story of the 1990s and beyond. A good title for that song might be: "Send in the Trolls."

6.4.2.1 Rent-Seeking Redux: A Troll Taxonomy

The Oxford English Dictionary, informative as always, tells us that "troll" is derived from the Old Norse *trolldómr*, a word with connotations of witchcraft, or magic-making. In Norse mythology, trolls are usually short, squat figures with unpleasant personalities. They are antisocial, found only in remote and isolated settings. They usually live in underground dwellings or caves. In sum, ill-tempered characters best left alone.

But patent trolls became very hard to avoid. The warm glow of big money – the billion-dollar *Polaroid* case, Lemelson's licensing paydays, the Texas Instruments save-the-company enforcement program,[153] and others – lured entrepreneurs into the patent business, and inevitably (given the business model) into the courtroom. There were many variations on the basic theme, as we see next. But they all earned their money through patent licensing demands backed by the threat of litigation. Often enough, the threat led to the deed. Patent infringement litigation boomed.

[152] Adam Goldman, Some claim inventor Lemelson a fraud, USA Today, August 21, 2005, available at https://usatoday30.usatoday.com/tech/science/discoveries/2005-08-21-lemelson-fraud_x.htm.

[153] Described earlier in this chapter.

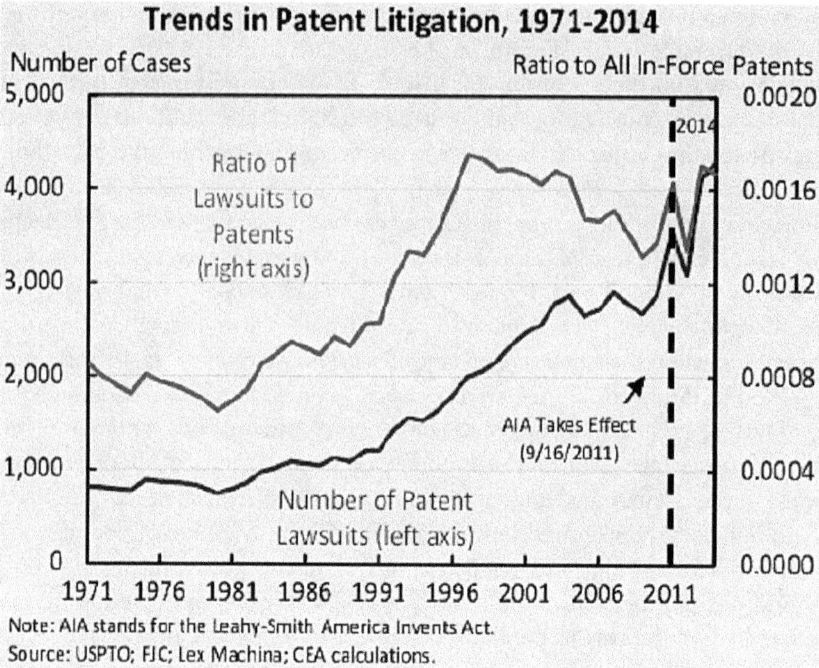

FIGURE 6.11. Patent lawsuit filings, 1971–2011
Source: Council of Economic Advisors Issue Brief, Office of the United States President, March 2016, available at https://obamawhitehouse.archives.gov/sites/default/files/page/files/201603_patent_litigation_issue_brief_cea.pdf, at p. 3.

Look at some data beginning in the 1970s. At that time, there were under 1,000 patent infringement cases filed in district courts each year. There was some modest growth pre-Federal Circuit (1982), but in the 1990s, case filings doubled. Then it was steady, rapid growth up until 2011 (an important year, as the AIA passed; see later). Figure 6.11 tells the tale.

The roughly 4,000 cases filed in 2011 represent a quadrupling of patent infringement suits since the 1970s. The right axis of this graph is a measure of the enforcement *rate* rather than sheer case numbers. It shows the ratio of lawsuits to the number of outstanding patents (the number "in force") in each year. Higher ratios indicate a higher enforcement rate. By this measure enforcement intensity peaked in the 1990s – signaling a rush to "monetize" as many in-force patents as possible.

Trends in case filings after 2010 are captured in Table 6.2.

But how many of these lawsuits were filed by patent trolls? That's where the taxonomy comes in.

50 SHADES OF TROLL In the early 1990s infringement suits were on the increase. One characteristic of troll litigation is that it typically takes aim at large, successful

TABLE 6.2. *Patent cases filed in US district courts, 2010–2019*

Year	*New district court cases*
2010	3562
2011	4031
2012	5614
2013	6270
2014	5114
2015	5852
2016	4619
2017	4050
2018	3658
2019	3573

manufacturers. Trolls typically file multiple lawsuits against a broad swath of companies. As trolling increased, the number of lawsuits against large, established companies took off rapidly. By one account, it was some lawyers at the pioneering computer chip company Intel who first used the "troll" label.[154] At this early stage, trolls were often given the more formal label "Non-Practicing Entity" or NPE. A fair bit of analysis and commentary emphasized that what delineates a troll/NPE from other companies is that trolls do not manufacture. They hold patents; seek out licensing royalties under those patents; and sue companies that refuse to pay up.

Around this time, many made the perfectly plausible point that patent law does not and should not favor patentees who happen to be in the business of manufacturing. In this they are entirely correct. We have seen throughout this book that as early as the 1810s, patent owners such as Ithiel Town – unquestionably a real pioneer in the design of wooden bridges – made money by licensing his patents, and not by building bridges.[155] We also saw that in the early twentieth century, the Supreme Court refused to require a patent owner to work or implement his or her patented invention as a condition to enforcing a patent (*Continental Paper Bag*, Chapter 4). And in general, some notable "idea shops" have emerged over the years. As a matter of fact, allowing non-manufacturers to enforce patents encourages talented inventors to do what they do best – an example, in the world of research, of Adam Smith's productive and efficient "division of labor."[156]

[154] See Joff Wild, "The real inventors of the term 'patent troll' revealed," Intellectual Asset Management Magazine, August 22, 2008, at p. 1 (attributing the origin of "troll" to one [or both] of Anne Gundelfinger and Peter Detkin of Intel, in 1993).

[155] See Chapter 2.

[156] See Robert P. Merges, A Transactional View of Property Rights; Ashish Arora and Robert P. Merges, Specialized Supply Firms, Property Rights, and Firm Boundaries (explaining how intellectual property protection can promote technological advances in specialized firms).

This explains why, during the steep run-up in troll activity, an observant scholar coined a more informative label: the Patent Assertion Entity (PAE).[157] In 2018, a team of scholars drilled deeper, and came up with seven categories of patent litigation plaintiffs, a definitive taxonomy based on a careful and comprehensive study of actual patent infringement suits. The seven are:

(1) University;
(2) Individual Inventor;
(3) Large Patent Aggregator;
(4) Failed Operating or Startup Company;
(5) Patent Holding Company;
(6) Operating Company; and
(7) Technology Development Company.[158]

Of these, (3), (4), and (5) can reasonably be classified PAEs. Some (but not all) are trolls. (Category (4) is especially tricky; see just ahead). In addition, some individual inventors appear to be small-scale PAEs or trolls (depending on the quality of their inventions, their litigation tactics, and what they do with licensing revenue). Category (3), large patent aggregators, consists of companies that buy up patents invented and originally owned by many disparate entities, combining them into subject matter-oriented portfolios, which they license to companies in various industries.[159] Category (5) is made up of

Some defenders of NPEs, those who object to the label "troll" altogether, rely on a willing buyer-willing seller construct to defend troll settlements. See, e.g., James F. McDonough III, Comment, *The Myth of the Patent Troll: An Alternative View of the Function of Patent Dealers in an Idea Economy*, 56 Emory L.J. 189, 190 (2006) (contending that PAEs "actually benefit society" by "act[ing] as a market intermediary in the patent market . . . provid[ing] liquidity, market clearing, and increased efficiency to the patent markets"). But not all voluntary markets are efficient (blackmail, contract killings, etc.), and a market economy relies on government institutions to shut down markets that undermine important public values and otherwise make no valuable contribution. See Robert P. Merges, *The Trouble with Trolls*, at p. 1583 ("The presence of willing buyers and willing sellers does not necessarily imply that social welfare is being served; at times, the legal system must shut down markets when the things being exchanged have no social value – as in the case of blackmail.").

[157] Colleen V. Chien, *From Arms Race to Marketplace: The New Complex Patent Ecosystem and its Implications for the Patent System*, 62 Hastings L.J. 297 (2010) (coining the term "patent assertion entity").

[158] Christopher A. Cotropia, Jay P. Kesan, and David L. Schwartz, *Heterogeneity Among Patent Plaintiffs: An Empirical Analysis of Patent Case Progression, Settlement, and Adjudication*, 15 J. Emp. Leg. Stud. 80, 93 (2018). For other breakdowns and analysis of the troll phenomena, see Colleen V. Chien, *Of Trolls, Davids, Goliaths, and Kings: Narratives and Evidence in the Litigation of High-Tech Patents*, 87 N.C. L. Rev. 1571 (2009); Michael Risch, *Patent Troll Myths*, 42 Seton Hall L. Rev. 457 (2012).

[159] See Christopher Cotropia et al., *Heterogeneity Among Patent Plaintiffs*, at p. 94 ("This [category] includes [the] Acacia companies, Wi-Lan, and Intellectual Ventures [, Inc.]"). Some of these companies are publicly traded, which makes it easier to see how much money

patent-owning companies typically organized as LLCs and owning one or only a few patents.[160]

6.4.2.2 The Special Case of Failed Product Companies

The tip of the spear in disputes over troll categorization is the debate over patents that come from failed product companies. These are companies that started life with the best intentions; their founders hoped they were creating the next Google, or Microsoft, or Intel. But as often happens with small companies, things did not work out as planned. Whether the intrepid startup never made a saleable product, or did, and was beaten soundly in the marketplace, the end result is the same: dreams of greatness died a certain death. What is left, when the battle is over and defeat is at hand, is often just a few loyal employees, some scattered assets, and (often) a great deal of debt.

Among the scattered assets left at the end, the firm's patents are often thought to have the most potential value. Sometimes this leads the failed product company to undergo a metamorphosis: It turns into a patent holding company, hoping to license its patents (and litigate if necessary, in service of the licensing campaign). Other times, the failed company sells its patents to another firm – perhaps an operating company, on the lookout for patents to bulk up its portfolio. Perhaps it sells instead to a patent aggregator, such as RPX or Intellectual Ventures. Or perhaps it sells to a PAE or an entity that looks for all the world like a classic patent troll.[161]

they make from the licensing-litigation model. See James Bessen and Michael J. Meurer, *The Direct Costs from NPE Disputes*, 99 Cornell L. Rev. 387, 403 (2014) (footnotes omitted):

> We obtained licensing revenue from disclosures by the 10 publicly listed firms that were predominantly in the patent-assertion business during the period from 2005 to 2010 (Acacia, Asure, Interdigital, Mosaid, Network-1, OPTi, Rambus, Tessera, Virnetx, and Wi-Lan) … These companies filed lawsuits against 1,450 companies during this period, accounting for about one-sixth of all PAE lawsuits filed in the … database [used in this research].

160 Ibid.

161 See Colleen Chien, *Startups and Patent Trolls*, 17 Stan. Tech. L. Rev. 461, 479–481 (2014):

> Some small companies have been able to sell or monetize their patent portfolios to support ongoing or new practicing business ventures … A successful patent assertion campaign can support the business, or help fund a transition, for example, to another operating company business model or full-time patent assertion. 4% of survey respondents [in a survey of startup companies] stated that they had monetized their patents. A handful explained that they had either sold the patents along with a product line, sold unused patents outright, or licensed their patents.
>
> … [Though most startups either never acquire patents or do not sell them,] [w]hen small companies do sell, the impact of such sales is not clear. Much of it depends on whether the company is healthy, e.g. selling to support a going concern, or in distress, e. g. in the process of dissolving, bankrupt, or restructuring the business to focus on patent assertion. Some monetization campaigns appear to fit the latter profile … However, it could also be that companies that sell or monetize their patents are not proud and

How should we feel about companies like this? Viewpoints fall along a spectrum.[162] On one end are operating companies who complain that the name says it all: these are failed companies. Failures. They did not deliver what society wants and needs, real innovations. Allowing them, after the fact of their loss, to extract money from the winners does no one any good. This is especially so, the argument goes, because these companies in general (they say) sue successful product companies for infringing patented inventions that the successful companies themselves invented on their own. Failed companies take advantage of the rule in the patent law that independent invention is no defense to infringement. So, the firms and people that end up holding the patents of failed product companies engage in lawsuits designed to extract rents from the companies that succeeded – on their own, without the help of the failed company – and transfer them to holders of patents that are the last, sad harvest of failure. This is rent-seeking, pure and simple: taking wealth from one who earned it and giving it to one whose business is to seek out well-deserved pockets of wealth and take some of it, without helping to create it or build it up.

On the other end of the spectrum on this issue are failed product companies who feel wronged in one way or another. They may feel that their ideas were in fact borrowed, or at any rate that they helped make possible some aspects of the technology that is now dominated by successful product firms.[163] At the extreme

> therefore unwilling to talk about them publicly. It's not "PC" to talk about patents in a positive way, was the sentiment of one serial entrepreneur, but the cash infusion can be helpful in several ways. The company can benefit by being able to dissolve rather than go bankrupt, or delay the death of a seller, one high-volume buyer stated. If a company is experiencing a transition when it decides to move away from a business line, it may also sell its patents, interviewees said.
>
> Indeed, in my companion survey of venture capitalists, companies that monetized their patents through NPEs reported having been able to "fund a business pivot (37%), pay for new hiring (20%), [or] help the company meet milestones (17%). (N=30)."

162 See Robin Feldman, Tom Ewing, and Sara Jeruss, *The AIA 500 Expanded: The Effects of Patent Monetization Entities*, 17 UCLA J.L. & Tech. 1, 40 (2013):

> Many of the individuals in the samples appeared to be inventors who had tried to operate companies and when they failed, switched to litigation as a way of monetizing their patents. We have heard a variety of narratives used to describe the transformation of such inventors. On one end of the spectrum is the narrative in which an individual inventor tries to develop a product, faces overwhelming competition from a well-entrenched larger entity that appropriates the inventor's idea and refuses to pay a licensing fee. The inventor is left with no choice but to go after those who are using the idea. On the other end of the spectrum is the narrative in which an individual inventor, whose own product attempts have failed, has turned to extracting settlements from successful operating companies, regardless of whether the claim has any merit. A number of narratives could be developed in between as well. For the purposes of our study the narrative is irrelevant. We are only examining whether the entity filing the patent infringement lawsuit is an operating company or a monetizer at the time the lawsuit was filed.

163 The flow of information around a technical field occurs in several different ways, some so subtle it can be hard to trace who had what idea when and how it ended up in a successful product. See Robert P. Merges, *A Few Kind Words for Absolute Infringement Liability in Patent*

they may feel that one or more big, successful companies stole their ideas outright. They may also feel that their ideas were in some ways superior to those championed by the now-successful firms – and that they lost out not due to inferiority but due to random developments or "path dependencies" early in the history of the industry that ended up rewarding the successful firms for essentially unimportant or random reasons. Viewing things this way, a failed product firm may feel it is no less meritorious than a successful company. And that at any rate, they should be paid for the unacknowledged contribution they made to the early development of the industry they worked so hard to create. Failure in the product market, in other words, does not mean total failure. And it ought not preclude these firms from getting some compensation for their valuable early contributions.

One team of researchers summarized the issue this way:

> Failed startups ... have little ongoing business. They may feel that the alleged infringer unfairly beat them in the marketplace. The alleged infringer may have the opposite view of the marketplace battle, and these underlying divergent views may affect the patent case. This divergence in views between failed startup plaintiffs and defendants may make disputes more difficult to settle, resulting in longer disputes. Failed startups also have investors who may desire some return, via the patent lawsuit, on their otherwise lost capital.[164]

The best study of these companies includes primarily companies that continue to manufacture some products, while also licensing patents that cover products these companies once made, but no longer do:

> Examples of formerly manufacturing entities include IBM, MOSAID (now Conversant), and General Electric. General Electric continues to make products, but also engages in extensive licensing of its large patent portfolio, including many patents covering technology that it does not manufacture. It is unsurprising, given the lack of precision in the rhetoric, that these companies have been attacked as "patent trolls," despite their past or ongoing commitment to manufacturing.[165]

Law, 31 Berkeley Tech. L.J. 1, 11 et seq. (2016) (summarizing studies of technical information diffusion).

164 Christopher A. Cotropia, Jay P. Kesan, and David L. Schwartz, Heterogeneity Among Patent Plaintiffs: An Empirical Analysis of Patent Case Progression, Settlement, and Adjudication, at p. 89. On patent sales as a way to earn back some money for investors, cf. Michael Risch, *The Layered Patent System*, 101 Iowa L. Rev. 1535, 1575–1576 (2016) (footnotes omitted):

> Venture capitalization, or lack thereof, is a potential source of concern for the failed startups [studied]. Not one of the failed startups [which were studied, and which litigated one or more patents] ... had venture funding. The reasons for this are unknown. The failed startups could have failed precisely because they had no financing, and venture-backed firms were savvy enough to sell their patents and remain in operation.

165 Kristen Osenga, *Formerly Manufacturing Entities: Piercing the "Patent Troll" Rhetoric*, 47 Conn. L. Rev. 435, 440 (2014) (footnotes omitted). See also David L. Schwartz, *On Mass Patent Aggregators*, 114 Colum. L. Rev. Sidebar 51, 52 (2014):

6.4.2.3 Failed Product Companies and Ex-Post Market Making

While, so far, I have mostly talked about failed product companies that sell their patents to third parties, another strategy is available. Some failed product companies may wish to license their patents rather than sell them. A number of studies on different types of patent plaintiffs find that there are a few companies that pursue this approach.[166] When it happens, the usual battle of competing narratives is joined – failed company scrapes the bottom of the barrel by becoming a troll; versus proud pioneer just wants recognition of its path-breaking innovations, which paved the way for its successors in the marketplace. Litigation of this type pits these narratives against each other. At stake is whether a failed company (a) was a true innovator and pioneer but was not skilled or just unlucky in the product introduction sweepstakes; and possibly (b) whether the failed company uses revenue from licensing patents from its first, failed incarnation to attempt a "second act," a new product development direction that might succeed where the first one did not. Again, though there are few bright lines in this taxonomy, the "troll line" is often defined with reference to these two factors: where the asserted patent came from (its significance in the field); and where the hoped-for patent royalties will be spent: to pursue innovation (good) or just to earn money for its own sake (not so good). Again, the key to the troll question is whether a tactic or company contributes to innovation (past or future). In other words: Trolls don't innovate, and true innovators are rarely trolls.

Failed companies can edge over the "troll line" if they turn into nuisance settlement firms, or if they overreach in other ways in their litigation tactics. Even so, patent litigation may sometimes be a reasonable way to award compensation in the wake of a frantic product development period. Patent litigation can be used, after the dust settles, to determine which patented inventions contributed to product

> While there are patent holders who abuse and exploit the patent litigation system, there also are patent holders with meritorious claims who have been unfairly denied compensation. This is true for companies that both do and do not manufacture. The critics also lump together a wide variety of seemingly different actors, including individual inventors, failed startups, research and development companies, mass patent aggregators, and Wall Street speculators who buy a single patent for purposes of enforcement. The correct analysis of the costs and benefits of patent trolls is quite complicated, and far beyond the simple narrative based upon whether the owner of the patent manufactures products.

166 See Christopher A. Cotropia, Jay P. Kesan, and David L. Schwartz, Heterogeneity Among Patent Plaintiffs: An Empirical Analysis of Patent Case Progression, Settlement, and Adjudication, at p. 94 (categorizing patent lawsuit plaintiffs):

> Failed Operating or Start-up Company: A company that originally invented the patent-in-suit and attempted to commercialize the technology. At present, the company sells no products and its primary business appears to be patent litigation. An example of the Failed Operating or Start-up Company is Broadband Graphics LLC.

Cotropia's data showed that failed companies brought 4 percent of such litigation in 2012. Christopher A. Cotropia, Jay P. Kesan, and David L. Schwartz, *Unpacking Patent Assertion Entities (PAEs)*, 99 Minn. L. Rev. 649, 692 (2014).

success during the all-out scramble for successful product development and market entry. But it does so after development is complete and the product market is established. This temporal decoupling – separating intensive development competition from a careful assessment of the contributions of individual patented technologies – can be a rational way to appropriately compensate the various contributors to a new product in fast-moving, technology-intensive markets.[167]

* * * *

In sum, the patent plaintiff categories summarized here are based on how the future patent plaintiff came by the patent or patents that are to be asserted. Firms in categories 3 and 5 often purchase patents on the secondary market.[168] The most egregious enforcement campaigns start with acquiring a broad but vague patent (sometimes out of bankruptcy) whose merits are dubious, then asserting it in hundreds of patent suits. The goal is to use the high cost and risk of patent infringement cases as a lever to extract a settlement – sometimes as little as a few hundred dollars: a classic nuisance suit business model.[169] Variations on this theme

[167] For a fuller account, see Robert P. Merges, *After the Trolls: Patent Litigation As Ex Post Market-Making*, 54 Akron L. Rev. 555 (2020).

[168] On the need for and value of the secondary market (the market where patents are bought and sold as distinct assets, not connected to an underlying product or technology) see Michael J. Burstein, *Patent Markets: A Framework for Evaluation*, 47 Ariz. St. L.J. 507, 508–509 (2015):

> [L]ike much in patent law, the effects of robust secondary markets are likely to vary with specific technological and business contexts. But at the very least, there are enough reasons to be skeptical of patent markets that we should proceed with caution when invoking them in policy debates about the contours of the patent system ... Taking seriously the analogy between patent markets and financial markets, I demonstrate that there are numerous circumstances in which even well-functioning patent markets will fail to promote innovation ... [L]iquid markets cannot be a panacea. We therefore need to have a different conversation about such markets, in which we seek empirical data about when their operation is socially beneficial, and in which we consider their merits alongside other proposals for patent reform.

On the notion that one major cause of complaints over trolls is an unregulated secondary market for patents, one where pieces of large corporate portfolios are sold off to multiple, dispersed patent owners, see Mark A. Lemley and A. Douglas Melamed, *Missing the Forest for the Trolls*, 113 Colum. L. Rev. 2117, 2117 (2013):

> Many of the problems associated with trolls are in fact problems that stem from the disaggregation of complementary patents into multiple hands. Our review takes us beyond labels and the search for "bad actors" and leads us to focus instead on aspects of the patent system that give rise to the problems, and on changes in patent law that will ameliorate them. These changes include updating standards for issuing patents and patent remedies, implementing measures to reduce abusive patent litigation, and heightened legal scrutiny of disaggregation of patent portfolios. We conclude that trolls are a symptom of larger flaws in the patent system and that those who have focused on trolls have, in effect, been missing the forest for the trolls.

[169] See Ranganath Sudershan, *Nuisance Value Patent Suits: An Economic Model and Proposal*, 25 Santa Clara Computer & High Tech. L.J. 159 (2009).

include using slightly higher-quality patents that might allow the plaintiff to at least survive a few rounds of litigation and claim a larger settlement. Many troll campaigns are based on software patents. Patents in this field were issued in broad form between the late 1990s and roughly 2010, so their claims potentially cover a wide technological space. This allows trolls to cast their enforcement net quite far. In the end, the low quality of troll patents is a primary reason many see this form of litigation as rent-seeking.[170] Extracting royalties on the basis of a weak patent, one which makes no real contribution, takes money away from product makers and gives it to patent litigation companies whose patent assets gave little or nothing to the progress of the industry.

If unworthy patents are one reason trolls are considered rent-seekers, another is that they do little or no R&D. They buy bad patents cheap, and if they bring in money, they don't spend it on improving any technology. Overall, these two factors explain most of the negative sentiment about trolls. Whatever the precise delineation, there is a commonsense line between innovative activities and rent seeking pursued under the guise of innovation. The overwhelming perception was that the American patent system was suffering from a deluge of unproductive litigation beginning in the late 1990s. From this was launched the patent reform movement of the same era. This reform, again like other rent-seeking episodes in history, activated both the Supreme Court and Congress. By 2011, both these primary actors in the patent system had worked gargantuan changes in the American patent system. We return to these reforms in Section 6.4.3.

6.4.3 *Growth of Defensive Patent Strategies*

After wading through the taxonomical bog, one fact remains. Some companies that specialize in patent litigation are engaged in rent-seeking, pure and simple. They do not innovate, and they are not even reaping today a harvest sewn yesterday. They extract (or extort) rents from manufacturing companies – rents they and the original inventors of their patents did little or nothing to bring into existence.[171]

[170] Unworthy patents and irritating litigation go hand in hand. Opposition to rent-seeking moments in the history of patent law are ultimately based on the perception that the patents held by trolls (or in the past, "patent sharks") are, from society's point of view, not worth the cost of enforcement. See Robert P. Merges, *The Trouble with Trolls*, at pp. 1588–1589:

> [T]he fundamental purpose of patent law is to encourage true innovation. [But at times,] there is a difference between a reward for true innovation and a legal instrument which permits rent-seeking activities. Only if there is a gap between what is truly innovative and what is permissibly patented and asserted is there space for the concept of a patent troll.

[171] On the social welfare costs of patent trolls, see Lauren Cohen et al., Patent Trolls: Evidence from Targeted Firms 4 (Harvard Bus. Sch. Fin. Working Paper No. 15-002, 2017), https://ssrn.com/abstract=2464303 [https://perma.cc/QUY7-VZN6]; Stephen Kiebzak et al., The Effect of Patent Litigation and Patent Assertion Entities on Entrepreneurial Activity 3-4 (June 16, 2015) (unpublished manuscript), https://ssrn.com/abstract=2457611 [https://perma.cc/Z5ZG-4TFS];

Nevertheless, troll litigation is an accepted part of corporate life, especially in the software and information technology industries. To protect themselves, companies in these industries have had to play defense: to devise strategies to pre-empt, offset, or neutralize troll litigation. Expenditures on defensive strategies represent patent-related investments that are quite different from traditional spending on R&D, product development, and the like. These traditional investments involve patents, as a way to protect or recoup innovation-related costs. Defensive strategies are on the other hand expenditures to *keep a company free from other companies' patents*. They are designed to assure "freedom to operate": the freedom to pursue corporate objectives without too much fear of interference from other firms' patents. This defensive motivation poses a challenge to traditional rationales for patents. It promotes innovation in the sense that it aims to remove obstacles to research and product development. It is in some ways like buying insurance against patent harassment rather than seeking out a positive reward for innovation.

Actually, defensive patenting has a long history among large companies. We saw evidence of it as early as the General Electric founding era and the heyday of the Big Three auto companies. Although acquiring patents does not in and of itself create a legal defense against infringement suits, it may provide an effective *practical* defense. If a company has enough strong patents to be confident that other companies in its industry (other makers and sellers of products) infringe some or many of those patents, that company can probably stop worrying about patent litigation with competitors.

The logic is the same as the overall situation with respect to nuclear weapons held by large countries. If both Country A and Country B hold large nuclear arsenals, neither one will ever use theirs against the other. That's because each country knows than an attack will be matched by a counterattack right away. So, because each country has destructive firepower – and because each country *knows* the other country has that firepower – neither will ever use the weapons. (Thankfully!)

In the same way, a company that has a large and effective patent portfolio in an industry (autos, or computers, or mobile phones) has little fear of being sued for patent infringement by one of its main competitors. Any lawsuit would instantly be met with a counterattack, "launched" out of the company's large patent portfolio. No one can really win in this situation, because each competitor has large-scale destructive patent "firepower" against all its competitors. So, the large portfolio serves as a "deterrent": it prevents the initiation of any litigation among large players in the industry. The result is a stable situation. Notice that this is reinforced by the fact that each company can easily find out about the other company's patent holdings. The fact that information about patents and their owners is public drives

Roger Smeets, Does Patent Litigation Reduce Corporate R&D? An Analysis of U.S. Public Firms 3-5 (April 28, 2014) (unpublished manuscript), https://ssrn.com/abstract=2443048 [https://perma.cc/S2UF-2UN7]. To summarize: trolls, at least the ones studied in these papers, suppress innovation rather than promoting it.

the deterrent effect of patent portfolios. A knows what B has; B knows what A has; and each knows that the other knows. This makes a pre-emptive "first strike" a pointless and destructive exercise. Neither can win, so nether starts a fight.

6.4.3.1 No Easy Defense against Patent Trolls

Patents make an effective deterrent against litigation from competing manufacturers and product sellers. If a manufacturer such as Company A brings litigation against competing manufacturer Company B, Company B can use its large patent portfolio to cause harm to Company A. The harm comes in the form of a counterattack: patent litigation by Company B against Company A.

Now consider a company that does not make or sell any products. Its *only* business is owning, licensing, and litigating patents. A manufacturer cannot threaten to sue this type of licensing/litigation (troll) company for patent infringement. This kind of company never infringes. It does not make, sell, or use any products that might infringe another's patent. If a company makes things, it might infringe the troll's patents; but a troll company will by definition never infringe anyone else's patents. So big companies get no help from their defensive strategies based on "mutually assured destruction" or counterattacks. This "one-sided" infringement scenario requires other defenses.

6.4.3.2 Anti-Troll Defenses

There are a number of ways companies defend against patent troll litigation. One way is to establish a reputation for being aggressive – for not settling troll cases, and for seeking attorney fees when it wins a lawsuit initiated by a troll.

Another way to defend against troll litigation is to seek out and acquire – directly or indirectly – the patents a troll might themselves buy. Many trolls acquire patents on the secondary market, so if a large company becomes active in the same secondary market it can buy up at least some of the patents that a troll might use to bring a lawsuit against it. Most true trolls are not failed product companies. They actively seek to buy patents developed and owned by others. If a company is willing to enter the secondary market, it might be able to take some important patents out of the hands of the trolls. The basic idea is to "vacuum up" loose patents (those not held by direct competitors) to remove them from the secondary market.

There are a number of ways to vacuum up dangerous patents. Several specialized companies have been founded in the United States to vacuum up patents not for a single company but for a group of companies. These are called "defensive patent aggregators," to distinguish them from large patent licensing/litigation (troll) companies that also buy large numbers of patents.[172] The defensive aggregators have

[172] For more detail, see Justin R. Orr, *Patent Aggregation: Models, Harms, and the Limited Role of Antitrust*, 28 Berkeley Tech. L.J. 525 (2013).

various structures. They also offer various defense plans to their member companies, depending on which patents a member wants to be protected from and for how long. One early defensive aggregator in the United States is called RPX (short for "rational patent exchange"), founded in 2008. The RPX service is sold on an annual membership basis. Any member who pays the required fee receives a free license to all patents held by RPX; this means RPX members cannot be sued for infringing any patents owned by RPX. The annual membership fees may increase as the RPX portfolio grows, but members who join earlier may pay less. There are also other defensive aggregators, including an organization called Allied Security Trust.

Despite the fact that it is producing companies (makers and sellers) that suffer most of the harm from licensing/litigation companies, it is producing company patents that are often acquired by trolls. This occurs because companies in the middle of financial difficulties will often sell off some of their patents to make it through difficult times. An alternative is for companies to undertake an aggressive licensing campaign, in hopes of earning substantial royalties from competitors. Licensing campaigns such as these must be backed up by litigation, typically. Because licensing and litigation can take several years, a company in severe financial difficulties may be tempted to simply sell some of its patents to raise cash. To block this tactic, a defensive tool has been worked out that prevents the patents a company sells from being used by patent trolls.

The technique involves joining a group of companies that all agree to place a binding restriction on the patents they file and receive as part of their normal business operations. The legal restriction is a "trigger": a legal mechanism that goes into effect if a patent litigation/licensing company (troll) ever acquires any patents that have been subjected to this restriction. When a troll acquires a restricted patent, a free license is triggered. The free license is available to all companies that have joined in the group. So, if company A is part of the group, which also includes companies B, C, and D, any sale of a company A patent to a troll initiates the trigger. The effect is that the troll cannot file lawsuits against companies A, B, C, and D, because the acquisition by the troll triggers the free license to these companies.

The best-known version of this technique is an organization called the License on Transfer (LOT) Network. License on Transfer is a description of the trigger: When a patent is transferred to a troll, the license to all member companies in the LOT network goes into effect. According to the official description of the LOT group:

> By joining the LOT Network, you agree to provide all other members with a license to your patents if, and only if, those patents fall into the hands of a [Patent Assertion Entity, or troll]. All traditional uses of patents – suing other companies and selling them – remain unaffected.

The LOT Network defines a licensing/litigation (troll) company this way:

PAE refers to a "Patent Assertion Entity." [That is, a troll.] The LOT Agreement refers to PAEs as "Assertion Entities," which is defined as an entity and its affiliates if more than half of their total revenue is derived from patent assertion in a twelve-month period, or if it has a plan approved by senior management to do so.

Currently, the LOT Network charges a fee for companies to join. Generally, small companies (under $US 25 million annual revenues) may join for free, and large companies pay an annual membership fee of approximately $20,000.

Though the LOT Network concept shows promise, it should be noted that the legal mechanism – the legal rules that constitute the license "trigger" – at the heart of the Network have not been tested in court. Because the law in this area is complex, there may be doubts about whether the conditions triggering a free license can be successfully "built into" each patent contributed to the Network. Do restrictions like the automatic LOT license "run with" a patent right, so that they apply to all future assignees of the patent? If and when a LOT patent is purchased by a troll and asserted against an infringer, a court will have to decide whether the automatic license obligation is valid against the troll who bought the patent.

When this issue arises in court, it will recapitulate an early chapter in the history of American patent law. As we saw in Chapter 2, courts in the early nineteenth century adapted the law of patent assignments to facilitate the business model favored by patentees at the time – the regional patent franchise. Will there be a similar adaptation to the law of assignments today: a ruling that the LOT restrictions do "run with the patent," thus preventing use of LOT patents by trolls? Such a ruling would facilitate the anti-troll tactic that advocates are trying to build into LOT Network patents. On the other hand, there has traditionally been solicitude for keeping property rights free of any restrictions modifying the original, basic property entitlement. The law disfavors creation of custom-modified property rights, preferring instead to preserve the standard property forms intact.[173] Any future challenge to the LOT concept, and the notion of privately modified property rights in general, will have to traverse these issues.

6.5 PATENT REFORM: FIRST THE SUPREME COURT, THEN CONGRESS

The quote at the beginning of Section 6.3.2 recalls the glory days of Supreme Court engagement with patent law: when national historical figures such as Abe Lincoln and Daniel Webster represented household name inventors such as Cyrus McCormick. But with the exception of a few procedure-oriented cases, the Supreme Court had by 1970 given up regular oversight of the field. This continued after formation of the Federal Circuit. As late as 2001, a patent scholar entitled a

[173] On this, see Thomas W. Merrill and Henry E. Smith, *Optimal Standardization in the Law of Property: The* Numerus Clausus *Principle*, 110 Yale L.J. 1 (2000).

review article "Patent Law in the Age of the Invisible Supreme Court."[174] This scholar concluded: "[T]he Federal Circuit is the de facto Supreme Court of patents."[175] By this era, the Supreme Court often deferred intervention into various fields of law unless and until there was an inarguable and persistent split of authority between the regional circuit courts.[176] Regional splits were of course nonexistent for patent issues: The unified national jurisdiction of the Federal Circuit was fashioned in part to eliminate them.

But a funny thing happened on the way to Federal Circuit apotheosis. The Supreme Court got interested again – at times, very interested – in patent cases. Beginning with the 2006 term, when *eBay*[177] came down, and ending in 2018, the Big Court took thirty-two patent cases.[178] It decided five more in 2019 and 2020, bringing the total since 2006 to 37.[179] The cases touched on many different parts and portions of the grand tapestry of patent doctrine. In some cases, the Court ran down stray rulings where the Federal Circuit had mangled the contours of general legal doctrines when applying those doctrines to patent cases.[180] In other instances, the Court was less interested in legal system uniformity than in exerting sharp corrections to the Federal Circuit's chosen course. These were the most important decisions: they put the Supreme Court back in the captain's chair when it came to high-level patent policy. Three major decisions from these years stand out.[181]

174 Mark D. Janis, *Patent Law in the Age of the Invisible Supreme Court*, in Symposium: Intellectual Property Challenges in the Next Century, 2001 U. Ill. L. Rev. 387 (2001).

175 Mark D. Janis, *Invisible Supreme Court*, at p. 387.

176 See Tejas N. Narechania, *Certiorari, Universality, and a Patent Puzzle*, 116 Mich. L. Rev. 1345 (2018).

177 *eBay* v. *MercExchange, LLC*, 547 U.S. 388 (2006).

178 See Tejas Narechania, *Patent Puzzle*, at p. 1365 n. 100.

179 The role of the "elite" and insular Supreme Court bar in this process is explored in Paul R. Gugliuzza, *The Supreme Court Bar at the Bar of Patents*, 95 Notre Dame L. Rev. 1233 (2020) ("[I]n patent cases, a cert petition filed by an elite lawyer [as defined] is three times more likely to be granted than a petition filed by a lawyer outside that group. And although elite lawyers account for only 16% of cert petitions filed in patent cases, their petitions account for a remarkable 40% of the petitions granted").

180 See Peter Lee, *The Supreme Assimilation of Patent Law*, 114 Mich. L. Rev. 1413, 1413 (2016):

> [T]he [Supreme] Court's recent decisions reflect a project of eliminating "patent exceptionalism" and assimilating patent doctrine to general legal principles (or, more precisely, to what the Court frames as general legal principles). Among other motivations, this trend responds to rather exceptional patent doctrine emanating from the Federal Circuit in areas as varied as appellate review of lower courts, remedies, and the award of attorney's fees. The Supreme Court has consistently sought to eliminate patent exceptionalism in these and other areas, bringing patent law in conformity with general legal standards.

One observer sees these "field splits" as a new target for Supreme Court supervision, taking a place alongside "circuit splits" as a consistent rationale for Supreme Court intervention. Tejas N. Narechania, *Patent Puzzle*, at p. 1365.

181 The Court issued another blockbuster in patent law in 1996, in *Markman* v. *Westview Instruments*, 517 U.S. 370 (1996). By holding that patent claim interpretation is a matter of

First, and probably most important, was *eBay*.[182] As mentioned earlier, this decision altered one of the keystone pro-patent doctrines the Federal Circuit had put in place in its first year of operation: the automatic injunction rule. In *eBay*, the Supreme Court rejected this rule. The majority opinion reads like an early example of the rejection of "patent exceptionalism"; it assimilated injunction standards in patent cases back into the mainstream of American remedies jurisprudence. But it was the concurrence, from Justice Kennedy, that laid out the business and economic rationale for denying patent injunctions in some cases:

> An industry has developed in which firms use patents not as a basis for producing and selling goods but, instead, primarily for obtaining licensing fees ... For these firms, an injunction, and the potentially serious sanctions arising from its violation, can be employed as a bargaining tool to charge exorbitant fees to companies that seek to buy licenses to practice the patent ... When the patented invention is but a small component of the product the companies seek to produce and the threat of an injunction is employed simply for undue leverage in negotiations, legal damages may well be sufficient to compensate for the infringement and an injunction may not serve the public interest.[183]

The Kennedy concurrence said, in effect: "this is a case about patent trolls, a problem which has this Court's full attention." Subsequent patent cases applying *eBay* show lower courts picking up Kennedy's substantive concerns. In most post-*eBay* cases where injunctions are denied even though a patent is found valid and infringed, it is precisely the factors Kennedy identified that dictate the outcome.[184] The message was sent, and received: The courts are not to actively aid the "industry

law for judges (not juries) to decide, the *Markman* case paved the way to an entirely novel litigation event in almost all patent trials: the *Markman* hearing. Claim interpretation determines the parameters of any patent trial (what is prior art, what structures infringe, etc.), so these hearings are now a crucial stage in patent infringement suits. See Peter S. Menell, et al., Patent Case Management Judicial Guide (Washington, DC: Federal Judicial Center, 3rd ed., 2016), at chapter 5, Claim Construction. Despite its massive impact, *Markman* was in essence a decision under the Seventh Amendment of the Constitution, concerning jury trials; and it was not motivated by any trends intrinsic to patent policy. It was, however, a product of its times in one respect: It originated with a demand for a jury trial, which as noted earlier is consistent with patent litigation in the Federal Circuit era.

182 *eBay* v. *MercExchange*, LLC, 547 U.S. 388 (2006).

183 547 U.S. 388, 396-397 (Kennedy, J., concurring).

184 See Christopher B. Seaman, *Permanent Injunctions in Patent Litigation After* Ebay: *An Empirical Study*, 101 Iowa L. Rev. 1949, 1988–1989 (2016) (footnotes omitted):

> PAEs rarely obtained a permanent injunction after prevailing on liability (16%; 4 of 25 cases), while other patentees are successful in obtaining injunctions in the vast majority of cases (80%; 154 of 193 cases) ... This finding appears to lend weight to the view expressed in Justice Kennedy's concurrence [in *eBay*] that district courts should be reluctant to grant injunctions when the patentee is using the patent "not as a basis for producing and selling goods but, instead, primarily for obtaining licensing fees." It also is consistent with prior studies finding that PAEs are rarely granted injunctions. Even in the rare cases where a PAE was granted an injunction, the patentee was generally a failing or

[which had] developed . . . primarily to obtain licensing fees," particularly where the licensing is based on holdup, that is, "undue leverage."

The second major doctrine the Supreme Court neatened up was nonobviousness under § 103 of the Patent Act. They chose *KSR International* v. *Teleflex, Inc.*,[185] a case about an adjustable, electronically monitored car accelerator, to slow the momentum of the Federal Circuit's loosening of patent standards: in effect, a doctrinal brake applied by way of a novel gas pedal. In the case, the Federal Circuit had applied the rule it had been developing for some time. This rule ran under the rubric of the teaching, suggestion, or motivation (TSM) test; it placed a new, heavier burden on patent examiners and courts when finding that a patented invention was obvious.[186] Under the Federal Circuit's rule, a patent challenger under § 103 could win only by proving that the prior art for an invention laid out an unobstructed roadmap pointing directly at the claimed invention. Without this roadmap – found in a "teaching, suggestion, or motivation" in the prior art – the claimed invention was considered nonobvious over the prior art, and therefore patentable. The practical effect of the Federal Circuit's standard was to make it easier to get and defend a patent.

Like a legal chiropractor, the Supreme Court in *KSR* reset the skeleton of nonobviousness doctrine with one decisive twist. The dislocation that was the TSM test was quickly straightened out, and application of § 103 was restored to the straight lines laid down in *Graham* v. *John Deere* in 1966. For its rationale, the *KSR* opinion said simply that the TSM was not good law because it was not Supreme Court law. It had no foundation in the approach taken in its many decisions delineating the invention (pre-1952) and nonobviousness (post-1952) tests.

failed operating company that had previously sought to commercialize the patent and thus was only a non-practicing entity at the time of the injunction decision.

See also ibid., at p. 1998 (footnotes omitted, citing *eBay*, 547 U.S. 388, 396 (Kennedy, J., concurring)) ("When a patent is found to cover a small component, district courts rarely grant an injunction, as reflected by the low odds ratio for this variable. Thus, it appears that district courts are heeding Justice Kennedy's advice to avoid injunctive relief '[w]hen the patented invention is but a small component of the product the [infringer] seek[s] to produce.'").

Christopher B. Seaman, *Permanent Injunctions in Patent Litigation After* Ebay; Ryan T. Holte & Christopher B. Seaman, *Patent Injunctions on Appeal: An Empirical Study of the Federal Circuit's Application of* eBay, 92 Wash. L. Rev. 145, 145 (2017) (Federal Circuit supports permanent injunctions more often than district courts; this tends to "lend support to claims by scholars and others that the Federal Circuit, as a specialized court with a large number of patent cases, is more pro-patentee than the generalist district courts").

[185] 550 U.S. 398 (2007).

[186] See *Teleflex, Inc.* v. *KSR Int'l Co.*, 119 F. App'x 282, 290 (Fed. Cir. 2005), rev'd, 550 U.S. 398, 127 S. Ct. 1727, 167 L. Ed. 2d 705 (2007) (vacating a grant of summary judgment that the patent had not been proven obvious; the Federal Circuit said in vacating the decision: "The correct standard requires a court to make specific findings showing a teaching, suggestion, or motivation to combine prior art teachings in the particular manner claimed by the patent at issue."). For the lower court opinion, see *Teleflex Inc.* v. *KSR Int'l Co.*, 298 F.Supp.2d 581 (E.D. Mich. 2003).

And between the lines, *KSR* said in no uncertain terms that there is only one Supreme Court of patents – and it isn't the Federal Circuit.[187]

Turf issues and doctrinal curlicues aside, the real-world payoff from *KSR* was a modest but noticeable tightening of the nonobviousness requirement. Patents, the Court said in effect, ought to be slightly harder to come by. From the available data, it seems the lower courts got the message. One study of post-*KSR* cases at the Federal Circuit found that the § 103 invalidation rate increased from 40 percent to 57 percent.[188] A study in 2018 confirmed that the impact of *KSR* has also been felt in the Patent Office. This study looked at invalidation decisions affecting patents issued both pre- and post-*KSR*, reasoning that the Patent Office might have gotten a bit tougher on obviousness after *KSR*, and therefore that more post-*KSR* patents would survive a validity challenge.[189] The data support that conjecture: 26.7 percent of the pre-*KSR* patents survived obviousness scrutiny at the preliminary stage of PTO patent invalidation proceedings; the figure for post-*KSR* patents was 37.8 percent.[190]

The third blockbuster in the current era of Supreme Court patent cases is *TC Heartland LLC* v. *Kraft Foods Group Brands LLC*.[191] A case about procedure, and more particularly venue; not on the surface good material for a legal epic. But in the pantheon of early twenty-first-century patent reform, *TC Heartland* had few rivals. The reason has much to do with the fluky intersection between a single entrepreneurial court and an expansive act of legal interpretation. Doctrine aside, it was, and was meant to be, a legal dagger, aimed quite intentionally at the city of Marshall, Texas, a semi-rural town of 25,000 located 150 miles east of Dallas and up close to the Louisiana border. Marshall – whose prior claim to fame was that it was the Fire Ant Capital of the World – had become the most important city in the world of American patent infringement trials. At one point it hosted roughly half of the annual portion of four thousand infringement suits filed each year. Marshall had a history of hosting big tort trials, and the local law industry shifted dexterously to

[187] See *KSR Int'l Co.* v. *Teleflex Inc.*, 550 U.S. 398, 419 (2007) ("[T]he TSM test is incompatible with our precedents. The obviousness analysis cannot be confined by a formalistic conception of the words teaching, suggestion, and motivation, or by overemphasis on the importance of published articles and the explicit content of issued patents. The diversity of inventive pursuits and of modern technology counsels against limiting the analysis in this way.").

[188] Ali Mojibi, *An Empirical Study of the Effect of* KSR v. Teleflex *on the Federal Circuit's Patent Validity Jurisprudence*, 20 Alb. L.J. Sci. & Tech. 559, 596 (2010). But see Jason Rananen, The Federal Circuit's New Obviousness Jurisprudence: An Empirical Study, Patently-O Blog, January 31, 2013, available at https://patentlyo.com/patent/2013/01/the-federal-circuits-new-obviousness-jurisprudence-an-empirical-study.html (finding the rate declined from 46 percent pre-*KSR* to 57 percent post-*KSR* as of early 2013).

[189] Calvin M. Brien, *An Empirical Analysis of Patent Validity in Inter Partes Reviews Through the Lens of* KSR, 46 Am. Intell. Prop. L. Ass'n Q.J. 413 (2018).

[190] Calvin M. Briem, *Empirical Analysis of Patent Validity*, at p. 435. The preliminary stage is called institution. Basically, the findings show that more IPRs were instituted for pre-*KSR* patents. Once instituted, the invalidation rate is quite high, so the author treats institution as the key step toward finding an invention obvious.

[191] 137 S. Ct. 1514 (2017).

patent cases with the coming of tort reform and the subsequent rise of the Federal Circuit. Beginning in the tort litigation era, Marshall had a reputation for quick trials and plaintiff-friendly juries. Texas Instruments had used the federal court in Marshall for some of its enforcement actions beginning in the 1990s, when TI milked its rich patent portfolio to try to fund a new generation of computer chips (see previously).

TC Heartland put an end to that. In its wake, patent case filings have migrated in large part to several high concentration district courts, including Delaware (where many companies are incorporated) and the Northern District of California.[192]

6.5.1 *Section 101 Patentable Subject Matter: A Failed Reform?*

A rapid-fire series of cases beginning with *Bilski* v. *Kappos* [193]in 2010 thrust the patentable subject matter requirement of § 101 onto the patent reform agenda. The four cases that made up this mini-movement centered on two technologies: computer software (particularly as employed in a business method) and life sciences. The two-step test that emerged was intended to weed out improper patents in all technical fields, but has proven to be vague and unpredictable. Though the intent of the cases might have been to allow courts to eliminate weak or overbroad patents with a minimum of fuss, they have caused significant consternation among patent lawyers, patent owners, and inventors.

Before 2010, § 101 was employed only rarely to invalidate a patent. The wording of the statute itself speaks of "any new and useful process, machines, manufacture or composition of matter" being eligible for patent protection. Cases such as *Diamond* v. *Chakrabarty* (1980) simply asked whether the claimed invention at issue fit within one or more of these broad categories. If so, after a cursory pass through the three "exceptions" the Supreme Court had announced over the years, the patent was upheld.

Cases going back to the nineteenth century had recognized several exceptions to the liberal reach of § 101: laws of nature, natural phenomena, and abstract ideas.[194] By the time the first computer program patent appeared before the Supreme Court in 1972, the "exceptions" to the patentable invention categories under §101 had been distilled into a simple three-part statement: "Phenomena of nature, though just discovered, mental processes, and abstract intellectual concepts are not patentable,

[192] Alexander S. Krois, *The Evolution of Patent Venue in the Aftermath of* TC Heartland, 34 Berkeley Tech. L.J. 1023, 1023 (2019).

[193] 561 U.S. 593 (2010).

[194] See, e.g.," (*Mackay Radio & Tel. Co.* v. *Radio Corp. of Am.*, 306 U.S. 86, 94 (1939) ("[A] scientific truth, or the mathematical expression of it, is not patentable invention"); *Funk Bros. Seed Co.* v. *Kalo Inoculant Co.*, 333 U.S. 127, 130 (1948) ("[P]atents cannot issue for the discovery of the phenomena of nature," the Court said, in a case where the inventor combined a series of natural bacteria into a useful combined product).

as they are the basic tools of scientific and technological work."[195] By 1980, the three "exceptions" had been slightly recast, into what are now the well recognized triad: "The laws of nature, physical phenomena, and abstract ideas have been held not patentable."[196]

In the *Bilski* case, mentioned earlier, claims to hedging investments made in the context of commodity supply contracts were found unpatentable as an "abstract idea." Then in 2012 the Supreme Court turned its attention to the life science. In *Mayo Collaborative Services* v. *Prometheus Labs, Inc.*,[197] a patent covering measurement of drug uptake, determined by measuring intermediate compounds produced as the drug is digested, was invalidated. The correlation of intermediate compound levels and drug uptake was, the Court said, a phenomenon of nature. Next came *Association for Molecular Pathology* v. *Myriad Genetics, Inc.* (2013).[198] The Court invalidated all patents to the isolated versions of naturally-occurring genes – reversing a practice dating from the earliest days of the biotechnology industry. Finally, there was *Alice Corporation* v. *CLS Bank International* (2014),[199] another invalidated business-oriented patent, this time to a way of protecting participants in automated trading markets (e.g., for investment bonds or futures contracts) from being deprived of payment when trading accounts are "netted out" at the end of a trading day.

In all these cases, the claimed invention was found to fall into one of the three "exceptions" to patentable subject matter – (1) laws of nature, (2) physical phenomena, and (3) abstract ideas. The four post-2010 § 101 cases, especially *Mayo* and *Alice*, have left patent law with a legal standard that is often-repeated, often-applied, but always hazy: the two-step test. A typical statement of step 1 is: "[We] look at the focus of the claimed advance over the prior art to determine if the claim's *character as a whole is directed to excluded subject matter*."[200] More simply, step 1 is said to ask: is the claim "directed to" an excluded category (law of nature, abstract idea, or natural phenomenon).[201] If the patent claim is not "directed to" an excluded category, then the claim is patent eligible, and the court need not move to step two.

As for step two, the post-Bilski cases require "something more," an "inventive concept" in addition to the subject matter that qualifies as a law of nature, abstract idea, etc. An "inventive concept" has been defined as "an element or combination

195 *Gottschalk* v. *Benson*, 409 U.S. 63, 67 (1972) (invalidating claim to a simple algorithm on the multiply dubious theory that software code is math and math is discovered, rather than invented).

196 *Diamond* v. *Chakrabarty*, 447 U.S. 303, 309 (1980) (upholding patent on combination of genetic material from bacterial plasmids).

197 566 U.S. 66 (2012).

198 569 U.S. 576 (2013).

199 573 U.S. 208 (2014).

200 *Affinity Labs of Tex., LLC* v. *DIRECTV, LLC*, 838 F.3d 1253, 1257 (Fed. Cir. 2016) (emphasis added; internal quotation marks omitted).

201 See, e.g., *Koninklijke KPN N.V.* v. *Gemalto M2M GmbH*, 942 F.3d 1143, 1149 (Fed. Cir. 2019) (quting from *Bilski* etc. cases).

of elements that is 'sufficient to ensure that the patent in practice amounts to significantly more than a patent upon the [ineligible concept] itself.' "[202] That said, "the contours of what constitutes an inventive concept are far from precise."[203]

As you might surmise from the vagueness of the two-step test, on a substantive level, the *Bilski-Mayo* etc. line of cases has all kinds of problems. The two-step test is a sordid morass of uncoordinated doctrinal tendrils and conflicting policy impulses.[204]

Yet there is another perspective from which the *Bilski-Mayo* etc. cases make more sense. The key is that courts have been applying the § 101 test very early in a patent case. It has become customary to consider § 101 in the form of a motion to dismiss by the accused infringer under Federal Rule of Civil Procedure 12(b)(6) – a motion prior to any hearings, discovery, or depositions. This turns § 101 into an important procedural tool: an early "weed-out" for bad patents. It is, in the patent realm, equivalent to the antitrust law "quick-look doctrine."[205] In the patent context, the quick-disposal potential for § 101-based 12(b)(6) motions is the emphasis of most who praise the *Bilski* line of cases.[206] The problem is that, even if it is helpful to quickly weed out a patent that should never been granted, the vagueness of the test ensnares many a reasonable patent, many a potentially valuable patent. Which is why, as a patent reform effort, it is probably less effective than other initiatives (such as the AIA).

6.5.2 *Patent Reform in Congress*

In 2005, at around the same time the Supreme Court awoke from its long torpor on patent matters, Congress took up patent reform. From 2005 onward, drafters drafted, lawyers argued, and lobbyists lobbied. Until in 2011, Congress waved through the capstone reform legislation of the early twentieth century, the America Invents Act

[202] *Alice*, 573 U.S. at 217–218 (quoting *Mayo*, 566 U.S. at 73) (brackets in original).

[203] *Synopsys, Inc.* v. *Mentor Graphics Corp.*, 839 F.3d 1138, 1151 (Fed. Cir. 2016).

[204] See, e.g., *PPS Data, LLC* v. *Jack Henry & Assocs.*, Inc., 404 F. Supp. 3d 1021, 1039 n.8 (E.D. Tex. 2019) ("The only thing clear about the appropriate test for patent-eligible subject matter is that it is unclear."); Gene Quinn, Judge Michel Says Alice Decision 'will create total chaos,' IP Watchdog Blog (August 6, 2014), www.ipwatchdog.com/2014/08/06/judge-michel-says-alice-decision-will-create-total-chaos/id=50696/ [https://perma.cc/FLF8-EKV4] (quoting former Federal Circuit Chief Judge Paul Michel); Robert Merges, Symposium: Go Ask Alice: what can you patent after Alice v. CLS Bank?, SCOTUSblog (June 20, 2014, 12:04 PM), www.scotusblog.com/2014/06/symposium-go-ask-alice-what-can-you-patent-after-alice-v-cls-bank/ (predicting that the Alice case will be very difficult to apply).

[205] See Edward D. Cavanagh, *Whatever Happened to Quick Look?* 26 U. Miami Bus. L. Rev. 39, 57 (2017) (describing history and current status of the "quick look doctrine" in antitrust law, which permits a court to take a quick look at the facts behind an antitrust claim; the quick look applies in an in-between situation, where there is no per se antitrust violation, yet a full-blown "rule of reason" analysis may not be required).

[206] Paul R. Gugliuzza, *The Procedure of Patent Eligibility*, 97 Tex. L. Rev. 571, 575–576 (2019).

of 2011, or AIA.[207] It was the biggest news in patent law, on the legislative front at least, in 175 years. Only the 1836 Act matches the AIA for the sheer magnitude of its impact. That's true because the AIA whisked into place a new cadre of patent professionals housed within the Patent Office – a cadre with profound implications for the patent system.[208] In 1836 the newly minted innovation bureaucrats were the patent examiners. In 2011, the new personnel were a group of administrative patent judges tasked with running full-scale adversarial trials on concerning patent validity. These trials were new in American patent law: an additional station stop, interposed between patent grant and district court enforcement, on the journey of a patented invention from idea to marketplace.

Administrative patent review was an old idea in the patent systems of the world. A procedure called patent oppositions had been available for many years in Germany, Japan, and the European Patent Office, and more recently in China, Korea, and many other major patenting countries. But for many years the American system preferred to maintain the venerable and durable two-part division of labor present as far back as 1790: patent examination and federal court enforcement. With a few exceptions, the sifting of patents, good from bad, was done with this simple two-stage process. Full-bore validity trials where patent challengers had a direct voice in the outcome were thought unnecessary. Or at least there had never been enough enthusiasm for PTO trials to overcome the status quo.

The stimulus that resulted in the AIA was the same as the one that pricked the Supreme Court out of its deep patent slumber: patent trolls. The administrative trials were aimed specifically at lowering the cost of invalidating patents. The goal was to remove some of the legal leverage trolls rely on to push defendants into settling infringement suits. A major source of this leverage was the high cost of defending patent infringement in a federal court trial. US federal civil trials are in many ways a model of due process. Every facet, from service of process to personal jurisdiction to the conduct of discovery and depositions, is conducted according to detailed rules, subject to court review under a vast body of case law. These trials are designed to result in a full, comprehensive, and fair outcome: in a word, justice, as far as that is possible. Justice is a virtue, no arguing with that. But it can be an *expensive* virtue. And that expense hangs over the head of every company threatened with federal court patent litigation.

207 The Leahy–Smith America Invents Act (AIA), P.L. 112–129, 125 Stat. 284 (2011), signed by President Obama on September 16, 2011.

208 At the time of its passage, another of the AIA's major provisions was hailed as highly significant. This was the end of the old "first to invent" standard for patent novelty and priority, which was part of US patent law from 1790 until the new "first to file" provision took effect in 2013. While important conceptually, and a major step toward world harmonization, the "first to file" rule does not change enough outcomes to register a large impact on the patent system. This is partly because, with first to file the standard in patent offices around the world, many sophisticated inventors had already adjusted their internal procedures to adapt to a first to file regime.

With more and more patents in force every year; with more and more companies post-1982 seeking to cash in on the increased market value of patents; and with the warm Texas hospitality of the federal court in Marshall (see earlier) encouraging patent owners to sue any and all potential infringers, it is no surprise that the patent system turned to administrative validity trials as an alternative to federal court patent litigation.

The main reason for the PTO to conduct a validity trial is that it saves a lot of money. An administrative patent trial is cheaper because it is much more limited in scope compared to district court litigation. It is also tried to a panel of special judges with patent expertise, rather than (as is typical in litigation) a generalist judge and a jury of average citizens.[209] PTO trials are also subject to a wide range of procedural guardrails and limitations designed to keep the cost down and the proceedings simple. These points were well-rehearsed in the patent literature for many years.[210] But it took the crisis of excessive patent litigation to spur the patent system into action.

The AIA launched no fewer than four new administrative procedures in the PTO. The new administrative trials are heard by the Patent Trial and Appeal Board (PTAB), a much-expanded version of the pre-2011 Board of Patent Appeals and Interferences. The most popular PTAB proceeding is also the most important: Inter Partes Review (or IPRs).[211] An IPR is an adversarial trial on the specific issues of novelty and nonobviousness for all patent claims raised by a patent challenger.[212] IPRs can be held any time during the life of a patent.[213] An IPR only allows evidence

[209] The Patent Office administrative forum is called the PTAB, see later. Its members are patent lawyers and former patent examiners, among others. See AIA, at § 6.

[210] See, e.g., Joseph Farrell and Robert P. Merges, *Incentives to Challenge and Defend Patents: Why Litigation Won't Reliably Fix Patent Office Errors and Why Administrative Patent Review Might Help*, 19 Berkeley Tech. L.J. 943 (2004) (emphasizing the role of administrative patent review in maintaining the incentive structures underlying the patent enforcement system); Stuart J. H. Graham and Dietmar Harhoff, *Separating Patent Wheat from Chaff: Would the US Benefit From Adopting Patent Post-Grant Review?*, 43 Res. Pol'y 1649 (2014) (pointing out one important contribution to overall welfare from administrative patent challenges: the patents challenged under IPRs and other administrative procedures that are not worth challenging in court).

[211] IPRs are conducted under Chapter 31 of the Patent Act, 35 U.S.C. §§ 311 et seq. For the full list of procedures and an introduction to each see Robert P. Merges and John F. Duffy, Patent Law and Policy: Cases and Materials (Durham, NC: Carolina Academic Press, 7th ed., 2021), at pp. 955–1021.

[212] The Patent Office attempted to limit IPRs to only those claims the PTAB decided to consider in response to a challenger's petition to institute an IPR. The Supreme Court said no; the PTAB must consider *all* challenged claims if it decides to institute an IPR. *SAS Inst., Inc.* v. *Iancu*, 138 S. Ct. 1348, 1355 (2018) ("The [PTO] Director's claimed 'partial institution' power appears nowhere in the text of [35 U.S.C.] § 318, or anywhere else in the statute for that matter.").

[213] This is one difference between an IPR and the other major patent validity trial authorized by the AIA: the post-grant review, or PGR. A PGR can only be declared within nine months after a patent issues. PGRs are much more wide-ranging: they permit evidence on any validity issue,

of prior patents and printed publications. By concentrating on the issues that prove decisive in most validity cases – § 102 and § 103, referencing only patents and printed publications – the IPR simplifies and streamlines trials on patent validity.

Despite its appeal, the first fruits of the IPR procedure left a bitter taste for some of the backers of the AIA. Early on IPRs were invalidating patents at an alarming rate.[214] But it was apparent after a short time that challengers had picked off the weakest patents first. Also, it took time for people in the patent system to digest the two-stage nature of the IPR proceeding, which is crucial to understanding data about IPR outcomes. The first stage in an IPR is a petition to the PTAB, asking that tribunal to "institute" (commence) an IPR. Institution will be granted if the judges assigned to the case believe there is "reasonable likelihood" the challenger can prove that at least one of the challenged claims is invalid.[215] One of many streamlining devices in the IPR statute prohibits the losing party from filing an appeal of the institution decision.[216] Once instituted, IPRs usually invalidate one or more claims, as you can see from Figure 6.12 (data through June, 2020).

The first bar shows total claims in all the patents challenged under IPRs. Over 37 percent of the claims in PTAB-challenged patents were not even challenged in IPRs. Of the claims cited in IPR petitions, close to 50 percent were excluded at the institution stage: only half the challenged claims wound up in a full validity proceeding. Of the 38,000 or so claims included in full IPR proceedings, almost 73 percent were invalidated. Though this latter figure seems high (only about one-fourth of all patent claims valid), it is misleading. Taking into account all the claims patent challengers hoped to cancel, IPRs yield an invalidation rate of just over 27 percent (97,710 challenged claims, 27,864 claims invalidated after full proceeding ending with decision).

PTAB trials in the PTO have fundamentally altered not only litigation but the many business negotiations and transactions conducted under the umbrella of patent law. Any private law arrangement that assumes or depends on the presence of a valid patent is now a candidate for an IPR. Even the threat of an IPR increases the bargaining leverage in licensing, supplier-customer relations, and a wide range

including enablement, written description, and so on. See Robert P. Merges and John F. Duffy, Patent Law, at pp. 62, 932–934.

214 Brian J. Love and Shawn Ambwani, *Inter Partes Review: An Early Look at the Numbers*, 81 U. Chi. L. Rev. Dialogue 93 (2014) (reporting that the PTAB invalidated all claims in 77.5 percent of the first 160 petitions instituted).

215 35 U.S.C. § 314(a).

216 See 35 U.S.C. § 314(d) ("The determination by the Director whether to institute an inter partes review under this section shall be final and nonappealable."). See also *Cuozzo Speed Techs., LLC* v. *Lee*, 136 S. Ct. 2131 (2016) (applying this provision). The non-appealability of institution decisions even reaches to procedural matters, such as whether the petition for institution came too late under the IPR statute of limitations. See *Thryv, Inc* v. *Click-To-Call Techs.*, LP, 140 S. Ct. 1367 (2020). This statute of limitations bars an IPR petition made more than a year after an infringement suit is filed against the party seeking to institute the IPR. 35 U.S.C. § 315(b).

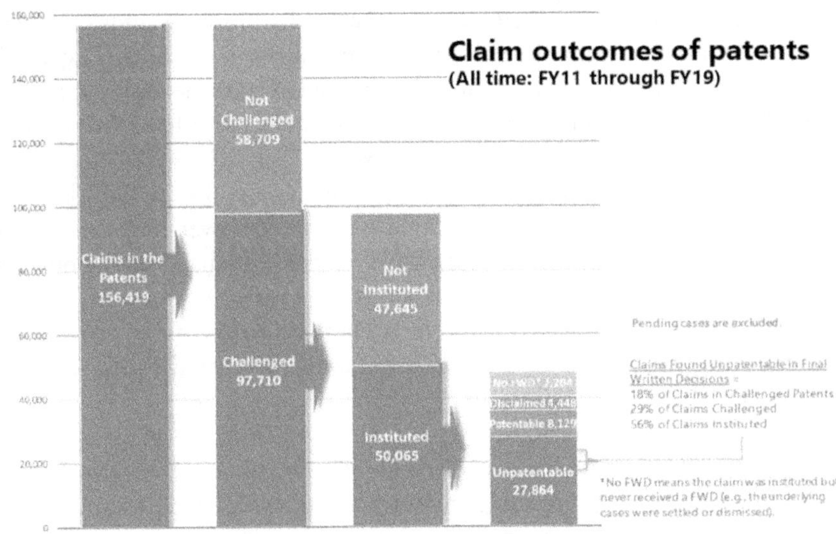

FIGURE 6.12. Outcome by claim, all AIA proceedings through June 2010.
Source: USPTO, Patent Trial and Appeal Board, Vice Chief Judge Michael Tierney, Lead Judge William Saindon, "Boardside Chat": New Developments, June 11, 2020, available at www.uspto.gov/sites/default/files/documents/PTAB_boardside_chat_new_trial_stats_sas_and_operational_faqs_06_11_2020.pdf.

of other business deals.[217] The threat of patent invalidation can be potent. And a patent challenger holds the initiative: unlike with federal litigation, he, she or it can seize the power of the first mover by filing an IPR at any time.[218]

6.6 LOOKING FORWARD

6.6.1 *Innovation in the Era of Big Platform Companies*

Five huge e-commerce companies have emerged in the United States as makers of mass-scale markets.[219] Many other companies, both in the US and elsewhere, are

[217] See generally, Robert P. Merges and Helen (Fang) Liu, IP Strategy for Business (text in English and Chinese), at pp. 128–130 (discussing the need to budget for administrative patent challenges in business deals involving patents).

[218] A case may not be brought in federal court until there is a real case or controversy. Under the case law on this Constitutional requirement, a potential licensee lacks standing to have the patent declared invalid until a patent owner makes a serious threat to sue for infringement. A clever patent owner can conduct negotiations without making a true threat, which eliminates the licensee's power to take the initiative. See *MedImmune, Inc.* v. *Genentech, Inc.*, 549 U.S. 118 (2007). As for filing an IPR, anyone may do it at any time. See 35 U.S.C.A. § 311("[A] person who is not the owner of a patent may file with the [Patent] Office a petition to institute an inter partes review of the patent.").

[219] Farhad Manjoo, The Upside of Being Ruled by the Five Tech Giants, *NY Times*, November 1, 2017, available at www.nytimes.com/2017/11/01/technology/five-tech-giants-upside.html?rref=collection%2Fsectioncollection%2Ftechnology&action=click&contentCollection=technol

working to put themselves in the middle of markets in all sorts of industries. The basic logic of network economics pushes these companies to continually expand in scale and scope. Scale means more buyers and sellers; scope means more markets served. What it ultimately means is this: The US economy has entered the era of the Big Platform.[220]

It is commonplace by now to worry about the massive size of Big Platforms. Competition and Antitrust Law experts will be battling it out over these issues in the years to come. Big Platforms have destabilized conventional assumptions and practices in fields such as employment law (Uber; Lyft; Didi in China), local regulation (Airbn'b), and taxation (Amazon). These new behemoths have resuscitated debates over the dangers of "bigness" last heard in the 1910s and 1920s, the trust-busting days.

At the same time, size and scale have their virtues. Tightly integrated operations on a massive scale can do some marvelous things: case in point, the elapsed time between "click to order" and opening the just-delivered box gets shorter and shorter. And big companies can at times do more than squeeze efficiencies out of current operations; they can innovate too. A solidly established school of thought says in fact that size (and the market power that comes with it) is the best friend that innovation could ever have. Even when big companies grow by swallowing up small ones, quite common in technology-intensive industries such as e-commerce platforms, there is a respectable school of thought that defends this growth by company

ogy&region=stream&module=stream_unit&version=latest&contentPlacement=58&pgtype=sectionfront&_r=0.

220 The word "platform" has taken on a constellation of meanings, which often vary depending on the subject matter specialty of the speaker. In business strategy, a common set of components that form the core of a machine, software system, or the like may be called a platform; an example would be Microsoft Windows. *See* Carliss Y. Baldwin and C. Jason Woodard, The Architecture of Platforms: A Unified View, in Platforms, Markets and Innovation (Annabelle Gawer. Ed., 2009). Many computer programs, sold by many different companies, can "plug into" the Windows operating system, making Windows a frequently-referenced "software platform." More recently, engineers and economists have reserved the word "platform" to refer to any physical or virtual thing, place or system that brings together multiple sellers and multiple buyers of products and/or services. These are often (and more properly) referred to as "two-sided platforms." Thus, a shopping mall (a building with multiple separate units for lease) brings together sellers and buyers of retail goods. Today, virtual platforms such as Amazon.com, Uber, and YouTube are much in the news because of their growing size and power. Amazon brings together buyers and sellers of a huge range of goods and services. Uber brings together (or "intermediates" between) independent drivers and riders. YouTube (along with Spotify and the like) brings together producers and consumers of content (video, audio, etc.). In a more general sense, all-purpose search engines such as Google also serve as two-sided platforms, bringing together advertisers and consumers, though in this and other cases of "ad-supported" content, ads are often an extraneous intrusion into the content or information sought by the consumer. These platforms might be said to bring together producers and consumers of information, in a format subsidized by advertisers. The advertisers use the platform to attract customers, even though the customers are (usually) not on the platform for the express purpose of looking at ads. These two-sided platform companies are the ones I concentrate on in this Article.

acquisition.[221] The buying up of talent, in the form of big companies acquiring smaller ones, is sometimes called "acqui-hiring,"[222] and is often praised as an effective way to encourage startup activity while supporting continued growth among big companies.

Good as it all sounds, there are risks in too much economic concentration. As with most technologies – revolutionary or mundane – online platforms are based on a wide range of innovations spanning many years and originating from many sources. The Internet itself, of course; but also mobile communications, data compression technologies, GPS satellites and mapping software, online payment systems, and many, many others. These innovations represent the successful harvest of many scientific and technological seeds planted at various times and in various places over the past 50 plus years. And the seeds for these technologies were planted in many different places: the public sector, universities, big companies, medium sized companies, and small companies too.

The pressing question is this: in the era of the Big Platform, will there still be room for such a varied innovative ecosystem? Will the trend toward "bigness" – and the "winner take all" nature of Platform markets – shut out the smaller innovators that have helped create the conditions for the platform economy to thrive?

Thinking this through should start here: From the point of view of innovation, *big is not always bad*. In fact, it can be pretty good. And when it comes to mergers and firm acquisitions, most (though again, not all) researchers conclude that *overall innovation* (as usually measured by number of patents)[223] improves after the merger. So, if overall innovation is all we care about, the case for the patent market looks shaky. There is more to the story, however. A consistent body of research also shows that *radical innovation* decreases with firm size. A newly acquired firm, in other words, becomes (by definition) part of a larger company; and large companies rarely succeed in paradigm-shifting innovations. We will return to the point about radical

[221] Peter Lee, *Innovation and the Firm: A New Synthesis*, 70 Stan. L. Rev. 1431 (2018).

[222] Andres Sawicki, *Buying Teams*, 38 Seattle U. L. Rev. 651 (2015); Samantha Nolan, *Talent for Sale: The Need for Enhanced Scrutiny in Judicial Evaluation of Acqui-Hires*, 67 Hastings L.J. 849, 849 (2016) (In " . . . acqui-hiring [,] [t]he buying corporation purchases the target, poaches its employees, jettisons its projects, and generally kills the company."; calling for shareholder protections for acquired firm).

[223] In most of the studies on mergers and innovation, innovation levels pre- and post-merger are measured by using various patent-related variables. Studies employ either the sheer number of patents before and after, or their quality (often determined, as is conventional, by the number of times the patents are cited in other patents and research studies). The simple objection to this measure is that it is usually large companies that make these acquisitions – bigger buys smaller. And bigger companies usually have a more aggressive mandate to build out their patent portfolios. The gains in numbers of patents, then, may show not a truly higher rate of innovation, but simply a greater propensity to acquire patents per dollar of R&D spent. As for the citation data, though it can often by helpful, citations are susceptible to a number of well-known limitations. It might well be that in many cases the higher number of citations come from the greater visibility that comes with patents issued to larger companies. It could mean quality, in other words; but it might also simply signal prominence.

innovation shortly. First, however, we need to understand why post-merger firms – and large firms in general – have been connected with increased innovation in so many studies.

One reason big firms are thought to foster innovation arises from the very market power that concerns antitrust authorities. What is known as the Schumpeterian Hypothesis, after economist Josef Schumpeter, turns this concern around. [224] High profit margins result from the oligopolies or monopolies enjoyed by big companies, and this, Schumpeter argued, provides money for increased R&D.

A second advantage bigness provides to innovation springs not from market power, but from the nature of technology; it is captured by the term "synergy." Multiple, related researchers working in proximity with each other combine findings and ideas in ways that increase the productivity of the entire collective group. Talented researchers, heretofore isolated in "silos," share ideas with others from related fields, a fertile formula for innovation. The whole of the combined research teams ends up being greater than the sum of its individual parts.

Schumpeter's argument for the benefits of bigness would generally regard mergers as a good thing. Typically, "mergers reduce . . . product market competition and [therefore] increase expected payoffs from employee innovations"[225] due to the increased size and market power of the post-merger firm. From this perspective, the market power that so concerns antitrust authorities is actually a benefit, because firms with market power are more secure in the pursuit of ambitious and long-term-oriented R&D.

A comprehensive study verified that there are benefits from integrating the R&D efforts of acquiring and acquired firms – that, in other words, there actually is something to the idea that acquisitions yield valuable "synergies."[226] This study found: (1) firms acquire other firms more often when the "technological overlap" between the two firms is high, when they are familiar with and can effectively

[224] Joseph A. Schumpeter, Capitalism, Socialism and Democracy (New York: Harper Brothers, 1942). *See also* Frederic M. Scherer, Innovation and Growth: Schumpeterian Perspectives (Boston: MIT Press, 1984). The idea that monopoly power leads to innovation is associated with the later writings of Schumpeter such as the 1942 volume just cited. This book includes the famous idea of "the perennial gale of creative destruction," which describes the "process of industrial mutation that incessantly revolutionizes the economic structure from within, incessantly destroying the old one, incessantly creating a new one . . . " Ibid., at 82–83. This "later" Schumpeter is often contrasted with an earlier st of writings in which he emphasized small firms and individual entrepreneurs. *See* Richard R. Nelson and Sidney Winter, An Evolutionary Theory of Economic Change, 39–40 (Cambridge, MA: Belknap Press, Harvard University Press, 1982), citing Joseph Schumpeter, The Theory of Economic Development: An Inquiry into Profits, Capital, Credit, Interest, and the Business Cycle (Cambridge, MA: Harvard University Press, 1936) as a good expression of "earlier Schumpeter."

[225] Paolo Fulghieri and Merih Sevilir, *Mergers, Spinoffs, and Employee Incentives*, 24 Rev. Fin. Stud. 2207, 2233 (2011).

[226] Jan Bena and Kai Li, *Corporate Innovations and Mergers and Acquisitions*, 69 J. Fin. 1923 (2014) (studying 1762 mergers from 1984 to 2006).

evaluate the quality of the acquired firm's R&D activity (an aspect of what is known in technology studies as "absorptive capacity");[227] and (2) acquisitions are dominated by big and successful companies: "larger firms, as well as firms with faster sales growth, better operating performance . . . and higher prior year stock returns, are more likely to engage in M&As as acquirers."[228] The logic of "bigger is better" is surely at work here. The larger a firm, the more products and research projects it has.[229] With more projects comes a greater chance for synergies.[230]

The downside of a merger is that the acquired entity ceases to be autonomous; the merger folds it into a larger structure (the acquiring firm). Acquisition, in other words, is a two-edged sword. It is a reward for *past* innovation. But according to a sizeable body of research, it is a damper on the *future*. The team that develops a technology will cash out nicely. But the autonomy and independence that created the context for the original innovation will be gone. Despite heroic efforts to preserve the best of both worlds, with the massive acquiring company usually pledging to "keep hands off" and "preserve the special culture" of the acquired company, acquisition brings an inevitable change. After all, if a large company could completely duplicate the culture of the startup, why wouldn't it do so from the outset, and develop the technology in-house? In the end, two stark facts usually stand out. The acquired company did what it did because it was plucky and independent. And after the acquisition it becomes part of a big company. That is the reality when

[227] Bena and Li, *Corporate Innovations and M&A*, at 1945.

[228] Ibid., at 1936.

[229] Synergies may add value, but the first finding is troubling. If mergers are more common in cases of a degree of technological overlap, mergers would be more likely to remove potential future R&D competition than product market competition. While this is good in one sense – short-term consumer welfare is enhanced by product market competition – it is worrisome in another: future innovative capacity is likely to be absorbed into larger and larger firms. Whether small companies aim from the outset to be acquired; or whether they simply fail to introduce meaningful product competition; their future innovative potential will be taken inside a large company. And so again the benefits of independence and autonomy will be lost.

[230] One aspect of the Bena and Li study presents a contrast with conventional Schumpeterian market power explanations of mergers, and so is worth noting. The authors find that "close rivalry in product markets has a negative impact on the likelihood of firms merging. As a result, the positive effect of technological overlap on the likelihood of a merger pair formation is reduced for firm pairs that also overlap in product markets." Bena and Li, Corporate Innovations and M&A, at 1949. Note that one study, based on an economic model (and not empirical data), provides support for this empirical finding (even though it contravenes Schumpeterian wisdom). See Paolo Fulghieri and Merih Sevilir, *Mergers, Spinoffs, and Employee Incentives*, 24 Rev. Fin. Stud. 2207, 2233 (2011), where the authors argue that mergers with direct market competitors eliminate one outside option for specialized employees, and that this may reduce employee incentives. Note that the (now fading) practice of "parallel R&D" groups was put in place to stimulate *intra-firm* competition, and at least some managers believed that this was effective. *See, e.g.*, Richard R. Nelson, *Uncertainty, Learning, and the Economics of Parallel Research and Development Efforts*, 43 Rev. Econ. & Statistics 351 (1961).

technology is acquired through acquisition of an entire company. Autonomy and diversity both exit the scene, never to fully return. [231]

6.6.1.1 For Radical Innovation, More Is Better and Small Is Big

A second major point regarding large firm acquisitions is that they reduce the chance for radical innovation. There are two reasons. First, they reduce the total number of separate firms in a given field. And second, they usually eliminate from the landscape precisely the sort of smaller firms that have often generated paradigm-changing innovations. In these two ways, and despite post-merger efficiencies, it is the loss of radical post-merger innovations that counts as the major cost of large firm acquisitions.

In its simplest form, a corporate merger executes a certain form of legal arithmetic: 1 + 1 = 1. Starting with two separate firms, we end up with one. Whatever gains this brings, in operations and in more efficient R&D, it entails a loss: an independent firm ceases to be. The consequences for future innovation are at once well understood, in an aggregate sense; yet very hard to pin down, in any individual case. Future innovation is by its nature hard to predict, hard to see in advance. But students of long-term innovation patterns are fairly uniform in their assessment of the optimal number of firms: more is better. It is impossible to quantify what is lost when fewer, rather than more, separate firms take part in the innovation sweepstakes. But something is (on average; over time; in general) surely lost.

6.6.1.2 Small Is Big

So far in this section I have been talking about why *more* firms might make for more innovation in a given industry. Now I will turn to a related issue: why more *small* firms might be good.[232] All the arguments below are variations on a single theme:

[231] Cf. Victor Luckerson, How Google Perfected the Silicon Valley Acquisition, Time.com, April 15, 2015 ("Oftentimes [after an acquisition] founders are rolled up inside another group inside of the company. They can't make decisions as freely as when they were entrepreneurs. That affects people's willingness to stick around.") (quoting Justin Kan, venture capitalist at Y Combinator and cofounder of Twitch).

[232] Definitions of "small" and "big" can of course vary, but in general small firms usually have fewer than 500 employees, and often fewer than 100, while large firms usually measure their workforces in the thousands. For a study of the very smallest firms and their ability to innovate, see Julian Baumann and Alexander S. Kritikos, *The Link between R&D, Innovation and Productivity: Are Micro Firms Different?*, 45 Res. Pol'y 1263 (2016) (Data on German micro-firms, drawn from 10,000 to 15,000 firms in a total sample of firms in Germany, between 2005 and 2012). The authors find that most micro firms are young: 53 percent of the smallest firms were younger than 15 years. Ibid., At 1266; that "larger [small firms] have a lower R&D intensity than smaller ones: ceteris paribus, small firms invest 36% more in R&D per employee, firms with 0–4 FTE employees invest 90.4% more in R&D per employee than medium-sized firms." Ibid., at 1267; R&D intensity increases process and product innovations for all sized firms

smaller firms are more resourceful, nimble, focused and productive, and hence more likely to come up with something new and different. As one study put it, summarizing a large literature: "Empirical research on innovation and firm size confirms that despite large firms' apparent advantages in scale and access to complementary assets and capabilities … small firms are more efficient at innovation, particularly radical forms of innovation."[233]

Business people and scholars have named three different benefits to smallness for purposes of generating innovations: (1) magnified incentive effects; (2) better focus, meaning simpler and more direct decision processes within firms; and (3) the preference of those with an "entrepreneurial personality" for greater autonomy, which is better satisfied in small firms. Let's take these one at a time.

One explanation for better innovation results is that small firms have more riding on their (relatively few) research projects. To begin with, they have fewer distractions. In addition, failure is more painful, because the future of the company may be riding on a single research project. But success is sweeter, because the individual researchers often own a significant chunk of their small company.[234] Some theorists have described how big companies can leverage these features of small firms, by entering into contracts that provide large rewards for project success. This is an example of the "high powered incentives" delineated by economist Oliver Williamson as an advantage of contractual exchange as compared to integration or ownership.[235] Large firms are much more diffuse; individual projects pale in comparison to the overall scale of the firm. And individual effort is dwarfed by the totality of collective effort, so there is less direct reward for extraordinary effort. Large

(which is to be expected). Ibid., at 1268; and that "Micro firms that do invest in innovation activities have 90% higher R&D expenditures per employee than medium-sized firms. Thus, firm size is negatively correlated with R&D intensity." Ibid., at 1271.

233 Todd R. Zenger and Sergio G. Lazzarini, *Compensating for Innovation: Do Small Firms Offer High-powered Incentives That Lure Talent and Motivate Effort?*, 25 Manag. Decis. Econ. 329, 329 (2004). As regards overall innovation efficiency, this conflicts with some of the studies cited in the preceding section. That might be explained by the fact that many of the studies showing greater overall efficiency for post-merger firms were published after this article was. The conclusion regarding radical innovation, however, has not been superseded in the intervening years.

234 Todd R. Zenger and Sergio G. Lazzarini, Compensating for Innovation, at 342:

> [T]he results [of this study of 352 engineers in Silicon Valley and Route 128 in the Boston area] … provide consistent evidence that outcomes are linked directly to differences in contract attributes, which in turn are related to firm size. Firms with more aggressive reward systems appear more successful in motivating high effort and in luring and retaining top talent. Engineers with larger equity shares and a greater variable component to their pay work longer hours and are more likely to bring work home. Strong norms of peer monitoring may further escalate effort in small firms. By contrast, engineers with small equity shares, those employed in contracts with weak incentive intensity and weak peer performance pressure are less likely to work long hours and bring work home.

235 This is an application of Oliver Williamson's transaction cost economics. *See* Oliver E. Williamson, The Mechanisms of Governance (Oxford: Oxford University Press, 1999); Robert P. Merges, A *Transactional View of Property Rights*, 20 Berkeley Tech. L.J. 1477, 1483 (2005).

companies can access these stronger incentives only indirectly – by contracting with small firms to supply research services or research-intensive inputs.[236]

A small team that puts all its energy into a challenging project, and that is under the pressure of a specific contract requiring the team to deliver, will on average work harder than a larger team embedded in a larger company. That at any rate is the idea of "high powered incentives" that accompany a contract specifying a discrete "deliverable." A researcher working in a research division of a large company cannot typically be motivated so directly. But a researcher or small team under pressure to deliver a specific result (and earn a contractual reward) can be expected to concentrate more and work harder: the downside of failure is greater (the small firm might fail or experience a very serious setback), and the upside of success is greater too, if the contract is written so as to reward success robustly.

The second reason some researchers say small firms are superior is their relative lack of bureaucracy. As one literature summary puts it, "[D]ue to some of the characteristics of large firms, such as a loss of marginal control or [a] high level of bureaucratic control, R&D performance … decreases."[237] The perils of large bureaucracies are well understood, of course. But they seem especially salient with respect to R&D activities, in which freedom from bureaucratic oversight is said to be especially important.[238] As one pair of researchers put it, "it is not the size of firms per se, but rather the internal processes activated as firms evolve in size that affect innovation outcomes."[239] To be more specific, in planning for innovation large firms typically gather more information as part of detailed analytical procedures. They "tend to make decisions in a more planned and more formal manner … than small firms."[240] This is partly a matter of organizational routines and styles, and partly due to increased monitoring: "as firms increase in size, managers become subject to closer monitoring by the firm's board of directors and shareholders, who expect decision making to be based on justifiable arguments."[241] Finally, with more

[236] See Ashish Arora and Robert P. Merges, Specialized Supply Firms, Property Rights and Firm Boundaries, 13 Indus. & Corp. Change 451 (2004). *See generally* Bo Carlsson, Zoltan J. Acs, David B. Audretsch, and Pontus Braunerhjelm, *Growth and Entrepreneurship*, 18 Indus. & Corp. Change 1193, 1222 (2009):

> There are two main reasons why small firms have become more important in recent decades. One is that small firms simply do certain things (such as certain types of innovation) better than large firms. As a result, through division of labor between small and large firms, the efficiency of the economy is increased. The other reason is that small firms provide the entrepreneurship and variety required for macroeconomic growth and stability …

[237] Negin Salimi and Jafar Rezaei, *Evaluating Firms' R&D Performance Using the Best-Worst Method*, 66 Eval. & Prog. Plan. 147, 148 (2018).

[238] *See, e.g.*, Clayton M. Christensen and Joseph L. Bower, *Customer Power, Strategic Investment and the Failure of Leading Firms*, 17 Strat. Mgt. J. 197 (1996).

[239] José Lejarraga and Ester Martinez-Ros, *Size, R&D Productivity and Decision Styles*, 42 Small Bus. Econ. 643, 644 (2014).

[240] Lejirraga and Martinez-Ros, at 646.

[241] Ibid., at 646–647.

layers of review and perhaps more competition over recognition and resources – that is, what are often called "company politics" – the personal agendas of corporate employees may come into play more often in large firms.[242]

Big firms recognize that their complex structures often fit poorly with the process of innovation. The spate of acquisitions by Big Platform companies and others attests to this; what the "bigs" cannot make, they buy. But it is also borne out by the institution of "skunk works," semi-secret or "unofficial" R&D projects within large companies that are conducted outside normal oversight and review procedures.[243] Indeed, complex oversight and approval seem anathema to successful R&D in whatever form. For example, a study of 464 R&D joint ventures in the telecommunications industry found that "Collaborative benefits [from these joint ventures] are diminished most by selection of governance that imposes excessive bureaucracy ... "[244] Whatever the industry, multi-stage decisions procedures and more complex organizational landscapes seem to be the enemy of important innovation.

In reviewing the advantages of small firms, we have so far touched on enhanced incentives and reduced bureaucracy. The final explanation relies less on the environment inside small firms and more on the personalities of those who found them and staff them. For many scholars, it is not firm size that shapes the entrepreneurial innovator; it is the entrepreneur, with his or her distinctive taste for autonomy and independence, who shapes the features of the small firm.

[242] See Tom Burns and G. M. Stalker, The Management of Innovation (Oxford: Oxford University Press, 1961), at 195–196 (quoting a research scientist brought into an industrial company to open an R&D lab):

What happens is that a plan devised in terms of changing the working organization [to include an R&D lab] fails to materialize because factors of status and politics play a determining role, and nobody realizes, or rather, admits, that these are real problems to be dealt with.

'The understanding was,' said the head of the laboratory, 'that I was needed by the firm, I was to take over their whole technical side and be responsible for technical development. My view now (after two years) is that this has been a wholly unsuccessful venture . . . . Everything I've put up has been blocked, it's met with deaf ears.

[W]hat they expect the lab to do is to hand over a blueprint of a new product, which the manufacturing side, the works manager, could put into production almost straight away . . . . They have no conception of what development work in this industry involves . . . .

See also Ibid., at 9 (describing R&D lab at one company):

Political conflict appeared to be clearly related to the particularism which was fostered by the separating out of the tasks of the firm according to specialist functions. Given a mechanistic system, changes of all kinds, including expansion, continually threw up new institutions within the firm which were intended to carry the whole of a new defined task and which themselves engendered political problems.

[243] "The designation 'skunk works' or 'skunkworks' is widely used in business, engineering, and technical fields to describe a group within an organization given a high degree of autonomy and unhampered by bureaucracy, with the task of working on advanced or secret projects." Wikipedia, "Skunkworks," available at https://en.wikipedia.org/wiki/Skunk_Works. The name was first used at Lockheed Aeronautics; it was taken from the old L'il Abner comic strip: in that comic series, it was the name of a moonshine liquor still. Ibid.

[244] Rachelle C. Sampson, *The Costs of Misaligned Governance in R&D Alliances*, 20 J.L. Econ. & Org. 484, 485 (2004).

According to some detailed research, engineers and scientists who have a strong preference for autonomy and challenging projects tend to work at startups, while those impelled by security and risk avoidance more often work at large companies.[245] These differing motivations produce different outcomes: put simply, the autonomy valued by startup researchers creates the right sort of environment for radical innovation. As the title of one journal article says, "*Being Independent Is a Great Thing.*"[246]

Small firms have their own pressures, of course. One is that venture capital finance, which makes startups possible, brings with it external monitoring and accountability. Another is that although it is exciting to choose one's career direction, it is also risky: going "all in" on a single project means little chance to deflect blame or soften the blow if it fails. Apparently, however, these negatives are outweighed (for some people at least) by the relative freedom from hierarchical oversight.[247] The simple act of choosing one's own course holds personal rewards.[248] But it also has ramifications for the larger economy. Small firms, founded out of a desire for personal autonomy, supply diverse and farflung sources of fresh, new ideas. They ensure that many minds attack technological problems from many different, uncoordinated starting points. By decentralizing decision making, they make it more likely that a small team "off the radar" of the established research paradigm will develop an unconventional or novel approach.[249] Just the type of approach that can lead to a radical innovation

6.6.1.3 Policies for a Healthy, Variegated Industry Structure

The point of this research is not to place a rigid limit in firm size. It's not to promote a one-size-fits-all prescription in favor of small firms. No, the point is to plan for a

245 Henry Sauermann, Fire in the Belly? Employee Motives and Innovative Performance in Startups versus Established Firms, Nat'l Bureau of Econ. Res., Working Paper 23099 (January 2017), available at www.nber.org/papers/w23099, at 14. But cf. Thomas Lange, *Job Satisfaction and Self-Employment: Autonomy or Personality?*, 38 Small Bus. Econ. 165 (2012) (finding that, based on survey data, the fact of autonomy explains higher job satisfaction among self-employed men and women better than measures of various individual personality traits; a preference for autonomy, in this study, is not treated as a personality trait in and of itself).

246 Bruno Frey and Mathias Benz, *Being Independent Is a Great Thing: Subjective: Evaluations of Self- Employment and Hierarchy*, 75 Economica 362 (2008).

247 Martin A. Carree and Ingrid Verheul, *What Makes Entrepreneurs Happy? Determinants of Satisfaction Among Founders*, 13 J. Happiness Stud. 371 (2012).

248 Cf. Robert P. Merges, *Autonomy and Independence: The Normative Face of Transaction Costs*, 53 Ariz. L. Rev. 145 (2011) (arguing that even if multiple small firms add a modest increment to transaction costs in a given industry, the intrinsic value of autonomy might make it worthwhile to tolerate and encourage some small firms in that industry's structure).

249 Each small firm also does its part to perpetuate the overall culture of small firms, the ethos and norms of this type of firm. By keeping this culture alive, even an unsuccessful small firm may sew the seeds of a future success. See Daniel W. Elfenbein, Barton H. Hamilton, and Todd R. Zenger, *The Small Firm Effect and the Entrepreneurial Spawning of Scientists and Engineers*, 56 Manage. Sci. 659 (2010) (researchers from small firms more likely to subsequently be self-employed).

variegated industry structure – one that includes a number of smaller firms – but also medium and large ones. This diverse industry structure gives the best chance for important future innovations, including radical ones, in platform-related technologies and elsewhere. As one study summarized it,

[T]he results show that larger firms enjoy greater advantages for incremental innovation performance ... but not for radical innovation performance on which large firm size has a negative non-significant effect ... Large firms rarely introduce radical innovation performance; rather they tend to solidify their market positions with relatively incremental innovations ... Large firms with strong knowledge bases may become so entrenched in existing technology trajectories that they might overlook emerging knowledge and technologies from new territories ... Large firms also discourage radical departures from the status quo, which would require a different set of rules and processes ... "[250]

Both these themes – increased overall innovation and decreased radical innovation – are apparent from a large-scale study of post-merger R&D in European companies. Because this study aptly summarizes many of the points I have been trying to make, I describe here in a bit of detail.

Economist Joel Stiebale studied 941 European mergers between 1978 and 2008 using data on the nationality of inventors listed on patent applications. The results show that after many mergers, inventive activity increases in the country where the acquiring company is located but decreases in the country that is home to the target (or acquired) company.[251] The study accounts for the fact that after a merger, consolidation of patent activities in the headquarters of the acquiring company is to be expected, and that therefore more patent applications will originate from the home country of the acquiring company after the merger. Stiebale adjusts for this. National-level inventiveness is tested not by patent applications originating in the acquiring and target home countries but by the domiciles of listed inventors on those patent applications. The patent department (and thus filing country) may change after an acquisition, in other words; but the inventors usually stay put. Stiebale finds that target company R&D productivity drops, as measured by the number of patent applications filed by target company inventors in the post-merger period.

Notably, for the point I am making, the larger the patent portfolio of the acquiring company (called the "knowledge stock" in the Stiebale study), the greater the drop in inventiveness in the country where the target firm is located. As the author says:

The asymmetry of [positive and negative inventiveness] effects between acquiring and target firms increases with pre-acquisition differences in knowledge stocks,

[250] Beatriz Forés and César Camisón, *Does Incremental and Radical Innovation Performance Depend on Different Types of Knowledge Accumulation Capabilities and Organizational Size?*, 69 J. Bus. Res. 831, 836 (2016) (summarizing literature; references omitted).

[251] Joel Stiebale, *Cross-border M&As and Innovative Activity of Acquiring and Target Firms*, 99 J. Int'l Econ. 1 (2016).

indicating a relocation of innovative activities towards more efficient usage within multinational firms ... [T]he larger the pre-acquisition knowledge stock of the acquirer, the more pronounced is the positive ... effect of international M&As on post-acquisition innovation in the acquirer's country. Hence, relocation of innovation seems to be most pronounced for large pre-acquisition differences in innovative capabilities ... [I]t is possible that the target firm's pre-acquisition knowledge stock is valuable to the acquirer's research program and that acquired knowledge is exploited in the acquirer's country rather than in both countries. The results are consistent with large technology-based firms acquiring smaller companies whose technologies are integrated into the acquirer's research program post-acquisition.[252]

From an overall efficiency standpoint, there is a good and defensible reason for this result. As the author himself says, "[it] indicates that innovation activities are not relocated from targets to acquirers per se but to the part of the multinational firm that is more efficient in innovation."[253] But even so, it matters that there is a loss of innovative vigor on the part of the target firm after these mergers. Efficiency is gained, while paradigm-stretching creativity may be lost.

Now, granted, this study (1) applies only to Europe and (2) documents a drop in inventiveness only for the trans-national, intra-European mergers studied. It is not beyond the realm of possibility that these results pertain to European mergers in some peculiar way. Aside from this, however, the study sounds a cautionary note. While the overall *volume* of innovation increases in the expected way after a merger, this seems to come at the expense of the innovative output of the acquired firm. While the gains in efficiency may outweigh the loss of a highly innovative independent firm, the theory and experience reviewed earlier tell us to be wary of the long-term effects. Multiple, rivalrous sources of innovation are still a good thing – even, one might say, a good in and of themselves. Losing many autonomous firms to the merger trend may generate serious costs in the long run.

Perhaps the best way to summarize what I have been saying is to quote from a classic historical study published in 1969, aptly entitled *The Sources of Innovation*,[254] which takes the long view regarding matters of industry structure and innovation:

> There will always be a wide range of unsatisfied needs more or less precisely defined (a cure for the common cold; a silent [airplane] engine; a typewriter which will operate from dictation [hello, Dragon Software!] ... an electric battery of much greater endurance [Tesla, anyone?], and so on through an almost endless list) and an equally wide range of hypotheses about how they might possibly be met.

[252] Stiebale, *Cross-Border M&Ss*, at 11.

[253] Ibid.

[254] John Jewkes, David Sawers, and Richard Stillerman, The Sources of Invention (2nd ed., 1969), at 211–12 (summary of the invention and development of 56 important innovations, including the ball point pen, catalytic cracking of petroleum, new polymers such as polypropylene, the transistor, etc.).

> It seems inconceivable that any one type of institution could properly explore every suggestion holding out some promise of success. There are not, and never will be, enough large firms to follow up every feasible idea. This is why the history of every large firm presents instances of its apparent failure to take up some idea which ultimately proved to be highly profitable. The big firm may well be wise not to spread its energies too widely . . .
>
> Thus the way may be left open for other, small organizations to try their luck. The differences in the sizes of firms may very well be associated with specialization in research. Some projects will threaten to be costly but offer a reasonable chance of success (as, for example, where 'systems' are concerned as contrasted with the possibilities of inventing smaller pieces of equipment). These may well be the lines of research which commend themselves to the bigger firms. Other projects will be more risky but explorable with much smaller outlays. This may be the proper field for the smaller firms or even firms brought into existence for the purpose of following up a single inventive idea.

As in 1969, when this study was published, and as in the times when the innovations studied were being developed, there is an important place for small firms in a healthy R&D-rich industrial ecosystem. That was true before Big Platform companies, and it is very likely to be true now as well.

6.6.1.4 Decentralized and Diverse Research Capabilities: New Research on the Role of Patents

The economic study of patents has undergone a gradual but thorough change over the past 25 years. As late as the 1990s, most economists understood patents as state-backed monopolies. Theoretical studies mostly featured a tradeoff model: losses from monopoly pricing were balanced against the societal benefits of new technologies. The lure of monopoly power called forth inventive effort, but the benefits of new inventions came at the expense of above marginal-cost pricing.

Call this the Incentive/Tradeoff (I/T) theory.[255] Tradeoff theory deals in highly aggregated terms: the costs and benefits of patents are modeled and discussed at the society-wide level. The total value of all new inventions called forth by patents is weighed against the total cost of supra-marginal pricing across all markets in an economy.

Roughly 25 years ago something new began to take shape in economic writing on patents. Just as in economics as a whole, classical microeconomics was being modified by a newfound interest in the various structural elements that together

[255] For a review of the Incentive/Tradeoff Model, and its role in patent scholarship, See Robert P. Merges, *Economics of Intellectual Property Law*, in The Oxford 2 Handbook of Law and Economics: Private and Commercial Law (Francesco Parisi, ed., 2017), available at DOI: 10.1093/oxfordhb/9780199684205.013.017.

determine aggregate economic activity (firms, transactions, property rights, and other "institutions"), so too with the literature on patent economics. Tradeoff theory was refined by inquiries into two new topics: (1) how patents affect the *locus* of inventive activity, and not just its aggregate level and (2) transactional solutions to problems of dispersed patent ownership. One frequent finding in these newer studies is that patents (and IP rights generally) promote firm specialization, and in this way, patents affect not just aggregate incentives but industry structure as well. For this reason, we might call the new approach the Specialization/Industry Structure (S/IS) Theory.

The basic insight from this literature is that IP rights can actually affect the location of firm boundaries.[256] The key to this new understanding of IP is to see it not primarily as something that affects overall incentive levels, but instead as an instrument that affects transactions – and hence the organization of production. Advocates of this view see IP as a way for small, specialized firms to protect against opportunism when contracting with larger firms. IP makes it easier for specialized firms to sell technology and know-how via arm's-length contracts, which permits specialized producers to exist as independent firms. IP rights can then be said to affect industry structure: Without these rights, specialized knowledge subject to opportunistic copying would have to be produced within large, vertically integrated firms. This in turn would mean a loss of the "high powered incentives" (to use Oliver Williamson's term)[257] available to independent firms who sell their output via contracts. The upshot is that IP at the margin may enable more small and independent firms to remain viable even in industries where multicomponent products are assembled and sold by large, vertically integrated firms.[258]

Put simply, it is not enough to celebrate the benefits of a variegated industry structure, or even to push for it through antitrust policy, such as stricter review of

[256] An early contribution is David Teece, *Profiting from Technological Innovation: Implications for Integration, Collaboration, Licensing and Public Policy*, 15 Res. Pol'y 285 (1986). Among legal scholars an early articulation of the idea is in Robert P. Merges, A *Comparative Look at Property Rights and the Software Industry*, in The International Computer Industry: A Comparative Study of Industry Evolution and Structure (David C. Mowery, ed., 1996), at p. 282 ("The Japanese software industry teaches some valuable lessons about the role of property rights in overcoming transaction costs. Without the security of a property right granted by the government, software suppliers in Japan would be loath to leave the protective contractual sphere they shared with their captive customer/patrons ["keiretsu"]. But with such a right, enforceable outside the context of an individual contract (that is, a right that is "good against the world"), these firms are free to sell to other customers."). See also Robert P. Merges, *A Transactional View of Property Rights*, 20 Berkeley Tech. L.J. 1477 (2005). An excellent overview of the literature that has developed around these ideas, with many important and original contributions of its own, is Jonathan M. Barnett, Innovators, Firms, and Markets: The Organizational Logic of Intellectual Property (Oxford: Oxford University Press, 2021).

[257] See Oliver E. Williamson, The Economic Institutions of Capitalism: Firms, Markets, Relational Contracting (New York: Free Press, 1985), at pp. 141–144.

[258] See Ashish Arora and Robert P. Merges, *Specialized Supply Firms, Property Rights and Firm Boundaries*, 13 Indus. & Corp. Change 451 (2004).

small firm acquisitions in markets dominated by the Big Platforms. Maintaining a viable patent system is important too. The new appreciation among researchers for the transactional role of patents adds to the conventional view that the patent system gives an important boost to new entrants and smaller firms in general.[259]

6.6.2 *Pharma Patents: The Good, the Bad, the In-between*

If there is one industry where the conventional "incentive theory" of patents is actually true, it is the pharmaceutical industry. As a result, it is equally well understood that eliminating or weakening patent protection in this industry could significantly reduce the volume of R&D and consequently the supply of new drugs.[260] In light of one consistent theme of this book, and despite appearances, the big pharmaceutical companies contribute in their way to a vibrant and diversified (but often hidden) drug therapy development ecosystem. Big Pharma is not big and isolated; the major firms rely on smaller firms, many founded on university research, that supply a rushing stream of new discoveries, science-based drug candidates, drug discovery techniques, and so on.[261] The best evidence of the diverse sources and general effectiveness of pharmaceutical research is the rapid development of COVID vaccines beginning in 2020 when the virus was first identified. Whatever its problems (and they are legion), the pharmaceutical industry in this instance delivered the goods.

Yet the other half of the pharma story is one of aggressive use of patents to reap and sustain profits for drug therapies that have proven effective. However essential *some* patent protection must be for the pharmaceutical industry, there is abundant evidence that after fulfilling its basic obligation (developing effective new therapies), the industry seeks to relentlessly extend profits for as long as possible, to the

[259] The secondary market for patents – in which a small firm for example sells part of its patent portfolio to others in the industry – can also play a role in maintaining the viability of specialist firms in platform-based markets. See Robert P. Merges, *Patent Markets and Innovation in the Era of Big Platform Companies*, 35 Berkeley Tech. L.J. 53, 53 (2020).

[260] Richard C. Levin et al., *Appropriating the Returns from Industrial Research and Development*, 18 Brookings. Pap. Econ. Act. (Special Issue) 783 (1987); Wesley M. Cohen, Richard R. Nelson, and John P. Walsh, "Protecting Their Intellectual Assets: Appropriability Conditions and Why U.S. Manufacturing Firms Patent (or Not)," Working Paper 7552, National Bureau of Economic Research, Cambridge, MA (February, 2000, revised 2004); Stuart J. H. Graham, Robert P. Merges, Pam Samuelson, and Ted Sichelman, *High Technology Entrepreneurs and the Patent System: Results of the 2008 Berkeley Patent Survey*, 24 Berkeley Tech. L.J. 1255 (2009) (survey of 1,332 small and start-up companies formed since 1998; finding that patents are much more important in biotechnology industry than in computer hardware and software).

[261] See Peter Lee, *Transcending the Tacit Dimension: Patents, Relationships, and Organizational Integration in Technology Transfer*, 100 Cal. L. Rev. 1503, 1572 (2012); Ronald J. Gilson et al., *Contracting for Innovation: Vertical Disintegration and Interfirm Collaboration*, 109 Colum. L. Rev. 431, 439 (2009); Gary P. Pisano, *The R&D Boundaries of the Firm: An Empirical Analysis*, 35 Admin. Sci. Q. 153 (1990).

detriment of many a cash-strapped patient faced with absurdly high prices on a drug he or she needs badly but cannot afford.

Drug company profit extension takes two forms: (1) huge investments in government lobbying, designed to protect existing advantages and tweak the current system so as to extend exclusivity or otherwise deter generic companies and (2) sophisticated deployment of detailed, technical rules and practices at the interface of drug approval (the Food and Drug Administration (FDA)) and patent law, all of which contribute to the goal of extending the "franchise" of a successful drug by eliminating, for as long as possible, competition from generic drug companies.[262] Examples of these tactics include acquiring numerous "secondary" patents (covering the proper dosage of a hit drug, or the combination of two pre-existing drugs), and using them to effectively protect the market for a drug long after the basic drug patent has expired – what is termed "evergreening."[263]

The high cost of patented drugs has become a major issue in discussions over the future of health care in the United States. This puts a spotlight on the patent system, and has prompted proposals to rein in pharma company power by adding extra stringent review to "secondary" drug patents.[264] The pharma industry argues that franchise extension supplies the working capital to invest in the many failed projects that precede a big hit. Meanwhile, patients see the immediate relief, in the form of lower prices, every time a drug goes "off patent," as well as the much lower cost of drugs in countries outside the United States. There is resentment too over the fact that the same drug can often be purchased outside the United States for much less than the US price. This is irksome especially because a fair number of developed countries with no domestic pharmaceutical industry and a small or nonexistent research infrastructure in effect rely on outside pharma companies, including those in the United States, to develop new drugs. When these new drugs are available at lower cost in countries where they were not developed, there is a feeling that American consumers[265] are subsidizing the rest of the world through the much higher prices required to fund the drug discovery process. Regardless of how the costs are allocated, the pharmaceutical development system remains a vital institution. On it depend many lives and deaths. When one considers the issue of

[262] See Scott Hemphill, Robin Feldman, Jay Lefkowitz, Sean Nicholson, and Judge William G. Young, *Assessing Strategies to Delay Generic Drug Entry*, 11 NYU J. Intell. Prop. & Ent. L. 60, 62 (2021).

[263] Robin Feldman, *May Your Drug Price Be Evergreen*, 5 J. L. & Biosciences 590 (2018).

[264] See, e.g., Michael D. Frakes and Melissa F. Wasserman, "Investing in Ex Ante Regulation: Evidence from Pharmaceutical Patent Examination," NBER Working Papers 27579, July 2020, revised May 2022, available at https://papers.ssrn.com/sol3/papers.cfm?abstract_id=3661071 (calculating net social benefit of extra stringent review of secondary drug patents). See generally Michael D. Frakes and Melissa F. Wasserman, *Does the U.S. Patent & Trademark Office Grant Too Many Bad Patents? Evidence from a Quasi-Experiment*, 67 Stan. L. Rev. 613 (2015).

[265] If this can be called a subsidy, consumers in other regions/countries that are home to large pharma companies – Europe, Japan, and a few others – also share in providing it.

intergenerational equity – fairness to future generations – it is crucial that whatever patent-related policies are adjusted to lower drug costs, it must be done in a way that does not seriously and permanently degrade the effectiveness of drug development.[266] It is the need for this balance – reasonable cost and universal citizen access to vital drugs, as against stewardship of an essential innovation ecosystem – that makes patent-related health policy so challenging.

6.6.2.1 Twenty-First Century Patent Political Economy: Infotech and Pharma

The leadup to the America Invents Act (AIA) of 2011 hammered home a fact about the patent system that was becoming more and more evident: the interests of pharmaceutical and biotechnology companies were often very distinct from those of other patent-owning companies. Of the non-pharma companies, those from the computer hardware, software, online platform, and consumer electronics industries – often grouped into the "infotech" constituency[267] – advocated most frequently and vociferously for reforms that were at odds with the interests of pharma.[268] It had been true at least since the Hatch-Waxman Act of 1984 that the patent system had incorporated a number of pharma-specific rules and procedures,[269] based on the special needs of the industry and the ultra-importance of individual patents in its business model.[270] Infotech is a high-volume,

[266] See Robert P. Merges, Justifying Intellectual Property (Cambridge, MA: Harvard University Press, 2011), at pp. 271 ff.

[267] The AIA was in some ways what drew infotech into patent policymaking and lobbying on a basis equal to pharma. R. Polk Wagner, *The Supreme Court and the Future of Patent Reform*, 55 Fed. Law. 35, 35 (2008) ("[Major trends today include] . . . the emergence of the technology industry (on the West Coast) as a major player in the political economy of the patent system.").

[268] See Congressional Research Service study from 2006. Wendy H. Schacht, Cong. Research Serv., CRS Report No. RL33367, Patent Reform: Issues in the Biomedical and Software Industries (2006). For background on the formation of patent reform lobbying groups centered in rival industries, see generally, Candace Lombardi, Tech Firms to Lobby for Patent Litigation Reform, ZDNet News, May 11, 2006, http://news.zdnet.com/2100-9595_22–148032.html; New Coalition Seeks to Protect American Innovation, IP Frontline, March 23, 2007, www.ipfrontline.com/depts/article.asp?id=14571&deptid=8 (illustrating the formation of the 21st Century Coalition for Patent Reform, an organization of pharmaceutical companies, some universities, and companies from other industries).

[269] On Hatch-Waxman, see Chapter 5.

[270] For one account of the stress and high stakes characteristic of drug development, as well as the incredible value of a basic patent on a blockbuster drug, see Barry Werth, The Antidote: Inside the World of New Pharma (New York: Simon and Schuster, 2014). Werth describes the massive drop in profits – and concomitant drop in stock price – that visits a pharma company when a patent on a blockbuster drug expires. See, ibid., at 195 (describing the "patent cliff" faced by drug company Pfizer when its patent on the cholesterol-control drug Lipitor expired in 2011, ending an exclusive position that earned it $12.5 billion annually pre-patent expiration. Ibid., at p. 195. Generic entry is known to reduce profits of the pioneer firm by as much as 80 percent.

low-value-per-patent industry, so there was a natural clash of interests. But the troll problem had grabbed the attention of many players in the patent system. With the legislative wheels turning, both pharma and infotech tried to load up the AIA on all the new rules they each thought would most benefit their respective industries. It was in this spirit that, beginning in 2005, infotech pushed for an apportionment of damages provision – something in the Patent Act to tamp down the potential for ruinous damages verdicts, which were emanating from jury rooms fast enough to take a large bite out of infotech profits.[271]

Pharma blocked any change in the rules on damages. The AIA says nothing about remedies at all. But this among other episodes leading up to the AIA showed that the patent field now had two interest groups, each powerful enough to block almost anything it strongly opposed.[272] It was fortunate in a way that administrative invalidity was favored by both, because without that it would not have been included in the AIA.[273] In general, the presence of two strong influence blocs makes legislative compromise difficult.[274] As in the past, however, the courts can implement patent policy themselves in the way they interpret, apply, and adapt court-made doctrine to newly arising problems in patent law. If contemporary political economy produces more legislative stalemates in the future, stakeholders in the world of patents may need to rely on this tradition of court-based policy making to adjust patent policy in light of changing conditions.

[271] See Joe Matal, *A Guide to the Legislative History of the America Invents Act: Part I of II*, 21 Fed. Circuit B.J. 435, 439 (2012) (Proposed legislation from 2007 to 2008 included "a requirement that reasonable-royalty damages be based on a patent's 'specific contribution over the prior art' and new substantive and procedural barriers to awards of enhanced damages").

[272] On "veto players" in political institutions such as Congress, and how these players may be influenced, see George Tsebelis, Veto Players: How Political Institutions Work (Princeton, NJ: Princeton University Press, 2002). On the ways that patent doctrine under our (superficially) unitary patent system adjusts to the needs of different industries, see sDan L. Burk and Mark A. Lemley, *Is Patent Law Technology-Specific?*, 17 Berkeley Tech. L.J. 1155 (2002).

[273] Administrative patent review undoubtedly helps infotech. It has in fact proven to be one of the most effective policy responses to the problem of excessive patent litigation (i.e., troll lawsuits). See Robert P. Merges, *After the Trolls: Patent Litigation as Ex Post Market-Making*, 54 Akron L. Rev. 555, 588 (2020) ("It is difficult to overstate the importance of the [Inter Parte Review procedure], how it has changed the dynamics of patent enforcement [and helped reduce troll litigation").

But pharma also supported it, though with some modifications. See Prepared Statement of Philip S. Johnson, Chief Intellectual Property Counsel, Johnson & Johnson, On Behalf of the Coalition for 21st Century Patent Reform, Before the United States Senate Committee on the Judiciary On "Patent Reform in the 111th Congress: Legislation and Recent Court Decisions," March 10, 2009, available at 2009 WL 599165, www.judiciary.senate.gov/imo/media/doc/09-03-10Johnsontestimony.pdf, at p. 10 (supporting inter partes "reexamination," later deemed IPRs).

[274] The two groups spent nearly $3.5 million lobbying for the AIA. See Amanda Becker, Capital Business: Patent reform measure ignited fierce lobbying effort, *Washington Post*, March 27, 2011, available www.washingtonpost.com/capital_business/patent-reform-measure-ignited-fierce-lobbying-effort/2011/03/25/AFzD9VkB_story.html.

6.6.3 *Same as It Ever Was: The Need to Police the Line between Helpful Incentive and Harmful Rent-Seeking*

In patent policy, every generation seems to encounter a different variant of the same basic problem:

> In the ideal world, patent law polices the boundary between legitimacy and overstretch, between rewarding innovation and inviting rent-seeking. [Today, we may call] this boundary the "troll line" – the line that separates beneficial from harmful patents and patent enforcement.[275]

The contemporary problems reviewed in this section are all versions of this classic line-drawing challenge. In platform markets, small innovators may need to rely on patents to stay viable in the face of huge industry-spanning competitors. In this effort, weak or ineffective patents will be no help. The threat of litigation may be needed at times to help patent-centric firms hold their place in the industry; quality patents, with a good chance of surviving invalidity review, are essential for this purpose. At the same time, as witnessed during the height of the troll litigation boom, excessive litigation can weigh down big companies to such an extent that it taints legitimate enforcement and prompts skepticism about overall patent quality.

In pharmaceuticals, profit-milking "evergreening" poses the same threat. And, intertwined as it is with the sensitive topic of overpriced drugs. The line-drawing exercise will be closely scrutinized. But, as we have repeatedly seen, that exercise has been the central theme throughout the history of US patent law.

[275] Robert Merges, *After the Trolls: Patent Litigation as Ex Post Market-Making*, 54 Akron L. Rev. 555, 587 (2020).

7

In Conclusion

CHAPTER OUTLINE

7.1 THE PRIVATE (LAW) LIFE OF PATENTS

Patents figure into all sorts of business arrangements. Businesspeople have used patents as a scaffolding around which a business can be built. From the earliest days, patents funneled investment into technology-centered enterprises. But soon after, businesspeople began subdividing patent rights along two dimensions. Patents served as a way to divide up ownership shares in flexible and customizable fractions. They were also subdivided by geography: A partial patent assignment can be used to confer exclusive rights to a new owner in a particular region, state, or city. In this way, patents anchored a network of exclusive regional franchises.

Over time, the scale of an average patent became too small to support an entire company. So, patents became specialized corporate assets. Though no longer the "glue" that held an entire company together, a firm's patents still might serve valuable purposes. During the late nineteenth century period of corporate consolidation, for example, patents served as bargaining chips. In the mergers that formed General Electric and AT&T, the constituent firms used patent portfolio value as one way to allocate ownership shares in the newly consolidated firm. Each constituent firm used its patent portfolio to represent the "technology quotient" it was contributing in the consolidation. Later still, patents became bargaining chips of a different kind. Patent portfolios were built and maintained to gain advantage in cross-licenses with other large firms, and to gain a seat in the formation of the occasional patent pool with other industry players. Finally, in more recent years, an active "secondary patent market" has grown up. Patent portfolios of various sizes are bought and sold by producing companies in service of various corporate strategies. They are also occasionally sold into the hands of patent "monetization" companies, some of whom are characterized as patent "trolls" (litigation-settlement specialists).

Some of these business techniques may have been planned and even encouraged by Congress. Certainly, the regional exclusivity idea was baked into patent law at an early stage, and partial ownership franchising was known from the time of Isaac Watt in Great Britain. Even so, most of the ways businesspeople employed patents for private ordering simply developed over time. They were unplanned, spontaneous adaptations that emerged from the demands of business. As a consequence, these practices are not reflected in the Patent Act, and they enter the case law only sporadically and in passing. Except for a small group of entrepreneurs, investors, and patent lawyers, the private law dimension of patents went largely unnoticed.

What this dimension means is close attention to how patents figure into various business transactions; what motivates those transactions; and how patents are folded into larger corporate strategies and industry development.

The policies embedded in the Patent Act and related doctrines will continue to be important. Every time a patent is challenged, and very often when it is enforced, its validity is put in play; and foundational policies are right on the surface of every invalidation attempt. [## public private]

7.2 LEGACY OF THE "DEMOCRATIC PROPERTY" DEVELOPMENT STRATEGY

We saw in Chapters 2 and 3 the success of the economic development strategy I referred to as "democratic property."[1] In the distribution of government land, the award of patent rights, securing of mining claims, and in other ways this nineteenth-century ideal combined a reliable government grant with private capital and individual initiative. When it worked, property was doled out where possible in small increments to a dispersed population. Anyone who qualified and could pay the (relatively modest) price set by a government agency could become an owner. And from there, a person could build a business enterprise on the foundation of the government grant. Multiple, dispersed owners did not present a problem in this arrangement; they were in fact the goal.

In the era of democratic property, government-backed entitlements were fairly well-matched to the scale of the average enterprise. A half section of land made a workable farm; a mining claim perfected with improvements was by design big enough to yield some valuable mineral but small enough for a small team to work by itself. Many early patents were broad enough to cover a viable enterprise: a steamboat, or flour mill, or a wooden bridge. True, even then, multiple machines, covered by multiple individual patents, sometimes had to be combined to equip a viable business such as a shoe or tool factory, but the number of machines, and the number of patents covering them, was manageable. A small businessperson could compare competing machines by cost, including the patent-related royalty burden they might carry with them. Limited complexity, and a usually manageable number of patents, meant that the principle of democratic property did not interfere too much with running a business.

Things are different now. First, the sheer number of issued patents is far, far bigger than in the nineteenth century. (If we count overseas counterparts to US patents – that is, patents issued in China, Europe, Japan, Korea, Brazil, Nigeria, Israel, etc. – the number is astronomically larger.) Second, these patents typically cover one aspect or part of one component, which is combined with many other components into a final market product. Each individual patent covers only a small piece of the final product. Just as the physical components of a market product must be integrated to put it in useable form, a large number of patents must be accounted

[1] I said in Chapter 2, and repeat here, that this means *relatively* more democratic (compared to other regimes, many in the past), not *optimally* democratic. The gap occurs because unprivileged creative people, with all the interest and even passion for creativity that people often have, fail to gain entry or find a welcoming space in patent-related institutions. Grade school, high school, college, grad school, research institute, university, R&D department, startup company – these are all unrepresentative institutions in American society. Until this is no longer so, US IP law can never claim to be truly democratic in fact. For many of us, remedying this remains a paramount goal. Structural distributive justice in IP law is the key to a balanced system that promotes creativity in a way open to all on equal terms.

for as well. Just as many modern products are far more complex than in the past, there are far more patent-related transactions taking place in the background both before and after that product hits the market. Put simply, in today's conditions the democratic property strategy brings with it quite sizeable transactional burdens.

It is therefore necessary today to conceive of patent law as a field that is centered on two equal concerns: (a) the initial grant of rights and (b) the transactional landscape into which those rights are born. Put simply, the field must strive to understand that today, the grant of rights aimed at conferring independence and autonomy are accompanied not just by the social cost of granting any exclusive right, but by another cost as well: the cost of complexity. The ways and means of assembling rights into viable units – in general, the post-grant transactional environment – is a core interest now. It is equal in importance to the contribution represented by a single invention, which is the heart of traditional patent analysis at the time of the grant. *Independent* patent rights in an *interdependent* economic scene pose problems specific to the contemporary economy. If it is to remain relevant and useful, those responsible for the future of patent law must grasp this. As we have seen, patent rules and institutions are constantly tested by the threat of rent-seeking. Under the rubric of innovation, wrapped in the mantle of the meritorious inventor, business people and lawyers find ways to divert a system designed for innovation into channels that are privately profitable but socially unproductive. This must be watched. And when it gets out of hand it must be stopped. We can point to individual episodes when "patent sharks" or "patent trolls" put pressure on the integrity of the system. And we can point to waves of patent reform that grew in response at different moments in history. But these episodes blend into each other, they blur together. So much so that in the end the history of the system looks like one continuous episode of expansion and contraction, invention and opportunism, progress and retrenchment.

7.3 FROM DEMOCRATIC PROPERTY TO SPECIALIZED CORPORATE ASSET

As I have tried to explain, the patent system has throughout history adapted to trends in technology, business organization, and the needs of business in general. From a functionalist point of view, this is to be expected and indeed desired; a patent system that did *not* adapt might be thought of out tune with its constitutional mandate, "to promote the progress of ... useful arts." Even so, one narrative might decry the movement from the democratic property strategy toward a patent system tightly connected with large companies and professional researchers. Patents as the foundation of individual enterprise and small business might be celebrated, while patents as a specialized class of corporate assets might have less appeal. Or it might even be seen as another example of how "corporatization" and huge-scale businesses have concentrated economic power and threatened democratic values.

There may be something to this. But there is something on the other side, too. The title of Section 6.6.1.4 points the way: "Decentralized and Diverse Research Capabilities: New Research on the Role of Patents." In that earlier section I explained how new research highlights the transactional role of patents, and argues that patent rights assist new entrants and smaller companies remain competitive, innovative, and viably independent. The recognition that patents play a special role when in the hands of small, highly motivated technical teams shows that patents are not *inherently* biased toward "bigness." They can do some positive things that work against centralization, consolidation, and greater scale.

7.3.1 *Into the Future: From Transaction Costs to Transactional Capabilities*

One impression left from a comprehensive overview of the history of American patent law is that patents have played a part in all sorts of business transactions and contributed in their own way to various organizational forms in the world of business. With an eye toward the promotion of autonomy, and with an understanding that greater complexity and a greater multiplicity of patents put a premium on solving transactional issues, it seems a good idea to peek ahead and imagine some new directions for patent-based transactions.

Many serious students of patents are well versed in the transaction *costs* that arise from the multiplicity of patent rights and the sometimes-conflicting private strategies of patent owners. The competitive nature of R&D, together with the modest scope of most patents, often results in a fragmented ownership structure.

Many technologies are made of hundreds or thousands of components. These must be integrated into a workable whole to make a marketable product, or to permit the technology to work. Integration can come in the form of a final manufacturer, an overall product assembler that pulls all the inputs together and produces a final product. For physical inputs, this can be complicated enough; that's what supply chains are for.

But parallel to the physical inputs there are often patent inputs at well. These inputs are scattered patent rights, held by widely dispersed owners. (Where a physical component seller also holds patents, the patent rights are usually transferred along with the component, so unless there is a breach in the supplier relationship, patent rights need not be dealt with separately.) Patents held by firms that do not supply physical components represent a separate and distinct "input stream" into the final product.

The market for these patent inputs is complex. One reason is that patent enforcement depends on the initiative of each patent owner. A patent owner who doesn't know about a certain infringement has no chance to initiate the market-making process. Even if an owner knows of a possible infringement, it is often not easy to decide whether and when to enforce a patent against a given firm. There is the normal cost-benefit analysis: probability of winning, cost of litigation, strategic considerations (such as, choosing not to sue a key customer or a company whose patent portfolio is so huge that counter-litigation is all but certain, etc.). It is also in many cases partly hidden from view.

Even when a patent owner's assertion of a patent leads to a license agreement, the terms of this agreement are often hidden from view. The market for patent rights is in a sense a shadow market, operating parallel to the market for physical goods, but in a far less visible way. Because most infringement cases settle, the relatively few cases that proceed all the way to a remedy (injunction, damages, or both) have immense influence. Court cases, plus whatever public information can be divined from press releases, financial disclosure documents, the rare public royalty rate statement (such as in a patent pool), and the like – these are the sources that determine the parameters of private licensing agreements. But the details of those agreements often remain confidential.

The shadow market for patent rights is also an expensive market to operate. That's because this market is structured and shaped by an expensive legal process. Courts, patent offices (reviewing validity), and lawyers are prominent players in the market; it is a market that is tightly intertwined with legal proceedings.

Typically, the owner of an "unattached" patent right (one not owned by a physical input supplier) brings that right to the attention of the manufacturer through a demand letter, a request to enter into licensing negotiations, or perhaps just a blunt infringement lawsuit. Because patents are complex instruments that cover (in many cases) complex technologies with elaborate histories, it can be quite expensive just to figure out if the patent is valid. These days the manufacturer is likely to file one or more challenges to some of the patent owner's claims in an administrative court run by the Patent Office. If the patent is not invalidated, the parties will then contest whether one or more of the patent claims cover some aspect of a manufacturer's product – often by pursuing (expensive) litigation in a federal court, at least through a few stages of the legal process.

The overall point is this: Because patent rights are complex (and legally contestable) inputs, the legal-process-structured market for this input is quite expensive. Firms in patent-intensive industries do find ways to lower transaction costs: cross-licenses between large patent holders; joint membership in patent pools; patent waivers and partial waivers; industry standard norms for licensing deals; and so on. But while these arrangements help, they are far from universal among patent owners. The more typical, legally intensive form of market making – particularly in the case of "unattached" patents – usually involves at least a few rounds of (costly) legal process. So, no matter how patent inputs are assembled, it is a complex process, shot through with heavy transaction costs.

These transaction *costs* are therefore quite familiar in patent law. But what about a patent's transactional *capabilities*? We hear less of those. In this book I have tried to remedy that. The question for the future is whether patents have anything to contribute to business models such as a more active "market for ideas," i.e., purchase, sale and licensing of disembodied knowledge assets, and if so, how to prevent rent-seeking under the rubric of such a firm. In addition, it remains to be seen if patent law can more fully promote new firm entry. The role of patents in helping small, specialized suppliers is of particular interest in this regard.

7.3.2 *Thinking of Patents as a "Shadow Market"*

The market for goods and services, even in the digital era, is a visible market. Sellers offer things out in the open, buyers haggle, deals are struck. Often price data is available to all.

Market exchanges in IP rights are less visible. As real goods move through the distribution chain and into the hands of consumers, IP rights often follow, though usually only the parties involved know whether any IP licenses are in place. Most goods can be tracked and accounted for. But patent transactions operate in the background. Deals are struck, but the terms, let alone the subject matter, are not transparent.

There are three reasons for this:

- The patent market is structured and, in some cases, conducted within a legal framework, which masks the operations of the market. The assignor of a patent or portfolio is a seller, plain and simple; the assignee, a buyer. But one must pierce through the linguistic fog and tone of the transaction to grasp its economic essence.
- Most patent-related transactions are confidential. They are not reported on an exchange, to a clearinghouse, or anywhere else. They are in this sense shadow transactions by design.
- Patent transactions are stalked by uncertainty. A patent owner may own multiple patents; these may or may not cover some feature of a product sold on the market; the only definitive way to know if any of those patents are valid, cover a feature, cover that feature in a way that confers economic value, and – if all these conditions are met – if this economic value makes the patent worth licensing: all these are preconditions to a market transaction. This uncertainty makes for a murky, shadowy market.

Odd as it may sometimes seem, this market has its uses. Inventors and investors who manage to navigate it do so for several reasons. As emphasized throughout this book, though large corporate patent holdings have their functions and utility, patents seem especially valuable when they make it possible for a new entrant to gain a foothold in an established market. When a small firm that would otherwise be squeezed out manages via patent to hold fast in the face of incumbent pressure, we count this a success. Few patents, in truth, serve this vital function. But those that do help justify the cumbersome aspects of granting and enforcing patents.

The shadow market for patents can also help offset the lopsided distributional effects of "winner take all" markets.[2] Patents can help a specialized component maker stay in business in an industry otherwise dominated by the logic of vertical integration. It can help an innovative firm that contributed to building a new technology yet lost out in the end user market for products incorporating that technology.[3] Money from the sale or licensing of patents can provide "pivot capital": resources that give a prior innovator a chance to monetize the patents acquired in its "first act," to take a shot at a "second act." Patent-related revenue can also permit a failed product company to shut its doors with dignity, providing at least a little salvage value to its disappointed investors. This is not the vision early investors have, of course; they would much prefer hard cash raining down in the wake of a record-breaking initial public offering. But some salvage value is better than none.

7.3.3 *Patent Portfolios and the Secondary Patent Market: Specialized Property Rights for Specialized Transactions*

One theme of this book is the flexibility of a patent as a transactional instrument. Another theme is the creative businesspeople and lawyers who found different ways to leverage federal patents into some business advantage. All the examples in this book are historical. But the process continues. Although it is new, the practice of buying and selling patents – mostly in portfolios – may indicate yet another way patents can be of use in furthering business strategy.

While it is convenient that a corporation can sell off a patent portfolio, this might not seem significant. After all, a company can sell a used machine or truck, or furniture or any other type of personal property. What is so special about patents? In one sense, nothing. Property in a patent is no different from other property.[4] So patents are just one of many things a company can sell when and if it chooses.

But in another sense, patents are different. An absolutely central quality of property is that it confers very broad control rights on an owner. As compared with

[2] On this, see Robert P. Merges, *Patent Markets and Innovation in the Era of Big Platform Companies*, 35 Berkeley Tech. L.J. 53 (2020).

[3] These common scenarios are described in Robert P. Merges, *Patent Litigation as Ex Post Market Making*, Akron L. Rev. (2021).

[4] Patents are exclusive rights, just as personal property is the right to exclude others from using an object:

> The right to exclude others is the essence of the human right called 'property.' The right to exclude others from free use of an invention protected by a valid patent does not differ from the right to exclude others from free use of one's automobile, crops, or other items of personal property.

Panduit Corp. v. *Stahlin Bros. Fibre Works, Inc.*, 575 F.2d 1152, 1158 n.5 (6th Cir. 1978). See also Michael H. Davis, *Patent Politics*, 56 S.C. L. Rev. 337, 386 (2004).

a contract, for example, in the sale of an asset that is subject to a property right, there is no need to write down in detail all the ways the buyer can use the asset in the future.[5] Legal academics say this wide discretion in deciding what can be done with an asset is the core feature of property: the simple "right to exclude" everyone else from using an asset leaves property owners almost unfettered discretion in determining how it may be used. Economists likewise think of property as an entitlement distinct from contract. For them, allocating rights and duties by contract is a basic feature of economic activity. But because it is difficult and expensive (and theoretically impossible) to specify *all* rights and duties pertaining to an asset as between two contacting parties, property rights are necessary, and crucial for economic exchange. Property gives an owner all *residual rights*: the right to all uses of an asset *not* specified in a contract.

So, from a legal and economic perspective, ownership means a wide and full scope of control over the uses – known and unknown; present and future – of an asset.

It is this feature of property rights that is so important for patents. A patent gives its owner control rights over all embodiments of a claimed invention. Technology is unpredictable. R&D leads researchers in many (often unpredictable) directions,[6] and so broad control rights over many variations on a basic theme, and over (as yet) unforeseen applications of a technique or design, are especially important for new technologies and R&D activity generally. This is exactly what you get with a patent.[7]

Thus, a company can sell a machine or truck, as well as a patent. The buyer of the machine or truck can do anything he or she wants with it (as long as the use is legal). So personal property in trucks and machines adds some value. It would be

5 See Henry E. Smith, *Property as the Law of Things*, 125 Harv. L. Rev. 1691, 1704 (2012) ("When O1 owns Blackacre, the exclusion strategy for delineating her rights, implemented through devices like the tort of trespass, protects a range of actions A1, A2, A3 ... without the law's needing to specify these actions.").

6 According to Henry Smith:

> The uses of an asset are not just risky (e.g., with a variance in outcomes forming a probability distribution), but uncertain, in the Knightian sense. That is, the set of uses of an asset may not correspond to a known probability distribution, and nonowners may not even know the members of the set. Property law helps manage this uncertainty by not making knowledge of the uses or even the probability distributions of their values relevant to dutyholders. In previous work, I have argued that Knightian uncertainty is more conducive to property rules than to liability rules, which do require more knowledge of probabilistic information by officials or courts.

Henry E. Smith, Institutions and Indirectness in Intellectual Property, 157 U. Pa. L. Rev. 2083, 2088 (2009) (footnote omitted), citing Frank H. Knight, Risk, Uncertainty and Profit 19–20, 197–232 (1921) (distinguishing "risk" from "uncertainty" by noting that "uncertainty" is immeasurable in principle).

7 On this, see Henry E. Smith, Institutions and Indirectness in Intellectual Property ("For property, and intellectual property especially, the discovery of options (rather than the measurement of the value of options based on known risks) is something that the indirect modular structure of property tends to foster.").

burdensome for the company to specify all the things the buyer can do with the truck or machine, and property makes this unnecessary. Yet in the case of a truck, for example, the list of future uses, though difficult, would not be intractable. Driving, carrying, delivering, etc. – the foreseeable uses of the truck are legion but not infinite. And the vast majority are foreseeable.

Patents are different. A patent on a mediocre glue might make "post-it notes" possible.[8] Invention of a nonstick coating for cookware might make rainproof but breathable cloth possible.[9] A patent on a mildly useful compound for one medical condition might open the door later to an effective treatment for a major disease or problem,[10] and so on.

The essence of a patent is an extrapolation from one or a few prototypes, successful experiments, or working models; those who draft patent claims work everyday in the realm of projection, extension, variation, and modification. Even within a single patent, the usual practice is to draft a set of claims that begin broadly and then become narrower. This pattern is repeated several times in a typical patent. Thus, from an economic perspective, the best way to conceptualize a patent is as a set of nested options. It is impossible to know for certain on the date a patent is filed, or on the date a claim is redrafted ("amended"), whether that claim will cover ("read on") a valuable commercial product ("embodiment") in the future. There is also a risk that a broader claim may encompass something known in the field before the claim was filed – making that claim invalid. (Patent drafters are forever navigating the eternal golden braid of validity risk, legitimate extrapolation ("enablement"), and future coverage.)[11] But the better the claims are drafted, and the more of them there are, the more likely that something of future value will be covered.

8 See Spencer Ferguson Silver, US patent 3,691,140 ("Acrylate Copolymer Microspheres"), issued September 12, 1972. For the story behind the invention of the post-it note, see www.post-it.com/3M/en_US/post-it/contact-us/about-us/.

9 A DuPont researcher named Roy J. Plunkett invented polytetrafluorethylene (PTFE), trademarked as "Teflon," in 1938. See Science History Institute, "Robert W. Gore," available at www.sciencehistory.org/historical-profile/robert-w-gore. One of Gore's co-workers was W. L. Gore, who left DuPont to develop new applications of PTFE – one of which (in research with Gore's son, Robert Gore) led to the surprising discovery that quick-stretching PTFE made a thin film that was air permeable but waterproof: Gore-Tex. Ibid. One early Gore-Tex patent is Robert Gore and Samuel Allen, US patent 4,194,041 ("Waterproof Laminate"), issued March 18, 1980.

10 See, e.g., Douglas Martin, "Guinter Kahn, Inventor of Baldness Remedy, Dies at 80," New York Times, September 19, 2014, at p. A21 (describing Gunther Kahn's discovery that a failed ulcer treatment called minoxidil was quite effective at stimulating hair growth). See also Charles A. Chidsey III and Guinter Kahn, US patent 4,596,812 ("Methods and Solutions for Treating Male Pattern Alopecia"), issued June 24, 1986. See generally Rebecca S. Eisenberg, *The Problem of New Uses*, 5 Yale J. Health Pol'y, L. & Ethics 717, 724 (2005) ("[C]linical trials showing that a drug works for a new indication may support a process patent on a new method of treatment, even though the same drug has previously been used for another purpose."); Kathryn Brown, *Repurposing Old Drugs for New Uses*, 28 DePaul J. Art, Tech. & Intell. Prop. L. 1 (2017).

11 For just one of the thousands of examples that could be cited, compare *Automotive Technologies Intern., Inc. v. BMW of North America, Inc.*, 501 F.3d 1274, 1282 (Fed. Cir.

Now remember that the real-world unit of analysis these days is not a single patent but a patent portfolio,[12] and note that most portfolios include pending patent applications, which, unlike issued patents, can still be amended – and therefore have even greater option value. (Their claims can be stretched, where legitimate, to cover products that have become viable or foreseeable in the interval between the filing of the original claim and the amendment.) Put it all together and this is what you get: a very large bundle of ownership claims over a multitude of technological options. The options cover embodiments that may be hard (or impossible) to foresee. And it is equally hard (or impossible) to predict the market value of these unpredictable embodiments.

These contingent ownership claims over uncertain future technologies and market products represent a uniquely indeterminate set of assets. Which makes exclusionary rights, or residual rights, uniquely valuable as a form of entitlement over them. It might be said that if property did not exist before, then the desire to transfer rights over future technological embodiments and R&D trajectories would have made it necessary to invent it. Put another way, the fit between the core feature of property – residual rights over unspecifiable uses – and the nature of a patent is exceedingly tight.[13]

2007) (In patent for side door airbag sensors, claim covered sensors with a movable mass, i.e., mechanical sensors, and that sense an impact due to changes in a magnetic field, i.e., electronically; the claim was invalidated, because the patent specification adequately taught only the use of mechanical sensors: "[T]he district court was correct that the specification did not enable the full scope of the invention because it did not enable electronic side impact sensors."); with *Hologic, Inc.* v. *Smith & Nephew, Inc.*, No. 2017-1389 (Fed. Cir., March 14, 2018) available at www.cafc.uscourts.gov/sites/default/files/opinions-orders/17-1389.Opinion.3-12-2018.1.PDF (disclosure of a single type of "light guide," a fiber optic light source, was adequate to support a claim to the use of any type of light guide in a surgical instrument invention).

[12] See generally Gideon Parchomovsky and R. Polk Wagner, *Patent Portfolios*, 154 U. Pa. L. Rev. 1, 31–32 (2005) (outlining a theory of patent value in which the worth of a patent portfolio is greater than the sum of its individual parts). This article describes two chief advantages of portfolios: (1) "scale" and (2) diversity:

> [A] well-conceived patent portfolio is in many ways a form of "super-patent," sharing many of the marketplace advantages conventionally attributed to individual patents (paradigmatically, rights to exclude others from the marketplace), only on a larger, broader scale. By aggregating the individualized value of a number of closely related patents, the scale-features of patent portfolios enable holders to realize true patent-like power in the modern marketplace to a degree which is impossible using individual patents alone.
>
> [At the same time,] the inherent diversity created by the aggregation of many different patents offers holders a range of benefits – such as the ability to address the risk and uncertainty fundamental to innovation – that cannot be easily achieved absent the creation of such structures.

See also Michael Risch, *Patent Portfolios as Securities*, 63 Duke L.J. 89 (2013).

[13] Henry E. Smith, *Property as the Law of Things* ("The modular theory is more explanatory than the bundle picture. It helps explain the structures we do not find, shows how property can be used to maximize option value, and demonstrates why innovation in property takes the institutional paths it does.").

7.3.4 *Patent Portfolios as Bundles of Assets: Relationship to Corporate Law Theory*

There are several ways to think about this. One is that patents represent investments in "unsticking" information assets from other, related assets. Another is that patents represent an internal form of asset partitioning. The literature on corporate law theory has given us a rich account of how the corporate form permits discrete assets to be cleaved off and moved into a distinct entity separate from the personal assets of the people behind the corporation. This is efficient: it allows company founders to put boundaries around a limited "stake" they are willing to place inside the corporation, without endangering the founders' separate assets.[14] This is an obvious corollary to the well-known feature of corporations, which is that they limit the liability of shareholders. The asset partitioning idea examines the asset side of the corporate risk equation: by drawing a conceptual circle around corporate assets, the corporate form permits a discrete set of assets to be placed at risk – and no others.

This provides a template for how to think about patent portfolios. These allow a form of asset partitioning too. But instead of limiting liability, they promote market efficiency. Patent portfolios allow a firm to place a distinct, related set of assets into a sellable bundle, an idea pioneered in the context of general corporate assets and contracts by Ken Ayotte.[15] Bundling in this form has numerous advantages that apply to R&D and patents – most notably, it encourages investment in complementary assets (e.g., related patents) and it prevents opportunistic holdup. Patent law requires bundling in some cases, so as explicitly to prevent holdup.[16] There is as well a general sense that parties to a patent transfer agreement have a duty to prevent

[14] Known as "asset partitioning." See Henry Hansmann and Reinier Kraakman, *The Essential Role of Organizational Law*, 110 Yale L.J. 387, 390 (2000) (defining asset partitioning, which the authors say is the central defining characteristic of the corporation as an organizational form). See also Giacomo Rojas Elgueta, *Divergences and Convergences of Common Law and Civil Law Traditions on Asset Partitioning: A Functional Analysis*, 12 U. Pa. J. Bus. L. 517, 554 (2010) (discussing elaborations and refinements of the asset partitioning concept).

[15] Kenneth Ayotte and Henry Hansmann, *Legal Entities as Transferable Bundles of Contracts*, 111 Mich. L. Rev. 715, 744 (2013) (Holdup is prevented by including all potentially overlapping contracts and assets in the bundle or portfolio that is sold.)

[16] Holdup could occur if the seller of a patent withheld one or more related, overlapping patents, so that when the buyer began making and selling a product based on the acquired patent, the seller could sue for infringement under the patent(s) that were withheld. Patent law includes a rule that formally overlapping patents (those technically subject to what is known as "double patenting") (1) must expire at the same time (through use of what is known as a "terminal disclaimer" of any term in a second patent that would otherwise extend beyond the term of the first patent) and (2) must be transferred together, as a bundle, to prevent lawsuits from multiple sources against use of a single invention. *See* In re Van Ornum, 686 F.2d 937, 948 (CCPA 1982) (double patenting doctrine seeks to prevent the possibility of multiple suits against an accused infringer by different assignees of patents claiming patentably indistinct variations of the same invention; "When a terminal disclaimer causes two patents to expire together(,) a situation is created which is tantamount for all practical purposes to having all the claims in one patent. Obviously, that thought contemplates common ownership of the two patents, which remains

holdup.[17] And parties can of course agree contractually to an anti-holdup provision.[18] In these ways, patent law encourages asset bundling. This works to cluster assets around a single, discrete R&D project. The bundle – the portfolio – can then in turn be cleaved off from the other assets of the firm and sold separately. Unlike classic asset partitioning, the patent portfolio does not cut down on the risk of liability; it enhances the ability of a firm to monetize an R&D project in the form of a discrete transaction. The remainder of the firm's assets stay put, and the firm goes on as before.

Because of this, patents represent a distinct set of property rights that exist inside the boundaries of a firm's otherwise undifferentiated assets. They are separated from the firm's other assets with recognizable legal boundaries. The legal form of the patent represents a standardized bundle of rights over assets, which – for all the reasons general to this feature of property – segregates these assets from the other, unsegregated, assets owned by a firm. Patents, or rather project portfolios, are therefore characterized by these attributes: (1) compartmentalization; (2) segregation

common throughout the life of the patents."); 37 CFR § 1.321(c), on "Statutory disclaimers, including terminal disclaimers":

> A terminal disclaimer ... must: (3) Include a provision that any patent granted on that application ... shall be enforceable only for and during such period that said patent is commonly owned with the application or patent which formed the basis for the ... double patenting [issue].

Second, parties can include a "non-holdup" provision in a patent transfer or purchase agreement.

17 See *Abraxis Bioscience, Inc.* v. *Navinta LLC*, 625 F.3d 1359 (Fed. Cir. 2010), cert. denied, 132 S. Ct. 115 (2011). This case involved a $350 million asset purchase by Abraxis including eight pharmaceutical patents. Seller company AstraZeneca agreed to "do, execute, acknowledge and deliver, or will cause to be done, executed, acknowledged and delivered, any and all further acts, conveyances, transfers, assignments, and assurances as necessary to grant, sell, convey, assign, transfer, set over to or vest in Buyer any of the Transferred Intellectual Property" described in the asset purchase agreement. 625 F.3d 1359, at 1369. It was subsequently discovered that a subsidiary company of the seller had failed to transfer ownership of relevant patents to the seller; this was remedied and the seller then transferred the patents to buyer Abraxis. Unfortunately, the transfer occurred too late to confer standing on the buyer Abraxis; so Abraxis's patent infringement action against another company, defendant Navinta, was dismissed. 625 F.3d 1359, at 1365. (On this, see Xuan-Thao Nguyen, *In the Name of Patent Stewardship: The Federal Circuit's Overreach into Commercial Law*, 67 Fla. L. Rev. 127, 169 (2015)). Nevertheless, the background to the case shows the general duty to transfer all technology or project-related patents, and therefore prevent patent-related holdup.

18 For an example, see Intel-Realnetworks Patent Portfolio Purchase Agreement, January 26, 2012 (Exhibit 2.1 to RealNetworks SEC Form 8K, filed January 30, 2012), available at www.sec.gov/Archives/edgar/data/1046327/000119312512029831/d290265dex21.htm, at § 2.9(f) ("Codec Intellectual Property Rights"):

> None of the Patents or Patent Rights retained by Seller after the Closing read on, relate to, or are otherwise infringed by the development or use of the Codec Assets (excluding the Codec Personal Property) in the manner in which Seller and its Subsidiaries have been developing such Codec Assets prior to the Closing and as reasonably anticipated in order to commercialize the Codec Assets.

or partitioning; (3) seperability or "unstickability"; and (4) (therefore) the potential for market fluidity.

It is crucial to recognize that a firm need not necessarily be active as a seller in the secondary patent market for it to benefit from that market. A firm's overall patent portfolio can be thought of as creating a series of options. Each project portfolio that goes into a firm's research program can be sold off if necessary. This gives the firm added flexibility.[19] In other words, just the possibility of project portfolio sales makes the firm nimbler. And, from an option theory perspective, more profitable. In theory, markets should recognize this though it is doubtful that the understanding of this feature has developed sufficiently for it to exert much influence on existing markets.

7.3.4.1 Are Patents Any Different from Other Assets?

In some ways, patents are not so different from other assets insofar as all the asset types mentioned are covered by different forms of property rights. The two attributes that are key to property are (1) that it permits a very wide range of uses for assets that are owned (i.e., it is a residual right) and (2) it creates duties of noninterference for everyone (it is "good against the world"). So, it is not necessary to specify in a detailed contract between a corporate seller and buyer all the things the buyer may do with the asset being sold, the machine, or truck, or land. The buyer can do anything he or she wants (so long as it is legal). And it is not necessary for the seller to provide that rights and duties pertaining to the machine, truck, or land attach to any subsequent buyer to whom the first buyer may transfer the asset. Succinctly said, patents are property, and come with all the features this entails.

On the other hand, there is a distinct difference between machines, trucks, land, etc., and the subject matter of patents, which is new inventions. The residual nature of property is *especially important and valuable* in the case of patents. That's because patents often cover technologies whose end uses and market value are especially uncertain, particularly when they have just been filed or very recently issued. The future trajectory of a given technology can be very difficult to evaluate, which means that contracts are a very poor substitute for property of this kind. While it might be possible to provide a list of future uses for a machine or truck, so that a contractual transfer would serve almost as well as the sale of property in these assets, the same is not true of inventions. The right to do anything that can be done, now or in the

[19] Gideon Parchomovsky and R. Polk Wagner, Patent Portfolios ("The broader scope of protection ensures that a wider range of technological possibilities will be covered, which both increases the possibility that the end result of the research and development effort will be covered, and diminishes the concerns of infringement of others' patents. This 'freedom of movement' – the ability to invent, implement, produce, and ship products with in-house resources – is increasingly viewed as an advantage in today's dynamic market environments, where speed and flexibility are economic imperatives." [footnotes omitted]).

future, with the technology claimed in a patent is a right that can only be reliably embodied in a property right.

Most corporate patent sales involve patent portfolios. Because the patents in these portfolios cover overlapping and interlocking aspects of the technology developed in an R&D project, they are a rich source of potential future uses and applications. The collective bundle of residual rights that accompanies transfer of a portfolio is an especially rich stock of residual rights.

Finally, there is even more flexibility built into these transactions. Patent portfolios almost always include pending patent applications as well as issued patents. Pending applications can be amended after purchase to cover uses, applications, and embodiments whose value is not yet apparent at the time the application is purchased. Assuming that the disclosure filed with an original patent application supports patent claims covering the later-added material, these later additions can be folded into pending applications. So, the purchase of a portfolio that includes these applications represents the possibility of an even wider (and hence more valuable) set of technological options than does the purchase of issued patents alone.

From the point of view of external investors, project portfolios allow investments in a set of property rights that represent discrete, "compartmentalized" corporate assets. Without patents, it would be expensive and difficult for an outside investor to gain ownership over these particularized corporate assets by themselves. The entire firm would have to be purchased, and then the particular assets of interest would have to be separated out and split off from the residual assets of the corporation. The particular assets of interest would have to be placed into some sort of separate ownership structure while the residual firm assets – all those assets owned by the original firm, minus the particularized assets of interest – would presumably remain in the old firm, which then would be sold off to another buyer, or shut down, or the like. This would all be difficult and expensive. The hidden value of the secondary market for patents is that it permits this sort of asset divestment to take place in a much more efficient manner. Patent portfolios comprise identifiable, discrete assets, which can be easily plucked out of the general corporate structure and sold off in well-recognized markets. The patents are themselves well-defined assets; when placed in a portfolio they represent legally distinct asset bundles that are conceptually separable from the other, undifferentiated assets of the firm.

Project portfolios make the firm's boundaries more porous or permeable to outside investors. Put another way, they increase liquidity for discrete assets without requiring messy and disruptive penetration of firm boundaries by outsiders. Assets from the guts of the firm can be surgically plucked out without messy and complex cordoning off and extraction operations. Internal assets central to the firm can be passed outside the firm's membrane in a clean and painless operation.

Secondary markets for patents thus play an important role in firm flexibility and liquidity. This in turn allows for quicker abandonment of failed innovation strategies, and thus a quicker pivot to other, more fruitful projects. For outside investors it represents a way to get hold of firm assets without penetrating and breaking up the firm. The "going concern" value of the overall firm is preserved while particular assets are extracted and sold off.

7.4 NORMATIVE THOUGHTS

In trying to tell the story of what happened in relation to patents and private enterprise, I came to see the transactional flexibility patents provide. There may be a lesson in this for patent policy. The value of patents as a foundation for private ordering has been overlooked, and this means that some patent practices and doctrines that have ignored this value might need to be revisited. I have in mind two in particular: (1) post-AIA patent challenges and (2) contractual (licensing) provisions restricting the licensee in various ways, either in market operations or compensation; or in agreements not to challenge the licensed patents.

The post-AIA regime of administrative patent challenges, in place since 2011, has in many ways been a success. These procedures lower the cost of challenging patent validity, which in turn reduces one of the major costs associated with patent enforcement. But, in patent litigators's never-ending search for a tactical advantage, excessive patent challenges threaten to make essentially every patent perpetually vulnerable. Weeding out bad patents is surely good; but society benefits little from the fifteenth or twentieth challenge to validity. And patent owners benefit not at all. This goes for the transactional partners of those patent owners too.

If society sees every challenge to a patent as an inherent good, then there is no reason for this tactical use of IPRs to cause any concern. Public interest aligns with private value. But suppose instead we agree to take account of the private cost of defending an IPR. Or imagine we agree that the additional social cost (in PTAB time and resources) of the fourth, or fifth, or sixth (etc.) patent challenge exceeds the marginal benefit from that challenge. In either case, we will arrive at the conclusion that it might be a good idea to place some limits on the number of IPRs that can challenge any individual patent claim. We might at least remove some forms of challenge, taking off the board some avenues of attack that have already been tried multiple times.[20]

Consider next contractual (licensing) provisions restricting the licensee in various ways, either in market operations or compensation; or in agreements not to challenge the licensed patents. The law has been very keen to limit the power of a patent owner to restrict a licensee, but as with excessive IPR requests, the private ordering value has been ignored.

[20] See Robert P. Merges and John F. Duffy, Patent Law and Policy (Durham, NC: Carolina Academic Press, 8th ed., 2021) (Chapter 10, section entitled "Towards Patent Incontestability?").

Supreme Court cases from the twentieth century consistently championed the importance of encouraging patent challenges. When there was a conflict between private contractual arrangements and the desire to encourage challenges, challenges won. It might be said that the pro-challenge cases placed the public law value of eliminating patent rights above the value of secure private ordering via contract.

Consider, for example, assignor estoppel: the rule that one cannot benefit from assigning a patent and then later attack the validity of that patent. This doctrine, either as an implied doctrine or in the form of an explicit "no assignor challenge" contract term, was rejected by the Supreme Court in *Lear, Inc.* v. *Adkins*.[21] Even before the AIA, *Lear* was criticized for its indifference to the needs of patent owners and entrepreneurs.[22]

General "no challenge" clauses in patent licenses have also been suspect ever since *Lear*.[23] The idea was that patent challenges were rare, and no potential challenger should be taken out of the running, particularly a contractual partner of the patent owner. Through their contractual dealings, the licensee might learn something that would help invalidate the patent. This is outdated, now that the AIA makes challenges so much easier and cheaper. Even in its day, the *Lear* rule prevented a patent owner from giving up something of value, e.g., a lower royalty demand, in exchange for an exemption from patent challenges on the part of the licensee. In effect, *Lear* undermines contractual trust from the start, in exchange for an outdated belief in the need to encourage every potential challenge to a patent.

Likewise, collection of post-patent-expiration royalties is strictly forbidden under *Brulotte* v. *Thys Co.*[24] and *Kimble* v. *Marvel Entertainments, Inc.*[25] One rationale for the rule is that if post-expiration royalties were permitted, patent licensees would have no incentive to challenge a licensed patent. Again, even before the AIA, this restriction on licensing arrangements was criticized.[26] As with the *Lear* rule, it makes

[21] 395 U.S. 653 (1969).

[22] The classic discussion is in Rochelle Cooper Dreyfuss , *Dethroning Lear: Licensee Estoppel and the Incentive to Innovate*, 72 Va. L. Rev. 677 (1986). For an update see Rochelle Cooper Dreyfuss and Lawrence S. Pop, *Dethroning Lear? Incentives to Innovate After* MedImmune, 24 Berkeley Tech. L.J. 971 (2009).

[23] See generally Michal S. Gal and Alan D. Miller, *Patent Challenge Clauses: A New Antitrust Offense?*, 102 Iowa L. Rev. 1477, 1484–1485 (2017). But see *Baseload Energy, Inc.* v. *Roberts*, 619 F.3d 1357, 1362–1364 (Fed. Cir. 2010); but compare *Flex-Foot, Inc.* v. *CRP, Inc.*, 238 F.3d 1362, 1370 (Fed. Cir. 2001) (voluntary infringement case dismissal and settlement: "Once an accused infringer has challenged patent validity, has had an opportunity to conduct discovery on validity issues, and has elected to voluntarily dismiss the litigation with prejudice under a settlement agreement containing a clear and unambiguous undertaking not to challenge validity and/or enforceability of the patent in suit, the accused infringer is contractually estopped from raising any such challenge in any subsequent proceeding.").

[24] 379 U.S. 29 (1964).

[25] 576 S.Ct. 446 (2015).

[26] See Harold See Frank M. Caprio, *The Trouble with Brulotte: The Patent Royalty Term and Patent Monopoly Extension*, 1990 Utah L. Rev. 813 (1990); Susan Mazurek, *Patent Licensing Tangled in the Brulotte Web: A Comprehensive Analysis of the Supreme Court's Opportunity to*

even less sense post-AIA. In effect the law restricts a plausible and sensible contractual arrangement, royalty payments that carry over in the post-patent period, with no offsetting benefit to society.

The point is not to promote per se legality for licensing restrictions that cut down on patent challenges. It is to recognize that IPRs have changed the incentive picture related to challenges. And maybe some of the private law restrictions can be revisited. After detailed analysis they may appear to be more beneficial on net than they were prior to the AIA.

Because these cases were all decided before the AIA, it is worth asking whether they still represent good policy. IPRs – and all the other AIA-based procedures – fundamentally shift the incentive landscape for patent challengers. It may no longer be necessary to support a pro-patent-challenge policy at every turn. Perhaps it is worthwhile to take another look at the private law function of patent-related contracts. With patent challenges so well served outside the context of infringement litigation, certain contractual restrictions might now be permissible. The key to this fresh look is that the private benefits – and the indirect public value of promoting patent-based business arrangements – might now be worth the reduction of incentives to invalidate.

7.5 A FINAL REMINDER: PATENTS IN CONTEXT

The phrase often used is "law is a seamless web." It is probably foolish to argue in detail what this means; better to hear it with an open mind and listen for the general teaching, which I take to be this: notice that things are interconnected. In steady states, see how parts cooperate and interact. In times of change, remember: A shift in one location might cause a slight lean in another, a nudge that crosses some delicate, almost invisible threshold. The seamless web teaching, in other words, holds a caution. The web metaphor serves as a kind of wreck buoy, a warning beacon for navigators on the seas of legislation, policy, and reform. Throttle back, feel your way along. Keep moving – but use care.

The way I think of patent law, it is enmeshed in two interlocking webs. The first is purely legal. Statutes, doctrines, cases, and official practices intertwine in a taut fabric weave. But this is just one fabric among many. Patent law is only one part of something much larger – a giant patchwork, made up of other institutions, communities, and practices. The blanket term is "innovation system": an aggregate of multiple components, linked together and influencing each other, related by the common purpose of creating and disseminating things that are new (often technologies). The tightly spun cords of patent law, then, occupy but one corner of a larger textile tableau whose other parts are finance, scientific research, education, training,

Reconsider a Fifty-Year-Old Precedent in Light of Widespread Criticism, 18 Tul. J. Tech. & Intell. Prop. 237 (2015).

government procurement, military spending, and many another policy swatch, patch, or emblem.

7.5.1 *Summing Up*

It is very difficult to place any kind of definite value on the aggregate of business arrangements facilitated by patents. Because of the creativity of lawyers acting in their capacity of "transaction cost engineers,"[27] it is possible that some of these same arrangements could have been made without patents. Even if a federal patent in the mix lowered the cost the parties paid to set things up as they wished, one could only guess at the costs saved in any particular deal. Aggregating all these savings into an overall figure is the stuff of economic models or ideal theorizing: a most excellent exercise, thwarted in its practical aspirations by the brute facts of inadequate data.

Yet for all that, it seems very likely that patents do add some *unique* value to the private law arsenal. It is difficult to duplicate the economic effect of a state-backed right "good against the world." These rights – property rights – provide a uniquely flexible foundation for a variety of transactions. And even when there are alternatives to patents, that is, other mechanisms for recouping R&D investments, these alternatives often require a large minimum scale: big companies, that is. To the extent there is value in having a diverse industry structure, a mix of big and small, integrated and specialized, patents may again contribute something unique.

Keeping all this in mind, it appears that patents did (and do) contribute some quantum of unique value as instruments of private ordering. They have been used so many ways, and persisted as a business tool for so long, that it's reasonable to conclude they add something to the mix.

However one might choose to measure this "quantum" or "something," the key is that it is there. And whatever its magnitude, when the topic is patent policy, it seems at best submerged, and more likely completely overlooked. To the extent there is anything akin to a grand cost/benefit ledger for patents, their role in private business arrangements is strictly "off the books." Outside the books might be more accurate.

If there is anything of value in this book, it will be to remedy that. Looking backward, what stands out are the many contributions patents have made since 1790 to private ordering in American business. This book is full of stories of the people who invented and invested in a new, better, or improved way of doing something. Not everyone had (or has) a great experience with the patent system. But looking backward it seems that for many, a token of recognition and potential in the form of a patent boosted them along.

[27] The catchy phrase is Ron Gilson's. See Ronald J. Gilson, *Value Creation by Business Lawyers: Legal Skills and Asset Pricing*, 94 Yale L.J. 239, 244 (1984) (describing the role of the business lawyer as a transaction cost engineer).

One consistent finding throughout history is that patents are associated with new firm entry and small firm survival. Indirectly, then, patents promote specialization and help small innovators protect margins and market share in markets dominated by large firms. The enigmatic polymer that held such fascination for W. L. Gore (PTFE, or Gore-Tex) was protected by a portfolio of patents, carving out a niche for Gore's small and specialized company after it spun out from behemoth DuPont Chemical. This in turn allowed the Gore family to experiment with a radically "flat" management structure designed to promote intra-company autonomy and equality. Their patents protected their ideas, and this protection made it possible for them to run their own company according to their own initiative, their own values. At their best, patents continue to encourage not just novel ideas, but novel companies and novel business models. To an individual business person, patents can be enormously frustrating. A single graduate thesis on a library shelf can invalidate a patent on a technology painstakingly developed over years; a slight new twist in component design or industrial process can permit competitors to take the heart out of a valuable invention because old patent claims can't be stretched to cover the new variation. And so on. For an individual patent, or a single case in litigation, the outcome can seem maddeningly arbitrary, the rationale byzantine. But in the aggregate, over time, patents have permitted enough new firm entry, and small firm survival, to justify their continuing place on the menu of legal entitlements. Maybe not always a satisfying dish, but on the whole a vital nutrient that some independent souls seem to thrive on.

Patents, when seen as private law entitlement, are in a sense passive instruments. They can be slotted into a variety of business structures. And they can be employed in a variety of business strategies. They are valuable tokens that can be deployed and moved around on a number of different game boards. As economic conditions change, so does the role of patents. Property rights are by themselves tightly bounded entitlements: see. e. g., patent claims. But the Chapters of this book show that while the legal contours of a patent are fairly tightly constrained, the things you can do with a patent are diverse, variable, open-ended. The legal scope of a patent is determined by all manner of complex validity requirements and boundary-defining rules. In its essence, though, it is simple: it confers ownership (exclusive rights) oven a discrete invention. But it turns out that this compact little right – call it the Lego of the entitlement world – can be plugged and slotted into a wide variety of business arrangements. From regional franchises in the 1820s to the experimental post-assignment property restrictions of the 2010s, meant to depress the market for patents usable in rent-seeking litigation, patents have proven to be highly flexible instruments in a wide variety of private orderings.

Looking forward, we must recognize that businesspeople may find other uses for patents. I outlined some that have emerged, tentatively, in recent years, in the form of a market for patent portfolios. And I described some speculative possibilities, ways patents might play into larger schemes for creating "thicker" markets for inventions, product designs, and other forms of disembodied but valuable information. My overall point is that whatever the new uses of patents might turn out to be, we will only appreciate them, and only fit them into the pattern of history, if we are on the lookout for them in the first place.

Index

Printed in the USA
CPSIA information can be obtained
at www.ICGtesting.com
LVHW050925010324
772918LV00004BA/252

9 781009 123419